MW01064666

The YMCA *of Middle Tennessee*

The YMCA *of Middle Tennessee*

THREE CENTURIES OF SERVICE

RIDLEY WILLS II

Managing editor: Alice Sullivan, www.alicesullivan.com
Designed by Mary Susan Oleson, BLU DESIGN CONCEPTS

Published in Nashville, Tennessee by Dunham Books. For information regarding special sales or licensing, please contact the publisher:

Dunham Books
63 Music Square East
Nashville, Tennessee 37203
www.dunhamgroupinc.com

ISBN: 978-0-9839-9066-6

Printed in Mexico.

Contents

Cornerstone from the Nashville YMCA building completed at the corner of Seventh Avenue North and Union Street in 1912.

THIS BOOK IS DEDICATED to Ralph L. Brunson, Adrian B. Moody, Clark D. Baker, and John Mark "Journey" Johnson—four men of ability and integrity, who, each in his own way, were instrumental in propelling the YMCA of Middle Tennessee to its present position as one of the finest YMCAs in the world. A commonality among these different leaders, with their different managerial styles, is that each had, as his centerpiece, a determination that the YMCA of Middle Tennessee would always reflect its Christian values.

Foreword

IT IS WITH MUCH PLEASURE that I write the foreword to Ridley's history of the Nashville YMCA. Ridley and his family are integrated into the fabric of what makes the place so great. I can hardly contain my enthusiasm for this opportunity to capture the emotion many of us share for this hallowed institution. It has endured and thrived in good times and in bad, and the thread that runs through the words so well crafted by Mr. Wills is its attention to mission. The words honor the vision and intention of the founders to adhere to the "common loyalty to Jesus Christ" and the persistence that was necessary to sustain its ministry.

I was caught by words and phrases used that today would need to be explained—recording secretary, boys work, reading rooms, gospel meetings, ladies auxiliary, physical culture, night law school, billiard room, correspondence room, radio club, community chest, Hi-Y. The names of the early founders and even the Y leaders of the day, read like the "who's who" of Nashville. Even the changing of the name from Nashville to Middle Tennessee shows the desire to be inclusive, to be open to change, and yet remain the same.

I am reminded of the financial struggles...and often say, "there is no mission without money," yet somehow the dream continued. There was always someone willing to sign a note, make a loan, write a check, or make a gift. Names like Brunson and Moody in recent times, conjure up stories.

If you follow the growth of the YMCA, you follow the growth of the city. Many have come through this Y on their way to leadership in the movement. There is no Y that has produced more staff who have taken leadership in major Ys across this country than those who passed through our halls. On a per-capita basis, there is no YMCA that can boost the growth in membership, depth of community service, creative programming, or philanthropy than this YMCA. "Changing Lives" is not just a slogan for a campaign—it's what the local Y does and is so well-captured in this book.

We love the colorful logo, the characters who come in and out of our buildings, the laughter around the coffee pot, songs around the campfire at Widjiwagan, and we are grateful for what Ridley Wills II has shared in these pages—the story of a mission well-lived.

I am proud to be part of what we call the Nashville YMCA Alumni Association—and know even now that new chapters are being lived.

—Clark David Baker
CEO/Nashville YMCA
YMCA of Middle Tennessee
1987–2001

CHAPTER ONE

The Early Years
1855–1875

IT TOOK LESS than eleven years for the Young Men's Christian Association to find its way to Nashville after its founding in London on June 6, 1844. In 1855, Nashville was a city of less than 15,000 people—4,196 miles and one continent removed from London, then the largest city in the world.

George Williams, a nineteen-year-old clerk for Hitchcock and Rogers, a London dry goods firm, founded the YMCA. On June 6, 1844, this "new boy come to town" invited eleven other clerks to meet with him in room 72 on the second floor of the firm.[1] Once assembled, he asked their help "to work to improve the moral and spiritual condition of young men in our great city." At that time, working hours in London were from 7 a.m. until 9 p.m. in the summer and from 7 a.m. to 8 p.m. in the winter.[2] These long hours, six days a week, left George, his friends, and their colleagues with little time for recreation or study. As a direct result of this inaugural meeting, Bible study classes and a "Young Men's Missionary Society" were initiated. These efforts were the beginnings of the Young Men's Christian Association.

At the time, Williams earned $750 a year as a dry goods clerk. Of that, he gave $250 to the YMCA he founded and lived on the rest.[3] From his inauspicious business start, Williams rose in the ranks of his company to become its head, and one of London's merchant princes. For years, he was president of the London YMCA Association. Because of his service to the world in organizing the institution, Queen Victoria knighted him in 1894. His life was characterized by his habit of "princely giving" to worthwhile causes.[4] When he died in 1905, Sir George Williams was buried in St. Paul's Cathedral in London. And at the time of his death, the YMCA had grown from a handful of young men in 1844 to an organization numbering 8,245 associations across the world with 699,213 members.[5] After World War I, a large stained glass window in Westminster Abby was dedicated to Sir George Williams, to the YMCA, and to the great work the association accomplished in the Great World War. The window features a red triangle, the symbol of the YMCA.[6] The triangle symbolized the unity between body, mind, and spirit.

The first YMCA in North America was organized at Montreal, Canada, on November 25, 1851. A few weeks later, on December 29, 1851, a thirty-year-old seaman and lay missionary, Captain Thomas V. Sullivan, founded the first YMCA in the United States at the old South Chapel in Boston. Sullivan had read about the London Association in the Boston Watchman & Reflector in October 1851. Captivated by the ideals of the fledging organization, he visited the London Association. Returning to Boston, Sullivan convened a meeting on November 15 of thirty-two Christian men from twenty Boston congregations. Seven men from that group were appointed to draft a constitution for the YMCA that was approved December 29.[7] Captain Sullivan said that the purpose of the new organization was "to combat vice, delinquency, crime, drinking and other evils to which young men are subjected." He also correctly predicted that the movement would sweep the land like a "manifest destiny" and that, "by the end of this century, there will be a YMCA in virtually every major city in this great nation of ours."

News of the Boston YMCA and its good work spread across America by sailing ships, steamboats, railroads, and stagecoaches. By January 1855, word of the movement had reached Nashville, where on January 31, 1855, a group of young men met to form an association. J. J. Toon, a dealer in books and stationery, was elected president; and a constitution was adopted by a desire to promote "the moral and religious welfare of the young men of the city." The stated object of the association was to improve "the spiritual, mental and social condition of the young men of Nashville by the ways and means to be hereinafter designated." Weekly prayer meetings were started on Tuesday evenings, and, soon, the fledgling YMCA rented space in a building on the Public Square at Cedar Street, where they had a reading room. At this early date, there was no physical fitness component to the YMCA's work.[8]

The other YMCA officers for 1855 were six vice-presidents: N. Davidson Cross, representing the Presbyterian Church; G. P. Ferriss, the Methodist Church; J. H. Nelson, the Baptist Church; F. L. Miller, the Christian Church; W. R. Moore, the Cumberland Presbyterian Church; and M. D. Myers, the Episcopal Church, W. T. Wheeless was elected recording secretary while W. Bryce Thompson was elected corresponding secretary; A. B. Shanklin, treasurer; and George Cowan, librarian. Members of the board of governors were also elected by Protestant denominations. The Baptist members were A. L. Whitaker and D. S. Wright. The Christian members were D. H. Eichbaum and W. H. Wharton. The Methodist representatives were J. H. Dodd and J. H. Washington. The Episcopalians were W. F. Orr and W. M. Reckless, while the Presbyterians were H. Hill McAlister and Robert Lapsley, and the Cumberland Presbyterians were S. Kirkpatrick and W. J. Porter.

In 1855, the Nashville association had five membership categories: active, associate, life, honorary, and counseling. Any white male between 18 and 39, who was a member of an evangelical church, was eligible for an active membership. Active members had voting rights upon payment in advance of $1 annually. The primary requirement to become a life member was "the payment in advance of a $20 annual fee." Honorary members were elected by the vote of two-thirds of the members present at any regular meeting. Counseling members were males over 40 who were members in good standing of an evangelical church. Their annual dues were $3, the same as for associate members, which were younger members.

• • • • •

Article III of the constitution stated that the committee on rooms "shall procure proper places for the meetings of the association," and that the committee on statistics "shall collect such facts as they may deem of interest to the association." Article IV called for the hour of adjournment to not be later than 10 p.m. Article VII called for the association to meet on the first Tuesday of each month, and for the annual meeting to be held on the first Tuesday evening of each October. Initially, there were six committees: finance, lectures, library and reading room, publications, rooms, and statistics. The constitution also stated that each meeting should open with scripture and prayer, followed by twenty minutes of introductions and general conversation. Miscellaneous business would follow and each meeting concluded with singing and prayer.

• • • • •

On May 5, 1855, the Nashville YMCA issued a formal and elegant invitation to prospective members to a meeting at the First Baptist Church on Summer Street. Later, the board of governors approved the committee on rooms' recommendation that the association rent space in a building on the public square at Cedar Street. The reading room established there and weekly religious meetings apparently constituted the entire work of the association for its first two years.[9] A reading room was important because educational resources were limited and the city had no public library.

• • • • •

In its first year, the Nashville Association adopted the following creed: "The Young Men's Christian Associations seek to unite those young men who, regarding Jesus Christ as their Lord and Savior, according to the Holy Scriptures, desire to be his disciples in their doctrine and in their life, and to associate their efforts for the extension of his kingdom among young men."[10]

• • • • •

In January 1856, William R. Moore, a twenty-four-year-old clerk at the Eakin Company, a merchandise house at 48 Public Square, became president of the Nashville YMCA. Moore, who had come to Nashville nine years earlier to enter the dry goods business, resigned in July 1856 to move to New York City. In time, he would return to Tennessee to establish the William R. Moore Dry Goods Company in Memphis.[11] One of Moore's associates in the YMCA in 1856 was Alexander Stewart, a mathematics professor at the University of Nashville. Having been exposed to the practices and precepts of the

YMCA in Nashville, Stewart founded the first college of the YMCA in the country at Cumberland University in Lebanon, Tennessee.[12] When Moore resigned in July 1856, D. S. Wright succeeded him as president of the Nashville Association, serving as president through the spring of 1857.[13]

On the second anniversary of the founding of the Nashville Association, a public meeting was held at McKendree Methodist Church. Brother W. J. Porter, a member of the board of governors, spoke as did Dr. John B. McFerrin, respected editor of the *Nashville Christian Advocate*. A few months later, Porter succeeded Wright as president.[14]

Recession and Rebounding

The economic recession of 1857 hammered Nashville and its YMCA. With unemployment rising, the association felt an obligation to expand its ministries beyond simply having a reading room and holding religious meetings for young men. The board decided to establish Sabbath schools in poor parts of the city. The constitution was rewritten to spell out the organization's structure in greater detail. Membership rules were tightened to be limited to males who were members in good standing with a church, were under the age of forty, and who had paid the initiation fee of $2 and the weekly dues of ten cents.[15]

The board of governors made another step toward permanency in 1858 by incorporating the Nashville YMCA by a general act of the General Assembly. When this happened on March 2, the association had moved to rooms rented on the second floor of a building at 53 1/2 Union Street that housed a grocery store on the ground floor.[16]

At the 1858 annual meeting on October 5, Bryce Thompson was elected president. He was very familiar with the association, having been corresponding secretary when the YMCA was founded three years earlier. That was particularly helpful as none of the six original vice presidents still held office. Their successors in 1858 were M. S. Stokes, Presbyterian; C. P. Wilson, Methodist; W. R. Stewart, Cumberland Presbyterian; L. S. Collins, Baptist; J. H. Farrar, Christian; and William Simmons, Episcopalian. R. G. Thorne was elected recording secretary replacing W. T. Wheeless, who became corresponding secretary. Hill McAlister, an original member of the board, became treasurer while Henry C. Shapard was elected librarian. The YMCA's programs in 1858 were Bible classes, lectures, and embryonic Mission Sunday schools. The members also had the use of the association's small library.

The year 1859 was a good year for the Nashville YMCA. Membership in the YMCA jumped from about 90 to 183. Henry Hill McAlister succeeded Bryce Thompson as president. A member of a distinguished Tennessee family, Hill's father, James A. McAlister, was a commission merchant with offices at the corner of College and Broad. Hill's future son, Hill McAlister Jr., would become governor of Tennessee. Hill, still a young man, would become a Nashville civic and religious leader after the Civil War. Upon stepping down as president, Bryce Thompson served as librarian, determined to make the association's reading room a true library.

In January 1860, the YMCA rented and furnished a hall over a store at 35 College Street, several doors north of Union Street. There, the YMCA housed its small collection of books, by then up to 400 volumes. A reading room was open daily to whomever wanted to come in and read the daily newspapers and periodicals. Books could be checked out, making the YMCA reading room the city's first public library. Board and monthly business meetings, weekly prayer meetings, and Sunday afternoon Bible classes were held in the hall, and mission work was enlarged to hold religious services in jails.[17]

Hill McAlister was reelected president in 1860 and 1861. Other officers in the latter year were P. L. Nichol, recording secretary; Nathaniel D. Cross, corresponding secretary; W. H. Morrow, treasurer; and Bryce Thompson, librarian.[18]

Secession and Southern Rights

Having weathered the recession of 1857, the Nashville YMCA had a larger worry-growing friction over slavery and states rights. Frequently, when prominent Nashvillians traveled to the East with their families in the 1850s, they were subject to harassment by northern abolitionists. John Brown's capture of the arsenal at Harper's Ferry in 1860 and his stated intent of provoking a slave resurrection intensified the hysteria. By January 1861, South Carolina had seceded from the Union and other deep-South states were poised to do so. Tennessee Governor Isham G. Harris called for a statewide plebiscite to determine whether or not to call a constitutional convention to consider secession. Tennesseans voted not to call a legislative session to consider secession. Tennesseans voted 69,675 against and 57,798 in favor of calling the constitutional convention. A large majority of Tennesseans wanted to avert war if possible.

Sentiment changed dramatically in April 1861 when,

three days before Fort Sumter fell, President Abraham Lincoln called for Tennesseans to furnish 75,000 volunteers to put down the insurrection in South Carolina. Governor Harris responded that Tennessee would not furnish a single man to attack South Carolina but would furnish 50,000 troops to defend Southern rights. Among the first to volunteer were YMCA members. Pro-secession rallies and parades were all the rage in Nashville and, on April 25, Tennessee declared its alliance with the United States null and void.

On May 6, the First Tennessee Infantry Regiment was organized in Nashville. A number of members of the YMCA joined the Rock City Guards Regiment. One of those was Matt B. Pilcher, newly named assistant quartermaster. Before the regiment left Nashville for camp at Allisonia in Franklin County, Pilcher organized a military branch of the Nashville YMCA, and conducted daily prayer meetings in the rooms of the YMCA. Other YMCA members joined the 20th Tennessee Infantry Regiment at Camp Trousdale in Sumner County. There, they demonstrated their Christian principles by doing religious work with the soldiers, such as Bible study.

M. B. PILCHER.

Matt B. Pilcher, Nashville YMCA President 1875–1877, 1886–1895

On June 8, a popular vote of the people of Tennessee ratified the state's secession when 104,913 Tennesseans voted to secede and 47,238 voted to stay in the Union. In Nashville, the vote for secession was 3,029 while the vote against was only 250.

After Nashville's sudden capture by Union forces in February 1862, chaos prevailed and there was no manpower or energy to maintain a YMCA. The association suspended operation, released its rooms, and sold its furniture. The Nashville Y's failure to survive the war mirrored what happened all across the South where only two YMCAs—one in Richmond and the other in Charleston, South Carolina—continued operations throughout the bitter conflict.[19]

To maintain a YMCA in occupied Nashville was impossible. Federals controlled the city from February 1862 until the end of the war in 1865. During the war, nearly all the young men from Nashville were with the Confederate Army of Tennessee. On December 4, 1864, on the eve of the Battle of Nashville, Maggie Lindsley, whose father, Adrian Van Sinderen Lindsley, was a prominent Unionist, wrote in her diary, "There is scarcely a family of any prominence in the city which is not represented by an officer of rank in his [General Hood's] army."[20] Many of these officers had been members of the Nashville YMCA before the war.

Rebuilding and Reorganization

When the Confederate soldiers returned to Nashville after the war, their focus was naturally on reestablishing their lives, dealing with reconstruction issues, and reacquainting themselves with their families. When some degree of normalcy had been established, a group of interested men, including Capt. Matt B. Pilcher and Hill McAlister, met at the lecture room at First Baptist Church on North Summer Street with the intent of reorganizing the YMCA. Hill McAlister presided while Pilcher was elected president. A new constitution was adopted. This happened on May 1, 1867. The YMCA rented a room over E. Wise's store on Union Street. The association held its first business meeting there June 10. However, on October 29, 1867, Pilcher and his associates disbanded the reorganization effort because of the highly partisan feeling between ex-Confederates and Unionists in Nashville.[21]

The inability of the Nashville YMCA to successfully resurrect itself after the war provided an opportunity for other organizations to do mission work. On November 16, 1868, Hill McAlister, president of the Nashville YMCA from 1859 until 1862, organized the Nashville Tract Society to distribute religious literature in both poor and affluent areas of the city. For several years, the society operated a Christian mission on Crawford Street.[22]

In 1872, Robert Weidensall, a former Union soldier, and the first national field secretary of the International

Committee of the YMCA, made a tour of the South that included a stop in Nashville. He came to revive the YMCA movement and pave the way for local and state organizations.[23] He came to Nashville from Clarksville, where he had met with the faculty of Stewart College and had interested them in forming an association. At Nashville he wrote in his diary, "There is no general office. I met with men who were identified with the association before and after the war. I did not attempt to organize for reasons that I cannot describe now for lack of space. Thence, I went to Huntsville where I easily succeeded in forming an operation."[24] Weidensall, realizing that Nashville had the potential to support a YMCA, returned in 1873. On his second visit, he met Hill McAlister, who told him about the Nashville Tract Society. Weidensall suggested to McAlister and John Lellyett, then president of the Tract Society, that they transform the society into a YMCA. They followed his suggestion and established a YMCA in the rooms of the First Baptist Church on North Summer Street on November 17, 1873. Five men affiliated with the earlier YMCA, some members of the Nashville Tract Society, and probably other young men were present. The new organization elected John Lellyett, president; Willis Bonner, vice president; H. W. Forde, treasurer; William M. Cassetty, corresponding secretary; and Frank P. Hume, recording secretary. The association seems to have accomplished little and lasted only until the following spring.[25] That period seems to have been consumed in structuring the organization, the members apparently having only a vague and indefinite idea of the work to be undertaken. The records of the association broke off abruptly with the minutes of March 10, 1874, and the YMCA evidently ceased to exist by mutual consent of the members.[26]

Messieurs Geo. A. Hall and Thomas K. Cree, sent out by the International Committee in 1874, to look after YMCA interests in the South, visited Nashville, as part of their attempt to revive associations in need. They found a prevailing skepticism among the old Nashville YMCA members as to the probability of being able to maintain an organization and some declined to become involved. Notwithstanding this, officers were elected, presumably on November 17. Nothing beyond this, however, seems to have been accomplished, and the Nashville YMCA appeared to be a thing of the past.[27]

When Weidensall returned in 1874, he found that the Nashville Tract Society had an office in a small room in the Exposition Hall, at the southwest corner of Spruce and Broad streets, where the Industrial Exposition had been held in 1873. He was pleased to learn that the room was also the headquarters of the Nashville YMCA.[28] Not long after Weidensall left, the Association seems to have become inactive as no records of its work are to be found from the time of Weidensall's third visit until the successful reorganization of the Nashville YMCA the next year.[29]

Meanwhile, a Nashville Library Association, founded in 1871, had assembled a library of several thousand volumes. These books were primarily donated by the Mechanics Association of Nashville and by private citizens. The library association occupied the main room in the old State Bank Building located on the corner of Union and Cherry Streets. The books lined the walls of the old bank building almost from floor to ceiling.[30]

Finally, on May 15, 1875, the Nashville YMCA, reorganized itself, and elected delegates to the National Young Men's Christian Association Convention, to be held in Richmond, Virginia, May 26 through 29, 1875. Soon thereafter, the directors of the Nashville Library Association offered to turn over their library and reading room to the YMCA on very favorable terms. If the transfer proved satisfactory, the library association agreed to make the transfer permanent at the end of three years without cost to the YMCA.[31] Not having succeeded in 1855, 1867, and 1873 in establishing a permanent YMCA presence in Nashville, the chances of success this time looked brighter.

• • • • •

The Nashville YMCA occupied this building from 1875 until 1882.

CHAPTER TWO

Seeking a Firmer Foundation
1875–1885

ON MARCH 19, 1875, The General Assembly of the State of Tennessee passed an act to provide for the organization of YMCAs and YWCAs and giving the directors of those organizations power to increase the number of directors of such associations to any number not exceeding 36. The act provided for "the encouragement, support and maintenance of YMCA and YWCA associations for the social, physical, intellectual, and religious improvement of young men and women."[32] Obviously, men interested in yet another attempt at establishing a YMCA in Nashville had lobbied members of the General Assembly to take action on their behalf.

In May, the evangelist team of Major D. W. Whittle and gospel singer Philip P. Bliss came to Nashville by train for a great religious revival. A small group of YMCA enthusiasts were on hand to meet them at the Louisville Depot and escort them to the Maxwell House Hotel. Ministers and evangelists preached morning, noon, and night. An estimated 4,000 people attended every service. Prayer services were also held at the Exposition Building, McClure's Hall in East Nashville, in several churches, and even in warehouses. When the revival ended on May 18, 1875, the preachers were escorted to the Chattanooga Depot by the YMCA group.[33]

Several days earlier, on May 15, 1875, 162 charter members met at the First Cumberland Presbyterian Church to organize the YMCA of Nashville and Edgefield.[34] After four speeches by local ministers, a committee was appointed to find suitable headquarters for the YMCA. Captain Matt Pilcher offered a prayer, and the meeting adjourned until eight p.m. the following Tuesday night at the Christian Church on Church Street.[35] The YMCA movement in 1875 was supported by the Baptist, Christian, Cumberland Presbyterian, Episcopal, Methodist, and Presbyterian churches.[36] Clearly, it was a Protestant organization.

Determined to get a better start than in 1867 or 1873, the founders met in the basement of McKendree Methodist, the largest Methodist Church in the city, on May 22, 1875 to elect directors. M. L. Blanton, R. L. Caruthers, L. K. Chase, S. D. M. Clark, Robert S. Cowan, J. E. Goodwin, Joseph B. O'Bryan, Matthew B. Pilcher, Major E. B. Stahlman, and J. M. Thatcher were elected directors.[37] Two days later, the directors met at Matt Pilcher's office on North Market Street. Captain Pilcher was elected president; S. D. M. Clark, the headmaster of MBA, was elected vice-president; J. E. Goodwin treasurer; Joseph B. O'Bryan, corresponding secretary; and E. B. Stahlman, recording secretary and librarian. Soon after the second meeting, a charter was obtained. Stahlman, the only paid employee, resigned a few days later. About June 1, 1875, J. Thompson Plunkett succeeded him. Mr. Plunkett later entered the ministry, serving some of the largest churches in the South. Soon, seven committees were appointed: boarding houses, churches, devotional, employment, membership, mission work, music, and visitation of the sick.[38]

Home Sweet Home: Liberty Hall

Matt Pilcher had been president of the YMCA when it tried to reconstitute itself eight years earlier. During the Civil War, he had been a captain in Company B of the Rock City Guards, First Tennessee Regiment, C.S.A. Wounded at the Battle of Franklin, he returned to Nashville after the war and entered the wholesale grain business. Active in the civic life of the city, he was a city alderman and later a councilman. He was also active in the First Baptist Church. In the YMCA's formative years, Captain Pilcher was considered the most outstanding member.[39]

On Pilcher's invitation, the YMCA met on June 5 at the First Baptist Church, where he was superintendent of the Sunday school. It was reported at the meeting that the Nashville Association had 200 members so a decision was made to broaden the YMCA's program. This meant that the YMCA needed a permanent place to meet rather than going from church to church. Accordingly, a committee to recommend a permanent meeting place was appointed.[40]

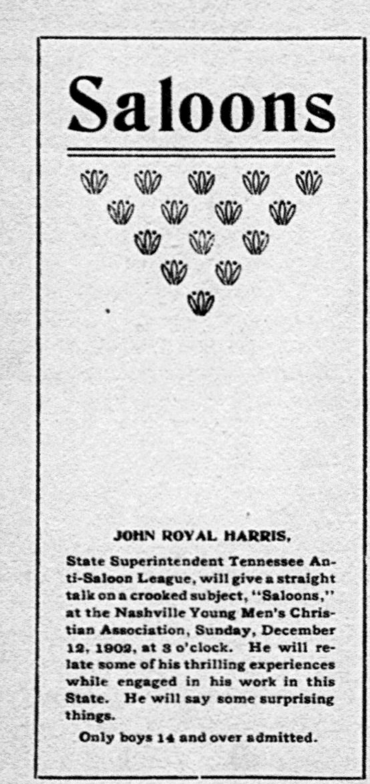

The YMCA's meeting selection committee quickly found an excellent home for the association in the Old State Bank Building on the NE corner of Union and Cherry Streets. The move took place on July 2. The Nashville Library Association had leased the main room in the building since 1871. Prior to that, the building had been the home of the Bank of Tennessee.[41] When the Library Association decided to go out of business, they freed up their reading room and a library that was jammed with 6,000 volumes and 62 newspapers. The directors of the Nashville Library Association made both rooms available to the YMCA on a three-year sublease under very favorable conditions. If, at the end of the three-year period, the YMCA wanted to stay, they would have an opportunity to do so. The elated YMCA leaders were thrilled to accept those terms, and renamed the building "Liberty Hall."[42]

The YMCA established in Liberty Hall not only a library but also a house of prayer "which was often made vocal with songs of praise." The YMCA's outreach broadened from what it had been before the war. It included open-air services conducted at four points in the city, and meetings held at the city and county workhouses, jail, and the women's mission home. Additionally, in Liberty Hall, a noonday prayer meeting began shortly after the YMCA moved in. The noon service was replaced in October by a men's prayer meeting held each Friday night. Bible classes and lectures were the responsibility of the general secretary.[43]

In 1875, the YMCA offered its members the following privileges: a chess and conversation room, a popular lecture course, social and musical entertainment, and (for full ticket-paying members) access to the circulating library of six thousand eight hundred volumes. Any person of good character could obtain an annual ticket, entitling him to all the above privileges (except to take books from the library), for $2.[44]

Liberty Hall, which the YMCA occupied until 1882, was nearly opposite Gen. Andrew Jackson's old law office on Union Street. Considered one of Nashville's historic buildings, the structure had massive proportions that set it apart from more modern buildings on Union Street. The YMCA opened the rooms daily from 8 a.m. until 10 p.m. The reading room, open to the public, featured newspapers and periodicals, writing materials, and a directory of good boarding houses. The librarian offered aid to young men seeking employment. Gradually, attendance increased.[45]

From the very beginning in 1875, the YMCA of Nashville and Edgefield struggled financially. The dues of $2 per year were insufficient to pay expenses. A thirty-six-member committee was appointed to look into the financial problems. Each member promised to solicit support from four people, each of whom was asked to contribute $1 per month to support the association. Fortunately the library, the only one in the city, was centrally located, commodious, and well lit with an attractive reading room adjacent to it. It contained some of the best American and English periodicals. Consequently, it was well patronized by young men and others. Because most of these young men were not being invited to accept Jesus Christ, the board of directors began to look for a general secretary to lead their Christian emphasis efforts.[46]

When President Rutherford B. Hayes visited Nashville in 1877, the YMCA wanted to identify itself with him on his well-known stand for the prohibition of alcohol. The board members were disappointed because their rented facilities were inadequate to entertain the President of the United

States. Nevertheless, two members, John Wheless and Col. Edmund W. Cole, were heavily involved in welcoming the President. Wheless was chairman of the reception committee while Col. and Mrs. Cole hosted an elaborate dinner for the president at their mansion, Terrace Place, on Church Street.[47]

In recording secretary Frank P. Hume's reminiscences, which appear to have been written in 1910, he stated that M. L. Blanton succeeded Matt Pilcher as president of the YMCA of Nashville and Edgefield in 1877. Blanton, an educator, served until J. B. O'Bryan was elected at the annual meeting on May 14, 1880.[48]

The Nashville and Edgefield Association called John H. Elliott, formerly the general secretary of the Augusta, Georgia Association, to succeed Frank P. Hume as general secretary. The transfer of responsibility took place on June 19, 1879. Hume remained as librarian until March 1, 1882. Elliott proved to be a good fit in Nashville. He inaugurated a men's gospel meeting held every Saturday night. This class persisted and was still in existence in January 1916 as a Saturday social supper and Bible class. Mr. Elliott also began a Bible training class to familiarize young Christian men with the use of the Word of God to better prepare them for Christian work. A committee was formed to distribute invitations to young men to join the association's religious meetings, "which resulted in much practical good." The library was also used as the members' parlor.[49]

Elliott's contributions also included the inauguration of a semi-monthly newsletter called the Association Bulletin. The first issue was published December 15, 1879. The Association Bulletin would become a monthly paper in January 1882. Free to YMCA members, it cost 25 cents per annum.[50] Despite the fact that Edgefield became part of the City of Nashville in February 1880, the YMCA would leave its name "The YMCA of Nashville and Edgefield, Tenn." until the constitution of February 1910 was adopted.[51]

Expanding the Mission

Meanwhile, as the YMCA matured in America, it began to change its emphasis, increasing the importance of the physical fitness and character-building aspects of the association's mission, and moving away from street preaching and mission work.[52] This idea was called muscular Christianity and would hold sway until 1920. Nashville would not adopt the idea until the association moved into its own building in 1889.

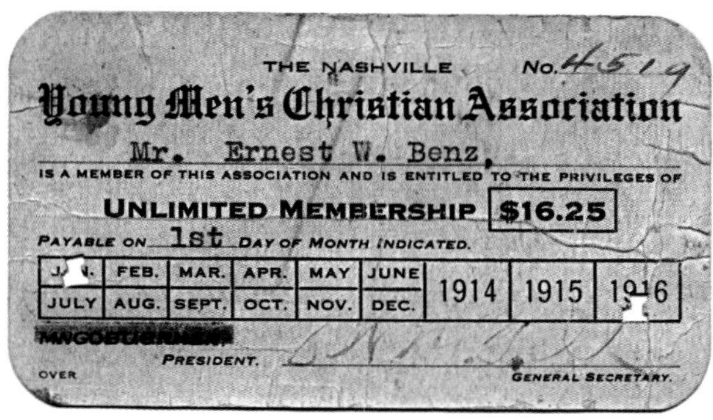

THE NASHVILLE No. 4519

Young Men's Christian Association

Mr. Ernest W. Benz,

IS A MEMBER OF THIS ASSOCIATION AND IS ENTITLED TO THE PRIVILEGES OF

UNLIMITED MEMBERSHIP $16.25

PAYABLE ON 1st DAY OF MONTH INDICATED.

JAN.	FEB.	MAR.	APR.	MAY	JUNE	1914	1915	1916
JULY	AUG.	SEPT.	OCT.	NOV.	DEC.			

PRESIDENT. GENERAL SECRETARY.

OVER

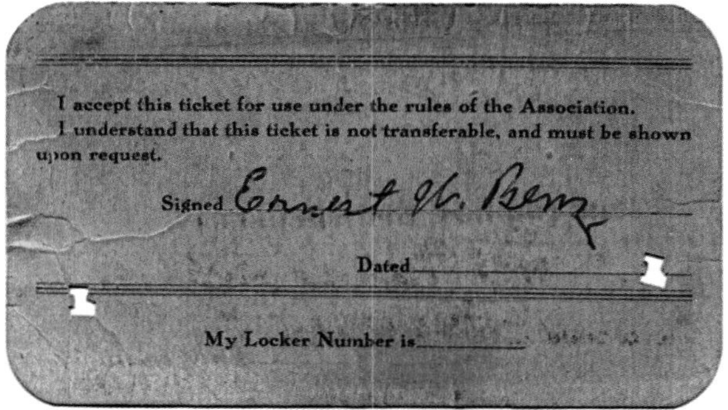

I accept this ticket for use under the rules of the Association. I understand that this ticket is not transferable, and must be shown upon request.

Signed Ernest W. Benz

Dated

My Locker Number is

With an increasing number of visitors to the reading room, the YMCA rented "the large room opening out of the library to the rear" in 1880. The association announced the opening of the new room and the fact that it was in the process of being attractively decorated for use as a members' parlor and reception room. Wallpaper and a new carpet were installed, a chandelier was hung from the ceiling, and new parlor furniture was ordered. In addition to out-of-town newspapers, the reading room featured writing material, a directory of good boarding houses, and aid in securing employment. The general secretary, John H. Elliott, used this room as his office and for all the smaller meetings of the association, such as classes and prayer meetings.[53]

The YMCA celebrated its fifth anniversary on Sunday evening, June 6, 1880, at First Presbyterian Church. President J. B. O'Bryan presided, and immediate past president M. L. Blanton gave a brief report on YMCA activities during 1879 when he was president. He said that during the year, an average of 91 people a day visited the reading room, employment was found for sixteen young men, thirty men were referred to rooming houses, 280 calls were made on young men, 131 daily prayers meetings and ten Association Lyceum meetings were held, and there were 670 meetings in total. Brothers

Association Bulletin.

Published by the Young Men's Christian Association, at Nashville, Tenn.

Vol. 1. DECEMBER 15, 1879. No. 1.

INTRODUCTORY.

AMONG the more active Young Men's Christian Associations of the country, it has come to be pretty generally believed that wherever indifference or opposition to the work of the Association exists, it is owing in a large measure, if not altogether, to ignorance concerning the character and work of the organization. To meet this difficulty, many plans have been resorted to, and perhaps none has succeeded so well as the Bulletin. Therefore, it is with a view of giving information in regard to our work that we begin the publication of the "Association Bulletin." We design to make it an interesting and welcome visitor to all who may read it, first, by its attractive appearance, and second, by keeping it full of fresh and sprightly church and association news.

OUR LIBRARY.

WE offer extraordinary inducements to the general public to become members of our Library, the terms of membership are moderate. An annual ticket is $5.00, and we have popularized the price of membership by giving a Library Member the privilege of taking a yearly ticket, and paying the amount in quarterly installments.

We keep many of the late works of fiction, history, etc., and as a special inducement we permit any of the following magazines, which we have in duplicate numbers, to be taken from the Reading Room, when fresh:

Harper's Monthly, Scribners Monthly, St. Nicholas, Lippincott's Magazine, Atlantic Monthly, Appleton's Journal, Popular Science Monthly, North American Review.

. . . We note with pleasure the increased attendance and interest at the Young Men's Bible Class on Sunday afternoons, at Library hall.

. . . MERRY CHRISTMAS!

. . . The McKendree Church congregations are still good. Dr. West is doing a noble work under great disadvantages.

. . . Rev. Dr. Graham, of Christ Church, is delivering a series of interesting discourses at his Sunday night church service.

. . . Have you ever heard the "Association Quartette"? If not, attend the Saturday night men's meeting and hear some good singing.

. . . When you buy your nice things for Christmas, don't forget that poor family that lives near you.

. . . Much to the regret of many young men Dr. Baird, of the First C. P. Church, has discontinued his Sunday night lectures on the books of the Bible.

. . . A full ticket to the association for one year costs only five dollars and entitles the holder to every privilege of the Library, as well as to every other privilege provided by the association.

. . . The only necessary qualification for active membership in the Y. M. C. A. is, that the applicant be a member in good standing of some evangelical church. Only active members are allowed to vote and hold office.

. . . Any man of good moral character, whether member of church or not, may become an associate member on payment annually in advance of two dollars. Full ticket entitling to full use of library, five dollars.

. . . An association has recently been organized at So. Pittsburg, Tenn. with Jas. Bowron, manager of "Southern States Coal, Iron and Land Co," as President. The company have promised to consider favorably the application of the association for a site and building for their use.

Caruthers, Elliott, and McGuire covered the literary, religious, and social work of the association. The approximately 500 members who attended the meeting also enjoyed hearing the voices of the YMCA's male quartet, In his report, the treasurer announced that the association had a balance of $235.50. By the fifth anniversary of the Nashville YMCA—only one year later—and the thirty-fifth anniversary of the founding of the YMCA in London, there were 2,400 YMCAs worldwide, including 1,000 in the United States and Canada, and 300 in Great Britain, Germany, and Holland. All the rest were in Europe.[54]

The YMCA normally closed for the first two weeks of July for housecleaning and rearranging the library.[55] In the summer of 1880, a number of new books were obtained. Concerned that the association's income was insufficient to pay for expenses, the board of directors hoped to enlist 150 sustaining members each of whom would make an annual payment of $10 each. Benefits of sustaining memberships were use of the library, free admission to lectures, and free attendance at German or arithmetic classes held at the YMCA.[56]

By January 1881, the most important work done at the Nashville YMCA was the young men's social religious meeting held at Liberty Hall at 8 p.m. every Saturday night. Counting library members, the membership of the Nashville YMCA was now close to 500.[57] Daily, except on Sundays, there were noon prayer meetings in the parlor. Women were invited to these meetings that lasted 30 minutes. On Sundays, the workers consecration meeting was at 8 a.m., the medical students meeting at 2 p.m. and the young men's Bible class at 3:30 p.m. in Liberty Hall.[58]

Space was tight in the old State Bank Building and Elliott felt the YMCA was ripe for a new building. Nationally, the YMCA was moving from renting space on the second floors of retail buildings downtown to having buildings of their own that included rooms for young single men who had moved to town. One thing that had not changed was the association's position on card playing, dancing, and going to the theater. The International YMCA had taken a stand in 1866 against these worldly temptations "so unscriptural in their influence as to be utterly inconsistent with our professions as Disciples of Christ." This position remained intact.[59]

In February, a few young men in the YMCA organized a literary society to be known as "Association Lyceum." It began meeting in the members' parlor on Tuesday nights. The president of the Lyceum was R. W. Lewis.[60]

Growing Pains

On April 1, the Association Bulletin announced, "Our General Secretary, Mr. John H. Elliott, has resigned his office at Nashville to accept a similar position at Albany, N.Y. His leaving the city will be deplored by all classes." Later in April, the YMCA honored Elliott with a reception. The rooms were crowded with his friends, who came to express their gratitude for his kindness and their regret that he was leaving. He would not allow them to say a word about him. Instead, he read scripture to the assembled group. Nevertheless, the board passed a resolution praising Elliott for having, in less than two years, established himself "in the confidence and esteem of the whole community." The resolution "Resolved that we truly recommend our brother Elliott as a safe counselor, a man of strict adherence to duty and principal-intelligent, industrious, and earnest in his work for the glory of God and the salvation of souls, in fullest confidence do we commend him to the brethren in his new field, and to all who love the Lord Jesus Christ."[61]

Elliott left the Nashville YMCA in reasonably good shape. Frank Hume acted as interim general secretary until a permanent replacement could be found.[62]

At the sixth annual meeting on May 13, eight men were elected directors and three men elected delegates to the International YMCA Convention to be held in Cleveland on the 25th. At the same meeting, YMCA president J. B. O'Bryan resigned and was succeeded by John Thomas Jr. J. W. Bonner was elected vice-president.[63] As the new president, John Thomas's immediate focus was on finding an outstanding general executive to replace the charming and earnest John Elliott. A significant problem was that there were few, if any, strong candidates in the South with YMCA general secretary experience. Having to look further, the Nashville and Edgefield YMCA search committee, chaired by M. L. Blanton, identified Raymond Rolph, the general secretary of the Ottawa, Canada, Association, as the man they wanted. He accepted the Nashville position in the fall. But even before he arrived, there seemed to have been misgivings regarding the choice. The Association Bulletin of October 15 said, "Our new general secretary, Mr. Rolph, of Ottawa, Canada, is expected to arrive on the 17th. He comes to us a stranger, not only to the members of the Association, but also to our people. But to the customs and habits of our Southern people, some time must be spent in gaining familiarity."[64]

Another uncertainty bothered the leadership. The Y board members, having recently learned that Liberty Hall had been sold, were impatient to know what this would mean to the YMCA. In December, additional uncertainty arose when E. W. Cole, the new owner of the building, announced that he planned to demolish the building to build "a handsome block" and that the YMCA would need to vacate Liberty Hall by February 1st. After a rushed search for new quarters, the Y found three connecting rooms in the old Olympic Theater Building at the corner of Summer and Union streets. The rooms were on the second floor and only one block away from the old Liberty Hall.

The premonition that the adjustment to a new general secretary from Canada would be difficult was an understatement. Despite coming from a YMCA that had no debt and had grown to nearly 400 members under his guidance, Rolph proved to be the wrong fit for Nashville. He resigned, effective March 21, 1882. Until a replacement could be found, a YMCA member J. O. Friend Jr. took his place. The ever-ready Frank Hume would soon replace him.[65]

A third challenge for the Nashville YMCA was that its relationship with the Nashville Library Association had become strained over the winter. Following the YMCA's move to the Olympic Theater Building, leadership of the two organizations met to try to resolve their differences. The result was that the YMCA formally surrendered all 6,000 books to Gates P. Thurston, president of the Library Association that was in disarray with only a few members. Thurston had the books packed in boxes and stored. This meant that Nashville had lost its only library. Fortunately, the YMCA still had about 2,000 volumes that they had either purchased or had been given. After the demise of the library association, the YMCA would rescue the books.[66]

During the winter, Mitchell M. Blanton, immediate past president of the Nashville Association, and some other Nashville YMCA leaders went to Chattanooga to assist that Association in reorganizing. Over $700 in subscriptions resulted from the effort and the Chattanooga YMCA began looking for a general secretary.[67]

When Frank Hume left in April to join Bradstreet's Mercantile Agency, C. C. Emery, of Atlanta, succeeded him. Perhaps stung by two general executives leaving in three months, and wary of making another mistake, the YMCA gave Emery the title of assistant secretary. He was described as "a warm-hearted, obliging fellow." A few weeks after Emery's arrival, the YMCA received its first telephone. It was placed in the reading room.[68]

The Nashville YMCA celebrated its seventh annual meeting May 12, 1882. So as not to conflict with the evening meeting, the Protestant Churches in Nashville cancelled their Sunday evening services that night. Five ministers participated in the service at McKendree Methodist Church, as did John Thomas Jr., who stepped down as president at the meeting. A. W. Wharton succeeded him. The association still did not have a general secretary as Emery seemed not up to the task.[69] At the time, the recently revived Chattanooga Association was the only YMCA in the state with a general secretary.[70] To perform the functions of a general secretary, the Nashville YMCA relied on one of its young members, J. O. Friend Jr., to manage the affairs of the association as best he could. During this time, the Nashville YMCA encouraged its members to subscribe to the *Watchman*, a semi-monthly published by the National YMCA in Chicago. A subscription cost $1 per annum.[71]

Realizing the Y was floundering, its board turned to the

International committee for assistance. In response, the National YMCA sent one of their best, Thomas K. Cree, to Nashville. He arrived in late January and stayed until the first of March. Cree's first contribution was to organize a YMCA ladies' auxiliary on January 30. Mrs. A. G. Adams, whose husband was an elder and trustee of First Presbyterian Church, was the first president. The auxiliary helped with entertainment, obtaining books for the library, and furnishing rooms. The auxiliary would valuably and faithfully support the YMCA for many years.

While Cree was in Nashville, the association moved to rooms on the second floor of the Allen Block at 26 and 1/2 Church Street, across from the Vendome Building. After twelve months of trying unsuccessfully to make the rooms in the Olympic Theater Building at the corner of Union and Summer streets work, the board of directors realized the move was necessary.

In March, about the time Thomas Cree left, the association employed Wesley T. Dunley, a paid general executive of the Detroit Association. The combination of two physical moves in twelve months, losing their library, and having no general secretary since April 1882, caused morale to plummet, and volunteer programs to slip badly. It was also difficult to convince members to accept positions of responsibility. This was the atmosphere Dunley confronted when he came aboard as general secretary. Under his aggressive leadership, the dispirited board was reorganized and new committees appointed. Meanwhile, warhorse Matt Pilcher was soliciting funds to help the association get rid of its debt. A. W. Wharton, an educator, was elected president to serve temporarily until the new organization was in place.[72]

At the eighth annual meeting in May 1883, James Bowron was elected president. He would serve three years.[73] In less than a year, Bowron and his board realized that Dunley was not effective as general executive as he was overly aggressive and lacking in Southern gentility. Dunley resigned in the summer of 1884, undoubtedly at the request of the board.[74]

Frank P. Hume returned to association work on November 1, 1884, when he accepted the general secretary position, replacing Dunley. He found the board fed up with operating out of rented rooms on the second floors of downtown buildings and also concerned about the association's finances. Accordingly, the YMCA began a quiet campaign to raise enough money to purchase a lot and erect a building as the permanent home of the YMCA of Nashville and Edgefield. The results were disappointing. In December, the association moved for the fourth time in its ten-year history, this time to the Noel Block on Church Street. The association had climbed out of debt but still needed more financial support if it was going to accomplish the work that needed to be done, and have its own building. Once again, the association called on the International Committee in New York for help.[75] In response, "Uncle Robert" Weidensall returned in January 1885. With his help, YMCA board members systematically canvassed the businessmen in town with encouraging results. The money needed to fund the 1885 budget was found. At this point, a decision was made to employ an assistant general secretary to help the general secretary, who had been spending a considerable amount of time raising money.[76]

On March 24, the Nashville Association found its man. He was Edgar S. McFadden, the young recording secretary and chairman of the committee on boys' work at the Murfreesboro YMCA and junior member of the firm McFadden and Son in that city.[77]

McFadden quickly proved to be particularly effective in working with young men and boys. Soon, more than 100 boys were enlisted in Sunday afternoon Bible studies, debating societies, and physical education. McFadden also established a twenty-eight-member Boys' Branch on April 26, 1885. Its first president was fourteen-year-old Matt Buckner and the boys enjoyed doing Bible study and going on excursions. Matt and another Boys Club member, Edgar Foster, would later become presidents of the Nashville and Edgefield YMCA. For some time, boys' work was done in the men's department.[78]

McFadden was definitely a step in the right direction, but the Nashville association still did not have the energy and confidence to take the needed and bold step of acquiring its own building. That energy would come from the greatest religious revival ever to hit Nashville.

• • • • •

CHAPTER THREE

Evangelism, a New Building, and a Fire
1885–1899

Throughout 1884, Nashvillians were reading and hearing about an amazing Georgia evangelist named Sam Jones. In city after city across the conservative South, he was stirring Christian churches with his plain manner of preaching, "his fearless rebuke of existing social evils, and his wonderful personal magnetism." When Jones visited Nashville briefly in March 1885, he left the city buzzing with religious fervor. As a result, an interdenominational committee of Protestant laymen and ministers invited him to return in May to hold a twenty-day revival. Upon his acceptance, a mammoth gospel tent, capable of seating seven thousand people, was erected on a vacant lot on the southwest corner of Broad and Spruce streets.[79]

In the first week of the revival, the *Nashville Banner* announced, "A religious movement is underway which promises to be the deepest and most far-reaching ever witnessed in the city."[80] So many attended the revivals, held three times daily, that many chose to remain outside the crowded tent to listen to the spellbinding Georgian. The best-known conversion that Jones made was that of Tom Ryman, one of the most successful steamboat captains in the South. After his conversion on the first night of the revival, Ryman decided not to renew the bar privileges on his steamboats when those concessions expired. This caused a considerable loss of revenue, but Ryman held true to his word. Not only

that, he conceived the idea of building a more permanent home for revivals, and became a leader in the successful effort to build the Union Gospel Tabernacle on Summer Street below the First Presbyterian Church.[81] When Ryman died in December 1904, Sam Jones and another evangelist, George Stewart, conducted the funeral in the Tabernacle. At the end of his oration, Jones suggested that the name of the Tabernacle be changed to the Ryman Auditorium.[82]

Many YMCA leaders attended Jones' revivals. Within that group, someone suggested that the YMCA enlist Jones' help in raising money to erect a building for the Nashville YMCA. They approached him with the idea, and found him receptive. He had already helped Henry Grady and others raise money to build the Atlanta YMCA.[83]

On Sunday night, June 7, 1885, Jones returned to Nashville and spoke to a crowd estimated at 5,000 at the same location he used in May. At the end of his address, he asked his audience to contribute generously to the YMCA's building fund, a project he said they had neglected. The crowd responded by pledging $22,000 that evening. On succeeding evenings, Jones repeated his plea on behalf of the YMCA. At the end of his revival, the building fund had grown to $37,000. Because of Sam Jones, the YMCA and the city's Protestant Churches all saw increases in membership, in Bible classes, and in enthusiasm.[84]

The YMCA celebrated the first anniversary of the opening of the boys' department on April 26, 1886, in YMCA Hall. The ladies' auxiliary served refreshments. And one month later, the eleventh annual meeting of the Nashville and Edgefield YMCA was held in the First Baptist Church on Sunday, May 30, 1886.

The annual report, made at the meeting, showed receipts for the fiscal year, that ended April 1, 1886, of $2,867.93, and disbursements for the same period of $2,779.31. General secretary Frank P. Hume's salary was set at $900 while assistant secretary McFadden's salary was $637.50. The building fund had $9,342.00. As of April 1, 1886, there were 250 active and 16 associate members. There were an additional 104 boys in the boys' branch and 62 members in the ladies' auxiliary. The board met 20 times during the year.[85]

To attract people to the weekly Gospel meetings, members scattered invitations around town nearly every Saturday night, and sang at the front door before the meetings started. Thirteen young men were converted during the year as a result of these meetings. There were also 35 open-air services with an average attendance of 140. They were held at Cheatham's Corner, Watkins Park, and the old cemetery in South Nashville. There were 22 services at the City Hospital, 22 at the County Jail and 13 at the County Asylum. The boys' branch held 49 devotional meetings with an average attendance of 44. During the year, 22 boys united with some church through the influence of the branch, of which Matt Buckner was boys' division president. Mrs. R. W. Brown was president of the ladies' auxiliary and Matt Pilcher was president of the board of directors. There also was a board of trustees of which E. W. Cole was president. The vice president of the board of trustees was Gen. W. H. Jackson, of Belle Meade. The board authorized the formation of a building committee. Its members were of J. B. O'Bryan, chairman; Matt Pilcher; Gates P. Thurston; H. A. Myers; Edgar Jones; and J. P. Wakley. Finally, there were five standing committees—devotional, social and literary exercises, employment, and visitation.

With 50,000 raised or pledged, thanks largely to Sam Jones, the YMCA was ready to consider sites for their proposed new building. Colonel E. W. Cole, who was planning to move from his palatial home on Church Street between Vine and Spruce Streets to an equally palatial home on Murfreesboro Pike, gave the YMCA a thirty-day option on his town house, that fronted on Church Street, at $250 a foot on July 2. The YMCA did not exercise the option; Cole subsequently sold his house to the Southern Baptist School for their offices.[86]

On October 11, 1886, the YMCA bought from Mr. and Mrs. Henry Sperry a lot fronting 68' on the south side of Church Street between Cherry and College and running back 105' to an alley. During the Civil War, the McNairy Building, used as the post office, occupied part of this lot. The purchase price was $12,496 with $4,166.67 paid in cash. The balance was to be paid by two promissory notes, each for $4,166.67 with 6 percent interest, due six and twelve months from the date of the contract. The lot was bounded on the east by the Nashville Athletic Club and to the west by the Nashville Banner building. To secure the promissory notes, a lien was placed on the property. Not having enough cash to build the building, the YMCA asked the subscribers to the building fund to go ahead and pay at least 20 percent of their pledges.[87]

By late 1886, Messrs. Smith and Sharpe, and Mr. George

W. Thompson, finished general designs for the new building. In February, the design submitted by architect George W. Thompson was accepted and, despite not having all the money they needed, the YMCA broke ground on March 23, 1887. Sixteen-year-old Matthew G. Buckner, president of the boys' division, presided. Nashville Mayor T. A. Kercheval was on hand to offer his congratulations. J. B. O'Bryan, chairman of the building committee, and Frank Hume, "the tireless and evidently uncomplaining general secretary," also spoke. Matt Pilcher threw the first shovel of dirt from a wagon provided for the purpose.[88]

As soon as plans were available, the YMCA published an etching of their proposed building. On the back, F. P. Hume, general secretary, and M. B. Pilcher, president, wrote, "The total amount of subscriptions to the new building has reached $50,293.25. Of this amount, $10, 614 has been raised since last March, and is the result of vigorous efforts on the part of the Association, and friends who have assisted. It was secured through the aid of circulars, personal canvas, statements made at various churches, at the annual and anniversary meetings, and through the efforts of Rev. Sam P. Jones and Maj. D. W. Whittle."

The members of the ladies' auxiliary and the boys' department contributed their fair share. The ladies raised $700 to furnish their room, while the boys collected $150 to help pay for furnishings for the three beautiful rooms assigned to them.

The building committee estimated that $15,000 in additional subscriptions would be needed to complete the building. They also reported that priority would be given to completing two rooms on the first floor first so that they could be rented for commercial use. The building committee estimate proved reasonably accurate as the total cost of the new building turned out to be $67,000.[89]

At the twelfth annual anniversary meeting held at First Presbyterian Church on May 1, president Pilcher reported that the Lyceum Society had suspended operations and that there were no funds available to purchase books for the overcrowded library. Nevertheless, he said the association was free of debt and had been since 1885. He then reported on the new building, saying, "We can state that the lot is bought and nearly all paid for, ground has been broken, and excavation begun."[90]

Several weeks later, on June 23, articles were deposited in the cornerstone box before John Oman, contractor for the cut-stone work, laid the cornerstone. The next day, *The Daily American* made the point, "By persistent effort and patient toil, the YMCA has raised itself out of a position of obscurity and neglect into a position that commands the community's respect. When the cornerstone of their proposed magnificent structure was laid yesterday afternoon, Governor [Robert Love] Taylor made the principal address, surrounded by solid men of Nashville. The building will cost about $30,000 and when finished will compare favorably with any public structure in the city."[91]

The construction did not go well as subscription money came in slowly and sometimes not at all. As a result, work stopped from time to time in 1887 and 1888 until more money was received.

Still, during the construction of the new building, the YMCA continued to operate out of their crowded rooms in the Allen Block. Because of a lack of space, the boys' gospel meetings had been held, since the beginning of 1888, at the Merchants' Exchange.

The YMCA's third quarter statement gave the status of the new building as follows: "The [first] two floors are about ready for occupancy, and are offered for rent. The basement of the building is being thoroughly drained, preparatory to finishing it. The building committee is making arrangements to give out shortly contracts for remainder of painting and glazing, plastering and plumbing, and also steam heating and glass for the windows. When these contracts are completed and the carpenter's work finished, the building will be finished, provided an additional fifteen thousand dollars is raised to accomplish this." The Y also needed another $6,000 to furnish the building.

The YMCA Building was sufficiently completed for the association to begin moving its library books and other furniture on December 31, 1888. For the next several months, all association work was done in the gospel room on the first floor and in the gymnasium.[92] Thanks to the volunteer leadership of Col. E. W. Cole, Gen. William Hicks Jackson, and Capt. Tom Ryman, nearly $50,000 had been raised at tent revivals and through other generous donations. Nevertheless, the YMCA would end up with $25,000 in debt. The last meeting held in the old rooms of the Association was the men's gospel meeting that occurred on Saturday night, December 29, 1888.[93]

Just as the association was moving to the new building,

E. S. McFadden announced, on December 26, 1888, that he was resigning as assistant general secretary to accept the call of the Augusta, Georgia, YMCA to become their general secretary. He left Nashville in January.[94]

Done but in Debt

Much of the four-story YMCA building of Kentucky sandstone was finished in January 1890. "On its first floor [the basement] were a small swimming pool, a bowling alley and locker rooms." The pool was one of the first indoor pools ever built in a YMCA building.[95] "On the second floor were offices, a library, a reading room, and a four-hundred-seat auditorium that doubled as a gymnasium. There was also space on this floor [that fronted Church Street] to be rented out for additional income. On the third floor were the dining room, committee rooms and clubrooms. The kitchen was on the top floor. A cupola topped the structure. No one thought to provide a separate entrance for boys or quarters for them. The new Nashville YMCA looked very much like others springing up across the country in such cities as Fort Wayne and Milwaukee."[96]

During 1889, vigorous efforts were made to reduce the building debt, but with only modest success. Consequently, the building was mortgaged for $20,000, leaving a floating indebtedness of between $2,000 and $3,000. The association also discovered that operating the larger building required a considerably larger expense than theretofore had been the case in the small rented rooms.[97]

The auditorium was used so much for social events that the YMCA physical fitness programs were forced to use the Hippodrome as well as the hall of the Nashville Laundry Company on Bridge Street for workouts. Classes, dominated by the Bible Study class that Mr. McFadden promoted, quickly grew to 200 people in attendance each week. Because the Bible study came to dominate all the other work of the association, the board felt their programs were unbalanced and appealed to the national office for guidance.[98]

Frank P. Hume, the general secretary, wrote the members in March encouraging them to use all the privileges in the new building—library, bowling alley, bathrooms, games, educational classes, lectures and other entertainments, and the gymnasium. He added, "We have at present only the library, but the other attractions mentioned will be in operation later in the year. We regret that the incomplete condition of the building, and the small amount of the building fund yet raised, prevents us from having all the departments of the work ready for use now." This was one of Hume's last letters to the membership as, on April 17, 1889, Charles E. Thomas succeeded him, becoming the association's first professionally trained secretary. Thomas got his training at the new YMCA School for Christian Workers in Springfield, Massachusetts, founded five years earlier by Jacob Browne, the father of professional education in the YMCA. By 1889, the YMCA School for Christian Workers had approximately 400 trained men with an average age of 29. After Thomas graduated, he served as general secretary of the Richmond, Virginia Association. Frank Hume, who remained with the Nashville YMCA, was given a new title of financial secretary.[99]

On August 15, the board felt good about the YMCA, having achieved a decade-long dream of owning their own building. In August, director R. E. Magill and Charles E. Thomas, general secretary, wrote a letter encouraging the international committee of the YMCA USA to hold its next conference in Nashville. They were aware that, in a few weeks, the secretaries throughout the country would make a decision on the conference site. Magill and Thomas wrote, "Tennessee stands well to the front in YMCA work in the South and, being the keystone state of the South, bordered by eight other states, the impetus the conference would give the work in Nashville and in Tennessee would be felt throughout this entire section." They went on to say, "We have from eight to ten thousand students from the South and Southwest in attendance upon our schools and colleges, and, through them, you would come in direct contact with the whole South." The Nashville officials promised a genuine, old-fashioned Southern welcome and mentioned the historic sites nearby. Despite having a strong case, the International Committee chose another city.

Luther Halsey Gulick made a name for himself in 1889 when he proposed the inverted triangle as the emblem of the association and the symbol of the unity between spirit, mind, and body in the Christian personality. He first discussed his belief in the importance of this unity in 1889.[100] One hundred twenty-two years later, the emblem still is instantly recognized as the YMCA emblem.[101]

In October, Matt Pilcher, president; Charles E. Thomas, general secretary; and F. P. Hume, financial secretary and librarian, wrote the following description of the interior of the YMCA Building:

> The hall for men's gospel meetings on the first floor of the new building and near the street has been neatly furnished with linoleum and folding chairs. The rooms on the third floor [are] arranged specially for social affairs. The Library and Reading Room have both been carpeted and furnished with new chairs and beautiful oak cases for the books adorn the library walls. Receptacles for the papers and magazines are being prepared and a correspondence table will be placed in the reading room. The association has leased the baseball park for a term of years for out-door athletic sports. The extensive repairs that the association had to make probably means the park will not be available until next spring. The bathing department was opened last June. The beautiful, spacious auditorium is being frescoed, and will soon be seated with comfortable opera chairs. A course of star entertainment has been arranged for the fall and winter to which all contributing members paying annually, not less than $10, are admitted free.[102]

The YMCA of Nashville celebrated its fifteenth birthday at 8 p.m. on May 11, 1890. Soon after, Charles Thomas employed Thomas Cornelius, of the Richmond Virginia Association, as the YMCA's first physical director. Cornelius quickly realized that the Nashville Y's gymnasium equipment was completely inadequate. Disappointed, he quit in September 1890 to accept the same position at the Baltimore YMCA.[103]

Undiscouraged, Thomas had far-ranging ideas for new programs. Volunteers and the small YMCA staff tried to keep up with Thomas. Frank Hume, who may have disagreed with how fast Thomas was changing things, resigned as financial secretary in November 1890 to accept a job as the general secretary for the Montgomery, Alabama, YMCA. He had fifteen years of service with the Nashville YMCA and had always been there when needed. Mr. Thomas resigned in June 1891 to accept a call from the Lansing, Michigan, Association to be their general secretary. He thought he had been called to the Nashville Association to initiate a balanced and expanded program and was frustrated that the board seemed hesitant in backing him.[104]

To replace Thomas, the Nashville Y turned to one of their own, E. S. McFadden, general secretary of the Augusta, Georgia, YMCA, who, less than three years earlier, had been assistant secretary of the Nashville Association.[105] McFadden came and gave untiringly of his time and energy in the work of the Association and, once again, held great influence on the spiritual life of the boys and men of Nashville served through the association.[106] He was helped considerably when the Nashville YMCA recruited J. T. Gwathney, "a superbly trained gymnast," to become the physical education director replacing Thomas Cornelius. Gwathney accepted and shared his time between the YMCA and Vanderbilt University, where he was instructor of the gymnastics team. In November 1891, McFadden got more help when he hired Charles Schall, formerly general secretary of the Brunswick, Georgia, Association, to become assistant secretary. Schall would resign in September 1893 to study for the ministry.[107]

A New Year

In 1892, the YMCA Building was a busy place. On New Year's Day, the ladies' auxiliary hosted an open house for four hundred young men, many of whom had moved to Nashville and were away from their families. That year, the boys' division was open to all Caucasian boys of good character between the ages of 12 and 16. Their rooms were on the third floor.

• • • • •

The following daily newspapers were available in the reading room on the second floor: *Atlanta Constitution*, *Chicago Inter-Ocean*, *Cincinnati Post*, *Denver Post*, *Louisville Courier-Journal*, *Memphis Appeal-Avalanche*, *Memphis Evening Scimitar*, *Nashville American*, *Nashville Banner*, *Nashville Herald*, *New Orleans Picayune*, *New York World*, *Philadelphia Record*, *Rome Tribune*, and the *St. Louis Globe-Democrat*. The library held 4,000 books.

• • • • •

The gymnasium, then in charge of W. J. Keller, physical director, was "well equipped with apparatus necessary for physical culture and systematic body-building, such as chest, rowing, and a variety of pulley machines, parallel and horizontal bars, ladders, ropes, bar-bells, dumb bells, clubs, etc." There were five baths, two with showers, and even a douche bath.[108]

Since moving in, the YMCA was open daily from 8:30 a.m. to 10 p.m. except on Sundays when the open hours were from 2 to 5 p.m. The criteria for membership had not changed very much since the YMCA reconstituted itself in 1875. Here are the requirements for membership in 1892.

> Who may join? Any young man of good moral character, without regard to religious belief or preferences. Any young man in good standing in a Protestant Evangelical Church may become an active member, and as such is entitled to vote and hold office. Any young man of good moral character is eligible to associate membership and is entitled to the same privileges as the active member, except voting and holding office. Any person who contributes annually the sum of ten dollars or upward may become a sustaining member. Ticket admits to all privileges of the association, except voting and holding office.

In 1892, the Nashville YMCA had 652 members of whom 315 were active, 91 associate members, and 246 sustaining members. There were 48,840 visitors to the building during the year, including 20,314 to the reading room. The most popular classes were the Sunday afternoon evangelistic men's meetings that averaged 48 in attendance. The second most popular class was the Sunday meetings for boys. Their average attendance was 40. The employment bureau had limited effectiveness. During the year, the YMCA found jobs for only 37 young men.

The Depression of 1893

Nashville and the rest of the country suffered through a severe depression that manifested itself in 1893. Its effects on the Nashville YMCA were sufficiently strong that between 1893 and 1902, the largest gift the association received was $2,000. The small staff and precarious income stifled growth. Turning inward, E. S. McFadden launched a series of men's Gospel meetings on Saturday and Sunday nights and additional meetings on Sunday afternoons. They were well-attended and brought some stability to the association.[109]

It seems remarkable that, in the depths of the 1893 depression, which hit Nashville's black population particularly hard, the YMCA had the energy, foresight, and progressiveness to talk to William Hinton, a young colored man, about the possibility of him moving to Nashville and establishing a Colored Men's Branch. In his visit, Hinton spoke to young colored men in the city. He was discouraged because there was almost no interest, a not-surprising development given that a large percentage of the city's young colored men were unemployed. Nothing came of the effort, but a seed was planted that would bear fruit later.[110]

One positive effort the YMCA made in 1893–94 was to bring in prominent speakers and musicals. Among those who spoke were E. B. Stahlman, publisher of the *Nashville Banner*; James H. Kirkland, the recently elected chancellor of Vanderbilt University; Reverend DeWitt Talmage; John Bell Keeble, one of Nashville's most prominent attorneys; and the Rev. Marcus B. DeWitt, a Cumberland Presbyterian minister who lived on Woodland Street. The Mozart Orchestra and the Schubert Male Quartet also gave performances during the year.[111]

By 1893, the YMCA board was well aware of the new building's deficiencies. Two related omissions were that the building had neither dormitory space nor a restaurant or cafeteria. Because the National YMCA had been pushing for both amenities before construction was started in 1886, it seems likely that "Uncle Robert" Weidensall had suggested the inclusion of these features, which were ignored, during his visit before construction started.[112]

W. S. Parks became physical education director in September. He stayed only six months, and was followed in 1894 by A. B. Barnard, who came from Pawtucket, RI, where he was the YMCA's physical director. An expert gymnast, with twelve years of YMCA experience, this gifted athlete also was interested in science. Under his leadership, social and physical activities increased, helping to balance the program that had always been heavily tilted to religious activities. Every Saturday morning, a wagon left the YMCA at 8 a.m. conveying Barnard and members to Williams' Grove for nature study and picnics. During Barnard's four years as physical director, he perfected a hot air balloon that flew over Nashville and was probably one of the first of its kind, a predecessor of the Zeppelin.[113]

Some good news came in November 1893 when Isidore Newman, of New Orleans, sent a major contribution to the Nashville Association. E. S. McFadden, Nashville's general secretary, wrote him a thank-you letter on December 1. A number of Nashville YMCA board members also wrote Newman, too many for him to thank individually. The Nashville Association needed some good news because bad news was on the way.

A Devastating Fire

A disastrous fire, discovered at 4:25 in the morning on October 5, 1894, badly damaged the association's five-year-old building. *The American* reported, "The YMCA Building near Church and Cherry streets was yesterday morning transformed into ruins and ashes. The front wall fell carrying telephone and telegraph wires along the south side of the street. Floor after floor went down and so did the roof."[114]

When the fire department arrived with all its horse-drawn engines, the handsome YMCA Building was a mass of flames. "Tongues of fire were issuing from the windows in the front and rear, and, at first glance, it looked as if the entire block was doomed. The fire started in the basement boiler room in the rear of the building and spread with great rapidity." Because the streets were blocked with people, Captain E. M. Carell and his men stretched ropes across Church Street to hold them back. Despite the heroic efforts of the firemen, the YMCA building, one of the most imposing in the city, was a mass of ruins. The library, one of the finest in the South, with 3,000 volumes, was completely wrecked, as was the gymnasium with all its paraphernalia."[115] Fortunately, the association had insurance on the building amounting to $27,500. The directors doubted it would be sufficient.

E. B. Stahlman, a YMCA director and publisher of the *Nashville Banner*, had more than one reason to worry. His newspaper was next door. The *Banner* building was saved, primarily because heavy fire doors separated the two buildings. The *Banner*'s editorial rooms on the fourth floor of the Y were heavily damaged, however, and all the files in those offices were destroyed. The Nashville Athletic Club, immediately east of the YMCA, was also saved,[116] and, by 6 a.m., the firemen had the fire under control. YMCA officials, standing behind the rope, didn't see much positive. The blackened walls remained standing, but the interior seemed to be gutted from basement to cupola. Their despondence grew as floor after floor gave away, each falling with a loud crash. The debris on the ground floor continued to pile up. The cupola was the last to catch fire and, when it did, it lit up downtown for blocks around. When the fire was at its zenith, it became obvious that the triangular-shaped front wall would soon give way and fall. Just after the firemen were warned to get away, the wall did collapse, breaking telephone, telegraph, and electric wires. The Western Union Telegraph Company's wires were hit with such force that two poles supporting them snapped in two just below the cross-arms. The Nashville Electric Railway's trolley wire was broken from Cherry to College Street.

Matt Pilcher probably felt the loss as badly as E. B. Stahlman. Pilcher had worked tirelessly to make the building a reality, and had been one of the most generous contributors to the building fund. It had been his one ambition to see the building completed. Now, only five years later, the building had, in a space of two hours, disappeared before his eyes. Tenants on the second floor—W. D. Gale, W. P. Rutland & Co., Fulcher & Dyas, Haddock and Ambrose, and Theo Cooley—lost all their furniture and suffered water damage. Thankfully, most had property insurance.

Through the courtesy of John M. Gaut, general manager of the Cumberland Presbyterian Publishing House, temporary quarters for the YMCA were secured on the first floor of the Cumberland Presbyterian Building at 154 North Cherry Street, and bathing facilities were made available in the basement.[117] On Saturday night, the men's service, held at the publishing house, was crowded and the Sunday afternoon boys' gospel service the next day had an unusually large crowd. Other citizens helped. Chancellor George Payne of Peabody College, and George Price, principal of the Nashville College for Young Ladies, both lent gym equipment until the YMCA could afford to replace what it lost. John H. Howe, manager of the Howe Ice Company, enclosed a $50 check with his letter of sympathy. He mentioned that he had been a member of the boys' department "when Mr. McFadden was in charge of that work." Many others wrote letters of condolence.[118]

The association used the insurance money to pay off their indebtedness. Unfortunately, this left the Y with a badly damaged building and no money with which to rebuild. The YMCA work continued, however, at the Cumberland Presbyterian Publishing House and in rented rooms. Contractors surveyed the damaged building and convinced the board that they could, with repairs, reopen the gymnasium, the swimming pool, and the offices and parlors. To pay for this partial restoration, the association put a mortgage of $10,000 on the property.[119]

The Nashville Association celebrated its 20th anniversary on Sunday, January 27, 1895, and the YMCA moved back to the partially restored building on the street-level floor in early February.[120] By then, the ladies' auxiliary was gearing up to refurbish the renovated rooms and parlors.

The gymnasium renovation was far enough along for it to be put back in use in April. The renovation of the swimming pool took seventeen months longer, partially because the YMCA board enlarged it to measure 15' wide and 50' long. When it reopened in August 1896, the pool proved to be very popular. According to a YMCA brochure from that year, the bathing facilities were called, "The best in Tennessee." Conversely, the third and fourth floors were too badly damaged to be repaired.[121]

E. S. McFadden and his directors were aware of the inadequacies of the Church Street building even before the fire. In truth, it was out-of-date soon after it was completed simply because the direction of association work nationally had radically changed. For example, boys' work in the early 1890s was scarcely known. By the middle of the decade, it had become one of the most important aspects of a modern YMCA. The lack of dormitory space and a separate entrance for boys, no restaurant facilities, an inadequate gymnasium, and insufficient space for the boys' department were annoying, particularly since cities no larger than Nashville were building imposing new buildings with such facilities. To compensate, in the mid to late 1890s, nearly all activities were held elsewhere. Meeting and programs were frequently held in parks and church basements. Cross-country runs became popular. Some of the boys' work was moved to the nearby First Presbyterian Church.

A longer-term solution was to sell the building for what they could get, and use the money to purchase a more commodious and desirable lot for the erection of an up-to-date building. This was impossible on their shallow inside lot on Church Street so the board of directors quietly advertised the building for sale.

Meanwhile, the ladies' auxiliary did what it could to make a bad situation better. Mrs. J. H. McClure, president, and Mrs. Will Manier, treasurer, raised $180 to provide a carpet for a room for boys' work. After the reading rooms were restored, the ladies also redecorated them.

The YMCA officers who had to deal with the somewhat crippled situation in 1896 were Henry Sperry, president, who succeeded M. L. Pilcher; A. L. Purinton, vice president; J. D. Hamilton, treasurer; J. U. Rust, recording secretary; E. S. McFadden, general secretary; and A. B. Barnard, physical director.[122]

Perhaps motivated by the revivalist Sam Jones' preaching in 1885 about the evils of alcohol and certainly by the presence of 175 licensed saloons and seven licensed billiard parlors in Nashville, 736 YMCA members visited five saloons and two billiard parlors on Saturday night, November 1, between 7:30 and 8:30. They urged, undoubtedly without success, the owners to close their places of business for the sake of the community. The YMCA leaders also asked patrons to quit patronizing immoral places. That was like stopping the flow of Stones River with a sieve.

Tennessee Centennial Celebration and the Spanish-American War

The Tennessee Centennial Celebration opened on the old West Side Park on April 1 and ran through September 1897. During the six months of the celebration, thousands of visitors saw Arthur W. Bernard, the YMCA's physical director, ride a bicycle suspended in the air from a cigar-shaped balloon that he built. Bernard propelled the bicycle by foot power. His initial performance was so well received that he repeated it a number of times during the Centennial.

During Mr. McFadden's administration, A. Allen Jameson became boys' secretary and the work of the boys' department flourished as in no other time in the history of the YMCA. Numerous activities were conducted for the boys and a large group of them met every Sunday afternoon in a religious meeting. In 1935, many Nashville men in their forties and early fifties spoke highly of the influence for good training they received in the boys' department during the time Mr. Jameson was secretary.

This year, the annual meeting was held January 7, 1898, in the directors' room at the YMCA. After supper, the directors elected Henry Sperry, president; J. U. Rust, vice president; J. D. Hamilton, treasurer; and W. W. Scoville, recording secretary. E. S. McFadden's general secretary report was distributed the next day to ten churches—Christian, Methodist, Presbyterian, and Cumberland Presbyterian. At each church, a YMCA layman gave the substance of the annual report.[123]

Just a few months later, the Spanish-American War, the biggest event since the 1893 recession, broke out in the spring of 1898. The National YMCA's work on army bases during the war led, that year, to the establishment of the YMCA's Army and Navy Department.[124]

The First Tennessee Regiment, recruited in Nashville in May, was the only Tennessee regiment to see combat service. Consequently, not too many YMCA members were temporarily lost to the war.

In the winter of 1898, E. S. McFadden was anxious to inaugurate a membership canvass and start work on repairing the swimming pool. Twelve days later, he was present at the annual meeting where Henry Sperry was reelected president. A. K. Jones was the physical director, having replaced Arthur Bernard.

While the board was meeting, an athletic contest was held in the gym with competition in four events: standing long jump, high jump, shot put, and pull ups. The winner of the high jump cleared 5'1."[125]

• • • • •

In 1899, the Nashville Association published a booklet describing how the YMCA was uplifting the spiritual lives of Nashville's boys and men:

- Evangelistic meetings for men, Sundays 4 to 5 p.m., October and November;
- Week of prayer the second week in November;
- Junior Department Gospel Services, every Sunday 2:30 to 3:30 p.m. October through December;
- Special Bible study classes Tuesday 7 to 8 pm, all year;
- Boys Bible Class Sunday afternoons 3:30 to 4:00 p.m., all year; and
- Youth Bible classes Monday afternoons, 4 to 5 p.m., all year.

• • • • •

The last year of the 19th century was one of the most successful in the history of the Nashville YMCA. Attendance at social meetings totaled 4,841. From September 1899 to May 1900, 5,948 people attended religious department events. The total attendance during this period was 44,649, or an average of 165 per day.[126] Tough times were ahead, however, as the deficiencies of the building became apparent.

• • • • •

NASHVILLE MEN

Published by The Young Men's Christian Association

VOL. 2 NASHVILLE, TENN., MAY 22, 1902. NO. 19.

W. D. WEATHERFORD.

The Tennessee College Y. M. C. A. Secretary, Mr. W. D. Weatherford, has received a call to the Southern student secretaryship of the International Committee, the place which has been filled by Mr. H. L. McIlhaney, of Virginia. Mr. Weatherford is also the physical director at Vanderbilt University.

He has many friends in Nashville who, while heartily congratulating him on his deserved promotion, will be right sorry to have him leave the city.

Passion Play.

The Bible class was fortunate in having a beautiful presentation of the Passion Play given complimentary to them last Tuesday.

The moving pictures were exceptionally fine, while the singing added materially to the value of the production. The lecture by Mr. Hutchings was of great interest, and was delivered with a beautifully clear voice. It is safe to say that not one present will ever forget this evening. The kindness of Messrs. Hutchings and Snyder was heartily appreciated. Some delicious frappe at the close was refreshing.

Railroad Meeting.

A meeting in the special interest of railroad men will be held at the First Baptist Church Sunday, June 1.

State Secretary McGill will speak on the Y. M. C. A. railroad work throughout the world. The story is a fascinating one.

Bible Class.

The attendance for the three Saturdays in May, notwithstanding the hot weather, was 173, an average of 58. This is a most remarkable number for this season.

Another class will be held on Saturday, although the class regularly closed the last Saturday in April.

Boat Excursion.

There were 244 paid tickets and 8 complimentaries taken for the steamboat excursion. Of the tickets taken 101 were cash at the boat, 30 were sold by the office, and 113 were sold by members. A few have not yet reported from the sale of tickets.

While the profit will be small, the excursion was delightfully successful.

A Handsome Gift.

An elegantly gotten up copy of the official history of the Tennessee Centennial Exposition has been placed in our library with the compliments of the N., C. & St. L. Railroad. It is a most valuable and highly appreciated addition to the library.

CHAPTER FOUR

Hanging Tough
1900–1903

THE YMCA BOARD of directors reelected Henry Sperry as president for his fifth consecutive one-year term in 1900. Other officers elected were James U. Rust, vice president; J. D. Hamilton, treasurer; and W. H. Sherman, recording secretary. Board members included Matt B. Pilcher, W. R. Manier, George M. Ingram, John D. Blanton, B. G. Alexander, and J. C. Cullom, Sperry and Hamilton were both trustees of Merchants Bank. James U. Rust was a partner in Jungerman and Rust Grocers.[127]

The members at the turn of the century continued to be young men and boys. The Y's principal attractions were its heated swimming pool and a gymnasium. Members could swim, play basketball, work out with barbells, and then take a shower. There were several basketball teams in 1900. Basketball had been invented nine years earlier by James Naismith at Springfield College in Massachusetts. Two of the teams, the businessmen and the seniors, played on March 12.[128]

Every Sunday afternoon, there was a spiritual meeting, optional for members and open to non-members. There were two weekly meetings for boys; one for boys between 10 and 13 and another for boys 14–16. These meetings were open to every Caucasian boy in the city.[129]

In an effort to attract new members, the YMCA held a reception for editors, reporters, printers, pressmen, lithographers, and bookbinders on January 23. The ladies' auxiliary produced the affair. The indefatigable Capt. Matt Pilcher was chairman of the event. The program, which consisted of musical and literary presentations, was warmly received. Refreshments were then served and a basketball game was played by two teams picked from members of the gymnasium class.[130]

For the first time in the Association's history, the Nashville YMCA opened a boys' camp. It was located on the south side and in the floodplain of the South Harpeth River at Allison's Mill in Davidson County's 14th Civil District. Immediately across the river from the camp was a spring flowing from the base of a high bluff. During the depression and later, there was a camp there called Clearwater Beach. The property, now known as Rau-Wood Retreat Center, was purchased by the Nashville Lutherans, Inc., a non-profit organization, in 1963 and was still owned by this group in 2011.[131]

On June 19, thirty-two boys left Union Station for camp, chaperoned by new boys' department director, A. Allen Jameson, and E. E. Ingram. A day before, wagons loaded with provisions were sent out to the campsite from the YMCA building. Another adult camp supervisor, C. C. Crutchfield, met the campers when they departed the train at Bellevue. The camp was named in honor of W. R. Manier of Manier, Dunbar and Company, and a YMCA board member. The intention was for the summer camp to become an annual program of the Y.[132]

Abbott Replaces McFadden

The biggest local association news in 1900 was the resignation of E. S. McFadden, the YMCA's excellent general secretary effective September 1. McFadden would later accept the general secretary position at the Macon, Georgia, YMCA.[133]

Board member B. G. Alexander acted as interim general secretary until the Nashville Association could find a permanent successor to McFadden. When Walter B. Abbott assumed the general secretary position on November 15, Alexander moved to Richmond, Virginia, to accept a position as assistant secretary at their association. In 1902, he would become the Knoxville Y's general secretary.[134] The YMCA welcomed Mr. Abbott with a reception at the association building given by the ladies' auxiliary. The YMCA orchestra furnished the music.[135]

Walter Abbott became immediately popular. Over six feet tall, and possessed of a contagious personality and a hearty laugh, he surveyed the association's programs and decided they needed more balance. Soon after arriving, Abbott decided to have a second season of summer camp at Allison's Mill. Eighteen miles from Nashville and about six miles from the railroad station at Bellevue, this would be a place where boys in short trousers and cotton stockings could enjoy the great outdoors by living in tents with no running water.

Abbott also establishing a large Bible class for men, and encouraged Y members to take part in civic affairs. Interested in physical fitness, he organized one of the first anti-smoking leagues for boys under sixteen years of age.[136] During the three years that Walter Abbott served as general secretary, "a spirit of comradeship and good will prevailed among the association members."[137]

Basketball, Boys, and Business

In Early December 1900, the Nashville YMCA basketball team challenged Vanderbilt to a game. Until then, Vanderbilt had only an intramural team. With a week's notice, Willis D. Weatherford, a graduate student, put together a Vanderbilt team that played the YMCA on December 15, 1900. Unaccustomed to the mesh wire backboards, the Commodores lost 22–19. Later that winter, Vanderbilt beat the YMCA team twice, 24–9 and 14–12.[138]

The 26th annual meeting of the YMCA of Nashville met in the Association building on Friday, January 25, at 6:30 p.m. At the meeting, Edgar Foster was elected president to follow Henry Sperry, who declined to serve a sixth term. The thirty-one-year-old Edgar Foster, business manager of the *Nashville Banner*, had been one of the charter members of the first boys' group organized by the YMCA in 1884 and had continued active in its ranks through his teenager years.[139]

The Nashville Association opened 1901 with a membership of 612. In April, there were 17 membership renewals and 28 new members, double the number than for all of 1900. Abbott's good work had a hand in this membership spike.[140] April also saw the introduction of a new association newsletter, *Nashville Men* that replaced the *Association Bulletin* that the association published two decades earlier. The first issue of *Nashville Men* appeared April 25, 1901. The subscription fee was twenty-five cents a year, payable in advance.

Secretary Abbott saw to it that *Nashville Men* kept the association members aware of the deficiencies of their own building and the fact that other associations, both larger and smaller than Nashville, had buildings planned or underway. The May 9 issue identified Asheville, NC; Augusta, GA; Colorado Springs; Joplin, MO; and Newark, NJ as planning or constructing new buildings. Abbott wrote in the same issue, "Ten years ago the Nashville Association conducted a splendid work in a $50,000 building. Today, it struggles along in quarters worth perhaps $20,000." Abbott also urged the association to pay off its $10,000 debt and to consider renovating the top two floors as dormitories. It was later determined that to do so would cost $5,000.[141]

In its second season, the Y's camp on the South Harpeth operated from July 2 to August 1. In 1901, the camp was renamed for the general executive, Walter Abbott. Camp Abbott had three sessions that summer with the youngest boys, called juniors, going from July 2 to July 11; intermediates from July 16 to July 25; and business boys from July 26 to Aug 1. Each division was limited to 22 boys. To reach Camp Abbott, the boys and their counselors assembled at Union Station at 6:45 on the day of departure. They took the train to Bellevue, and, from there, went by wagons the seven miles to the camp. Allen Jamison was in charge of the camp, and Dr. D. B. Blake returned as camp physician. A Bible, tennis shoes, fishing tackle, and musical instruments, for those who had them, were some of the items taken. No swimming was allowed except during swimming hours and in the presence of a leader. Cots were provided for sleeping in tents.

Despite having an outstanding boys' program, a steam-heated indoor pool second to none in the city, an attractive reading room, and one of the best equipped gymnasiums in Nashville, the YMCA was faulted for allowing its building to fall into decay. The top two floors were uninhabitable. The headline of an article in the June 6 issue of the *Nashville Men* was, "Nashville Has Suffered its YMCA to Grow Backward." The same issue had, on its front page, an illustration of the front of the building that proved the point. The next issue declared, "The building is a reproach to the city."

Despite the building's shortcomings, there were 25 basketball teams playing in the winter of 1900–1901, including the YMCA team that played Vanderbilt. Five hundred members used the gym during the previous fiscal year and total attendance at the Y was 13,400. Enough members were playing handball that handball rules were spelled out.[142]

In 1901, up-to-date books, magazines, and illustrated papers were to be found in the reading room. *The Bowen Blade*, *The MBA Bulletin* and the *High School Echo* were popular with the alumni of those schools.[143] Adjoining the reading room was the ladies' auxiliary parlor, where the women demanded absolute silence. The downstairs business office contained a number of illustrated magazines, papers and an assortment of newspapers.

Magazines available were: *Harper's*, *Century*, *Scribner's*, *Review of Reviews*, *Outing*, *Leslie's*, *Munsey's*, *McClures*, *Cosmopolitan*, *Current Literature*, *World's Work*, *St. Nicholas*, *Home Magazine*, *Recreation*—all monthly. The weekly magazines available were *Saturday Evening Post*, *Harper's*, *Scientific American*, *Public Opinion*, *Collier's*. *Illustrated London News*, *Puck*, *Judge*, *Ladies Home Journal*, *Outlook*, *Ram's Horn*, *Sunday School Times*, and *Interior*—a pretty impressive collection.

In 1901, physical director, A. K. Jones, and Allen Jameson published a five-page brochure on the boys' department. One page each was devoted to the junior section, the intermediate section, the business boys' section, and the advanced section.

The rapid growth of the boys' department, from 188 in 1900 to 279 in 1901, caused the addition of a fourth session. The growth also prompted the department to employ, for the first time, an assistant, John E. Dodge of Galesburg, Illinois. This accomplished athlete and gymnast began work October 1. The opening gymnasium classes in 1900 numbered 102. A year later, the number had skyrocketed to 150.[144]

Nineteen hundred and one ended with receipts exceeding outlays by 24 cents. The membership fees of $10 for men, $5 for boys and $1 for women were the chief sources of income. Paying the 5 percent interest on the association's $10,000 debt was difficult as large gifts were as rare as hens' teeth. In its twenty-six-year history, the largest gift the Nashville Y ever received was $2,500.[145]

In mid-October, the Nashville YMCA basketball team played the Chattanooga Association team, winning 21–16. The game was publicized as the first inter-association game of the season.[146]

• • • • •

In 1901, James E. Caldwell, president of the Cumberland Telephone and Telegraph Company, took what may have been the first public stand against the evils of smoking by a Nashville businessman. On December 1, he wrote his employees the following letter: "We desire to direct your special attention to the company's rule prohibiting cigarette smoking on or off duty. A violation of this rule will prevent you being considered for advancement, and may result in your dismissal from the company's service. There is no successful future ahead of the cigarette fiend.[147] Caldwell's letter was published in the *Nashville Men* because a number of YMCA members worked at the telephone company.

• • • • •

The Y's physical department was so proud of its success that it produced a brochure for the 1901–1902 season. It included photographs of the gymnasium, the director's office, the examining room, and A. K. Jones, the physical director. That winter the department hosted 25 classes, including five for boys. Lock boxes with combination locks were available for 50 cents a year. The subscribed uniforms for men featured black quarter-length shirts, full length gray pants with a black stripe on the outside seam, and black slippers, and, for boys, black quarter-length shirts, black knee tights and black slippers. There were nineteen showers and seven porcelain tubs. The pool was 15x50 feet in length with a depth of 3 feet 6 inches in the shallow end and 6 feet 6 inches in the deep end. The annual fee was $10, paid in advance.[148]

Neither a Church nor a College

In January 1902, the Nashville Association issued a statement about what the institution was and what it was not. The statement read: "The YMCA is not a church although it saves souls; it is not a college although it educates; it is not a sanitarium although it promotes health and cleanliness; it is not an inn or saloon although it does furnish both comfort and pleasure. It is a young men's home downtown, where opportunity is given for recreation, education, physical training and religious instruction."[149]

At the Nashville Association's 27th annual meeting, the board adopted unanimously a much-deserved tribute to Captain Matt B. Pilcher. The resolution read,

> Whereas Capt, M. B. Pilcher has been longer identified with the YMCA of Nashville than any person now holding membership in the organization, his connection dating back to the pioneer organization which existed a few years prior to the war, and, during his service in the Confederate Army, he was active in conserving the moral and spiritual welfare of his comrades in arms, and, on the organization of NashvilleAssociation in 1875, he became one of the charter members and was elected the first president of the new association, and, whereas his interest in the welfare of the association has never flagged during the years that have followed, for he has stood nobly by the work during days of adversity as well as prosperity, and has contributed largely of his time and means to the advancement of the work, and has served the association for ten years as president during the twenty-seven years of its existence, therefore be it resolved, by the members assembled in the twenty-seventh business session, that in grateful appreciation of his earnest efforts and wise counsels, Capt. M. B. Pilcher is hereby elected a life member of the YMCA of Nashville, and an honorary member of the board of directors.[150]

On February 10, 1902, the board held its first meeting of the new year and re-elected the following officers: president, Edgar M. Foster; vice president, J. U. Rust; treasurer, J. D. Hamilton; and recording secretary, Matt G. Buckner.[151]

Spirits at the Y were lifted when Sam Jones returned to the city in March. This time, his revival was held in the Union Gospel Tabernacle. At one meeting, a reported 8,000 men showed up with some even sitting on window ledges. Some YMCA members in attendance squirmed in their seats as Jones admonished the Nashville YMCA for its inadequate building and for giving more emphasis to physical and social programs than to Bible study. Jones bluntly said, "The Y, which is no more than a gymnasium, with a little seasoning of moral restraint thrown in, is not living up to its name." Jones felt that the name "Christian" in the Y's name meant that all other departments should be subordinate to the work of leading young men into a saving relationship with Christ." As a result of this rebuke, the YMCA revitalized the religious work committee, and men's meetings were again conducted on Sunday afternoons.[152]

Allen Jameson, YMCA's physical director, must have attended the revival. Some time later, he learned that the owner of a penny slot machine on Sumner Street was showing obscene pictures. Jameson had the man arrested.

At the trial, the man was found guilty, fined $100, and put out of business.[153]

When Jameson came to Nashville, there were 125 members in the boys' department. By 1902, there were 308 and the department was considered one of the best in the country. At a national boys' conference in Boston in January, Jameson had been besieged with questions asking what his secret was in keeping fifteen- and sixteen-year-olds involved in Y work. He had been particularly successful in grading the department into the junior, intermediate, and advanced grades. In recognition of Jameson's splendid leadership, the boys gave him a $100 Remington typewriter and a $35 oak desk.[154]

Sometime after St. Louis financiers agreed to pay for the expansion of Jere Baxter's Tennessee Central Railroad to Nashville in 1901, Jameson realized that, upon completion of the road, there might be a great opportunity to move his boys' camp to a favorable site on or near the railroad somewhere east of Nashville. By the time the Tennessee Central officially opened from South Harriman to Nashville on June 2, 1902, Jameson was ready.[155] He had secured a site at Bluff Springs, two miles from Gordonsville, 65 miles east of Nashville, and only one-half mile from the railroad. Camp Felder, named for Thomas J. Felder, a warm friend and supporter of the Nashville YMCA, was located on a bluff above the Caney Fork River. The expense for the ten-day camp, including railroad fare, was $7.50. Parents had no problem in entrusting their boys to Jameson, who, in five years of running boys' camps, had never had a serious accident or mishap.

Each day began with a bugler awaking the campers at 6 a.m. Breakfast was at 7 followed by a devotional by the river. During the morning, the boys divided into small groups to hike, wade and hunt frogs in the creek, play games, swim, fish, row, or hunt for clams in the Caney Fork. After lunch at noon, the boys could relax on their cots in their tents until 1 p.m. when they gathered to play baseball, hold sham battles, or engage in some other form of athletics. On the Fourth of July, the Camp Felder baseball club got walloped by the Gordonsville team 14–8. The bugler attracted the boys to supper each day at 6. About 7, a bugler sounded assembly and the boys gathered around a great bonfire to sing songs, tell stories, and listen to a short evening service. The boys then retired to their tents where taps ended the evening.[156]

The boys returned to Nashville on Thursday evening. During the ten days at Camp Felder, they did not complain and stayed so well that the camp physician, Dr. D. B. Blake, "grew weary of his enforced idleness." The last day of camp, the entire group was given free passes by the Tennessee Central Railroad to ride on the train to Monterey where they had a free dinner at Hotel Cumberland. A wrecked train at Buffalo Valley delayed them by several hours. Fortunately, Thomas J. Felder had sent along 80 bags of salted peanuts that saved the day. The delay forced the boys to have to stay overnight at the new hotel. That afternoon, they walked through Monterey Park and played games on the hotel grounds. Thursday morning, the party returned to Camp Felder at 5 a.m. They spent the day breaking camp and returning to Nashville. The boys were particularly enthusiastic in their praise of Mr. Jameson, who was "a past master" in the management of a group of boys. On July 12, a new group of 58 boys arrived at Carthage Junction and ran across the fields to the camp.[157]

In 1902, *Nashville Men*, YMCA's weekly newspaper, began to call for a new building to replace the partially burned-out building that it still occupied. The newspaper's columns were filled with pleas such as these: "Without an assembly room for meetings, the Association is endeavoring to conduct religious work. Without rooms for class work, it struggles through with classes. Without separate accommodations, it is trying to conduct definite work for boys." *Nashville Men* also pointed out that more than 800 men and boys were using bath and toilet facilities barely adequate for half that number. The economy was bad, money was scarce, and the paucity of financial support was discouraging. The newspaper changed its focus to plea for funds to meet the association's day-to day expenses. When the Nashville Y raised its dues from $10 to $12, membership slipped from the 615 it had been on January 1st.[158]

To compensate for not having an adequate building, the YMCA stressed activities that could be held elsewhere such as the boys' camp, boat excursions, minstrel shows in church basements, watermelon cuttings in parks, and cross-country runs that started at the end of the St. Cecelia carline, crossed the new bridge over the Cumberland, and continued along the east side of the river.[159]

Despite a tough financial situation, the Nashville Association built an addition on the back of the building. It was badly needed to accommodate the growing boys' department. By the end of the year, it was finished except for the boys' bathrooms and still needing some furniture for the new educational classrooms. Wm. W. Scovel, chairman of the building committee, was lauded for his "painstaking and faithful work," that had been set back about a month by a strike. Forty-one of the older boys pitched in $1 each in the fall to help furnish the annex.[160] In March, the Y also got a new barbershop.

A Lack of Large Gifts

There were two new staff members in 1902: R. E. Bartlett Jr., physical director, and Eugene R. Howard, membership secretary. Bartlett, a graduate of the Springfield Training School, replaced A. K. Jones, who went to the Indianapolis Association. Howard came from the Knoxville Association. General secretary Abbott had been able to recruit them despite the fact that the damaged YMCA building was still burdened with a $10,000 mortgage. Although Nashville was a wealthy, cultured city, and the Y was doing more than associations in most cities its size, it galled Abbott that the Nashville Y had never received large gifts.[161]

• • • • •

Basketball was all the rage in 1903. That winter the Y had fifty-two men playing on six teams.[162]

• • • • •

The association's 28th annual meeting was held January 29, 1903, "in our new room," meaning the annex. There was no change in the officers, and E. M. Foster was re-elected president. It was reported at the meeting that membership on January 1 was 506 men, down considerably from the 612 a year earlier. On a more positive note, the treasurer reported that the association showed a positive balance at year-end, "the second time in many years that this happy announcement has been made."[163]

The YMCA launched a successful membership campaign in March, with 103 men present for the closing banquet at the Tulane Hotel, each man wearing a "get one" button on his lapel. Governor Benton McMillin and Governor James B. Frazier spoke. Abbott said, it was "easily the greatest social event in our history and probably never surpassed by any YMCA in the South." Three hundred new members were enrolled.[164]

General secretary Abbott kept up the pressure on the directors to take the necessary steps to build or acquire a new building. In the April 24 issue of *Nashville Men*, he showed a photograph of the Knoxville Y. That association had recently acquired the four-story Palace Hotel and converted it into their headquarters. It had, on the upper floors dormitory rooms that could house 40 men. In the next week's issue, Abbott showed pictures of new YMCA buildings in Memphis and Chattanooga.

In late June, having gotten wind that Walter Abbott, the well-respected general secretary of the Nashville Association, was about to accept the call from New Orleans, a large number of disappointed Nashville members met to see if they could avert this. Charles Gilbert presided. Many members spoke of their appreciation for what Mr. Abbott meant to them. One said, "There was never a general secretary of any association who won his way into the hearts and lives of the young men and boys of a city more completely than has Mr. Abbott." Strong resolutions were adopted urging Mr. Abbott not to leave. Twenty-seven people sent him personal telegrams. Abbott responded with a telegram sent from New Orleans. It read, "Telegrams greatly appreciated. N. O. too strong, however. Have accepted."[165]

The YMCA's camp in 1903 was again held at Camp Felder. This year, boys from the Nashville, Murfreesboro, and Bowling Green YMCAs attended. The 60 campers ranged from 12 to 15 years of age, and each boy paid $8 that included the all expenses from Nashville to camp and back. Once again, the boys slept on cots in tents pitched on the bluff overlooking the river. There was a counselor and six boys per tent, a physician on duty, and a first class cook. The boys affectionately called Allen Jameson the "general." Someone said, "Every boy and man who has been in one of his camps will testify that he is all right. Good-natured, mindful of everything necessary for the campers' comfort, thoughtful, willing, and strictly up-to-date, he makes sure that every body has a fine time."[166]

One of the first steps, E. M. Foster took in his efforts to secure the best possible successor to Walter Abbott was to contact the International Committee of the YMCA in New York City. In response, C. L. Gates, the Southern field secretary for the committee, came to Nashville where he was helpful in identifying Burtt S. Fenn, general secretary of the Roanoke YMCA, as an excellent candidate. Gates also identified two more staff candidates, Fred West, who subsequently accepted the position of physical director and John K. Taylor, of Brooklyn, NY, who would come as his assistant.[167]

E. M. Foster could not attend much of the state convention on the 30th as, in the middle of the day, he and the other members of the Nashville board were interviewing Burtt Fenn for the open position in Nashville.

The feeling of the directors, following the meeting, was that Fenn, considered one of the bright stars in YMCA work, was almost certain to be called.[168]

On Sunday before Walter Abbott left for New Orleans, he was honored at a surprise going-away party. Edgar Foster, the president of the Y, introduced Charles Gilbert, who paid a heart-felt tribute to Mr. Abbott and then presented him with "a solid gold watch, chain, and Masonic charm, together with a beautifully-bound and embossed book containing the autographs of nearly all the persons connected in any way with the association." The watch was engraved with the monogram "W.B.A." on the case and the following inscription: "Presented to Mr. Walter Brooks Abbott, a Christian gentleman, August 2, 1903, by the Nashville YMCA members. General Secretary, Nashville, Tenn. YMCA, Nov 15, 1900 to July 31, 1903."[169]

Charles Gilbert may have written these words about Walter Brooks Abbott.

> Nearly three years ago an unassuming, genial stranger came into our midst. Last week this gentleman, beloved and honored by hundreds of Nashville people, departed. His cordiality, his culture, his refinement, his manliness, his ability, his frankness, his broadmindedness, his spirituality soon caused him to be recognized as a superior man. His conception of Jesus Christ as a man of courage, and valor, and strength, as well as possessing all the gentler qualities, was imparted to those with whom he came in contact. Many learned from him that 'A merry heart doeth good like a medicine,' while many others imbibed the truth of his teaching, 'If any man hath not the spirit of Christ he is none of his.' He will live long in the lives of his Nashville friends. He is one of the choice men of the earth, and a Christian gentleman, Mr. Walter Brooks Abbott.[170]

• • • • •

Oakdale was a railroad junction on the Cincinnati Southern Railroad in Morgan County, TN.

CHAPTER FIVE

The Burtt Fenn Years

1903–1906

HAVING ACCEPTED THE CALL of the Nashville Association early in August, Burtt Fenn arrived in Nashville on October 16, 1903. When he stepped off the train at Union Station, a crowd of one hundred YMCA members were there to give him a rebel yell and accompany him to the YMCA where a reception was held in his honor.

A native of Missouri, Fenn was a thirty-year-old bachelor when he became general secretary of the Nashville Association. Trained at the Chicago Training School, his first YMCA job was at the Springfield, MO, Association. From there he went to Roanoke, Virginia, where he had five productive years as their general executive. When he arrived at Roanoke, the membership was 117 and the association worked out of a small building that afterwards sold for $500. When Fenn left Roanoke in 1903 to accept the Nashville call, the membership was over 500 in a city of only 23,000. Five of his board members thought enough of the work he was accomplishing that they each gave $1,000 to the association's building fund.[171]

In January, the Nashville Y received a visit from two men from New Orleans—

> Mr. A. H. Ford and Edwin A. Neugass. Ford was vice president of the New Orleans Association and financial agent of New Orleans philanthropist, Isidore Newman. Neugass was Newman's son-in-law. It seems possible that Walter Abbott, the general secretary of the New Orleans YMCA told them about the good work being done at the Nashville Association. At any rate, Ford and Neugass seemed pleased with what they saw and took a special interest in the Y's work with boys. Earlier, Mr. Newman had sent the Nashville Y a check for $1,000 to build baths and toilets for boys in the first floor annex.[172]

Isidore Newman's name is well-known across the country because the school he founded in 1903, Isidore Newman School, is where pro-football player Peyton Manning went to high school. Located on Jefferson Avenue in uptown New Orleans, it began with one building and was founded to educate children living in the Jewish Orphans Home on St. Charles Ave. From the beginning, Newman stipulated that neighborhood children could also attend. Today, Newman is one of the most respected independent schools in New Orleans.[173]

The board met at noon on January 27 to elect officers for 1904. Elected were E. M. Foster, president, for his fourth term; J. U. Rust, vice-president; Dr. M. G. Buckner, secretary; and J. D. Hamilton, treasurer. The evening before, four directors were elected for a term of four years. Two, Dr. M. G. Buckner and E. Bright Wilson, were reelected while Leland Hume and John H. Burt were elected as new members. After the elections, Mr. F. M. Richardson urged the members to pitch in to raise at lease $1,000 to meet 1904 expenses. Immediately following the meeting, waters and chocolate were served and the YMCA orchestra played.[174] General secretary Burtt S. Fenn, who was also the editor-in-chief and business manager of *Nashville Men*, wrote in the February 19 issue, "Few associations are fortunate enough to have as President a man of the ability and activity of Mr. Foster, and none surpass him."

Wednesday Doubleheaders

In January and February, basketball double-headers were played every Wednesday night in the YMCA gym. The first week MBA beat Bowen 7–3 and Fogg High School defeated Wallace 27–4. Later, MBA and Fogg played for the

YMCA cup, with MBA winning 11–6. Later, in the city prep championship, the Maroons were upset by Fogg.[175]

In mid-January, the Nashville Athletic Club team defeated the YMCA 17–13, and Vanderbilt defeated the University of Nashville 32–6. Four intramural YMCA teams, "The Rough Riders," "The Westerners," "The Abbotts," and "The Stars" played at the YMCA gym, as did the four city league basketball teams mentioned above. Vanderbilt won the championship and received a loving cup presented by the Nashville American. Fred West deserved much of the credit for the success of the basketball season.[176] Unsatisfied, he proposed organizing a baseball league and holding an amateur athletic carnival in the Horse Show Coliseum at the State Fairgrounds in April. Events were proposed in gymnastics, intercollegiate track, novice track, open track, and a quarter mile event for boys. Teams from Alabama, Georgia, Kentucky, Mississippi, and Tennessee were invited to participate.[177] If that wasn't enough to keep him busy, he planned to take several boys in the boys' department to see the World's Fair in St. Louis in June. West and his boys left on June 8 for their trip to St. Louis. They took the NC and St. L. Railroad's "World Fair Route" through Martin, Tennessee, where they connected with the Illinois Central for the rest of the trip.[178]

Jameson and West organized the high school and preparatory school baseball league at the YMCA in the winter. Its governing board consisted of Jameson and West, the YMCA physical director, and a representative from each of the interested schools. The board arranged a schedule of games with the champion receiving the A. A. Jameson Cup. MBA, Fogg High School, and Bowen were represented at the meeting, with the high school claiming the championship over MBA by a score of 17–11.[179] West, also engineered and launched, in early January, a city basketball league consisting of teams from Vanderbilt, the YMCA, the university of Nashville and the Nashville Athletic Club. The Nashville American agreed to offer a silver trophy to the winning team.[180]

A Lack of Harmony and a New President

Japan's declaration of war on Russia on February 8, 1904, caught the world by surprise. Few could believe that an Asian country would have the audacity to take on Tsar Nicholas II's Far East Fleet at Port Arthur with a surprise attack hours before declaring war. The Russians and Japanese had both sent troops into China as part of the eight member international force to quell the Boxer Rebellion. The Japanese were incensed that the Russians had not left and were consolidating plans to take over Manchuria, having already acquired and fortified the warm-water port of Port Arthur. Feeling that Korea and Manchuria were essential buffers to stop Russian expansion to the east, the Japanese struck. When the Rev. W. B. Nance spoke on the war at the Nashville YMCA on February 20, he may have had knowledge from serving in that part of the world as a missionary. That February, no one knew who would win the war, but YMCA leaders were curious to see what Nance had to say about it.[181]

At the June 20 board meeting, Edgar Foster, who was in the middle of his fourth term as president of the YMCA of Nashville and Edgefield, resigned due to of the press of business affairs. The board issued the following statement: "Mr. Foster has been a faithful officer and member of the board of directors and his resignation was accepted with sincere regret."[182] The day after his resignation, an article in the *Nashville Banner* stated, "This resignation follows closely upon several others that have occurred recently. It is known that the official machinery of the organization has not been in smooth running order for some time, and it is said that Mr. Foster's resignation is due to the lack of harmony that has prevailed of late."[183]

At the same board meeting, the board elected Dr. Matt G. Buckner to succeed Foster as president. Although only thirty-four years old, Dr. Buckner had been a prominent worker in the association ever since he was president of the boys' department in 1886. When elected to the presidency, he was recording secretary for the board. Already a prominent and beloved physician, Dr. Buckner had also proved himself as an effective worker at First Presbyterian Church, where he had served as a deacon for five years and where, in 1904, he was elected an elder. Dr. Buckner was an 1893 graduate of Hamilton College, where he played football for two years, and an 1896 graduate of the medical department of the University of Nashville, where he was the top student in his 40-member class. While in medical school, he played a third year of football for Vanderbilt. In 1894, the proprietary medical school served both universities.[184] Beginning in the fall of 1904, Dr. Buckner would give physical exams in the physical director's office each Monday, Wednesday and Friday afternoon from 4:30 until 5:30.[185]

Camp Felder

For the third consecutive summer, the boys' department's summer camp was held at Camp Felder on the Caney Fork River. Once again, the boys rode the Tennessee Central to Carthage Junction, this year on June 30. The eighteen campers returned by the cars on July 9. The camp was under the direction of physical director Fred West and director of boys' work, Vallie C. Hart Jr. Dr. A. R. Halley was camp physician. The cost, including train fare, was $8, the same as in 1903.[186]

While in camp, West and Hart were considering offers from Walter Abbott to join him in New Orleans as physical director and assistant physical director of that association, respectively. When the directors heard about this possibility, they registered a strong protest. West accepted his offer while Hart declined only to accept in September an offer from the Woodford County, Kentucky, YMCA to handle association work there.[187]

Around Labor Day, J. S. Ford officially became physical director of the Nashville Association. He was an 1898 graduate of the Training School of Chicago, and had six years of experience with the Brooklyn and Chicago Central YMCAs. At the same time, the Nashville Y welcomed J. G. Hamaker as its new boys' department secretary, replacing Allen Jameson, who had brought the department a national reputation. Jameson left to accept the position as secretary of Boys' Welcome Hall in Brooklyn, NY.

Before leaving, Mr. Jameson gave the boys' department a large inscribed bevel-edge French Plate glass mirror. Jameson's replacement, J. G. Hamaker came with five years of YMCA experience.[188] The YMCA staff was much more professional than it had been twenty-five years earlier.

The boys' bathroom, that Isidore Newman so generously funded, was complete in September. It contained six showers and featured new dressing rooms with ample toilets and lockers. The old men's showers in the basement were replaced, and the dressing rooms there spiffed up.[189]

A Facelift for the Gym

The 26th annual State YMCA convention was held at Bristol October 13 to 16. At the time of the convention, the Nashville Association had four fulltime employees—Burtt S. Fenn, general secretary; J. S. Ford, physical director; J. G. Hamaker, boys' work director, and George W. Gore, colored secretary, and two open jobs, membership and assistant secretary. State secretary S. Waters McGill announced that there were seven associations in the state at Nashville, Chattanooga, Memphis, Knoxville, Bristol, Morristown, and Murfreesboro, where the general secretary job was unfilled.

Additionally, there were student associations at the University of Tennessee, Vanderbilt, Maryville College, and Hospital College in Memphis. There was also a railroad YMCA in Knoxville at the Southern Railroad yards. McGill said an overture had been made to the Nashville, Chattanooga, and St. Louis (N.C. & St. L.) management in Nashville to establish a YMCA for their 3,000 workers, but nothing had materialized. McGill was also working to establish small town YMCAs at Smithville, Tullahoma, Sweetwater, and Harriman.[190]

The open assistant secretary slot at the Nashville Y was actually filled while the state convention was underway. James H. Anderson arrived in town that week from Brookfield, Missouri, where he was general secretary. Like many of the younger YMCA secretaries, he was a graduate of the Chicago Training School.[191]

When physical director J. S. Ford began classes in October, there were new cluster lights in the gymnasium and a new coat of paint had been applied both to the gymnasium walls and the entrance. There were also six new lights over the pool. The staff was doing its best to make the building as attractive as possible. In the winter of 1904–05, handball was one of the most popular sports at the Y. For that reason, two new courts were fitted up on the third floor.[192] By the second week in January, one of the courts was in working order in the gymnasium. The court was 14 feet high and ten feet wide, "faced with hard beech wood and slick as glass."[193]

Burtt Fenn followed in Walter Abbott's footsteps in more ways than one. As Abbott had done, Fenn pushed for action on the association's damaged building. In October, he wrote this editorial in *Nashville Men*: "Can we not raise enough to complete the building we have? The room is needed so badly and the unfinished condition of the upper story has such a dilapidated appearance that strangers are apt to form a bad opinion of our people."[194]

• • • • •

Early in November, the YMCA night school opened in the association building at 8 p.m. on a Wednesday night. Courses taught were business and commercial law, English, penmanship and spelling, shorthand, typewriting, arithmetic, and bookkeeping. The night school's purpose was to help young men help themselves.[195]

• • • • •

Late in December the YMCA basketball team had two exciting games. On the 22nd, the Y team defeated Vanderbilt 24–22. On the 30th, the YMCA boys played Cumberland University at the YMCA gym. Cumberland won 13–12 when a last second goal by the YMCA team was ruled by the referee to have left the boy's hand after he blew his whistle ending the game. Said to have been the "most exciting game that has been played this year," the YMCA team considered appealing the loss to the Amateur Athletic Union.[196]

At the annual YMCA meeting held January 26, Dr. Buckner, president, announced that the number of YMCA members jumped from 496 on January 1, 1904, to 563 a year later. Bible class attendance went from 1,179 attendees in 1903 to 1,960 in 1904, and attendance at the men's meetings doubled from 1,762 in 1903 to 3,521 in 1904. Only, the number of junior members showed a decrease, dropping from 278 to 164.[197]

In the winter, the YMCA orchestra was reorganized with nine pieces but still lacked a drummer.[198] Unfortunately, the orchestra's music was sometimes muffled by blasting on Church Street in front of the building for a new sewer.[199] Nearby construction caused "terrifying noise and shock," as well as access problems for six months. During that period, the YMCA building was almost cut off from the public because of the erection of Marshall and Bruce's new building and the 12-story First National Bank Building on adjacent lots on Fourth Avenue North.[200]

A board committee charged with looking into the feasibility of erecting a sign on the building, reported in January. They recommended that the association erect an electric sign consisting of four letters "Y M C A." with each letter being flashed on separately and off. The sign was ordered through Standard Electric Company, and was erected by the Nashville Railway and Light Company.[201]

Dr. George J. Fisher, secretary of the physical work of the YMCA of North America, visited Nashville in February to meet with the physical directors of the Tennessee YMCA associations. The meeting's purpose was to raise the standards of athletics in the state.

For the year ending April 30, 1905, the membership stood at 550 up 45 from a year earlier. Bible Class attendance for the year was 1,348. There were 53 men's meetings during the year with an attendance of 3,889. In May, the board approved an increase in annual dues from $10 to $12.

Possibly as a result of Dr. Fisher's visit, the Nashville

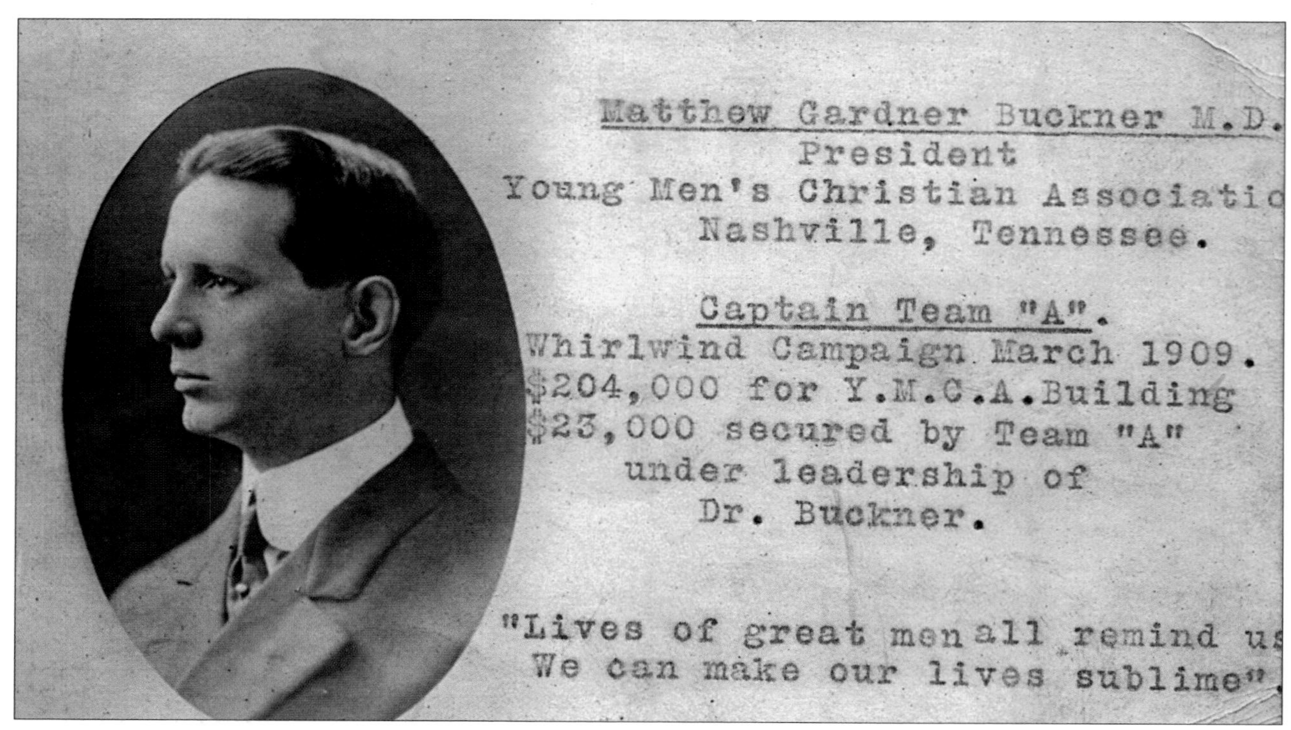

Association acquired grounds just across the river for outdoor sports. Tennis courts were included as well as a baseball diamond. Dr. Buckner, who once won the city tennis singles championship, undoubtedly played tennis there, possibly as part of the YMCA's tennis team. The facility proved to be very attractive to other members as well. Through the kindness of the Prewitt-Spurr Manufacturing Co., who donated the lumber and furnished the site, a bathhouse or dressing room was planned, and members could swim in the Cumberland.[202]

In May, J. G. Hamaker, secretary of the boys' department, announced that the boys' camp in 1905 would be on the Piney River in Hickman County. He said that the camp would be for ten days and that the scenery was beautiful with rugged cliffs across the river, and plenty of fish in the stream. Within two miles of camp, there was a large iron ore mine and smelter that the boys could visit. There was also a small playing ground where the boys could play baseball and other games.[203]

Here are the instructions Hamaker gave the campers' parents. The boys should "wear an old suit of clothes, a suit of underwear, old shirt or sweater, cap or soft hat, old pair of shoes with heavy soles. Bring one double or two single blankets, your Bible, an extra pair of trousers, coat, old outing shirt, another suit of heavy underwear, extra stockings, two towels, pillow case, two yards white table oilcloth, safety pins, comb, soap, tooth brush, metal plate, deep dish and cup, tablespoon, knife and fork. If you have a raincoat, musical instruments, camera, ball, bats, rubber soled shoes or gymnasium suit, take them along. Pack all your camp articles (except blankets and oil cloth) in a cracker box 12 x 12 x 20 with a hinged lid, which you may secure from a grocer, equip it with a padlock and two keys. Mark your name on the box clearly. Trunks or heavy boxes not allowed." The boys also took along a boat they built in the carpenter shop on the YMCA's third floor.
When the NC & St. L. train unloaded its cargo of boys at the little town of Nunnelly at 10:30 a.m. on June 21, the citizens were all agog. It was but a mile and one-half from the station to the camp at Vernon, Tennessee.[204]
The daily camp schedule was as follows:

6:30 a.m. Morning Call
7:00 a.m. Breakfast
7:45 a.m. Camp Inspection
8:00 a.m. Bible Study
8:30 a.m. Recreation, Games, Fishing and Rowing
11:00 a.m. Swimming
12:00 noon Dinner
4:00 p.m. Swimming
6:00 p.m. Supper
8:00 p.m. Twilight Talk
8:30 p.m. Bonfire
10:00 p.m. Taps

Just as college YMCAs were popular around the turn of the century, so were railroad YMCAs. The first railroad YMCA was established in Cleveland, Ohio in 1872. Memphis and Knoxville had railroad associations and new ones were opened at New Decatur, Alabama, at the L & N yards and at Oakdale, Tennessee, in Morgan County, Tennessee, on the Queen and Crescent Railroad.[205]

At home, the work of remodeling the two down-stairs rooms was almost completed in June. Burtt Fenn announced, "The offices will soon be on the first floor, and everything more convenient and inviting than before." He added that the ladies' auxiliary provided the funds for remodeling and papering these rooms. As part of the move, the *Nashville Men* office moved from the second to the first floor. That meant no more climbing stairs. An extra room on the ground floor was converted to a reading room, while the general secretary's office was in a cozy little room to the left as you entered the building.

In 1905, the Nashville boys' department was considered equal to any in the South. In membership, it ranked 5th in the South and 67th in North America. The boys' department held its first annual banquet to celebrate its success.

At the annual meeting on February 13, YMCA president Matt Buckner appointed a committee of three to revise the association's constitution. At a board meeting on March 6, Dr. Buckner was reelected president. Fred J. Fuller was elected vice president, E. E. French recording secretary, and J. D. Hamilton, treasurer.[206] The new constitution was discussed, approved and adopted at a called board meeting on March 19.[207] Interestingly, the new constitution kept the original name of the association, "Young Men's Christian Association of Nashville and Edgefield, Tennessee," even though Edgefield had been annexed by Nashville in 1880.

The new constitution included the new position of second vice president. At a regular board meeting the next day, Messrs. Garland Tinsley, Whitefoord R. Cole, J. B. Morgan and P. B. Jones were elected to the board. A month later, Howell E. Jackson Jr., and Percy Warner were named new board members, and James H. Parks was elected to the new position of second vice president.[208] The YMCA sponsored a basketball team in 1906 that played other institutions. On January 5, the Y team defeated the Vanderbilt Sophomore team 27–15.[209]

The boys' director decided to hold the summer camp much closer to Nashville than it had been since 1901. He chose a location on the Big Harpeth River about twenty miles from Nashville. The plan was for twenty boys to go to camp on July 10 for ten days. Because transportation costs would be less, the cost of the camp was reduced to $7.[210] When not enough boys signed up by June 14, Mr. Amaker called a meeting of all boys interested in going. Pleased with the turnout and the enthusiasm shown, he felt optimistic that the camp would be successful.[211]

With campaigns underway in Chattanooga and Memphis to build new buildings for those sister associations, officers of the Nashville YMCA were increasingly confident that they could raise the $200,000 thought to be needed to build a building in Nashville.

A more immediate problem was the resignation of Burtt Fenn, who resigned in the fall to accept a similar position in St. Joseph, Missouri, a much smaller city.[212] Mr. H. M. Giddings, the genial membership secretary, also left to become general secretary of the Railroad Association at De Soto, Missouri. These men were succeeded by Mr. William S. Frost and Mr. T. M. Sawrie, membership secretary.[213]

When Mr. Frost came to the Nashville to interview for the general secretary position, he realized that the YMCA could not stay long in its temporary quarters at the Chamber of Commerce Building, where the association had recently moved at least some of its functions, and hoped that, within a few months, the clamor for a new building would be irresistible. Offered the position, Mr. Frost accepted and moved his family to Nashville from Columbia, Tennessee, on November 1. He made a deal to secure the house that Burtt Fenn lived in at 2004 Arena Place in Murphy's Addition.[214]

When the State YMCA opened its annual convention in Columbia, Tennessee, on October 12, the Nashville and Edgefield Association brought a large delegation. Columbia was near Nashville so the roundtrip railroad fare was only $1.85. Another reason for the larger than usual number of Nashvillians attending was the fact that the Columbia general secretary W. S. Frost would become general secretary of the Nashville Association immediately following the convention.[215]

Born in Northern Illinois near Chicago, William S. Frost graduated from the University of Michigan. His first job was as a telegraph operator with the Chicago and Northwestern Railroad. Dissatisfied with his work, he entered the University of Chicago School of Law, graduating in 1888. He then moved to Knoxville, Tennessee, to enter practice. There, he joined the YMCA and, from 1898 to 1902, served on that association's board of directors. For the last two of those years, Frost was secretary of the Knoxville board. Having decided that he wanted to make the YMCA his life's work, he accepted an offer from the Kentucky State Association to become a traveling secretary, working out of Louisville. His next step was to accept the general secretary position of the Columbia, Tennessee YMCA, a position he held through the State YMCA Convention in October.[216]

"The policy of the Nashville YMCA," said Mr. Frost, "will be to stimulate social life and through it largely increase interest in the distinctive religious work of the association." "It will be our endeavor," he added, "to demonstrate the absolute need of a new YMCA building in Nashville by putting so much life into the present quarters that they will be inadequate for the work." He continued by saying, "From experience in the general field in association work it can be safely said that no finer opportunity for taking the front rank among the institutions of the city is offered than Nashville presents at this time." Mr. Frost said he believed the association that had 600 men and 200 boys as members could be increased to 1,000 by the end of the year 1907 and that efforts to reach the 1,000 mark "would be started at once."[217]

• • • • •

CHAPTER SIX

A New Building in Their Sights
1907–1910

ONE OF THE THINGS William Frost learned soon after accepting the Nashville general secretary position was that the YMCA board of directors had, for years, been quietly trying to sell their building. Several potential purchasers had inspected the half-burned structure but declined to make reasonable offers. One option was to tear down the old building and erect an expensive high-rise, steel structure on the small lot. Even when finished, this still would be less than ideal. The other option was to sell the property and use the proceeds to purchase a larger lot more appropriate for use as a YMCA. Half a dozen local real estate agents offered their opinion that the building was worth no more than $40,000.[218]

The Nashville Association turned to the national office for help. The International YMCA sent their financial

The new YWCA building on 7th Avenue North, 1911.

expert, Levi B. Mumma, to Nashville to survey the situation and make a recommendation. Mumma said that, before launching a fund-raising campaign, the board should do some groundwork, including conducting a feasibility study. The board reluctantly accepted his advice and the initial enthusiasm for jumpstarting a campaign languished.

Matt Buckner, the association president, had made up his mind. He felt that the YMCA building was impossible, and that to renovate it would throw good money after bad. It was not in the right location and was poorly situated, being in the middle of a block. He was convinced that the Y needed to be on a corner lot where men and boys could have separate entrances. "Slow winds bring the ship to harbor," he said. Still, Dr. Buckner wanted to proceed cautiously. Other board members were less restrained. A financial campaign to raise $200,000 was urged. There was a rumor, confirmed in October 1910, that John Hill Eakin, a wealthy philanthropist and former board member, who died in 1904, had put the YMCA in his will for a considerable amount of money. The amount of his bequest turned out to be $119,500, some of which was available for the building fund. Mr. Eakin actually gave his wife a lifetime interest in the property that, on her death, would go to the YMCA. With the permission of the YMCA, she sold the property and gave the proceeds to the YMCA, retaining a life annuity interest for herself.[219]

On January 2, 1907, the YMCA board sold their building on Church Street to the Board of Trade for $40,000, its appraised value.[220] This necessitated a series of moves to temporary quarters until a new building could be built. The first was on Sixth Avenue between Church and Commerce. It was small with only a lounge and a room for a library. The YMCA also rented office space in the Chamber of Commerce Building. With money in its pocket, the YMCA was in a position to take advantage of an unusual opportunity eight days later, when its board bought, for $21,000, from McKendree Methodist Church, a choice site for a new building on the northeast corner of Seventh Avenue North and Union Street.[221]

The sale of the YMCA Building impacted many programs, including basketball. The last basketball game played in the old building was on New Year's Eve 1906. Until a new building was built, basketball games were played at either the Nashville Laundry Hall or the Hippodrome on West End.[222]

The pressure to keep up with sister YMCAs in Bristol, Chattanooga, Knoxville, and Memphis must have pushed the Nashville YMCA to purchase the lot on Seventh Avenue. In the March 2 issue of *Nashville Men*, an article pointed out that Memphis, Chattanooga, Knoxville, and Bristol all were planning or had under construction new buildings or building expansions, ranging in cost from $60,000 at Bristol and $70,000 in Knoxville to $200,000 for Memphis and $150,000 for Chattanooga. "Who says Nashville is going to play tail-ender in this game?" said the article. In May, after 15 days of fund-raising, the Chattanooga Association had raised $159,241 in subscriptions, prompting the mayor to say, "This campaign was the greatest event in the history of Chattanooga."[223]

The Nashville YWCA was also feeling the pressure to build a new building. During March, twenty-five young women were turned away from the local YWCA as "it was impossible for the association to provide room for them." A movement was underway for the YWCA to build a $50,000 building on a lot they owned on Seventh Avenue North across the street from the lot the YMCA purchased two months earlier.[224]

Keeping Up with Memphis

In April, after only six months on the job, Mr. Frost threatened to resign. In his report to the YMCA board that month, Mr. Frost said, "Had I any idea of the conditions facing the Nashville Association, I would never have consented to get under such a load…I found a membership torn by dissention, and eager to know whose side the new secretary was going to be on, no real association spirit, and many of the old-time workers out all together." Frost's unfavorable feeling about the state of the YMCA was shared by many others in the community. In a later report to the board on religious matters, Mr. Frost said that "after twice being locked out" by the theater management, "we are now obligated to discontinue religious meetings" held in the theater.[225]

Realizing that he needed some outside help to pull off a capital campaign, Mr. Frost spent several days in Memphis in mid April, talking to Mr. C. S. Ward, the International Secretary in charge of building campaigns, who was in charge of a fifteen day capital campaign for $200,000 then underway in that city. The Memphis campaign, which ended about the first of May, was a disappointment, succeeding in getting subscriptions for $125,000. Mr. Ward surely suspected the campaign outcome that when he and Mr. Frost met on or around the 22nd of April. Regardless of the fact that the Memphis canvass was lagging, Frost asked Ward, who was an experienced fundraiser, to direct the Nashville campaign. Mr. Ward agreed to come to Nashville as soon as the Memphis campaign was over and correctly predicted that it would be easier to raise $200,000 in Nashville than it was in Memphis.[226]

The Nashville capital funds drive, then called a capital funds subscription, was scheduled to kick off on May 1 with a goal of $200,000. The plan called for YMCA members to call on Nashville businesses for donations. They would also conduct a house-to-house solicitation. The workers would be instructed to tell their prospects how exciting the new building would be. It was then envisioned as being a handsome six-story, fireproof structure. On the main floor, there would be a large lobby where the general secretary would have his office. Adjoining the lobby would be a reading room and a library. Also, convenient to the lobby, there would be a café, where light lunches and soft drinks could be served. The second and third floors would be devoted to the gym and rooms for physical training. The upper floors would be dormitories for young men and, on the roof, there would be a large roof garden. The swimming pool and bathrooms would be in the basement.[227]

The board realized, however, that sufficient groundwork had not been done, released Mr. Ward, and delayed the subscription until early November when Ward's services were again secured.[228]

Possibly anticipating that there would not be a boys' camp in 1907, the boys' department took a four-horse wagon trip to The Hermitage on June 8. The group left the association quarters at 9 a.m. and returned about 8 p.m. The cost was 50 cents. For those who wished to see the inside of the house, there was an extra charge of 25 cents. On the way out, the boys stopped for a swim in Mill Creek. That same month, a YMCA Bible class held its first meeting at the end of the Woodlawn car line, and two gymnasium classes were discontinued for the summer.[229]

With Ward on board, nothing happened as money got tighter and the subscription was delayed again, this time indefinitely. Ward was, once again, released. The senior membership that had stood at 611 on April 1, 1907 had dropped below 500 once or twice. Eighty-eight memberships expired in February 1908 alone. Of those, 20 young men left the city, 15 were out of work, and 26 others could not spare the money to rejoin. The YMCA board realized they were still not ready for a major fundraising effort.[230] Another problem was the loss of key staff members and the possibility that Mr. Frost might change his mind and quit. H. M. Giddings, the association's genial membership secretary, had resigned the previous February to become general secretary of the Railroad Association in DeSoto, Missouri. In May, Mr. J. G. Hamaker, the boys' secretary, accepted a call from Camden, NJ, to become their boys' secretary on June 1. Then, in mid-June, H. L. Thomas, office secretary for the previous year, tendered his resignation to become general secretary of the Vandalia, Illinois, YMCA. Thomas said a factor in his decision was the fact that "our own work will be much restricted until we can go in a new building."[231] No one knew how long that would be.

On December 12, it was reported that the campaign to raise $200,000 for a magnificent new building would likely start about the first of February. General secretary Frost had just returned from a trip to New York, Philadelphia, and Washington, where he inspected handsome association buildings in those cities. He was now optimistic that the Nashville Association could raise the needed funds in thirty days.[232]

The YMCA board was probably a little envious when the Young Men's Hebrew Association (YMHA) opened their handsome new building with a reception on New Year's Day. Located on Union Street across from Polk Avenue, the two-story building cost $22,500.[233]

Railroad YMCAs were all the rage in the first decade of the 20th century. They were normally built in small communities where there were railroad workers who needed housing and amenities. A large one was located in Oakdale, TN. In 1902, S. W. McGill, the State YMCA general secretary, spoke in Nashville of the importance of YMCA railroad work throughout the world. It took until January 1, 1908 for his message to bear fruit in the state capitol. On that day, the Nashville Street Railway and Light Department of the Nashville YMCA was organized with McGill's help. By April 1, it had 441 members, had held 18 meetings, and had 18 men profess their belief in Jesus Christ. In 1909, J. U. Rust was chairman and the Railroad Department offices were at 315 Cedar Street.[234]

Working without a building was difficult and one real possibility, as 1908 began, was that the YMCA might have to suspend operations until the new building could be erected. At one point, the board was pointing in this direction, but it was decided to continue to operate as best they could. The association's affairs were, however, not in the best shape, and the February start date for the campaign came and went. About the only thing working well, other than the Railroad YMCA department, was the Saturday Night Bible class. Its growth was so rapid that the members had to secure the use of the bucket shop "at the rear of our rooms."

A new physical director helped revitalize the Physical Department that almost closed in 1907. Eight different YMCA basketball teams played during the 1907–08 season. Games were held in the Nashville Laundry Club Hall on Bridge Avenue thanks to the Nashville Laundry Company. The YMCA's top basketball team, coached by Dr. Walter Hutchinson, lost to Vanderbilt twice and the Nashville Athletic Club once.[235]

In May, Mr. Frost reported to the board that a new spirit of cooperation pervaded the organization. He must have had no idea what was coming. In a dramatic and seemingly desperate cost-saving move, the YMCA board decided to go with a volunteer management team, and dispensed with its entire salaried staff, including Mr. Frost.[236] A volunteer management committee assumed responsibility for carrying on the work of the association during the subscription phase and until the completion of the new building. The YMCA was not entirely without professional help as they appealed to the state committee to free up their excellent general secretary, S. Waters McGill, to devote such time to the Nashville Association as might be needed for him to organize and lead the capital funds drive for the new building. In response, the state committee graciously acceded to the Nashville association request.[237]

The YMCA and YWCA boards met and discussed the possibility of conducting a single campaign to raise the money needed to build the two buildings. A study convinced both boards that it made sense to undertake two separate campaigns, under common leadership, with the YMCA launching a sixteen-day drive to raise $200,000 immediately followed by a seven-day YWCA drive to raise $100,000.[238]

With Waters there to guide them, the YMCA Board, on November 24, 1908, authorized President Matt Buckner to appoint an executive committee of twelve prominent citizens to (1) conduct the capital funds drive, (2) erect a new building, and (3) secure a new charter, constitution and by-laws. Dr. Buckner named himself, Whitefoord R. Cole, T. L. Herbert, John W. Love, Percy Warner, Joseph H. Thompson, John B. Ransom, A. M. Shook, A. H. Robinson, Major C. T. Cheek, P. T. Troop, and S. Waters McGill to the committee.[239]

This proved to be a wise move as all gave liberally of their time and means to their task. They first met on November 27 at which time Colonel A. M. Shook was elected chairman; Mr. Thompson, vice-chairman; A. H. Robinson, treasurer; and S. W. McGill, secretary, and following this meeting, the committee met regularly in offices E. B. Stahlman let them have in his new Stahlman Building. There, they laid out their campaign plans.[240]

The Executive Committee had also met with YWCA leaders and agreed that, as soon as the 15-day YMCA campaign ended on March 31, they would conduct an equally enthusiastic 7-day capital campaign for the YWCA with $100,000 as its goal.

In January 1909, the YMCA had scattered operations in several buildings. In an effort to consolidate, the association rented the first floor of the Exchange Building at 411-413 Union Street. The basement was used as a gym while swimming classes were held at Merton's Bathhouse.[241] Baths and lockers were available at Merton's while a reading room was set up in the Exchange Building. The management committee also hired an office secretary.

• • • • •

The YMCA basketball team was known as the "Brownies" in the 1908–1909 season. By New Year's Day, they had a nice win streak that they extended on January 2 when they blasted the YMHA team 29–4. Later in the season, the Brownies won over Winthrop at the University of Nashville gym.[242] Believe it or not, the YMCA also had an indoor baseball team that winter. Games, such as the one in which the YMCA played the Knights of Columbus, were played in the Hippodrome.[243]

• • • • •

By March the campaign committee had named three important subcommittees: a citizen's committee, headed by Joseph Thompson; a businessmen's committee, headed by Edgar Foster; and a young men's committee, chaired by Arthur Ransom. Mr. C. S. Ward, the international secretary in charge of building programs, was reengaged with Mr. McGill, of the state committee, to provide professional leadership.[244]

The YMCA launched its drive on Friday night, March 12 at a businessman's dinner at the Maxwell House Hotel attended by about 130 men. Joseph H. Thompson, who presided, announced that board members had already pledged $10,000 to the subscription.

On Saturday afternoon, at 12:30, the members of the various campaign committees met at campaign headquarters on Third Avenue North opposite the Stahlman Building. This was the first of a series of mid-day report luncheons that would be held daily until the successful conclusion of the sixteen-day campaign. After lunch, Mr. Thompson reported to the fifty businessmen present that, in addition to the $10,000 reported the night before, three individual subscriptions of $5,000 each had been received. They were from himself, A. H. Robinson, and Percy Warner. Mr. Ward complimented these men and spoke of the splendid start. Next, Edgar Foster, chairman of the businessmen's committee, handed out pledge cards.[245]

On Sunday a much larger meeting took place at the Vendome Theater. There, the theme for the campaign was announced, "200,000 in Sixteen Days." The featured speaker was George F. Tibbetts, whose talk had the title, "The Battle of the Strong." His lecture was highlighted by stereopticon slides, the power point of the day. The program went over so well that the campaign committee repeated it the following Sunday night at First Presbyterian Church, and later at the homes of Mr. and Mrs. Gates Thurston and Mr. and Mrs. Arthur Ransom.[246]

In addition to the daily reporting luncheons, the campaign featured banquets, as well as parades. To keep up interest and show the progress of the campaign, a gigantic clock was painted on the side of a building at Third and Union. Each day, the hands of the clock were repainted to show exactly how much had been raised. On Tuesday, March 16, the second day, the hands of the clock indicated that they were ahead of schedule. Elated, the campaign leaders encouraged their team leaders to push their workers to even greater heights. The team leaders did so and the men responded beautifully.

By March 26, the 12th day of the campaign, $17,957 in new subscriptions was reported and the campaign total reached $122,260. The workers entered the four-day home stretch with determination to success and prove Edgar Foster correct when he said, "Nashville has often been weighed in the balance but has never been found wanting."[247]

On the final day of the sixteen-day campaign, March 31, the canvassing teams met for dinner at the campaign headquarters in the Chamber of Commerce Building. Reports were made and the exhilarating clock showed the final total to be $202,503, or $2,503 over the $200,000 goal. Mr. Ward's prediction that it would be easier for Nashville to raise $200,000 for a new building than it was for Memphis, proved true. The executive committee members expressed their deep appreciation for the great work done by everybody involved, and for the nearly 5,000 citizens who made gifts or pledges.[248]

The support of the boys' department was special. These young people convinced the Fisk Jubilee Singers to donate their services for a victory concert. Miller Manier, boys' department president, and his young troops then tirelessly sold tickets to the concert.

The momentum of the successful YMCA campaign carried over the next week by encouraging the YWCA workers to reach and exceed their goal of $100,000. In seven days, they raised $111,474 in gifts and pledges. The twin campaigns, chaired by the same 12 members of the YMCA executive committee, proved to be one of the finest hours in the history of the two organizations.[249]

With the successful subscription, the YMCA building committee recommended that the association employ the Chicago architectural firm of Shadduck and Hussey to plan and supervise construction of the new building.

Breaking Ground

On May 17, ground was broken. Mayor James S. Brown presided while Dr. C. W. Byrd gave the primary address. Surrounded by his colleagues on the executive committee, Percy Warner turned the first dirt with his silver shovel. Excavation work began shortly thereafter.[250]

The steel contract for the new building was awarded in June to Foster, Creighton, Gould, of Nashville, a firm that had been the subcontractors for the steel work on Nashville's new Jefferson Street and Sparkman Street bridges.[251]

The *Nashville Banner* reported on July 28 that sealed bids were to be in the hands of the secretary of the building committee not later than August 16, and that, after that date, plans and specifications could be seen in the architects' local office in the Cumberland Presbyterian Building on Fourth Avenue North.

It turned out that 25 to 30 contractors and subcontractors, mostly local, bid on the various aspects of the project. When the bids were opened on the afternoon of the 16th, architect W. F. Shattuck was in Nashville, having brought with him twelve sets of drawings. The bids totaled $190,000 for the YMCA building and $90,000 for the YWCA.[252] It was thought that the contracts for the erection of the YWCA would be awarded very quickly.

Late in August, the YMCA building committee reluctantly concluded that the bids they received were so high that the money they raised would be insufficient to build the building. The committee decided to consider only local bids, and asked the local contractors who submitted bids to lower them. The committee also voted to eliminate a few features, and cut back on others to get the total cost down to something they could deal with. The contractors complied.

Meanwhile, the YWCA didn't have quite the smooth sailing they thought. Because their bids were also higher than expected, they scrapped plans for an auditorium, agreed on a cheaper grade of brick, substituted maple flooring for the terrazzo originally planned, and agreed to use metal lathes instead of tile. With these changes, the cost of the new YWCA building dropped to within their $90,000 budget. A worry was that $5,000 of the YWCA subscriptions was past due. Nevertheless, in early September, the contracts were let. Some wonderful news came when a generous benefactor gave the YWCA $6,000, enough to allow them to build the auditorium after all.

In August, YMCA officials heard a rumor that the City of Nashville would take some property off the back of the YMCA's lot for the widening of the alley from Church Street to Union Street, facing the State Capitol. This proved true. In mid-August, the city council passed an ordinance to widen the ten-foot wide alley by thirty-five feet on each side. The building committee realized they had three choices: (1) purchase the adjoining McWhirter lot on Seventh Avenue, North, and redraw building plans, (2) go ahead and build on the present constricted site, a lot smaller than the YMCA lots in Chattanooga or Memphis, or (3) abandon the present site and look for a larger one.[253]

While deliberating what to do, Percy Warner, Dr. Buckner and T. L. Herbert visited YMCAs in Dayton, Ohio, and Indianapolis and South Bend, Indiana the second week in September. The trip proved to be insightful. During this difficult time, the executive committee was fortunate to have, on a half-time basis, S. Waters McGill to provide leadership. Although he was not yet forty years old, McGill was experienced in technical construction matters, a good fund-raiser, an eloquent speaker, and genial. He had come to Tennessee twelve years earlier to reactivate the State YMCA that Robert Weidensall had organized in 1879. McGill, who was highly regarded across the state, was of enormous help in guiding the YMCA building committee through the project. With him on hand, confidence that the project would yet be brought to a successful conclusion soared.[254]

After a lot of soul-searching, the YMCA executive committee unanimously voted at their December 15, 1909, meeting, to purchase George McWhirter's house for $17,500. He had paid $10,000 for what was known as the old Samuel Crockett house when he purchased it from McKendree Methodist Church after they abandoned plans to build on the site.[255]

Plans had to be redrawn for the building, whose footprint had changed significantly. The building committee met on February 18 and approved the revised plans submitted by Mr. Hussey. Having fulfilled every requirement dictated by the building committee, he began drawing the detailed plans so he could provide the contractors with the changed specifications. At this point, the excavation work was almost finished and the foundation work was about to begin.[256]

Meanwhile, the city offered the YMCA $6,100 for the 35' it condemned—far less than the YMCA had to pay for the Crockett House and new plans. The YMCA, not having decided whether to contest the amount in court, did not accept the offered amount.[257]

In 1910, the Y moved its temporary location from the Exchange Building to three leased rooms in the Cole Building on Union Street at $420 per year. This was the site of Liberty Hall, which the YMCA occupied from 1875 until 1882. Some of the programs were administered from the Cole Building, while others were administered from a house that stood on Fifth Avenue North behind the Jackson Building. A frame structure behind the house was used as a gymnasium.

John B. Ransom, one of the city's most charitable, liberal, and likeable citizens, died on January 5, 1910. He was head of the John B. Ransom Lumber Company, probably the largest hardwood lumber concern in the South, and was the first member of the YMCA executive committee appointed in November 1908 to die.[258]

On February 28, 1910, Hallum W. Goodloe, Tennessee secretary of state, recorded the new Constitution and By-Laws of the Nashville Young Men's Christian Association. The incorporators were Joseph H. Thompson, P. T. Troop, W. R. Cole, A. H. Robinson, M. G. Buckner, T. L. Herbert, Percy Warner, John W. Love, C. T. Cheek, and S. W. McGill. Finally, the name Edgefield was removed from the organization's official name. Members were required to be members in good standing of an evangelical church to be interpreted in accordance with the definition approved by the International Convention of the YMCA.[259] Section 1 of Article X of the new constitution dealt with amendments. It stated that the provisions of the constitution in Article 2, sections 2 and 3, by which none but members in good standing of evangelical churches may become active members shall never be annulled, and no amendments shall be made which shall allow the said provision to be annulled. In the 1875 constitution, directors were elected by denominations. This was no longer the case although, under the 1910 constitution, not more than six of the nineteen directors could be members of the same religious denomination. The standing committees under the new constitution were 1. executive, 2. finance, 3. house, 4. membership, 5. boys' work, 6. educational work, 7. employment work, 8. physical work, 9. religious work, and 10. social work.

Preparatory School Basketball at the Y

Because of the inadequacy of the improvised gym in a house behind the Jackson Building that Mrs. Buckner's family owned, the YMCA found a new gym with a good gallery and improved bathing facilities. By January 6, the athletic department was in the process of equipping the gym for basketball, handball, and physical fitness programs. With the larger facility, the Y started an in-house basketball league of four teams from each section of town—North, South, East, and West. The teams would compete for the YMCA championship. After the championship game in February, an all-star team would be selected to play local and out-of-town teams.

In response to the growing interest in basketball, the Y proposed to the local preparatory schools that they establish a prep school basketball league and play their games at the Y. The schools agreed to this and play began. In the second prep school game, on February 8, Bowen School played the High School.[260] The athletic department, then under the charge of O. J. Kellerhalls, assisted by Ed Nesbitt, William Andrews, Allen Jameson, and Robert Brown, showed considerable initiative.[261]

The first meeting of the board of directors of the Nashville YMCA held, after the adoption of the new by-laws, was on April 7. The following officers were elected: Dr. M. G. Buckner, president; A. H. Robinson, treasurer, and S. W. McGill, general secretary.[262] The YMCA had, with the permission of the state committee, employed him fulltime. Mr. McGill was a Presbyterian minister, a Mason, a member of the Booster and Commercial clubs, and a golfer. The following fall, he employed E. L. Spain as house secretary. A native Nashvillian, Spain had spent his early years in San Francisco, before returning to Nashville.

The YMCA basketball team, consisting of the top players from the YMCA league, played its first game on February 10 against the University of Nashville, winning 36–16 behind the scoring of center and captain R. B. McGee, a former Vanderbilt player. The YMCA also played Cumberland University and, in the final game, had a return match with the University of Nashville, who turned the tables on the YMCA team 24–11.[263]

Unpaid Pledges Pose a Problem

Because of the considerable delay experienced in completing the plans for the Association building as a result of the construction of Capitol Boulevard, the cornerstone of the new YMCA was not laid until September 10. The colorful ceremony was presided over by Col. A. M. Shook, chairman of the executive committee. James I. Vance, pastor of First Presbyterian Church gave the address. Dr. Buckner, president of the YMCA, read the list of contents to be placed in the cornerstone, while Percy Warner, chairman of the building committee placed the box in the cornerstone.[264] In the box were a 1910 map of Nashville, photographs of several YMCA leaders, a contemporary YMCA booklet, the September issue of *Confederate Veteran*, a memorial tribute to John B. Ransom, the by-laws of Cumberland lodge No. 8 F and A.M. adopted June 10, 1907, and two copies of September 10, 1910, issue of the *Nashville Tennessean* and the *Nashville American*, that had a photograph of the YMCA executive committee.[265]

Much energy was expended in November in trying to collect the $26,000 due and unpaid on YWCA pledges, and the $88,000 due and unpaid on the YMCA pledges. The delay was seriously delaying the completion of both projects. After A. M. Shook decided, "to insist on immediate settlement of unpaid pledges in cash or by note," the names of unpaid subscribers were divided up among the board members of both the YWCA and YMCA, and personal calls were made. At the time, the YWCA building was nearing completion, and steelwork on the YMCA building was nearing the third floor. Already, people walking on Seventh Avenue North could see that handsome stone and brickwork of the YMCA on its imposing first floor. The expectation was that the building would be completed in the fall of 1911.[266]

Because of "the considerable" number of unpaid pledges, the YMCA directors realized that, without the $119,500 Eakin bequest, "it would have been impossible to have erected the building upon its present proportions." With the building well underway, Dr. Buckner announced in February the appointment of a special furnishing committee, chaired by Leland Hume. Three days later, most of the board went to the Ryman Auditorium to hear Williams Jennings Bryan speak as a guest of the YMCA. In a later speech to the legislature, Bryan argued for the direct vote of U.S. Senators, and the guarantee of bank deposits. He also attended the YMCA's Saturday night Bible class. Although twice defeated for President, Bryan was "still the foremost and most influential citizen of the nation."[267]

Monk Sharp and His "Ramblers"

Around Christmastime 1910, Henry "Monk" Sharp and a few friends started a basketball team called the YMCA "Ramblers." Their first opportunity to play a game came on Friday, January 13, 1911, when a doubleheader was scheduled at the Sixth Avenue gym between the four YMCA teams—East, West, North and South. When the North team did not show for the second game against the East Leaguers, by common consent, the newly organized Rambler team was allowed to substitute. The Ramblers won that game 27–23. Their starters were Carl and Ernest Benz at the forwards, Monk Sharp at center, and Mason Hunt and Will Schlattner at the guard spots. Basil "Old Folks" Ridley entered the game for the Ramblers as a substitute and scored a game-high eight points.[268] Monk Sharp, the captain, would play for the Ramblers until the team disbanded following the 1930 season. Scores from the 1911 season show losses to Vanderbilt, Branham & Hughes, BGA, and the Preps. Wins were recorded against the YMCA East team, the Franklin Athletic Club (twice), MBA and the YMHA.[269]

The game with Vanderbilt on February 3 at the Vanderbilt

gym was a slaughter by the "bigger, heavier, faster, and more skillful" Commodore team, who won 74–22. Starters for the Ramblers that night were almost entirely different than for the East game three weeks earlier. On the 3rd, Halcomb and Smith started at forwards, Jim Priest at center, and Basil Ridley and M. Priest at guards.[270]

As the Y no longer had use of the baseball/tennis facility in East Nashville, the physical work committee signed a contract with James E. Caldwell's Nashville Railway and Light Company to build six tennis courts and two baseball diamonds at Glendale Park that the company owned. The Railway and Light Company agreed to install lights for night play and allow the Y to use an existing clubhouse. Association members would pay $2.50 for privilege of using the athletic facilities for the 1911 season.[271]

Having a baseball diamond didn't mean the YMCA was relaxing its conservative feelings about morals. In September, the YMCA issued a statement deploring the Nashville Baseball Club playing games on Sundays in defiance of law and violating promises that they would not do so. The YMCA also found fault with the city officials being unwilling to enforce the law.

Steel Girders Up to the Fourth Floor

By March, steel for the YMCA building was up to the fourth floor. Anxious to raise the $45,000 needed to furnish the building, the furnishing committee announced naming opportunities—$10,000 to have a benefactor's name on the library in the boys' department, and $5,000 to name the auditorium or gymnasium. Meanwhile, the physical work committee, one member of which was Vanderbilt football coach, Dan McGugin, was raising money to equip the new gym. Delinquent pledges had been trimmed to $65,000, most of which were two years in arrears. After having mailed at least fourteen requests, asking for payment, the association turned them over to a collection agency.[272]

The YWCA moved to its new building, appraised at $175,000, in April. Just as the YMCA building would, the YWCA included dormitories for young women. There were 76 of them and the waiting list was already up to 40. Unsurprisingly, the major benefactors of the YWCA were the same men who generously supported the YMCA.

Having been without a boys' camp since 1906 or 1907, the Association made it known, in the spring, that it greatly needed a suitable location for a summer camp.[273] No one stepped forward with an appropriate site, however, and another summer passed without one.

In May, Julius Rosenwald, president of Sears-Roebuck & Company, of Chicago, made the startling announcement that he would give $25,000 to any YMCA in America if they would match it with a $75,000 gift themselves to build a colored men's YMCA building. The Nashville board knew he was serious because he had already given $100,000 to build a YMCA near the Sears-Roebuck factory in Chicago. Rosenwald explained why he made the offer. "You might think it is funny for a Jew to encourage the building of YMCA buildings, but I do not believe there is better work done anywhere in the world, so far as I know, than the work done by the YMCA. I do not believe I am less a Jew because I am willing to see summer camps. There is already a strong demand for this work to be undertaken by the Nashville Association."

With the steel girders high in the sky and the first brick laid June 30, 1911, the YMCA gave thought to its program goals once in the new building. The following were listed:

1. A Railroad YMCA for the lines entering Nashville;
2. Student YMCAs in all high schools, prep schools, colleges and universities, both black and white (seven had already been organized);
3. A centrally located Colored Men's YMCA Building to meet the needs of 350 to 500 members;
4. An East Nashville branch;
5. A West Nashville branch;
6. A North Nashville branch;
7. A South Nashville branch near the Vanderbilt Medical and Dental Departments;
8. An athletic park;
9. An active boys' club;
10. Playgrounds in various sections of the city;
11. A summer camp; and
12. Support for a YMCA worker in a foreign field.[274]

At a board meeting in mid-June, the building committee gave an encouraging report. They hoped to have the first floor ready by the September 18 visit of President Taft, to be ready for occupancy, at least in part, by November 1, and to be completely finished by January 1, 1912. The furnishing committee reported that Mrs. H. H. Corson had contributed $1,000 for the cafeteria as a memorial to her father. Mr. J. Harry Howe contributed $500 as a memorial to his son.[275] The gym was named for board member Percy Warner. The plaque read:

DEDICATED TO THE PHYSICAL WELFARE OF THE YOUNG MEN OF NASHVILLE AND NAMED IN HONOR OF MR. PERCY WARNER IN APPRECIATION FOR HIS FAITHFUL AND EFFICIENT SERVICE AS CHAIRMAN OF THE BUILDING COMMITTEE OF THE NASHVILLE YOUNG MEN'S CHRISTIAN ASSOCIATION

When the YMCA started its Night Law School on September 6, 1911, the trustees had no idea that the school would be in existence nearly a century later. The school was started to benefit those unable to attend law classes during the day, and those who could not afford to attend private law schools, such as Vanderbilt. Initially, there was no tuition and the faculty lectured for free.[276]

At the board meeting on September 12, it was announced that the committee of management, that had been conducting the work of the association at their quarters on Sixth Avenue North, would relinquish their duties on October 1, and turn the property over to the board of directors. The board adopted a resolution praising the committee for their unselfish services over the previous two years (actually since 1/1/1909) during which the work was entirely under their jurisdiction.[277]

Possibly because the YMCA Board thought they might get possession of the new building by the time of President Taft's visit on November 11, 1911, they did not extend their lease on their temporary quarters in the Chamber of Commerce Building. For whatever reason, the YMCA moved to a new location at 140 Sixth Avenue North on October 10. The board of directors met there for the first time that day. At the meeting, the treasurer announced that a balance of $40,000 was still outstanding on the building fund pledges. The furnishing committee reported that same amount was still to be raised to furnish the new building. It was decided, however, not to launch a renewed effort to raise $40,000 for furnishings until the impending Galloway Memorial Hospital campaign was finished.[278]

At this time, Dr. A. S. Keim was director of the physical education department. His focus was on body-building, and corrective and recreational exercises. Keim would be associated with the Y for many years. Other new staff members, who came in the fall, were W. E. Willis, director for religious work, and E. J. Filbrey, education work director.[279]

• • • • •

The *Better Nashville* issue of November 3 mentioned that, some time before, an enterprising student drew an emblem for the YMCA on the back of someone's coat. The triangle indicated the three-fold nature of the association work for the spiritual, intellectual, and physical nature of man. In the center was an open Bible with the scripture text John 17–21 "that they all may be one"—the prayer of Christ for Christian unity. The Bible and the triangle were held together by the Greek letters XP for Christ. The circle stood for the worldwide extent of the work. The emblem spoke of the three-fold work in the name of Christ for the young men of the world.[280]

• • • • •

Two weeks after the *Nashville Tennessean* ran an editorial praising the munificent gift made to the YMCA in the will of John Hill Eakin, the YMCA board voted to establish the John Hill Eakin Institute through which the educational work of the association would be conducted. The entire third floor of the new building would be devoted to the institute that would have a School of Commerce and Finance, a night high school course, the YMCA Law School, and a vocational course.[281]

The new YMCA building, nearly finished, was a growing source of pride to Nashvillians. Thomas W. Wrenne, a visitor to the city, was so impressed that, once home, he wrote Mr. McGill to say, "It has been my pleasure to see a large number of the buildings erected by the YMCA in the several cities of the country, and particularly in the South. I regard yours as one of the best, and I think it is easily the most attractive in appearance in the South."[282]

One of the last pieces of the YMCA puzzle to take place was to fill the big swimming pool in the new building with water. This took place on December 23. The first person to dive in the pool did so unofficially. He was an English carpenter, who worked on the building. He was said to have held several swimming records. The honor of being the first person to officially swim in the pool went to twelve-year-old boys' department member, Alfred T. Adams. Having recently learned the Australian crawl, Alf was anxious to demonstrate his mastery of the stroke and did so before an audience of 200 Boy Scouts who were spending the night at the YMCA, sleeping on mats in the gymnasium.[283]

• • • • •

CHAPTER SEVEN

The Largest YMCA in the South

1912–1915

ON NEW YEAR'S DAY 1912, S. W. McGill left Nashville by train for Trenton, New Jersey, to see Gov. Woodrow Wilson. McGill made the trip to personally invite Wilson to come to Nashville on February 24 to dedicate the new YMCA Building. McGill hoped to take advantage of Wilson's ties to Middle Tennessee. His brother Joseph R. "Joe" Wilson was a graduate of Southwestern Presbyterian University in Clarksville and a writer for the *Nashville Banner*. Joe's daughter Alice would attend Ward Belmont during Wilson's first term as president. Woodrow's father, Dr. Joseph R. Wilson, who died in 1903, had been the founding head of the School of Theology at Southwestern in 1884, and was, in earlier years following the Civil War, considered one of the three most important figures in the Presbyterian Church, U.S. Woodrow Wilson actually spent part of his youth in Clarksville. McGill may have told Governor Wilson, who was a Democratic presidential candidate, that there

The new YMCA building at the corner of 7th and Union

The 1912 Ramblers

was a "Wilson For President Club" in Nashville. In late, January, Governor Wilson accepted the invitation to be the guest of honor at the official opening.[284]

The day McGill left for New Jersey, the YMCA Building was sufficiently complete for the association to move in.[285] Ironically, about this same time, the YMCA's old building on Church Street had come into the hands of someone who put a saloon in it. Not only that, a so-called Athletic Club, organized for the purpose of promoting prize fighting, secured quarters there. The general manager, McGill, wrote, "This has been made possible by reason of the fact that the State Legislature, which did many good things, in an unconscious moment, legalized a brutal sport heretofore prohibited."[286]

The board first met in the new building on January 9. Mr. Hume reported for the building committee that four rooms in the new building had been given in honor of H. H. Corson (the Inside Inn), J. Harry Howe (the College Club Room), Will Nelson (the Game Room), and Joseph H. Thompson (the Reading Room). The Finance Committee reported that unpaid pledges had been knocked down to $36,692.08 and that $75,000 was still needed to finish the building. The House Committee chairman reported that 116 rooms had already been rented. The tight financial condition made it difficult for the Nashville YMCA to respond to cable from F. S. Brockman in Shanghai that reported that the YMCA associations in China were in imminent danger of financial ruin, and asked the Nashville YMCA for a $1,200 gift.[287] If a gift was sent, it was small.

The new boys' work director, Henry G. Hart, must have been introduced at the January 9 board meeting. A native Tennessean and a graduate of the University of Tennessee, Hart had spent the previous four years working for the South Side Association in Chattanooga. Standing 6' 2" tall and looking every inch an athlete, he seemed an ideal person to oversee the boys' department.[288]

With the enthusiasm that the new building engendered, this was an opportune time to gain new members. A campaign to gain 2,000 members in ten days was launched January 10. When the campaign stalled at 900 members, it was extended to February 1.[289] The end result was 1,200 members, well short of the goal and nearly 1,000 members short of the 2,118 members of the Memphis Association. A week later, the Nashville total climbed to 1,300.[290]

January also saw Dr. Buckner reelected president, a position he had held since June 1904. C. T. Cheek and Joseph H. Thompson were elected was elected vice presidents; A. H. Robinson, treasurer; and W. E. Ward, secretary, presiding at the dedication on Sunday afternoon. At a February board meeting, the treasurer reported a deficit in 1911, with expenses of $62,740 and receipts of $58,178.75. It was also reported that the cost of the new building was $410,045, a deficit of $75,045.48.[291]

The YMCA senior basketball league opened its season February 10 with a game between the "Giants" and the "Ramblers." According to scheduling committee members Dr. A. S. Keim, Henry "Monk" Sharp, and Will Pollard, the four teams in the league would play twelve games, all taking place on Thursday and Saturday nights. The other two teams were the "Athletics" and the "Cubs." The public was invited to attend all the games with free admission.[292]

During the ten-day celebration period following the opening of the new building, from February 15 through the 25th, Dr. Buckner presented G. A. Schrock, superintendent of construction, with a gold watch at a reception for mechanics and contractors who had worked on the building. Earlier, McGill said Schrock's outstanding work "merits the praise and gratitude of every association member." The 19th was designated "Ladies Day." The afternoon reception and the evening program were produced by the ladies' auxiliary.[293]

The highlight of the ten-day celebration was the dedication dinner held in the gymnasium on February 24. Four hundred people listened to Governor Wilson speak as did a scattering of ladies, who watched the proceedings from the balcony. Dr. Robert Lewis, secretary of the National YMCA, was the only other speaker. His remarks were sufficiently inspiring that the Nashville YMCA agreed to support, along with the Louisville YMCA, Rupert H. Stanley, a missionary who would sail to China on November 9 with his wife. During the evening, G. A. Schrock gave President Matt Buckner a key to the new building.[294]

The eight floors of the new building were originally arranged as follows:

> Basement: Barber shop, billiard room, employment bureau, laundry office, pressing club, public lavatories, tailor shop, and Turkish baths.
>
> First floor (Capitol Boulevard): Boys' department with amusement room, assembly room, check room, class rooms, dressing room, gymnasium, lavatories, locker room, offices, reading room, and swimming pool.
>
> First floor (Seventh Avenue): Men's baths, café, check room, correspondence room, cozy corner, directors' room, lavatories, library, main lobby, men's locker and dressing rooms, offices, reading room, sustaining members' club rooms, swimming pool, and visitors' gallery.
>
> Second floor: Bible class rooms, chess club, college club room, committee rooms, gymnasium, ladies' parlor, leaders' club room music room, physical director's room, private exercise room, state office, and Wilson auditorium.
>
> Third floor: Auditorium gallery, clubrooms, educational classrooms, educational director's office, dormitories, and study hall.
>
> Fourth, fifth, sixth, and seventh floors: Association apartments, baths and lavatories, special corridors, and trunk storage rooms.
>
> Eighth floor: Laundry and roof garden, outdoor gymnasium.

Because of the deficit that had grown to $80,000 more than the YMCA had in pledge payments and outstanding pledges, Dr. Buckner, Judge John A. Pitts, and Edgar Foster agreed to serve as general chairmen of yet another fundraising effort to make up the difference. The campaign used a clever advertising slogan, "White Elephant," copied from a Memphis YMCA "White Elephant" campaign in 1910, to refer to the debt. Posters bearing a picture of the white elephant were pasted on streetcars and posted on telephone polls. A life-size cutout of the white elephant was placed at the Seventh Avenue entrance. The *Nashville Banner* ran cartoon pictures of it on their front page on February 26 and 28. The caption read:

OPPORTUNITY

YOUNG
MEN'S
CHRISTIAN
ASSOCIATION

$80,000

SHALL WE LET THE $80,000
WHITE ELEPHANT
BLOCK NASHVILLE'S
"DOOR OF OPPORTUNITY"?

The cartoon on the 26th was accompanied by a full-page advertisement in which the YMCA described the cost overrun caused by the Capitol Boulevard project, the $25,000 in unpaid subscriptions, and the need for an additional $80,000 to finish the project. The advertisement then spoke of the YMCA's work that addressed the social, physical, educational, and religious needs of Nashville's young men. It made clear that the erection of a larger building was made possible by the Eakin gift of $119,500, and appealed to the community to provide the balance of the funds needed so that the association could be of the largest service to the city.[295]

The White Elephant campaign, to last twelve days, was launched at a luncheon on February 26. Each of the three campaign leaders had captains responsible for recruiting workers. As an incentive, it was announced that $17,500 of the $80,000 goal had already been subscribed.[296]

At a subsequent dinner meeting on the 3rd, Senator Luke Lea spoke to the 250 workers present. He reminded them of the great opportunities available to young men and of the advantages offered by the YMCA.[297] Unfortunately,

S. W. McGill, one of the association's most effective fund-raisers, was not available to help. He was ill and bedridden. During his absence, Dr. Buckner assumed his role as general manager. Another problem was that the campaign suffered, from the start, from a lack of workers. Because the campaign failed to reach its goal, the campaign was extended one week, to March 16. The week didn't help much as the goal seemed to remain as elusive as ever.[298]

In contrast to the unsuccessful fund-raising effort, the programs at the Y were going "full blast." In the first month that the new building was open, 1,330 young men enrolled as members, many taking advantage of the Physical Department, capably led by Henry G. Hart. By mid-June, that number would jump to 1,700. The association's religious emphasis was still strong as an average of 85 members attended the weekly Saturday night Bible class. Each morning, the staff gathered for a devotional service before beginning their duties. The fully accredited night high school was offering a four-year course, and it was announced that the new library would be named for W. B. "Sawney" Webb, as a result of gifts made or pledged by Webb alumni.[299] The Library was considered an asset even though the city had, since 1904, a wonderful public library only a block away on Union Street at Polk Avenue. The Public Library was made possible by a gift from Andrew Carnegie.

In 1912, the Nashville YMCA had five branches: the Central Department, the Student Department, the John Hill Eakin Institute, the Street Railway Department, and the Colored Men's Department.[300]

In the spring of 1912, 180 men were living in the apartments on the fourth, fifth, sixth, and seventh floors. The YMCA House Committee published a House Committee Bulletin for the men who were referred to as "our Double A members." The first bulletin said, "The supreme purpose of the Association apartments is the development of Christian character." The second bulletin urged the Double A men to conduct themselves properly, to get to know their neighbors, to be economical in the use of soap, towels, and water, to become involved with some form of Christian service through the Y, and to join the 3,000 Club by helping the YMCA enroll 3,000 members by January 1, 1913.

A new innovation at the Y was a Turkish bath on the Capitol Boulevard floor next to the swimming pool. To take the bath cost members fifty cents and non-members seventy-five cents.[301]

• • • • •

The YMCA made a progressive move in April when it employed William N. Sanders, an African-American, to work among the young colored men in the city.[302]

• • • • •

For the second consecutive summer, tennis courts with electric lights, an outdoor basketball court, a baseball diamond, and shower baths were available for members at Glendale Park. This came about in 1911 as the result of an arrangement worked out by YMCA Advisory Board member James E. Caldwell, whose Nashville Railway and Light Company owned the park.[303]

The youth in the boys' department were excited when they learned in May that, for the first time since 1906 or 1907, there would be a summer boys' camp. It would be held on the farm of A. P. Jackson about four and one-half miles from Ashland City on a horseshoe bend of Sycamore Creek where the stream was backed up by an eighteen-foot-tall stone dam that had been built by the Sycamore Manufacturing company in 1898 to furnish power for its mills, then under the supervision of Major E. C. Lewis.[304]

Accessible by the Tennessee Central Railroad as far as Ashland City, the camp was considered ideal for boating, fishing, hiking, and swimming. Henry G. Hart, boys' work director, who had been instrumental in finding the campsite, conducted the two-week camp that also offered basketball, baseball, tennis, and track. The schedule was reveille at 7 a.m., swimming at 11:00 a.m., dinner in the mess tent at noon, swimming at 4 p.m., supper at 5:30 p.m., baseball, rowing and fishing at 6:30 p.m. and taps at 9.

The boys slept in tents, with eight boys and "an older fellow" in each one. Fifty boys left for camp on the Tennessee Central at 8:05 a.m. Wednesday, June 12. The cost was $10, two dollars more than camp cost in 1906.[305]

Another change in 1912 was the name of the E. S. McSpadden Debating Club. It was renamed the YMCA Literary Club, suggesting a broader purpose. The association would, however, continue to have a debating club.[306]

The board was pleased with the quality of its new YMCA Night Law School that had opened in the autumn of 1911. It provided almost the same classes as those offered

Baseball grounds at Camp Sycamore, 1913

by leading law schools. Two years was required to complete the course. This did not mean graduating, however, as the school did not grant degrees until 1927. Many of those who completed the course before then went on to get law degrees at Cumberland University in Lebanon. The founders of the YMCA Night Law School were Morton B. Adams, William P. "Billy" Cooper, Lee Douglas, and Robert Selph Henry, all graduates of the Vanderbilt Law School. They had heard that the YMCA had launched a national program of night schools offering legal training, including schools in Boston, Cincinnati, Houston, and San Francisco. When the YMCA offered them space for classes on the third floor of the new YMCA building, they jumped at the chance.[307]

The faculty members of the John Hill Eakin Institute in the fall of 1912 included Edwin Lee Johnson, Ph.D., Vanderbilt, instructor in Latin and Math; Henry Meler, M.S., Vanderbilt, instructor in physical geography and Spanish; William Hume Jr. L. L. B. Vanderbilt university, instructor in law, W. T. Naïve, Cumberland Telephone Company, instructor in mechanical drawing; and J. Byron Naïve A.B. Peabody, instructor in chemistry.[308]

In October, C. R. Towson, International Industrial Secretary of the YMCA visited Nashville on a Southern tour to promote YMCA work in industrial companies. In addition to speaking to the YMCA board, he spoke to employees of two industrial companies and the engineering students at Vanderbilt. In November, the ladies' auxiliary held a bazaar at the general office for three days to benefit the YMCA.[309]

Over the winter of 1912–1913, the boys' department sponsored Class A and Class B basketball leagues, each with six teams, and the feared YMCA Ramblers continued their success. On Thanksgiving, the Ramblers traveled to Huntsville, Alabama, where they easily defeated the Huntsville YMCA 49–30. Later in the winter, the Ramblers beat archrival Vanderbilt 47–38 before the largest crowd of the season. The win clinched the city championship.[310] The Ramblers' record for 1913 was 13 wins and a single loss. Their starters were Benz and Donelson, forwards; Monk Sharp, center; and Emerson and Hutchison, guards.

Finally, at the November board meeting, the YMCA board reluctantly voted to take legal action to receive a fair settlement from the City of Nashville for the damage done by the appropriating of association property for the

Capitol Boulevard project. The city's meager offer did not come close to offsetting the expenses the YMCA incurred. The expense of redrawing architectural plans and buying the McWhirter property cost $20,000. In addition, construction costs increased and "practically an entire season's work in the new building was forfeited." The city's argument that Capitol Boulevard would increase property values of property owners along the boulevard did not help the association as much as it did other owners because the YMCA was a tax-exempt organization.[311]

The Year 1913

It was hard to believe that the association had occupied the new building for a full year when 1913 came along. At the first anniversary celebration that month, three charter members of the Nashville YMCA established in 1855 were on hand—R. S. Cowan, Edgar Jones, and R. G. Throne. The 300 Club that hoped to have 3,000 members by January didn't make their goal but did report that the association did have 2,300 members, a record high. When the Webb Memorial Library formally opened on January 24, Professor Webb spoke. Tennesseans had just elected Mr. Webb, who was the oldest member of the State YMCA Committee, to the United States Senate.[312]

In March, the House Committee decided that it had a lapse in judgment when it put pool and billiard tables in the basement. Perhaps the members were influenced by a December revival in Nashville to reconsider the matter in March, and remove the tables and use the space for Bible classes.[313] At the same board meeting, the House Committee reported that the number of men living in building apartments had jumped to 270.[314]

The focus on gaining 3,000 members which, had the YMCA reached this goal, would have put the association in the top 15 largest associations in North America, caused the Y to take its eye off the need to collect unpaid subscriptions. The large unpaid balance was causing the directors to have to pay large interest charges. Consequently, another notice was served on those whose subscriptions were in arrears.[315]

Late in May, Boys' Work Director Henry G. Hart sent postcards of the baseball diamond at Camp Sycamore to prospective campers. The message on the back read: "The annual boys' summer camp will be held June 10 to 24. The price is $10 including all expenses and railroad fare." Parents of campers were told that they could mail letters to their sons at Camp Sycamore, Route 2, Ashland City, Tennessee, and that, if they needed to talk to their sons, they could call long distance to Mr. A. P. Jackson's residence, on whose 1,700-acre farm the camp was located, one mile upstream from the old Sycamore Powder Mills dam. Sixty-one boys attended.[316]

June 6 was the 69th anniversary of the founding of the YMCA in London on June 6, 1944. The Nashville YMCA celebrated with a ladies' auxiliary produced Founder's Day dinner at which the Hon. Thomas R. Marshall, vice president of the United States, was the guest of honor and speaker.

• • • • •

The Boys' Division adopted a creed in September 1913 that read:

We believe it is better
To train him than to restrain him;
To form him rather than to reform him;
To prevent him rather than to punish him;
To lead him rather than to drive him;
To make him rather than to break him;
To use him rather than to abuse him.
Nashville YMCA[317]

• • • • •

Confident in the Future

At the September board meeting, the directors faced the future with confidence. The indications were that the 1913–1914 fiscal year would be the greatest season in the history of the Nashville Association or any association in the South. At the same meeting, the House Committee chairman reported that his committee was implementing a self-governing organization among the apartment men, with two men from each floor to be elected to a self-governing board. The Physical Department chairman reported that the outdoor gym on the roof of the big gym would be open in ten days. When completed, the outdoor gym would have a tennis court, three large handball courts, a volleyball court, and, possibly, a basketball court. The area would be lit for night play.[318]

In October 1913, Professor Clarence B. Wallace was chairman of the Educational Committee. He had three outstanding Nashville attorneys teach in the Law School—W. P. Cooper, Charles L. Cornelius, and Lee Douglas.[319]

The second annual membership banquet featured

United States Senator, W. R. "Sawney" Webb as special guest and speaker. Three hundred fifty men were there to hear him. That evening, some of the directors must have talked privately about the 502 subscribers to the Building Fund who had paid nothing, and the 1,100 subscribers who had paid their pledges in part. The amount unpaid was still at $42,000. The YMCA's attorney, Pitts and McConnico, had reminded the board that, under no circumstances, could the association divert funds designated for other purposes, to pay off the debt. The question was whether to bring suit against any of the delinquent subscribers.[320] On the other hand, the directors were grateful for the 3,780 subscribers who had paid their pledges in full. The three largest individual contributors were all directors—A. M. Shook, Joseph H. Thompson, and Percy Warner.[321]

Disappointing news came in November when the Commissioners of the City of Nashville offered $3,500 to settle their dispute with the YMCA. As this represented only ten cents on the dollar, the board rejected the offer. Two weeks later, the city came back with a $6,100 offer. Although disillusioned that the city had earlier said the YMCA would suffer no loss on account of Capitol Boulevard, the board decided to accept the amount in order to have closure.

As Christmas approached, the White Elephant Campaign, nearly twenty-two months old, had raised $62,179 in subscriptions. Despite its failure to raise $85,000, the board considered the campaign to have been a success and thanked Dr. Buckner, Edgar Foster, and Judge John Pitts for their diligence.[322]

The YMCA published an anniversary statement early in January 1914 to highlighted significant occurrences during the preceding year. More than 36,000 people passed through the YMCA doors in 1913. During the year, the YMCA brought Woodrow Wilson, William Jennings Bryan, and vice president Marshall to Nashville. During the year, 226 young men found employment through the employment section. Over 30,000 men and 22,346 boys enjoyed the swimming pool. There were 234 boys in the Boys' Department at year-end and the total attendance in that department was 37,400. The association membership at year-end was 2,300.[323]

Realizing that some cities officially recognize their YMCAs by giving them annual subsidies, Dr. Buckner and S. W. McGill, on behalf of the board, wrote the Davidson County Quarterly Court on January 14, asking for a $1,000 appropriation for 1914 using the argument that the YMCA performs a community service through its ministry to the boys and young men of Davidson County. In their letter, they mentioned the 368 boys the local association gave such services as free room and board, train tickets, food, and jobs. They also pointed out the number of Davidson County boys who come to town on huckster wagons and other means and who are welcomed at the Y anytime day or night. Upon receipt of the petition, the matter was referred to a committee on charitable institutions. That committee reported at the April Session that they had met with YMCA officials and had carefully gone through the facts but had made no decision and asked for more time.[324]

The YMCA officers for 1914 were Dr. Matt Buckner, president; Maj. C. T. Cheek and Joseph H. Thompson, vice-presidents; Joseph T. Howell, treasurer for the building fund; Garland S. Moore, recording secretary; and W. E. Ward, treasurer for the current fund. There were nine professional secretaries: S. W. McGill, general secretary; H. G. Hart, boys' work director; J. M. Stickney, business secretary; D. W. Gordon, cashier and publicity director; C. E. Lovett, educational director; E. L. Spain, house secretary; Dr. A. S. Keim, physical director; S. M. Cowles, Membership Secretary; and E. L. "Gene" Philpot, religious and social work director.[325]

Much to Celebrate

All the directors and profession secretaries had much to celebrate in 1914. Despite having not reached their ambitious goal of 3,000 members or that of making the tough White Elephant Campaign goal, the Nashville YMCA and its boys' division were both the largest in the South, and the association had the best equipped YMCA in the South. Earlier, the Louisville and Memphis YMCAs had larger memberships. More people lived in the Nashville YMCA than in all the hotels of the city combined. As someone said, "The YMCA is running a hotel, a restaurant, a club, a theater, a church, a school, an employment bureau, a relief agency, and a library, all combined into one. Branches are maintained for street railway men, students, and colored men."[326]

The board was also proud that George T. Motlow passed the Tennessee bar Exam on January 23. He was the first graduate of the John Hill Eakin Law Institute to do so. Born near Lynchburg, George was a member of the famous Motlow family known for making Jack Daniel Whiskey. A graduate of Peoples and Morgan's School, he had just begun practicing law with Thomas J. Tyne in the Stahlman Building.[327]

The Ramblers had an even better record in 1914 than they had in 1913. For the season, the YMCA team had 17 wins and a single loss.

Early in the spring, the Colored Men's Branch had succeeded in raising $33,806, nearly all in pledges to partially match the Julius Rosenwald offer of $25,000. The Colored Men's Branch was looking for the Nashville Association to raise the balance of the match, nearly $42,000. Unfortunately, the timing was awful as the Nashville Association was still trying to collect $40,000 in subscriptions made five years earlier to the Building Fund.[328]

Camp Beckett

Because it did not work out for the two-week summer camp to return to Mr. A. P. Jackson's farm on Sycamore Creek, arrangements were made for the 1914 camp to be held on the east side of the Cumberland River north of town. Camp Beckett was accessible from Nashville on the Gallatin Interurban Railroad. It consisted of eleven tents in a row with a wooden dining hall at one end. On the other side of an open quadrangle, there was a smaller wood building that served as the camp hospital. A flagpole flew in the center of the quadrangle. There were two other small tents, a tennis court, and a creek that had been dammed. The boys swam in the river from a sand bar and also canoed on the Cumberland. The Y also used the site as a weekend camp for boys who worked during the weekdays. In June, a number of boys' club members hiked to the camp for the night.[329]

Another group of Nashville YMCA boys attended the YMCA Southern Student Conference in Blue Ridge, NC, from June 12 to 21. They traveled to Black Mountain, NC, in a special N.C. & St. L. sleeping car that left Nashville at 9:30 p.m. on the 11th and arrived at Black Mountain the next afternoon at 3:05 p.m.[330]

During August, the boys' work division reached a record-breaking 400 members. For the second year, an annual prep school football banquet was held the first Friday night in November with Vanderbilt Coach Dan McGugin and Coach Wood, of the University of Virginia as featured speakers.[331]

The religious work committee was also active in 1914. It sponsored a series of Sunday afternoon meetings for men that began November 8 and went through December. The speakers were mainline Protestant ministers and the chaplain at the Tennessee State Prison.[332]

A six-day campaign for new members in November resulted in 795 new members. The December 14 issue of *Better Nashville* was devoted to a list of their names.

Dr. Matt Buckner Steps Down

At the annual meeting on January 12, Dr. Matt Buckner stepped down as president and was succeeded by W. O. Tirrill. Dr. Buckner, a busy physician with a wife and three daughters, had served for ten years, since June 1904, the longest tenure of any YMCA president since its founding in 1875. He had seen the Nashville YMCA grow to be the largest in the South and to have, as its headquarters, possibly the most handsome YMCA building in the South. Appropriately, resolutions were adopted expressing appreciation for his service. Mr. McGill, the general secretary, gave his annual report, "which showed gratifying progress along all lines of association work."[333]

President W. O. Tirrill was with Graham Printing Company. A member of the Commercial and Rotary Clubs, he was a director of the Boys' Club, a Master Mason, and a deacon in the Broadway Presbyterian Church. A good golfer, Tirrill was a member of the Nashville Golf and Country Club.[334]

January was always an appropriate time to reevaluate the association's needs. In 1915, the Y needed a Central Association Building without a debt, a Colored Men's YMCA Building, a Railroad Men's YMCA Building, a YMCA athletic field, and a YMCA summer camp.[335]

John R. Mott, associate general secretary of the International Committee of the YMCA visited Nashville in January to deliver the principal address at the laying of the cornerstone of the Association college, established for the training of men for YMCA service. A friend of both W. D. Weatherford, the International Student Secretary for the South who lived in Nashville, and Nashville general secretary W. S. McGill, Mott became, in 1915, the second general secretary of the International Committee.[336]

Something else significant happened in January. After carrying in its budget the cost of the Colored Men's Branch for three years, the YMCA board voted to discontinue that support and count on the Colored Men's Branch to provide their own funds to make their budget.[337]

• • • • •

CHAPTER EIGHT

The War to End All Wars

1915–1918

JANUARY 1915 SAW A CHANGE at the top. W. O. Tirrill succeeded Dr. M. G. Buckner as president of the Nashville YMCA. The only other change in the officer ranks was the election of J. H. Allison as first vice-president. He replaced Maj. C. T. Cheek, who was too ill to serve another term. Allison, H. A. Davis, L. H. McDill. G. S. Moore, Arch Trawick, and J. H. Thompson, all directors, were re-elected for terms expiring January 1, 1916. During the meeting, resolutions were adopted, expressing appreciation for Dr. Buckner's service during his eleven years as president[338]

General secretary S. W. McGill, showed gratifying results in the annual report in 1914 with progress in all areas of outreach. McGill was particularly pleased with the gains in membership.[339] He informed the board, but may not have put in the report, that, over the past few months, the Y had been literally overwhelmed with requests for food and shelter from young men in need of temporary relief. The Y was responding, McGill said, as best it could with limited resources.[340]

The YMCA Ramblers announced an attractive schedule of home basketball games in January. Included were two games with Vanderbilt, and single games with Union University, Kentucky State, Chattanooga, and the University of Georgia. In the second Vanderbilt game, the Commodores won 43–31 to claim the city championship.[341] The Ramblers' record for the season was fourteen wins and four losses.

The Nashville Rotary Club, founded in 1913, wanted to celebrate the 10th anniversary of the founding of the first Rotary Club in Chicago in 1905. Because more than 60 percent of their members, including W. O. Tirrill, were also members of the Nashville YMCA, it seemed natural for the Rotary Club to hold that meeting in the new YMCA building. The splendid event, that included wives, took place in the YMCA's Wilson Auditorium in February.[342]

An innovation in 1915 was the establishment of a central committee, composed of eighteen young men, whose purpose was to promote the activities of the Central YMCA on a more aggressive and comprehensive scale than was ever done before. Toward this end, the committee had two goals. One was to make membership so attractive that many more young men would want to join. The second goal was aggressively go after the delinquent subscribers to the capital campaign.[343]

The YMCA suffered a blow in March with the death of Maj. C. T. Cheek, one of the original incorporators of the YMCA when it reorganized in 1908. During the building period, when he and the other members of the executive committee met so frequently, he was always there. Very clear in his convictions, Major Cheek was, nevertheless, always courteous and respectful of the opinions of others. He was liberal in his support of the YMCA both with his wise counsel and financial means.[344]

Major Cheek's death meant that the ranks of the old guard were thinning. Major E. B. Stahlman and Robert S. Cowan were the only two surviving members of the original board of ten members elected at the reorganization in 1875.[345]

An important step taken during the year was the purchase of a lot on the northeast corner of Cedar and Park Place as a site for the Colored Men's branch of the

YMCA. Immediately across the street from the Capitol grounds, the site was also close to the colored business district. fundraising started immediately for a building on the site that was suggested by Nashville YMCA board member, Joseph H. Thompson.[346]

Plans for the annual summer camp were announced in May. It would be held June 11 to 24 in the woods along the headwaters of the Caney Fork River about four miles north of Clifty, Tennessee, a small mining town at an elevation of 1,600 feet. The site, on property owned by B. H. Johnson, was reached by the Sparta-Clifty branch of the N.C. & St. L. Railroad. The camp would be under the direction of Henry G. Hart, boys' work secretary. The river was shallow, from three to five feet deep, with a sand bank and rock bottom. Ideal for swimming, and fishing, boating was also available.[347]

On June 11, "forty young men left Union Station in a special coach with an attached baggage car for Clifty and Camp Peyton, named for John Howe Peyton, president of the N.C. & St. L. Railroad." Upon arriving, they walked four miles over a rough road to camp.[348]

Not long after the boys' camp was over, Henry G. Hart resigned as boys' work secretary to enter the missionary field. He, with his wife and daughter, would sail for India on October 1. The Nashville Association, because of the high esteem with which Hart was held, underwrote his $2,000 annual salary as a missionary. J. Young Todd succeeded him as boys' work secretary.[349]

Because of the popularity of the Business Men's Health Club, spaces formerly occupied by the barbershop and tailor shop were given to the health club. The barbershop moved to the foot of the stairs off the main lobby while the tailor shop relocated to the large room beneath the boys' lobby, accessible by either the elevator or the Capitol Boulevard entrance.[350]

The big news in September was a fire that badly damaged Percy Warner Gymnasium. Fortunately, the association had sufficient insurance to rebuild and improve the facility. The renovation was underway in November, and a smaller gym with handball courts was added.[351]

A baseball league was organized in November under the guidance of league president, Dan McGugin. In the spring there would be two leagues with eight teams each. Each team would have nine players, a captain, and a manager.[352]

The YMCA Debating Club met semi-monthly in 1915 and 1916. At the first December meeting, on Monday night, the question debated was, "Resolved, should Capital punishment be abolished?" Some topics transcend the decades.[353]

On December 29, the Nashville YMCA celebrated the 60th anniversary of the association's founding in 1855. An article written for the occasion said, "Little written or printed data remains of the earlier years of the Nashville YMCA previous to the year 1875." Although a few of the original members were still alive in 1915, they gave conflicting statements about YMCA events in the mid and late 1850s and were of little help in writing the article.[354] Unquestionably, however, in 1915 the Nashville YMCA considered itself as having been founded in 1855—not 1875.

The board members in 1916—all well-known Nashville citizens—were T. F. Bonner, Dr. Matt Buckner, A. Cayce Jr., Kendrick C. Hardcastle, Joe T. Howell, W. L. Looney, H. McClelland, L. H. McDill, S. W. McGill, Garland S. Moore, W. J. O'Callaghan, John A. Pitts, A. B. Ransom, Joseph H. Thompson, W. O. Tirrill, Arch Trawick, Clarence B. Wallace, and William E. Ward. Advisory board members were C. H. Brandon, Whitefoord R. Cole, Leland Hume, John Peyton, Harry Ransom, E. B. Stahlman, A. M. Shook, P. T. Troop, and Percy Warner—an impressive group.

Because the restoration of the gymnasium took until the first of February, the Ramblers played their early games away from home. In January, they went to West Tennessee to play Union University, and the Jackson and Memphis YMCAs. On February 25, the Ramblers won their second straight game with Vanderbilt 25–23 with Captain Monk Sharp scoring the winning goal. With this victory, the Ramblers claimed the Southern championship.[355] The repairs to the Percy Warner Gymnasium cost $2,880, of which $1,000 was a contribution from President and Mrs. Tirrill.[356]

In February, the average age of the young men living in the YMCA apartments was twenty-two. The average room rate was $2.25 per week. The boarders embraced the Baptist, Catholic, Christian, Episcopalian, Methodist, and Presbyterian faiths, and there were, naturally, a number of boarders with no church affiliation.[357]

In April, three baseball leagues were in full swing—an indoor league and two YMCA junior leagues. The Y also

YMCA swimming pool, 1916

had a swimming team that lost to the Memphis YMCA in May. The YMCA swimming pool was something the association was proud of. The pool, 60' by 20', was flooded in light from a skylight over the entire room. The walls were white enamel brick and ceramic tile with borders in colors.[358]

March brought a letter from Henry G. Hart, then in Lucknow, India. At this time, the International Committee's policy was to send missionaries, including Hart, only to countries where they were invited by missionary bodies in those countries. In India's case, the United Missionary organization in Madras, India, first asked for the services of an association secretary in 1888.[359]

Nearly two years after the World War erupted in Europe, the impact on the United States and the Nashville YMCA was minimal. One indication of how ill-prepared the country was for war was the fact that, for some period of time in the spring of 1916, 298 of 412 applicants for the U.S. Army and U.S. Navy were rejected, many because of "cigarette hearts caused by cigarettes."[360]

Because the Nashville YMCA had no permanent campsite, it moved again in 1916. That year, it was to be held in June on the Elk River about twelve miles southeast of Fayetteville. Campers could reach camp by riding on the L & N Railroad to Brighton, a small station about four miles south of the campsite that was on a ridge overlooking the river. The camp had formerly housed the summer camp of the Lincoln County Game and Fish Preserve. J. Young Todd, boys' work director, and E. W. Dance, assistant physical director, were camp co-directors. A short time before the camp opened, Dance took several of his tent leaders to the site "to get everything ready." While there he caught enough fish to feed all the campers. Dance would resign from the Nashville Association at the end of the year to become the physical director of the Norfolk YMCA.[361]

The membership drives in the fall of 1915 and 1916 featured imaginary train and automobile trips. In 1915, it was a 1,500-mile trip by rail that covered six Southern cities. For every dollar turned in, the train went one mile. The four cars in the train represented the four membership teams. The Dixie-Jackson Highway trip in October 1916 worked much the same way. At the beginning of the 1916 campaign, the Nashville Y had 2,123 members, and its boys' department was still the largest in the South.[362]

After having been pressured by state and private officials to sell the Park Avenue lot because it was too close to the State Capitol, the YMCA directors' purchased the old Duncan Hotel in December for the home of the Colored Men's YMCA. The purchase price was $70,000 with $10,000 paid in cash and with the second payment due May 15.[363] The Nashville Association did this despite not breaking even financially in 1916 when expenses totaled $72,147 and income only $67,488. This fact and the $50,000 of debt on the YMCA Building made the possibility of raising $70,000 for the Colored Men's Branch increasingly unrealistic. In response, the directors approved a 1917 budget of $68,025, less than a one percent increase, and projected $67,325 in expenses, a decrease of $4,822.09 from what was spent in 1916.[364]

In January, Willard O. Tirrill, who was with Graham Paper Company, was reelected president of the Nashville YMCA. He would continue to serve selflessly and with intelligence. Mr. Tirrill, who lived on Richland Avenue, would be tested in his third term as president.[365]

During Tirrill's tenure, he had good counsel not only from his board, and a board of advisors, but also from a ministerial board that, in 1917, consisted of Rev. Allen Fort, pastor of First Baptist Church; Rev. L. E. McNair, pastor of Moore Memorial Presbyterian Church; Rev. H. J. Mikell, rector of Christ Episcopal Church; Rev. Carey E. Morgan, pastor of Vine Street Christian Church; Rev. T. C. Ragsdale, pastor of McKendree Methodist Church; and Rev. T. A. Wiggington, pastor of Broadway Presbyterian Church.[366]

The sight of the YMCA Building, standing on a hill, must have been impressive and a source of pride to its staff and board. Eight stories tall, the building featured on its roof four giant letters "Y M C A" that were lit at night by electric bulbs and a battery. It would have been fun to have the lights blink on and off but Tirrill figured it would have seemed frivolous to spend money on that given the association's debt, the need to build a home away from home for boys, the obligation to raise money for the Colored Men's Branch, and other pressing needs.[367]

The Ramblers hoped to repeat as Southern basketball champions in 1917 but it was not to be. A February loss to the University of Georgia 26–24 dispelled that dream. Still, the team carved out a solid 10–4 record and were the champions of Middle Tennessee.[368]

An eight-day membership drive was held in March was headed by Vanderbilt football coach Dan McGugin, who had been president of the YMCA baseball league a year earlier. The campaign goal was $165,000. If successful, they intended to use $75,000 to pay for the Colored YMCA building, $49,000 to pay off the mortgage on the YMCA building, $25,000 for accumulated indebtedness, and $16,500 to cover YMCA operations for three years. This was an ambitious goal even for a coach whose football team at Vanderbilt had a 7–1–1 record.[369] The results, announced on March 30, proved disappointing. Despite having extended the drive, the amount raised in subscriptions was $110,663, nearly $55,000 less than its goal. Surprisingly, the Colored Men's Branch did better than its white counterparts as 1,482 colored citizens subscribed $18,517—92 percent of its goal. Only 577 white citizens made gifts or pledges. The white subscription total was $92,146 or 63.5 percent of their goal.

So what went wrong? There were several factors. One was that white people were unenthusiastic about the purchase of the old Duncan Hotel for the Colored YMCA branch, feeling that it was completely unsuitable, having no gymnasium, no swimming pool, and no auditorium. Julius Rosenwald felt the same way for the same reasons. He was adamant that not one dollar of his would go to pay for the Duncan. There were also campaign failures in communications and a lack of understanding regarding the association's priorities. Although the campaign leaders voted to extend the campaign, it had lost its steam and collapsed entirely when the United States declared war on the Axis powers in April.[370]

The War to End All Wars

Immediately after America entered the war on the side of Great Britain and France, a recruiting office was set up in the Capitol Boulevard lobby. When Camp Andrew Jackson, a mobilization camp, was set up late in April where the Belle Meade Boulevard entrance of present-day Percy Warner Park is today, the Nashville Association put and staffed a tent there. By May 5, a noncommissioned officer of the Tennessee National Guard was conducting a military training class three days a week at the Y. By May 18, forty Nashville YMCA members had enlisted in the army or the navy. President Tirrill urged the members to encourage others to join the

Colored Men's Branch, ca. 1917

association to fill the gaps. That same month, S. Waters McGill, the YMCA's able general executive, accepted a request to become supervisor for the South in a nationwide campaign to raise $100,000,000 for the American Red Cross's war work. Nashville and Tennessee's goals were $100,000 and $650,000, respectively. Within a month, boys' work secretary C. A. Witherspoon, was performing Red Cross work in Jackson, Mississippi. C. C. Beasley, membership secretary, was doing the same thing in Nashville, while Dr. A. S. Keim, physical education director, left for New York to serve as one of thirteen physical education directors responsible for directing all the physical activities of the YMCA in military training camps across the country. Interestingly, three years earlier in 1915, Keim had organized the first city park baseball league in Shelby Park.

Back home, the Red Cross campaign was hugely successful. By June 1917, Nashville had exceeded its goal by raising over $180,000. McGill had come back to Nashville from Atlanta to head that effort and reassume his duties at the Nashville YMCA.[371]

Despite its preoccupation with the war, the Nashville YMCA planned a summer camp in 1917. It was to be held in Cumberland County, 117 miles east of Nashville on the Tennessee Central Railroad. Near a 325-acre lake at 2,200 feet above sea level, the camp dates were to be June 18 through June 22, provided a sufficient number of boys signed up. Because boys' work secretary Witherspoon went to Jackson, Mississippi, in June to do Red Cross work, the camp seems likely to have been cancelled.[372]

In August 1917, General John Pershing asked the North American YMCA to undertake the management of all Army canteens. John R. Mott, general secretary of the International Committee, accepted the challenge despite knowing that it would be difficult to get supplies or men experienced in handling, distributing, selling, and accounting for supplies. Nevertheless, with thousands of YMCA secretaries helping, the YMCA stepped up to the plate. "From June 1918 to April 1919, the YMCA handled in France alone upwards of two billion cigarettes, thirty-two million chocolate bars, eighteen million cans

Father and Son Banquet, 1916

of smoking tobacco, fifty million cigars, sixty million cans of jam, twenty-nine million packages of chewing gum, and ten million packages of candy."[373]

Crippled by its loss of secretaries and members, the Nashville YMCA officially abandoned all its regular programs in September 1917 and dedicated itself to war work. That month, sixty soldiers were living at the YMCA waiting to be sent to mobilization camps. Staff members established a program of religious and social work for their benefit. The Y was also home for a recruiting office and the headquarters for five separate exemption boards. In their spare time, YMCA secretaries were also furnishing blankets and bedding for soldiers in the local camps. By September, the Nashville Y had established branch YMCAs at both Camp Andrew Jackson and Camp Kirkland on the Vanderbilt campus where most of the male students were in the Student Army Training Corps.[374]

On October 30, 1917, Robert S. Henry, a member of the Nashville Association, wrote Nashville YMCA general secretary S. W. McGill from Camp Wheeler in Macon, Georgia.

> While I do not believe that anyone who has ever lived in a camp before and after the YMCA buildings were opened could doubt the great value of the YMCA to the soldiers. The association here has just finished rendering one of those conspicuous services which call attention to the fact that they are rendering a splendid day-by-day service also. During the past few days we have received from other camps about 10,000 men, and every man of them, as soon as he was unloaded from the train, has gotten sandwiches and coffee at a YMCA tent set up by the railroad track. The military authorities have simply turned over to the YMCA that important part of the reception of the troops, and it has been most successfully handled.
>
> Yours truly,
> Robert S. Henry[375]

In November, office secretary McBride left to do Army YMCA work in Augusta, Georgia. That same month, the YMCA undertook responsibility for managing all post exchanges on U.S. Army bases to free enlisted men and officers to go to France to fight. In Nashville, a second National Red Cross drive kicked off, this time to raise $50,000. Nashvillians responded beautifully and before month's end, $55,193.66 had been raised. This was called the most popular financial campaign ever conducted in Nashville.

Despite the loss of men to the services, the Nashville YMCA had 1,757 members in November 1917, making it still the largest YMCA in the South. That distinction may have ended abruptly as, by mid-December, the Nashville Association had lost 264 men to military service and the membership had declined to 1,424 men and 278 boys. By then another secretary had left. Paul Daugherty, boys' division secretary, went to Washington, DC, to enlist. He was replaced by Arthur C. Tippens.[376]

When 1917 ended, Nashville had distinguished itself by holding five separate war drives—two Liberty loan drives securing $11,024,250, the Red Cross drive for $184,000, the Army YMCA drive for $58,500 and an Army YWCA drive for $13,500. In every drive, the city surpassed its goal by an astonishing 143.9 percent, raising a total of $11,280,250 against a collective goal of $7,839,850.54.[377]

The 1918 New Year's Open House was possibly the best one ever held in the new building. There was entertainment throughout the day. Conspicuous in the crowded lobby were "war mothers" whose sons had been YMCA members before entering military service. The formal entertainment started at 5 p.m. when a motion picture was shown. Throughout the day and evening there were handball and volleyball games, gymnastic classes, gun drills, relay races, and basketball games. The 225 young men residing in the apartments hosted the dinner in the YMCA café.[378]

With the YMCA giving its all for servicemen in Nashville, it is surprising that, for 1917, the Nashville Association managed to run a balanced budget. The officers elected for 1918 were Willard O. Tirrill, president; James H. Allison, vice-president; Dr. R. W. Weaver, vice-president; Joseph T. Howell, treasurer; and William E. Ward, recording secretary.[379]

Despite the war, the Ramblers were still rambling with Captain Monk Sharp hitting from the corners and sharp shooting guard Jake Petway in the lineup. On January 18, the Ramblers defeated the visiting Memphis Boys Club team 53–32.[380]

By February, Nashvillians were aware that the Federal Government planned a huge powder plant in Jones Bend of the Cumberland River. The Nashville YMCA quickly offered the use of its facilities to the War Department and to those in charge of the great undertaking. The Secretary of War wrote the YMCA thanking the association for its offer and saying that the government would advise the workers of the recreational opportunities and facilities available to them. On Sunday afternoon, February 24, the YMCA held a musical in the YMCA lobby with a local vocalist singing familiar religious songs around the piano. The Association hoped to attract some of the men flooding into the city to work at the munitions plant.[381]

• • • • •

The Nashville YMCA still had an active ladies' auxiliary in 1918, thirty-six years after it was founded. The president that year was Mrs. C. C. Beasley.[382]

• • • • •

As a diversion from the war and in an effort to showcase local grammar and high school gymnastic talent, the YMCA hosted a demonstration of physical work in the gymnasium on March 22. Representatives from Hume-FoggHigh School, Peabody Demonstration School, the YMHA, as well as boys from the YMCA, and girls from the YWCA participated in dancing, gymnastics, games, gun drills, an acrobatic act, and wrestling and boxing exhibitions. L. K. Gordon, the YMCA's physical director, supervised the affair with the help of his counterparts at the other involved organizations.[383]

To help reduce its debt, the Nashville YMCA began offering its members, late in the spring, $50,000 worth of YMCA Liberty Investment Bonds in denominations of $500 each. The bonds, which paid 6 percent interest, were secured by a deed of trust on the YMCA building. In a month, $30,000 of the bonds had been sold.[384]

Early in July, immediate past YMCA president, Capt. Matt Buckner, then forty-seven years old, left Nashville for Anniston, Alabama, to head a ward at the Fort McClellan base hospital. When he wrote his wife, Elizabeth, he often did so on Army and Navy YMCA stationery that featured the YMCA Triangle and the American flag.

Three more directors, Moore, McDill, and Trawick, left not much later.[385] Another Nashvillian, Murray E. Hill, became the youngest YMCA secretary with the armed forces.[386]

In September, the Nashville YMCA manned service stations at the State Fair, providing writing paper, drinking cups, information, and literature free of charge. As this was the largest attended State Fair in history, the YMCA volunteers had their hands full.[387] African-American soldiers received less help in Nashville as there were only three showers and a limited number of rooms available at the Colored YMCA for the large numbers of African-American soldiers passing through town.[388]

In the midst of coping with wartime conditions, the Nashville Y did not need controversy but that's what it got, largely through its own action. Stung by criticism from the Nashville Association that the Colored Men's Branch was practicing elitism and nepotism, the African-American trustees of the branch raised money to take over their mortgage and successfully petitioned the national YMCA to receive an independent charter.[389]

The YMCA Wins Respect at the Front

One of the principal battles at the close of World War I was the first American major offensive under General Pershing. Over a three-day period, from September 12 to 14, 1918, the Americans drove the Germans from the St. Mihiel salient that the enemy had held since 1914. Just before they were ordered to "go over the top" from their entrenched position, a company of American soldiers noticed a civilian in their midst with a huge pack on his back. He did not explain his presence but some of the men had noticed that he had whispered a word to their company commander who nodded approval. When the order to advance came, he went with them. At the first pause, when the soldiers were sheltered behind a small rise of ground, the YMCA man made his way from soldier to soldier, giving each a cake of chocolate and a pack of cigarettes. When he ran out, he disappeared to the rear only to return a couple of hours later with more chocolate and cigarettes. He did this all day. Right there, the YMCA won its place in the hearts of a company of American soldiers.[390]

In October, there were sixteen YMCA units in Nashville an amazing number. They were the boys' branch; central branch; Fisk University; Old Hickory Plant; Old Hickory Colored; Peabody College; Meharry Medical; Railroad branch; State Normal; Street Railway; Tennessee Industrial School; Vanderbilt Academic, Biblical, Dental, and Medical; and Walden University.[391] The Y was stretched pretty thin.

Realizing how stressed financially the Nashville Association was, President Tirrill made a $10,000 contribution to the Central YMCA in October, a magnificent gift for that day. That month, another director, Henry C. Hibbs, left for Army YMCA work. Three new directors, George E. Bennie, Vernon S. Tupper and Edward B. Craig Jr. were appointed to fill trustee vacancies. Paul Harris, director of religious and social work, resigned in November to accept a job with the Boy Scouts of America in Memphis.

The bloodbath of the Great War ended November 11, 1918, when Germany surrendered to the Allies. Yet much remained to be done by the YMCA in Europe.

In December, the National War Council of the YMCA called on "a few of the outstanding general secretaries of the United States and a few of the leading ministers to go overseas at once to conduct evangelistic services among the soldiers." Among those called were Dr. James I. Vance, pastor of Nashville's First Presbyterian Church, and S. W. McGill, general secretary of the Nashville YMCA. Both went, McGill having been granted a six-month leave of absence by the YMCA board.[392]

Remarkably, the YMCA membership grew during the war. The Nashville Y stood 2nd in membership in the South in June when its membership was 1,995. Officers in 1918 were Willard O. Tirrill, president; W. E. Ward, recording secretary; J. T. Howell, treasurer; and S. W. McGill, general secretary.[393]

The national YMCA, that operated 1,500 canteens in France, had been asked in 1918 to provide private transportation across the North Atlantic of supplies to France. This naturally added to the cost of items for sale in the canteens. The YMCA was criticized so heavily, that it asked for a government investigation. The government did so and cleared the YMCA of any wrongdoing. High-ranking military officers testified that the YMCA had done a wonderful job, despite its shortcomings. Soon, national sentiment turned in favor of the YMCA, setting the tone for the YMCA's successful efforts in Nashville and elsewhere in the 1920s.

• • • • •

CHAPTER NINE

The Aftermath
1919–1921

YMCA Graduate School at 21st Avenue South

IN DECEMBER 1918, W. C. McAlister, chairman of the military examining board, wrote the Nashville YMCA to thank the association for providing his board with comfortable quarters in which to conduct their business during the war. Other organizations wrote similar letters.[394]

At the YMCA board of directors' annual meeting on January 8, W. O. Tirrill did not stand for reelection. Having served "in a most faithful and self-sacrificing way for the past four years," he felt it was time to step aside. In his place, the board elected John P. W. Brown, a Vanderbilt Engineering School graduate, then forty-four years old. Shortly after his election, Brown would be promoted to general superintendent of the Nashville Railway and Light Company with responsibility for the railway and electrical divisions. He and his wife, the former Annie Crockett, had seven children.[395]

The directors learned, possibly at the same January 8 meeting, that their general secretary S. W. McGill had landed safely in Europe, following his voyage by steamship from New York. While he was gone, D. W. Gordon served as interim general secretary.[396]

In January, the board voted to offer free memberships for three months to all military men on their being mustered out of service. By June, over 500 men had accepted the offer.[397]

When the 114th Field Artillery and the 115th Field Artillery of the 30th Infantry Division returned to Nashville, they were welcomed home by parades on March 31 and April 5, respectively. Wanting to do its part, the YMCA offered the doughboys free baths, stationary, and "lounging headquarters." E. L. Spain, then membership secretary, helped supervise the feeding of the soldiers at the Hippodrome.[398]

• • • • •

Summer camp, discontinued in either 1917 or 1918, was reinstituted. It was held from June 23 to July 19 on the Rocky River at Rock Island in Warren County less than a mile upstream from the Tennessee Power Company Dam at the junction of the Collins and Caney Fork rivers. The camp, affectionately called "The Best Camp Ever," was the longest ever run by the association and the most heavily attended in history. It was under the supervision of boys' work director C. W. Abele. The cost was $22.50, not including railroad fare that was $6.71 roundtrip.[399]

• • • • •

Early in April, the U.S. Army released the YMCA from its responsibility of running Army Exchanges for the American Expeditionary forces. Back in Nashville, the staff hoped Mr. McGill, Dr. Buckner and other YMCA guys would be home soon. McGill landed in New York on June 27, while Dr. Buckner was discharged on July 13.[400] While McGill was gone, the YMCA had suffered considerable hardships.

When McGill returned, the YMCA vacation school was in session and would be until August 15 three weeks before public schools opened. Faculty members were Nashville Public School teachers. The vacation school offered both grammar school and high school classes.[401]

Early in August, A. Waters McGill resigned as general secretary. He had a long run, having served full-time since May 1, 1910, and having been heavily involved before that when he was splitting his time between the Nashville and Edgefield YMCA and the state council. He had performed remarkably well, as testified to by the six months leave of absence he was given before his resignation.[402] Nevertheless, being without a general secretary for most of the time since the previous December, the Nashville YMCA took a step backward.

A new general secretary, Charles W. Bush, arrived in September from Camp Wheeler, Georgia, where he had been involved in war work. One of the challenges he faced was to adjust the YMCA's programs to fit the post-war period. Called by a reporter a "live wire," Bush started off fast.[403] Under his aggressive leadership, the Y accelerated its programs, hired more employees, and increased activities in every department. He and President Brown supported a national trend of decentralizing YMCA services by establishing a presence in industrial plants, schools, and churches. The idea was that these units would evolve into branches of the Central YMCA, a hope that would not materialize for more than two decades.

The YMCA's indebtedness, the failed campaign, the inability to effectively decentralize, an unbalanced budget, and the continuing free services offered to military men, such as the 900 marines who enjoyed the pool, showers, and other services while on a three-day midsummer pass, combined to cause great concern. The directors even voted to accept an offer from the National Baptist Convention to buy the Colored Men's Branch YMCA Building for $100,000, but that came to naught when the Colored YMCA board successfully sued to prevent the sale. This strained relations between the YMCA and its Colored Men's Branch even more than they were. Fortunately, as far as the board knew, the association's weak financial condition was not public knowledge. As one source of help, the YMCA applied to the Community Chest for financial support. Presumably, it was given.[404]

New staff blood arrived with the recruitment of John F. Baggett as religious work director in October, and C. L. Boynon, director of membership and religious work, who came in early December.[405]

The spirit at the Central Y in December was festive. There were big Christmas trees in the boys' lobby, and in the main lobby for the men in the apartments. On New Year's Eve, members and their lady friends celebrated the traditional open house. The public was also invited.[406]

Another positive note that winter was the continuing success of Captain Henry "Monk" Sharp and his YMCA

Rambler basketball team. Three other team stars were "Slick" Welsh, Ivo Burton, and "Emma" Thompson. Slick joined the Ramblers after graduating from Hume-Fogg High School where he was a three-sport athlete and basketball starter for three years.[407] By defeating their archrival Vanderbilt in March, the Ramblers won the city championship. It was their second win over the Commodores that season.[408]

The Central Federated Board

In the week after Christmas 1919, there was an unusual meeting at the Central Y of what was called the Central Federated Board. It consisted of representatives of all the separate YMCA entities in the city—the Central YMCA, the YMCA Graduate School, the Street Railroad YMCA, the state committee, and the student YMCA. The heavy hitters, including J. P. W. Brown, W. D. Weatherford and Dr. O. E. Brown, were trying to determine how much money would have to be raised to carry on the work of the YMCA in Nashville in 1920 and how to prevent duplication of work.[409] This meeting led, in February, to the board approving a Federated YMCAs of Nashville campaign of $63,300 to meet the association's needs relating to "work with men and boys, citizens and students, white and colored, Association Workers Training agencies, and Nashville's part in the work for men and boys in Tennessee, North America and foreign lands." Stalwarts Dr. Matt Buckner, Kendrick C. Hardcastle, and Arch Trawick directed the February 17–23 drive under the overall leadership of H. G. Hill. The drive succeeded in raising $31,753.95. Even though the campaign did not reach its goal, it was considered a success from several standpoints, including rekindling interest in the YMCA and clearing up some misunderstandings. While this was going on, the association's indebtedness had risen to an alarming $144,000 and income could not keep up with expenses.[410]

The Commercial Baseball League kicked off its season in April with Dr. S. A. Keim, YMCA physical director, as league president. This was the league's sixth season. An indoor baseball league had eight teams signed up by early May. As had been done in 1919, the Y offered free swim lessons from April 26 to May 8. The first day, 370 boys showed up. The YMCA Vacation School kicked in on June 14. W. S. Perry, of Hume Fogg, was principal of the school as he had been in 1919. The YMCA also had a boys' swimming team that swam against several area teams, including Peabody.[411]

On June 6 the International YMCA was seventy-six years old. As part of the celebration in Nashville, Major Stahlman and R. S. Cowan were honored as the only surviving original directors of the Nashville YMCA when it was organized in 1875.[412]

Henry G. Hart, who had returned to Nashville from India to accept the position as state YMCA's boys' work secretary, assisted Dr. Keim with physical education. Keim's most lasting contribution to the Y was to organize a health club that would last for 40 years. The most acrobatic staff member was Ludlow "Doc" Gordon, a muscular and gifted acrobat, who joined the staff in 1912. He celebrated his birthday each year by standing on his hands on the ledge of the roof over the YMCA building's eighth floor. He would continue to do this until his seventieth birthday.[413]

In June, it was announced that the boys' division of the State YMCA had secured a large tract of ruggedly beautiful forest on the Cumberland Plateau about five miles from Crossville for a summer camp site. The location was at Meadow Creek Falls in Cumberland County. Henry Hart, the camp director, invited the Nashville Association's boys to use the camp from July 6 to August 21, possibly with campers from other associations. Naturally, the Nashville Y was delighted to accept. Hart's focus was on woodcraft, defined as the art of overcoming the daily obstacles of life. The camp cost was $7 per week plus $8.40 for the roundtrip from Nashville to Crossville on the Tennessee Central Railroad. Boys could swim, play woodcraft related games, relax around bonfires and hike. To qualify, the boys had to be twelve years old or older.[414]

There was also an eight-week YMCA vacation school at the Y in the summer. Experienced Nashville public school teachers were in charge. In 1919, there had been 165 students, both girls and boys. The 1920 session attracted more than 200.[415]

William P. Cooper, a founder of the law school and its presiding spirit, became dean in 1920. He would leave in 1926 to return as a substitute lecturer until 1939 when he returned full-time. He would not retire until 1946.[416] Another innovation was the introduction of free evening school classes for ex-servicemen, funded by a grant from the National War Council. Less than two miles away, on the Vanderbilt campus, W. D. Weatherford, president of the YMCA Graduate School, opened his college for the second year. It was one of the three colleges in the country training future YMCA secretaries. The other two were in Chicago and Springfield, Massachusetts. Dr. Weatherford expected an enrollment of 84 students. Being in Nashville, Weatherford continued to give generously of his time to the Nashville YMCA.

Frank P. Bond, a pioneer of the Nashville YMCA, died in October. He had been the Association's first recording secretary in 1875 and held that position for most of the following four years. He resigned in the summer of 1879 but remained as assistant secretary until 1882. In 1884, he was elected general secretary and held that position until 1889 when he resigned to focus on the association's finances and its library that he managed. In 1890, Bond resigned to accept the position of general secretary of the Montgomery, Alabama, Association. He performed his duties with the Nashville Association faithfully during its difficult early years and received justified recognition at his death.[417]

H. G. Hill: A New Director

At the annual meeting on December 7, 1920, six new directors were elected, each to serve a three-year term. They were K. C. Hardcastle, Henry C. Hibbs, H. G. Hill, Henry McClelland, A. M. Souby, and Arch Trawick. Recommended by a three-man nominating committee, the new directors were elected by the vote of all members over sixteen years of age, who were in good standing in the association. The returning board members were tried and true—J. P. W. Brown, Dr. M. G. Buckner, George E. Bennie, E. B. Craig Jr., Dr. W. J. O'Callaghan, Joe T. Howell, W. H. Lambeth, and G. S. Moore.[418] Earlier, in November, John P. W. Brown had been reelected president of the Nashville Association.

H. G. HILL 1921-1934

Membership in 1920 rose slightly with 1,737 members as opposed to 1,708 in 1919. Three hundred twenty men were living in the apartments at the Central YMCA and another 101 were living at the Colored Men's Branch YMCA. The apartment men came from nineteen states.[419]

The YMCA lost the services of assistant secretary D. W. Gordon, who, for several years, had been editor of *Better Nashville*. In early January, before Gordon left for his new job with Southwestern Presbyterian University, then planning to move to Memphis, the board adopted a resolution, expressing their appreciation for his nine years, less one month, of service. The board praised his energy, unfailing patience and courtesy.[420]

The State YMCA, which had not met since 1914, held its 32nd annual convention in Nashville. After the war, the state association's work had two focuses: (1) assisting city, railroad, industrial, county and student associations, and (2) conducting their summer vacation and recreational camp. Some attention was also paid to promoting a better understanding between the two races in Tennessee. This effort, launched in 1919, had resulted in 58 committees being established across the state. The annual report said that "Tennessee leads the Southern states in the absence of mob violence" and that, through the work of interracial committees, it was hoped that this record would be maintained.[421]

In the area of athletics, there was a buzz about the 1920–21 Ramblers. Earlier it had been learned that Tommy Zerfoss, the star Vanderbilt guard and medical student, who had been found ineligible to play for the Commodores because of having played a year in Kentucky before transferring to Vanderbilt, would join the Ramblers J. L. Ray, a *Nashville Banner* sportswriter wrote an article with the lead, "Meet Mr. Zerfoss, Ex-Commodores Star." Another of his articles said, "Sad things await the foes of the Ramblers. The Memphis Y is in mourning." Already, the YMCA Ramblers were one of the strongest teams in the South.[422]

When the Ramblers were not playing in the YMCA gym, other teams were. In March, Hume-Fogg upset MBA 24–22 in the YMCA gym to win the State High School Basketball Tournament. There was a fight between partisans of both schools after the game. To defuse the situation, Dr. Keim locked both teams in his office until control could be reestablished.[423]

Basketball was a fast-paced game, but there was an exciting new game in town, infinitely faster. It was called "radio." In March, the YMCA board voted to allow the Nashville Radio Club to hold their meetings in a room on the 8th floor. The club members, mostly teenagers, installed a short wave receiver to receive messages from amateur and ship radios. They installed a two-stage amplifier that allowed the weakest signals to be easily heard without the use of headphones. Stations in Bordeaux, France, at the Eiffel Tower, and in Rome, along with others in

North America could be heard. Part of the equipment was "an apparatus in a box, one foot square and one foot deep attached to a wire 40 feet long and 25 feet high above the roof." This was soon replaced with the best and highest aerial in the city—85 feet long and 140 feet above the street. With it installed and with the purchase of a Magnavox loud speaker, the club hoped to invite YMCA members to listen to President Harding's inaugural address. The sound could be heard as far as Church Street.[424]

As the Nashville Radio Club room wasn't finished until the first week in April, the boys probably were unable to broadcast the president's message. Once, the room was ready in April, five club members, Hales Broughton, John Cain, Percy Cullum, Jack DeWitt, Julius Lowenstein, and Owen Morris—all teenagers—gave lectures on amplifying transformers, telephone receivers, generators, grid leaks, and oscillating circuits. When the American Radio Relay League, Inc., of Hartford, Connecticut, appointed the Nashville Radio Club an official relay station, the boys were thrilled. This put the station on par with the most important stations in the country and allowed it to receive and forward messages from all across America.[425]

In March, it was announced that the 1921 State YMCA's boys' camp would be on the Collins River at Rock Island near where that river, its tributary, the Rocky River, and the Caney Fork all came together to form Rock Island Lake. The site, three miles from the railroad station at Rock Island, may have been where the summer camp had been held two years earlier. Chester A. Kerr, state boys' work secretary, would direct the camp. One of his assistants would be C. A. Abele, Nashville YMCA boys' work secretary.

In May, Kerr's State YMCA campsite failed to materialize but he quickly found another site two and one-half miles above the Tennessee Power and Light Company Dam at Rock Island on the Caney Fork River. It included 163 acres, half timberland. Kerr went up there with a group of older boys and worked hard to lay out a quarter mile track; baseball diamond; basketball, tennis and volleyball courts; and build a dock and boat house, together with a diving tower and a chute for a fleet of boats. One wonders how and if he got all that done when the first campers arrived June 1. Fortunately, a majority of the campers didn't arrive until June 14 when a party of 40 arrived from the Nashville YMCA. That summer, boys at the camp hiked to the top of 1,800 foot Mount Cardwell 12 miles away. Another group paddled up the Caney Fork as far as they could go.[426]

Mass Resignations

On June 8, 1921, subscribers to the *Nashville Tennessean* were surprised to read that the executive committee of the YMCA board of directors had taken control of the association, effective immediately. The day before, resignations from the entire executive and clerical staffs, with one exception, were received. That exception was E. L. Spain, an associate secretary had had done a beautiful job of managing the dormitories and who had been a calming influence at the Y where personality conflicts were rampant. He was placed in full charge of all YMCA activities by the executive committee that consisted of H. G. Hill, John P. W. Brown, George H. Bennie, and Arch Trawick. Effectively, Spain became general secretary, replacing Charles W. Bush, whose resignation was effective July 1. Mr. Hill, spokesman for the committee, said, "although the association will not be able to conduct as full a program as in the past, they will be able to retain all the essential parts, and the plans of the executive committee when completed would no doubt work for the benefit of the association in every way."[427]

Other resignations, also effective July 1, were received from John F. Baggett, religious work director; C.L. Boynton, membership secretary; Dr. A. S. Keim, physical director; W. E. Jones, assistant physical director; C. A. Abele, boys' work director; Stanley Hamilton, high school boys' secretary; and B. A. Roller, assistant boys' secretary.[428]

What caused the executive committee to take such drastic steps? Personality conflicts and other internal dissention, the inability to pay down the association's $144,000 debt, the difficulty in paying interest on the debt, the recent loss of staff members, and a long-standing monthly deficit were primary causes. Until recently, the board had been unaware or indifferent to the fact that the Nashville public was aware of their problems. The directors were shocked into an acute awareness of their precarious financial position by the fact that it was public knowledge.[429]

Sometimes, several important things happen all at once. This was true in June 1921 as the prominent African-American group running the Colored Men's Branch obtained a charter incorporating the Colored YMCA as an independent entity. The reaction of the executive committee was that they had anticipated the move and were not regretful. Later in June, the YMCA executive committee sold the Colored YMCA title to the Duncan Hotel for $6,935. After that, all relationships between the two associations ceased.[430]

At the October 15 board meeting, H. G. Hill was elected president, succeeding John P. W. Brown, who had served two years. Hill, the immediate past president of the Commercial Club, was the CEO of H. G. Hill Grocers, a rapid-growing grocery chain.[431] He immediately implemented cost savings in every department. Hill also met privately with C.A. Craig, Ridley Wills, and Tom Tyne, all senior National Life and Accident Insurance Company executives, as soon as he was elected. They made an offer to buy the YMCA Building for the home office they so badly needed because of the State of Tennessee taking their crowded home office building across Union Street. Horace, who knew the three men well, listened to their offer and said he would get back after taking the matter to his board. The board declined the offer, and Horace turned his administrative skills into restoring the YMCA to a viable, healthy organization.

• • • • •

Horace G. Hill *(1873–1942)*

Horace G. Hill, the oldest of ten children of G. M. and Hulda Rogers Hill, was born at River Hill near Sparta in White County, Tennessee, September 21, 1873. His parents brought him to Nashville when he was five years old. He attended local public schools and Montgomery Bell Academy. After next taking a course at Draughon's Business College, he worked as a bookkeeper for three years at his father's small grocery on Market Street near the Murfreesboro Turnpike. With that experience and possessed of an entrepreneurial spirit and ten dollars, Horace, at age twenty-two, went in business for himself in November 1895. He opened a store at State and McTyeire [18th Avenue, North] streets. In a 1925 interview with Walter H. Seely, editor of *Success Magazine*, Mr. Hill explained how this happened. He said, "You see, a fellow grocer had failed and I bought his stock on credit." Mr. Hill also explained to Seely some of his business philosophy. "We expect all of our employees to be polite and courteous to the trade at all times, and we do not allow any loud boisterous talking, profane or ungentlemanly language in our stores."

In 1897, Horace married Miss Mamie Wilson, a daughter of Robert H. Wilson, a prosperous East Nashville druggist. Horace and Mamie had three children: Elizabeth, Horace G. Jr., and Frances, and were members of the Presbyterian Church.

Two years later, Mr. Hill decided to operate on a strictly cash basis and build a chain of groceries. When he told his father, Mr. Hill predicted, "You are going to starve to death." Mr. Hill's prognosis was wrong. The H. G. Hill Grocery and Baking Company was incorporated in March 1907 with a capital stock of $100,000. By 1913, Horace operated twenty-eight H. G. Hill Grocery Stores in Nashville, one in Columbia, Tennessee, and six in Birmingham, Alabama. At that time, he also owned considerable farm property as well as property in Nashville, and was considered one of the city's most successful men. H.G. Hill Co. set a trend for local grocery stores by eliminating grocery delivery service in 1917 and continuing to operate on a cash and carry basis.

In the first decade of the twentieth century, Nashville operated under a set of "Blue Laws" that were in effect most of the century. Hill followed those laws faithfully, closing his stores on Sunday and refusing to sell beer at all. He was innovative, implementing such retailing innovations as self-service, cash-and-carry, and newspaper price advertising. He preferred to own the land on which his stores were located and enjoyed investing and dealing in real estate.

Active in business and community affairs, Mr. Hill was president of Nashville's Commercial Club from 1919 to 1920. He served two successive terms as president of the Nashville Chamber of Commerce, and was also elected head of the Nashville Industrial Corporation that took over the Old Hickory powder plant after the war.

In 1921, Mr. Hill was elected chairman of the Nashville YMCA Board and served in that capacity until 1934. Had it not been for his conservative and able leadership, the YMCA may well not have survived. Mr. Hill also served on the boards of the Tennessee Central Railroad, Peabody College, The Masonic Widows and Orphans Home, and the Fourth and First National Bank. He additionally served as president of the Nashville Navigation Company and the Phillips-Trawick Company, a wholesale grocery company that he bought about 1915 when other wholesalers refused to sell groceries to his stores.

Mr. Hill was able to wear so many hats while steadily growing his own company largely because of his indefatigable energy. He also possessed unflinching honesty, keen judgment, and a strong desire to succeed. In 1926, Mr. Hill founded the H. G. Hill Realty Company to buy real estate all over Middle Tennessee. That same year, he personally bought property on a dirt road overlooking the Collins River at Rock Island, Tennessee. Mr. Hill completely renovated a dilapidated house on the property that had been used by the Tennessee Electric Power Company administrators when building the Rock Island Dam in 1915 and1916. The house that family members still call the "big house" has been used by the Hill and Caldwell families as a summer home ever since, except during World War II when gasoline rationing prevented Ma May [Mrs. Hill] from making the trip from Nashville with her children and grandchildren.

The H. G. Hill Company and the realty company both weathered the depression. In 1933, Horace purchased the Nashville Trust Company that was in financial difficulty and served as chairman of its board until his death. By then, he had gained a well-deserved reputation as a philanthropist as well as one of Nashville's wealthiest men.

When H. G. Hill, whom his grandchildren called Papa, died in October 1942, he was survived by his wife; three children, Horace G. Hill, Jr., Elizabeth (Mrs. William) Penick, of New Orleans, and Frances (Mrs. Wentworth) Caldwell; and four grandchildren, May, Anne, Frances and Wentworth, Jr.

• • • • •

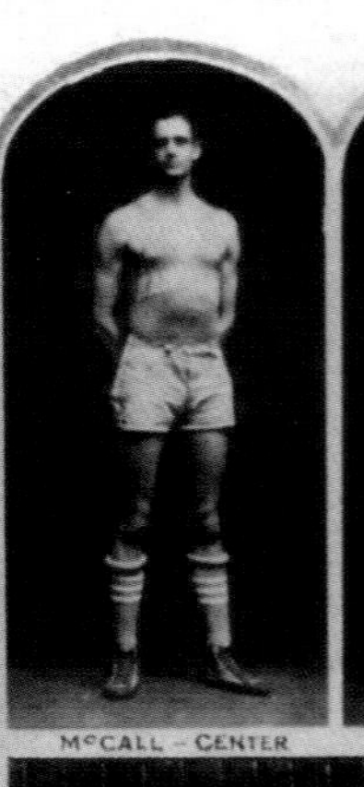

RAMBLERS

1923–24

Record

Ramblers.	55.	Franklin Athletic Club.	30.	Ramblers.	29.	Vanderbilt University.	19
Ramblers.	25.	Mexico City Y.M.C.A.	17.	Ramblers.	36.	Chattanooga Rail Lites.	23.
Ramblers.	32.	Mississippi A&M College.	28.	Ramblers.	32.	Chattanooga Rail Lites.	39.
Ramblers.	25.	Vanderbilt University.	17.	Ramblers.	38.	Y.M.H.A.	51.
Ramblers.	26.	Memphis Y.M.C.A.	25.	Ramblers.	21.	Memphis Y.M.C.A.	34.
Ramblers.	23.	Y.M.H.A.	21.	Ramblers.	34.	Cumberland University.	21.
Ramblers.	44.	Southwestern Pres. Univ.	25.	Ramblers.	46	Michigan City Y.M.C.A.	24
Ramblers.	35.	Chattanooga Rail Lites.	46.	Ramblers.	38.	Y.M.H.A.	29

CHAPTER TEN

H. G. Hill and Camp Sycamore
1922–1926

THE LAST WEEK in January 1922, H. G. Hill represented the Nashville Association at the State YMCA Convention held in Nashville. A lot was going on in Nashville that winter.

Chester A. Kerr, boys' work secretary for the state, reported on the state camp for boys established the previous summer. He said that the camp had been financed by a group of Nashvillians and praised Ken Hardcastle of the Nashville Association, in particular, for his help on behalf of the camp. Kerr urged the six associations in the state with their own summer camps to do so "as a character building enterprise."

Gypsy Smith was holding a month-long revival at the Ryman while the YMCA Ramblers, after losing their first two games, went on a long winning streak only to be defeated 19–13 on January 26 by an underrated YMHA Pep team. The Ramblers, having whipped such college teams as Marquette and Baylor universities, overlooked the upstart Peps. The Ramblers redeemed themselves by defeating Vanderbilt twice. After the second victory over the Commodores, Captain Monk Sharp claimed the city championship for the Ramblers, their seventh such title in ten years. They still had, however, one piece of unfinished business—to revenge their loss to the Peps. They did so, convincingly, in February, winning 40–18.[432]

The Nashville Association issued its 1921 annual report in February. C. M. Patterson, membership secretary, reported that membership as of January 1, 1922, was 1,695 exclusive of 792 regular members of the boys' department and 109 free memberships still being given servicemen. Aggregate attendance during the previous year was 131,677. Patterson also reported that there were 315 men living in the apartments, and that 700 beds were given out during the year to men and boys who were temporarily out of funds.

The Hi-Y work over the winter and spring was under the auspices of the Southern YMCA College run by Dr. W. D. Weatherford—not the Nashville Association. Approximately 50 boys from Central, Duncan, Hume-Fogg, Peabody, and Wallace attended the Hi-Y banquet at Wesley Hall. One of them was Coleman Harwell, future editor of the *Nashville Tennessean*.[433]

In May, A.B. Richardson, of the State Association, announced that the State Y camp would return to Rock Island on a bend of the Collins River near the Tennessee Power Company Dam. The camp was scheduled to open on June 16 and stay open until September 1. As had been the case the summer before, the boys would stay in tents. Two Nashvillians, Jesse M. Overton and K. C. Hardcastle, key camp committee members, served as president and treasurer respectively. The day after the State "Y" camp was announced in the *Nashville Banner*, the Nashville Y announced that it would open its own camp on a 500-acre farm on the bend of the Harpeth River between Newsom Station and Pegram Station, seventeen miles from the city. The matter was decided at a meeting of the association's camp committee consisting of Horace G. Hill, John P. W. Brown, and E. B. Craig Jr. The Nashville Association camp's first two-week session would begin June 16. The boys would sleep in tents on iron cots with mattresses. The dining hall was screened, and there were at least four canoes for use on the river. The new site had an athletic field, part of which was reserved for the YMCA Ramblers and another Y basketball team. Two secretaries would direct the camp that was

E. L. Spain (L) with a group at Camp Sycamore. H. G. Hill is in the center with his tie tucked into his shirt.

named for H. G. Hill in recognition of his interest in and his work on behalf of the YMCA boys. Dr. Matt Buckner and Dr. Robert Brown would share duties as camp physician.[434]

The H.G. Hill Camp opened three days late due to heavy rains. Forty boys were there for the first session. Throughout the summer, the YMCA gave free camp experiences to several groups, including winners of Sunday school contests at various churches, and newsboys from the *Banner*. The "Newsies" traveled to camp by trucks as, by 1922, rural roads, though still bad, were somewhat improved and trucks and cars more commonplace than before the war.

Community Chest Campaign

Because the YMCA changed its priorities dramatically during the Great World War and promoted many new activities, the international committee held a conference at Niagara Falls in July to chart the future direction of the YMCA. O. E. Brown, of Vanderbilt, and a key member of the YMCA Graduate School board, was one of the speakers.[435]

One outreach of the Nashville Association that had existed since the Y's reorganization in 1875 was the holding of weekly religious services at the city jail. During July, the religious work committee held five such services there,[436] attended by 525 prisoners. There were also 23 shop meetings at the N.C. & St. L. Railroad during the month attended by 920 men.

Good news came in 1922 when the first Community Chest campaign benefited 39 local social welfare agencies, including the Nashville YMCA. This positive event, having their own summer camp, and Mr. Hill's leadership elevated the self-esteem of the YMCA board and staff. Maybe, they were turning a corner.[437]

One of the least noticed staff additions came late in 1922 when William C. E. Terry, a young colored boy, applied for a job as a porter. He was hired on a temporary basis for "a couple of weeks." William did such a conscientious job that the weeks stretched into a permanent job. Terry would work at the Y for 50 years and gain the respect and love of all the members for his genial nature and willingness to do anything. When he and Everett J. Gilbert, who began his career in 1925, died in 1980, their photographs were displayed in the Downtown Center.

By secret ballot, the members of the Nashville YMCA elected eighteen directors on December 5. This was the first election of an entire board of directors since the reorganization a year and one half earlier. The members elected were George Bennie Jr., H. O. Blackwood, John P. W. Brown, Dr. Matt G. Buckner, E. B. Craig Jr., George R. Gillespie, Henry C. Hibbs, H. G. Hill, K. C. Hardcastle, Carl Howe, Garland S. Moore, Dr. W. J. O'Callaghan, Frank M. See, Henry "Monk" Sharp, Arch Trawick, Professor Charles J. Turck, Vernon S. Tupper, and the Rev. J. J. Walker. The members were elected for one-, two-, and three-year terms.[438]

In the first board meeting of the New Year, held January 11, 1923, Horace G. Hill was reelected president. Vernon S. Tupper, a University of the South graduate and general manager of the Nashville Roller Mills, was elected first vice-president. H. O. Blackwood was elected second vice-president; Carl Howe, recording secretary; E. B. Craig Jr., treasurer; and E. L. Spain, general secretary. There were only three other paid professionals on the staff at the time—R. J. Foster, boys' work director; Jonas Coverdale, physical director (part-time); and H. A. Davis, membership director. Each gave positive reports. The best possible news delivered was that the association had whittled down the size of the building debt. Mr. Craig was delighted to report that all current bills were being paid and some unpaid accounts totaling $20,000 settled, and $5,000 paid on the mortgage. Mr. Davis reported that the association gained 110 new members and received renewals from 19 members during December, bringing the association membership to 2,604.

Jonas Coverdale reported that, during December, 12,908 men and boys used the pool and or the gymnasium.[439] Three months later, Hume-Fogg and MBA used the Y gym for their fourth basketball game of the season, Hume-Fogg had won two of the first three and this one was for the city championship. Hume-Fogg won 43–15 before what was described as a record-breaking crowd. The game was extremely rough with both teams fouling constantly. Feelings were high and, as the crowd began to file out after the final whistle, a fight broke out between partisans of the two teams. The *Nashville Tennessean* described the fight as a riot saying that, "before police stationed in the building could prevent it, the entire gymnasium floor was a veritable Shiloh of young Jack Dempseys with each lad belligerently defending the honor of his alma mater." Doc Gordon defused the madhouse by locking the Hume-Fogg and MBA players in his office.[440]

Most seasons, the Ramblers scheduled one non-traditional foe as an exhibition game. In 1923 it was a home contest with the professional New York Celtics. The Ramblers lost but pulled in a $600 profit. The Ramblers went on to lose the state championship but win the city championship by swamping the Peps.

The Nashville YMCA's 1923 boys' summer camp was held at the same site the 1912 and 1913 camps had been held. The camp on Sycamore Creek was one mile upstream from the old Sycamore Manufacturing Company's gunpowder factory and flour and saw mills. In 1873, the Dupont Company acquired an interest in the plant and operated it until 1904.[441] Located a mile or two off Hyde's Ferry Road, four and one-half miles north of Ashland City, and twenty-two miles from Nashville, Camp Sycamore could be reached by Hyde's Ferry Pike or by train to Ashland City. From there visitors were instructed to continue on Hyde's Ferry Pike one mile north of town where the road forks. A camp sign there pointed the way along the remaining three and one-half miles to camp over an unpaved and rough road. As had been the case in 1912 and 1913, the camp was leased from A. P. Jackson.

There were four camp periods, each being two weeks long. That summer, boys slept on metal beds with real mattresses in eight 16' by 16' tents pitched in a row along a tree line that divided two athletic fields that consisted of about 20 acres in total. Six boys and one leader slept in each tent. For the first week of camp, forty boys, who had come by train, were present. A permanent dining hall, 40 by 50 feet and properly screened, had recently been completed. The boys, all of whom were ten or older, were served their meals cafeteria style. Parents were invited to write their sons at Camp Sycamore, Route 2, Ashland City, TN.

The beach on Sycamore Creek was about 200 feet from the athletic field. A new swimming dock and diving board were available. On the other side of the creek, there was a picturesque bluff. The camp had one or two small flat-bottomed boats and five Indian canoes.

Highlights of the sports program were junior and senior division canoe races. In the senior races, the distance was a little more than one-half mile. In the junior races, the distance was reduced to about a quarter of a mile. One of the winning canoeists was Buddy Hackman, a future football star at MBA and the University of Tennessee. In 2011, Camp Sycamore Hills, owned by the Cumberland Valley Council Girls Scouts of America, occupied a 1,300-acre site about two miles downstream. The girl scouts acquired the property in 1958, when Camp Sycamore was still owned by the YMCA but no longer used as a camp.[442]

Raymond J. Foster, director of boys' work, was Camp Sycamore director. Jonas Coverdale was his assistant. How Coverdale became a YMCA director of physical activities is interesting. He was an outstanding high school basketball player at Hume Fogg, and a prized recruit for Josh Cody's Vanderbilt basketball team. The problem was that Vandy didn't offer basketball scholarships and Coverdale couldn't afford to pay the tuition. Consequently, he got a part-time job at the Nashville YMCA while attending Vanderbilt. After the first term examinations in the 1923–24 schoolyear, he was ruled ineligible.

Cartoon of H. G. Hill in *"Lookin' 'Em Over" Prominent Business Men of Nashville* by D. H. Grant.

During the first week of camp, H. G. Hill, George Gillespie, Ferriss Bailey, and other YMCA members visited the camp. They deemed it one of the best boys' camps in the state. Two of the few drawbacks were that the boys had to haul drinking water a quarter of a mile, and the road to the camp from Hyde' Ferry Pike was so rough that cars had difficulty navigating it.[443]

During 1923, the YMCA's physical department served 113,821 individuals. Health club attendance was nearly 20,000 and 41,385 individuals were served by the religious department. The gymnasium was used by 14,926 men and boys, and a total of 57 outside agencies, including churches, fraternities, the State YMCA, the Boy Scouts of America, railroad organizations, the YMCA Law School, high schools and Hi-Y clubs, used the building.

Finally, a Permanent Boys Camp

Thanks to a gift from YMCA president Horace G. Hill, the Nashville YMCA bought Camp Sycamore from Mr. and Mrs. A. P. Jackson for $2,000 on December 31, 1923. Jackson, who had been superintendent of the Sycamore Powder Mills in the 1890s, had owned the property since 1909, five years after the powder mills closed. The deed gave the YMCA the right to raise the dam on the creek, to have ingress and egress to their site from the main road, the use of a spring on the Jacksons' property, and the right to pump water from that spring to the camp. The YMCA now owned, for the first time in its history, its own boys' camp.[444]

A few weeks earlier, the YMCA Ramblers announced an attractive 1923–24 slate. In pre-season practices, Coach John D. Barrow stressed defense to his team that included Chin Johnson, Slim Embry, Bowser Chest, Blair and Hughes at guards. Embry, a newcomer, played for the Commodores in 1922 and 1923.[445] At forward were Monk Sharp, Slick Welsh, Lallie Richter, Jonas Coverdale, Julian Thomas, and Harrison. John McCall, at 6'4", was the center. After opening with the Franklin Athletic Club, an easy win, the Ramblers defeated a short and inexperienced but surprisingly good Mexico City YMCA team 25–17.[446] Next was Mississippi A & M College, the 1922 Southern champions. The Ramblers won 52–28. Four nights later came Vanderbilt. Jonas Coverdale, a YMCA employee, wanted to play against

Vanderbilt but Coach John D. Barrow thought it would show bad sportsmanship to allow him to do so given the fact that Jonas had just been ruled ineligible at Vanderbilt for playing for the Nashville YMCA.[447] The Ramblers, without Coverdale, won 25–17 and then eased by the Memphis YMCA 26–25 before a one-point loss to the YMHA Peps.

A win over Southwestern Presbyterian University set the stage for a game with the Ramblers' bitter rival, the Chattanooga Rail Lites. The Chattanooga boys won 46–35. The Ramblers then defeated Vanderbilt for the second time and avenged their earlier loss to the Rail Lites, winning 36–23. In a match with the Rail Lites, the Ramblers lost 39–32. The Ramblers played poorly in the next two games, losing for the second time to the YMHA Peps and to the Memphis YMCA. The season ended on an up-tick with wins over Cumberland University, the Michigan City YMCA, and the YMHA.[448]

Between high school and Rambler basketball games, the Y hosted a supper for 350 underprivileged boys from the Nashville Boys' Club. Fourteen Nashville debutantes served as waitresses.[449]

The same evening, the YMCA Graduate School hosted the employed officers' conference of the State YMCA in Wesley Hall at Vanderbilt. John Barrow, then the acting general secretary of the Nashville YMCA, was on the arrangements committee.[450]

After the close of the 1923–24 fiscal year at the end of February, the Y reported on its previous year's activities. The religious department served 41,385 people in nine shops and industrial plants. The total number of people using the physical department was 113,821. This included 14,180 people who attended city league and high school games, and nearly 50,000 who used the pool. A total of 57 outside agencies used the building during the previous year. They included churches, fraternities, the State YMCA, Boy Scouts, railroad YMCAs, and the Boys' Club. Nearly 50,000 men and boys used the pool. In the last month of the fiscal year, 6,250 people ate in the YMCA café, and 1,716 men visited the health club.[451]

To acquaint Nashvillians with what was going on at the YMCA, the association held an open house on May 27. John D. Barrow, back in his regular job as physical education director, was on hand that day to orchestrate various physical activities for the visitors.[452]

Now owning a beautiful fifteen-acre summer camp along beautiful Sycamore Creek, the Y made substantial improvements before the 1924 camp season opened June 16. First, the staff solved the water-hauling problem by having a 60-foot well bored and installing an automatic gasoline pump. They also built a storage tank house of large cedar logs. Pure, cool water was piped from the pump house to all the camp buildings and to several drinking fountains conveniently spaced across the camp.[453]

Through the generosity of George R. Gillespie, vice-president of the YMCA, the camp also had a new gasoline-powered craft each capable of carrying a good number of campers. The boat was christened the "George R." in honor of him. During the summer, the "George R." and another motor-powered boat, the "Lizzie," made regular runs between the camp landing and a substantial new landing dock just above the dam at the old Sycamore Powder Mills. Comfortable rustic benches were placed on the dock. A new nature trail along Sycamore Creek was extended that summer to provide an even more delightful hike. The trail ran along the base of the cliff across the creek through a magnificent hardwood forest and native wild flowers. Finally, the camp had a library and a camp store.[454]

The first weekend in June, Mr. Hill, Mr. Spain, and a number of other board members spent a night at Camp Sycamore in the new lodge built to accommodate camp visitors. They must have been thrilled as clearly this was, by far, the finest summer camp the Nashville YMCA had ever had. They decided to come back, in smaller groups, once camp started.[455]

Fifty-seven boys arrived in camp as scheduled on June 16. They came by trucks and automobiles, accompanied by E. L. Spain and Charles Curren. Where Hyde's Ferry Road crossed the creek, the boys were ferried up stream to the campsite in the "George R." and the "Lizzie." Other boys drifted in, upping the total number to 65. Additionally, there were 18 adults, led by J. Ray Foster, camp director, back for his second year; Jonas Coverdale, director of activities; and J. P. Abbott, who doubled as director of educational classes and camp reporter. E. L. Spain's son, E. L. Spain Jr., was there that summer teaching bird lore. Emanuel Buford, the African-American camp cook, was beside himself with his large, new range, and hot and cold running water.[456]

One tennis court was available all summer while a second one became available some weeks later. On the athletic field, there was also a baseball diamond and a volleyball court.[457] There were four two week sessions in 1924 with the last one ending August 14.

For boys not in camp, the YMCA had a swimming team that summer. The distances swum were much shorter than they would be later in the century. For example, there were 20 and 40-yard freestyle and backstroke events.[458]

In October 1924, the YMHA and YWHA (Young Women's Hebrew Association) dedicated their four-story steel, brick, and concrete building on Union Street at Polk Avenue, separated by an alley from the National Life and Accident Insurance Company building. Called the Jewish Center of Nashville, the new structure, a joint effort of the two Jewish organizations, cost $250,000. It featured the Rachel Morse Gymnasium, where the YMHA Peps played, and the Joseph Eskind Auditorium, which seated 900 people.[459] With the construction of the National Life and YMHA buildings, the YMCA was now in a completely commercial area. Within a one-block area of downtown Nashville stood the homes of the YMCA, YWCA, and YM-YWHA.

Basketball season at the YMCA kicked off in November with four teams, composed of ten men each, competing in a "Turkey Loop" League. As soon as this league finished before Thanksgiving, another league kicked off.[460]

The Ramblers began their season with a win over a travel-weary Baylor University team 32–22. First year coach A. S. Keim's squad was raw with only one member, Count Blair, returning from the previous year. Starters were Lallie Richter and Ray Foster at forwards, Ewell Costello at center, and Blair and Bowser Chest at guards. Costello was big but too passive to suit Lallie Richter. To toughen Ewell up, Lallie taught him how to box. That helped. The Ramblers' record was good but not great. In one of the last games of the season, Vanderbilt held the YMCA five to three field goals, in clinching the city championship.[461]

Jonas Coverdale, having regained his eligibility at Vanderbilt, rejoined the Commodore basketball team for the 1924–1925 season. Before the Tulane game in January, Coach Josh Cody said, "Jonas Coverdale has been going great all season and should make a good showing tonight." Elected captain for the 1925–26 season, Coverdale dropped out of Vanderbilt after playing only one year, depriving him of being captain. Nevertheless, he felt that his sports experiences at Vanderbilt shaped his life. He said, "It taught you how to work as a team, to accept defeat and hard work as facts of life."[462] With Coverdale not available, the Ramblers relied heavily on Lallie Richter and Ewell Costello. In an easy victory over the Jackson YMCA on January 12, these two combined for 56 of the team's 60 points.[463]

Hill's Guidance and Business Acumen Praised

At the 1925 annual meeting, held on January 15, the directors unanimously reelected Horace G. Hill president. They were grateful for his wise guidance and splendid business acumen that had been instrumental in clearing the association of much of its indebtedness. He paid close attention to every phase of YMCA work, particularly that dealing with boys. The other officers elected were the same men who held office in 1924. They were George R. Gillespie, first vice-president; Vernon S. Tupper, second vice-president; Ferriss C. Bailey, treasurer; and E. L. Spain, general director. Other directors were former presidents Dr. Matt Buckner and John P. W. Brown, Charles L. Cornelius, W. R. Elam, W. Dudley Gale, Henry C. Hill, Dr. John L. Hill, Dr. W. J. O'Callaghan, Hunter Perry, Frank M. See, Henry Sharp, the Rev. J. J. Walker, and H. B. Wilkerson. Advisory board members were Maj. E. B. Stahlman, William R. Manier, John D. Blanton, George Cole, and Joel O. Cheek, who had not yet made his fortune.[464]

The reports on 1924 activities made it clear that the Y had "one of the most successful years of the decade." A total of 41,363 men attended 1,021 religious meetings and 52,390 individuals were served by the physical department. The boys' division membership was 2,241 with the total number of visitors 22,614. Other boys' department activities included silent moving pictures of an educational nature and a father and son banquet. Ninety-one different outside agencies used the building with 9,924 people attending. During the year, there was an average of 265 regular roomers, and the association furnished free beds to 1,256 men. There turned out to be 270 boys at Camp Sycamore with 19 leaders and 265 visitors.[465]

The women's auxiliary, that had been inactive since before the Great War, was reorganized at the end of January when Mrs. W. H. Sherman was elected president. She and her fellow members pledged themselves to "promote the welfare of the men in the building, to create a greater interest in the work of the association, and also to sponsor social activities."[466] The auxiliary must not have lasted very long as it never appeared in newspaper articles of the 1930s.

During the winter, the boys' division, under the direction of A. Raymond "Ray" Hunt was busy. Ray divided the boys into junior A and junior B classes. The boys played basketball and other games, drilled, and swam. The boys division also organized, in collaboration with counselors from the YMCA Graduate School, a group of students at Tennessee Industrial School.[467]

At the March board meeting, the directors noted that the newly organized women's auxiliary, working with the social committee, had put on a Valentine's party that everyone enjoyed. Prizes were given to the winners of competitive games, During February, 2,630 people attended religious services, and 1,790 men used the health club. In the boys' department, 2,977 members took advantage of YMCA privileges.[468]

John R. Mott returned to Nashville on March 23 to speak to 300 business and professional people on the Ward-Belmont campus. Invited by the school and the YMCA Graduate School, his talk brought out all the local YMCA leaders, including Dr. Weatherford; H. G. Hill and E. L. Spain, of the local YMCA; Howard Hubbell, general secretary of the State YMCA; and Dr. O. E. Brown, dean of the Vanderbilt School of Religion and chairman of the State YMCA executive committee.[469]

• • • • •

In the late spring, the YMCA swimming team led by the talented Richter brothers, kicked off its season. An early meet was with Vanderbilt, who prevailed 38–34. May also saw the YMCA-YMHA Players close out their season with the production of a mystery play, *The Thirteenth Chair*, in the Eskind Auditorium at the YMHA.[470]

• • • • •

E. C. Faircloth, chairman of the YMCA camp committee, announced in mid-May that the summer camp at Sycamore was ready for its opening on Monday, June 22. Mr. Spain would handle camp operations, including reservations, transportation, and supplies. Working closely with him would be camp director, Jonas Coverdale, the Y's physical director. Coverdale would be assisted by Raymond J. Hurt while J. P. Abbott, of Vanderbilt would handle educational classes. Bird lore and woodcraft would be taught, once again, by E. L. Spain Jr.[471]

The biggest improvement at camp in 1925 was the replacement of tents with bungalows with screened porches. The bungalows could accommodate 100 boys, and on opening day, 95 were there.[472]

Two days earlier, a group of 43 men, including board members, leading Nashville businessmen, educators, and ministers inspected the camp as happened in 1924. After a fish fry, the men tried out a new fleet of ten boats and some went swimming. Mr. Hill and Mr. Spain also pointed out the new grading of the camp road, improvements to the ball grounds, several new buildings, and new tennis courts.[473]

Thanks to Mr. E. C. Faircloth, the boys came to camp in trucks. Included were twenty-two boy scouts from a troop sponsored by First Presbyterian Church. The fact that E. L. Spain was their scout leader explains their presence. Various Sunday school groups also enjoyed camp that summer, as did a group of boys from the YMHA who spent a week there in 1924 and two weeks in 1925 as guests of the YMCA. The YMHA boys had the camp to themselves from July 20 to August 4. The camp chef, Buford, was at camp for the full eight weeks. The large number of boys who asked for seconds spoke to his popularity.[474]

Jonas Coverdale planned a spectacular Fourth of July celebration. He kicked it off with a morning dip in Sycamore Creek, followed by sitting up exercises. There was also Bible reading, and a lecture. More fun for the boys were water polo games, a tennis tournament, baseball and soccer games, and a track meet. The dedication of a flagpole 60 feet high with an American flag five by eight feet flying above it was a highlight. The flagpole, that had an 8-inch bronze ball at the top, was at the end of the row of cabins. Balloons were released and medals awarded in the afternoon. The boys also took part in a patriotic march, watched by many of their parents. A watermelon feast in the late afternoon and a fireworks display that evening capped off the ceremonies.[475]

Monk, Slim, and Slick

The big event of the fall was the State YMCA Convention held September 18–20. This was always a good opportunity for President H.G. Hill and general secretary E. L. Spain to talk with their counterparts from other Tennessee cities.[476]

The Ramblers launched their 1925–26 season on December 11 in the Warner Gymnasium. Dr. A. S. Keim, who had earlier been the Hume-Fogg basketball coach, led the Ramblers to their opening victory over Union University, still located in Murfreesboro, 34–12, despite having lost several key players. Jonas Coverdale, who had played for Keim at Hume-Fogg, and, having dropped out of Vanderbilt, returned to the Ramblers, and, as he had been in the 1923–24 season, was a star. Against Union, he was the high scorer with 16 points. Other starters that winter were Monk Sharp, Slim Embry, Frank McCall, and Slick Welsh.[477] A few weeks later, about 100 boys gathered at the Y and organized basketball leagues under the name of the Y-City Basketball Association. Each team could sign up ten players.[478]

At the annual meeting in January, all the officers were re-elected. The total membership of the association was 1,704 and there were 555 in the boys' division. It was also reported that, during 1925, meetings at industrial plants had been attended by 26,765, and that 292 professions of faith had taken place.[479]

First Membership Drive Since 1921

H. G. Hill announced on February 21 that the YMCA would launch their first membership drive in five years. The goal was to get 1,000 new members. Mr. Hill chaired the whirlwind campaign that kicked-off at a noon luncheon on Monday and closed Wednesday night. Three hundred business and professional men participated in the drive that stressed the work accomplished by the boys' division in reaching out to a large number of Nashville youngsters. Mr. Hill felt the boys' division had reached a peak of activity never before attained by the YMCA. An innovation was that the campaign workers invited large Nashville companies into buying group memberships for their employees.[480]

The campaign netted 429 new members when it officially closed at the Wednesday noon meeting of workers. The result was pronounced "very gratifying." J. P. W. Brown was awarded a barrel of flour donated by Mr. Hill to the division chairman who brought in the largest number of new members. Brown also won a handsome, silk flag for having the most division workers in attendance. Mr. Hill, who unavoidably missed the meeting, asked Mr. Spain to express his deep appreciation for the work done by the volunteers. Mr. Lambeth, campaign vice chairman, told the workers that he counted it a privilege to be associated with them. They gave him a rising vote of thanks for his leadership.[481] Mr. Hill felt the drive, despite not reaching its lofty goal, would give the Association momentum for the balance of the year.

• • • • •

CHAPTER ELEVEN

Rambling Ramblers and Good Times
1926–1928

Camp Sycamore campers in Sycamore Creek, 1926. Photo courtesy of Forrest Cooper.

TWO HIGHLIGHTS of the Rambler's 1926 season were their crushing victories over the Chattanooga Rail-Lytes and the Vanderbilt Commodores by scores of 41–27 and 25–8, respectively. The game with the Rail-Lytes was covered by *Banner* sportswriter Ralph McGill, who went on to fame as publisher and editor of the *Atlanta Constitution*. Jonas Coverdale was the Rambler's most consistent scorer that year.[482] He didn't play the night the professional world champion New York Celtics came to town. They defeated the Ramblers 37–18 and could have beaten them much worse had they cared. The huge crowd roared with delight at the Celtics' pinpoint passing, dribbling wizardry, and withering speed. The spectators also got a kick out of the trademark yellow ball the Celtics used.[483]

The Ramblers tied with the Burk Terrors for the city championship. Monk Sharp, the Rambler captain, however, did not acknowledge the Terrors as a legitimate co-champion, still miffed that they had pirated four players off the 1925 Rambler team: Lallie Richer, Bowser Chest, Ewell Costello, and Petty.[484] At the end of the season, Slick Welsh retired after seven years as a Rambler. He later became a well-known men's clothing salesman on Sixth Avenue North.

BASKET BALL

Vanderbilt vs. Ramblers

Y. M. C. A. GYMNASIUM
TUESDAY NIGHT, FEBRUARY 2, 1926
GAME CALLED 8 P. M.
50 CENTS

Vanderbilt won this game 21–12. Photo courtesy of Forrest Cooper.

Camp Sycamore opened for its third eight-week season on Monday, June 21. A week earlier, E. L. Spain took four board members on an inspection tour to make sure everything was ready. Jonas Coverdale was camp director for the second year. Associate camp director R. S. Bowron, boys' work director, assisted Coverdale. That summer, a counselor and eight campers slept in each 16' by 16' bungalow. The large dining hall accommodated 200 boys. Two new tennis courts had been added, and the baseball diamond enlarged, made level and rolled "to perfection." There was a new swimming pier that extended to the middle of the creek. There were also springboards and a 30-foot chute. Two new buildings were completed during the session, bringing the total number to sixteen.[485] That summer, the campers received shoulder patches with "Sycamore Camp Y" in white felt on a blue felt background.

The tradition of inviting Nashville business and religious leaders to visit the camp continued in 1926. The group of thirty-five came out on July 15 for the day. Mr. Hill served as their host for a fish fry before they returned to Nashville late in the afternoon. Among those who came were Lewis Pope, who would run for governor in 1928; Tony Sudekum, the theater chain owner; Banker A. E. "Ed" Potter Jr., president of Commerce Union Bank, and newspaperman, James G. "Jimmy" Stahlman. This was wonderful exposure for the camp.[486]

Other special occasions were a track meet on June 28 and the awarding of camp emblems to the camp's most outstanding boys, based on their development spiritually, mentally, and physically.[487]

The Ramblers began working out regularly in November. The players were grown men, often ex-high school stars. The veterans back for the 1927 season were all the starters from the previous winter—"Slim" Embry, "Monk" Sharp, "Red" Currin, Frank McCall, and Ray Foster. To insure that he had the depth he needed, Keim recruited several new men. They were Dixie Roberts, McEwen, Templeton, and Redd, all former MBA stars; and George O'Callaghan, formerly of Hume Fogg. In addition to having lost "Slick" Welsh, Jonas Coverdale's retirement left a big scoring void.[488]

• • • • •

The 1920s will forever be called the "roaring twenties" because of its association with jitterbugging, flappers, camel hair coats, cigarettes, and wild parties. The national YMCA was alarmed at the decadence of the decade and reacted by declaring war on petting and flappers. One of its strategies to counter the frivolity and decadence was to publish and distribute nationally a flyer whose title was "Petting is mock love." Somehow, this probably didn't do much to restrain the parties along fraternity row at the University of the South.[489] The Catholic Church also looked askance at the YMCA because of its entirely Protestant orientation.

• • • • •

Despite being one of the youngest Rambler teams, A. S. Keim's charges had some notable wins in 1927, including victories over the Chattanooga Rail-Lites, the Memphis YMCA Triangles twice, the Atlanta YMCA, and a split with Vanderbilt. The Y also sponsored one or more teams in the City League composed of less skilled players.[490]

Boys' Division Sets Record

Horace Hill was reelected president in January for the seventh time. His fellow officers were also veterans—Gillespie first vice president, Vernon Tupper second vice president, Ferriss Bailey treasurer, and Spain general secretary. The only new board member was Joseph W. Rowland, president of Bransford Wholesale Furniture Manufacturing Company. Returning to the board, along with the officers, were John P. W. Brown, Dr. Roger T. Nooe, W. H. Lambeth, Henry C. Hibbs, Dr. W. J. O'-Callaghan, Henry Sharp, H. B. Wilkerson, Dudley Gale, Charles L. Cornelius, W. R. Elam, Dr. John L. Hill, and Hunter Perry. The executive committee remained Messrs. Hill, Gillespie, Tupper, Brown, and Spain.[491]

The work of Mr. Hill and the executive committee were praised at the annual meeting as was the work done by Dudley Gale, chairman of boys' work. That division had

716 members at year's end, the largest in history. George Appleby, religious work director, reported that the lives of 14,329 people were touched in 1926. Dr. O'-Callaghan reported on the association's work in the city's industrial plants including National Casket Company, L & N Shops, L. L. Cohn, Radner Yards, and Hardwood Flooring Company.[492]

Mr. Spain reported that the men's division had 1,096 members at year-end and that 9,503 visitors were accorded privileges during 1926. He also said that the total cafeteria attendance during 1926 was 3,820, and that 4,480 transients spent a night in the Y building. The number of men who found jobs through the employment department was 128.[493]

Later in January, George C. Appleby, assistant secretary of the Nashville Association, died suddenly and unexpectedly of a heart attack. He had been associated with the Nashville YMCA for fourteen years, and was highly regarded. The executive committee adopted a memorial resolution a few days after his death that spoke of his graciousness and sincerity during his years of service.[494]

On March 10, 11, and 12, the Tennessee Inter-Scholastic Athletic Association (T.I.A.A.) held its basketball tournament at the YMCA. Hume-Fogg defeated MBA to win the championship. The referees for the *Nashville Banner* sponsored state tournament were Jonas Coverdale and Slick Welsh, former Rambler stars and YMCA men.[495]

The Rambler's last game came on the 15th when they played the archrival Burk Terrors, a team sponsored by Burk & Company. At stake was the state championship. The Terrors won 33–23 to avenge an earlier two-point loss to the Ramblers.[496]

In March, a group of Nashville businessmen, including William C. "Will" Weaver, a future YMCA president, enjoyed playing volleyball each day at noon in the Warner Gymnasium.[497]

An innovative use of the gymnasium came about in May when the Tennessee gallery rifle championship was held there. The event was sponsored by the Bon Air Gun Club of the soon-to-be-opened Camp Bon Air for Boys in Bon Air, Tennessee, just over 100 miles east of Nashville on the Memphis-Bristol Highway. What is interesting is that E. L. Spain was president of both the gun club and the camp. The camp vice president was Dr. A. S. Keim, of Rambler fame; and the treasurer was none other than Ferriss C. Bailey, treasurer of the Nashville Association. It seems surprising that the YMCA board sanctioned Spain opening the camp, which was likely to be in competition with Camp Sycamore. In a January press release, Spain announced that the camp would be the official summer school of the School of Engineering at Vanderbilt and that 50 engineering students would be at the camp from June to September.[498] Later, Mr. and Mrs. Spain converted Camp Bon Air into a camp for girls, eliminating any conflict of interest.

• • • • •

The YMCA Law School of Nashville, Inc. was established as a non-profit corporation in 1926 and given the authority to confer the degree of Doctor of Jurisprudence. The school's 1926–27 catalogue said this took place "in order to take care of the increased number of students and to provide more extensive facilities." The diminished effectiveness of the Cumberland Law School in Lebanon also was a factor in the progressive move by the YMCA law school that was under "the direct supervision of the Central YMCA." An executive committee, chaired by H. G. Hill Sr. was empowered to select the Law School faculty. On the faculty at the time was Nashville attorney Littell Rust, who had joined the boys' department in 1895 at age nine. He would teach at the Law School for 36 years before retiring in 1962. Littell would also serve as treasurer of the Y board for 25 years.[499]

• • • • •

Between 50 and 60 boys left the YMCA building in trucks for Camp Sycamore on June 21. W. M. Wakeford, boys' work secretary and R. E. Johnson, boys' physical director, were in charge. Mr. Spain also went. The first night at the campfire, Charlton Rogers talked to the boys on the value of camp life. The boys were probably more excited about finding that six new canoes arrived in camp earlier. Emanuel Buford, the "chef de luxe," was back for a third season in the kitchen. One of the new counselors was Sartain Lanier, who had been a camper two years before. When camp closed, it was said that every boy who stayed the entire season had a lump in his throat when the big passenger transport bus provided by the Nashville Railway and Light Company pulled away from camp to take them home.[500]

A week after camp closed, George R. Gillespie, who had given the camp the motor-powered boat, the "George R." in 1924, died. He had been vice president of the

Camp Sycamore boys saluting the flag, ca. 1926. Photo courtesy of Forrest Cooper.

Nashville Association. George had a great love for boys and Camp Sycamore, and would be missed.[501]

The "Iron Duke" at His Best

Ralph McGill, the *Banner*'s sportswriter gave sports fans an insight into how tightly wound Rambler's coach Dr. A. S. Keim was as he impatiently waited for the 1927–28 season to open. McGill wrote that Keim's ambition for the Ramblers "makes Napoleon's or Macbeth's look puny." He said that Keim was so impatient for the season to start that "he can hardly restrain himself." An aggressive recruiter, Keim had lured Jim Stuart, Vanderbilt's All Southern center in 1926–27 to join the YMCA and become a Rambler. McGill further described Keim as a big man, someone kind to his family but a competitor who has "no good will for his foes."[502] Unfortunately, Stuart must have changed his mind as his name does not appear in any of the box scores of Rambler games that season.

In their first major test, the Ramblers lost to the Rail-Lites in Chattanooga. They didn't improve, losing, in January, to the Burk Terrors, and the YMHA Peps. The Ramblers then righted their ship and avenged all three of these losses. After defeating the Terrors to clinch the city championship, McGill marveled that Keim, whom he called the "Iron Duke," did a remarkable job coaching.[503] The normal starting five for the season were brothers Frank and John McCall at forward and center, respectively; Duck Roberts at the other forward; and Red Currin and Bernard Spain at the guard spots.[504] Particularly pleased with his team's turnaround, Dr. Keim decided to call it quits and retire after coaching the Ramblers for five highly successful years. His successor would be Jonas Coverdale, his former player at Hume-Fogg and on the Ramblers.

In 1928, the Y sponsored City League teams were scattered from the Una Independents to the southeast to the Goodlettsville Independents to the northwest. The American National team was naturally called the "Bankers." The "Y" Terrors, coached for the last time by Jonas Coverdale, won the championship.[505]

A front-page headline of the *Nashville Banner* on January 12 read, "YMCA Board Re-elects Hill." Early that afternoon, eighteen members of the YMCA board unanimously elected the prominent Nashville grocer to his eighth consecutive term as president. Vernon Tupper returned as second vice president as did Ferriss Bailey as treasurer. The directors asked former president John P. W. Brown to come back as first vice-president. He did so. The only new board member elected was M. D. Anderson who filled the vacancy caused by Gillespie's death.

At the annual meeting January 12, it was announced that the association had substantial growth in "its general activities" in 1927 and that the year had been one of the most successful in the YMCA's history. Most importantly, the Y had lived within its budget. All the department heads gave their reports.

"March Madness" in Nashville in 1928 came in the form of two interscholastic state tournaments, both held in the YMCA's Warner Gymnasium. The Tennessee Interscholastic Athletic Association (T.I.A.A.), primarily composed of the state's prep schools, came first. MBA won that tournament. The next week, the Tennessee Secondary School Athletic Association (T.S.S.A.A.) brought their largely public school tournament to town. Purdy H.S. in Hardin County outclassed Nashville's Cathedral School to win the T.S.S.A.A. championship.[506]

Camp Sycamore opened Monday, June 18, when eighty enthusiastic boys arrived in time for dinner at noon. They gave Emanuel Buford, the camp cook, a standing ovation, and later in the summer named him an honorary member of the camp fraternities. Wallace Wakeford, boys' work secretary, was camp director. He was assisted by R. E. Johnson, athletics director; Eugene "Chin" Johnson, Rambler star and newly appointed assistant physical director; and about thirteen others. On the first Friday, H. G. Hill hosted his annual fish fry for all his fellow board members and a large group of Nashville businessmen.[507] In talking to campers, the board members realize how much the boys were anticipating field day and how much they enjoyed swimming and baseball, the most popular camp activities. The competition between the bungalows for the flag awarded daily to the best-kept lodge was probably less spirited. During the second week, the finals in all competitive events were held as was field day. After that week, the first group of boys regretfully returned to Nashville to be replaced by an equally enthusiastic second group of 80.[508]

Back in Nashville, J. Gilbert Lackey, a member of the faculty of the YMCA Law School, awarded diplomas to seven men and one woman. Other faculty members that year were Ferriss Bailey; O. W. Hughes, dean; Miller Manier; Littell Rust; Frank Siemonds, and future chancellor William J. Wade. Manier would teach there for twenty-seven years.[509]

The Ramblers opened their 1928–29 season on Sewanee Mountain against the University of the South. Rambler starters were Duck Roberts, Maynard Eaton, Ewell Costello, Butts Gentry, and Chin Johnson. Roberts, Gentry, and Johnson had played for Sewanee's Coach, Lucian Emerson, when he was coach at MBA. The Ramblers won 28–21. The YMCA team played twice more in December, winning both handily.[510] The year 1928 had been a good one.

• • • • •

Camp Sycamore swimming hole, ca. 1930s

Prosperous Years Turn Lean
1929–1933

THE HEADLINE on the front page of the *Nashville Banner* on December 30, 1928, was "Financiers Forecast Prosperous New Year." Little did financiers, or H. G. Hill, or anybody else know what was going to happen to their world the next October.

In January, Mr. Hill was reelected for the eighth consecutive year as president of the Nashville YMCA. His fellow officers in 1928 were also reelected—J. P. Brown, Vernon Tupper, Ferriss Bailey, who was Mr. Hill's lawyer and fishing partner, and general secretary E. L. Spain. Board members were also the same as in 1928. Treasurer Bailey reported that the association was operating within its budget, that all current debts were promptly being paid, and best of all, that the building debt had been greatly reduced.[511]

Mr. Spain's report for the previous year showed there were, at year-end, 972 members in the men's department and 528 members in the boys' division for a total membership of 1,500. Interestingly, that number was 800 less than it was in January 1923 when the association had its highest membership in history—2,300.

In the men's department, 70,838 men used the baths and swimming pool and 614 outside agencies used the building. The employment department secured 200 jobs for men while 1,257 men were given charity beds during the year.[512]

In the boys' division, 23,674 attended group and club meetings, while 4,397 boys used the privileges of the division. Eight outside boys' groups used the facilities and 604 gymnasium classes were conducted.[513]

On the basketball court, four losses in January put the Ramblers behind in the city race but, as happened the previous season, they came back to whip the Rail-Lites, the Burk Terrors, and Vanderbilt to get back in the middle of the title chase.[514] After defeating the Peps, the Ramblers captured the city championship for the second straight year. Monk Sharp did not play that evening as he was a player and coach in 1929, playing for the Ramblers and coaching the Peps. The Ramblers' only important game remaining was with the Rail-Lites. Their player-coach Bill Redd, embarrassed by their early season loss to the Ramblers, brought in two Midwestern ringers, and won the game and the state championship 55–27.[515]

Dr. A. S. Keim, whose association with the YMCA went back to 1911 when he was employed as physical education director, announced in February that he was giving up his position as director of the YMCA Health Club to start his own health club. Keim had seen the YMCA Health Club grow tremendously since he assumed its helm six years earlier. The Keim Health Club would be in a building to be constructed on Fifth Avenue North between Commerce and Church streets.[516]

For the third straight year, the *Banner*'s T.I.A.A. State Tournament was held at the YMCA. Nashvillians read in the *Banner* that the teams would "eat, sleep, and play" in the YMCA. That was partially true. Some slept in the Y while others stayed in a nearby hotel. The teams certainly played in the Y and the association furnished referees for the third consecutive year. This year, the referees were holdover Jonas Coverdale and newcomer Chin Johnson, two of the best referees in the state. The teams, faculty members, and coaches may have had breakfast at the Y but they also ate in one of the city's best cafeterias.[517]

With basketball season finally over, Coverdale hosted an

indoor track meet in the Warner Gymnasium for the Nashville Boys' Club the last week in March. Four days later, he and everyone else who read the *Nashville Banner* sports pages were upset to learn that Ralph McGill was leaving the *Banner* to accept a sports-writing position with the *Atlanta Constitution*. McGill, who frequently covered Rambler games, would be missed.[518]

• • • • •

The YMCA Law School held their annual graduation exercises in June. Dean O. W. Hughes, for the first time, presented law degrees to a husband and wife. Vincent and Grace Bohannon graduated together, intending to practice together in Nashville.[519]

• • • • •

Summer of '29

Camp Sycamore opened in mid-June with seventy-five boys in the first session. Mr. Hill's annual fish fry and camp inspection was successful. The boys were glad to see the visitors as they got to participate in the festivities, including the fish fry. The Round Table initiated fourteen boys. Junior and senior tennis singles championships were held with Whitehall Morrison winning the junior championship. That evening after supper, the boys played a seven-inning baseball game. Earlier, they had enjoyed some fine watermelons brought down by Mr. Spain in the trunk of his automobile.[520]

The 1929 camp season may have been shorter than usual as, on July 7, it was announced that, on the following Monday, seventy members of the Nashville Boys' Club would leave for Camp Sycamore for a week's outing. They would take over the entire camp under their own supervision. The expenses for thirty-nine of the boys would be paid for by the Community Chest. The Optimist Club, the American Legion, and the Forty and Eight Club, paid for most of the rest. The cost per boy was $6.[521]

Camp Sycamore shoulder patch. Photo courtesy of Forrest Cooper.

No one in that hot summer of 1929 had any idea that the stock market would crash on "Black Thursday" October 24. By then, Roger Caldwell's Caldwell & Company was already in trouble. With the crash, he became increasingly desperate and began scrambling for cash. Soon his empire would crash.

Nashvillians didn't have as much disposable income to buy groceries in H. G. Hill's stores, even in the new one at the corner of Twenty-First and West End in the heart of one of Nashville's most affluent areas. The Fourth and First National Bank was forced to merge with the American National. The symphony would fold in 1930. Still, these things didn't happen all at once but slowly, and in 1930, there were not that many "doom and gloom" stories in the local newspapers.

Despite concern over his stock market loss, Horace Hill was not about to jump the YMCA ship. He decided he would stand by the YMCA and, if asked to serve as president again in January, he would do so. At the annual meeting on the 14th, he was reelected president, supported by his veteran cast of officers—John P. W. Brown as first vice-president, Vernon Tupper as second vice-president, Ferriss C. Bailey as treasurer, and E. L. Spain as general secretary. Elected to the board for one-year terms were Ferriss C. Bailey, Dudley Gale, Dr. John L. Hill, E. E. Murrey, Dr. Roger T. Noone, and Henry Sharp, the veteran Rambler basketball player. Elected for two-year terms were J. P. W. Brown, H. G. Hill, Dr. W. J. O'-Callaghan, Hunter Perry, Vernon S. Tupper, and H. B. Wilkerson. The three-year class consisted of M. D. Anderson, Charles L. Cornelius, Wade Elam, Henry C. Hibbs, and J. W. Roland.[522]

The State YMCA still had its offices in the Nashville YMCA building in 1930. On February 2, they announced that their annual meeting would be held at Murfreesboro's new James K. Polk Hotel. Francis S. Harmon, president of the National YMCA Council, told the attendees, "We must realize that our local branches are only forts and no army ever achieved anything by simply holding a fort." It seems clear that he was calling for the YMCAs to go where the people lived and not expect them to come to us. Although there were some branch YMCAs in 1930, including Cincinnati's Hillsboro Branch, Nashville would not create one until 1945.

In February, the Nashville YMCA issued a call for all boys (meaning white boys) in the city to meet at the Y to form a swimming team. Bill Trabue Jr. would be their coach.[523]

Although the name "March Madness" was unheard of in 1930, March that year was a very busy basketball month in the YMCA's Warner Gymnasium. The first week of the month, the Ramblers stumbled through their final game of the season, losing to the Idea Aces. Expected to have another good team, the Ramblers ended up with four wins and eleven losses, their worst record in history. They were unable to beat a single one of their traditional adversaries. Next, the T.I.A.A. held its fourth consecutive state championship at the YMCA from the 6th to the 8th. This time, Baylor School defeated McCallie to win the crown. The final acts of the post season were two championship games at month's end to determine the winners of the Methodist League's men's and women's championships.[524]

E. L. Spain was honored in early June when he was elected president of the Affiliated Exchange Clubs of Tennessee. He was then in his second year as president of the Nashville Exchange Club.[525]

A Poor Economy

June meant camping season. For the eighth consecutive summer, the YMCA outing was held at Camp Sycamore. Fifty-six boys were there for the opening session; fourteen less than attended the first session in 1929. The decrease was attributed to the poor economy. Jim Way, the camp director, organized the boys into two tribes, the Cherokees and the Mohawks, with an equal number in each. Each tribe had two coaches.[526]

When the second week at Camp Sycamore opened on Monday, June 30, fifty-seven boys were present. That morning, the junior Mohawks defeated their Cherokee counterparts in volleyball. The senior Mohawks held up their part of the contest by routing the Cherokees in soccer 7–2. That afternoon, the juniors played soccer while the seniors competed in volleyball. Two camp features were the morning salute to the flag and the evenings spent around the camp fire, singing songs, listening to ghost stories, and performing impromptu stunts. The regular camp closed on Sunday the 6th. The next day, the Nashville Kiwanis Club occupied the camp.[527]

While the YMCA boys were at Camp Sycamore, some of the Nashville Association secretaries were at Blue Ridge attending the annual summer school for YMCA secretaries, sponsored by the YMCA Graduate School. Some of the courses available were on administration, boys' work, the life of Christ, membership, and race relations.[528]

December brought a huge change. First, it was announced on November 30 that it was uncertain whether or not the Ramblers would field a basketball team in the city league. A few days later, it was obvious that the fabled Ramblers had folded their tent. By early in December, Rambler players signed up with two of the four remaining teams—the Ideal Aces and the DuPont squad. Ewell Costello, the Y's player coach in 1929, Bowser Chest, Bobby Worrall, and Teaks Eaton were grabbed by the Aces—Chest, Worrall, and Eaton as players and Costello as coach. Chin Johnson, Duck Roberts, the best player in the league, and John McCall joined the DuPont club. John "Monk" Sharp, who had played for the Ramblers at least since 1913, retired. A memorable athletic era seemed to be over.[529]

Hill Reelected

The Nashville YMCA Board met on December 17 in the directors' room at the YMCA. H. G. Hill was reelected to his tenth consecutive term as president, the other three officers—Brown, Tupper, and Bailey—and the general secretary Spain, were also reelected. The board members paid tribute to Mr. Hill for his "safe counsel and able leadership" in directing the politics of the Y and "extending its various and helpful influences to thousands of Nashville boys and young men." In turn, Mr. Hill thanked the board for their loyal support and cooperation. Two new board members were welcomed—F. C. Haller and William C. "Will" Weaver. Mr. Weaver, a wholesale hardware merchant on Second Avenue, had been a YMCA Health Club member for a number of years, having just concluded a term as president of the health club.

This year, Mr. Hill's executive committee, included himself as president, Messrs. Brown, Perry, Tupper, and Wilkerson, and E. L. Spain as secretary.

Mr. Spain gave a lengthy report on activities for the first eleven months of 1930. The largest numbers were in the boys' department, he said. The total number of boys using the pool and playing games was 56,388. Outside groups using the facilities included various scout groups, Sunday School classes, and several basketball leagues. The total attendance in gym classes was 21,384.

Mr. Spain also reported that, during the eleven-month period, 248 members joined the YMCA and that the showers and swimming pool were used more than 44,000 times. This figure was down from more than 70,000 in 1929. The number of outside groups using the building was 147, also down. Conversely, the use of charity beds in the apartments was up from 1,257 to 1,428. These figures reflect the increasing impact of the recession. During 1930, religious services had been held on Tuesday mornings for the staff, Friday afternoons for workers, and Tuesday evenings for apartment men. There were also weekly services for businessmen.[530]

In January, YMCA board member Dudley Gale was elected president of the Nashville Kiwanis Club, while former YMCA president Dr. Matt Buckner was named president of the State YMCA, both indications of the prominence of the YMCA board members and their involvement in a broad array of civic causes. The State YMCA met, as usual, in the YMCA building in January. Twenty-five YMCA organizations were represented by 75 delegates.[531]

The T.I.A.A. state basketball tournament was held in early March at the YMCA. Leo Long's Father Ryan team won the state championship over MBA before an overflow crowd. The tournament was described as the T.I.A.A.'s best ever.[532]

Of great importance to the Nashville Association was the resignation in June of Jonas Coverdale, the YMCA's capable physical director since 1925. He left to accept a position as principal of the Junior School and physical director at Castle Heights Military Academy in nearby Lebanon. He would assume his new duties in the fall. Eighteen years later, Coverdale and Paul Reddick, intramural director at Castle Heights, would resign to become co-managers of BGA.[533]

For the eighth consecutive year, the Nashville Association held its annual boys' camp at Camp Sycamore. The 1931 session was abbreviated, lasting only two weeks. The junior and senior campers were equally divided into two groups—the Cherokees and Mohawks. Robert L. King, the third camp director in three years, introduced a new game of batball that the boys seemed to enjoy. There were also the customary track meet, baseball and volleyball games, tennis matches, hikes, swimming, and fishing.[534] By this time, there was a walking bridge over the creek just below the dam that the boys enjoyed.

In early July, the camp was turned over to the Lion's Club that brought seventy underprivileged boys from seven social centers in Nashville to Sycamore for a week.[535]

The Nashville YMCA's religious work committee observed the annual week of prayer, celebrated world-wide, by holding prayer services in the library of the Seventh Avenue lobby level each morning from 9:00 to 9:30. Each of the six services, to which the public was invited, was preceded by a song period. A different Protestant minister spoke each day.

A New Year and New Opportunities

Nashville YMCA president H. G. Hill was unanimously reelected president for 1932. His management team changed with the retirements of John P. W. Brown and Vernon S. Tupper as first and second vice-president, respectively. They were succeeded by E. E. Murrey, vice-president of the Nashville and American Trust Company; and J. Frank Jarman, who had, in 1924, founded Jarman Shoe Company. Jarman was a new board member as was Robert S. Cheek, son of Joel Cheek. Others elected included indefatigable treasurer, Ferriss Bailey. Robert S. Spain was reappointed general secretary for the twelfth consecutive year, having, before 1921, served an additional nine years as secretary.

In his annual report, Spain mentioned that, for the first time in many years, the YMCA would resume publication of a bulletin. The first issue of the *Central Y*, he said, had just come from the press.

The demise of the popular Ramblers a year earlier created a void at the YMCA as the Ramblers had an avid following. A problem developed quickly because the Ideal Aces and the Burk Terrors of the Major League played their games at the YMCA. This caused a problem for YMCA members who could only play handball, racquetball, and pick-up basketball games at night. When there were Major League games in the Warner Gymnasium, they could not exercise and told Mr. Spain that unless something was done, they were going to drop their memberships. He told the two outside teams that they would have to find another place to play.[536]

The association still sponsored two lower-level basketball

leagues—one for men and the other for women. The men's league featured teams from First Lutheran Church, Hermitage Mills, Lockland Baptist Church, Jarman Shoe Company, Judson Methodist Church, Keith Simmons, and A.U.A. Season tickets were on sale at the YMCA at 75 cents for adults and 10 cents for children.[537]

• • • • •

Julius Rosenwald, the Jewish philanthropist from Chicago, who had, in 1911, offered to give $25,000 to any YMCA in America that could match the offer with an additional subscription of $75,000 to build a Colored Men's YMCA, died in January. I was estimated that during his lifetime, he had given away $25 million. Although the Nashville YMCA had been unable to raise the needed subscription to build a colored YMCA branch building, Rosenwald's foundation gave Meharry Medical College $250,000 and Tennessee A & I School $150,000.[538]

• • • • •

Despite the depression, the Nashville YMCA board remained one of the city's strongest, as it had been throughout its existence and as it would be for another eighty years. In October, there were photographs of three YMCA board members—Robert S. Cheek, J. Frank Jarman, and Dr. John L. Hill—in the Nashville Banner in recognition of their work for the 1932 Community Chest drive.[539]

The Nashville YMCA had a swimming team in the winter of 1932–33 as it did a year earlier. Among the team members were John A. Ball, son of MBA's headmaster Isaac Ball; the Richter brothers; and Paul and Ernest Spain, sons of E. L. Spain, the general secretary. The 1932 team had an attractive schedule that included trips to Atlanta, Chattanooga, Knoxville, and Memphis to swim against their YMCAs.[540]

In the annual meeting, held on January 17, 1933, Mr. Spain was reelected president for the thirteenth year and E. L. Spain was reelected general secretary for his twenty-second year. In the history of the Nashville YMCA, no president or general secretary has served so long. These records would stand well into the twenty-first century. Also elected were E. E. Murrey, J. Frank Jarman, and Ferriss C. Bailey as first vice-president, second vice-president, and treasurer, respectively. They directors having recently voted to increase the size of the board from eighteen to twenty-four, elected eight new directors—W. W. Dillon; Dr. I. W. Gernert, minister at First Lutheran Church; Benjamin H. Johnson, a dentist; Norman McEwen, president of McEwen Laundry; Ed Potter Jr., the thirty-four-year-old president of Commerce Union Bank; Littell Rust, and attorney; Hubbard F. Srygley, superintendent of city schools; and James G. "Jimmy" Stahlman, young publisher of the *Nashville Banner*. The board reelected fifteen existing board members, leaving one vacancy. After the election of officers and directors, Mr. Hill named his committee chairman—finance, J. Frank Jarman; religious work, Dr. John L. Hill; house, H. Burton Wilkerson; health club, W. W. Dillon; and employment, Dr. W. J. O'Callaghan.

In his annual report, Mr. Spain said that the YMCA was used more than 175,000 times in 1932 and that 14,225 people watched basketball games. He also listed his priorities for 1933—extension of Hi-Y programs, organization of unemployed boys into groups, development of hobby and craft work for boys, introduction of a leaders training course, development of Torch Clubs, stepped-up publicity, education of parents, and more programs for boys.[541]

The Growth of Boys' Programs

During 1933, there were 2,781 boys in the boys' division. They attended 1,244 sessions with a total attendance of 12,737. During the year, 229 outside groups used the pool, and 340 new boys were received as members. A total of 4,360 boys used the pool during the year, and 94 swimming tests were passed.

From January through December 1933, members took fencing, tennis, archery, riflery, wrestling, boxing, and advanced gym classes. They also played basketball and handball, exercised individually, took life saving tests, received swimming instructions, sun bathed, and used the pool, and the health club. During the summer, the Nashville Association, in cooperation with the Nashville Baseball Club, arranged for 4,057 boys and girls from city and county high schools to see Nashville Vols Southern League games free of charge.

The 1933 annual report also indicated that Camp Sycamore was used, during the summer, without cost by First Presbyterian Church, the Vanderbilt YMCA, Howard School, East High School, Duncan School, and class groups from the Central YMCA. No mention was made there or in the *Nashville Banner* of the regular boys camp that may have fallen victim to the YMCA's carefully planned entrenchment program put into operation in 1932.[542]

Swimming continued to be heavily emphasized in 1933. That summer, 187 boys were taught how to swim at the YMCA pool, considered the finest in the city. All of Davidson County's white grammar school boys were invited to take advantage of this opportunity. The YMCA eleven-man swimming team was very competitive in its meets with other YMCAs across the state. Thirty-six boys passed junior life saving classes, and became members of the YMCA's Whale Club. In the Warner Gymnasium, the Y hosted a citywide indoor tennis tournament for boys and girls.

Cooperating with the Boy Scouts of America, the swimming pool and gym were used for the passing of all scout tests. Y staff members assisted the scoutmasters in this work. During the year, three Boy Scout groups with 128 members were headquartered at the Y with all the privileges of the association.

Two hundred nineteen students from nine prep and high schools were in Y-sponsored Hi-Y clubs during the year. The high schools were East, Central, Hume-Fogg, Peabody, Isaac Litton, and Duncan. The grammar schools were Clemons, Cavert, and Tarbox.

With the depression gradually deepening, the YMCA intensified its program of providing non-resident transients with showers, shaving facilities, a place to wash their clothes, assistance in making contact with welfare agencies, a place to play games, write letters, and send telegraphs, and above all, clean beds. During 1933, 2,260 free beds were given to homeless men and boys. To accommodate these guests, the Y equipped a room with twenty beds. The homeless also had their own showers. To assist the Y in coping with the homeless, the Communications Workers of America provided supervisory manpower.

The Nashville YMCA employment service worked, hand-in-glove, with other agencies of the Community Chest in trying to find employment, permanent or temporary, for the jobless.

The good news was that, during the early 1930s, the YMCA's Businessmen's Club was self-sustaining. Between 1931 and 1933, 534 men enjoyed its benefits. Those amenities were Swedish massage, steam baths, electric baths, dry heat baths, ultra-violet ray, infra-red ray, vibrators, rowing machine, electric horse, bending mats, chest weights, swimming pool, corrective exercise, volleyball, and handball.

In December, Mr. Spain reported that the YMCA was carrying on its membership roles for 161 deserving boys whose limited means were such that without this free service, they would not have been able to enjoy the benefits of the Association. This included boys from Monroe Harding Children's Home. Additionally, the Hume-Fogg wrestling and boxing teams practiced at the Y three times a week without charge. The state high school boxing and wrestling championships were held at the Y. The Hume-Fogg administration, mindful of the free use of Y facilities by their students and of the relief work the YMCA was doing with underprivileged Nashville boys, gave the association 450 old Hume-Fogg uniforms to distribute as Mr. Spain saw fit.

The 22nd annual report of the Nashville Y, published in December, was twenty-three pages long. On page one, the Y staff wrote, "our Association should move definitely and with great urgency, as far as hundreds of Nashville boys are concerned, in the direction of becoming even more largely a place of fellowship for boys and young men using their leisure time together creatively and sharing an increasing variety of vital life interests.... As we come to the New Year with its numberless opportunities, we welcome the privilege of sharing in a movement that is concerned with the fundamental principles of life—the building of character. Through conscientious effort, it is our purpose to make 1934 a year of genuine achievement in serving the boys and young men of our community."

• • • • •

Where There's a Will There's a Way
1934–1938

THE Y CELEBRATED the beginning of 1934 with its annual New Year's Day open house. Most of the officers and staff members came with their spouses, including Mr. and Mrs. Hill and his soon-to-be-elected successor William C. "Will" Weaver and Will's wife, Irene Morgan Weaver. Mr. Hill and Mr. Spain, the general secretary, welcomed their guests with the hope that the New Year would bring a revival of prosperity to the city.

Horace Hill was ready to step down. He was seventy years old and had been YMCA president for a record-setting thirteen years. At the annual meeting on the 17th, William C. Weaver, the forty-eight-year-old president of McWhorter-Weaver and Company, was elected president. A Davidson County native, and a member of a prominent local family, Will was a Rotarian and a member of Arlington Methodist Church. He had been on the YMCA board since 1931 and had experienced officers to work with—E. E. Murrey, J. Frank Jarman, Ferriss Bailey, and E. L. Spain, who was elected for his twenty-third consecutive year as general executive. Having agreed to stay on the board, Mr. Hill was reelected with twenty-two other directors.

During the meeting, Dr. John L. Hill praised Mr. Hill for his dedicated years of service as president. He emphasized two highlights—Mr. Hill's love of boys, manifested in so many ways, and his fiscal responsibility, particularly in 1922 and during the most recent years when the economy was so distressed. Dr. Hill then unveiled a life-sized oil portrait of Mr. Hill, painted by Miss Edith Fisher, a Nashville artist. The portrait would be hung, he said, in the lobby of the YMCA building as a reminder to future YMCA leaders that, had it not been for Mr. Hill's leadership, the association might not have survived. In his response, Mr. Hill told the directors that, while much had been accomplished, "unlimited opportunities still exist and there are places of usefulness and importance awaiting each member of the board."

Mr. Spain's 22nd annual report stated that, during 1933, the association lived within its budget. He reported that, in the boys' division, 13,160 boys attended 7,871 classes, and that, in the men's division, attendance in classes reached 38,188, a new record. He spent some time speaking about the services rendered to homeless young men and boys because of the terrible economy.[543]

The Nashville Association had another member of the W. C. Weaver family making news in January. William C. "Bill" Weaver Jr., the 6'5" son of the new YMCA president, was

the starting center on the rejuvenated YMCA Rambler basketball team. After not fielding a team since the 1929–30 season, the Ramblers were once again in what was, in the 1933–34 season, called the Major League. Despite having a brand new and inexperienced team and a new player/coach, Lallie Richter, the Ramblers held their own. In a loss to the Hermitage Feeds team in January, Weaver was the leading Rambler scorer with seven points. A week later, Bill scored a game-high 15 points as the Ramblers decked the Knights of Columbus Kay See outfit 46–30.[544] The Ramblers ended the season in second place in a five-team league after the Hermitage Seeds dropped out because one of their players was ruled ineligible.[545]

In early February, the TSSAA, that included most public high schools, held their district boys' and girls' tournaments at the YMCA.[546] The Y also continued to open the gymnasium free of charge for church league basketball games. Under this arrangement, 268 boys and girls, who were members of Baptist and Presbyterian Churches, played in Warner Gym weekly. On some nights, as many as five games were played at the Y's two gyms.

New athletic director Paul Toombs also oversaw the second annual Gattis-Richter Independent basketball tournament. The Nashville Business College girls' team, a future powerhouse, also played their home games in Warner Gymnasium. Their league's tournament in mid-March was also hosted by the YMCA.[547]

If basketball wasn't enough, there were weekly boxing and wrestling matches at the Y. Amateur boxing was a much bigger sport in the 1930s than it would be eighty years later.

In April, Nashville's second indoor tennis tournament and the 17th annual demonstration of physical training of youth at the YMCA were the big events. There were sixteen entries in the tennis tournament, double the number in 1933. Half of those were members of the Vanderbilt tennis team. The physical training exhibition featured acrobatics, wrestling, fencing, and dancing. The crowds for this free event were described as moderately large.[548]

• • • • •

The YMCA Night Law School, under Dean W. O. Hughes, had eighteen graduates in June. Judge John B. Aust, former chancellor in Davidson County Chancery Court, was the featured speaker.[549]

• • • • •

Lean Years

The Nashville YMCA was helped in adjusting to the lean years of the depression by being a recipient of funds from the Community Chest. In 1934, one of the city and nation's biggest problems was unemployment. This put even more pressure on the YMCA's employment service. During the year, 44 positions were secured for the unemployed and membership was furnished free to 92 deserving boys who, otherwise, could not have afforded to join. The annual learn-to-swim campaign for grammar school boys was continued, enabling 157 boys to learn to swim.

Under the new regime, the Nashville Association continued its "Christian" emphasis through noonday religious services held at industrial plants in Nashville and at the county jail. Religious meetings were also held regularly at the YMCA building for staff, apartment men and members.[550]

The Ramblers fielded a team in the 1934–35 Nashville Major Basketball League that had six teams—the Ramblers, the YMHA Peps, the Ideal Aces, the Knights of Columbus Kay Sees, Pat's Place, and the Big 4's. The team had a competitive season but did not draw as well as it had in the 1920s. Bobby Worrall was one of the mainstays. As had been the case for a number of years, there were fewer high school games played at the Central Y gym, as there were forty high school and college gymnasiums in Davidson County.

At the annual meeting in January, the board reelected W. C. Weaver as president, E. E. Murrey as first vice-president, Frank Jarman as second vice-president, Ferriss Bailey as treasurer and E. L. Spain as general secretary. In his report, Mr. Spain mentioned that only one of the YMCA officers in 1875, when the association revived, W. H. Ford, was still alive. He had been treasurer in 1875.[551]

In January, the YMCA announced the most ambitious winter swimming program ever to be held in Nashville. C. W. Batey, the coach, said that home and away meets had been arranged with YMCAs in Chattanooga, Knoxville, Louisville, and Memphis as well as with the Maryville College swim team. The boys had been working out two nights a week since early December.

The weekly boxing and wrestling matches picked up again in January. On the 15th, there was also a fencing exhibition, and a performance on the flying rings. One of the wrestlers that week was Dick Given, the YMCA wrestling instructor, who was a former Southern amateur welterweight champion. Heaven help his opponent.[552]

February saw the Nashville YMCA Swim Team travel to Knoxville to take on their Y. Nashville came out a 41–39 victory. In March, the third annual city pingpong tournament was held in the lobby. Later in the month, the Health Club sponsored its volleyball tournament. The two finalists were Kendrick Peterson and Joe Folk. They also met in the 1934 finals.[553]

There was no publicity in the *Nashville Banner* in the summer of 1935 regarding Camp Sycamore. It undoubtedly opened that summer as did several other boys camps, including Camp Bon Air, operated by YMCA general secretary E. L. Spain at Sparta; Camp Boxwell, the Boy Scout camp; and Camp Overton, run by the State YMCA at Rock Island.[554]

In July, the *Nashville Banner* carried a picture of African American children from the Hadley Park and Napier areas at a swimming pool. This was part of a learn-to-swim program, sponsored by the YMCA and the Nashville Chapter of the American Red Cross.

William C. "Will" Weaver was elected to his third term as president in January 1936. He renewed his pledge "to broaden the scope of association work for Nashville boys and young men." Also reelected, E. L. Spain, general secretary, was beginning his 25th consecutive year with the association. E. E. Murrey, Frank Jarman and Ferriss Bailey were the other officers elected at the annual meeting.

Mr. Spain reported that the association had a balanced budget in 1935 and mentioned the needed additions and improvements had been made to the building. He said that the use of the facilities was up from the previous year.[555]

The Ramblers were still in the Major Basketball League but didn't make a great impression. In mid-January, they were mired in fourth place among the six teams. A later loss to the last place Peps didn't help. YMCA athletic director Paul Toombs started at guard and tried to rally the squad, but not with much success.

The boxing and wrestling season in 1936 culminated in a tournament in March with nine bouts waged. In the feature duel of the evening, former Vanderbilt gridder Oscar Noel won by a decision over John Berry of Hume-Fogg. A young man needed to think twice before getting in the ring with either of the Noel brothers. There were fifty-six entries in the tournament and medals were presented to the winners and runner-ups. Plans were formulated to make this an annual event.[556]

• • • • •

On June 18, 1936, The Nashville YMCA board of directors recognized its very popular general secretary E. L. Spain for his 25 years of faithful service to the Nashville Association by giving him a plaque that his grandson, Forrest Cooper, owned in 2011.

• • • • •

Weatherford's Disappointment

The big news in 1936 was the announcement that the YMCA Graduate College was closing. Organized by Dr. Willis D. Weatherford in 1919 as a professional educational venture working with Vanderbilt, Peabody and Scarritt, the Graduate College had a $500,000 plant and an annual budget exceeding $100,000. The end came when the school could no longer meet payments on the $167,000 mortgage that had been placed on the building in 1933.[557] The prestigious school's closure was a serious blow to the entire YMCA movement as the school had been a matter of pride locally and to the national YMCA. Had the post World War I prosperity continued through the thirties, the YMCA Graduate School and the Nashville YMCA would undoubtedly have both achieved steady growth. That was not to be. The YMCA persevered despite lagging subscriptions and cancelled memberships. The Graduate School, despite Weatherford's heroic efforts, was not strong enough to make it. Vanderbilt, by necessity, foreclosed on its mortgage.[558]

Despite having just accepted a position on the school board, W. C. Weaver agreed to serve as president of the Nashville YMCA for the fourth consecutive year. He was elected at the annual meeting on January 15, 1937. At the same meeting, E. L. Spain was elected general secretary for his twenty-sixth year. Four new board members were also elected—E. M. Kirby; Dr. Thomas C. Barr, associate minister of First Presbyterian Church; Warren C. Brown; and E. W. Turnley. Beside Mr. Weaver, twenty-one other returning board members were reelected. Mr. Murrey, Mr. Jarman, and Mr. Bailey returned as first and second vice-presidents and treasurer, respectively.

The secretary and the treasurer then gave their annual reports. The latter report showed that the budget for 1936 balanced and the building and equipment were in good shape.

Mr. Spain went over the activities for 1936. He reported a substantial increase in the use of the building in both the boys and senior divisions. In the former, 8,664 boys in 6,054 classes had a total attendance of 70,444. In the senior division, 31,437 men in 28,813 classes had a total attendance of 158,590. The grand total was 229,044. Mr. Spain reported that the renovation of the building and improvements in equipment, begun in 1935, had been completed with the result that the building was thoroughly renovated, inside and out.

In the winter, ten-year-old George Cate Jr. was first introduced to the YMCA when he came downtown from his home in East Nashville to participate in a learn-to-swim program in the Y's pool.[559] Over the next seven decades, George would serve the Nashville YMCA in a myriad of ways, including two terms as president.

The Ramblers were in the Major Basketball League in 1937, finishing third under player/coach Paul Tombs. Crowds were mostly disappointing.

Camp Sycamore was open for twelve weeks in 1937. Camp director was Gilbert McLemore, boys' work secretary, who had ten assistants. The first week, twenty-two newsboys and nine boys sponsored by the Kiwanis Club spent a week there.[560] In addition to swimming, the boys took a six-mile hike, played softball, had a track meet, and enjoyed campfire programs each evening. An innovation that summer was the organization of a camp orchestra under the direction of Allen Miller. When camp closed in August, 549 campers had enjoyed its pleasures, none more than another group of twenty-five or so newsboys who were there in August, thanks to a grant from the Community Chest.[561]

In December, the City Basketball League, that the Ramblers had been in since its inception, decided to call it quits, as only three teams—Old Hickory, the Bulldogs, and the Aces—were ready to play. A month later, the Burk Terrors and YMHA Peps decided to give it another try, and the five-team league made it through the season, but without the Ramblers, whose player coach, Paul Toombs, moved over to the Aces.[562]

The Nashville YMCA had a wrestling team in 1938. In late February, the YMCA boys defeated the Wesley House Boys Club 28–8 as one in a series of matches that evening.[563] On March 18, East High won the Nashville Interscholastic wrestling championship at the YMCA, defeating T.I.S. by a single point. Central finished third.[564]

Paul Toombs, the YMCA's physical director, put on a splendid basketball tournament the same week. It featured 24 of the best independent teams in Middle Tennessee. The Linden, Tennessee Independents won the tournament. Their star was Jim Murdaugh, the scoring leader in the Mississippi Valley Conference for the season just ended. Murdaugh scored 126 points in the YMCA tournament.[565]

In early April, Mitchell Filbert, a Vanderbilt pre-medical student from New York, won the Nashville table tennis championship at the YMCA defeating W. H. Cox. Earlier in the year, Filbert won the Vanderbilt table-tennis crown.[566]

The next evening, the YMCA sponsored the 21st consecutive physical education demonstration in the Warner Gymnasium with more than 200 boys and girls taking part in the mammoth demonstration. Teams from the YMCA, Ward-Belmont, Peabody College, West End High, East High, and Hume-Fogg participated.[567]

Camp Sycamore was still operating in 1938 and 1939, although there was no notice of it in the *Nashville Banner*. Conversely, the Boy Scout camp, Camp Boxwell, got considerable publicity.

On Tuesday evenings in the spring, the YMCA's fellowship group met in the library. On April 19, the Rev. Dayton A. Dobbs, pastor of the Russell Street Presbyterian Church, spoke on "And Peter." Following the talk, Collin Winter, of the YMCA staff led group singing. E. L. Spain, general secretary, presided.[568]

In 1938, the Supreme Court of Tennessee established a rule, to go in effect in September of that year, that required applicants for a law degree and certification to the state bar examination to have two years of college education before beginning the study of law. Theretofore, only a high school education was required to attend law school. This new rule had an immediate and decidedly negative impact on the YMCA Night Law School. As a result, in September 1938, the number of first year students dropped to 30. For the ten years previous the first year Night Law School class had averaged about 60. The YMCA Night Law School began its 29th year on September 6, 1939. There were eight instructors, four for students in the first year class and four who taught in the combined second and third year class. Tuition was $100 per year.[569]

During the year, a new physical director and two new assistants in the boys' division were added to the staff. Despite the recession, the program had continued to expand, and the association continued to live within its budget. Will Weaver's administration had five productive years.

War Clouds Materialize
1939–1943

THE YMCA RAMBLERS resurrected themselves for the 1938–39 season. The only familiar name on the team was Paul Toombs. On January 5, the Ramblers upset DuPont 39–35 by scoring 14 points in the last four minutes. The write-up in the *Banner* was tiny as college and N.I.L. basketball were much bigger draws.[570] This would be the Ramblers' last hurrah!

The *Nashville Banner* reported on January 27, 1939, that the YMCA board of directors had, at its annual meeting on the 26th, elected Dr. W. J. O'Callaghan as president, replacing W. C. "Will" Weaver, who had served in the position five years. Dr. O'Callaghan was the long-time U. S. postmaster for Nashville, who had been on the YMCA board since 1923, when it was reorganized. His title of "doctor" was no nickname, as he was a graduate of the medical school of the University of Tennessee, and was known as "a scholar among postmasters." Back in 1927, *Time* magazine had devoted more than a column to Dr. O'Callaghan's efficient work in educating the Nashville public in proper methods of mailing. In one of his many messages to Nashville businessmen, he wrote,

East YMCA dance during WWII

not many years after the Scopes trial, "Your granddad was either a man or a monkey—take your choice—but, if you write to the man, give us the street and number, and, if you write to the monkey, give us the tree and limb." Accordingly, Nashville's mail service was famed "from the Ellis Island to the Golden Gate," at least according to the good doctor.[571]

Littell J. Rust was elected first vice-president; Dr. John L. Hill second vice-president; and Grady Huddleston, treasurer. E. L. Spain, was reelected general secretary. In accepting his first term as president, Dr. O'Callaghan pledged himself to work to make the privileges of the association available to a still larger number of young men and boys—a familiar refrain.

Grady Huddleston gave a report at the annual meeting on the financial status for 1938. He said that the Y had operated well within its income and that numerous improvements in building and equipment had been accomplished.[572] It was reported that B. R. Allison had been employed as physical director and that two new workers for the boys division had been added to the staff.[573]

The YMCA presented its annual sports carnival in May with 60 boys and young men participating in an exhibition of indoor athletics. The fifty-member YMCA band, under the direction of John W. Kendle, furnished music for the performance. L. K. "Doc" Gordon, secretary of the YMCA Health Club, supervised the gymnastics and tumbling events that included hand-balancing acts by James McGowan and young Tom Hanvey, and performances on the parallel bars and vaulting horse by twelve others. There were two clown stunts, and the Nashville Bar Bell Club showed its muscle when its two strongest and biggest members grunted and groaned lifting heavy weights. Boxing and wrestling were still part of the program and levity was provided by a comical baseball game. Twenty boys from the YMCA boys' department gave a demonstration of physical education.[574]

• • • • •

The Night Law School had earlier been decimated by the

rule that incoming students had to complete two years of undergraduate work before being qualified for admission. By 1940–41, the number of students would drop to 27.[575]

• • • • •

Mr. Spain reported in August 1939 that there had been over 15,000 visits annually to the YMCA swimming pool. Through a gift from the Community Chest, 60 boys were being given Y memberships free of charge. Mr. Spain said that other Community Chest agencies frequently sent boys to the YMCA for help with lodging, memberships, and use of facilities. In speaking to a reporter on the YMCA's emphasis on boys' work, Spain expressed his simple philosophy, "If you can keep a boy wholesomely occupied, you have no problem. Toward this, we utilize every type of activity in our boys' division. By this I mean that boys do not come for gym work or swimming alone, but participate in everything we have to offer...If the people of Nashville could see, particularly in the little fellows from less privileged sections of the city, the very definite results of the YMCA's influences, they would realize what an asset the 'Y' can be in building of good citizens of tomorrow."[576]

In October, the Nashville YMCA joined 1,289 other branch associations in the United States in celebrating Founder's Day, the 95th anniversary of the YMCA and the 50th anniversary of its world service program.[577]

In preparation for the fall and winter program, many improvements were made throughout the YMCA building including new badminton, squash, archery and four-wall handball courts as well as open handball courts. The Y also built a fifty-foot rifle range for a rifle club organized in January as an affiliate of the National Rifle Association. The range was open every night of the year for target practice.[578]

Groups using YMCA facilities would, during the fall and winter months, be under the supervision of ten directors. In addition to the sports just mentioned, the weekly schedule offered regular gym work, swimming, Red Cross examinations, badminton, fencing, archery, boxing, wrestling, volleyball, tennis, basketball, weight lifting, and advanced gymnastics. These activities were open to holders of membership cards without additional cost. The YMCA sponsored the high school Hi-Y clubs at Duncan, West, East, Central, Cohn, Isaac Litton, Highland Heights, Waverly-Belmont and East Junior High.[579]

The excitement of the New Year was dimmed in YMCA and other circles by the death of former YMCA president John P. W. Brown. On December 29, nearly 1,500 people gathered at his home on a cold and bleak day to pay tribute to this friendly man whose modesty was born of service, love, and affection for his fellow man. He had remained a member of the YMCA board and executive committee until his death.[580]

Dr. W. J. O'Callaghan was reelected president of the Nashville YMCA and head of the board in January 1940. E. L. Spain was reelected secretary. Other officers elected were Littell Rust, first vice-president; Dr. John L. Hill, second vice-president; and Ferriss C. Bailey, treasurer. The following board members were reelected for a one year term: W. Dudley Gale, E. E. Murrey, Dr. Thomas C. Barr, Robert S. Cheek, Vernon Tupper, Dr. John L. Hill, and Grady Huddleston. A thirty-page report indicated several major improvements during 1939. Included were the refurbishing of rooms in the association building, and the four new four-wall handball courts in the physical department. Mr. Spain also reported that the association had operated within its income for 1939. The following new members have been added to the staff: E. C. Register, membership and supervisor of Hi-Y clubs in the prep and high schools; A. K. Gardner, assistant secretary; and Ramon Jones, assistant in the physical department.[581]

The annual Nashville YMCA learn-to-swim program began the second Monday in June at the Central YMCA. The five-day program was for white boys 7 to 14 with no requirement that they be YMCA members.[582] Camp Sycamore functioned for six weeks that summer.

In January 1941, Dr. W. J. O'Callaghan was reelected president for his third successive term. Robert S. Cheek was elected first vice-president, and E. W. Turnley second vice-president. E. L. Spain was renamed general secretary to begin his forty-second year while Ferriss Bailey continued his stalwart service as treasurer.[583]

The Impact of War

With Europe at war, and Japan on the rampage in China, thousands of American boys were pouring into military training camps over the winter as President Roosevelt pondered how long America could stay out of the conflict. The war seemed a little more personal to E. L. Spain and other YMCA staff members and volunteers when they read in the *Nashville Banner* on January 22 that the building in St. Paul's Churchyard in London, where Sir George Williams founded the YMCA in 1844, had been destroyed by fire following the bombing of the city by the Germans.[584]

There was not nearly as much organized basketball at the YMCA in 1941 as normally as only junior high teams used the gym. High schools, like Hume-Fogg, Isaac Litton, MBA and East, now had their own gyms, while Vanderbilt played its home games at the Hippodrome.

The YMCA hooked up with the YWCA late in the winter to hold an open forum for boys and girls to discuss what a girl should expect of a boy and what a boy should expect of a girl. Held in the YMCA auditorium, David Camp, YMCA boys' work director, and his YWCA counterpart, Miss Louise Brown, were in charge. A month later, youth leaders were invited back for a three-session course on "boy and girl growth and behavior."[585]

In April, the YMCA board of directors, after considerable deliberation, granted permission for the Warner Gymnasium to be used for dances for servicemen. This would be the first time in history that a dance would be held in the downtown building. The board had earlier approved amending house rules to allow servicemen to use the swimming pool and showers on Sundays, and voted to install in the building a soldiers and sailors' lounge with ping pong tables, a radio, and a nickelodeon. The next step was a meeting with representatives of the Women's Club, the Junior League, the American Legion, the Rotary Club, and three Vanderbilt women's auxiliary groups in a collaborative effort to sponsor dances, open by invitation only, to be held at the YMCA, the YMHA, the YWCA, and the Knights of Columbus Hall. Hours would be from 8–11 p.m. and Mrs. Clark Akers, chairperson of the dance committee, would make sure there were plenty of chaperones.[586]

In June, D. C. Camp, the boys' work secretary, had a day camp for boys 7–10 at the Y on Monday, Wednesday, and Friday mornings, and another one for boys 11–13 on Tuesday and Thursday mornings and Saturday afternoons. The older boys could also sign up for a softball league. Camp worked out still a different program for high-school boys. The YMCA pool was open for neighborhood groups each Saturday morning and there was a swim club.[587] High School students could also take arithmetic that summer under Professor James A. Tate, who ran a boys' school in Shelbyville until it closed in 1933. Adult members could hear prominent speakers—one of whom addressed "world conditions" while the other spoke on "Christianity's problems."[588]

Camp Sycamore opened on June 24, 1941, with 40 boys arriving that morning from Nashville. Under the direction of Gilbert McLemore, the camp lasted six weeks with all the usual outdoor activities—swimming, canoeing, first aid, fishing, lifesaving, baseball, crocket, horseshoes, tennis, and volleyball. When summer storms appeared, the boys could focus on ping-pong, woodcraft, beadwork, and leatherwork.[589]

In early October, as war seemed more probable, an ecumenical home hospitality committee was announced. The group met at the YMCA to map out plans for the fall. Mrs. Akers announced that the dances would continue through the winter, sponsored by the civic clubs, and that there would be one each Saturday night for draftees and enlisted men. The dances would continue to be held at the YMCA, YMHA, YWCA, and the Knights of Columbus Club. Camp Forrest and Camp Campbell were already open and pouring soldiers into Nashville on weekends. Many of them headed for the YMCA's soldiers' and sailors' lounge, now staffed with hostesses. It was conveniently located on the main floor of the Y.

The YMCA staff in the fall of 1941 was led, as had seemed to be the case forever, by E. L. Spain. Under him were David C. Camp, director of boys' work; F. J. Warren, supervisor of adult gym classes; Robert E. McInturff, devotionals; Charles Holt, fencing and archery, boxing and wrestling; Thomas Hanvey and Francois Cordier, men and boys' swimming. There were also two assistants—Stuart Perrin, and E. L. Hixon. When physical director B. R. Allison left, the Y must have divided up his duties. The staff turnover had been considerable.[590]

The Nashville YMCA celebrated the 97th anniversary of the founding of the YMCA in October. Mr. Spain took advantage of the occasion by officially remembering the 120th birthday of founder George Williams.[591]

There were extensive Christmas activities at the Y in 1941, possibly because, for the first time since the Great War, Nashville expected an influx of soldiers over the holidays. The attack on Pearl Harbor by the Japanese Empire on December 7 made that certain. The Nashville festivities were coordinated with the USO, as was the case nationwide.[592]

Before the annual meeting on December 16, Dr. O'-Callaghan announced that he would not consider a fourth consecutive term as president. Consequently, W. Dudley Gale, a long-time member, was elected to take

Dr. O'Callaghan's place, effective January 1, 1942. Dudley knew his two-year term would be different and difficult.[593]

Gale, a local general insurance executive, was well prepared, having eighteen years of experience as a board member. Six board members were elected to serve three-year-terms They were W. C. Weaver, H. G. Hill, H. B. Wilkerson, Leonard Sisk, Dr. Roger T. Nooe, and Dr. I. W. Gernert. E. L. Spain was reelected general secretary.[594]

It seemed appropriate that the City of Nashville and the YMCA participated in a universal week of prayer that began on Monday, January 5. At 10 a.m. there was a meeting of the Nashville pastors' Association at the YMCA, Dr. Roger T. Nooe, president of the association and pastor of Vine Street Christian Church, presided. The topic "Our churches during the war" was discussed by four association members—Dr. Thomas N. Caruthers, rector of Christ Episcopal Church; Dr. King Vivion, pastor of McKendree Methodist church; Dr. Harrell, pastor of West End Methodist Church; and the Rev. Edward T. Ramsdell, of Vanderbilt.[595]

Mr. Spain announced in February that about seventy-five engineers working on the Smyrna Army Air Force project were living on the second floor of the YMCA building. To accommodate them, Spain had to move a bunch of soldiers, who had been sleeping there for ten months, to the former dressing room of the health club where he had put comfortable beds and some cots.[596]

With the Induction Center on Thompson Lane and the Smyrna Army Air Field both on line, the military needs for weekend housing and recreation continued to accelerate. In May, the *Nashville Banner* reported that the entire first floor of the YMCA building was being converted into a service men's club. The Rev. Pickens Johnson, chairman of the citizen's committee on servicemen for the local defense council, reported on the 9th that the YMCA-USO servicemen's club, sponsored by the USO and subsidized by the Community Chest, "will be complete with recreation room, lounge, library, snack bar, showers and swimming pool." When finished, the city, he said, would have six such centers for white soldiers and one for Negro soldiers. Between January 1 and May 4, 1942, 12,810 servicemen came to Nashville by train or bus for weekends. Others arrived by automobile. The YMCA dances were the most popular in the city with 1,281 soldiers attending them.[597]

Francis Cordier, the YMCA swimming director, directed the learn-to-swim program for boys in 1942, mindful that this might be the last time he could do so until the war ended. Sessions were held each morning for a week and there was no charge. Boys were assigned to classes by age and swimming ability. Earle Whittington, director of boys' work, pitched in to help.[598]

Despite the war and the USO's welcomed encroachment on the YMCA for space, the YMCA Law School opened on September 9, 1942, for its 32nd session. Its mission, unchanged since its founding in 1911, was to afford men and women unable to attend law school during the day with an affordable opportunity to study law at night. Classes met on Monday and Thursday evenings from 7 p.m. to 10 p.m. Annual tuition was $100, payable in installments. The course of study took three years and complied with the rules of the State Supreme Court and the Board of Law Examiners for the State of Tennessee. There were eight faculty members in 1942. The school met on the first floor but may have later moved as the military and USO gobbled up floor space.[599]

Sadly, Horace G. Hill, 69, died of a heart attack Saturday afternoon, October 18, 1942, at his home on Harding Road. Funeral services were held Monday afternoon at the residence with Rev. Thomas C. Barr and Rev. John E. Phifer officiating. Mr. Hill's death was an enormous blow to the YMCA. He had been its biggest benefactor, and served longer as president than anyone else. Survivors were his wife, the former Miss Mamie Wilson; his son, Horace G. Hill Jr., then stationed at Fort Oglethorpe, GA; two daughters, Mrs. W. E. Penick, of New Orleans, and Mrs. Wentworth Caldwell, of Nashville; six sisters; two brothers; and four grandchildren.[600]

The YMCA survived the first full year of the war and Gale was game to have another go. He was reelected president for 1943, along with Robert S. Cheek, vice-president; Edmund W. Turnley, vice-president; Ferriss C. Bailey, treasurer; and E. L. Spain, general secretary.[601]

During the first quarter of 1943, more than 200 volunteer hostesses were on duty at the YMCA-USO servicemen's lounge in the YMCA every week—150 regulars and another 50 volunteers in the library. The lounge hostesses were trained by Mrs. Marguerite Shannon and a few others to know the facilities offered by the YMCA, entertainment activities at the lounge, places of interest in the Nashville area; Army camps in the vicinity; restaurants, hotels and rooming houses that provided official sleeping accommodations for soldiers; bus and train schedules;

location of churches; and how to obtain aid in emergencies, including addresses and telephone numbers of the American Red Cross, Traveler's Aid, Military Police, and other agencies. A few of the hostesses even knew the Automobile Club in Bordeaux also was a popular dinner and gambling establishment. Hopefully, they kept that information to themselves. They were instructed to send AWOL soldiers to the Army Air Center (AAFCC), and to tell soldiers that, to prevent being AWOL, they should report to the nearest army post which was at the classification Center on Thompson Lane. The hostesses were also told that knowing the answers to these questions was not the main test of a good lounge hostess. The thing, above all others, that made a service men's lounge successful was their attitude.[602]

In early June, E. L. Spain made an urgent appeal to Nashville residents to make their homes available for lodging purposes to service men in town over the weekend. With Army maneuvers then underway in Middle Tennessee, thousands of service men were visiting Nashville each Saturday and Sunday, Spain pointed out. He said, a total of 22,516 men in uniform registered at the Y in just one week.

Only seven months after H. G. Hill died, the Nashville YMCA lost another one of its presidents. W. C. "Will" Weaver died on June 14 at age 58 of cancer. President of the YMCA for five years, beginning in 1934, three of his honorary pallbearers were E. L. Spain and YMCA board members Dr. John L. Hill and Dudley Gale.[603]

A War-time Balancing Act

One of the YMCA's balancing acts during World War II was to try to maintain some aspects of a normalcy while devoting most of its time and effort to helping the war effort on the home front.

In June, the Y kicked off its annual learn-to-swim campaign. E. C. Collins, who replaced Earle Whittington as secretary of boys' work, conducted the program with instructors from the Y staff as well as the American Red Cross. In total, 275 boys from the ages of 8–12, received free swimming instructions.

Although Camp Sycamore had been closed since the war began, probably due, at least in part, to gasoline rationing, YMCA officials were determined to retain camp life in some fashion. During the summer, the Y offered five home and citizenship training camps for boys ages 8–11. E. L. Spain explained the camps' purpose. They were, he said, "to give training in healthful exercise, teach hobbies and crafts, life studies and Christian citizenship." He added that the counselors were encouraging the boys to help with victory gardens at home. Registration for the camps was $1. Because most of the YMCA building was occupied by the USO, other war-time offices, and soldiers, the camps were held at junior and senior high schools, and Buena Vista, Centennial, and Shelby parks. The fee of $6 entitled participants to swim at Cascade Plunge and use all summer facilities at the Y.[604]

In 1943, the YMCA experimented with taking the YMCA to the people rather than inviting them to come downtown, where there was no room for programming anyway. Edmund Turnley, vice-president of the Nashville Y, chaired a steering committee to explore the idea with W. H. Oliver, the highly respected principal of East High School; and a group of East Nashville business and civic leaders. They were receptive to the idea of bringing activities not just to children in East Nashville but to entire families. The plan was implemented and functioned for five months. This fragile and short-lived effort would be the genesis of the East Nashville YMCA Branch.

The YMCA Night Law School continued to be heavily impacted by the war. There were only three graduates in June. Twenty members of the 1943 graduating class had been called into the armed forces.[605]

Following his father's death, Horace Hill Jr. assumed the presidency of the H. G. Hill Company. In July 1943, he was elected to the board of the Nashville YMCA. Although a young man, Horace was already a director of the Nashville Trust Company and a member of the board of the George Peabody College for Teachers.[606] Naming him to the YMCA board would prove to be a very wise move for the association then struggling to stay afloat in a world of turmoil.

A typical week's schedule in the servicemen's lounge in the summer of 1943 looked like this: Tuesday—sketching class, Thursday—open house for servicemen and their families; Friday—art group meets; Saturday night—an enlisted men's dance in the gymnasium and a dance for officers in the library; and Sunday—an afternoon open house.[607]

YMCA staff members, volunteer hostesses, and others were sensing that many of the soldiers they were dealing with were under stress. The National YMCA also recognized that stress was a growing problem. The Army and Navy Department of the YMCA decided to act by sponsoring a lecture series at YMCAs across the country. One was held at the Nashville YMCA the last three days of September. Dr. Russell L. Dicks, of Dallas, Texas, led it. Following these seminars, the Nashville Y opened a room, comfortably furnished, where service men and women could come for personal advice on an individual basis. A minister or chaplain was on duty daily.[608] At a time when the military was focused on defeating the Axis powers, little therapy was available in the Army or Navy. This undertaking by the national YMCA, while imperfect, was a start.

An even bigger problem was the woeful lack of weekend housing for the soldiers pouring into Nashville each weekend from the Smyrna Army Air Field, Camp Campbell, Camp Forrest and the Barrage Balloon Training Center at Camp Tyson in Henry County. One soldier even knocked on the front door of the governor's residence on West End Avenue, asking if it was a rooming house. The author remembers coming to the first Presbyterian Church on Sunday mornings and finding soldiers sleeping everywhere, including on the top of a piano in the chapel. The YMCA Housing service was formed to deal with this problem. In October, Mr. Spain expressed appreciation for the volunteer women and girls who devoted their Saturday afternoons and evenings to help coordinate the housing effort. Many of them worked at the Methodist Publishing House, Southern Bell Telephone and Telegraph Company, and the Nashville secretaries' association. Spain reported that, on an average weekend, some 200 servicemen were being provided sleeping quarters in private homes and sometimes the number had been as high as 400.[609]

Still another problem for Nashville was the rise in juvenile delinquency, partially caused by so many fathers being in military service. An increasing number of young boys were roaming the streets of downtown Nashville. The YMCA, the Nashville Boys Club and the city police department teamed up to implement a plan approved by the Juvenile Court to curb this. The YMCA offered free membership to needy boys and cooperated in other ways.[610]

In November, Mrs. Paul Bell Thompson succeeded Mrs. Marguerite Shannon as hostess of the YMCA-USO service men's lounge, opened in 1942. She assumed responsibility for training and supervising the work of 300 volunteer junior and senior hostesses, planning the weekly programs, and supervising the various lounge activities. A Sweetbriar College graduate, Mrs. Thompson taught at Tarbox School before her marriage. A past president of the Fannie Battle Social Workers, she was a member of the Nashville Junior League and active with the PTA.[611]

Mrs. Thompson's first assignment was to host an open house for veterans of World War I. A day later, the lounge observed the 168th anniversary of the United States Marine Corps' founding with members of the corps being special guests during the day. The first marine to enter that day was given a free, long-distance telephone call to his home.[612] Upcoming Christmas and New Year's Eve celebrations and dances gave the hostesses little breathing room.

Mr. Spain and Mr. Gale were shocked, embarrassed, and dismayed when they read in the National YMCA Year Book, the official roster of the National YMCA, that the Nashville YMCA had been suspended for having failed to meet one or more of its obligations to the national office. The Nashville YMCA would remain off the roster for six years. It seems likely that the local association failed to make the mandatory annual payment to the national office. Spain and Gale probably thought the national office should have waived the fees as the Nashville YMCA had, for all practical purposes, turned its building over to the USO and the U.S. Army. Most traditional sources of income were gone. The suspension was a source of great embarrassment as nothing like this had happened since the Nashville YMCA, always a proud institution, closed during the Civil War.[613]

The Nashville YMCA, depleted of so many of its members, and not completely in control of its own ship, ended a hard year by participating in sending gift packages to American soldiers in German prisoner of war camps under the auspices of the War Prisoners Aid Division of the International YMCA.[614]

• • • • •

General Secretary Ernest L. Spain and Nashville YMCA President Edmund W. Turley presenting service pins to USO volunteers, YMCA-USO Lounge, 1945. Photo courtesy of Forrest Cooper.

CHAPTER FIFTEEN

Peace and the First Branch YMCA

1944–1947

DUDLEY GALE WAS ELECTED to a third consecutive term as president at the annual meeting on January 25, 1944. Other officers elected were Edmund W. Turnley and Robert S. Cheek, vice-presidents; Ferriss C. Bailey, treasurer; and E. L. Spain, general executive. Other directors for the new year were Dr. Thomas C. Barr, Dr. I. W. Gernert, Horace G. Hill Jr., Dr. John L. Hill, Grady Huddleston, Dr. B. H. Johnson, E. E. Murrey, Dr. Roger T. Nooe, Dr. W. J. O'Callaghan, Littell Rust, Alden H. Smith, Leonard Major Sisk, Tony Sudekum, Vernon Tupper, and H. B. Wilkerson, twenty in all.[615]

In February, the Nashville YMCA authorized a $4,000 expenditure to launch a year-round recreational program at junior and senior high schools in the eastern and southwestern parts of the city, areas the YMCA had targeted for program expansion. Messrs. Gale and Spain met with the City Board of Education on February 28 to seek approval. That night, the Board of Education appointed a committee to study the program that requested the use of school facilities for after-school programs designed to combat juvenile delinquency. The committee recommended that no such use be made of schools until after the school year ended in June. This closed the door, at least temporarily, on the YMCA plan.

Not content to be dependent on the actions of the Board of Education, and desirous of systematically establishing YMCA branches in the east and southwest, E. L. Spain called a mass meeting for 8 p.m. at East Nashville High School on March 28. The Y mailed more than 300 letters to East Nashvillians, advising them of the meeting, the purpose of which was to organize a branch YMCA in East Nashville and elect officers of that branch. The audience was fully supportive of the plan and George Cate Jr., a young attorney, whose father had earlier chaired the City Board of Education, presented a constitution and by-laws that were adopted that night by unanimous vote. J. W. Jakes, vice-president of the Nashville Trust Company, was elected president of the new organization and six men were named to the board of directors—Jakes, H. G. Alford, H. W. Crook, L. O. Hardaway, Lynn C. Teal, and Edmund W. Turnley, the latter representing the Nashville YMCA board.[616]

A month later, The City Board of Education voted to appropriate $7,000 for the purpose of carrying out the summer program proposed by the YMCA but modified to better suit the Board of Education. Dudley Gale wrote Board of Education chairman William Hume to advise the board that the YMCA declined to participate in the eleven-week summer recreational program because of "our continuing conviction that the YMCA should offer the community our four-fold program—physical, mental, spiritual, and social—on a year-round basis."[617]

Meanwhile, plans for the East Nashville branch were going full-speed ahead. Spain had cleared, with the Community Chest, the idea of having a membership and enrollment drive for the East YMCA. It would start May 10 and last ten days. This would be the first YMCA drive in "a score of years," Spain said.[618]

The Nashville YMCA celebrated the 100th anniversary of the founding of the first YMCA in London in 1844 with an all-day open house on June 6. There was a musical program, directed by Mrs. Charles Ragland at 4 p.m., followed by a reception in the servicemen's club. In advance of the big event, the board asked nine prominent YMCA leaders to each write a paper on some aspect of the Nashville YMCA's history. Littell Rust's paper was titled, "The Local History of the YMCA." Dudley Gale was given the cumbersome title of "The Forward Movement of the Local Organization into communities of the City and County." Dr. Joseph Roemer's title was the broadest—"One Hundred Years With the YMCA." Henry Hart, who had served as a missionary in India in 1916, wrote on "The World Service Program." John Hill did so on "Maintaining the Strong Spiritual Emphasis" while the Reverends Gernert and Barr, quite naturally, wrote on "Relations of the YMCA to the Churches." Dr. W. D. Weatherford's paper was "Development of the Association Profession and Secretarial Training" which he knew more about than almost anyone in the country. E. W. Turnley's selection was "The USO and the YMCA." The last paper, given by Dr. Walter L. Stone, was optimistically titled "The YMCA and the Post-War World." Additionally, 10,000 pamphlets were distributed in Nashville churches emphasizing the close relationship that the YMCA enjoyed with Nashville churches. Finally, Governor Prentice Cooper issued a proclamation designating 1944 as YMCA Centennial Year in Tennessee.[619]

With the membership and enrollment drive, led by East Nashville physician Cleo Miller, successfully completed, the next order of business for the East Nashville Branch was to find a location from which to operate. A possibility was a community center building on the corner of South 10th and Fatherland streets. Built in the 1920s, the brick building, owned by the city, was underused, primarily serving as an election site and for occasional community meetings. An East Nashville Businessmen's Club held the lease on the property, paying the city $1 per year in rent. Jakes and other YMCA leaders found that the club board was agreeable to turning over their lease to the YMCA. When that was accomplished, the city agreed to give the YMCA a five-year lease with the understanding that the YMCA would spend a considerable amount of money equipping the center and building an outdoor playground. An announcement was made that the deal was struck on June 30.[620]

The YMCA's finances eased enough in 1944 for the association to finish making payments on the indebtedness accumulated over the past three decades. Hopefully, the Y could also resume making annual payments to the national organization. Progress was being made and hopes were high that the war would end in 1945.

With Camp Sycamore unused since early in the war and not in good shape, E. L. Spain was anxious to provide an overnight camping experience somewhere else for the new generation of boys growing up in the YMCA orbit. In late August, fifty deserving Nashville boys left by bus for a week's stay at the State YMCA camp in the Cumberland Mountains. There, under the direction of the State boys' division staff, they enjoyed swimming, boating, fishing, and the usual outdoor sports. The boys selected were kids who otherwise could not have afforded camp. Either the state or local association, or both, picked up the cost.[621]

Sgt. Preston S. Abbott was the 2 millionth service man to use the YMCA-USO lounge. A veteran of ten months' overseas combat, Abbott was then convalescing at the Thayer Army Hospital on White Bridge Road. A radio operator and top turret gunner on a BN-24 Liberator bomber, he held the Distinguished Flying Cross, the Air Medal with three Oak Leaf Clusters, the Purple Heart, and the European Theater of Operations ribbon with campaign stars. Shot down over Austria, Abbott managed to make his way back to his base in Italy. One Saturday in October, he became the center of attention at the YMCA's servicemen's lounge, where he was greeted by city, county, state, and civic leaders and a trumpet fanfare and told that he was the 2 millionth service man to visit the center. The surprised Abbott was then escorted into the lounge and introduced to Gov. Prentice Cooper and an admiring crowd. There was a tea dance that afternoon with Beasley Smith's orchestra providing the music. That evening, Frank Pickens' swing band played for a formal dance that lasted until midnight.[622]

The formal opening of the East Nashville Branch took place November 18, 1944. W. Jakes, president of the branch board, presided and introduced the five speakers—Mayor Thomas L. Cummins; County Judge Litton Hickman; East High principal William H. Oliver; Dr. W. L. Caldwell, minister of Woodland Presbyterian Church; and Edmund W. Turnley, chairman of boys' work at the Central YMCA. Mr. Jakes also introduced his board—H. W. Crook, vice-president; Leslie O. Hardaway, secretary; H. G. Alford, treasurer; Lynn Comer Teal, the new director of the East Nashville Branch; W. A. Alexander, and George Guy.[623]

The East Nashville branch got off to a good start. During the first 22 days of January, 1,514 boys used the facility that consisted of a reading room, where arts and crafts were taught, and a large gymnasium. Outside, the playground wasn't finished but would be by early spring. Comer Teal had not arrived yet as D. J. Cummings was acting director, assisted by Carnie R. Burcham. Cummings said that, the big draw was obviously the gym, particularly on cold winter afternoons. He also commended the work of the Hi-Y, Gra-Y and N-Y clubs, adding that there were fourteen in East Nashville alone. On February 8, Mr. Spain told the press that the YMCA "is now operating six Negro YMCAs." He must have meant the YMCA was conducting programming at six Negro schools, churches, or community centers.[624]

One of the young professional people who enjoyed playing basketball at the 217 South 10th Street Y was George Cate Jr. Decades later George remembered that, at the time the gym there was one of the few gyms in East Nashville available to young adults.

Dr. Matt Buckner, who had served as president of the Nashville YMCA for eleven years, almost lived long enough to see the Second World War end. He died April 10, 1945 at age 75.[625] Dr. Buckner was the only person to serve as president of the boys' division, president of the Nashville YMCA, and, in the early 1930s, as president of the State YMCA. During his presidency of the Nashville YMCA, the new building was built and the Nashville Association was the largest in the South.

Peace at Last

The war in Europe ended on V-E Day, May 8, 1945. An armistice with Japan was signed August 14 and Japan formally surrendered on September 2. On Saturday night, July 28, when the outcome of the war was pretty certain, the USO service men's club at the YMCA celebrated with a victory dance. The party theme was red, white, and blue and flags of the United Nations were displayed. The orchestra was composed of enlisted men from the medical detachment at Smyrna Army Air Field. At a predetermined point in the evening, dancing ceased and all present bowed their heads for a moment of silent prayer. Then, the orchestra played the national anthem. After six years, the war was within weeks of being over.[626]

During the fall and winter of 1945, the YMCA struggled to maintain its building that had taken enormous wear and tear during the war. The elevator was in such bad shape that it had to be replaced. The dormitory rooms and most of the class and clubrooms had to be refurbished. The vending machines, the tailoring shop and the equipment in the shoeshine stalls were worn out. In the middle of the restoration effort, Mr. Spain had to tell the contractors to stop as the cost exceeded the money available. The renovation would not be completed until 1948. The dismal condition of the building cost the association a loss of $4,000 in income.[627] Because relations were still strained with the national YMCA, they could not be counted on to help.

Beasley Smith and his orchestra played in November at a Saturday afternoon tea dance while a military orchestra came in later to play for the dance that night. All World War One veterans in the Nashville area were invited to attend. On Thanksgiving, November 23rd, there were two events held—the tea dance at 5:30 p.m. and the Harvest Ball at 9 p.m.[628] Later in the year, Brooks Kirk's Orchestra played for the New Year's Eve dance sponsored by the YMCA-USO service men's club.[629] YMCA-USO social events, such as dances, would keep on going through the second quarter of 1946.

In April 1946, between 700 and 800 soldiers from Camp Campbell and Camp Forrest were still coming to Nashville every weekend.

Amazing Statistics

The annual meeting in January was a luncheon on January 22. At the meeting, a recap was given on the number of servicemen who used the facilities from April 1941 through December 1945. The answer was 2,291,201, of whom 147,660 slept there in beds or cots, 436,169 took showers, and 133,033 enjoyed the swimming pool. During 1945, 60 local organizations made free use of the library, pool and clubrooms, and 73,451 beds were occupied, of which 23,362 were used by transients, 322 to regular occupants, and 482 to charity transients. A total of 90,351 sports sessions were conducted during the year by the men's physical department and 9,689 attended health club sessions. The boys' department's total attendance, including those at outside activities was 99,813. Boys attended 4,503 individual sessions.[630]

• • • • •

L. K. "Doc" Gordon was director of the Health Club until his retirement in 1949. Sometime, during the 1940s, a muscular young man challenged Doc to see which of the two of them could be the quickest to climb one of the two ropes hanging from the ceiling of the gym, touch the metal disk at the top and rappel down the rope to the gymnasium floor. The challenger, decades younger than Doc, may not have known whom he was competing with. Before he could reach the top and strike the medal plate, Doc Gordon was already back on the floor.[631]

• • • • •

The theme of the annual Hi-Y conference in early February was "Christian Youth in the post-war era." E. L. Spain served as toastmaster. The chief feature of the conference was Saturday afternoon when the delegation of 132 met in the Senate Chamber and House of Representatives to receive instruction in citizenship and governance. Governor Jim McCord spoke to the group. This was the beginning of the youth-in-government program that later would flourish in Tennessee, particularly in Nashville.[632]

All of the new staff members served either in the U.S. Army or worked at USO clubs at military bases during the war. The one who would make the greatest impact on the Nashville Association was Charlie Gray. A native of Walker County, Alabama, he graduated from Auburn Polytechnic Institute in 1920 and immediately took a job with the Huntsville YMCA where, at age twenty-five, he became acting secretary. Three years earlier, he married Miss Virginia Dunaway of Orrville, Alabama. They would have two daughters. In 1926, Charlie accepted a call to become director of the boys' division of the Birmingham YMCA. In his fourteen years in the "Iron City," Gray became noted for his personal understanding of boys and was able to develop a program that attracted thousands of them.

Gray left Birmingham in 1940 to become program secretary for the YMCA's Southern Area Office in Atlanta. In 1943, he began splitting his time equally between the Southern Area Office and the USO in Atlanta, where he was regional supervisor. With the war over, Charlie was ready for a new challenge and accepted the call in August 1946 to come to the Nashville Y, an association he was familiar with, as secretary for the boys' division.[633]

In August, Comer Teal, most recently in charge of recreational activities at Warner Robbins, Georgia, also accepted a call to the Nashville Y to work with the East Nashville extension program. Earlier, he had been a high school football coach in his native Alabama. In Nashville, Teal would quickly demonstrate a remarkable ability to relate to children.

Comer Teal quickly set about implementing the YMCA outreach program. He established Gra-Y clubs at Bailey, East, and Highland Heights junior highs and a Hi-Y Club at East High School. He also established baseball, basketball and softball leagues, resident and day camps, teen conferences, leadership courses, parties, and dances. His impact on East Nashville teenagers would be life changing.[634]

Anticipating a growth in students following the war, the YMCA Night Law School enlarged the faculty by three and named longtime instructor Ferriss C. Bailey as the school's new dean. He replaced Owen Hughes on September 4, 1946.[635]

Beginning October 1, a new schedule of activities at the Central YMCA was implemented. Four nights a week were reserved for basketball league play. Other sports on the winter schedule were swimming, badminton, handball, squash, racketball, boxing, wrestling, and "bar bell" work.[636]

One of the first persons to use the handball courts was Don McGehee. This muscular young man gave of himself, as a volunteer for the YMCA and for the Nashville Boys' Club, almost as much as Comer Teal would do for the YMCA as a professional. Older YMCA members still can recall watching Don play handball in the 1990s. His impact would last for half a century. In about 1993, Don founded a YMCA program called "I am somebody" to install values in children who had little parental guidance.[637]

Edmund Turnley was elected to his third consecutive term as president of the Nashville YMCA on January 17, 1947. His supporting cast remained unchanged. This would be Bailey's twenty-fourth year as treasurer, and Spain's twenty-seventh year as general secretary. The board was particularly pleased that, in 1946, boys' work picked up tremendously as the energy devoted to the welfare of soldiers had begun to abate. Spain said that, under Charlie Gray, the Nashville Y "now has the most spacious and beautifully furnished boys' division in the South." The men's health club was also touted as "thoroughly modern, splendidly equipped, and well-staffed."

In January, the Nashville YMCA also organized a Phalanx Fraternity, the purpose of which was "to unite young men in cooperative effort to practice and to extend Christian standards and ideals." A successful application for a charter was made the following week and Jack Irwin elected fraternity president.[638]

A final manifestation that the war was really over came in July when the USO finally released its space in the YMCA building. At once, the Y began to lease the vacated space to take advantage of the shortage of office space in Nashville. This happened because all non-essential construction had been curtailed during the war. Five rooms were leased to the U.S. Corps of Army Engineers on the second floor while one-half of the lobby was leased to the Reserve Corps of the War Department. Smaller spaces were allocated for Nashville businesses, including the Chamber of Commerce. The net result was that the building was still crowded. Some badly needed revenue was coming in, however.[639]

CHAPTER SIXTEEN

New Leadership
1948–1953

AFTER SERVING AS TREASURER for twenty-four years, Ferriss Bailey finally got his chance in January 1948 to become president of the Nashville YMCA. He was elected at the annual meeting on January 12. Bailey had joined the YMCA board in November 1922, a year after he graduated from Vanderbilt Law School. A member of the Nashville, Tennessee, and American Bar Associations, Bailey began teaching at the YMCA Night Law School shortly after graduating from law school, and had been dean of the school since 1946. He had also been a member of the County Board of Education since 1942.[640]

Dr. B. H. Johnson became the first new treasurer in many years, and H. G. Hill Jr. and Robert S. Cheek were re-elected vice-presidents. Horace and Ferriss had been classmates at Vanderbilt and Bailey had provided legal services to Horace Sr. and Horace Jr. and their business interests. E. L. Spain was re-elected general secretary despite his questionable health. George Criswell was employed as physical director. Later in his career, Criswell would become the CEO of the Charlotte, North Carolina, YMCA.

• • • • •

Mr. Spain gave attendance figures for 1947 that were as follows: health club 13,282, men's physical department 105,755, boys' department 189,810, use of gymnasiums 28,950, showers 18,546, pool 16,200. He also reported that 26,591 people had attended meetings held either at the central building or at the South Tenth Street branch.

• • • • •

The board members read in March that maneuvers would be held at Camp Campbell in May with 25,000 troops. This brought up the possibility that the USO lounge in the YMCA Building might need to be reopened. As practically all the recreation equipment was still there, this would work.[641]

In the spring of 1948, the YMCA announced plans to expand the East Nashville YMCA as a project separate from the Association board. By July, there was general agreement that the idea of building a new East Nashville Branch YMCA, sponsored, financed, and administered by citizens of East Nashville made sense. The forty-two-member East Nashville board enthusiastically agreed to undertake a door-to-door campaign to recruit members. Jakes was confident they could pull this off. "We feel," he said, "we can provide most of the necessary funds" to build the branch. "Heretofore," he added, "all funds except for an initial $500 contribution during the first year, have been provided by the central organization." Comer Teal, executive secretary, knew the need was real. He reported that "more than 5,000 visits are made monthly" to the inadequate facility on South Tenth Street by East Nashville boys.[642]

Eleven law students were awarded degrees by the YMCA School of Law in June. Chancellor William J. Wade, a member of the faculty, presented the degrees.[643]

None of the 433 boys enrolled in the YMCA's two-week learn-to-swim program knew how to swim before enrolling. When the annual program ended on June 19, 256 boys passed the final test of diving in the pool and swimming its 20' foot width.[644]

The board got a shock in 1948 when the City of Nashville mailed the general secretary a $40,000 bill for taxes. The board simply did not anticipate that there were tax repercussions for a non-profit agency renting space for profit. The YMCA appealed the assessment and, four years later, the indebtedness was rescinded. The staff and board had learned a lesson.[645]

Attorney and civic leader Ferriss C. Bailey was reelected on January 10, 1949 to his second term as president. H. G. Hill Jr. and Robert S. Cheek returned as vice-presidents, Dr. B. H. Johnson as treasurer, and E. L. Spain as general secretary. Dr. King Vivion, pastor at McKendree Methodist Church, joined the board.[646]

The secretary's annual report showed that health club membership for 1948 was 11,434, down from 13,282 in 1947; that the men's physical department showed 99,126 visits, down from 105,755 in 1947; and that the boys' division attendance, including both downtown and at East, was 169,977 down from 189,810 in 1947. Over 25,000 people attended community service programs in the Central YMCA building during 1948, only marginally down from the 26,591 who did so in 1947. The best news was that the YMCA had operated within its budget for the year.[647]

In May, Mr. Spain announced that Don McGehee had been appointed director of the YMCA health club succeeding the aging L. K. Gordon. McGehee, a Marine Corps veteran and Nashville native, had extensive experience as a physical instructor. That month was also time for the annual membership drive to be launched.[648]

The progress in East Nashville came quicker than Bailey anticipated. In May, Jakes and his group launched a three-week campaign to put the East Nashville YMCA "on a community-sustained basis." Since it was founded in 1944, it had operated on an annual budget of $7,500 with most of the money coming from the Community Chest. The idea was to gain 1,000 new members who would each pay an annual fee of $10. As an incentive, for each $10 membership, members could subsidize the annual membership of a deserving boy. Plans were also underway to knock out the rear wall of the East Branch on Fatherland Street in order to enlarge the gym to a standard size.[649]

June was the traditional month for boys' camps to open. Although the YMCA still owned Camp Sycamore, the association did not use it. Instead, the Y arranged for 50 boys between the ages of nine and twelve to go by bus daily to camp at Montgomery Bell State Park beginning June 20 and ending July 1. A second session lasted from July 5 until Saturday, July 16. Jimmy Barrick was camp director. Fishing, swimming, and nature craft were the camp offerings. Back in town, 784 boys participated in the YMCA's learn-to-swim campaign. Physical director George Criswell ran that program in 1949 and would do so again in 1950.[650]

A Great YMCA Leader Steps Down

On the advice of his physician, E. L. Spain submitted his resignation as general secretary, effective October 31, 1949. He was named general secretary emeritus by a board grateful for the thirty-nine years he had devoted to the Nashville Association.

Spain had come to Nashville in the fall of 1910 to become house secretary under S. Waters McGill. He succeeded Charles W. Bush as general secretary on July 1, 1921. A leading worker and leader in many worthwhile causes, Spain was particularly active in Community Chest and Red Cross drives in Nashville. A Nashville native, he and Mrs. Spain had five children who were all solid citizens, and six grandchildren. They lived in a spacious log home on Glendale Lane that their sons built. He was a deacon of the First Presbyterian Church, a Mason, and past president of both the local and state Exchange Clubs.[651]

During his career with the Nashville Y, Spain was instrumental in paying off a $140,000 mortgage, in addition to eliminating numerous other debts, and had a big hand in restoring the organization's credit to normal. Since the end of World War II, he had had the building completely renovated, and increased the membership from approximately 800 to a total of 2,353 in 1947.[652]

In addition to his other duties, Spain gave much of his time and money to Camp Bon Air for Girls on the Cumberland Plateau near Sparta, which he organized with Mrs. Spain in 1927 as a welfare corporation. Through this work, Mr. and Mrs. Spain enabled many underprivileged girls to attend camp in the summers.[653]

Mr. Spain had worked tirelessly during World War II and was instrumental in the USO collaborating with the Nashville YMCA to operate the lounge for servicemen from 1942 until 1947. Spain was for many years a member of the Southern Area Council of YMCAs.[654] A giant in YMCA circles, who had worn himself out with tireless work, was passing from the scene. When he retired, Mr. Spain was presented with a bound book, which contained letters of praise from board members, the city's leading ministers, civic leaders with whom he worked, and YMCA employees. Reading the letters makes one realize how popular he was. Because he had been a fixture at the helm of the YMCA so long, board members had difficulty accepting the fact that he would no longer be there. Ezell Craig, president of Brandau-Craig-Dickeron Co., wrote, "You served the YMCA well and we look upon you as the best YMCA man in the South."[655]

Several weeks after retiring, Spain wrote Ferriss Bailey, president of the Nashville YMCA, asking him to thank all the board members for their loyalty and help "during my long and happy experience at the Y." Spain said he often thought of the struggle the Y had "in getting back into the good graces of the community," back in 1921 and 1922 when he was the only paid executive. He expressed great confidence in the future of the Y before going on to praise his successor, Charlie Gray, writing, "You are fortunate in having Charlie Gray take over. I think a lot of him and have greatly enjoyed working with him in pleasant harmony since he joined our staff. He is fundamentally sound in association work and is the best boys' work secretary in the South so why shouldn't he become the best general secretary?"[656]

Charlie Gray was named acting secretary to succeed Mr. Spain. He had big shoes to fill. In addition to his education at Auburn, Charlie spent two sessions at the YMCA Graduate School in Nashville and also studied at Blue Ridge Conference Center.[657] He had also visited the Nashville YMCA when he was on the YMCA staff in Atlanta. If Gray performed well, he would be elevated to full-time general secretary. In 2009, George Cate Jr., remembered Gray as being very conservative, a Southern gentleman, and a Type B personality.

In December, the Nashville YMCA made formal application for reinstatement as a full-pledged member of the National YMCA. The local Y agreed to submit annual reports and to support the national YMCA financially on the same basis as every other accredited YMCA did, that is, by sending the national office an annual check based on percent of the Nashville YMCA's income. The application was approved and the embarrassment was over.[658] It would have been nice had that happened before Mr. Spain's retirement.

Summer Fun

Ferriss C. Bailey was reelected president of the Nashville YMCA for a third term at the annual meeting in January 1950. Also elected were Horace G. Hill Jr., and Robert S. Cheek as vice-presidents, Littell Rust as treasurer, and Charles M. Gray as general secretary. The board members elected had all served the previous year. Charlie Gray, in his annual report gave attendance figures for 1949: health club 12,022, men's physical department 71,352, boys' division 78,746, East Nashville Branch YMCA 49,470. More than 20,000 people attended meetings in the two YMCA buildings free of charge. Mr. Spain also announced a membership enrollment drive to start in February.

June meant swim lessons and day camp. The former were held at the Central YMCA and were for boys eight to fourteen. The six-session course cost fifty cents. George Criswell, YMCA physical director and a certified aquatics instructor, was in charge.[659] Meanwhile, Comer Teal arranged with the Nashville Park Board to hold six weeks of day camp at Shelby Park in the summer. Teal divided the camp into three sections of two weeks each. Archery, hiking, softball and swimming were Shelby Park activities while story telling, airplane modeling, woodworking and leather working took place at the Y.[660]

There was an unusually large turnover in directors in 1951. On January 23, seven returning directors—Bailey, Barr, Cheek, Gale, Horace Hill and Dr. John L. Hill, and Littell Rust—and thirteen new directors were elected. The new board members were William M. Blackie, General Shoe Company; Russell W. Brothers, Velvet Ice Cream Company; Sam F. Coleman, Coleman Construction Company; George S. Hastings, of Aladdin Industries; John S. Herbert, R. D. Herbert & Sons; Neal O. Jones, Moore-Handly Hardward Company; Clifford Love Jr., Love Insurance Agency; David L. McQuiddy, McQuiddy Printing Company; Ernest J. Moench, Tennessee Tufting Company; James H. Reed III, Jim Reed Chevrolet; J. Donald Ross, Castner-Knott Dry Goods Company; Lem B. Stevens, Seventh Avenue Motors; and Joe Thompson Jr., Northwestern Mutual Insurance Company.[661]

The next week, officers were elected. Horace G. Hill Jr. succeeded Ferriss C. Bailey as president. It had been eighteen years since his father, H. G. Hill Sr., stepped down from the same position. The new vice-presidents were Stirton Oman and Charles W. Waterfield. Littell Rust returned as treasurer as did Charles M. Gray as general secretary. Dr. Roger T. Nooe, who had been a board member since 1926, welcomed the new board members. He said that the YMCA's most important task was that of "spreading good will and teaching the whole world to recognize the importance of human dignity." Littell Rust

YMCA campers at Montgomery Bell State Park, 1950

reported that the association had raised $600 for foreign rehabilitation. Although still owning Camp Sycamore, the new board discussed plans for a summer camp to be held at Montgomery Bell State Park for boys 7 to 14 years of age.[662]

Jim Reed III, one of the new board members, chaired the annual membership drive launched in April. His goal was to obtain 496 new members in ten days.[663]

In August, Charles Gray, by then general secretary of the Nashville YMCA, was elected vice-president of the Kentucky-Tennessee Association of YMCA Secretaries at the closing session of the group's convention in Lexington.[664]

The 100th anniversary of the establishment of the first YMCA in the United States in Boston was celebrated in November. During the week, a series of events were held at the YMCA building in observance, which also had been set aside by both the YMCA and the YWCA for prayer and world fellowship. Nashville churches joined in the program. A father and son supper on Thursday night and an open house for civic clubs were two of the events planned by E. W. Turnley and his committee.[665]

In January, H. G. Hill Jr. was elected to his second one-year term as president of the Nashville YMCA. Stirton Oman and Charles W. Waterfield were re-elected vice-presidents, and Littell Rust was re-elected treasurer. Charles Gray continued as general secretary. The only board members not to return were George Hastings, Neal Jones, and Ernest Moench. Five new board members ware named to take their places and fill two vacant slots. The new members were Mark Bradford Jr., George Green,

Henry Horrell, Robert Payne, and J. Haskell Tidman.[666]

Retired general secretary E. L. Spain may have been too sick to read about the reelection of Horace Hill Jr. as the YMCA's president. Ernest had been ill for several months and died on February 2, 1951, of a heart attack. He would have been pleased, however, as he had worked so closely and harmoniously with Horace's father, H. G. Hill, for all the years the senior Hill was president of the association.[667]

During 1951, the report stated that the Y paid off more than $8,000 of its indebtedness. Particularly welcome to the apartment men was the installation of a laundry room in the central building. Gray predicted that the laundry, that cost $5,000, would pay for itself in three years. New asphalt tile floors were laid in the locker rooms and in the young businessmen's room. A lounge for residents was opened on the sixth floor and the USO Information Center began operation off the lobby. During the year, world service contributions totaled $800 up from $600 in 1950.[668]

In the fall of 1951, the Y launched a citywide football league. Given the popularity of the sport, this made sense. Probably, Charlie Gray knew that professional football had its origins in the YMCA. Two of the earliest professional teams were fielded by the Latrobe, Pennsylvania, and Dayton, Ohio, YMCAs. The latter team was named the Dayton Triangles.[669]

At the 1952 annual meeting, the board reviewed the record for 1951. It showed that more people than ever before participated in YMCA programs. New president Hill called this "a remarkable record." Particularly outstanding was the record of the East Branch where 37,421 boys participated in Y activities. Membership at East totaled 1,265.[670]

One item of new business was that furniture dealer Robert Payne was named to succeed W. H. Oliver, East High School Principal, as chairman of the East branch activities. Looking ahead, the board also approved the following program for 1952:

1. Increased emphasis on boys' work activities;
2. Expansion of volunteer leadership and group activities in the physical department;
3. Installation of a luncheonette in YMCA building;
4. Redecoration of the lobby, apartments and rooms;
5. More emphasis on Christian brotherhood among members;
6. Increased staff so membership can be correspondingly increased;
7. And obtaining stronger financial support.[671]

George H. Cate Jr., young Nashville attorney, who had worked at the East YMCA each summer during his school years, was named vice-president of the branch. The YMCA board reelected Horace G. Hill Jr. to his third term as president on January 28, 1953. Also reelected were Stirton Oman, vice-president; Littell Rust, treasurer; and Charles M. Gray, general secretary. E. E. Murrey was elected to the other vice-president position, succeeding Charles W. Waterfield, who stepped down to head the 1953 Red Cross campaign. New board members were Thomas P. Henderson Jr., Merrill K. Hovey, Wilson Sims, Harold Buchi, and Joe C. Carr.[672]

In 1953, the YMCA boys' camp moved from Montgomery Bell State Park to Standing Stone State Park beside a three-acre lake. The Y brought 70 boys to camp for the first two-week session that began June 7. The third and last session ended July 19. Camp director Norfleet Hawkins, boys' work secretary, divided the campers into two Indian tribes to compete against each other. Among Hawkins' counselors were Jim Gore and Jim Sasser, later a U. S. Senator and Ambassador to China. One of the campers was Bob Clement, the son of Gov. and Mrs. Frank Clement, and a future congressman.[673] The newly located camp, named Camp Widjiwagan in 1953, featured swimming and canoeing, tennis, miniature golf, and archery. There was also a fully equipped craft lodge where boys could learn to carve.[674]

On May 12, the Nashville YMCA launched its annual membership enrollment campaign and, with it, the association's first capital funds drive since 1914. Board member Joe C. Carr was chairman of the drive to raise $24,000, of which $15,000 would be used to build a new social recreation lounge for teenagers complete with a lunch counter and soda fountain, Carr said. The remaining $9,000 would be for other improvements in the downtown center. The membership goal was to increase the number of members from 600 to 900.[675] At the kick-off, attended by fifty business and professional people, H. G. Hill Jr. pledged $1,000 to what was called the "Building for the Future" Campaign.[676]

Despite the *Nashville Banner*'s editorial endorsing the drive, the campaign failed to meet its goal at the end of the twelve-day fundraising effort.[677] Predictably and properly, the board extended the campaign. On May 29, the total secured in gifts and pledges reached $17,213 with 186 new adult members having been recruited. This was not what the campaign leadership had hoped for, as even with the new members, the adult membership at the Y was still well short of the 1,096 members in 1927. H. G. Hill Jr. said, "About $3,000 in new pledges still was outstanding."[678]

If the capital campaign was only partially successful, a new YMCA program launched in the spring was very promising. This was Nashville's first Youth-in-Government program. Nashville teenagers in grades eight through twelve met at the state capitol where they assumed roles ranging from governor to lobbyists and argued current issues as a mock legislature.[679] Nashville had been briefly exposed to the national Youth-in-Government program four years earlier when four "boy" governors from California, Idaho, Oregon, and Washington stopped in Nashville on their way home from the Boys' Governors' Conference in Washington, DC, to visit Governor Gordon Browning and the Nashville YMCA.[680]

The Indefatigable Comer Teal

Comer Teal was indefatigable in reaching out to boys in East Nashville. His day camp in the early and mid 1950s included a devotional service, playground activities, hiking, swimming and nature study at Shelby Park and woodworking, leather craft, movies and story telling at the East branch. The camp traditionally closed with a picnic at Shelby Park.[681]

The fall schedule at the YMCA included the usual gym and swim classes. Dick Hinch coached a YMCA swim team that competed with other Southern YMCAs. In the craft shop in the boys' division, boys worked with a lathe, wood-burning equipment and plaster to produce such novelty items as rolling pins and plaster Santa Claus figures. Norfleet Hawkins, the boys' work secretary, even organized a junior leaders club to assist him in planning, promoting, and conducting the activities of the boys' division.[682]

• • • • •

H. G. Hill Jr.
(1901–1993)

Born in Nashville in 1901, Horace G. Hill Jr. was the son of Horace Greeley and Mamie Wilson Hill. Educated in the Nashville public school system in grammar school, Horace graduated from Duncan Preparatory School and matriculated at Vanderbilt University in 1917, where he joined the SAE Fraternity, and where he was the starting center on the Vanderbilt football team for three years. After graduating in 1921, Horace did graduate work at Yale University, before returning to Nashville to join his father's company, H. G. Hill Company. Horace was a bachelor until the fall of 1961 when he and his long-time girlfriend, Edith Caldwell, married.

Horace worked for the H.G. Hill Company until early 1942, when he resigned to enter the U.S. Army as a private in the Quartermaster Corps stationed at Fort Oglethorpe, GA. In October of that year, his father, H. G. Hill, Sr., died, creating a leadership vacuum at the H. G. Hill Company. Because of the firm's importance as a food supplier for the war effort and the fact that Horace was forty-one-years old, he was honorably discharged so that he could succeed his father as president of the H.G. Hill Co. He soon sold the company stores outside Tennessee and consolidated the small grocery stores in the state into supermarkets.

Horace inherited the house at Rock Island, Tennessee, that the H.G. Hill Company owned. In the summers, Horace and Edith spent two weeks of August there, as well as the 4th of July and Labor Day weekends. He would often invite close friends to house parties there. His sister, Francis, her husband, Wentworth; and their children—May, Anne, Frances, and Wentworth Caldwell Jr., stayed at the "Little House," also owned by the company. Mrs. Caldwell and the children did so from the time school was out through Labor Day. Wentworth came on weekends. "Gunkle," as Horace was called by his nieces and nephews, would give the children rides on the Collins River in his elegant Chris Craft motor boat. He also enjoyed fishing with friends on the Caney Fork, Collins and Rocky rivers that converged at Rock Island.

During his long business career, Horace devoted most of his time to his business, as he had no hobbies. By 1955, the H. G. Hill Company was operating 31 supermarkets in Nashville and many more in the mid-state. By 1960, the company had 27 Nashville stores and 13 outside Nashville and $30 million in annual sales.

Mr. Hill was a member of Belle Meade, Bluegrass, and Hillwood country clubs, the Cumberland and Rotary clubs, and Hillwood Presbyterian Church. He also was extremely generous with donations of time and money to worthwhile Nashville organizations. A great friend of education, he was chairman of the board of George Peabody College, where he headed its 1977 capital funds campaign. A philanthropist, his gifts of several millions of dollars to Peabody helped keep that school alive.

Horace Hill Jr. was a long-time member and enormously generous benefactor of the Nashville YMCA that his father was instrumental in saving in the early 1920s. He was vice-president of the Association in 1948, 1949, and 1950 before being elected president in 1951. He served in that capacity for three years, and returned as president from May 1965 until May 1967.

In December 1967, Mr. Hill, president of the H.G. Hill Company and the H.G. Hill Realty Company, gave eight acres of land in Green Hills on Hillsboro Circle to the Metropolitan Nashville YMCA to be the site of the Southwest Family Branch. The tract valued at $225,000 was the largest gift ever presented to the Nashville Association. Mr. Hill said, "We are making this gift to repay at least in a small part the tremendous benefits that have come to the H. G. Hill Co. and its personnel and to the H.G. Hill family." In 1980, the H. G. Hill Co. made a contribution of $500,000 to the Nashville YMCA for a family center in Brentwood, doubling the size of the 1967 gift.

After Edith Hill died in 1971, Horace married her first cousin May Buntin Murray. She was the widow of Shade Murray. Horace and May lived in a small house on West Hillwood Drive until he built the beautiful two-story home at 4820 Post Road. Deeply committed to his business and his employees, Mr. Hill worked for H. G. Hill Co. for over seventy years and was in his office the Friday two days before his death on September 5, 1993 at age 92.

Fred Russell, sports editor emeritus of the *Nashville Banner*, became friends with Horace in the 1920s when Russell worked part time as a cashier in the senior Hill's first drugstore on the site of the Downtown YMCA. Russell said of Hill, "He was one of the truest gentlemen in every sense of the word. He was an extremely private person who avoided publicity."

• • • • •

East Nashville YMCA

CHAPTER SEVENTEEN

Shorter Term Presidencies
1954–1959

AFTER SERVING THREE years as president of the Nashville YMCA, H. G. Hill Jr. stepped down in January 1954, making way for Ennis E. Murrey, who had been on the board for a decade, to fill his enormous shoes. Murrey's team consisted of Stirton Oman and Russell Brothers, vice-presidents; Littell Rust, treasurer; and Bryan Jones, president of the East Nashville Branch YMCA. Four stalwarts retired from the board. They were Mr. Hill, Ferriss C. Bailey, Robert S. Cheek, Dudley Gale, and Dr. John Hill—all tried and true.[683]

With kids in school, February was a good time to hold lifesaving and water safety classes at the Y for adults. These classes were held on Monday and Friday evenings from mid-February until the end of April. National life-saving cards were presented those who successfully completed the class.[684]

April brought youth legislators from across the state to Nashville for the annual Youth Legislature meeting. The young people met in the YMCA building. On the last evening the boys were honored at a banquet given at the Hermitage Hotel at which former governor Jim McCord spoke and awards were given to outstanding mock legislators.[685]

W. Paul Alexander joined the staff in the spring with responsibilities for developing activities for the young men who lived in the building and for young men generally between 18 and 25. Alexander seemed well prepared, as he had been general secretary of the Anniston, Alabama YMCA. Soon, he launched a summer program for young men just out of high school.[686]

There was a membership drive in 1954 with George Green Jr. as chairman. Concurrent with the fund-raising effort was the annual learn-to-swim program at the indoor pool, orchestrated by Jimmy Burdette.[687]

Despite the fact that the cost of a modern, air-conditioned youth center had jumped from the initial estimate of $15,000 to $20,000, the Y had somehow found the money to fund it. Completed in July, the room on the lower level of the YMCA was 55 by 70 feet, complete with a dance floor and soda fountain. Mr. Gray said that it was patterned after ones in Los Angeles and several other metropolitan areas.[688]

Lots of older Nashvillians in 2010 could remember with fondness the youth center at the YMCA during the mid-1950s. Charlie Gray said, "It is one place in Nashville where young people can come and dance to good music where no intoxicating beverages are sold or allowed." Certain nights were reserved for various groups. In 1954, Tuesday night was the regular night for students of Nashville Business colleges.

At the time, the Nashville Business College occupied the entire third floor of the YMCA Building. The Nashville Business College had a female basketball team that was better than the Ramblers, winning 12 national titles, and traveling all over the world. Their coach was John Head. Dr. Cleo Miller traveled with them as team physician. At the time, Dr. Miller owned Miller Clinic in East Nashville. Nera White was the Nashville Business College star. In 2010, she was still remembered as the one of the greatest female basketball players in the world. She also was All American many times in the fast pitch softball league.[689]

E. E. Murrey served as president of the Nashville YMCA

George Volkert presenting Gra-Y football awards at Sylvan Park, 1957.

for one year. In January 1955, the board of directors elected Stirton Oman to succeed him. Oman, who was president of the Nashville Rotary Club, had been vice-president of the YMCA for four years. Five new directors were elected: Andrew Benedict Jr., G. Daniel Brooks, Herbert Luton Jr., Alfred Sharp, and Elmer Bryant. Ferriss Bailey also returned to the board after a one-year absence. Russell Brothers and George Green were elected first vice-president and vice-president respectively while Mark Bradford Jr. succeeded Littell Rust as treasurer. Russell Brothers gave the annual report. He said, "For the past few Saturdays," more than 1,000 people participated at YMCA activities at 7th and Union, and that the Nashville association's contribution to the world service program had nearly doubled in five years—from $651 in 1950 to $1,234 in 1954. A goal of $1,500 was set for 1955.[690]

In February, Charlie Gray announced the employment of the best-known athletic figure to head the physical education department since Jonas Coverdale vacated that job in 1931. With the departure of physical director Jimmy Burdette, Gray employed William C. "Bill" White effective March 1. White was familiar to all Sewanee men. From 1946 through 1953, he had been head football coach at Sewanee, where his teams won 38 games, lost 23, and tied one. In 1947 and 1948, the Tigers had 6–1–1 records, the best since the football team of 1909. One of the reasons White's teams won so many games was that his players were more afraid of him than they were of teams from such schools as Hampton-Sydney and Mississippi College. In 1954, White left Sewanee not because of any failing on his part but because his wife suffered from a severe depression and delusions of being persecuted. The Sewanee community was simply unable to cope with her problems. White moved to Birmingham where he was head football coach and athletic director at Howard College for the 1954 season. When White left the YMCA after three years and four months as physical director, sportswriter F. M. Williams wrote this about him in the *Nashville Banner*: "With his leaving goes a certain athletic dignity that only a man who has known all the thrills of winning and all the heartbreaks of losing can give."

Feeling good about his hire of White, and reasonably pleased that the United Givers Fund had allocated $27,640 to the YMCA, Gray was sufficiently confident of his staff's ability to fill in for him that he asked the board in April for a two-month leave of absence in July, August and September so he could take Mrs. Gray to the YMCA's 32nd World Conference in Paris, where a new YMCA constitution would be voted on. Gray's request was granted, and they, and John T. "Buddy" Fisher Jr. a member of the YMCA Bible study group, had a great trip. On their way, the Nashvillians were guests of the Denmark YMCA in Copenhagen.[691]

The first week of June saw YMCA kids from Nashville, Franklin, Murfreesboro, Livingston, and Springfield head to Camp Widjiwagan, the YMCA camp at Standing Stone State Park. Wilson Sims, chairman of the camp committee, said that 350 boys attended the camp that he called "one of the most successful in the history of the Nashville YMCA." Norfleet Hawkins was camp director. Meanwhile, about 500 boys signed up for the summer learn-to-swim program at the Y.[692]

Four new handball courts were built and some decorating work was done in the summer on the new youth center at the YMCA. At teen night in August, 500 boys and girls crowded into the facility to socialize, play ping pong, enjoy ice cream sodas at the soda fountain, dance and listen to rhythm and blues music blaring from the juke box. Larry Johnson, WKDA disk jockey, who helped promote the affair, handed out five theater passes.[693]

Undoubtedly, the most colorful staff person at the YMCA in the years during and following World War II was Ludlow "Doc" Gordon, the director of the health club, who, on his 78th birthday in 1953, stood on his head atop a 120-foot tall smokestack. On either this or another occasion, Doc and a friend were going to climb the smokestack at the City Water Works. The other man, much younger than Doc, lost his courage, quit halfway up, and climbed back down. Doc went on to the top and did a handstand before safely coming down. In 1955, Gordon could still do cartwheels and fancy dives. Having been with the Nashville YMCA since 1925, he would be 81 on September 6.[694]

If Doc Gordon was the most colorful character at the YMCA, George Cate Jr. was one of the most effective young volunteers. He had returned to Nashville in 1954 to begin the practice of law after serving in the U.S. Army for two years with the Judge Advocate General program. In 1955, George organized the "Magalops," a group of young men dedicated to the development of physically, spiritually and morally well-rounded young men. They had luncheon meetings once a month and discussion meetings weekly. Several years later, George said, "our main purpose is to get young business and professional men to take part in civic interests and to help in any way we can to promote Christian growth in the youth of Nashville."[695]

Across the river, "teen town" had outgrown the limited space it had occupied in the basement of the East Nashville Public Library for the past three years. With approval from the Board of Education and Mayor Ben West, the popular program, sponsored by the East Nashville YMCA, moved to the cafeteria of East Nashville High School, where it met on Tuesday and Thursday nights. The Board of Education also approved the use of Bailey Junior High School gymnasium by the East Nashville YMCA for its church basketball league.[696]

Senator Albert Gore of Carthage, the school's most distinguished alumnus, was the guest of honor and speaker at the annual alumni breakfast of the forty-four-year-old YMCA Night Law School on November 26. That morning, assistant district attorney R. B. Parker Jr. made the surprise announcement that a Billy Cooper Scholarship Fund had been established that would provide education for two law students by 1956. W. P. (Uncle Billy) Cooper, surprised at the honor, was speechless. He had been a founder of the Night Law School in 1911, and had taught there ever since. J. G. Lackey Jr. took over as dean of the school in 1955. Under his leadership enrollment would grow steadily.[697]

The elections of officers and board members for 1956 were held January 25. The YMCA board re-elected its officers to serve another year. They were Stirton Oman, president; Russell Brothers, first vice-president; George M. Green Jr., second vice-president; and Mark Bradford Jr., secretary. Elected to three-year terms as new board members were James M. Ward, with WLAC; Thomas E.

Baldridge, owner of the Sportsman's Store; A. Battle Rodes, president of Franklin Builders Supply; and Ernest J. Moench, president of Tennessee Tufting Co. Moench had previously served on the board in 1951–52. Charles M. Gray was reelected as general secretary.[698]

The YMCA Night Law School alumni met on June 16, 1956, to elect new officers and generate enthusiasm for fully endowing "The Billy Cooper Scholarship Fund for the YMCA Night Law School." Approximately $1,000 had already been contributed without any solicitation. Dean Lackey also reported the 25 students were enrolled the previous September and that he expected an even larger enrollment in the fall.[699]

For the fourth straight year, the Nashville YMCA held its summer boys' camp at Standing Stone State Park. The activities began on June 17 when a large crowd of boys left the YMCA at 7:30 in the morning for camp.[700]

As had been the case for several years, the annual life-saving course was held at the Central YMCA in June with one class for boys 13 and 14 and another for boys 15 and older. The summer program for boys at the Y began on June 18 and continued through Labor Day.[701]

In mid-November, the YMCA kicked off its New Industrial League made up of fourteen basketball teams from Nashville businesses—Braid Electric, Commerce Union Bank, Cullum & Ghertner, First American National Bank, First Church of the Nazarene, General Shoe, Hoover Express, Nashville Electric Service, Purina Company, Third National Bank, Victor Chemical Company, Washington Manufacturing Company, Western Electric, and Woodbine Presbyterian Church. These games, all played at the YMCA, were open to the public free of charge.[702]

November saw George Horton take his YMCA weightlifting team to Chattanooga where they won the AAU weightlifting championship. A week later, the Nashville YMCA was host for a handball tournament for juniors.[703]

H. G. Hill Jr. Rejoins Board

At the annual meeting on January 26, 1957, Russell W. Brothers Sr. was elected president. Other officers named were George M. Green, first vice-president; Dr A. L. Currie, pastor at Westminster Presbyterian Church, second vice-president; Mark Bradford, treasurer; and Charles M. Gray secretary. Brothers was an active layman at First Baptist Church, president of Rock City Ice Cream Company, and an officer in M. P. Brothers Grocery Co. A fine athlete, his hobbies included playing handball at the YMCA and golf at the Belle Meade Country Club. He was a past president of the Nashville Exchange Club, and, as a boy, had gone to the YMCA's Camp Sycamore.[704]

Horace G. Hill Jr. rejoined the board in 1957 after being off for three years. Charles H. Warfield, and Robert C. Taylor were the other new members. Also reelected to the board were Mark Bradford Jr., Russell Brothers Sr., Joe Carr, Dr. A. L. Currie, George M. Green Jr., and Hubert Luton Jr. Sam F. Coleman rotated off after six years of service.

Realizing that Charlie Gray needed more assistance, the Nashville YMCA board employed an associate general secretary, effective February 1. His name was Clifford E. Backstrom, a Kansas City native, who came to Nashville from the Fort Wayne YMCA where he had been in charge of boys' work and camping for six years. Soon after arriving, Backstrom told the board that he soon hoped to establish a Y Indian Guides program. He explained that this national YMCA program "would give the small boys of Nashville, who are too young to attend downtown meetings, a way of getting to know their dads and a way for fathers to get to know their sons."[705] The result was that the 'Y' Indian Guide program came to Nashville at least by the fall of 1957 when a Y Indian Guides program was launched at Parmer School.[706]

The Nashville YMCA ran three camps in the summer of 1957. Camp Widjiwagan, for boys 8 to 14, opened at Standing Stone State Park on June 16 and closed on August 10. The Central YMCA also had a day camp at Montgomery Bell State Park. It ran from August 19 until August 30. The East YMCA day camp was open from June 10 to August 2. It was for boys 6 to 15 and may have been at Shelby Park.[707]

For the seventh straight season, the YMCA ran a city-wide Gra-Y football league in 1957. Sylvan Park won the championship with a 5–0–1 record and played a Gra-Y All-Star team at MBA's Frank Andrews Field on November 16.

Several weeks later, YMCA George Horton's weight lifting tournament was held Saturday night, December 7 with entries from Atlanta, Birmingham, Chattanooga, Knoxville, Memphis, Montgomery, and Nashville.

There were 16 teams in two divisions in the YMCA

Industrial basketball league in 1957. As of November 27, First American Bank led the Red League while Attorneys Title was in first place in the Blue League. George Volkert, former Litton and Georgia Tech gridiron star, was a member of the Nashville Gas team.

There was also a handicap handball tournament at the Y the first week of December. Ex-Vanderbilt football star Bud Curtis was in charge of the event that brought two national handball champions to Nashville—John Jones and Jim Jacobs.[708]

A New Slate

George M. Green Jr. was named president of the YMCA board of directors in 1958, succeeding Russell Brothers Sr. Other officers elected were Mark Bradford Jr., first vice-president; Dr. Dr. Armand L. Currie, second vice-president; and James C. Barbour, treasurer. Green was president and general manager of General Truck Sales and executive vice president of Thompson and Green Machinery. Currie was pastor of Westminster Presbyterian Church, and Barbour was trust officer for Third National Bank.[709]

Seven new board members were elected at the annual meeting. They were Dr. Robert Foote, Charles J. Sanders Jr., Fred Webber, George H. Cate Jr., James C. Barbour, James Booker, and Dick Dance. Foote, a North Dakota native, graduated from Vanderbilt with both B.A. and M.D. degrees. Sanders was with Charles J. Sanders Co., a Lion Oil distributor; Webber was with the Nashville Bank and Trust Company and on the Board of Stewards at West End Methodist Church. Cate, active in the YMCA since he was a teenager, would, in 2010, have the distinction of having served on the Nashville YMCA Board for fifty-two years. Barbour had a B.A. degree from Vanderbilt and an M.A. from Tufts. He also was a member of West End Methodist Church. Booker was the southern sales manager for DayBrite Lighting, Inc. and a deacon at Woodmont Christian Church. Dance was an attorney with Associates Finance Corporation and a Cumberland University graduate.[710] One of the board members to rotate off was Merrill K. Hovey, who had served two three-year terms.

Board members of the East Nashville YMCA hosted 250 East Nashville, Madison, and Inglewood businessmen at the cramped East Branch at 10th and Fatherland. William H. Oliver, the former principal of East High School, since promoted to be superintendent of the City School System, was the principal speaker. He summarized the program at the East Y, saying that an average of 154 boys a day came there. Many of these men had teenagers who participated in the Y-sponsored "teen town" dances held weekly at the East High School cafeteria. Oliver explained that these popular and drink-free affairs were the place to be on Friday nights in East Nashville, attracting between 300 and 500 boys and girls. Oliver reminded his audience that the East Y also sponsored three Hi-Y clubs and a church basketball league using the Y gym, and the gyms at East and Bailey schools. Through the help of the Central Y the East Y building had undergone a $4,000 repair and improvement program, including interior painting, a new floor for the gymnasium, and construction of a downstairs game room and snack bar. Teal said that because "Teen Town" was so popular, the East Branch had initiated a Saturday night "co-ed" dance using a record player and the gymnasium floor. Because growth was so restricted at the present location, Teal also spoke of the five-year goal of the East Nashville YMCA to build a fully equipped, conveniently located East Nashville YMCA with all the facilities of the Central Y.[711]

Charles M. Gray announced three new members of the YMCA staff in August. They were Armand B. Ball Jr., boys' work secretary; Jack Morris, physical director; and Bob Courtenay, adult program director. Ball, a native of Dubach, Louisiana, was a graduate of Louisiana College and the Southwestern Baptist Seminary in Ft. Worth. Morris, formerly of Norfolk, Virginia, had been athletic director for the Norfolk Y for five years. He had ten years of YMCA experience and was a graduate of the University of Richmond, where he was a football star. Morris replaced Bill White who was a hard act to follow.[712]

Two weeks after arriving in Nashville, Armand B. Ball Jr., the new boys' work secretary, announced that registration would begin for the boys' division fall schedule. He said the program would include bodybuilding, wrestling, volleyball, badminton, basketball, gymnastics and swimming.[713]

On October 6, 1958 the *Nashville Banner* broke the story that the Nashville YMCA had bought 6.13 acres of land on Gallatin Road in the 11th Civil District from Biscoe Griffith and his wife, Inez Carroll Griffith. The cost of the land was $112,500 of which $25,000 was paid in cash. The balance, $87,500, would be paid in seven promissory notes in the amount of $12,500 each, the first note to be payable on January 1, 1960, and one note payable on the first day of each January, thereafter, until seven payments had been made. The YMCA's intention was to build its first family branch on the site, realizing that its present location at 10th and Fatherland was at best a stopgap solution. The YMCA would take possession of the property within 90 days.

For the past 6 months, the East Nashville branch board, headed by chairman J. Clyde Thomas, had been working to develop a plan for a location that would more adequately serve the entire East Nashville area. Dr. James Hudgins, chairman of the special building committee, recommended the Griffith property as an ideal site halfway between Isaac Litton and East High schools. The Griffith home, a colonial frame house, would be torn down. Charles Wheeler, Nashville architect, was retained by the East Nashville YMCA board to develop plans for a building on the site.[714]

The East Nashville branch had a membership in October 1958 of 2,750. The branch provided a summer day camp each year and had the past summer had 311 day-campers with an average daily attendance of 120. Comer Teal and his staff had done a splendid job with very limited facilities. In recognition of his accomplishments, he was named "Man of the Year" by the East Nashville Exchange Club. Known familiarly and affectionately as "East Y Teal," the tall, gray-haired former Alabama school teacher, had come to Nashville in 1946 to develop YMCA programs and a facility in East Nashville. Since that time, the cramped community building, leased from the city for one dollar a year, had been both recreational and Christian leadership headquarters for thousands of boys.

During his twelve years in Nashville, Teal organized basketball leagues, day camps, baseball leagues and weekly "teen towns" in addition to the Hi-Y and Gra-Y clubs developed in East Nashville schools. He challenged the Exchange Club to join with YMCA leaders in pushing the Y's newest project, a community YMCA for all of East Nashville, to successful conclusion. He exuded excitement over the recent purchase by the YMCA of the Griffith property as the future home for a $600,000 East YMCA building.[715]

George M. Green Jr., was reelected president of the Nashville YMCA board of directors for his second year. Mark Bradford Jr. was reelected first vice president, and Clifford Love Jr., succeeded Dr. A. L. Currie as second vice president. Similarly, John H. Hanson Jr., took James C. Barbour's place as treasurer; Clifford Love Jr., second vice-president; Charles M. Gray, general secretary.[716]

In 1959, Jack Morris, physical director at the Downtown YMCA, said, "handball is fast becoming one of our most popular sports, and for a body developing activity, this highly competitive game can't be topped. This sport has made such strides that the National championships were played at the Nashville Y this year." Among the members regularly playing handball were Russell Brothers Sr., Bud Curtis, Tom Henderson Jr., Don McGehee and Joe Morrissey. Less popular was weight lifting. Most high school football coaches, including Howard Allen at MBA, still did not encourage their players to lift weights, erroneously thinking that doing so would diminish the athletes' flexibility. Nevertheless, a volunteer organized the "Triangle Bar Bell Club."[717]

In the winter of 1958–59, Tom Henderson Jr. would load up eight to ten Woodmont School fifth and sixth grade boys, including his son, Tom Henderson III, and take them to the YMCA to practice or play basketball. The boys' team, the Woodmont Hawks, won the city championship that winter in the YMCA gym. Naturally, the eleven- and twelve-year-old boys explored as much of the YMCA building as they could, including climbing up the metal fire escape to watch Mr. Henderson and his friends play handball. They also overcame their inhibitions by swimming naked in the YMCA swimming pool where a sign read "No Running, No Yelling, No Suits." They could play ping-pong in the basement without being harassed. These were fond memories for Tom and his buddies that included Ed Anderson, Norman Carl, Paul Clements, and Tom Weaver Jr.[718]

Members of the boys' department had two camping options in 1959. Camp Thunderbird, the YMCA's new day camp for boys began June 15 at Ray's and Marrowbone lakes in northwest Davidson County. The camp, that could accommodate 40 boys, ages 7 to 13, operated for four two-week periods. Swimming, camping, fishing, and canoeing were camp activities.[719]

The YMCA's Camp Widjiwagan also operated for eight weeks, in four two-week segments, beginning June 14. It was still at Standing Stone State Park. Out-of-camp trips were made to the Great Smoky Mountain National Park and Mammoth Cave. On July 7, thirty-five boys were at Camp Widjiwagan.[720]

The fall program of the YMCA boys division begin September 17, Armand Ball, boys' work director, announced. The new program offered a 45-minute gym period of instruction and play in various sports, gymnastics, and physical fitness. Don McGehee of the YMCA Health Club taught the fundamentals of wrestling while other classes included one on lifesaving.[721]

D. H. Vardell, chairman of the building committee, announced in September that a major gift from the H. G. Hill interests had been received and would be used for the outdoor recreational area and swimming pool of the proposed $675,000 East Nashville YMCA. The development, he said, would be named "The Horace G. Hill Recreational Grounds" in memory of H. G. Hill Sr. In announcing the contribution, H.G. Hill Jr. said he always had a special regard for East Nashville because he and his sisters grew up at their parents' home on Boscobel Street. His was the first contribution to the campaign.[722]

In November, John H. Hanson Jr., Fred Hinton, John S. Herbert, John O. Jackson, Clifford Love Jr., Dortch Oldham, and Edmund W. Turnley were elected to the YMCA Board of Directors. Turnley, a former president, was returning after a several year absence. Members re-elected were Thomas Baldridge, Richard Dance, the Rev. Thornton Fowler, A. Battle Rodes, and James M. Ward.

On November 15, 1959, George Barker wrote a long article in the *Nashville Tennessean* on Comer Teal. The article described the East Nashville YMCA as "a shabby landmark in a tired neighborhood. The only thing new is a pool room which glowers at the Y from across the street." The clientele at the two places, the article said, were separated only "by the vigilant will of a wiry-haired fifty-three-year-old professional recreation worker named Comer Teal." Teal was known by most of the 6,000 kids who lived in the area between Isaac Litton and East high schools. He considered the poolroom across the street as a symbol of the things that were working against him. The East Y's shoestring operation is, Teal said, "more like a tight rope." Police motorcycle officer David Lee Thompson told an amusing story about Teal and his hold on East Nashville boys. Thompson caught a boy speeding in a hotrod a few weeks earlier and offered the offender his choice of getting a speeding ticket or facing Teal. "Gimme the ticket," the boy said "and for Pete's sake, don't tell Teal."[723] Teal's popularity made it hard on Charlie Gray, who did not have the same outgoing personality.

Two days later, the YMCA announced definite plans to develop Nashville's first "family-style" branch YMCA at 4401 Gallatin Road. Development of the tract would be done in three phases with the first stage to include an outdoor recreational area behind the building that would initially include an indoor swimming pool, game rooms, lounge, offices, kitchen and space for a future gymnasium. The East Y, construction of which would start within a month or two, was expected to provide a blueprint for future branch facilities.[724]

At the same meeting, it was also announced that an executive committee headed by H. G. Hill Jr. and Dr. James M. Hudgins, would direct planning for the new East Nashville YMCA facility. Despite its limited facility, the East branch YMCA had a total membership of 3,750 with 175 groups including 72 team organizations, and Gra-Y and Hi-Y programs with a total enrollment of 2,990. In addition, the Y also provided activities for 5,200 non-members during 1958. Much of this work was subsidized as 55 percent of the East YMCA's total operating budget of $20,381 was provided by funds from the United Givers Fund.[725]

The planned East Nashville community YMCA moved a step closer to reality on December 14 when 75 section chairmen, division managers, team captains, and team members met in the old East Y building to map the 1960 campaign for a new $675,000 East Branch Building that would include clubrooms, game rooms, an indoor swimming pool and off-street parking. The new branch, on a six-acre site at 4401 Gallatin Road, would be "one of the most modern in the United States" according to a brochure then being prepared for distribution.[726]

• • • • •

Gra-Y basketball

A Top 50 P.E. Department and Racial Unrest
1960–1964

THE NASHVILLE YMCA elected Mark Bradford Jr., president; Harold Buchi, and George H. Cole Jr., vice-presidents; and John Hanson Jr., treasurer at the annual meeting on January 8, 1960. Charles Gray was reelected general secretary at the same meeting. In all, six board members were reelected and new members were elected, including prominent automobile dealer, Alvin D. Beaman. The board also approved leasing 50 acres on Old Hickory Lake as a site for its day-care activities.[727]

The official kick-off for the capital funds drive to build the $675,000 family YMCA in East Nashville took place on January 14 at a banquet at East High School. Presiding were J. Clyde Thomas, president of the East Branch, and Comer Teal, the East general director. Famed guitarist Chet Adkins provided the music. Dr. Cleo Miller, advance gifts committee, was there. His clinic was just down the street. The principal speaker was Ray Evans, an outstanding YMCA layman from Chattanooga. All three Nashville TV stations—WSM, WLAC and WSIX—carried a thirty-minute television simulcast on Sunday afternoon publicizing the campaign. Campaign executive committee co-chairman H. G. Hill Jr. and Dr. Jim Hudgins both spoke on the simulcast. Hudgins said, "It is our hope to have the new facilities constructed and in operation within the next three years or less and this type of new YMCA facility will serve as a model for other similar projects in other areas of Nashville and Davidson County. Dick Battle devoted his City Hall column in the *Nashville Banner* on Friday to push for support of the project. He had grown up in East Nashville. The campaign also had the enthusiastic support of Mayor Ben West, County judge Beverly Briley and Governor Buford Ellington.[728]

At the first reporting session, on the 19th, $176,506 had been raised. In a speech to the Nashville Sertoma Club a week later, State Senator Richard Fulton, a member of the East Nashville YMCA Board, emphasized, "Nashville wants a program for the entire family." By then, $290,000 had been raised, despite snow and sub-freezing temperatures.[729] The momentum continued to build as on the January 29 report meeting, $364,550 in gifts and pledges was reported.[730]

Progress slowed at this point and, at the next report session on the 2nd, the total subscription climbed only $30,000 to $396,813. This was the last session before the campaign windup on Thursday. Oliver, Dr. Hudgins, and H. G. Hill Jr. urged the 250 workers present to make "every minute count."[731]

Workers reported at the final report session that they had raised $470,437, including nearly $75,000 the past four days. Despite having raised more money, perhaps, than had ever been raised in East Nashville, the campaign was still about $200,000 short. Two days later, Horace Hill Jr. and Dr. Hudgins announced the campaign would continue through the following Thursday.[732]

The last week in March, Mark Bradford Jr. and Charlie Gray met with United Givers Fund representatives to apprise them of the YMCA's current program and future plans. They said the YMCA board had approved investigating ways and means to develop a "YMCA Health Club" with new and fully equipped quarters by combining the present Health Club and the young businessmen's department. The expenditure of $2,000 was approved to obtain initial architectural and engineering estimates and sketches for construction of new facilities by roofing over the area above the swimming pool. Joe Booker, a board member, said it was thought that the area between the two wings of the YMCA could be designed to add two floors that would contain all the necessary facilities for a modern athletic club sustained by probable membership fees of $100 per year. The board also had under advisement a proposal of the East Nashville YMCA directors to give priority to full-scale development of the outdoor facilities on the site of the proposed new branch. This would enable them to build the outdoor pool, athletic fields, outdoor playgrounds, and parking areas.[733]

Kilcrease Breaks New Ground

The Nashville sit-in demonstrations of two years earlier lasted from February 13 to May 10, 1960. The non-violent campaign to end racial segregation at lunch counters in downtown Nashville was coordinated by the Nashville Student movement and the Nashville Christian Leadership council, founded by the charismatic Rev. Kelly Miller Smith, pastor of First Baptist Church Capitol Hill. Sit-in participants, primarily black college students, were systematically abused both verbally and physically. On the day when African-American attorney Z. Alexander Looby's home was bombed, nearly 4,000 people marched to City Hall to confront Mayor Ben West. When asked by Diane Nash, one of the student leaders, if he thought the city's lunch counters should be integrated, the mayor answered "yes." This was a pivotal moment and his statement paved the way for subsequent negotiations between store owners and protest leaders that led to an agreement under which, on May 10, the lunch counters in downtown Nashville were desegregated.[734]

The YMCA and nearly all other organizations in Nashville remained segregated in 1960. That fall, Nashville postal worker Irvin Hugh Kilcrease Jr. applied for admission to the YMCA Night Law School. Dean J. G. Lackey Jr., who was also chairman of the board of the school, rejected his application "because the school does not admit Negroes." Kilcrease said, "I'm not bitter about it. I hope to be admitted someday."[735] A year later, Kilcrease tried again. Lackey again declined to accept him. This changed in the fall of 1962 when the school accepted Kilcrease and two other African-Americans. Kilcrease recalled that they were "well received." One of the three did not complete the course but Kilcrease and Thomas Linston Smith Jr. would graduate on June 8, 1966. In 1980, Governor Lamar Alexander would name Kilcrease as Davidson County Chancellor. He was the first African-American to preside over a Tennessee Chancery Court.[736]

The Tennessee Youth General Assembly, with 353 delegates, took over the lawmakers' seats in the legislative chambers one day in April. Proposals providing for giving eighteen-year-olds the right to vote, and reapportionment of the Tennessee legislature were two of the questions debated.[737]

The YMCA announced in April that they would operate nine weeks of camp this summer at Camp Widjiwagan, 103 miles from Nashville at Standing Stone State Park. Boys could attend for 2, 4, 6, or 8 weeks. While in camp, they would live in groups of seven with one counselor to a cabin. The camp fee of $55 would cover food, lodging, and insurance for a thirteen-day period. Much emphasis would be placed on outdoor living with overnight trips. A new feature would be a two-week camp designed exclusively for high-school students. This was planned in cooperation with the Fellowship of Christian Athletes under the guidance of Hank Duvier, Bob Taylor, and Bill Wade. Another new feature would be one six-day family group session.[738]

The new camp period for high school boys at Camp Widjiwagan was particularly attractive, as Armand Ball, camp director, had lined up a number of noted coaches and athletes on the staff. Included were John Oldham, basketball coach at Tennessee Tech; Wilburn Tucker, football coach at Tennessee Tech; and Jim Carlen, freshman football coach at Georgia Tech.[739] Another milestone came that summer when Reiner Dauder, of Boblingen, Germany, became the first foreign counselor at a Nashville YMCA camp. Dauder came under the auspices of the International Committee on Friendly Relations.[740]

The YMCA's new day camp on Old Hickory Lake began its first two-week period on July 11. The camp was on a 55-acre site adjoining the Easter Seal Camp and had approximately one and one-half miles frontage on Old Hickory Lake. The boys lived in tents during the day with eight boys assigned to each adult counselor. Activities included swimming, archery, hiking, cookouts, canoeing, crafts and nature lore. A new access road and swimming dock were ready when camp opened.[741]

• • • • •

On August 19, 1960, Charlie Gray, general secretary of the Nashville YMCA, was honored with a forty-year service certificate at Blue Ridge for his years of YMCA service. Gray was at Blue Ridge attending a meeting of the Association of Secretaries of the YMCA. The veteran executive, who lived at 1921 Eighteenth Avenue South in Nashville, had been with the Nashville YMCA fourteen years and had been general secretary since 1949.[742]

• • • • •

When the Nashville Chamber of Commerce vacated its leased space in the YMCA building, two Health Club members, Harold Buchi and Joe Booker conceived the idea of establishing an Athletic Club in the vacated space. The old Health Club was still functioning but was hampered by limited equipment and the absence of a professionally trained staff. In October, Booker and Buchi met with other interested members of the proposed Athletic Club at Mark Bradford's home. At that meeting, Booker agreed to serve as chairman of the effort to establish an athletic club with Charlie Creagh as co-chairman. With board approval, they made studies of other athletic clubs before retaining Hart, Freeland, and Roberts as architects, and Fred Wright as contractor. Equipment was purchased for approximately $130,000. The YMCA paid for this by borrowing $130,000 from the National Trust Company. In less than a year, the Athletic Club was functioning and 1,000 new members had joined the YMCA, a majority of whom used the Athletic Club facilities. Jack Morris was physical director and Lloyd Wood assisted him. Among the Athletic Club features were whirlpool treatment, judo classes, ultra-violet solarium, nap room, and oil massages.[743]

At the annual meeting, held November 28, Mark Bradford Jr. was re-elected president with Harold U. Buchi and George Cate Jr. as vice-presidents. Ten members were elected to the YMCA board. They were Frank Gorrell, attorney with Bass, Berry, and Sims; Olin West Jr., General Shoe Company; former presidents Russell W. Brothers Sr. and George M. Green Jr.; George Volkert, Nashville Bank and Trust Real Estate Co.; Joseph Booker, George Cate Jr., Fred Webber Jr., Harold Buchi, and James Wyatt. Bradford told the board members, "The Nashville YMCA has experienced great growth in the past year." He pointed out that Gra-Y and Hi-Y programs throughout the city and county almost doubled in the number of boys enrolled in the past twelve months, and mentioned that ground would be broken in the next few months for the East Nashville branch.[744]

Charles Gray, general secretary, learned in early December that the Nashville Y's physical education department was honored as being one of the top fifty in the nation. Sharing his pride in the honor were Frank Gorrell, chairman of the new athletic club; Jack Morris, physical director; and Joe Booker, building chairman of the new athletic club.[745]

Frank Gorrell announced in December that a portion of the 2nd floor of the YMCA Building would be remodeled for a newly organized athletic club. The remodeling project and new equipment were expected to cost about $100,000, Gorrell said. The Athletic Club was to be self-governing and operated as a branch of the YMCA. Gorrell added, "We plan to start work in January and that there would be separate rooms for steam baths, heat treatments, massages and various exercise activities. Memberships are $100 a year and more than 200 men have already joined the club."[746]

During the winter, the YMCA offered instruction in gymnastics, trampoline, rope climbing, and traveling rings. There was also a beginning class for swimmers and a competitive swimming team coached by Tom Kenny, Vanderbilt swimming coach.[747]

Comer Teal, executive secretary, announced on February 15 that construction would start on the East Nashville Branch YMCA building on March 1. Teal said the first phase would be a one-story brick building at 2624 Gallatin Road containing "three administrative offices, five clubs rooms, snack bar, kitchen and an all-purpose room." Kennon Construction Company got the contract with a bid of $258,951, while the architect was John Charles Wheeler. Teal said the unit was expected to be completed in eight months and that the entire project would be completed in five years. The second phase would include an indoor pool, locker rooms, showers, gymnasium, and an outdoor recreational area containing handball courts, swimming pool, baseball diamond, tennis and volleyball courts and a picnic area.[748]

The groundbreaking ceremonies for the new East Nashville Branch YMCA were held Saturday afternoon, March 18, 1961, at the site on Gallatin Road at Delmas Ave. More than 100 people listened as D. H. Vardell, chairman of the building committee, presided. Mrs. Elton Sowell, the first woman to serve on a Nashville YMCA board of directors, manned the shovel. She had recently been elected to the East Nashville YMCA board. Comer Teal, executive director of the East YMCA and J. Clyde Thomas, president of the East Y board, also participated in the ceremonies.[749]

The YMCA Night Law School got a boost in February when it was announced that Judge Benson Trimble of Family Court had joined the faculty to teach domestic relations, beginning in early March. Trimble was the second judge on the Night Law School staff, the other being Judge

Charles Gilbert, retired Criminal Court jurist. Gilbert was teaching criminal law at the school that had 150 students, the largest enrollment in its fifty-year history.[750]

YMCA's second day camp season at Camp Thunderbird on Old Hickory Lake ran from June 26 to July 7. Any boy who had completed the first grade was eligible, said Max Cook, camp director.[751] Camp Widjiwagan was again held at Standing Stone State Park. For the second consecutive year, there was a foreign counselor there. That summer it was Owe Schweltzer, of Wuppertal, Germany. He was a college student at the University of Cologne.[752]

Nelson Discovers Racquetball

Nelson Andrews was introduced to the YMCA in about 1961. Years later, he recalled, "About this time I joined the YMCA, which basically was a one entity downtown enterprise. My first exercise was joining a bunch of basketball enthusiasts at lunchtime." Nelson, an advocate of "no blood, no foul," did not like the frequent basketball arguments over alleged fouls that became chronic and the tempers that got out of hand. Consequently, he looked for some other physical activity and was introduced to racquetball, a sport he fell in love with. "The original racquetball courts were primitive at best," Nelson said. "They consisted of three regulation-sized courts that the hand ball players called their domain, with a smaller court suitable for squash. To access the courts you went up as far as the elevator would take you, climbed out a window, crossed a tar roof, then back through another window to the courts. No heating or air conditioning—cold in winter, miserably hot in summer. I didn't care. I had found a new love."[753]

In the spring of 1960, Nashvillian Frank Burkholder graduated from the University of Kentucky and returned to Nashville, where he started working for Equitable Securities. Frank first went to the YMCA when his friend James O. "Jim" Bass Jr., invited him to go there. Jim never really bonded with the YMCA but Frank did. Burkholder recalled in 2009 that, starting about 1961, he played racquetball with Nelson Andrews at the YMCA four times a week for 25 years. He said that Nelson won about 2/3 of the time and he won about 1/3 of the time. "Age and cunning won over youth and running," Frank said. Nelson said that he often won because he could usually anticipate Frank's next move.[754]

Racquetball players were not allowed to use the handball courts between noon and 2 p.m. and between 4 and 6 p.m. as those prime times were reserved for handball which was more popular. Because Nashville Sporting Goods stores did not carry racquetball paddles, Tommy Henderson Jr., a regional manager for National Life and Accident Insurance Company, and a former three-sport athlete at Vanderbilt, would buy them for $12 each when he was in Houston on company business and bring them home where he sold them at cost to his fellow racquetball players. At that time, racquetball paddles were modified wood tennis racquets that had the handles cut down by 12 inches and a string grip installed at the end of the handle that went around the player's wrist. Because the heat on the courts was so stifling in the summer time, the players pooled their money and bought three air conditioners to go in three of the courts. Conversely, in the winters, there was no heat but this was no big problem as heat reached the rooms from lower floors. The players also put a rubber mat on the fire escape because it became very slippery when it rained.[755]

While YMCA members such as Nelson Andrews, Frank Burkholder, Tom Henderson Jr., Don McGhee, Joe Morrissey, and Walter Knestrick became addicted to racquetball, other members, including Bob Stone, the city's top handball player since 1957; Charles Creagh, who reigned as city champion for many years; Jack Morris, physical director at the YMCA; and Art Guepe, Vanderbilt football coach, remained loyal to handball. The Y had four of the ten standard handball courts in Nashville.[756] Other YMCA members were just as committed to running. In the early 1960s, jogging became popular and a 100-mile marathon was organized. For several years, about 30 men completed the 100-mile run. Bob Brown led the way, running nearly 300 miles in the allotted time.

Gov. Buford Ellington, Mayor Ben West, and Frank Gorrell, president of the board of directors of the YMCA Athletic Club, formally opened the new facilities on 7th Avenue North. The air-conditioned clubrooms would be under the supervision of Jack Morris and Lloyd "Woody" Woods.[757]

Armand Ball, youth secretary, announced in October that two new staff members had been employed: Jerry Shaw, who had been associate youth secretary in Winter Haven, Florida, and Mark Owen from Owensboro, a graduate of Kentucky Wesleyan University. Jerry would work with the greater Hillsboro YMCA community committee, established to explore the possibility of a branch YMCA in that area while Mark was hired as youth physical director to direct all classes and activities for boys in the central building.[758]

A Shift in Emphasis

The new 1962 leadership team of the YMCA was elected on December 12, 1961. Harold Buchi was elected president, Clifford Love and George Cate Jr., vice presidents; and Charles Gray, executive secretary. At the board meeting, five new members were installed. They were attorney and former YMCA president Ferriss C. Bailey, investment banker Harold "Cotton" Clark; real estate developer Sam F. Coleman; lumber firm president Merrill K. Hovey; and Clark Hutton Jr., who was with Life and Casualty Insurance Company of Tennessee.[759] Bailey, Coleman, and Hovey had all been on the YMCA board before.

During the Gray years as general secretary, there was a shift in emphasis at the Nashville YMCA from the evangelistic approach of earlier years with frequent men's Bible study to discussions bearing on contemporary life. Still, however, Bibles were placed in every room and the staff held devotional services at the beginning of each day. Board meetings continued to be opened with prayer. The YMCA annually sponsored prayer breakfasts and had a solid alignment with the YMCA World Service program. The Y also had a relationship with the Fellowship of Christian Athletes.[760]

Early in the year, YMCA youth director Armand Ball conducted a survey to gauge the demand for a Y in the southwest area of Davidson County. When the results were positive, dedicated layman John Jackson recruited a southwest suburban community committee to explore the feasibility of establishing a YMCA branch in the area.[761]

The YMCA announced in February 1962 that Camp Widjiwagan would offer a ten-day canoe trip to the north woods of Minnesota and Canada the following summer. The special trip, conducted by Armand Ball, was open to boys 15 and older who had swimming skills. The canoe trip would start at Camp Widjiwagan in Ely, Minnesota.[762]

The Nashville Y's Camp Widjiwagan was named for Camp Widjiwagan, Minnesota, by a St. Paul boy who visited the Nashville YMCA day camp in 1952. Maybe it was retribution that, in October 1962, the St. Paul YMCA successfully recruited Armand Ball to join the staff of the St. Paul YMCA as executive secretary of their Camp Widjiwagan branch in Ely.[763]

YMCA's Camp Thunderbird on Old Hickory Lake had four two-week sessions during the summer. The first session began June 11.[764]

The southwest community committee of the Nashville YMCA took its first step toward addressing the needs of that community by beginning June swimming classes for boys and girls between six and twelve years of age at four private pools near several county grammar schools, including Parmer, Woodmont, and Julia Green. Mrs. John Napier and Richard Shaffer served as instructors.[765]

Grady Looney came on board in November as the Nashville YMCA's new citywide youth director, succeeding Armand Ball. Looney, a twenty-seven-year-old native of Montgomery, Alabama, had been citywide youth director of the Montgomery YMCA for five years. A graduate of Birmingham-Southern College, Looney would also assume Ball's responsibilities as camp director.[766]

Kelly Miller Smith's Challenge

Clifford Love, owner of Love Insurance Agency, was elected president of the Nashville YMCA board of directors in December, succeeding Harold Buchi. Officers elected were George Cate Jr., vice mayor elect, first vice president; Merrill Hovey, owner of Old Hickory Box and Lumber Company, second vice president; Charles Gray, secretary; and John Hansen, CPA, treasurer. Re-elected to three year terms on the board were Charles Creagh, Metropolitan Life Insurance Co.; J. Vaulx Crockett Jr., attorney; and Henry Gillespie, a local realtor.[767]

Eleven new members were elected at the meeting. They were: Douglas Henry Jr., assistant general counsel, National Life and Accident Insurance Company; James Ward, WLAC sales staff; A. Battle Rodes, Franklin Builders Supply Co.; Robert L. Freeman, partner Harvey Freeman and Sons; Robert Albergotti, vice president of Neeley Coble Co. and Leasco Inc., H. A. "Hank" Duvier, Tennessee Products and Chemical Corp.; Ben R. Murphy, Baptist Sunday School Board; and Roupen Gulbenk Jr., vice-president of Gulbenk Engraving Company.[768]

In October 1962, Kelly Miller Smith reported to the press that efforts by the Nashville Christian Leadership Council would be directed toward St. Thomas and Baptist hospitals, the YMCA and the YWCA. He said the hospitals would be asked to admit and serve members of minority groups, and that the YWCA and the YMCA would be asked to desegregate all their facilities.[769]

In January, John Robert Lewis, a Fisk student and chairman of the Nashville Non-violent committee, and three Tennessee State students tried to register to spend the night at the YMCA. The night clerk turned them down and, on instructions from Charlie Gray, had them arrested at the Y for "unlawful conspiracy to obstruct trade and business." They were paroled that night to their attorneys, Avon Williams and Z. Alexander Looby, and instructed to be in Judge John T. Boone's general sessions court on February 26 for trial.[770]

On February 24, 1963, a Sunday, a pro-integration group of about 60 people, led by the Nashville Christian Leadership Council, marched the two and one-half blocks from the First Baptist Church Capitol Hill to the YMCA building to protest the association's segregationalist policy. Most of the marchers were older with a sprinkling of younger college students. A majority were African-Americans but some were Caucasians. After the marchers assembled on the sidewalk in front of the YMCA across from the Downtowner Motel, the Rev. Kelly Miller Smith read a short statement: "The YMCA is not alone in practicing segregation. But it was selected for this demonstration because it symbolizes that fact that segregation still dominates the scene in downtown Nashville." The group sang hymns and heard prayers from several of their leaders. After twenty minutes, they quietly dispersed and walked back to the church without incident. Rev. J. Metz Rollins, regional field director of the United Presbyterian Church, was one of the protestors. He said, "We wanted to show there still is substantial adult leadership interested and active in these matters." Charles M. Gray, the general secretary of the Nashville YMCA issued a statement. He said, "the YMCA Board decided the previous October to reaffirm their policy of segregation and, to my knowledge, the board has not been contacted since that time about possible negotiations."[771]

On the 26th, Judge Boone found John Lewis and his three co-defendants guilty and fined each of them $25 plus court costs, bringing the total to $41. The boys appealed the verdict in Criminal Court. There, Judge John Draper delayed their trial indefinitely. His reasoning was that "the case should not be set for trial until some initial disposition is made on the motion for a new trial for eight Negro students convicted last week on the same charge at B&W Cafeteria."[772]

A week later, several African-American students integrated the Downtown YMCA lunch counter without incident. Y officials said later that the Negroes were served due to a mistake. Approximately 24 students, both white and African-American, entered the downstairs lunchroom about 5:30 p.m. and asked to be served. John Lewis, who led the group, said they were served "without any trouble at all, but that it could have been a mistake on the part of the waitress." "It was," said Charles M. Gray, when told of the incident. "As far as I know," Gray added, "there has been no official agreement that we will serve Negroes." Gray also said, "If I had been there, I would have had to deny them service." Clifford Love Jr., president of the YMCA board of directors, confirmed that "no change has been made in the segregationist policy of the association." "We are giving this problem continuous study," Love said, "but as of now, the policy is the same as it has been."[773]

Leo B. Marsh, the first African-American to be elected president of the Association of YMCA Secretaries, and a member of the staff of the National Council of the YMCA in New York City, monitored the situation at the Nashville YMCA through Katherine Jones, executive director, Tennessee Council of Human Relations. In response to his request for information, she wrote Marsh the following letter in March 1963.

> Leo B. Marsh
>
> National Council of the YMCA
> 291 Broadway
> New York City 7, N.Y.
>
> Dear Mr. Marsh:
>
> This letter is in response to your request for additional information regarding the arrest of young Negro students in Nashville whose attempt to gain access to the YMCA resulted in their arrest.
>
> On the second warrant, signed by the YMCA executive secretary, and charging obstruction of trade, the students came to trial on February 26. As the enclosed clipping indicates, the four students were fined $25 and court costs, or a total of $41 each, plus attorney fees. The harshness of the punishment and the vigorous prosecution has stirred the Negro community to new efforts for eradication of discriminatory practices in Nashville stores, restaurants, hotels, etc. A withdrawal of trade from Nashville merchants is now underway; it is too early to determine its effectiveness.
>
> The case is being appealed to criminal court, but has not been set for hearing. Judge Draper, mentioned in the second page of the clipping, will be on the Bench in Criminal Court, and therefore the outcome is not promising.

> You will also note that the service granted at the YMCA lunch counter on March 1 was termed a mistake by the executive secretary, and confirmed by the president of the board, Mr. Love.
>
> The students are represented by Mr. Avon Williams Jr., attorney, 327 Charlotte Ave., Nashville. Mr. Williams and his partner, Mr. Z. Alexander Looby, are able attorneys and handle a great many civil rights cases throughout the state.
>
> The students and their addresses are John R. Lewis, Fisk University, Nashville 8, Tenn; Lester G. McKinnie, 920 28th Avenue North, Nashville 8, Tennessee; Frederick Leonard, 920 28th Ave. North, Nashville 8, Tennessee, and Vincent Horsley, Route 1, Box 227, Old Hickory, Tennessee.
>
> The following explanation of the YMCA resistance to desegregation was given me by a man in the community. I have no other confirmation of it, but you may find it helpful in understanding the situation. About 10 years ago, the YMCA was in serious financial straights. A group of young businessmen got together and sought to underwrite its continued existence by establishing a health club there. From their own resources, they invested considerable money in health equipment, and it is used rather extensively by them. They apparently consider this a private club, and are resistive to desegregation since this would open the facility to Negroes. It is hard for me to comprehend the reasoning which allows a tax-exempt institution, in a highly favored location, to be considered a private club with selected membership. I have also heard that the YMCA Board wished to drop the legal charge by the time of the February 26 trial, but the district attorney would not agree.
>
> We are encouraged by your concern and interest.
>
> Sincerely yours,
>
> Katherine Jones,
> Executive director
> Tennessee Council of Human Relations
> 2011 Grand Avenue
> Nashville 12, Tennessee

It seems more than coincidental that the YMCA offered, early in May, a three-month course in marksmanship and firearm safety. Mark Owen taught the course, open to boys in grades one through eight. Why the Y targeted boys so young for the course seems strange.[774]

Protests, sit-ins, and pickets continued in 1963 and 1964 until the Civil Rights Act of 1964 ended overt, legally sanctioned segregation nationwide. Because of strong leadership, Nashville escaped most of the violence that flared up in cities across the South. For example, in June 1963, the Nashville Metropolitan Human Relations Committee announced that the Nashville Hotel-Motel Association and a number of downtown restaurants had agreed to desegregate their facilities. James O. Bass Sr., chairman of the Nashville-Motel Association, stated, "the bulk of tables in downtown eating establishments now are offered on a desegregated basis."[775]

In the early 1960s, certainly during the 1963 sit-ins at the YMCA, Charlie Gray's health was failing. Accordingly, his secretary, Martha Wiggins, made more and more of the daily decisions. Clifford Love Jr., the YMCA president from 1962 until 1964, also took some of the responsibility that the CEO would normally assume.[776]

Early in 1964, Mr. Gray became seriously ill and was forced to submit his resignation as general secretary that was reluctantly accepted. Despite his willingness to be an agent for social change at the end of his long and productive professional career, he was beloved for his dedication to young men. Mr. Gray would soon develop Alzheimer's and die in 1969. In February, the Y suffered two more staff losses when Jack Morris, the physical director, resigned to accept the position as executive of the Alexandria, VA, Branch of the Washington, DC, YMCA, and Mark Owen, boys' physical director, accepted a job in Clinton, Iowa. Fortunately, Lloyd Wood, the athletic club director, was willing and able to assume the role of physical director.[777]

In February 1965, under a new executive director, Ralph L. Brunson, the Board of Directors of the Nashville YMCA resolved to reaffirm its long-standing policy:

> Services of the Nashville YMCA are rendered without discrimination or segregation because of race, creed, color, or national origin.
>
> It is the policy and practice of the Nashville YMCA that its Board of Directors and its committees are open to representation from all segments of the public. It is further the policy and practice that there be no discrimination with regard to hiring, assignment, promotion or other conditions of staff employment.

Youth activity at YMCA's Camp Thunderbird, June 1965

CHAPTER NINETEEN

Ralph Brunson Arrives
1964–1965

WHEN A *NASHVILLE BANNER* writer interviewed Comer Teal in January, 1964, Teal said his dream had half come true with the new facilities at the East Nashville YMCA and that the other half would come true when the rest of the facility—an indoor swimming pool and a gymnasium—materialized. "I've got ten more years before I retire," Teal said, "and I hope to leave a $1 million plant with the staff hired and program underway. We're going to get it too because the people out here are going to build it." Teal's determination and enthusiasm had been the spark behind the East YMCA since general secretary Charles M. Gray hired him in 1944. Twenty years later, the East YMCA was a $500,000 plus facility that offered families a complete recreation center. Perhaps the most popular program was the Saturday night Teen Town that drew an average of 500 youngsters to the Y weekly. The outdoor pool, opened in the summer of 1963, boosted membership 100 percent.

Teal, 57, explained his mission, "Our job is to help young people, and, though we may not be doing enough, we're doing what we can. I believe the YMCA helps by giving them a Christian atmosphere in which to have fun. If we couldn't make them better for coming, we wouldn't be trying to get them here."[778] Years later, Teal recalled that Nashville's ex-mayor Bill Boner was one of the East High School teenagers who took full advantage of the programs at the East branch. According to Teal, Boner was a wonderful dancer who was sufficiently self-poised, as a high school freshman, to dance with senior class girls at Hi-Y dances. Former mayor Richard Fulton was an East YMCA board member in its early years. In 2010, the Richard and Sandra Fulton Teen and Senior Center would be opened at the center in their honor.

At the January 1964 board meeting, the 1963 financial report showed that the association ended the year with a surplus of $5,799.49, an improvement over 1962 when there was a $16,396.03 year-end deficit. Frank Gorrell, membership committee chairman, announced that a sustaining membership enrollment would be held with a goal of gaining 100 new century members at $100 each. Robert Freeman gave the status of the Donelson site, saying that the State of Tennessee was ready to sell the property and that a fund-raising effort in the community was underway.[779]

In February, the Nashville YMCA took a big step toward developing a branch YMCA in the Donelson area by purchasing the 11.8-acre tract on Lebanon Road from the State. The property fronted Lebanon Road for about 600 feet and was more than 1,000 feet deep. Located just past the Tennessee School for the Blind, the property adjoined the old Cloverbottom Mansion. The Donelson YMCA community committee, headed by Bob Freeman, was working toward eventual development of a complete facility there that would serve every member of the family. To purchase the property, the YMCA borrowed $23,000 from the Nashville Bank and Trust Company.[780] Four months later, the YMCA purchased a small triangle of land needed to increase the frontage on Lebanon Road from the State of Tennessee for $1,700,000. The triangle measured .59 acres.[781]

While Bob Freeman was shepherding the process of developing the YMCA's presence in Donelson, Roupen Gulbenk, chairman of the YMCA's southwest committee, was working hard in Green Hills. The previous fall, Roupen spent nearly every Saturday afternoon visiting Frank "Nick" Becker, who lived on his family's 4.9-acre

Robert L. "Bob" Freeman, Nashville Metropolitan Board President 1971–1972

farm on the north side of Richard Jones Road in Green Hills adjacent to Hillsboro High School. Roupen told Ridley Wills II in 2009 that he and Nick would sit on Nick's front porch and churn homemade ice cream. Roupen was trying to convince the Beckers to give their small farm to the YMCA. For weeks, Becker was non-committal. Finally, he told Roupen, "We are not going to give you the farm but we will lease it to you for 99 years for a nominal annual fee." Roupen was delighted. The YMCA board learned about the opportunity at the May 1964 board meeting when Tom Baldridge reported that the Becker farm could be leased on a ninety-nine-year basis at a cost of $250 per month.[782] YMCA's Metropolitan Board approved the lease.

All this time, YMCA board members were reflecting on the legacy of their general secretary, Charlie Gray, who would retire on July 1. They instinctively thought of his devotion to his job, his great interest in boys, and the broader vision he encouraged with respect to the YMCA World Service Fund and the International YMCA. During his years as general executive, gifts of $500 to the YMCA World Service Fund began to materialize, several foreign students visited the Nashville YMCA to participate in summer camps, and Nashville YMCA members took a European tour in 1962, sponsored by the Southern Area YMCA office in Atlanta.[783] Gray had also started the East branch, a big programming success. Unfortunately, during his last years as general secretary, his health and energy lagged and his mental condition deteriorated. Without a strong, active leader, the physical condition of the building slipped, and the Y slipped into mediocrity.

George H. Cate Jr., chairman of the eleven-man general secretary search committee, reported at the March board meeting that his committee had narrowed its prospect list to five men, three of whom had been invited to Nashville. A promising finalist, Ralph L. Brunson, visited on April 6 and 7 with his wife, Willie Belle.[784]

Following the visits, the committee quickly decided that Brunson, the experienced and highly regarded general secretary of the Lexington, KY, YMCA was whom they wanted. Ralph, who was forty-nine, accepted the challenge of becoming the CEO of the Nashville YMCA for a salary of $12,000 annually with a $500 increase annually until his salary reached $15,000.[785]

Clifford Love, president of the Nashville YMCA, made the announcement of Brunson's appointment on May 11. He told the board of the Victoria, Alabama native's background and experience. Brunson, Love said, was a 1940 graduate of Howard College in Birmingham, who served four years in the Navy during World War II. He had begun YMCA work while still in high school, and became camp director and Hi-Y secretary for the Birmingham YMCA after his discharge from the Navy. Brunson, Love continued, was later named general secretary of the Columbus, Miss., YMCA where he served more than three years, doubling the association's annual budget and tripling its program and services. In recognition of his work there, Brunson was named Columbus' "Man of the Year." Ralph moved to Louisville in 1953 as associate general secretary of their Metropolitan YMCA board. He was named general secretary of the YMCA of Greater Lexington [KY] on May 19, 1957. Love also said that Brunson was past president of the Southern Association of YMCA Secretaries and had been active in many civic organizations. He and his wife, the former Willie Belle Wills, had three sons ages twelve, seven, and four. A Baptist, Brunson had been a Sunday school teacher and active in other church work. He had also served on the boards of the Red Cross, PTA, Kiwanis Club, and the Ministerial Association.[786]

On the eve of Charlie Gray's retirement, the Nashville

YMCA had 1,412 members, including 511 in the Athletic Club, 206 regular members, and 695 boy members.[787]

Having seen through the process of employing a new general executive, Clifford Love decided that it was appropriate for him to step down from the YMCA presidency. Accordingly, at the June 22 board meeting Love resigned and George H. Cate Jr. was elected president. Until 1964, officers were normally elected in December with their terms to begin January 1. Merrill Hovey and Jim Ward were elected vice presidents, and Ben R. Murphy, of the Baptist Sunday School board, was elected secretary-treasurer. New board members elected included Nelson Andrews, Mark Bradford Jr., and Horace Hill Jr. Bradford and Hill were former members and presidents. Also reelected to the board were George A. Volkert, Russell W. Brothers and Frank C. Gorrell. The new officers took office July 1 and would every year thereafter.[788]

Clifford Love had one last task, which was to properly honor Charles M. Gray Jr. Love and his successor, George Cate Jr., who was also vice-mayor of Metropolitan Nashville, presented Gray with a plaque honoring his forty-four-year service with the YMCA and eighteen-year service with the Nashville YMCA. Gray was also honored at a dinner. He had served diligently.[789]

In the summer, Camp Widjiwagan was operated at Standing Stone State Park for six weeks with 175 campers. Grady Looney Jr. was camp director. Other groups used Camp Widjiwagan after the YMCA camp closed in early August. Camp Thunderbird, the YMCA's day camp on Spencer Creek in Old Hickory Lake, operated for eight weeks, ending August 6.[790]

Ralph L. Brunson arrived in Nashville on August 1 to assume his new post. Characteristically, he spoke candidly, saying, "People in Nashville have shared with me their belief that the YMCA is old, out-of-date, and should move in force on an expansion program in Nashville. It has been suggested that a new Y be established in Donelson, Southwest Nashville, and other areas of need. There is a good program in East Nashville, but other areas are lacking in YMCA facilities and influence."[791]

When Charlie Gray met Ralph, Gray warned him, "This job you are taking will involve eating a lot of chicken sandwiches and potato chips while you hold meetings at lunchtime." George Cate Jr. accompanied Brunson when the new general executive first inspected the YMCA building, that the board was contemplating selling.

George H. Cate Jr., Nashville YMCA President 1964–1965; Metropolitan Nashville YMCA President 1969–1970

When Ralph walked in the lobby, he turned to George and said, "It looks like a fraternity house without a house mother." The lobby even had spittoons, Brunson noticed. Very quickly, Ralph got rid of the spittoons and had the lobby repainted and refurbished to present the right impression. When he was through, the beige and white lobby looked spotless. George recalled this series of events in 2009 and also remembered that he and Ralph would meet weekly, late in the afternoon, for a two-hour session. They also drove around town to help Ralph familiarize himself with the city and assess needs for YMCA outreach. George said, "Ralph didn't think I had anything else to do."[792]

It seems unbelievable that at a board meeting on August 19, 1964, only eighteen days after his arrival, Brunson offered the board a seemingly endless number of observations and recommendations. The board members rolled their eyes when his list of recommendations went on and on. There were seven typewritten pages of recommendations in seventeen different areas. Brunson was not lacking in self-confidence.[793]

Not long after arriving in Nashville, Ralph realized that

the YMCA building was being used to its utmost capacity. In 1964, "bed night" occupancy totaled over 50,000 with 9,819 different men in residence. The wear and tear on the forty-two-year-old building was obvious. Ralph recommended that the building be refurbished. The ensuing renovation was nerve-wracking and time-consuming but the result pleased the board members who felt the more than $40,000 cost definitely worth it.[794]

At his first board meeting, Ralph suggested that the southern and national YMCA offices be invited to scrutinize the local program. He told the board members, "Let's expect to achieve success." He said many people had told him the Nashville YMCA needed a new image. "It can be created," he commented.[795]

Ralph also felt that the Y needed more direction, having, in his opinion, been more reactive than foresighted. Accordingly, he and the board agreed to form a long-range development committee to chart all future expansion. One of the results was the adoption of new by-laws. Attorney J. Vaulx Crockett led this effort. The Nashville YMCA board was soon replaced by a thirty-six-member Metropolitan Board of Directors in which was vested the overall management of the association and its branches. The Metro board was Ralph's idea. The idea came about one day when Ralph said to George Cate, one of the architects of Nashville's new Metro Government, "Nashville has Metro. We need Metro."[796] Ralph also told George, "We need more presidents on our board and not as many vice-presidents." They set about working on that.

Ralph arrived in Nashville near the height of the racial segregation controversy, In an effort to make its position known, the YMCA, with Ralph's strong backing, adopted a strong resolution reaffirming its policy of rendering service without regard to race, creed, color or national origin. The resolution's wording seems strange as only seventeen months earlier, Charlie Gray said the Nashville YMCA's policy was to uphold segregation. Undoubtedly, the national YMCA had a non-discrimination policy considerably earlier than did Nashville. Three years later, the Metropolitan Nashville YMCA Board signed the Equal Employment Certificate.[797]

Bob Freeman Leads at Donelson

Just after Labor Day, Max Cook, the newly appointed executive secretary of the Donelson Branch YMCA, announced preliminary plans for the construction of a $1 million facility for the Donelson Branch YMCA. It would be a two-story building housing executive offices, a gymnasium, numerous clubrooms, and an outdoor pool. More than half of the cost to complete the project had already been raised by the Donelson YMCA youth committee headed by Bob Freeman. The balance of the funds would be raised by a capital funds drive, Cook said.[798] Until the YMCA on Lebanon Road could be built, the Donelson Branch YMCA would meet in the Freeman Building, from which it conducted community programs.[799]

The Nashville YMCA board of directors voted on September 16 to develop the YMCA extension program in Donelson into a permanent branch. The Metro Planning Commission had approved plans for a $1 million structure for the Y on its Lebanon Road site. The new facility would be only the second such addition to the YMCA program since it began in 1875. The East Nashville YMCA was the first in 1962. At Donelson, more than 1,200 youngsters were engaged in YMCA-sponsored activities in 1964.

• • • • •

A native of Mayfield, Ky., Max Cook has been with the YMCA since 1959, and was a George Peabody College graduate.[800]

• • • • •

One of the many recommendations, Ralph Brunson made soon after arriving in Nashville was to organize an endowment committee. This became a reality in September when the Y organized an endowment committee with attorney Ferriss Bailey its first chairman.[801]

Ralph Brunson and the Nashville YMCA's new president George Cate Jr., got an early test in October, when William A. Dansby Jr., a young African-American student at Tennessee A & I University, applied for membership. He was greeted cordially by Cate and Brunson and asked to return on Saturday to meet with them and the physical director, Lloyd Wood. At that meeting, Cate told Dansby that he did not think the time was ripe to integrate the Downtown Center, and suggested that he withdraw his application and come back 3 or 4 years later when the YMCA would likely have open an integrated branch in North Nashville. George said this because he was afraid the YMCA board would reject Dansby's application, something Cate did not want to happen. Dansby's response was that he would like to leave his application on the table, and that he would accept the directors' decision. Cate and Brunson agreed to go forward.

Since Dansby had told them that he had been a member of the Ft. Wayne YMCA, Brunson wrote John Lehman, the Ft. Wayne, general secretary, for a character reference. Lehman wrote back that Dansby would be "a good member to start with." Ten or twelve days after he submitted his application, the YMCA board chairman sent Dansby a letter informing him that he had been accepted for YMCA membership without a dissenting vote. Thus, Dansby said, "I became the first Negro to be admitted as a member of the Downtown YMCA." A decade later, in 1975, Dansby, then minister of Gay-Lee Christian Church in North Nashville, wrote Lloyd Armour, editor of the *Nashville Tennessean*, telling this story and complimenting the Nashville YMCA for its achievements on the occasion of its Centennial Celebration, titled "100 Years, Putting It All Together." In the last paragraph of Dansby's letter, he wrote, "The last ten years I have been a member have been enjoyable years. Mr. Ralph E. Brunson has done and is now doing a remarkably wonderful job, has a concern and interest in people regardless of their identity. He has done more for the community in ten years than had been done in the first ninety years of existence. Maybe the time was not ripe, but, thanks to God, it is ripe now, and juicy ripe, and Mr. Brunson helped ripen it."[802]

The Association's highlight in December was the YMCA's third annual Old Hickory Handball Tournament. In the doubles competition, youngsters Jack Pirrie and Art Demmas came from behind to defeat veterans Tommy Henderson and Charlie Creagh for the championship.[803]

Spring of 1965

The personal highlight for Ralph in December was going coon hunting with George Cate Jr., and his father, George Cate Sr. The Cates would pick Ralph up after supper in Mr. Cate's four-door sedan that would have two or three coon dogs in the trunk. The three men would drive to Ashland city, cross the river on State highway 49, and hunt coons on the ridge dividing Cheatham and Dickson counties till 10 p.m. or so. Ralph grew to love coon hunting as much as the Cates did and once wrote up his coon hunting experiences in a national YMCA magazine.[804]

In early March, the Nashville YMCA held an open house to announce plans for a million dollar Southwest Nashville Family Center scheduled for construction near Hillsboro High School. Grady Looney, YMCA Metropolitan Youth Director, said the family center would be built on land leased by the YMCA on the corner of Richard Jones Road and Hillsboro Road one block south of the high school. The five-acre center was leased from Frank Niederhauser, a double first cousin of the Beckers, at $1,750 a year for 99 years. Those attending the meeting included Ralph Brunson, Gulbenk, and George Cate Jr.[805]

Hermitage Gra-Y football team, 1964

George Cate Jr., presided over the last meeting of the Nashville YMCA board on June 30, 1965. He closed the meeting early so that the Metropolitan Board that would replace the Nashville YMCA board, and the Downtown Branch board could have their initial meeting. The downtown building would no longer be referred to as the Central YMCA, but as the Downtown Branch. Horace Hill Jr., who had been president of the YMCA Board from 1951 to 1953, agreed to serve as the first president of the newly established Metropolitan Board. Naturally, he was elected. Additionally, Bill Earthman was elected vice president, Ben Murphy treasurer, and Thomas Baldridge secretary. George Volkert and Lloyd Wood became chairman and executive secretary, respectively, of the Downtown Branch. At the session, 20 new metropolitan board members were named. They were F. Murray Acker, Andrew B. Benedict Jr., Harold U. Buchi, Col. Gilbert Dorland, the Rev. Frank Drowota, Guilford Dudley Jr., William Earthman Jr., Clark Gower, Wayne Hudson, Franklin M. Jarman, Stirton Oman, James H. Reed III, A. Battle Rodes, J. Donald Ross, Fred Russell, Leroy O. Seltz, Lemuel B. Stevens. Overton Thompson Jr. William C. Weaver Jr. and Frank G. Witherspoon. A number of these men had served before. At the meeting, Delwyn H. Bardell was named the 1964–65 Nashville YMCA "Man of the Year"; Roupen Gulbenk received the

Service to Youth Award; and H. G. Hill Jr. received the first Order of the Red Triangle plaque, the highest of all YMCA awards.[806]

In his report, Mr. Brunson said that the YMCA was growing rapidly and that, during 1964, the membership reached 19,508. The general executive also said that a shortage of funds would prevent the association from beginning any building projects "right away" but added that the Southwest property had been acquired for use as a future branch site. In the meantime, Brunson said that the Richard Jones site was being graded as he spoke and that it would be used for a day camp that summer.[807]

At the June 30 annual meeting, the Metropolitan board voted, without dissent, to accept applications from two more Negroes for membership in the downtown branch. "This brings to three the number of Negroes who have been approved for membership in the last few months," said Brunson. A racial barrier had quietly been broken.[808]

Roupen Gulbenk's Finest Hour

Insurance executive Joe Thompson Jr. presided over the first board meeting of the new Southwest family branch, held in September at the First American National Bank in Green Hills. Roupen Gulbenk, vice-president of the Metropolitan Nashville YMCA Board, who had been instrumental in the organization of the Southwest Y, spoke on the needs and aspirations of the Southwest Y. Board members and officers were elected. As far as the Southwest family branch board knew, a building would sometime be built on the five-acre Becker track and they expected it to include a swimming pool, gymnasium, club and game rooms, administrative offices, meeting rooms for males and females, snack bar, banquet room, reading and study room, TV lounge, reception room, and rest rooms.[809]

An area YMCA study team recommended, on October 2, 1965, that a $5 million, eight-branch expansion program be implemented over a period of eight years to provide Y services throughout the entire metro area. A three-man team from the Southern Area Council of YMCAs made the report at the request of the Nashville YMCA. In addition to the downtown YMCA, the branches suggested were in the downtown north, downtown south, southeast, southwest, Donelson, Northwest and Northeast service areas. The study team said the scope of the project would require a $4.25 to $5 million capital funds drive over five to eight years.[810]

The Green Hills community was clearly excited about the likelihood that YMCA would be built on the five-acre site on Richard Jones Road. On about October 1, the Woodmont Kiwanis Club presented the YMCA with a $1,000 check earmarked for payment of rent on the site just south of Hillsboro High School. By this time, the grounds had already been improved and more than 1,600 young people in the Green Hills area were involved in the activities of "Y" Indian Guides, Gray-Y, Hi-Y, and resident and day camps.[811]

Joe Porter was named physical director of the Nashville Metropolitan YMCA, effective October 25. He succeeded Lloyd Wood, who earlier had been promoted to executive secretary of the downtown branch. Porter had been physical director of the Norfolk YMCA for seven years.[812]

At the October 27 meeting of the Metropolitan Nashville YMCA board, the directors voted to adopt the Metropolitan Atlanta YMCA plan for financing the Metropolitan Nashville YMCA operation. The three primary components of the plan were for the Metropolitan Nashville Y to receive:

- All sustaining membership fees from Metropolitan Nashville YMCA board members;
- A 3 percent Fair Share from all branches in line with area and National YMCA Fair Share Plan; and
- All remaining necessary funds from the united Givers Fund allocation.

There was a lively discussion at the October meeting concerning the future of Camp Widjiwagan that had lost money for a number of years. Brunson's motion to continue the camp for another season but with changes in fees and management was declined, and the question was referred to the executive committee. In November, approval was granted by the executive committee and board to continue the camp for one more year. At the board meeting that month, Jim Henson was approved to become branch secretary for the Southwest branch.[813]

The long-range development committee presented an important report in December. It recommended to the Metropolitan YMCA board that an extensive study be conducted by the downtown board concerning the feasibility of razing, rebuilding, or relocating the Downtown YMCA with a minimum of expenditure suggested for the present building until the time that the study is completed. The study was expected to take one year or less.

The long-range development committee also recommended to the Metropolitan YMCA board that a capital funds campaign with a goal not to exceed $4,000,000 be conducted in 1969. All the long-range planning committee recommendations were approved at the December 22, 1965 Metropolitan Nashville YMCA Board meeting.

In 1971, Ralph Brunson wrote down his remembrance of highlights of 1965—his first full year as CEO of the Nashville YMCA. They were, (1) the organization of the Donelson-Hermitage Family Branch; (2) the rehabilitation of the Downtown YMCA building at a cost of $45,000; (3) a city-wide YMCA needs survey with help from the Southern Area Council in Atlanta and the establishment of long-range goals; (4) The organization of the Downtown Branch; (5) the organization of the Metropolitan YMCA board structure, (6) the first city-wide membership enrollment campaign; (7) the revision of all association procedures and practices; and (8) an expansion of budget and programs.

This was an ambitious start. This is unsurprising given that Ralph's philosophy was to always aim high.

• • • • •

RALPH E. BRUNSON
Nashville YMCA General Secretary (1964–1980)

During his senior year at Phillips High School in Birmingham, Alabama, Ralph E. Brunson worked at Stockton Valve Company YMCA in Birmingham.

That fall, in 1936, he entered Howard College, where he graduated in 1940. Next, he became assistant boys' secretary at the Downtown Birmingham YMCA. On June 22, 1941, Ralph married Willie Bell Wills in Alpharetta, GA. She was a graduate of the University of Georgia with a major in home economics. They would have three sons, William Thomas, Alan Ralph, and David Wills.

Brunson left Birmingham in 1941 to attend George Williams College in Chicago. He entered the U.S. Naval Reserve in 1942 as a Third Class Petty Officer. Ten months later, Ralph received the rank of Ensign. He later saw action in the South Pacific from New Caledonia through Bougainville, and had become, by 1945, a Lieutenant senior grade.

After being honorably discharged in January 1946, after four years of antiaircraft and amphibious duty with the Navy, Ralph returned to Birmingham as camp director and Hi-Y Secretary for the Birmingham YMCA. On May 13, 1947, Ralph was officially certified as a secretary of the YMCA. The certification was granted by the chairman of the board of Certification of the YMCA of North America after examination of Ralph's education, personality, Christian purpose, and qualities of leadership. A year later, Ralph was named secretary of the Southern Association of YMCA Youth Secretaries. He would later become president of that organization.

After three and one-half years at the Birmingham Y, where he worked in all phases of youth work, Ralph accepted the position of general secretary of the Columbus, Mississippi, YMCA; He was vice-president of the Mississippi Association of YMCA secretaries in 1951 and was president in 1952. During his tenure as general secretary of the Columbus Y, its annual budget doubled and its program and outreach tripled in size. A member of the Kiwanis Club in Columbus, Ralph was nominated for 1952 Columbus Man of the Year. In 1951, while living in Columbus, Willie and Ralph's first son, William Thomas was born. Ralph was chairman of the Columbus Red Cross Disaster Committee in 1952 and taught Sunday School at the Baptist Church where he and his family were active members. Just at the end of his years in Columbus, Ralph was program chairman of the Southern Association of YMCA secretaries at their annual conference held in Blue Ridge, NC.

In June 1953, Ralph joined the Louisville, Kentucky, Metropolitan YMCA as associate general secretary. Ralph served four years at the Louisville Y, giving direction to the planning and construction of new branches, development and organization of new branches, and working in program and financial development for the entire Louisville Association and its seven branches. He continued his church activities by teaching Sunday School at his church in Louisville. In 1956, the Brunsons had a second son, Alan Ralph.

In May 1957, when Alan was 10 months old, Ralph was invited to become general secretary of the Greater Lexington, Kentucky, YMCA. He accepted and thoroughly enjoyed his seven years in Lexington.

In 1964, he wrote of his Lexington years as "one of the finest and busiest experiences in my more than 23 years as a YMCA secretary." In 1959, Willie and Ralph completed their family when David Wills, their third son, was born.

During Brunson's seven-year stretch, the Greater Lexington YMCA advanced from almost a non-entity in the community to an organization of considerable strength, having gained respect and prominence throughout Central Kentucky and having achieved a very high rating among the YMCAs in the country.

While in Lexington, Ralph and Willie gave back to the community in many ways. He was a first vice-president and board member of the PTA, president of the Lexington Social Agency Executives Association, first vice president and president of the Southern Association of YMCA Secretaries, secretary of the local ministerial association, worked in various capacities for the annual United Community Fund campaigns, served several years as a member of the Juvenile Court Advisory Committee, served as Secretary of the Southern Area Council of YMCAs and was on the boards of the Lexington Red Cross and the North American Association of YMCA Secretaries. He also served as a deacon at his church, and was, in 1964, on the boards of the Blue Ridge Assembly and the University of Kentucky YMCA. In his letter of resignation to Y president Ben Cowgill in April 1964, Brunson said the decision to leave "was the most difficult one I have ever made in my Y work." His last day in Lexington was July 31.

Within days after Ralph Brunson's resignation as General Associate of the Greater Lexington YMCA to accept the position of general secretary of the Nashville YMCA, an editorial titled "Brunson's Leadership Was Invaluable" appeared in the *Herald-Leader*. It said that Ralph could look back on his years in Lexington "with complete satisfaction. His leadership during this period was invaluable and he rendered outstanding service not only to the YMCA but to the whole community."

Brunson, whose life motto was "Make Big Plans," was fully prepared to tackle his next challenge in Nashville.

• • • • •

CHAPTER TWENTY

Downtown-North: A Reality

1966–1967

WHEN THE METROPOLITAN NASHVILLE YMCA board of directors met on January 25, Grady Looney Jr. gave the opening prayer and devotional, following a long-standing tradition. The most important piece of business came when Dr. James H. "Jim" Hudgins presented to the Metropolitan Board a proposal to complete the construction of the East Nashville Branch YMCA by the Metropolitan Board borrowing approximately $300,000 for approximately three years for the purpose of constructing a 75' long by 25' wide indoor pool and locker rooms.

All four branches held membership drives in 1966. The Downtown Branch was most successful, enrolling 337 members and exceeding its goal of $25,000 by $3,000.[814]

Despite his busy schedule, Ralph Brunson set a physical fitness example for local YMCA members by running a mile and one-half six days a week on the YMCA track. He also completed the 100-Mile Marathon organized by the Downtown Branch physical department, an event won by Bob Brown who ran 315.19 miles in 72 days.[815]

The Metropolitan Nashville Board executive committee meeting in March featured a momentus step in the process of integrating the Nashville Association. George Cate Jr. made a motion, seconded by Roupen Gulbenk, that the executive committee recommend to the Metropolitan Board that the president and staff work with the Southern Area YMCA staff in the organizing of a Downtown North Branch YMCA, cooperating with the present Colored YMCA and using the recommended procedures made by Dunbar Reed, associate secretary of the Southern Area Council of YMCAs. The motion carried.

Roupen then submitted a recommendation from the Southwest board of managers "that the Metropolitan Nashville YMCA board of directors be requested to employ the services of the National Council YMCA Building and Furnishings Services and the architectural firm of Taylor and Crabtree for developing plans leading to construction of the Southwest Family Branch YMCA building." The motion carried subject to the approval of the Metropolitan property committee and the insertion of the word "preliminary" before the word "plans" in Mr. Gulbenk's motion.

The Metropolitan Nashville YMCA board approved both of the above-mentioned proposals at the March 23 meeting with the additional approval of the selection of Kennon Construction Company as the contractor for the East Family Branch project at a maximum cost of $295,770. By May 25, construction had begun on the indoor swimming pool and locker rooms that were scheduled for completion in 180 workdays weather permitting. Without any additional cost, the East Family Branch would also establish a Horace Greeley Hill Memorial Park behind the East Branch building to be completed by June 1. It would have two tennis courts, volleyball courts, a baseball diamond, two shuffleboard courts, a horseshoe pits, tetherball rings, and a picnic area.[816]

By 1966, the YMCA annual budget had grown to $114,140.40 in expenses and $128,988 in income. During 1965, the association had experienced a $2,803 deficit with Camp Widjiwagan being one of the poorest performers.[817]

The long-range planning committee was busy planning for the capital funds drive, tentatively scheduled to be conducted between November 1968 and May 1969. A

Horace G. Hill Jr. receiving resolution presented by Roupen Gulbenk (R) at the Nashville Association's 92nd Annual Meeting, May 23, 1967.

goal of between $2 million and 2.5 million was being contemplated.[818]

With the approval of the organization of a Downtown North Branch YMCA in his pocket, George Cate Jr., vice-chairman of the long-range development committee, convened a meeting of key Metropolitan YMCA players and their counterparts at the Colored YMCA. Cate filled in the Colored YMCA leaders on a development survey that showed that a branch in the colored area of the city north of downtown was viable and that the project had executive and Metropolitan Board committee approval. The Colored YMCA representatives were enthusiastic and said that they would discuss the matter with their board and report back.[819] At the April Metropolitan Nashville Board Meeting, five days later, Roupen Gulbenk reported on the special meeting, stating, "harmony was the keynote of the meeting."

• • • • •

Robert S. Cheek, a former board member, was eighty-eight years old in 1966 when he was recognized as being the oldest living member of the YMCA, having joined in 1887 when he was nine years old. He was given a Plaque of Honor at the June 22 board meeting.

• • • • •

With camp season just around the corner, a new camp called Arrowhead was being organized by the Southwest Branch board on Russell Brothers' farm off Highway 100 sixteen miles from Green Hills. This addition increased to four the number of day camps then in operation. The other camps were Tsagali, established in 1965 on Hillsboro Road for boys and girls 5 through 7; East; and Thunderbird operated by the Donelson Branch YMCA. The one resident camp was, of course, Widjiwagan at Standing Stone State Park.[820]

Construction was underway in late April on the East Nashville Branch swimming pool. At Southwest, a land use plan and preliminary drawings for the branch building were in-hand. The Donelson Branch board was frustrated by the fact that a Board of Zoning Appeals question concerning their zoning was under advisement by a judge.[821]

Colored YMCA Embraces North Nashville Branch

Mark Bradford Jr., chairman of the nominating committee, nominated the following officers for 1966–67: Horace G. Hill Jr., president; William F. Earthman Jr., first vice-president; Roupen M. Gulbenk, second vice-president; Ben R. Murphy, treasurer; and Thomas E. "Tom" Baldridge, secretary. The slate was unanimously elected. Bob Freeman, chairman of the Donelson Branch board of managers, submitted a recommendation from his board that the titles of all YMCA secretaries be changed to that of "Directors" in line with the recent change made by the National Council of YMCA's at its annual meeting. The local staff titles would be, he said, executive director, Metropolitan Board; executive director for each branch board; physical director, camp director, youth director, etc. The motion was unanimously approved.[822]

The 91st annual meeting of the Metropolitan Nashville YMCA was held May 25, 1966 with 167 members present. Nine nominees for re-election to the board were elected and installed as were the new officers. Clifford Love Jr. received the Order of the Red Triangle, while George Cate Jr. was honored as YMCA Man of the Year.[823]

The mid-year news from the East Family Branch was mixed. A cost overrun on the swimming pool and locker room project to $307,936 was the bad news. The good news was a flattering article on the East Branch written by Virginia Keathley in the *Nashville Tennessean* on May 29.[824]

In July, the Southwest Branch YMCA board of managers discussed the value to the YMCA of the current lease on the Richard Jones property. They concluded that the question should be carefully evaluated in the event this site was appropriated by the Board of Education as looked likely. Their property committee was already looking at alternative sites.[825]

T. B. Boyd Jr., president of the board of directors of the Colored YMCA, wrote Ralph Brunson in July saying that his board fully discussed the Metropolitan YMCA's plans for organizing the Downtown North Branch YMCA and the idea of the Colored YMCA cooperating in this effort. Boyd said his board voted approval of the suggestion that the Colored YMCA amend its charter and discontinue use of the name Colored YMCA and also approved the suggestion that all members of the Colored YMCA, as individuals, cooperate and support the metropolitan Nashville YMCA in its plan to organize the Downtown North Branch YMCA and that in the future, this organization will consider making financial contributions to the overall Metropolitan progress. How thrilled Ralph Brunson, George Cate Jr., Roupen Gulbenk, and others who hoped for this answer were. Immediately, the Metropolitan Board voted to invite Dunbar Reed, of the National staff, back to Nashville to assist in the immediate organization of this branch. He came on September 12

East Branch YMCA outdoor pool, summer 1967

Clyde Keltner, H. G. Hill Co, passing the deed to Ralph L. Brunson and William C. Weaver of the YMCA for the 8.5 acres of land in Green Hills for the Southwest Branch on December 31, 1967.

and 13 and spent that time with Ralph Brunson selecting a board and doing other organizational work.[826]

The integration of the two Nashville YMCAs was a very progressive step for a Southern city. For example, "the black Y" in Evanston, Illinois, and the Evanston Y in a city that boasted of its diversity did not merge until 1969.[827]

There was more exciting news. Camp Widjiwagan, a continuing financial drain on the Metropolitan Board, saw a dramatic increase in campers in 1966, jumping to 240 boys in 1966 from 160 in 1965. The camp committee recommended that a professional, whose primary responsibility would be the operation of the camp, be employed before the 1967 season.

Mark Bradford Jr., chairman of the nominating committee, nominated Dr. Walter S. Davis, president of Tennessee A & I University, and Col. Jesse L. Fishback, U.S. District Engineers, to two-year terms on the Metropolitan Board. When they were approved, Davis became the first African-American to serve on the Metropolitan Nashville YMCA Board. Roupen Gulbenk then moved the approval of twenty African-Americans—18 men and two women—to become the initial board for the Downtown North Branch YMCA. This motion was adopted. Soon, seven white members were added to the Downtown North Board.

In other action, Larry Thomas was approved as part-time worker in the Southwest Branch YMCA and full time director of Camp Widjiwagan.

Finally, President Hill named an eighteen-man campaign executive committee that he would chair. It included representatives from each branch and such heavy hitters as businessmen William C. Weaver Jr. of National Life, and Ben R. Murphy, Director of the Office of Management Services at the Baptist Sunday School Board.[828]

The first meeting of the Downtown North Branch YMCA Board of Managers met at the downtown YMCA building at noon on September 26. Metro Chairman Horace G. Hill Jr. welcomed the group and wished them well in their service to North Nashville. At the meeting, Dr. Thomas E. Pogue was named temporary chairman of the Downtown North Branch.[829]

Without a branch building, Frank Bellar and Max Cook at the Donelson YMCA, had put a lot of energy into Gra-Y clubs. In the fall, Donelson had fourteen different Gra-Y clubs with an enrollment of over 300.[830]

A Challenging Year

The year 1966 was difficult, strenuous, and challenging though much was accomplished. There was a thorough appraisal by the Southern Area Council. One of the results was an overhaul of the YMCA's bookkeeping system, policies, and practices. The Downtown building, allowed to run down over the past few years, was unattractive, even to the point of being dismal. During the year, it received a $42,000 facelift that created a much better image. The Donelson Branch acquired four additional acres, increasing their site to sixteen areas, plenty for a new building. The Y conducted its first citywide membership drive in February and March, enrolling over 450 new members. Brunson now had a professional staff of five—an executive for each of the three branches—and a fourth man assuming the role of Metropolitan Program director. A fifth man was employed as physical director of the Downtown Branch. The percentage of funds received from the United Givers Fund dropped from 26 percent in 1963 to a little over 16 percent for 1967.[831]

At the Metropolitan Nashville YMCA Board meeting on November 30, the 1967 budget of $538,000 was approved. Mr. Hill announced to the directors that he had appointed Dr. Thomas Poag, who had been serving as temporary chairman of the Downtown North Branch, as permanent chairman of that board for a one-year term. Mr. Hill also reported that the YMCA Law School was interested in having a floor reserved for their use in the proposed YMCA building downtown. The YMCA Law School alumni, he said, would raise the money for the project. At some point in the meeting, J. Vaulx Cockett read a memorial resolution celebrating the life of Ferriss Bailey, who died earlier in the year.[832] During his decades of association with the local YMCA, Ferriss had many roles—that of teacher in the Night Law School, legal and financial advisor, working member and long-time treasurer of the board of directors and, finally, president.

The election of new members and the reelection of existing members took place on December 5. This included Metropolitan board members as well as members of the boards of managers of the Donelson, Downtown, Downtown North, East, and Southwest family branches.[833]

Early in 1967, Ralph Brunson invited the Most Reverend Joseph A. Durick, D. D. Apostolic Administrator of the Diocese of Nashville, to tour the YMCA and to give the invocation at a YMCA committee meeting. In a wonderful ecumenical display of unity and openness, the Diocese of Nashville fully endorsed Catholic membership in and support of the Metropolitan Nashville YMCA after Brunson readily agreed to two conditions: (1) that each Catholic member of the YMCA be encouraged to be faithful to the practices and teachings of his Communion, and (2) that it be mutually agreed that the YMCA would honor and promote the cause of religious freedom in a manner that would respect the convictions and worship of each Catholic communicant.[834] Another significant barrier had been broken, largely through the efforts of Ralph Brunson.

The 1967 citywide membership drive resulted in 933 members and $60,554 in dues. The Downtown Branch was the only one to exceed its goal, achieving 102 percent and 107 percent of its member and cash goals.[835]

The third Monday of April saw Nashville YMCA members Sam Brashear and Bob Brown, and staff members Wayne Blackwelder and Lloyd Wood complete the 71st Boston Marathon. Blackwelder was a new Southwest staff member while Wood was executive director of the downtown branch. Brown had the best time, finishing in three hours and thirty minutes. Soon, the YMCA runners adopted the name "Nashville Striders" and sponsored several runs annually.[836]

At the April meeting of the Metropolitan Board, the

directors approved a motion to change Article VII, Section of the bylaws to have three vice presidents instead of a first vice president and a second vice president. The board also approved the employment, effective June 1, of Julius Jones as executive secretary of the North Nashville Branch YMCA.[837]

The long-awaited new indoor swimming pool, an enlarged gymnasium and better locker facilities for men and women were formally opened at the East YMCA on Sunday, May 21. East members and guests toured the building and also the "Horace G. Hill Memorial Park" behind the building. In the first ten days that the pool was open, 3,224 people enjoyed using it.[838]

At the 92nd annual meeting of the Metropolitan Nashville YMCA, held at the East Nashville Family Branch on May 22, 1967, Roupen M. Gulbenk was elected president, succeeding Horace G. Hill Jr., who had served two years, having earlier served as president from 1951 to 1953. Also elected were Wallace R. Bunn, vice-president; Thomas Cummings Jr., vice-president; Rev. Frank F. Drowota, vice president; James M. Ward, secretary; and Ben R. Murphy, treasurer. Ralph L. Brunson would begin his fourth year as executive director.

Roupen Gulbenk presented Mr. Hill, the first president of the Metropolitan Board, with a framed resolution expressing appreciation for his wide range of contributions during two exciting and ground-breaking years. Clifford Love Jr., winner of the Order of the Red Triangle Award in 1966, presented Edmund W. Turnley Sr. with this award for 1966–1967.[839]

Three campers sit by a campfire with the honorable Frank Drowota and Camp Director, Mark Weller

At the meeting, Ben Murphy, treasurer, gave the financial report. He said that, for the year ending December 31, 1966, Y income was $476,789 while expenses were $473,223. Assets stood at $1,670,994 at year-end. During the calendar year, total attendance was 619,232, Murphy said, with 16,929 different members enrolling during 1966. A total of 10,7984 sessions were held at various YMCA locations.[840]

Nineteen men and two women were elected as charter members of the new YMCA Foundation Board of Trust. Overton Thompson Jr., who wrote the charter, was elected president. Among his fellow trustees was Edward Potter Jr., chairman of the board of Commerce Union Bank, who had wrestled, swam, played handball and lifted weights at the Central YMCA for twenty years. His involvement in George Horton's barbell club contributed to Potter's life-long obsession with weight lifting.[841]

Finally, the board paid tribute to Ennis E. Murrey Sr., who died May 17. Mr. Murrey had been president of the Nashville YMCA in 1953–54 and was the retired founder and chairman of the board of First Mortgage Company.[842]

The 1967 Board Report was dedicated in his memory.

• • • • •

CHAPTER TWENTY-ONE

A Tough Capital Campaign

1967–1969

ROUPEN GULBENK was elected president of the Metropolitan Nashville YMCA at the June 28, 1967, board meeting.[843] His leadership team consisted of Wallace R. Bunn, Thomas L. Cummings Jr. and the Rev. Frank Drowota, vice-presidents; James M. Ward, secretary; and Ben R. Murphy, treasurer. Earlier in the meeting, Horace G. Hill Jr., chairman of the campaign executive committee, spoke of the impending capital campaign and then deferred to Clifford Love Jr., who made a motion that the Nashville Association conduct a capital funds campaign in 1969 for a goal of $2,985,999. The funds, if raised, would be distributed as follows:

Donelson $575,000
Downtown $525,000
East $300,000
North $575,000
Southwest $725,000

The remaining $285,000 would be spent on campaign costs, including shrinkage of pledges. The motion carried unanimously.[844]

In July, the North Nashville Branch YMCA established its office on the second floor of the Frierson Church Development Foundation Building at 1310 Jefferson Street in the heart of Nashville's African-American community. Although there was no signage to indicate the building was a YMCA, a husky young twelve-year-old Orlando Westbrook walked in a few days later and said, "I want to join the YMCA."[845]

There was tremendous use of the swimming pool at the East Branch in the summer of 1967. At Donelson and Southwest, private pools, and, in Donelson's case, also ones at motels were utilized to teach children to swim. In July, there was an Association fish fry, similar to ones held by Horace Hill Sr. in the 1920s and 1930s at Camp Sycamore. Proceeds from the fish fry went to sponsor worthy boys at Camp Widjiwagan.[846]

The highlight of the August Metropolitan YMCA executive committee was the approval of the drafting of preliminary drawings by the National YMCA Building and Furnishings Services for the proposed Downtown Branch building. Metropolitan YMCA president Roupen Gulbenk made the announcement. He said that the Board of Education had released their claim on the Richard Jones property, making that land available for a branch building. Gulbenk also informed the board that the total assets of the Association had climbed to $2,1001,964. He pointed out, however, that there were notes payable amounting to $406,000, of which $310,000 was at the East Branch, where the pool had been completed. The East Branch was running a deficit although the Association had an annual surplus of a little over $11,000.[847]

At the September board meeting, Owen Ferrell, chairman of the Camp Widjiwagan committee, recommended that the resident camp be given branch status with full privileges effective January 1, 1968. The motion was unanimously approved.

The program service committee chair reported that the YMCA, possibly for the first time in history, was working with the Juvenile Court to provide recreational services for boys incarcerated in the Juvenile Detention Center. Horace Hill Jr. reported that Hal Gibbs, capital campaign director, was pleased with progress to date on the capital campaign.[848]

Bob Freeman announced the good news at the October 1967 Metropolitan Nashville YMCA board meeting that the Board of Zoning Appeals had approved granting the YMCA a land use variance on the Donelson branch property, paving the way for the construction of a permanent branch building there.

Dr. Thomas E. Pogue announced the organization of a Y Men's Club for the Downtown North branch and a meeting to be held that evening at the Tennessee A & I cafeteria. Downtown North would have 47 members by year-end, he predicted. Jack Patterson, who gave the Southwest report, said that this board had been reorganized and revitalized during the past several months.[849]

Lloyd "Woodie" Wood announced in October that he would be leaving in February to become executive director of the Bethesda-Chevy Chase YMCA. He had come to the Nashville YMCA in 1961 as assistant physical director and became executive director of the newly organized Downtown Branch on July 1, 1965. Largely through his efforts, the Athletic Club had grown from 300 to over 750. Wood would be replaced by Gene M. Miller, the associate executive director of the Champaign, Illinois, YMCA. Earlier in his career, Miller had worked for Ralph Brunson at the Greater Lexington, Kentucky, YMCA.[850]

Fall was highlighted by YMCA Gra-Y football teams at East, Donelson, and Southwest. Before the Clinic Bowl on Thanksgiving Day, four Donelson Gra-Y teams entertained the crowd, then mostly parents, with two games of their own. The big news downtown was the most successful Old Hickory Handball Tournament in history. The YMCA's Jack Pirrie, a former Vanderbilt basketball star, made it to the semi-finals competing in a very strong field.[851]

The Largest Gift Ever

The Metropolitan Nashville YMCA annual membership meeting was held December 5. Members of the boards of management for each of the six branches (East, Donelson, Downtown, North, Southwest and Camp Widjiwagan) were elected as were directors of the Metropolitan board. The Downtown North Branch was by this time called the North Branch YMCA.

In December, Horace G. Hill Jr., president of the H.G. Hill Company and the H.G. Hill Realty Company, gave eight acres of land in Green Hills on Hillsboro Circle to the Metropolitan Nashville YMCA to be the site of the Southwest Family Branch. The tract valued at $225,000 was the largest gift ever presented to the Nashville Association. Hill said, "We are making this gift to repay at least in a small part the tremendous benefits that have come to the H. G. Hill Co. and its personnel and to the H.G. Hill family."[852]

The *Nashville Banner* praised Mr. Hill for his magnificent contribution to the forthcoming capital funds drive. The editorial read in part, "As did his father before him, he [Horace G. Hill Jr.] has worked and given in behalf of the 'Y' program as an institution of basic human benefit. His tenure as YMCA president and later as president of the Metropolitan board was an assignment of important civic responsibility to able hands. He has shared the vision, and helped materialize it, which is establishing family branches in suburban areas. His was the initial capital gift which helped make the Nashville East Y a reality."[853]

In January, Roupen Gulbenk announced that Nashville civic and business leader John S. Bransford had been named general chairman of the 1969 multi-million dollar building fund campaign. Bransford, vice-president of Bransford, Sharp and Wallace and Company, said, "I am especially grateful for the opportunity of working with my life-long friend, Horace Hill Jr., whose unselfish and unlimited devotion of time and means will unquestionably serve as an inspiration to those of us assisting in this most worthy cause." Bransford, a long-time YMCA member, had played handball at the Y when his offices were downtown.[854]

Questions regarding what to do with the Richard Jones property leasehold, the repercussions of future flooding of Sugar Tree Creek on the H. G. Hill Jr. property, and the appropriate location for a North Branch YMCA dominated the February meeting of the property committee. Decisions were made to study the Richard Jones property lease, to conduct a flood study of the Hill property, and to recommend that the North Nashville branch be built in Bordeaux, not North Nashville. The latter was done because of the existence of other welfare and social service agencies in North Nashville, and the lack of the same in Bordeaux.[855]

The capital campaign was about to heat up. Beginning in March and lasting until September, there would be an intensified effort to solicit gifts from the top 350 to 400 prospects. A public relations campaign also kicked off.[856]

In 1968, a number of people, who had made significant contributions to the Nashville Association, were recognized. Usually, they were high-profile people like William C. "Bill" Weaver Jr., whose father first brought him to the

YMCA when he was six years old. Every once in a while, however, someone well down the chain of command was also recognized. This happened to Charles Toms, the seventy-year-old African-American deluxe masseur at the athletic club, whose services Bill Weaver Jr. so long enjoyed. Charles had started working part-time at the YMCA in 1915. For forty years he held a regular job as a U.S. mail carrier moonlighting at the YMCA so that he could send his five children to college. The YMCA recognized him in 1968 "as a living example of what a man can do in America by hard work and a deep faith in God."[857]

• • • • •

In April, Ralph Brunson, Gene Miller, Julius Jones, and Grady Looney Jr. met with Judge Richard Jenkins, of the Juvenile Court, to propose two new ways the YMCA might effectively work with young boys in the Juvenile Court Detention Center. For six months, the Y had provided instruction in arts and crafts and proposed in April to work more intensively with first offenders and provide speakers once or twice a week.[858]

• • • • •

The 1968 annual meeting of the Metropolitan Nashville YMCA was held at the First Presbyterian Church on May 21. Roupen Gulbenk was reelected president. Robert K. Eby, manager of the Ford Glass Plant, was elected vice-president as were Rev. Frank F. Drowota and John M. Mihalic Jr., of Avco. James M. Ward was elected secretary and Ben R. Murphy was elected treasurer. Ralph Brunson was reelected also. Now, however, he was general executive not executive director. His title change, that took place in February, was the second such change in two years. Until 1966, the CEO's title had been general secretary.

The 300 people attending the annual meeting were surprised and pleased when John S. Bransford made the announcement that John Jay and Henry Hooker had pledged $175,000 to the capital campaign. The pledge followed the earlier gift of land valued at $250,000 from the family of Horace G. Hill Jr. In his brief remarks, something unusual for John Jay, he said he considered "the greatest gift of God the power to give and the power to share." The fourth recipient of the Order of the Red Triangle was announced that evening. The winner was Mark Bradford Jr.[859]

The gift of eight and one-half acres by the H. G. Hill Company made the Richard Jones property obsolete as a site for the branch building. Because the Southwest board had been unable to sub-let or sell the leasehold, the lease and tax payments were creating a financial burden. Accordingly, the Metropolitan board voted unanimously to take them off the hook by assuming responsibility for such payments.

Summertime at the Y

There were active summer programs at all the YMCA branches in 1968. Day camps and church softball leagues

Men's noon basketball game, Nashville YMCA

DonMcGhee (L) and Russell Brothers (R) playing handball

were two of them. One of the best was the Southwest private pool program that was conducted at eight homes, those of the W. A. Scanlon, Dr. W. Scott Jr., John Cobb, Ernest Perry, Cawthon Bowen, Benson Trimble, Eugene Wager and J. F. Hathcock families.[860]

One of the North YMCA branch's strongest supporters in 1968 was the same young man who was arrested five years earlier with three others for trying to spend the night in the downtown YMCA. How attitudes had changed over that short span of time. In 1968, thanks largely to the leadership of Ralph Brunson, the Metropolitan Nashville YMCA was considered one of the most progressive in the South.[861]

By September, the North Branch YMCA had $12,000 in membership pledges. Unfortunately, only about half that amount had been paid. As a result, the branch had a deficit through August of $3,500, an amount that the North board felt would get worse. They asked the Metropolitan board to consider building an outdoor pool and some recreational areas by the next summer, thinking that these additions would solve many of their problems.[862]

Hal Gibbs and his associate Carroll Lewis were back in town on September 21st to set up a campaign office in the old youth division of the Downtown Branch building. They employed 10 women who helped process 20,000 prospects. Approximately 1,800 volunteers would have to be recruited and trained. Within a few days, Gibbs had established a campaign budget of $74,300. Gibbs' expectation was that he would be in Nashville for seven months.[863]

Having already employed one staff member, Gene Miller, who had worked for him before, Ralph Brunson employed Jim Rayhab, then a young staff member at the Louisville YMCA. Ralph knew Rayhab when Jim worked for him in 1953 at the Louisville Y. In 1962, Ralph invited Jim to join his staff in Lexington, Kentucky. Jim accepted but changed his mind and stayed in Louisville. When Brunson offered Jim the opportunity to come to Nashville to fill the new position as business director for the Metropolitan YMCA, he warned the energetic Kentuckian not to accept if he was going to change his mind again. At the time, Jim was executive director of Louisville's St. Matthews Branch YMCA. Jim accepted and he and his wife, Delores, drove to Nashville, where his first day on the job would be January 1. When they crossed the Cumberland River and drove up Charlotte Avenue, Jim saw the vacant Colored YMCA at Fifth Avenue North. Afraid it might be the Nashville YMCA, he said to Delores, "I'm not moving to a place like this. We're going back to Louisville." Quickly, Jim realized that the Nashville YMCA was not on Charlotte but at 7th and Union. When Jim joined the Nashville YMCA, the organization had six professional staff members and only 25 employees.[864]

Camp Widjiwagan also had a new director—Robert Giesy Jr. He had been a boys' program worker at the Wesley House Center in Nashville.

The Metropolitan YMCA executive committee authorized the purchase of property next to Cumberland High School in Bordeaux on Hydes Ferry Road as the site for the North Branch for $100,000. At closing, the YMCA made a down payment of $21,000 and then paid another $29,000 on January 1, 1969. The remaining $50,000 would be paid in $5,000 annual payments at a 6 percent interest rate.[865]

A major personnel change also took place on January 1. Comer Teal, who had come to Nashville twenty-two years earlier with a dream for a YMCA family center in East Nashville, was promoted to a new position as assistant to general executive Ralph Brunson. His dream for the East Nashville Branch had come true after many years of hard work. When Teal left to join the Metropolitan YMCA staff, the branch was considered one of the finest family YMCA centers in the country. Teal was loved by literally thousands of people in East Nashville.[866]

Thanks largely to the efforts of George Cate Jr., chairman of the Christian emphasis—world service committee, and the staff, the local association reached its 1968 world service goal of $7,500—the highest ever attained by the Metropolitan Nashville YMCA. Countering this positive note, the year-end financial report that showed the Metropolitan YMCA had a $10,748.62 deficit for 1968, the first since Ralph Brunson arrived.[867]

The last order of business meeting was to approve a recommendation from the personnel committee that William "Bill" Portman, an ordained Baptist minister, be employed as executive of the East Branch. He had been executive director of the Marietta, Georgia YMCA.[868]

Julius Jones got news he wanted to hear in February when the long-range planning committee approved a change in the building plans for the North Branch building to include an outdoor swimming pool to be finished by June 1, 1969.[869] At the February Metropolitan board meeting, the Donelson Branch YMCA was granted permission to do some grading, develop outdoor recreational areas to the rear of the property, and proceed with the parking areas. Because the Donelson YMCA had no pool, its board, with the approval of the Metropolitan board, purchased for $50,000 the Hickory Bend Swimming Club on Stewart's Ferry Road, from Cousins Properties, Inc.[870] Horace Hill Jr. spoke on the campaign, saying that pattern gifts were about as expected but that large gifts had so far raised about $500,000 and "are lagging somewhat." This was the same point Gibbs had made. The public campaign kickoff was scheduled for April 8.

At the February meeting, tribute was paid to Edmund W. Turnley, who died at age 80. He had been president of the Nashville YMCA from 1945 to 1947 and had, during the war, served as president of the Nashville USO.[871]

Physical director George Horton attended the board meeting where he was given an award by Bill Weaver Jr. for his thirty-five years of "devoted and unselfish service to the YMCA by helping young men develop their bodies." Horton explained that it was a mistake to consider bar bell exercises as "weight lifting." He explained that bar bell workouts were simply calisthenics with enough weight increased gradually to develop portions of the body that needed strengthening. The only remuneration Horton received was the $5 annual fee each young man paid.[872]

The drain of $6,100 annually in taxes and lease payments on the Richard Jones property caused the Metropolitan board to give a high priority to negotiating with the Becker/Neiderhauser family to either rewrite or sell the lease.

At the March Metropolitan YMCA board of directors meeting, Mr. Hill and Mr. Gibbs both reported on the campaign which they guardedly said was going "reasonably well." Two problem areas were the failure to recruit a satisfactory number of solicitors, particularly in the big gifts division, and the slippage in that part of the campaign.[873]

Because the Donelson YMCA had no pool, its board, with the approval of the Metropolitan board, purchased for $50,000 the Hickory Bend Swimming Club on Stewart's Ferry Road, from Cousins Properties, Inc. George Volkert, the Nashville representative for the Atlanta Company, facilitated the purchase.[874]

The public campaign kicked off April 8, 1969 with the final report day scheduled for three weeks later. Mr. Hill reported for the Champaign Executive Committee to the full board on the 29th. He said that the Victory banquet would be held in one week, that pattern gifts had gone over its goal with $139,000 in gifts and pledges, but that big gifts had raised only $650,000. Hal Gibbs reported some sizeable gifts but expressed disappointment that only 250 of the 1,100 workers had made reports. There had clearly been a breakdown.

The 94th annual meeting of the Metropolitan Nashville YMCA was on May 15, once again at First Presbyterian Church. Roupen Gulbenk presided and spoke of some of the highlights during the past year. Mark Bradford presented the new officers for 1969–70 who had been elected at a board meeting held immediately prior to the annual meeting. They were George H. Cate Jr., president; John S. Bransford, Shade Murray, and James M. Ward, vice-presidents; Overton Thompson, treasurer; and Robert L. Freeman, secretary. Robert Eby, manager of the Ford Glass Plant, highlighted the 94th annual report, pointing out that the association enrolled 18,740 different members during the year and had 981 different groups use the facilities with a total attendance in 1968–69 of 730,578.

Mr. Hill briefly highlighted key events in the recently completed capital funds drive. He said that, as of May 13, the campaign had raised $2,328,000 of its $2,850,000 goal. Campaign chairman, John Bransford, presented campaign service awards to Ed Shea, Kirby Primm, Walter Ketchum, John Hanson Jr., Bill Wade, Mrs. George Cate Jr., and Dr. Thomas E. Poag. Following Bransford, Hal Gibbs and Carroll Lewis presented a 3' by 6' check to Mr. Hill for the amount raised in the campaign. Hill, in turn, presented going away gifts to Mr. and Mrs. Gibbs and Carroll Lewis.

The 1969 Capital Funds Drive, the first major campaign since 1955 when the YMCA conducted a drive to raise funds to build the East YMCA branch, failed for several reasons. One was an inability to get enough dedicated workers to make the calls. Another was the failure of the big firms division to come through. Another possibility was that the goal was overly ambitious. Of the key campaign workers, none was more disappointed than Kirby Prim, a dedicated fundraiser, particularly for the United Givers Fund. He felt the campaign failure reflected both on him personally and on Commerce Union Bank where he was a senior officer. Despite not reaching its campaign goal, the YMCA continued to progress in 1969.

Outgoing president Roupen Gulbenk had played an important role in his two years as president. More than anyone else, with the exception of Mr. Hill, he made Southwest YMCA happen. Appropriately, he received the Order of the Red Triangle, the YMCA's highest honor.[875]

Donelson-Hermitage YMCA, August 1971

Donelson and Southwest
1969–1971

THE OUTDOOR POOL at the North Branch YMCA opened on July 12, 1969. Six weeks later, more than 200 boys and girls were taught to swim there. The large swimming pool fostered the hope that more family groups and adults would use the North facilities. The enthusiasm was dampened, however, when someone threw a Coca Cola machine in the pool. The Coke machine had been inside the bathhouse that had been converted into an office and program area. This so upset Mr. Hill that he voted to withdraw support from the branch. The Metropolitan YMCA board seldom if ever challenged Mr. Hill but in this instance, they overrode his vote and voted to continue the support of the North branch.[876]

Two months before the North branch outdoor pool opened, the Donelson branch acquired the Hickory Bend pool. This caused a spike in memberships because as many as 30 family memberships were being purchased in a single day to use the pool. The private pool program at Southwest was also having another fine year.

Homer B. Gibbs Jr., Nashville YMCA president, 1974–1975

At the July Metropolitan Board meeting, Mr. Hill and Mr. Bransford reported that campaign calls were still being made and that the campaign total had risen to $2,389,804.77, an increase of $23,000 in a month. President George Cate Jr. then called on Roupen Gulbenk to report on the Richard Jones property. Since the YMCA had decided not to use the property for their Southwest branch, as was originally intended, the Becker and Neiderhauser families wanted it back. After discussion, the board approved a motion that the YMCA explore possibilities of doing that or subleasing the property, possibly to the school board. Above all, the Y would try its best to reach an agreeable settlement with the Becker/Neiderhauser family. Homer Gibbs Jr. reported for Downtown that Bill Hearn had been employed as public relations director for the branch.

Toward the end of the meeting, Ralph Brunson, who had just completed five years as CEO of the Nashville Association, expressed his gratitude for the cooperation of all the boards. He then asked President Cate to appoint a committee to consider how the association should celebrate its 100th birthday in 1975.[877]

The Metropolitan YMCA gave the Charles W. Hawkins III Company a ninety-day option to purchase the ninety-nine-year lease of the Richard Jones property. The company did not exercise the option, however. About the same time, a subcommittee was appointed to employ architects to design the Donelson, North, and Southwest branches.

Sixteen members of the Nashville YMCA's professional staff held a retreat in September at Montgomery Bell State Park. The theme was, "The Nashville YMCA In Years Ahead." One of the assignments was for each person to submit his personal goals.[878]

In September, the Metropolitan Board approved a new five-year lease of the building at 10th and Fatherland.

This extension of the East Y served over 400 youngsters in summer day camp, sponsored fifteen Gra-Y clubs reaching approximately 500 boys, and had been used during the previous school year for skating, basketball, parties, and other recreational purposes.

Harold Buchi, chairman of the new building committee, recommended three architects to design the three branch buildings. They were L. Quincey Jackson and Associates (North), Morgan and Isaac (Donelson), and Taylor and crabtree (Southwest). George Cate discussed the Southwest branch lease and the possibility of an Extendicare Center being built there. He said that negotiations with the Becker and Neiderhauser families had stalled. He would keep trying, however, as the Y certainly didn't want a lawsuit.[879]

At a building committee meeting a day before the September board meeting, chairman Buchi announced how much money from the capital funds drive was available for each branch. Donelson would get $460,000, East $240,000, Downtown $420,000, North $460,000, and Southwest $580,000. Local banks would have to make loans to fill in the gaps. Meanwhile, the branch boards were working with the building committee to plan final space budgets, with the National YMCA Building and Furnishings Service functioning as a consultant.[880] Already, the Donelson Y had purchased 16 2/3 acres on Lebanon Road and the five-year-old swimming pool on Stewarts Ferry Road for a combined cost of $82,000. The North branch had bought the 9.5 acres just north of Cumberland High for $100,000, while the Downtown Y had bought the site for its new building on McLemore for $250,000.[881]

The National Life and Accident Insurance Company sponsored the YMCA's Old Hickory Run in Warner Park on October 5. The event had grown to the point that there were three courses with distances of 11.2, 5.8, and 1.56 miles. Andy Russell, a former David Lipscomb College distance runner won the 11.2 with a time of 1 hour, 16 minutes, and 11 seconds.[882]

During the fall, Gra-Y football, Hi-Y, Jr. and Hi-Y clubs, Indian Guides, women's programs, and fitness classes were popular. In December, church basketball leagues stepped forward. The newest project was the establishment of a residence center pilot program downtown for

Tennessee Governor Winfield Dunn and admirers at the Southwest dedication, August 15, 1971

delinquent boys primarily between 15 and 18 years of age. The Urban Village, which had been started a year earlier in cooperation with the State Vocational Rehabilitation Division, was on the top floor of the YMCA building. The boys received vocational and academic training, varying from attending Pearl High School to barber school to welding.[883]

Recommendations were made at the October board meeting for approval to move forward on building plans at Donelson, North, and Southwest. The gymnasium at Donelson would be designed in such a manner that a track could later be suspended above the playing floor. The North Y would have approximately 100,000 cubic feet of space while the $300,000 building at Southwest would include a gymnasium. All three recommendations were approved.[884]

After considering two options to sell the ninety-nine-year lease on the Richard Jones property, the board voted unanimously to accept a $30,000 offer for the property with the purchaser paying the real estate fee. Before the vote, President Cate said he had been assured there would be no lawsuit. After discussion, Harold Buchi, a, member of the budget and finance committee, moved that a 1970 budget of $823,000 be accepted. The motion carried. Finally, the board approved salary increases for the next year and the retirement of the legendary Comer Teal.[885]

The big story in December was that the Old Hickory Handball Tournament chaired by Dr. Jim Wilson was a huge success and deemed one of the best in the South. In addition to 70 of the top players in the Nashville area, participants came in from across the country. Nashville YMCA members Lloyd Wood and Jack Pirrie won the doubles championship.

At year-end, the YMCA Foundation, the name of the YMCA endowment fund since 1967, had gifts totaling nearly $7,000. A number of those had been made in memory of Charles M. Gray, general secretary of the Nashville YMCA from 1949 until his retirement in 1964. He had died recently. At the December board meeting, a resolution was adopted lauding Gray for the inspiration and leadership he demonstrated during his fifteen-year tenure as general secretary.[886]

The Most Meaningful YMCA in the Southeast

The deficit concerns, expressed at the December board meeting, were real. When the year-end financial reports came out in January, the association had a deficit of $13,116. The directors realized that last-ditch efforts to avoid annual deficits did not work. Deficit problems had to be addressed much earlier in the year.

President Cate wrote a January letter to members and supporters of the YMCA in which he looked forward with confidence to the challenges of the new decade. The board members all received a detailed report of the accomplishments of the last decade and goals to be accomplished in 1970 and by the centennial year of 1975. The theme of being strong in "Spirit, Mind and Body" was emphasized.

The first week in February, Ralph Brunson received a cherished letter from Richard W. MacMorran, executive director of the Southeast Region of the YMCA in Atlanta. MacMorran wrote, "I wanted to tell you that from where I sit the Nashville YMCA is becoming the most meaningful YMCA in terms of modern issues that we have in the Southeast Region. I appreciate it personally and feel that your example gradually will spread to many others who have similar opportunities but apparently lack the courage or insight to take advantage of them." One of the issues MacMorran had in mind was the Nashville YMCA's courageous embrace of integration since Ralph became general executive.[887]

The 1970 membership drive directed by Y staffer Bill Hearn, went over the top, reaching 104 percent of its goal. Chairman Douglas Henry Jr. and more than 100 fellow volunteers got it done.

Willie Caruth, who had been the motivating force behind the Urban Village since its inception, officially assumed responsibility for its operation. Soon thereafter, the Metropolitan board approved a contract between the Tennessee Vocational Rehabilitation Department and the YMCA to jointly run the Urban Village.

Bob Giesy took over responsibility for the Camp Widjiwagan branch in March. Over at Southwest, a pavilion was nearly completed, construction had begun on two tennis courts, and a road was being built into the property. The Southwest leadership was disappointed when a Louisville firm withdrew its offer to purchase the Richard Jones property lease. Fortunately, the local Harpeth Land Company stepped up with a similar offer. Unfortunately, that fell through also.[888]

In March, the nominating committee presented the following slate of officers for the 1970–71 year: James M. "Jim" Ward, president; John S. Bransford, Beverly W.

Landstreet III, and Thomas E. Baldridge, vice-presidents; Overton Thompson, treasurer; and C. Raymond Thombs, secretary. The slate was accepted by acclamation.

At the April 22 board meeting, the directors delegated authority to the general executive and the president to act as they deemed best with regard to the sale of the ninety-nine-year lease on Richard Jones. The board was clearly ready to dispose of it. The Metropolitan Board also gave Welty & Woods, of Atlanta, an option on the Downtown branch property for 120 days. Before the option expired, Welty & Woods made an offer. Their project would include a Hyatt-Regency Hotel with an adjoining parking garage. Stipulations were that the YMCA would have air rights over the garage where the association could build their new building, and that, until Welty & Woods broke ground, the operation of the downtown YMCA would not be interrupted. The Y voted to sell the property to Welty & Woods for $550,000. Mr. Hill dissented. He felt the YMCA should remain on its present site for several more years and then move to the Church and McLemore site when they had more cash.[889] Welty & Woods came to the YMCA's attention when board member Overton Thompson Jr., called Ralph Brunson one day and asked, "Are you really interested in selling the Downtown building?" Brunson replied, "We certainly are." Thompson then said, "I'm sending a couple of gentlemen, Messrs. Welty & Woods, developers from Atlanta, up to see you." They came and talked with Brunson and the "ball then began to roll."[890]

At the YMCA's 95th annual meeting on May 14, 1970, a memorial service was held for three YMCA stalwarts—Robert Creighton, Shade Murray, and Charles Gray. Creighton, a member of the board, had been big gifts chairman of the 1969 capital funds campaign. Ray Thombs, secretary of the association, said of Gray, "He went about doing a lot of good, salvaging the lives of countless men and boys who sing his praises." Shade Murray was remembered for his enthusiasm and hearty laugh. He had been a vice-president.

Awards were also given to the living—Order of the Red Triangle to George H. Cate Jr., and others, including man of the year, service to youth, and community service. The new officers, led by James M. Ward, were installed.

During the meeting, Horace Hill Jr. moved that Homer Gibbs Jr. be elected to serve a three-year term on the Metropolitan board. Already a member of the finance committee, Homer would still be active, as a member of the YMCA Foundation board 40 years later. In December 2010, he and his wife, Barry, would receive the H. G. Hill Philanthropic Award at the Heritage Club dinner.[891]

It was hard to believe that 1970 would be the 17th season that Camp Widjiwagan had operated at Standing Stone State Park. The Camp Widjiwagan board held a fish fry to raise money for camper scholarships.[892]

Then in June, Grady Looney Jr., resigned from the YMCA staff to accept the position of general director of a new independent YMCA in Hendersonville, TN, that had been chartered by the national association on March 2. Over the previous seven years, Grady had made many friends and contributions to the association and Camp Widjiwagan. Grady would find the Hendersonville assignment would be extremely difficult. In 1972, the association disbanded with some of its programs taken over by the East YMCA.[893]

Ralph Brunson received a letter of intent in 1970 from the State Department of Vocational Rehabilitation to continue the Urban Village. The behavioral modification program seemed to be working. Chuck Harris, a Vanderbilt Divinity School graduate, ran the village. As soon as Harris came aboard, he realized that everyday he was coming face to face with a drug problem not only with the boys in his Urban Village but also on the streets of Nashville. To learn how to better deal with this problem, he attended a Drug Abuse Conference in Birmingham in May 1971.[894]

Finally, on July 7, the Southwest branch began construction on its family branch YMCA. The contract for $157,875 went to Alexander & Shankle. Included would be club and committee rooms, boardroom, lounge, central offices, program director's and executive director's offices, lobby, and locker and shower rooms for men and women. When another $86,000 could be raised, they would build a gymnasium. Already constructed were a pavilion, two tennis courts, an athletic field, and an outdoor running track. Jim Henson was executive director.[895]

The Donelson family center facility did not get off the starting block as fast as Southwest. The lowest bid came in at $104,000 higher than the architect's estimate. This resulted in a redesign that set the project back several months. When financing was worked out, the Metropolitan board gave Donelson the go ahead and, in September, approved awarding of the contract to Alexander & Shankle for $207,469.[896]

In August, the YMCA learned that it had prevailed in Chancery Court on the issue of the association's legal right to sell its leasehold on the Richard Jones property. This opened the door to sell the leasehold for $50,000. There should have been a standing ovation. A funding plan to pay for the gymnasium at Southwest was also approved thus allowing the construction of the gymnasium to go forward.

The Donelson board recommended in October that the name of that branch be changed to the Donelson-Hermitage Family Branch to better reflect where its members lived. The motion was approved as was a motion by Allen M. Steele, chairman of the Metropolitan personnel committee, to adopt salary ranges for all YMCA employees.[897]

The continuing financial strain at the North Family Branch YMCA forced the board and its chairman Dr. Thomas E. Poag to make changes to alleviate the growing problem. Effective September 1, Julius Jones was appointed director of Urban Services while continuing to carry responsibility as executive director of the North branch. Poag said other staff reductions and realignments would be put in effect. In October, the branch board asked the Metropolitan Board to 1) close the existing office on Jefferson Street; 2) change the name of the branch to the Bordeaux Family YMCA and to change their constituent area from North Nashville to north of the Cumberland River; and 3) construct outdoor recreational and fitness areas such as a running track, tennis and basketball courts, and a softball diamond. If approved, responsibility for serving North Nashville would go to the Urban Services Department of the Metropolitan YMCA. The Metropolitan board approved the proposal in principal and asked the appropriate committees to implement the changes.[898] The name "Bordeaux Family YMCA" did not last long. By June 1971, the branch was referred to as the "Bordeaux-North Family YMCA."

Donelson had its funding plan together by November to pay for their gymnasium, shower and dressing rooms. The Metropolitan board approved the $85,000 project with the stipulation that the need for $32,000 in furniture and fixtures be re-examined.

The annual membership enrollment to begin January 18 and conclude February 12 was particularly important because 1970 had been an extremely tough year financially. The year-ending deficit was $50,769.56 increasing the accumulated deficit to $69,951.46. This would be the largest deficit in Ralph Brunson's long career in Nashville. The strains and stresses of a tough economic year, coupled with challenges of raising money in a year following a successful capital funds campaign, losses at East and Bordeaux, where medium household incomes were much lower than at any of the other branches, and a shrinking membership caused a difficult financial dilemma that took months to turn around. Major adjustments were made and the association would show a $12,732 surplus in 1971.

Mr. Hill Declines Honor

The 1971 membership goal was to enroll 2,090 new and renewal members.[899] The four-year-old YMCA Foundation had slowly grown to $9,645, largely through small memorial gifts in memory of deceased YMCA members.[900]

At the January board meeting, the general secretary announced the results of a poll taken by mail on whether or not to name the new Southwest Family YMCA building for Horace G. Hill Jr. The result was unanimous in favor of naming the building for Mr. Hill. Nothing came of this, however, as Mr. Hill would not agree to the change. Planning was also underway for the celebration of the association's 100 anniversary in 1975. Mr. Hill's sisters, Mrs. Wentworth Caldwell and Mrs. William E. Pennick, made generous gifts to underwrite the cost of an appropriate person writing the history of the Metropolitan Nashville YMCA. The idea was for the book to be published during the Centennial year, which would be named *All Together, A History of the Nashville YMCA 1875–1975*.[901]

By February, progress on the Donelson-Hermitage Family YMCA building was moving along nicely. All pre-stressed concrete beams were in place and most of the outside brickwork was completed. The building was targeted to open June 15. The Southwest branch building was a little further along with its opening date scheduled for mid-May. By then, Gene Miller, Downtown branch executive, had also assumed responsibility for the Southwest Branch. Wayne Blackwelder, of the Downtown staff, also joined the Southwest branch temporarily to help get it open.

Because the Southwest and Donelson branches needed help in paying for the construction and furnishing of their new buildings, the Metropolitan Board approved the borrowing of a sum not to exceed $400,000 to accomplish those objectives. The board assigned all pledges to the capital funds drive as collateral. With an existing loan of $183,000, the indebtedness totaled $583,000. At the same meeting, the board approved a motion that: "We reaffirm our commitment to the allocations to branches originally established, as reduced proportionally by shrinkage in payments." This was done because of a concern that all building fund pledges would be "locked up" by the banks to cover the loan for the construction of the Southwest and Donelson branches.[902]

• • • • •

After the successful Old Hickory Invitational the previous October, the Nashville Striders, the Downtown YMCA and the National Life and Accident Insurance Company teamed up to jointly sponsor the inaugural Music City Open on April 10 in Percy Warner Park. Runners could choose any of four distances from 1.56 miles to a 26-mile marathon that would include both the Park roads and Belle Meade Boulevard.

• • • • •

Ralph Brunson decided to bring together quarterly the senior leadership of the Metropolitan board and all branch boards to work on common objectives and help solve some of the difficult problems facing the association. Those invited included the top volunteer and professional staff members from each branch. When they first met in March, Ralph told them "The YMCA looks at problems and sees opportunities." Brunson also urged his team to "batten down the hatches" with regard to expenses. He named the group the "First President's Council.

In its first sixteen weeks of existence, the Urban Village was gaining traction. By the placement of a number of boys in jobs, the program was garnering the respect of State and Metro probation officers. Rusty Yeoman came on board to replace Scott Davis as counselor of the 20 boys then housed on the 7th floor of the Downtown branch.[903]

Welty & Woods and the YMCA met and agreed on new terms for the sale of the Downtown YMCA facility. In a letter to Ralph Brunson, dated May 26, an attorney for Welty & Woods spelled out those terms:

- Welty & Woods would complete the outright purchase of the YMCA property for $800,000; and

- The YMCA would have the right to remain on the premises until May 1, 1972.

At the board of directors meeting, held in the Southwest Branch at 6 p.m. Thursday, May 27, 1971, prior to the association's 96th annual meeting, a motion was passed that the "board approve the recommendation of the Property Committee that we authorize the sale of the downtown property for $800,000, retaining title to any equipment in the building needed in the new building, with a contract to be entered into within ten (10) days, closing by August 15, and earnest money of $40,000."

The Nominating Committee then submitted the following slate of officers for 1971–72: Robert L. Freeman, president; Thomas E. Baldridge, president elect; Homer B. Gibbs Jr., vice-president; Beverly W. Landstreet III, vice-president; Sydney F. Keeble Jr., treasurer; and C. Raymond Thombs, secretary.

The slate was accepted by acclamation. Six men were re-elected to serve for three years and nine new board members were elected. They included Dr. Dorothy Brown, a well-known and highly respected African-American physician, and Mrs. Alex "Chippy" Pirtle, a civic leader and former president of the Junior League. They were welcomed as the first women elected to the Nashville YMCA Board of Directors in its 96th year history.[904]

The new officers were presented at the annual meeting, the highlight of which was a multi-media film dramatization, If You Are Not Part of The Solution, You Are Part of The Problem. This presentation highlighted the Nashville YMCA's urban programs.[905]

Camp Widjiwagan began its 1971 session on June 21. There were three two-week sessions during the summer with a total capacity of 240 boys. Scholarship campers accounted for 93 of the 231 campers enrolled as of the first week in June.[906]

Despite having agreed to vacate the downtown site at 7th and Union Street by May 1, 1972, the Metropolitan YMCA Board was still undecided whether to build at McLemore and Church Street or build at 8th and Union on property owned by the National Life and Accident Insurance Company. The board had given up on the idea of building on top of the hotel parking garage.

The Bordeaux-North board felt left out without a building and not knowing where they would get the $214,000 it would take to build one, not counting furniture or a gymnasium. Nevertheless, they were determined to serve their community and to never give up or lose sight of their building goals.

CHAPTER TWENTY-THREE

New Downtown Center Becomes a Reality

1971–1974

BERT HAYWOOD, chairman of the Downtown branch board, probably surprised some Metropolitan board members when he advised them at the July 7, 1971, board meeting that the Downtown Branch recommended that the YMCA build on the lot at the southwest corner of Union and Eighth Avenue North owned by National Life. The life insurance company, when approached earlier by the YMCA about the possibility of buying that lot, said that they would trade the Union Street property for the land the YMCA owned on McLemore and Church Street as they felt the two properties were of equal value. In addition, National Life agreed to contribute $50,000 to the Metropolitan Nashville YMCA. One of the factors that led the Downtown Branch to its decision was the fact that 82 percent of the people who came to the Downtown YMCA walked and that the 8th and Union site would be a shorter walk for nearly all of them. Mr. Haywood's motion to build on the National Life property, received a second. After an energized discussion, a substitute motion was made to refer the issue to the Metropolitan board property committee. This motion carried. Before adjourning, a decision was made to have both properties appraised. Bob Freeman had survived his first board meeting as president.[907]

The Metropolitan board decided to hold the dedications of their new buildings at Donelson-Hermitage and Southwest on the same day—Sunday, August 15, 1971. George Cate Jr. gave the dedicatory address at Donelson-Hermitage at 4:30 p.m. while Gov. Winfield Dunn did the same at Southwest at 2 p.m. There were tours of both buildings following the ceremonies.[908]

Southwest YMCA, August 1971

After the 1971 camping season at Camp Widjiwagan, its director, Bob Giesy, resigned to accept a camp position with a Methodist Church in Alexandria, VA. His last YMCA camp was one of his most successful with 244 campers.

In August the executive and finance committees grappled with the problems at the Bordeaux-North branch due to low incomes, racial concerns, and the fact that the branch received no support from the white community. There were no longer any white people on the Bordeaux-North board and the branch board members felt they were unable to afford the size of the mortgage they would need to build a new center. Their conclusion was that the property should be sold or the Metropolitan board put it to whatever use they liked. At the joint committee meeting, someone pointed out that there was an obligation by the Nashville community at large to help disadvantaged youth in the Bordeaux-North service area. A motion was passed that the YMCA should meet with the people in the area before reaching a decision.[909]

With unfinished buildings, considerable indebtedness and a need to expand into neglected areas in greater Nashville, the Metropolitan board authorized Bob Freeman and Ralph Brunson to seek permission of the United Givers Fund to hold another capital funds drive in 1975, the 100th anniversary year of the local association.

In the meantime, it seemed prudent to refinance the YMCA's debt. The board approved doing so in August, authorizing a mortgage loan not to exceed $225,000 at 8 percent for twenty years from Fidelity Federal to refinance present obligations and pay for the construction of a track and outdoor pool at Southwest. The board also voted to increase the family membership fee at Southwest to $200 a year, effective immediately. Within a month, the Southwest branch board changed its mind about the pool, deciding that an indoor-outdoor pool would be much more helpful in attracting new members than an outdoor pool. This would cost an additional $30,000 and could be ready by January. After much discussion, the Metropolitan board approved the change in September.

The board had already approved in August spending up to $15,000 for the design of the proposed downtown building at McLemore and church Street.[910] So, the decision regarding which site to select had finally been made. By October, detailed drawings were well underway and scheduled for completion by November 1. Contract documents were to be completed by December 1 and bids let December 15.[911] Sometime before plans were set, Dr. Thomas F. Frist Jr. offered to fly Kent Rea to Dallas to look at Kenneth Cooper's Clinic there. Kent met Dr. Frist at the Nashville airport at 6 a.m. the next morning. Dr. Frist piloted his plane that got back to Nashville before supper.[912]

Wayne Blackwelder had performed sufficiently well at Southwest that, effective October 1, he was named acting executive director of the branch, allowing Gene Miller to give 100 percent of his time to the Downtown branch.[913]

The Christian emphasis committee was active in 1971. Its chairman was the Rev. Robert H. Spain. In September the committee asked all the branches to implement the following policy:

- Appoint a committee to carry on Christian emphasis and World Service program;
- Work with churches in each branch area through YMCA members who are members in those churches;
- Have an annual banquet or special event to promote world service or the Christian emphasis programs; and
- Display the Christian flag, along with the American flag, in each branch.[914]

The YMCA still had not closed with Welty & Woods on the downtown property causing the anxiety level to rise in the Metropolitan YMCA boardroom. Attorneys for the firm assured Brunson that they would close by October 15.[915] Their plan was to build a twenty-seven-story Hyatt Regency Hotel on the site. The hotel construction was expected to take two years.

Watching developments at Southwest energized the Donelson board to want to make their new facility a full-service facility. Consequently, they petitioned the new building committee to recommend an overhead running track in the gymnasium, two saunas, two tennis courts, a handball court, exercise equipment, and further development of the outdoor recreational area at Donelson-Hermitage. The building committee and the Metropolitan board approved a mortgage loan of up to $150,000 to pay for these additions. This inflated the amount the YMCA owed banks to $432,000.[916]

One hundred twenty runners participated in the 3rd annual Old Hickory Invitational at Percy Warner Park, sponsored by the Downtown YMCA and National Life. MTSU won the college division.

Over in East Nashville, a Leaders Club was formed at the 10th and Fatherland outpost. They conducted classes in tumbling, weightlifting, and basketball. Gra-Y football leagues were active at several branches. Donelson-Hermitage had 16 teams in the league.

Welty & Woods requested a thirty-day extension on the close date due to a problem with the title to adjacent property they were buying from Castner-Knott Department Store. This request was approved. The board also voted to sell a five-foot strip of land along Hillsboro Circle Road to the Metropolitan Government as part of a road-widening project. The board additionally authorized having an appraisal made of the Donelson-Hermitage branch's Hickory Bend Swimming pool in anticipation of selling it and using the proceeds to build needed facilities at the center. Finally, the board asked each branch to establish a building maintenance program.[917]

Toward year-end, the YMCA Foundation reported that two recent wills and other gifts brought the total under management to $21,000. A trend was set when Roupen Gulbenk, former president of the Metropolitan YMCA board, was named chairman of the foundation board.[918]

One Step Closer

In January, Mrs. Bess (E. Louis) Cochran began gathering facts, pictures, and old records in preparation for writing the one-hundred-year history of the Metropolitan Nashville YMCA. Mrs. Cochran, who once wrote a column on advice to the lovelorn for the Memphis Commercial Appeal under the name Cynthia Gray, also wrote, in 1968, the twenty-five year history of Nashville's Woodmont Christian Church. To facilitate her research, she was given an office in the Metropolitan YMCA offices. She guessed that she would actually begin writing in September and that it would take her twelve months to complete the task.[919]

About the same time, the State Department of Vocational Rehabilitation evaluated the YMCA Urban Village and concluded the YMCA was still providing excellent rehabilitative services to the community.[920]

When Nashvillians read the *Nashville Tennessean* on February 16, 1972, they learned that the Downtown YMCA was one step closer to reality with the awarding of the construction contract to Alexander & Shankle, whose bid of $1,074,000 was the lowest of eight submitted. Robert L. Freeman, president of the Metropolitan Nashville YMCA said, "We've been in the heart of Nashville for over 61 years and our new building will keep us here. Hopefully, plans can get underway in time

Douglas Henry Jr. (R) presenting the YMCA Man of the Year Award to James M. Ward (L) on May 27, 1971 in the Southwest Branch's new building. Photo courtesy of Grannis Photography.

to vacate the existing facilities by September 15 of this year." The four-story brick structure would have, at street level, a lobby, administrative offices, and athletic clubs. There would be eight handball courts, twice as many as in the current building, and a large gymnasium on the second floor. Two of the handball courts would have glass walls for spectators. An indoor track would rim the gymnasium. Finally, there would be a swimming pool and an outdoor track on the roof. There would be no residential apartments for the first time since 1912.[921]

A week later, the executive committee opened bids for the Bordeaux-North's new building. The low bid of $246,596 was considered too high so the members voted to ask the architect L. Quincey Jackson to scale back the plans so that new bids could be obtained in two weeks.[922] A month later, CTC Construction dropped their bid by $15,000 to $232,332, prompting the executive committee to accept it.

On March 1, the Metropolitan Nashville YMCA bid goodbye to Julius Jones, associate general executive and acting executive of the Bordeaux North YMCA. He had accepted an appointment as the executive director of the central branch of the Washington, DC, YMCA. Jones had been a trailblazer in his almost five years in Nashville. He had been the first African-American to hold the executive directorship of a branch at a YMCA in the Southeast. With help from Ralph Brunson, Jones had organized the board, developed a program from scratch, changed the image of an old, impaired Colored

YMCA to a Bordeaux North Family YMCA, and represented the Nashville YMCA well on the Southeast Region and National YMCA Councils, boards and committees.[923] Jones was replaced by Milton Ivy as executive director of the Bordeaux North YMCA.

A proposed lease between the YMCA Law School and the YMCA was discussed and approved at the April board meeting. Under the agreement, the YMCA Law School would pay the YMCA $50,000 in advance to pay for finishing up space in the basement for the law school that would lease for twenty years at an annual rental of $4,800 annually.

Taylor and Crabtree made an inspection of the progress of the construction on the Downtown branch on May 12. They reported to Ralph Brunson that most concrete columns had been poured on the second floor, that the retaining wall from Church Street to the building had been poured, and that the electrical work in the second floor slab was in progress. All in all, Floyd Bowles, of Taylor and Crabtree, said the project was progressing extremely well.[924]

Kenton "Kent" Rea succeeded Ralph Reynolds as the YMCA's physical director on May 2, 1972. A Sewanee graduate in the class of 1957, Kent began his YMCA career at the Louisville YMCA in 1959, where his first job was coaching the Y's new wrestling team. From there, he went to the YMCA in Covington, Ky., his hometown. Kent's next stop was in Jacksonville, where he was physical director from 1966 until 1972.

Ralph Brunson convinced Kent to come to the Nashville YMCA to open and manage the new downtown center's physical fitness center under fellow Kentuckian Jim Rayhab, director of the Downtown facility. Brunson promised Kent that, if he did well, he would promote him to associate general director, which happened.[925]

The 97th annual meeting and awards dinner was held at the Hillwood Country Club on May 16, 1972. Andy Holt, the popular past president of the University of Tennessee, was the featured speaker. The officers and board members for the upcoming 1972–73 season were presented and awards for the previous year given. The new officers were: Thomas E. Baldridge, president; Sydney F. Keeble Jr., president-elect; Dr. James M. Brakefield, Homer B. Gibbs Jr., and V. E. New, vice-presidents; C. Ray Thombs, treasurer; and among the new officers was Mrs. Alex "Chippy" Pirtle Jr., secretary. Chippy thus became the first woman ever elected an officer of the Metropolitan Nashville YMCA.

Russell W. Brothers presented Dr. James M. Hudgins, M.D., with the Order of the Red Triangle Award at the annual meeting. Dr. Hudgins had been an active member of the YMCA Foundation Board since its inception in 1967, served on the Metropolitan board of directors for several years, and been a diligent campaigner and generous donor during the East Family Branch campaign in 1960 and the Metropolitan Nashville YMCA campaign in 1969. He had served as chairman of the East Family Branch and had served on virtually every committee at the East branch.[926]

Andy Holt thoroughly enjoyed speaking at the YMCA annual meeting. A week later, he wrote Ralph Brunson, "I am quite sincere when I express the opinion that no city in our land has a finer YMCA program than yours. It was a real pleasure to witness the enthusiasm of your staff and members and to see at least a few of the marvelous fruits of your labors."[927]

Concerned that the YMCA's Urban Village would be without a home on September 15, 1972 when the association had to vacate the building at 7th Ave. North and Union Street, Bob Freeman agreed to purchase the vacated Episcopal Church of the Advent at 17th Avenue South and Edgehill that the YMCA could lease for a year with an option to renew the lease for another year at a cost of $600 per month. The lease would also include an option clause that would allow the YMCA to purchase the property anytime during the two-year period for $75,000. The directors gratefully accepted Mr. Freeman's generous offer. At the time, the Rev. Bill Sherman, minister of Woodmont Baptist Church,[928] was chairman of the Inner City committee that supervised the Urban Village. Chuck Harris and Rusty Yeomans, both graduates of Vanderbilt Divinity School, ran the project with dedication and skill. In 1974, with help from the State Division of Vocational Rehabilitation and a Federal grant, the Nashville YMCA was able to buy Urban Village from Bob Freeman's brother, Richard Freeman.[929]

Juvenile Court referee Wendell S. Cooke Jr., referee of the Davidson County Juvenile Court, wrote Rector George J. Kuhnert, rector of the Church of the Advent, urging him to sell the property to the YMCA. He wrote that few people or institutions are willing to take a chance on delinquent youngsters once they reach the age of sixteen or so but that the YMCA was doing exactly this through the Urban Village and that the continuance of the program was important to the community.[930]

As the contractor's newest projection was that the

YMCA would not be able to move into their new building until December 15, the bigger problem was where the Downtown branch would move for the three months they would be without a home. National Life once again stepped forward by advising the YMCA that they had available space in their old building having moved to their new thirty-one-story building next door. The YMCA, grateful for the offer, accepted at a cost of $550 per month. The move date was September 9.[931]

The YMCA changed its board structure in 1972 by creating four councils: Budget-Finance, Financial Development, Operations, and Program Activity. In a related move, the Downtown Board would have the following functions: Athletic Club operations, Urban Village operations, and public relations.[932]

• • • • •

For the first time in history, the Metropolitan Nashville YMCA combined its Widjiwagan Camp program with that of another Metropolitan YMCA. That summer, Nashville YMCA boys went to the Chattanooga Association camp Ovoca on the Ocoee River. This meant that Camp Widjiwagan after 20 years of operation at Standing Stone State Park, had completed its long run. The move was expected to save money.[933]

• • • • •

Despite the three-month delay in moving in the new building, things were beginning to fall in place. Members of the YMCA Law School presented their check for $50,000 to complete their rooms in the new building. A decision was made to name the general executive's office for former general executive Charles M. Gray. The Urban Village moved on September 1 and 2 to its new location at 17th and Edgehill. A week later, the downtown and metropolitan offices moved to the 9th floor of the old National Life Building. A little chagrined by their debt load, the executive committee voted to not construct any more buildings until the money was in hand to build them. The board was already committed to borrowing an amount not to exceed $700,000 for the construction of the Downtown and the Bordeaux-North branches.[934] Because the YMCA's policy was to rotate its bank accounts between the city's three major banks, Sydney Keeble Jr., recommended that all three banks—First American National, Commerce Union, and Third National participate equally in the loan.[935]

A physical education committee was authorized in October 1972 by the Metropolitan YMCA Board of Directors. Staff member Kent Rea would advise the committee. One of the committee's components was a physical fitness-testing program, temporarily set up in the YMCA, for all members. The committee also sponsored the annual Old Hickory Run that had, in 1972, a record 220 participants and saw all course records broken.[936]

Some of the year's major accomplishments were these:

- Plans were laid for a $2–2.5 million capital funds drive;
- The YMCA sold the Downtown building for $800,000;
- The YMCA moved its Metropolitan and Downtown offices to the new building in December; and
- The YMCA exchanged the Donelson-Hermitage's outdoor pool on Stewart's Ferry Road to Hooper Realty Co for an indoor-outdoor pool and bathhouse beside the new Donelson-Hermitage Building.[937]

Thankfully, the Metropolitan Nashville YMCA had a small surplus for 1972 of $3,543.14, reversing a discouraging trend. Brunson was relieved.

One bit of unfinished business at the old YMCA building, then nearly demolished, was to remove the cornerstone and move it to an adjacent parking lot where it was opened. This took place on November 3. Present were Thomas E. Baldridge, president of the Metropolitan YMCA; E. M. "Bert" Haywood, immediate past chairman of the Downtown branch; Mrs. Louis (Bess White) Cochran, YMCA historian and future author of *All Together, A History of the Nashville YMCA 1875–1975*; and Robert L. "Bob" Freeman, chairman of the Metropolitan new building committee. Found in the cornerstone were a 1910 city directory, a history of Nashville up to 1910, a photograph of the ground-breaking ceremony in 1910, two copies of the September 10, 1910, the *Nashville Tennessean*, a September 1910 issue of the *Confederate Veteran*, a memorial tribute to John Bostick Ransom, a booklet about the YWCA, and a YMCA booklet entitled "The Making of a Man."[938]

Ninety-Seven Years of Service

When the New Year dawned, the Metropolitan Nashville YMCA had been in continuous existence for 97 years. The 98th year was special in that, for the first time, the association had an approved budget that exceeded $1 million. Income and expenses for 1973 was approved at $1,221,275 each.[939]

At the December meeting of the Metropolitan board, a decision was reached to move from monthly to quarterly

Outgoing Nashville President Robert L. Freeman accepting the gold key to the old downtown building from Mrs. Jesse E. "Ellen" Wills on January 28, 1973. Ellen's father, Dr. Matt G. Buckner, had been given the key when the building was dedicated on February 24, 1912.

meetings. With a strong board, active committees and competent staff members, twelve annual meetings were deemed unnecessary.[940]

Another innovation came about on January 1 when the Nashville YMCA began operating under a new management policy that allowed family members of all branch YMCAs to use any other family branch under one management plan. The only requirement was that a member must join the YMCA Family Branch in his or her own geographic area. The four centers involved in this plan were Bordeaux-North, East, Donelson-Hermitage, and Southwest.

January was exciting. First, Jimmy French's membership drive was wonderfully successful. On December 26 when the physical fitness center opened, the Downtown branch had 824 members. By January 11, this number had jumped to 1,204. In a little over two weeks, the Downtown YMCA received 317 new members and 63 renewals for a total of 380. It should be said that some of those new members were actually former members who dropped out for the nearly three months when the Downtown branch was without a building. A little later in the year, the membership climbed to 1,400.[941]

The other good news came when William C. Weaver Jr., Chairman of the Board of the National Life and Accident Insurance Company, announced that the company would begin immediately subsidizing the memberships of company employees in the YMCA, YWCA, and YMHA on a sliding scale. After five years of employment, National Life would pay 25 percent of all dues. After ten years of employment, the company would pay 50 percent of the dues, and, after fifteen years of employment, 75 percent of the dues. In a cover letter to Ralph Brunson, Weaver, a former YMCA board member and the son of a YMCA president, said, "my father took me to the YMCA when I was a small boy and I have participated in its many programs practically all of my life. I can say without qualification it has had a real influence on my life and I have gotten much more out of the program than I have contributed to it."[942]

When the New Year dawned, the Metropolitan Nashville YMCA had been in continuous existence for 97 years. The 98th year was special in that, for the first time, the association had an approved budget that exceeded $1 million. Income and expenses for 1973 was approved at $1,221,275 each.[943]

Chuck Harris' Urban Village, in its fourth year of operation, was going strong, and was, by January, a complete rehabilitation program for boys from 15 to 18 years of age, who were referred to Urban Village from the juvenile courts. The former sanctuary had been converted into a gymnasium and the parish house into a dorm with lounge, kitchen, dining, and office facilities.[944]

On a rainy January 28, a group assembled in the open courtyard of the new YMCA at 1100 Church Street to insert the same cornerstone [actually a metal box] that had been placed 62 years earlier in the old building, in the wall of the new Metropolitan YMCA building. This was followed at 3 p.m. by a formal dedication service in the gym, and an open house. YMCA Metropolitan Board President-elect Sydney Keeble Jr. presided. Ralph Brunson spoke as did Lloyd H. Griffin, chairman of the Downtown board of managers. Dr. Nat Winston, the Freeman Trio, and Fred Waller provided the music. Richard W. MacMorran represented the Southeast Regional Council in Atlanta at the event. Robert L. "Bob" Freeman, chairman of the new building committee and immediate past president of the Metropolitan Board, formally accepted the new building when Bill Alexander, the contractor, presented him with the key to the building. Ellen (Mrs. Jesse E.) Wills, daughter of Dr. Matthew G. Buckner, YMCA president from 1904 to 1914, was present. She had donated glass cabinets to display memorabilia collected throughout the YMCA's history. The cabinets were placed at the end of the first floor hallway in the new building. The area was set up as a memorial to Dr. Buckner. A plaque was placed on the wall in his memory.[945] Alf Adams gave his reminiscences of the opening of the old building in 1912. R. L. Wagner, president of the National Life and

Accident Insurance Company, and a Metropolitan YMCA board member, gave the dedicatory address.[946]

One person who was not at the dedication was Horace G. Hill Jr. A very conservative man, he still vigorously opposed selling the old YMCA building and building the new one on Church Street at McLemore. Mr. Hill hated debt, which the YMCA had incurred to finance numerous projects, and was nowhere to be seen on dedication day.[947] Horace would feel better in 1979 when his nephew Wentworth Caldwell Jr. was elected to the Metropolitan board.

The Metropolitan YMCA and the Donelson-Hermitage YMCA board members were jolted when they received the news that Robert L. "Bob" Freeman killed himself on April 10. That Bob had been suffering from depression for some time was not known to most of his friends. His widow, Ginny, eulogized her husband with these words, "I believe that in God's divine plan, men are destined to do certain things. Bob was given a large assignment and he did it well. He worked overtime and finished early…Bob did more in his allotted 45 years than most could do in twice that time." In addition to being chairman of the Donelson YMCA board, which branch he helped found, and president of the Metropolitan Nashville YMCA, Bob was chairman of the new building committee that oversaw the construction of the YMCA's magnificent new building. In 1972, he was the 1971–72 Nashville YMCA "Man of the Year." He also had been in the real estate business for 25 years, winning Realtor of the Year awards in 1961 and 1968.[948]

The following officers for the 1973–74 fiscal year were nominated in April: Sydney Keeble Jr., president; Homer B. Gibbs Jr., president-elect; Dr. James Brakefield, Dr. Elbert Brooks, and Stanley D. Overton, all vice-presidents; William "Bill" Henderson, treasurer; Mrs. Alex "Chippy" Pirkle Jr., secretary; and Mrs. Lipscomb "Florence" Davis Jr., assistant secretary.[949] Mrs. Pirtle, an excellent committee person, had recruited Florence to join the board in 1972 and to become her assistant.

Supporting the volunteers under Ralph Brunson, who was responsible for the Operations Council, were three associate general directors: Jim Rayhab, responsible for the Financial Administration Council; Gene Miller, Financial Development Council; and Kent Rea, Program Activity Council. These four operational areas had been organized into councils earlier in the year.[950] Gene Miller later left the Y but Jim Rayhab and Kent Rea would spend their entire careers with the Y.

Kent Rea welcoming guests at the opening of the Nashville YMCA Center, January 28, 1973

The long-awaited dedication of the Bordeaux-North Center was held May 12. An open house for approximately 300 people was held on the 12th and 13th. Located at 3700 Ashland City Highway, the beautiful new center would help the Bordeaux-North board take on membership and program challenges.[951] The facilities included an outdoor swimming pool and bath house, outdoor athletic area, and the following rooms inside the new building: lobby, lounge, offices, a general purpose room, kitchenette, three committee and club rooms, and an enclosed golf driving range. The Bordeaux-North Family Center had also been given 34 acres on Kings Lane to be used for day camp.[952]

The 98th annual meeting of the Metropolitan Nashville YMCA met at the Hillwood Country Club on May 16. Described as one of the best ever, the meeting saw the nominated slate of officers elected, and winners of the annual awards—Order of the Red Triangle, YMCA Man of the Year, Service to Youth, and Special service awards—were recognized. Twenty-four employees were recognized for their long service, including Everett Gilbert, 47 years, and C. E. Terry, 50 years. Bob Freeman won the Order of the Red Triangle Award posthumously.

There was a change in leadership impacting the Southwest and East branches when Wayne Blackwelder resigned as executive director at Southwest. Reluctantly, Bill Portman moved over from East to take his place. Replacing Bill was Charles Cleveland, who had been program director at East. Those moves were completed by August 1.[953] Portman proved his worth by quickly improving programming and finances at Southwest, both of which had badly deteriorated. Portman's new physical director at Southwest was Richard M. "Rick" Erdenberger, a graduate of George Williams College. Not long after he came on board, Rick asked Kent Rea to rent a flame-thrower for him to use at Southwest. Although puzzled why Rick would want such a thing, Kent found one and took it to Erdinberger who used it to clear brush off the back of the Southwest Y's property.[954]

The first YMCA-sponsored citywide swimming meet was held on August 18 at the Southwest center. Kent Rea, Nashville YMCA physical director, directed the event that drew 175 youngsters from 8 through 17 years of age. All the centers had entrants.[955]

The fifth annual Old Hickory Run was held on Saturday, October 6 at Percy Warner Park. There were a record 242 participants, twenty more than in 1972. The run continued to be sponsored by the National Life and Accident Insurance Company, the Nashville YMCA and the Nashville Striders. Other fall activities included Gra-Y football leagues at Donelson-Hermitage, the East Branch's first Indian Guide program, a tumbling class for children at Southwest, and judo classes in the Downtown Center.[956]

Plans for a twenty-eight-week capital campaign for $2 million in 1976 were firmed up a little with the visit of Robert H. Apgar, executive director of Campaign Associates, the fund-raising arm of the National YMCA. Apgar agreed to furnish a campaign director, who would be onsite for twelve to fourteen weeks. He also recommended the association conduct a pre-campaign cultivation, by then a standard practice. After his visit, Mr. Apgar reported that the cost of a full campaign for $2 million would cost approximately $80,000.[957]

Bill Henderson, treasurer, gave a detailed analysis of the YMCA's financial situation at the October board meeting. He projected a year-end deficit of $36,109 and explained why that seemed likely: the loss of the Model Cities program, continued losses at Bordeaux-North; and losses at Southwest although Bill Portman was making great progress there in addressing the problem. A "hard-hitting December" enabled the association to end the year with a slight surplus of $126.00, a pleasant surprise to Henderson and to Brunson.

The Metropolitan YMCA changed directions in November by interviewing Hal Gibbs, who had been director of the 1969 capital funds drive, for a position on the Nashville YMCA staff as associate general secretary responsible for current, capital and endowment development. Gibbs, who was financial development director of Chicago's Bethany Hospital, accepted the offer made by the executive committee.[958] This decision seems a little strange given the troubles the 1969 capital campaign suffered. Gibbs planned to come to Nashville in February when he expected to present a plan of action.

The YMCA Foundation's officers for 1974 included George Cate Jr. as chairman of the board and two female officers: Mrs. George M. Green Jr. as vice-chairman, and Mrs. Henry Foutch as secretary. At the foundation's December 1973 meeting, Ralph Brunson thanked out-going foundation chairman Roupen Gulbenk for his two and one-half years of dedicated service.[959]

Hal Gibbs came in February as associate general secretary responsible for current, capital and endowment development and immediately delved into campaign planning, meeting with branch executives and volunteer leaders, discussing strategies for raising money for the Urban Village and the Foundation, and asking key leaders to identify prospective large donors.[960] The tentative campaign goal was set at $2 million.

Nashville YMCA handball and racquetball championships began April 22 and ended May 31. There were three divisions—open, senior 35–45, and master 45 and older. Jim Rayhab won the senior racquetball title.

• • • • •

Thanks largely to the work of the Rev. Bob Spain and his Christian emphasis-world service committee, the Nashville YMCA qualified as the first International YMCA in the South.[961]

• • • • •

Centennial Year Plans

Plans for the 1975 Centennial Year Celebration and Capital Campaign were in full swing by the summer of 1974. The National YMCA board would hold its annual meeting in Nashville in October 1975. The Nashville Chamber of Commerce would hold a breakfast on October 31 in observance of the Centennial and the National YMCA Basketball Tournament would be held in Nashville in March. A Centennial Committee was formed to coordinate all the centennial events. Its honorary chairman was Horace G. Hill Jr. Other members were Tom Baldridge, general chairman; Rev. Bob Spain, special observances; Roupen Gulbenk, historical; James Ward, promotion/publicity; Dr. Bill Sherman, religious emphasis; and Tom Griscomb, public relations.[962]

Another first was the first annual meeting ever held by the Heritage Club. Held at the University Club on August 14, sixty-five members and their spouses attended. To qualify they had either included the YMCA in their estate planning or had made a substantial gift to the endowment program.[963]

The new officers for 1974–75 were installed at the July 31 board meeting. They were: Homer B. Gibbs Jr., president; president elect Charles L. Cornelius Jr., vice presidents Clarence H. Berson, of National Life, and Rev. Robert H. Spain; secretary Mrs. Lipscomb Davis Jr., and treasurer, Mrs. Alex Pirtle Jr.[964]

The 100th annual meeting and awards banquet was held at noon on September 11, 1974, in the President's Room. As usual, the meeting opened with an invocation. Plans were discussed for the Centennial Celebration to be held May 13, 1975 when the speaker would be Dr. Nicholas T. Goncharoff, Director of International Education and Cultural Affairs for the National Board of YMCA's. Assignments were made for various subcommittees.[965]

Present at the September executive committee meeting, held at the Urban Village, was Homer Sparks, general director of the Lebanon, Tennessee, YMCA. He came to ask for assistance from the Nashville YMCA, and specifically to request guidelines for affiliating with the Nashville YMCA. The executive committee promised to consider the request.[966] Ridley Wills II, a member of the Urban Services Committee, reported that the Downtown board had relieved Chuck Harris of his day-to-day activities at the Urban Village, so he could spend three months studying the feasibility of an expanded Urban Services program. Rusty Youmans would take up most of Chuck's workload, Ridley said, and a part-time counselor would be employed to cover Rusty's duties. In response to Ridley's request for approval, a motion was passed supporting the study with the stipulation that the expenses not exceed $1,200.[967]

A little later in the 1970s, after Ridley succeeded Rev. Bill Sherman as chairman of the Urban Services Committee, he became acutely aware the boys there were considered a nuisance by their neighbors. Ridley got the bright idea of inviting the neighbors to a grievance session at the Downtown YMCA. That was not only a mistake but was the most unpleasant meeting Ridley ever moderated. The next-door neighbor, Mrs. Scott, was particularly irate because the boys continued to pee out of the upstairs windows. In response, the Urban Services Committee made a number of recommendations, including adding two neighborhood representatives as non-voting members of the Urban Services Committee, and putting up a chain link fence with slats between the Urban Village building at 1200–02 17th Avenue South and Mrs. Scott's house.[968]

Bill Bailey, Bordeaux-North board chairman for 1974–75, gave the report for his branch. He said a survey in the community showed that a lack of physical fitness programs made it difficult to get more family memberships. By October, plans were underway for a physical fitness program to start in November.

The Old Hickory Invitational Run on October 5 drew 349 runners from 12 states. Nine course records were broken. The runners ranged in age from a six-year-old to a seventy-year-old man. With one hundred more entrants than in 1973, the 6th annual run was the largest ever.[969]

Jim Ward and Maryland Farms

The first recorded conversation about a branch building in Williamson County came in October when board members of the emerging Southeast branch discussed the idealistic possibility of having their own building in Maryland Farms. This might work, they thought, if the City of Brentwood would give them some land on which to build it. Hal Gibbs volunteered to speak to Jim Ward, who developed Maryland Farms, about the possibility.[970] Bill Portman, the able executive for the Southwest Family YMCA, was asked to additionally take responsibility for the newest YMCA branch. Temporarily, the new branch would be headquartered in the Southwest Family Center.[971]

In November, Mrs. Jesse Wills gave the YMCA the key to the 1912 building given to her father, Dr. Matt G. Buckner, at the dinner celebrating its opening. Dr. Buckner was president of the Nashville YMCA at the time. The hope was that Mrs. Wills' gift would encourage others to bring old photographs and YMCA memorabilia to the Y for the Centennial Celebration only weeks away.[972]

In 1974, the Nashville YMCA had served 14,500 members and an additional 40,823 non-members in registered programs, and another 87,127 persons in non-scheduled classes. The total attendance was 448,909. The Y taught 4,245 people to swim. There was a 34 percent increase in program participation over 1973 and a 35 percent increase in Gra-Y and Tri-Gra-Y teams.[973]

The YMCA organization looked forward to an even greater 1975 and the celebration of the YMCA's 100th anniversary.

Metropolitan Board Officers for 1975–1976. From left to right: Charles L. Cornelius Jr., President; Whatley S. Scott, Vice President; Florence Davis, Secretary; and William I. Henderson, Vice-President.

CHAPTER TWENTY-FOUR

The Centennial Year
1975

IN JANUARY, the executive committee responded to the Wilson County YMCA's request to become affiliated with the Metropolitan Nashville YMCA. The committee suggested that the Wilson County YMCA do the following to merit consideration for joining the Metropolitan Nashville YMCA:

1. Develop corporate planning;
2. Conduct financial and program audits;
3. The general executive set forth personal business goals; and
4. The association placed the financial structure on a sound basis.

At the same executive committee, a motion was approved to print 1,500 copies of *All Together A History of the Nashville YMCA 1875–1975* written by Bess Cochran.[974]

The Metropolitan Nashville YMCA was, by the mid-seventies, active in Hendersonville with Gra-Y basketball teams sponsored by the East Nashville Family Center. The Y also had its new Southeast branch in Brentwood. The Wilson County YMCA benefited through money raised by the Nashville YMCA designated for the Wilson County operation. This meant that the Y had a presence in four Middle Tennessee counties—Davidson, Sumner, Williamson, and Wilson.

The citywide membership drive kicked off on February 9, 1975. The goal was to enroll 2,400 members and raise $289,750. A victory celebration was scheduled for Sunday afternoon, March 9. By February, the overall theme for the Centennial capital campaign was adopted:

Nashville YMCA
100 Years (1875–1975)
"Getting It All Together"
Spirit–Mind–Body

The financial development committee, having conducted a marketing study but, more importantly, having learned from the 1969 campaign mistakes, made five recommendations to the Metropolitan Board for the 1975–76 Centennial Campaign. They were:

1. That a campaign goal of $2,750,000 be established;
2. That needs be prioritized and that the #1 priority be to eliminate the present indebtedness;
3. That the allocation of funds be based on some sort of ration;
4. That an adequate amount of funds be on hand before building or renovating a facility; and
5. That no long-term mortgage or indebtedness be incurred for construction or renovation.

By March 20, the citywide membership drive had achieved 83 percent of its goal or $238,475. Two centers, East at 116 percent and Southwest at 124 percent were over the top.

March also saw the YMCA host the largest racquetball tournament ever held in the Southeast, a national YMCA men's basketball tournament featuring sixteen YMCA teams, and the 6th annual Music City run. The Southern Regional Racquetball Tournament saw 175 players played in 200 matches over three days. Co-chairmen Jerry Bryant and Frank Burkholder were praised for pulling off such a success.[975] The basketball tournament received excellent publicity because it honored the famous

YMCA Rambler teams of old, and featured a group of ex-Vanderbilt players on the Nashville YMCA team, including Ray Maddox, Rudy Thacker, and Tommy Hagan. The aging Ramblers' biggest problem was walking up steps. Kent Rea, who ran the tournament, recalled in 2010 that Nashville YMCA team finished third.[976] The Music City run attracted 279 runners.

By the early spring of 1975, the capital [campaign] planning committee, chaired by Roupen Gulbenk, was meeting monthly with Hal Gibbs. The kickoff date was established as April 1976, and a calendar of campaign events was published. Already, a YMCA song, written by Country Music Hall of Fame member Jim Fogelsong, was being played on the radio and the YMCA had written the manager of the Hyatt Regency Hotel, asking that a historical plaque be placed on the hotel's exterior near the corner of Seventh and Union. The wording would say that the Nashville YMCA occupied the site from 1912 to 1972.[977]

Unfortunately, the YMCA's Centennial Year was also a period of economic upheaval with spiraling prices in the cost of gas, oil, and electricity. During the first two months of the year, YMCA expenses were up and income down. Brunson felt "almost trapped." In response, he wrote a memo to his entire professional staff, outlining a wide-ranging austerity program that included no new programs or services unless funding was available, eliminating part-time jobs, and not filling vacant positions unless absolutely necessary. "We must," he wrote, "operate within our budgets."[978]

In 1975, the still emerging Southeast Family YMCA identified its service area as Crieve Hall, Oak Hill Estates, Brentwood, and Brenthaven.

On the last day of March, Clifford Harrison Jr., chairman of the 100th anniversary membership enrollment, was delighted to report that the drive was very close to its goals, having raised 95 percent of its monetary goal of $289,000 and 93.5 percent of its 2,400-member goal.[979] Seventeen days later, the totals had climbed to $278,119 in income and 2,291 members.

At the April board meeting, Dr. Elbert Brooks, Superintendent of the Public School System, made the motion that the Southeast Family YMCA be made a part of the Nashville Association. The motion carried and David Booth, the first board chairman at Southeast, was notified. Next, officers were nominated and elected for the 1975–76 year. They were: Charles L. Cornelius Jr., president; Rev. Robert M. Spain, president-elect; William I. Henderson, William H. Keinath, and Whatley S. Scott, vice-presidents, J. P. Foster, treasurer, Mrs. Lipscomb Davis Jr., secretary; and Mrs. Alex Pirtle Jr., assistant secretary. New and old board members were also nominated. By April everybody was anticipating the 100th annual meeting of the Metropolitan Nashville YMCA on May 13th at the Hillwood Country Club. The featured speaker would be Nicholas T. Goncharoff, Ph.D. Still, other business had to be addressed. Bill Henderson moved that the YMCA request $125,000 from the United Way for 1976—an 8.7 percent increase. The motion passed. One of the new services that came out of Chuck Harris' three-month investigation was the decision to provide a recreational director at the Juvenile Detention Center. The director of the center wrote Harris in the spring to say that the YMCA's Harry Dickey was doing a marvelous job there.

The capital campaign was coming together with Clifford Love Jr., James Ward, Russell Brothers, and George Cate Jr. all accepting leadership positions.

The 100th annual meeting was, without a doubt, at least in Ralph Brunson's mind, the greatest annual meeting ever held in the history of the Nashville YMCA. Over 400 people attended, new officers and board members were presented, annual award winners announced, and employees recognized. One thing the meeting lacked was brevity. Tom Baldridge received the YMCA Order of the Red Triangle, and two employees, C. E. Terry and Everett Gilbert were presented plaques for their combined total of more than 100 years of devoted service. Dr. Goncharoff, director of International Education and Cultural Affairs for the National YMCA, spoke on "We are in the people business." Copies of *All Together, A History of the Nashville YMCA 1875–1975* were presented to each family in attendance. One thing the meeting lacked was brevity. That day, a Metropolitan Nashville Historical Commission marker was dedicated by vice-mayor David Scobey on the front of the Church Street Branch of First American National Bank. This marked the site of the first YMCA in Nashville following the Civil War.[980]

YMCA leadership visited United Way officials on July 16 to officially receive clearance for the $2,750,000 Centennial Capital Fund Campaign. Sam Friedman, Chairman of the United Way board of trustees, wrote President Charlie Cornelius on July 25 giving that approval with the stipulation that publicity and promotion not start

Publicity shot taken on the roof of the 7th Avenue building. Larry Stumb (middle) and George Cate Jr. (far right) are running and William S. "Bill" Cochran is in the foreground pretending to be asleep.

until the close of the United Way campaign on November 15.[981] Soon thereafter, a campaign budget of $70,830 was proposed.

The YMCA Foundation's Heritage Club held their second annual dinner on August 13 with seventy-two people in attendance. Not much progress had been made in the previous twelve months with no increase in the 50 people who had already included the Y in their estate planning. The total value of all commitments was approximately $350,000. Still, the foundation hoped to have 100 new members by year-end.[982]

Another extension of Urban Services' outreach was the "cool-in-the-pool" program sponsored by the YMCA and National Life and Accident Insurance Company for inner city children. When the program ended, 576 children had participated, 176 more than had been anticipated.[983]

In October, YMCA officials were still worried about avoiding deficits and cutting expenses. It helped immensely that the Southwest board approved giving the Metropolitan Y $10,000 from its anticipated 1975 surplus to meet critical needs in the inner city. Jim Rayhab assured the executive committee that all possible cutbacks had been made, including implementing a group purchasing policy and more economical use of electricity.[984]

The last day of October, budget concerns were temporarily forgotten as Nashville Mayor Richard Fulton proclaimed October 31 as "YMCA Day in Nashville," The long-awaited day kicked off with a Chamber of Commerce breakfast honoring the YMCA at the University of Tennessee Nashville Center. That evening, the Centennial banquet was held at the National Life Center. Former governor Winfield Dunn was master of ceremonies, the Rev. Frank Drowota gave the testimonial, and Art Linkletter, the Emmy Award-winning host of the Television show *People Are Funny*, was the featured speaker. During dinner, the Suzuki Violin Players from Blair Academy performed thanks to new board member Ann Potter Wilson. Earlier in the day, Linkletter appeared on local television and radio stations. Among the huge crowd at National Life were YMCA executives from across the Southeast and members of the National YMCA board, who held their annual meeting in Nashville that day. You can believe that they, their spouses, and Linkletter received tickets to the Grand Ole Opry that night. The celebration banquet drew rave reviews. One man said, "Superb. We felt it was one of the most enjoyable evenings we have ever spent." An out-of-town attendee wrote Ralph "a brief note to thank you and your associates for the wonderful week-end in Nashville. We enjoyed every minute of it and returned North with a new and warm appreciation for Nashville and your YMCA."[985]

In December, D. M. Robie, a member of the Knoxville YMCA board of directors, wrote a letter to his counterparts in Nashville praising the recent Old Hickory Handball Tournament at the Downtown YMCA. "As usual," he said, "your handball club did an outstanding job. Some of the local participants were Tommy Henderson III, Mac Husband, and Dr. Jim Wilson. Robie also complimented the Nashville YMCA on its beautiful facilities. Earlier participants in the 7th annual Old Hickory run were equally effusive in their praise of how well Ken Rea ran that event.[986]

Homer Gibbs Jr.'s big gifts campaign kicked off on December 3 with 174 workers. Thirty-four women under the indomitable Ellen Hofstead's leadership kicked off the women's division campaign two days later. Solicitations of board members were also underway with 47 percent of its $275,000 goal secured by December 18.

The board of directors met on New Year's Eve to approve objectives for 1976 and hear reports from the centennial and property committees, and the financial administration council. Reporting for the council, J. P. Foster said that 1975 had been a difficult year but added that, despite having a $2,300 deficit for November, he anticipated the month of December "will bring us out of the red." J. P. was correct. The Association ended the year with a $564.49 surplus, but only because the entire staff worked hard, even on New Year's Eve, to make that happen.[987]

Statistics for the year showed that the association had 14,658 members at year-end with the largest family branch being Southwest with 4,391 members. In 1974, East had been the largest center. There were 64,085 program participants during the year, up more than 20 percent over 1974. Of these, 3,648 were in Gra-Y and Tri-Gra-Y programs.[988] Total attendance for 1975 was 256,818, up from 233,182 in 1974. Finally, 4,256 people learned to swim during the year.[989] Homer Gibbs Jr. and Charlie Cornelius Jr. could feel good about the Centennial year that they shared as president.

• • • • •

CHAPTER TWENTY-FIVE

Another Disappointing Campaign
1976–1977

THE CENTENNIAL YEAR had been a huge success but it was stressful. Soon after the executive meeting on January 15, Ralph Brunson found himself in the hospital where he was operated on for a troublesome disk. After a month recuperating at home, he returned to work in March. At the January executive committee of the year, the members heard from Jim Rayhab that the association's cash flow was in a good position. They also approved a recommendation that the YMCA return to the U.S. Army Corps of Engineers the 55 acres they had leased for some years on Spencer Creek.[990]

Despite the extensive publicity the YMCA received during the Centennial year and reasonably good attendance at key campaign meetings and kickoff events, campaign director Hal Gibbs was increasingly alarmed at the indifference and apathy that had followed. Five months after the board solicitation kickoff on September 23, only 70 percent of the board members had made a commitment for a total of $129,000, or 51 percent of their $275,000 goal. As happened in the 1969 campaign, the big gifts division was lagging, having raised by mid-February only 19 percent of its $577,000 goal, and only 57 percent of the big gifts committee members had made their pledges.

On the 19th, Hal Gibbs and his associate, Erv Holth, wrote the executive Committee that, unless there was a big change, the campaign would fail. Gibbs asked that big gifts workers turn in their unsolicited cards by the 25th and they would be reassigned. The pattern gifts division, that solicited gifts of $10,000 and more, was doing somewhat better, having received $331,150 in commitments. As that division had the largest goal, $1,400,000, it was imperative that additional prospects be developed, Gibbs said.

The State racquetball tournament, held at the Downtown Center in February, was a great success with well over 100 entries, including several of the top racquetball players in the United States. The Nashville Association had two state championship teams—Frank Burkholder and Jerry Bryant in senior doubles and Joe Morrissey and Harold Hitt in master doubles. The International Racquetball Association had recently moved its headquarters to Memphis as they considered Tennessee to be the top racquetball state in the country.[991] Not to be outdone, the YMCA handballers would host the state handball tournament in April.

At the March executive committee, Ralph Brunson announced a $75,000 gift to the YMCA Foundation from the Gannett Foundation and tried to fire up the troops for the campaign that would officially kickoff at the National Guard Armory on March 23. President Charlie Cornelius Jr., presented Florence Davis with a framed certificate thanking her for her many services to the Y, especially as chairperson for the Centennial Celebration banquet. With the capital campaign still lagging, Erv Holth made a desperate plea for more workers in the general public campaign. At that point, only 650 of the 1,600 workers needed had agreed to make calls. At the March meeting of the board of directors, Ralph Brunson challenged the board to work even during the public phase that kicked off a week earlier. Bill Henderson, financial development council chairman, said that, to date, pledges and cash received totaled $739,132 or 27 percent of the goal.

George Cate Jr. was re-elected president of the YMCA Foundation at its April meeting. With the addition of the $75,000 Gannett gift, the foundation assets had jumped from $31,763 in 1974 to $111,686 in April 1976. On the recommendation of the executive committee, the foundation board approved the establishment of a pooled income account at Third National Bank. Before the addition of the Gannett gift, a majority of the assets ($17,483) had been held in cash.[992]

The new officers for 1976–77 were presented at the 101st annual meeting and awards banquet held at the Hyatt Regency on May 11. The Rev. Robert H. Spain, pastor of the Belle Meade United Methodist Church was elected president for the 1976–77 year. Other officers elected were Bill Henderson, president elect; Cliff Harrison Jr., William H. Keinath, and Whatley S. Scott, vice-presidents; J. P. Foster, treasurer; and Florence Davis, secretary.[993] Dr. George K. Schweitzer, PhD., professor of chemistry at the University of Tennessee and a committed Christian, spoke to the 420 people in attendance on the relationship between science and religion. Officers were elected and awards presented. Homer Gibbs Jr. won the Order of the Red Triangle.

A Fundraising Disappointment

Embarrassed, frustrated, and disappointed with his inability to manage a successful capital campaign in Nashville, Hal Gibbs informed Ralph Brunson in early April that he was resigning effective June 15 to accept the vice-presidency of the Milwaukee YMCA. Brunson read the letter at the April executive committee meeting when it was reported that, with only two weeks to go, the campaign had raised $785,239 of which $230,930 was in cash. Of course, it was too late to salvage the campaign. The final report, written on May 20, told the sad story: $834,679 had been raised, only 36 percent of the goal. Despite a lot of hard work, the report, written by Gibbs, said that a negative attitude and apathy permeated the whole campaign and it was not a top priority for either board members or staff. Many workers didn't attend report meetings and many calls were not made. There was never an urgency on the part of the board and this, Gibbs wrote, infected the entire campaign. The board and staff pledged $147,000 against a goal of $412,000. The largest board gift was $5,000. The many other events during the Centennial Year seemed to have been a diversion from the campaign rather than a stimulus, the report concluded.[994]

Despite having failed in Nashville twice, once in 1968–69 and again in 1975–76, Hal and Betty Gibbs made many friends while living in Nashville for two and one-half years. They felt richer from knowing them. Ralph Brunson was gracious in his public statement, saying "Hal Gibbs has made an outstanding contribution to the Nashville YMCA. He not only is especially gifted and experienced in development but is the embodiment of what a YMCA professional should be."[995] Before he left, Gibbs suggested that the YMCA inform the United Way that a sizable list of companies solicited during the campaign had deferred making commitments, and ask the United Way for permission to continue the solicitation of those gifts. He hoped that an additional $100,000 might be raised through such a follow-up. A painful job that summer was the reallocation downward of campaign funds expected to be received by the various branches.

Although Camp Widjiwagan had been closed since 1971, there were plenty of day camps to take up the slack. In 1976, the "Keep Cool in the Pool" program taught 600 inner city youth to swim at the Bordeaux-North, where Ray Parks was the director, and at the East Family Center. At the Downtown Center, "YMCA Camp Downtown" offered 60 children ages 7 through 13 a unique opportunity to learn more about their city. Swimming, tennis and T-ball were among the favorite summer programs at the family centers. The Hickory Bend pool, which had never been sold as anticipated, was still being operated by the Donelson-Hermitage Family YMCA and was popular. Women's dance and exercise classes at Southwest were at record highs. The Brentwood-Crieve Hall center saw day camp increase from 2 sessions with 20 kids to 8 sessions with 200 youngsters. They were held at St. Matthias Episcopal Church on Nolensville Road. The East Branch, under Charles Cleveland's leadership, showed a 10 percent increase in swim lessons while tennis instruction was offered for the first time at Bordeaux-North. Usually 20 to 25 people attended each session.[996]

On July 28, the Metropolitan Nashville YMCA board adopted operating goals for 1977 through 1981. A new one was to work cooperatively with other organizations to strengthen family structures, youth from broken homes, children with special needs, and youth and adults alienated from society. Other goals dealt with having adequate maintenance, creating opportunities for Christian living, and maintaining standard fiscal policies. While these goals were worthy, they were not specific enough to be adequately measured.[997] The same month, the Wilson County YMCA made formal application to become a family center of the Metropolitan Nashville YMCA. Their board realized that there future was in jeopardy without the help of their YMCA neighbor. After the Nashville YMCA took the matter under consideration, they gave the Wilson County Association more benchmarks they would have to clear to be eligible to affiliate with the Metropolitan Nashville YMCA.

Factors arguing against adopting the Wilson County YMCA as a family center were the almost desperate financial condition at Bordeaux-North and a deficit situation at East almost as bad. To the north, the independent Hendersonville YMCA had a board that was nearly defunct. Brunson felt the only responsible thing to do was to ask the Hendersonville YMCA to surrender its charter. He was not anxious to add another ailing center to his organization that, except for Bordeaux-North and East, was in excellent condition.[998]

A Dark Cloud

Hugh Hurst Jr. joined the Nashville YMCA staff on August 15 as associate general executive responsible for financial development. He had been in Salisbury, NC. Hugh's first assignment was to assist Bordeaux-North and East with their financial problems.

A dark cloud hovered over the Urban Village in September when the YMCA received a letter from the State of Tennessee Vocational Rehabilitation Department that funds for the Urban Village would be terminated on November 1 because of a change in Federal laws and the loss of Federal funds. A meeting was held with the assistant commissioner to see if anything could be done to save the funds. Apparently, this was an exercise in chasing the wind, as the YMCA reluctantly closed the worthwhile program as scheduled. The youth living there were placed elsewhere.

A crisis at the YMCA Night Law School reached a climax in 1976 when two-thirds of the graduates failed the state bar exam. Discontent flared with Dean Lackey receiving much of the heat. Some good came out of this as some faculty members accused of poor teaching departed, and new research and legal writing courses were introduced.[999]

The eighth annual Old Hickory Run was held October 2 at Percy Warner Park. Growing like topsy, it attracted a record-breaking 667 runners in twelve divisions over the 1.6, 5.8, and 11.2 mile courses. Twelve states were represented on a beautiful fall day.[1000] A sponsor for the eighth consecutive year was the National Life and Accident Insurance Company. October also saw Frank Burkholder and Mac Husband win the city racquetball and handball championships, both held at the YMCA.[1001]

• • • • •

Miss Janine Cox became the first female professional director in the 76 years that the Nashville YMCA had been in existence. She worked for Charles Cleveland at East, where, in October, she received her senior director certificate.

• • • • •

Sadly, for the first time in memory, the possibility of two lawsuits against the YMCA arose due to the drowning of a child earlier in the summer at Northwest and the injury of another child at Southwest in a trampoline accident.[1002]

At the financial development committee meeting on October 27, Ralph Brunson gave an update on the follow-up for the Centennial Campaign. In the five months since the campaign officially ended, he said an additional $54,000 in pledges had been received. This was far short of the $100,000 Hal Gibbs felt was out there. The new totals as of October 15, were $889,176 in pledges of which $328,286 had been paid. Follow-up continued and by December 13, the campaign total had reached $954,610 with 250 additional gifts.[1003]

With advice from Bo Hardy, the new YMCA Regional consultant, the YMCA's long-range planning committee, under the direction of Dr. Elbert Brooks, Director of the Metropolitan Nashville School System, was active. At the request of the executive committee, Dr. Brooks' committee conducted a goal-setting study similar to one conducted in 1964–65. It would focus on the ensuing five to ten years with an emphasis on personnel, facilities, programs and planning. Bo would be of help to the Nashville YMCA for years to come.[1004]

The Metropolitan YMCA gained another female staff member in the fall when Suzanne Briggs started her new job as program director at Southwest. That fall, ladies fitness classes were held at Southwest and Brentwood-Crieve Hall. Over at Donelson-Hermitage, Gra-Y and Tri-Gra-Y basketball was in full swing. At East, a women's heath and fitness center opened in mid-October with 100 women enrolled. At Bordeaux-North, daycare for children 3 to 5 was the big program. It was a joint effort between the State Department of Human Services and the Bordeaux-North branch and was designed to allow low-income parents the opportunity to become employed while their children were in a protective learning environment.[1005]

The YMCA Foundation got a late fall boost when 5.34

acres of land on Murfreesboro Road at Town Park Drive was given to YMCA by Eugene Pargh and Gerald Averbush. It was suggested that the site be developed for a day camp, particularly since adjoining property was expected to be available for YMCA use. The gift, valued at $80,000, brought the current value of the foundation at year-end to $170,676.[1006]

As 1976 came to a close, the Metropolitan Nashville YMCA had seven units serving the metropolitan Nashville area. Four were family centers—East, Bordeaux-North, Donelson-Hermitage, and Southwest in Green Hills. Brentwood-Crieve Hall did not yet have a facility but was conducting programs and activities in its area. The other two units were the Metropolitan Center at 100 Church Street and the Urban Services Center at 1202 17th Avenue South.

The 13th annual Old Hickory Handball Tournament was held at the YMCA Physical Fitness Center December 3–5 where 129 players competed in six divisions. Tom Henderson III, Dr. Jim Wilson, Mac Husband, and Dr. Ron Bowers, who finished fourth in open singles, held their own.[1007]

An important feature of the Christmas season were the devotional programs held at noon, December 20 and 21 at the Downtown Center lobby. This was done in connection with the Fellowship of Christian Athletes.

The Metropolitan Nashville YMCA ended the year with a surplus of $1,431, thanks largely to the $27,543 surplus at Southwest. The 1976 budget totaled $1,361,563, the largest in history. At year's end, 16,154 members were on the roll, a 9 percent increase over 1975. Overall, there was a slight trend toward more adult and family memberships and fewer youth members.[1008]

YMCA-YWCA *Merger Discussed*

Bill Moynihan, Director of the Council of Community Services, met with the YMCA's long-range planning committee in early January to review with the board the results of a 1973 study that identified the relative importance of the many social services in the community. Mr. Moynihan said that he had been asked by the United Way to do this to make the YMCA aware of where they stood in rankings of various community social services. He said that the activities of the YMCA were ranked in the bottom of the five categories used. The services ranked in the higher categories tended to deal with drugs, rehabilitation, health care, and critical human needs. He added that a later study showed that the YMCA had moved up to the middle category. Moynihan brought up the possibility of the YMCA and the YWCA merging, a subject he said had arisen several years earlier. After many questions, and expressions of appreciation from Moynihan for the responsible leadership the YMCA had always displayed in the city, he left. If the long-range planning committee members did not already know why the percent of funds the YMCA received from the United Way had been steadily decreasing over the years, they certainly did on the 6th of January. The meeting with Bill Moynihan was timely as his committee was developing long-range goals for the association with results to be presented in June. This was the first detailed study since 1964–65.[1009]

• • • • •

Charles L. Toms Sr.'s death in January caused sadness at the Downtown Center where he had been a full-time masseur from the time of his retirement from the post office in 1965 until 1975, when he retired from the YMCA at age 80. Even earlier, he had worked at the Downtown Center part-time. In recognition of his outstanding service and a life lived honorably and purposefully, the executive committee adopted a resolution honoring him at its February 16 meeting. One day a couple of years before Charlie retired, Kent Rea noticed a series of black spots on the white massage room walls about chest high. At the time, Mr. Toms was sitting in his straight-back chair against the wall. When Kent asked him about the spots, Charles sheepishly admitted that he used black shoe polish to dye his white hair and that, sometimes, he leaned back against the wall. It was no trouble to remove the shoe polish.[1010]

• • • • •

Early March was a good time to be inside. What better place to be than at the first Annual Music City Racquetball tournament held March 4, 5, and 6 in the Downtown Center. The hospitality room was welcoming and people enjoyed the matches even if Memphis dominated the tournament. An exception came when Harold Hitt and Joe Morrissey of Nashville won the master doubles.[1011]

At the March 23 board of directors meeting, the Metropolitan board members approved a request from Southwest to build two tennis courts at a cost not to exceed $25,000. The branch's existing surplus would be used to pay for the courts. It didn't hurt that Southwest was running well ahead of its 1977 budget.

April brought warmer weather to Nashville and a new look to Southwest with painting and a general cleaning. During the month, over 300 boys and girls signed up for soccer at the Green Hills center with more coming in. This would be the Southwest program's most successful season ever in the Nashville area.[1012]

On March 26, 552 runners competed in the YMCA's 8th annual Music City run. The record crowd surpassed the 1976 record by 128 runners. The men and women came from 20 states, including 10 from San Diego, and broke six records. The Music City Run was the annual spring event while the YMCA's Old Hickory Run came each fall.[1013]

fundraising On My Mind

At the April executive committee meeting, Hugh Hurst Jr. reported on the 1977 Sustaining Funds drive and said that $27,666 had been raised and that he anticipated that total reaching $50,000. As the goal was $95,000, it was obvious the Nashville YMCA had not yet mastered fund-raising. Also, at the executive committee meeting, a resolution was passed deploring the death of Stirton Oman, a business, civic, religious, and social leader who had been president of the Nashville YMCA in 1955–56.[1014]

Ralph Brunson often had fund-raising on his mind, particularly when sustaining membership drives were lagging. When in this mood, he usually grabbed Jim Rayhab and Kent Rea and urged them to make some more calls. One day, Brunson gave Kent Frank Burkholder's card. Kent took it because Frank was easy to find as he played handball at the Downtown Y nearly every day. Kent approached Frank in the men's locker room and made his pitch. Frank gave him $25. Little did either man know how generous Frank would be with the YMCA in later years.[1015]

Clyde Lee, former Vanderbilt and NBA star, was the speaker at the 102nd annual meeting at Hillwood Country Club described as "the best ever." Clyde talked about his experiences as a child at the YMCA. Gene Steakley's testimonial, "What the YMCA Means to Me" was also inspirational. President Robert H. Spain presented the new officers elected to serve for a year, beginning July 1, 1977. They were William I. Henderson, president; Dr. Elbert Brooks, president-elect; Florence Davis, Clifford J. Harrison Jr., and Whatley S. Scott, vice presidents; William J. Jeffares, treasurer; and Walter Knestrick, secretary. James M. Ward won the Order of the Red Triangle. Jim was keenly interested in all phases of the YMCA, including serving for many years on the Camp Widjiwagan board. He had also served on nearly every YMCA board committee, including the executive committee.[1016]

Walter Knestrick would become the Metropolitan Nashville YMCA President in 1985.

Hugh Hurst's prediction that the sustaining membership campaign would raise $50,000 was optimistic. It only generated $37,000 or 39 percent of its original goal. Budgets would have to be adjusted because of the shortfall. The YMCA got 40 percent and the State of Tennessee got 60 percent. Rusty Yeomans, who had been at the Urban Village, moved over to the Southwest Y as physical director.[1017]

In June, Kent Rea reported the results of a three-year dropout rate study for the Physical Fitness Center. In 1974, '75, and '76, the highest dropout rate was among those in the 25–29 age group. The lowest dropout rate was among those 66 and older.[1018]

Max Cook, Donelson-Hermitage executive, reported to the executive committee in June on the progress the Wilson County YMCA was making toward becoming a branch of the Metropolitan Nashville YMCA. Surprisingly, it was encouraging. Max was running the Wilson County program with the help of a program director. They had an office in Lebanon, and four private pools had been secured for the "learn-to-swim" program. An event called "Day of

Dedication" was planned for November 30 when 30 members each from the Wilson and Metropolitan Nashville YMCAs would gather in Lebanon to hear Nashville Mayor Richard Fulton speak. The special event was planned to raise budget money for 1978 and pay off current debt.[1019] A total of $35,303 would be raised from approximately 300 donors and the Lebanon-Wilson County Family YMCA, temporarily at 233 Gay Street in Lebanon, would, on November 30, officially qualify to become the newest unit of the Nashville YMCA with a full-time director. A month or so later, the search began to find an executive director.

Sharing top billing with the Lebanon event was Dr. Elbert Brooks' long-range planning committee's recommendation of six long-range goals for the association. Approved by the Metropolitan Nashville YMCA on July 27, the "splendid set" of goals resulted from the committee's long and arduous work from October 1976 until July 1977.[1020]

The biggest area of concern continued to be the continuing and, so far, unsuccessful struggle to operate the Bordeaux-North Family Center in the black. Dr. Frederick S. Humphries, president of Tennessee State University since 1975 and a new YMCA executive committee member, suggested that the Bordeaux-North board study the problem and make a written report to the executive committee in October, outlining steps to be taken to remedy the situation. The motion passed. With the demise of the Hendersonville YMCA, the East Y was operating programs in Hendersonville and asked for $10,000 in funding from the Sumner County United Way.[1021]

In July, Bert Haywood, reporting for an ad hoc committee to consider expanding programs and services at the Metropolitan Nashville YMCA physical fitness center, submitted his report. It concluded that, "In light of recent court decisions in other jurisdiction requiring that physical fitness facilities of the YMCA be opened to women

Donelson YMCA pool ca. 1970s

as well as men, the committee felt it advisable to refer this matter to the long-range planning committee for study."[1022] This subject clearly wasn't going to disappear.

Ralph Brunson reported at the board of directors meeting on July 27 that the reports to the board for the past thirteen years had been bound. This was an important move since, before 1964, the board minutes and reports could not be found. Having all reports since 1964 would be an immense help to Ridley Wills II in 2010 when he was writing the history of the YMCA of Middle Tennessee.[1023]

After struggling for 16 months after the official close of the capital campaign, the total pledged finally edged past the $1 million mark with $1,037,120 pledged through September 16. This was 63.3 percent of the goal. Homer Gibbs Jr. deserved credit for spearheading the campaign cleanup effort that would continue to inch upward to $1,057,620 by year-end.[1024]

A week before Labor Day, the YMCA and YWCA executive committees got together to discuss their relationship, something that the Council of Community Services had recommended nineteen months earlier. Charlotte Brooks, the YWCA president, and the wife of YMCA president-elect, Elbert Brooks, stated candidly that it was a "sad day" when the YMCA opened their membership to women and girls. The possibility of the YWCA using YMCA facilities was addressed and quickly rejected by the ladies. YMCA president Bill Henderson, having read reports that the YWCA was floundering, asked in what direction the YWCA had decided to move. Mrs. Brooks replied quickly that what he read was not "entirely correct." Anne Gulley, a past YWCA president, then said that the YWCA was emphasizing "fitness, health, family enrichment, preventive programs, services to single women, information and referrals." Mary Anne Jackson, the YWCA executive director, added, "We may ease out of the health and physical education field and let the YMCA take that over." The meeting ended with a resolution that the presidents and executive directors of the two organizations appoint committees to meet regularly to coordinate program planning. Given the sometimes-tense give and take at the meeting, the possibility of meaningful cooperation seemed dubious. Gertrude [Mrs. Ben] Caldwell, who went on the YWCA board that year and who worked for the YWCA for seventeen years as associate director for development, said, in 2010, that she could not remember any subsequent meetings between the YMCA and the YWCA regarding coordinate programs.[1025]

The 9th annual Old Hickory Invitation Run was a huge October success with 847 runners despite rainy weather. Kevin Harper, a University of the South sophomore, set a course record on the 11.2-mile course with a time of 58:25.[1026]

At the December executive committee meeting, David Furse, a Vanderbilt professor and three graduate students presented the Vanderbilt Bordeaux-North management report. Phil Smartt, of the Lebanon YMCA board, came to the same meeting to express his appreciation for the help of all the Nashville YMCA members who helped make their Dedication Day so successful. Smartt said they raised $37,000 in cash and pledges. Ralph Mosley, a Brentwood-Crieve Hall board member, reported that his branch had obtained an option on Concord Road property and that plans for a building were being developed.

Tennessee was in 1977 one of the countries' most obese states, no different than would be the case thirty-four years later. Nationally, over 50 percent of deaths were due to cardiovascular-related diseases. The YMCA's response was to test over 2,000 people during the year for blood pressure, pulse rate, and percent of fat in a series of mini-health fairs at all the centers.

Ralph Brunson breathed a sigh of relief when he learned in January that the Metropolitan Association ended the year with a surplus, even if it was only $55. He was even happier about the association's nearly 28 percent growth in membership that jumped from 16,154 at year-end 1976 to 20,631 as of December 31, 1977. Total attendance in all activities went from 535,454 in 1976 to 728,475 in 1977. During the year, 3,194 people volunteered their services to the YMCA.[1027] In his year-end report, President Bill Henderson reported that the association's operating budget was the highest ever—$1,525,614 and that approximately 92 percent was financed internally from memberships, program fees, tuition and the like, leaving only 8 percent to be provided by the United Way. He added that, in the past twelve years, "the support we received from the United Way has declined from 20.3 percent to 8 percent." All of this, he pointed out, was used to provide needed services to boys, girls, men, and women who were financially unable to pay for them. Bill expressed his gratefulness for the responsiveness, creativity, and hard work of the YMCA staff that contributed to the association's outstanding achievements.

• • • • •

Basketball at the Northwest YMCA

Growing Pains
1978–1979

THE LAST RESOLUTION passed by the board of directors of the Metropolitan Nashville YMCA in 1977 was to establish a Family YMCA in Lebanon and Wilson County to be operated under the corporate charter and by-laws of the Metropolitan Nashville YMCA. The effective date would be January 1, 1978. Later in the meeting, Clarence Berson, chairman of the personnel committee, moved that David "Butch" Hannah be elected as executive director of the Lebanon and Wilson County YMCA. The motion carried.

No longer having an Urban Village, Urban Services decided that its emphasis in 1978 would be on their juvenile detention recreation program, learn-to-swim, Buddies, daycare, and CETA.

Hugh Hurst Jr. announced in January that the 1978 sustaining membership campaign would begin in two weeks with a goal of $87,000.[1028]

An important new program introduced in February 1978 was the Youth Basketball Association that combined the joint efforts of the NBA Basketball Players Association and the YMCA to establish a "values in youth" basketball program. Twenty teams of boys and girls would be in full operation the next winter, and already the program was thriving in the Bordeaux-North branch. The program would also focus on the inner city.[1029] In all centers, the winter season was the busiest with Gra-Y and Tri-Gra-Y basketball and fitness classes among the major programs. In March, the 9th annual Music City Invitational was run with the YMCA, the Nashville Striders, Castner Knott, and the Athlete's Foot the sponsors. It turned out to be the biggest and best run in Nashville's history with over 900 runners.[1030]

The recommendations of the Bordeaux-North YMCA management report, submitted by graduate students at the Vanderbilt University School of Management, were approved by the Bordeaux-North board and passed on to Bill Henderson, chairman of the Metropolitan Nashville board of directors in March. Among the eleven recommendations were ones to define priorities and establish goals, conduct income and expense evaluations on program activities, strive for a family oriented program, move toward the acquisition of a gym, and develop more volunteer help under the direction of a full-time assistant director with professional experience in programming.[1031]

The United Way allocation for the Metropolitan Nashville YMCA was $131,464 for 1978 or 7.67 percent of the association budget of $1,704,274. The allocation would be $146,464 for 1979. The Y also received $10,000 each in 1978 from the Sumner and Wilson County United Way organizations.[1032]

The YMCA Foundation was also growing. Assets in 1978 would increase by $48,725 to $414,741 and the Heritage Club grew to 124 members. Gifts of property, starting with the Una gift of 4.34 acres, since graded into two athletic fields, and the Gasser property in Madison helped swell the total, although the Una site proved unsatisfactory and it would be put on the market.

Jerry Clower, Mississippi's gift to the Grand Ole Opry, was the featured speaker at the 103rd annual meeting and rewards dinner at the Opryland Hotel on April 20. Clower told some of his "coon hunting" stories to an audience that came close to "rolling in the aisles." Clower came with his wife, Homerline, and their next-door neighbors, Marguerite Hill, a Lebanese Catholic and her husband, an Indian Chief who, Clower said, had taken up the Church of Christ religion. Clower added that the Hills didn't like a lot of fanfare but he expected "they'll go for a gathering of Christian folks." Because Ralph Brunson was known for having long annual meetings, Tom Baldridge, chairman of the annual meeting committee, had promised the board in March that they would be out by 9 p.m. There was considerable applause.

At the annual meeting, board members were elected and new officers for the 1978–79 year presented. They were: Dr. Elbert Brooks, president; Whatley S. Scott, president-elect; Florence Davis, J. P. Foster, and R. Sidney Koonce, vice-presidents; William J. Jeffares, treasurer; and William Moss "Bill" Wilson, secretary. Charles L. Cornelius Jr., received the Order of the Red Triangle.[1033]

The YMCA held its ninth annual Good Friday breakfast at the Downtown Center for staff, board members, sustaining members, and friends. Mr. Leonard Moody, minister of music at the Beacon Baptist Church led the service with his wife.[1034]

The 9th annual Music City run was conducted on Saturday, March 18. Over 900 runners participated, a record that would be broken in the fall when the Old Hickory Run, still sponsored by National Life, attracted 1,200 runners.[1035]

The Brentwood Crieve Hall YMCA took a big step in April when its chairman Ralph Mosley reported that the center had purchased for $38,000 a site on Concord Road that was in the flood plane of the Little Harpeth River.[1036]

Chuck Harris reported at the same meeting on the 25th anniversary meeting of the Tennessee Youth In Government program. He said that the Nashville YMCA had assumed administrative responsibility for the statewide program. At the time, Urban Services' biggest splash was its "Cool-in-the-Pool" program that had spread from Bordeaux-North to lower East Nashville and, in 1978, to West Nashville.[1037]

In recognition of the great work he had done leading the Urban Service program, Chuck Harris, 31, was named the first full-time executive director of the Brentwood-Creive Hall YMCA, effective June 26. Two months later, Chuck watched the property on Concord Road being graded and prepared for athletic fields.[1038]

Up in Flint, Michigan, a young YMCA outreach coordinator named J. Lawrence read in a YMCA vacancy list that there was a vacant position at Nashville's Bordeaux-North Branch. He applied for the position in a letter to Ralph Brunson. Some days later, J. got a phone call from Jim Rayhab, the Nashville YMCA executive responsible for financial administration. Rayhab told J. that the Bordeaux-North position had been filled, but they needed a director of Urban Services to replace Chuck Harris. J. was interested and flew to Nashville to be interviewed for the position. He recalled in 2010 that Bill Wilson and Ridley Wills II were among those with whom he talked. J. got the job and had a wonderfully productive and life-changing career at the Nashville YMCA.[1039]

By 1978, the Metropolitan Nashville YMCA was a much more sophisticated organization than when Ralph Brunson arrived fourteen years earlier. For example, planning for the 104th annual meeting to be held in April 1979 was pretty much in place the previous July. Four annual meeting committees were active; Phil Woosnan, commissioner of soccer for North America, had already accepted the invitation to speak; and a ballroom had been secured at the Opryland Hotel. With soccer the Nashville YMCA's fastest growing sport, the choice of Woosnan as speaker was appropriate.[1040]

Despite the fact that an ad hoc committee at the Donelson-Hermitage YMCA was again considering the possibility of selling Hickory Bend pool on Stewart Ferry Pike two or three miles from the center, it seemed imprudent to do so until a pool could be build at the center itself. The inconvenience of the Hickory Bend location must not have been significant as, by June 26, 1,000 members used it.[1041] Nevertheless, the idea didn't die and the center was granted permission in November to draw preliminary plans for construction of an outdoor pool on the Donelson-Hermitage YMCA property.[1042]

With memories of the failed 1976 capital campaign still on their minds, the leadership at the Nashville YMCA were thrilled that the 1978 sustaining membership campaign was a big success. Bob Philp, chairman, reported in July that it raised $119,618, a record amount. Three centers, Donelson-Hermitage, Downtown, and Southwest exceeded 100 percent of their respective goals.

Frank Bailey, chairman of the Bordeaux-North Family Center, was excited to announce in September that Edward Hargrave, of Washington DC, had been employed as the long-sought program director at the center on Hydes Ferry Pike. Hargrave seemed to have all the right credentials. A graduate of Howard University, he had spent three years working for the International YMCA in Monrovia, Liberia. Highly recommended by Julius Jones, the former Bordeaux-North executive director, Hargrave was the son of the general executive of the Washington, DC, YMCA where Jones was associate general executive.[1043]

At the fifth annual Heritage Club meeting, held at the lovely home of Buzz and Florence Davis in September, it was announced that there were 126 members, including eight couples who joined in 1978.[1044]

Over at Southwest, there were growing pains. The center had simply outgrown its space. Bill Portman, Bob Sheehan, and Bill Scott presented a $1,250,000 expansion plan to the executive committee in October. The idea was to have a capital campaign at the end of 1979 to raise the money. The executive committee approved the proposed plan subject to review.[1045]

As an organization with more than 3,000 volunteer workers, Ralph Brunson knew the value of recognizing veteran leaders. Consequently, he held an event on October 11, the birthday of Sir George Williams, to recognize five YMCA stalwarts who had collectively given 117 years serving the local association. They were A. Battle Rodes, 22 years; Dr. James M. Hudgins, 22 years; Dan Ewing, 34; Thomas E. Baldridge, 24, and Clarence Berson, 15. Another long-time member was Walter Bell, who was a regular on the indoor track at the Downtown Center. Walter was famous for yelling out "25 in 5," which meant that he had run 25 laps in 5 minutes. This was clearly not true as Walter was far past his prime as a runner and even at his best could probably not break an 8-minute mile.[1046]

At the quarterly meeting of the Metropolitan Nashville YMCA Board on October 25, Homer Gibbs Jr. reported that he and a dedicated few were still collecting funds for the 1976 Centennial Capital Campaign. Through November 15, the total pledged had slowly climbed to $1,068.210 with $828,898.62 paid.

The Bordeaux-North YMCA held a Day of Dedication on November 29, copying the similar event in Lebanon. This was a fund-raising event that raised $11, 049 in cash and pledges to go toward the center's 1979 operating budget. Some 110 people attended.[1047]

There were two important staff changes late in the year. Charles Cleveland resigned as East Center executive to become executive of the Five Points Branch in Birmingham. Charles had given the association seven years of "extremely fine service." Butch Hannah, Cleveland's counterpart in Lebanon, also resigned to become physical director of the Metropolitan Physical Fitness Center, that, in its six years of operation, had developed a top-notch program with 2,330 members. Plans were then in the works to allow women to use the center. This was controversial, and had to be managed carefully. Hannah would be replaced as the Lebanon-Wilson County executive by Jim Latchford of Danville, VA.

In November, Elbert Brooks announced the resignation of president-elect Whatley Scott from the Metropolitan board of directors. Scott resigned to take a new position in Birmingham with South Central Bell.[1048] Florence Davis was elected to take his place. Ralph Brunson immediately wrote her to express his pleasure that, the following July 1, she would become the first woman ever to serve as president of the Nashville YMCA. To reassure her, he said that women and girls constituted 46 percent of the YMCA's membership.[1049]

To clear the way for two development plans—the Southwest capital campaign in 1980, and an approved plan of approaching selected corporations for the next ten years for capital funds to be designated for individual centers—the long-range planning committee voted in November to seek the permission of the United Way.[1050] Hopefully, it would help that Ridley Wills II, a downtown member, was United Way campaign chairman.

In December the budget and finance committee finalized the 1979 Metropolitan YMCA budget at $1,922,629. To cover deficits at East and Northwest, they used surpluses from other centers. The 1978 calendar ended with a surplus of $22.

In his year-end report, Dr. Elbert D. Brooks, YMCA president, said, "We are now one of the largest and most active YMCA movements n the United States with our Metropolitan Center, six Family Centers, Foundation Board and Metropolitan Board." He added, "Our 1978 membership of 21,640 represents an increase of more than 1,000 members, and 43,458 were active in YMCA-sponsored programs."[1051] Indeed, 1978 had been a good year.

Good Press

The importance of good communications and public relations was not lost on the Metropolitan Nashville YMCA in 1979. The plan for that year was to send a steady flow of releases and articles to the *Nashville Tennessean* and the *Nashville Banner* and to offer a feature article to each paper about once a quarter. This strategy would be duplicated for the suburban newspapers. There would also be an in-house citywide publication for members. Public service announcements would be sent to radio and television stations quarterly and the Y would try to get articles in *Nashville!*, *Advantage*, *South*, and Southern Living during the year. There would also be a press appreciation luncheon.[1052]

February was supposed to be devoted to securing new and renewal memberships with a goal of enrolling 2,275 members. Of course, it took a lot longer than that. At the Metropolitan Nashville YMCA board meeting on July 25, Sidney Koonce said that the drive should exceed the goal of $141,000 and possibly reach $150,000 by year-end.

Yoga, ladies fitness, and water exercise were the most popular winter programs at Southwest. There was also a disco dancing and disco fitness class there. Across town at East, a scuba diving class received an overwhelming response. Non-traditional programs seemed to be in vogue.[1053]

The 104th annual meeting was held at the Hillwood Country Club on April 17, 1979. The principal speaker, Phil Woosnam, commissioner of soccer for North America, was described by *Sports Illustrated* as "a Welshman with the tongue of a spellbinder and a bulldog's persistence." At the event, officers for 1979–80 and board members were introduced. Florence (Mrs. W. Lipscomb) Davis was elected president; J. P. Foster was elected president-elect; Walter G. Knestrick, Don Knobler, and R. Sidney Koonce were elected vice-presidents; Edward A. "Ted" Adams was elected treasurer; and William M. "Bill" Wilson was elected secretary. Florence was the first female president in the Association's 104 years. Two of the new board members—Lee Barfield and Ridley Wills II—would, in time, become president of the YMCA Board. The Order of the Red Triangle was awarded to A. Battle Rodes.[1054]

Foreign exchanges were becoming more frequent. In the summer of 1979, an international camp counselor from Finland worked in all the day camps, and the Donelson-Hermitage YMCA took a group of soccer players on a two-week trip to Egypt, Greece, France, and England. Ralph Brunson and Mike Frith accompanied the group. Nashville YMCA members also hosted 55 foreign students in their homes. Not surprisingly, our association was named as an International YMCA for the fifth consecutive year.[1055]

The *Tennessean* reported on July 5 that Rusty Yeomans, associate executive director of the Southwest YMCA Family Center, had been named Southwest Region YMCA Leadership Commissioner. Yeomans would work with leaders' club composed of youth ages 13 to 18, who volunteer their services in exchange for training, fellowship and fun. He would also serve on three national or regional committees.[1056]

On July 25, Ralph Mosley urged the Metropolitan YMCA board to stop foot-dragging on the issue of allowing women to use the Metropolitan physical fitness center and move forward by addressing the matter quickly. New board president Florence Davis told Ralph that she felt that, within a few months, there would be something concrete to report.[1057] The board went ahead and commissioned Shockley Research to conduct a study on probable female interest in using the facilities, and, concurrently, asked Lee Barfield, chairman of the law committee, to look into the legal aspects of the matter. In September, Lee reported that the Y was not in violation of any state of federal laws by not allowing women in the center, but that the possibility of a lawsuit did exist. Granbery Jackson, chairman of the Downtown board, had earlier reported that the fitness center was only 20 members under capacity, so that, too, was a problem.[1058]

• • • • •

In the fall, it was learned that past-president Bill Henderson would soon leave Nashville to accept a job in Houston. Before Bill left, he was awarded the Order of the Red Triangle, the association's highest award.[1059]

• • • • •

The 11th annual Old Hickory Invitational Run was held in Warner Park on October 6. Described as the best ever, with approximately 2,000 runners in 25 events, this was the oldest and biggest run in Nashville. Sponsored by the NLT Corporation, the parent company for National Life, the race had as its honorary starter Rusty Wagner, chairman of the board of NLT.[1060]

Still without a center of its own, the Brentwood-Crieve Hall Center planned, for the second straight winter, to use the use the Lipscomb School gym. Needing space of its own, the center requested permission to purchase for $10,900 a modular office-program committee building to be placed on their Concord Road property.[1061]

H. G. Hill Jr. Recognized

The Heritage Club had a great meeting at the home of H. G. Hill Jr. on October 21. Composed of 137 people who had either made direct contributions to the foundation or included the YMCA in their estate plans, the Heritage Club welcomed new members and recognized Mr. Hill for his 53 years of leadership and service to the YMCA. Homer Gibbs Jr., president of the YMCA Foundation, reported that its assets were $469,902.97.[1062] At year's end, the foundation turned over approximately $13,000 to the Metropolitan board.[1063]

By far the most serious topic at the October 24 Metropolitan board meeting was Ralph Brunson's report on the Northwest Family YMCA Center, since October 1978 the name for the old Bordeaux-North branch. First, Ralph circulated a sheet summarizing the finances of the center for the past thirteen years. It showed that, for nine of those years, the Northwest branch had run a deficit, cumulatively amounting to $137,989. This happened in spite of the center receiving, over those thirteen years, $382,886 from the United Way, 47 percent of the total received by the Association. Ralph then, his voice wavering with emotion, spoke of the countless, strenuous efforts made over the years by both the Northwest board and staff and the Metropolitan board and staff to correct the problem. He said these efforts were largely unsuccessful, as the deficits increased year after year, being made up annually from surpluses from the Downtown Fitness Center and the Southwest Center.

Influenced by these failures, spiraling inflation and the slackening economy, Brunson recommended that the president appoint an ad hoc committee from the Metropolitan board to work with an ad hoc committee from the Northwest board to work toward correcting the financial problems of the center. He further recommended that, if the problems could not be resolved within a six-month period, that the center be sold. A motion to accept Mr. Brunson's recommendation was made, seconded, and passed. Jim Wilson and Dr. Samuella Junior, the mother of future Alabama football star E. J. Junior, immediately asked to serve on the committee. Frank Bailey, the chairman of the Northwest board since 1978, who had poured so much of his energy and time into the center, spoke of how desperately he wanted the Northwest Center to survive. As no one had any interest in dealing with other, seemingly less important issues, the meeting adjourned.[1064]

In November, the Shockley report was received. It showed little female demand for programming at the physical fitness center. In December, the Downtown board adopted a policy that the center would conform to the National YMCA policy concerning providing program services to women. A problem was that the answers Lee Barfield received to questions he had asked Chris Mould, attorney for the National YMCA, seemed vague. Brunson was frustrated and concerned. He verbalized his concern over the attitude, spirit, and apparent lack of concern of the Downtown board for the Metropolitan organization. He thought the Downtown board members were slow in increasing rates; worried about the lack of growth in members there, and the lack of a surplus. Without a surplus from the Downtown board, Brunson stated that it was impossible for East and Northwest to balance their budgets due to their locations in low-income areas. In summary, he urged all centers to work together for the good of all—not as separate units apart from each other.[1065] Probably, Ralph felt a little better when, in December, the Metropolitan board approved the participation by women in the Downtown center, and established a task force to implement the decision. This decision was made despite the fact that the fitness center was in compliance with local, State, and Federal laws, and a number of members, including Bert Haywood and Douglas Henry Jr., were adamantly against doing so. Duck Roberts didn't want ladies on the running track to see how out-of-shape he was.

Boris Kazimiroff, executive director of the YMCA's Men International/U.S. Area, spoke of his YMCA experiences in Korea and Ceylon at the Nashville YMCA Voting Members luncheon on December 5 in the YMCA Law School room. During the meeting, Martha Wiggins, who would retire on December 31 as Mr. Brunson's secretary, was recognized for her twenty-nine years of service to the Association. On behalf of the Metropolitan board, Ralph told her that her retirement gift was a paid vacation in Hawaii.[1066]

During 1979, the membership was at an all-time high—25,062, an increase of 3,422 over 1978. The total number of program participants was 54,268, a 10,830 increase over 1978. The Metropolitan YMCA managed another miniscule surplus, this time $855. Deficits were rung up at Donelson-Hermitage, East, Northwest, and Youth & Government. On the other hand, Southwest and Downtown had solid surpluses that tipped the scales to the positive side for the Metropolitan Y. A special sustaining membership push in December made the difference. One year, possibly this one, Mr. Brunson was so intent on balancing the budget that he sent Kent Rea and Jim Rayhab out on New Years Eve to solicit memberships. Rayhab called on Shade Murray, who happened to be hosting a New Year's Eve party. Mr. Murray was cordial and made a gift, undoubtedly realizing that Jim did not come of his own accord. The Centennial Capital Campaign follow-up also officially closed with $1,068,210 in pledges and $946,868 paid.[1067]

Awards ceremony with Sydney F. Keeble Jr., Florence Davis, Ralph L. Mosley, and J. P. Foster

CHAPTER TWENTY-SEVEN

Ralph's Last Year
1980

ON JANUARY 5, 1980, Ralph Brunson wrote Florence Davis, president of the Metropolitan Nashville YMCA, to announce that, in accordance with the Association's retirement policy, he would resign "at age 65 plus six months," on December 31, 1980. Ralph wrote of having spent nearly forty-five years serving the YMCA in six cities and each was a growing experience but that his greatest pleasure was the sixteen and one-half years he served as general executive in Nashville.

With the announcement of Ralph Brunson's impending retirement, a selection committee was quickly appointed. Chairman Charles Cornelius Jr. quickly secured the help of Ron Kinnamon, executive director of the Southeast Regional Office and got to work.[1068]

YBA basketball was extremely popular in the winter of 1980. At Southwest alone, there were 62 teams with approximately 560 boys and girls playing, possibly the largest group at any branch YMCA anywhere. Association wide, there were 185 teams with 1,885 players.[1069]

In February, the Metropolitan Nashville YMCA executive committee gave the Brentwood-Crieve Hall Center approval to proceed with their $1 million capital campaign and to employ Bill Beck, of campaign Associates, to run it.[1070] At the same meeting, Granbery Jackson III, chairman of the Downtown Board, said that part of the Church Street side of the first floor would be converted to accommodate 150 women at a cost of $93,000. This would be paid for by a $100,000 loan. Walter Knestrick, chairman of Metropolitan sustaining enrollments, reported that the 1980 Association goal was $197,393, a $32,000 increase over 1979. No one who knew the out-going Walter doubted that the campaign would be successful.

Finally, new officers of the Metropolitan Board were elected for the 1980–1981 year. They were J. P. Foster, president; Robert L. Bibb Jr., president-elect; Walter G. Knestrick, William M. Wilson, and Dr. Robert H. Crumby, vice-presidents; Edward A. "Ted" Adams Jr., treasurer; and Wentworth Caldwell Jr., secretary.[1071]

At the March 26, Metropolitan YMCA board meeting, William C. E. Terry, an employee of the Association for 57 years was honored. He gave an inspiring devotional. This was a timely event as Terry died in June. At the same meeting, Granbery Jackson III reported that a minimum of 150 applicants needed to join the women's health center before remodeling would start. The women would be required to pay a $50 nonrefundable earnest money deposit. This fee would be credited toward their $275 annual membership fees. Women were expected to begin using the facilities in December.[1072] By May, 136 women had signed up, and approval was expected soon from the United Way to allow fund-raising for the project to start.

The State Handball Tournament returned to the Downtown Physical Fitness Center on March 21–23 with 60 players participating. Nashville had finalists in 6 divisions and had 6 runner-ups.[1073]

Soon after the March executive committee meeting, Ralph Brunson entered the hospital for cardiac surgery for four bypasses. Ralph had known that he had at least one blocked artery for many years, but his daily habit of running regularly had built up his collateral circulation so that he was able to function well for a long time. However, a back injury and an arthritic condition "slowed me down to a walk" and a recent arteriogram showed considerable deterioration, necessitating the bypass surgery.

Ralph was out of the hospital by mid-April and back at his desk in May.[1074]

The statewide Youth and Government program, directed by Chuck Harris, was held in Nashville on April 18 with 360 participants.

On April 25, the Southeast Region YMCA Assembly met at the Radisson Hotel. This was a good opportunity for Nashville board members to learn more about regional activities. It was a shame that Ralph Brunson was still recuperating from his surgery and unable to be there to receive the first International Distinguished Service Award given to a YMCA staff member in the Southeast. Florence Davis accepted the award for him. It seemed appropriate that, in his final year as the Nashville YMCA's general executive, Ralph Brunson was recognized for the special interest he had long taken in the YMCA's International work. Ralph had been a member of the International Division for eleven years. In both 1978 and 1979, the Nashville Y was number one of 173 YMCAs in the Southeast in World Service giving. Nashville was also the first association in the Southeast Region to qualify as an International YMCA and had qualified for seven consecutive years.[1075]

Florence Davis called a special meeting of the Metropolitan Nashville board of directors on June 18 to hear the report of Mr. John E. Kuhlfah, from Campaign Associates, who had just concluded a feasibility study to ascertain the probability of success of what was termed a ten-year $10 million financial development plan. He recommended that the board move forward and implement the development program. Mrs. Davis was also excited to announce that the H. G. Hill Company had made a

Florence Davis, first female President of the YMCA of Metropolitan Nashville, 1979–1980

pledge of $500,000 to the capital drive. The H. G. Hill gift primarily consisted of a five-acre tract of land on Franklin Road at Williamson Road in the heart of Brentwood. Mrs. Davis said, "This is the largest gift ever made to the local association." Back in 1967, when the H. G. Hill Company gave property worth $225,000 for the Southwest Center, the same statement was made. With the gift, the YMCA decided to build the Harpeth Center on the Franklin Road site and use the Concord site for an athletic field.[1076]

In June, George Cate Jr. reported to the executive committee for the ad hoc committee studying the Northwest problem. George stated that, for 1980, the center was expected to do better on its budget and that the Northwest board had developed a 1981 budget that balanced. He asked that the plan for rejuvenation he presented be accepted. After lengthy discussion concerning the viability of the plan and what the consequences of its failure would be, the committee accepted the plan and asked the ad hoc committee to monitor progress every three months and report to the executive committee every six months.[1077]

At the July 16 executive committee meeting, it was reported that six finalists, out of 58 candidates, had been interviewed, two local and four from outside Nashville. The committee was charged with recommending a successor prior to September 1, 1980.

At the quarterly Metropolitan Nashville board meeting on July 23, Elizabeth Craig Weaver, the widow of William C. "Bill" Weaver Jr., accepted from out-going president Florence Davis, the Order of the Red Triangle on behalf of her late husband. Before his death on March 6, 1979, Bill Weaver was retired board chairman and chief executive officer of NLT Corporation and the National Life and Accident Insurance Company. He had been one of the first Metropolitan board members, had served as chairman of the property committee, and was a prime factor in his company's generous contributions to the YMCA—a level of corporate support second only to that of the H. G. Hill Company.[1078]

The selection committee found their man in August. The committee's final choice was Adrian B. Moody, 45, vice-president of the YMCAs of the Greater Houston Area. Before joining the Houston staff in 1977, Moody had served for eight years as the general director of the family YMCA in Bristol, TN-VA. The resolution to offer Mr. Moody the position, effective January 1, 1981, was unanimously adopted.[1079]

Meanwhile there was work to be done to get the women's facility on-line at the Downtown Center. Ridley Wills II made a motion at the August board meeting that the United Way be asked for a four-week extension of fundraising for the project, that construction begin when $60,000 in cash and hard pledges had been made, that that the contractor be asked to wait for one year before expecting to receive the final $7,000, and to purchase up to $18,000 in furnishings and equipment on time. The motion passed.[1080]

The fund-raising efforts for the women's center at the Downtown Fitness Center made progress over the summer. By September 9, $59,545 had been raised, only $455 short of the amount needed to let contracts. Consequently, the Metropolitan board gave approval for the contract to be signed by September 15, construction to start immediately thereafter, and completion set for December 1.[1081] One of the champions of the women's center was Florence Davis, an excellent president who would remain active on the Metropolitan board for decades to come.

A report from the ad hoc committee monitoring the Northwest YMCA situation, given in September, said that the center's deficit through July was $17,887 and that the budgeted deficit for the year was a little less, $16,350. Contributing factors were high unemployment and spiraling inflation. Dr. Jack Tarleton, a Northwest board member, was leading the effort to cut the amount to $12,887 by year-end. Unless that was accomplished and a balanced budget approved for 1981, the executive committee voted to either close the center or change its program to operate within its existing funds.

As Ralph Brunson moved through the twilight months of his illustrious YMCA career, a serious deficit situation plagued him, with the four biggest problem areas being Downtown, Harpeth, Lebanon, and Northwest. Ralph's new theme was "Be Tough, Be Tight and Work Hard."

October 7, 1980, was proclaimed "Ralph L. Brunson Day" by Mayor Richard Fulton. That evening, at the Hillwood Country Club, Brunson was honored at the Association's 105th annual meeting and recognition banquet. Approximately, 375 people were there to hear Solon Cousins, executive director of the National Council of YMCAs in New York, speak. Following Mr. Cousins' message, George Cate Jr., chairman of the recognitions committee, introduced Ralph's family—Willie Belle, their sons Bill and Alan and Bill's wife,

Nashville YMCA General Executive Ralph Brunson at his desk

Claudia. The youngest son, David, was in college and could not attend. A number of awards and gifts were then given to Ralph, including a garden planter from the Lexington, KY, YMCA, and the governor's Outstanding Tennessean Award. A bound book of letters from YMCA friends and the keys to a new Chevy Chevette virtually left Ralph speechless, but not for long. After regaining his composure, he reminisced about the past. Dr. Robert H. Spain concluded the evening with a beautiful benediction.[1082]

Walter Knestrick reported in October that the sustaining membership drive, then at 87 percent, would make its goal. Walter declared victory at the December executive committee meeting when the total hit $187,910, or 101 percent of the goal. It would edge up to 103 percent by December 26. Meanwhile, the Southwest capital campaign's co-chairs, Bob Meyer, of Third National Banks, and Bob Devlin, of Life and Casualty, were first focusing on gifts from the Southwest board, who had pledged $30,000 although one-third of the board had not yet given.[1083]

Although bids had been received, contracts to build the women's center had not been signed in October. Consequently, it was obvious that the center would not be open by December 31. Because the women's membership fees were needed to balance the Downtown budget, a plan was adopted to begin serving women in the fourth quarter. By December, 151 women had signed up for memberships and the opening had been postponed until the early spring.[1084]

Walter Robinson, president of NLT, was honorary starter for the 12th annual Old Hickory Run, sponsored by NLT. Over 1,700 runners took part.

The budget situation that Brunson worried so much about was more acute in 1980 than in a decade. Cuts were made and other last minute measures tried, but to no avail. The association had its biggest deficit since 1970—a loss of $49,907. Only one profit center—Southwest—had a surplus. It was $24,382, nearly $4,000 better than budgeted. Bill Portman should have been congratulated and surely was. The biggest deficits were at Lebanon-Wilson ($20,236), Harpeth ($19,000), and Northwest ($17,287). How to deal with Northwest and Lebanon would be two of new president Adrian Moody's immediate challenges.

Goodbyes

On December 23, on his last day in office, Ralph wrote an open letter of appreciation to the YMCA membership family. He penned these words, "The last sixteen years in Nashville have been the most interesting, exciting and gratifying in my forty-five-year career with a great movement, the Young Men's Christian Association. You have been among the finest, most interested, dedicated YMCA lay leaders I have ever known and with whom I have had the privilege of working."

Ralph was both successful and respected in Nashville. The Nashville YMCA was an infinitely stronger organization when he left than when he came. It had grown enormously. While it took the Nashville Association ninety-eight years for its annual budget to reach $1 million, it only took seven to reach $2 million.

One of the highlights of his career was surely the courageous and assertive leadership he demonstrated in integrating the Nashville YMCA and in bringing back into full partnership the members of the Colored YMCA in 1966, only three years after John Lewis was arrested for trying to integrate the Downtown Center. For 45 years prior to that, the Colored YMCA had its own charter and were independent of and estranged from the Nashville YMCA. Ralph was clearly ahead of his time. Above all else, Ralph Brunson was a dedicated Christian man who gave everything he had to his job and did it well. When he retired, the Nashville YMCA was nationally respected. That was not the case when he arrived.

• • • • •

CHAPTER TWENTY-EIGHT

"Changing Lives" Campaign
1981–1983

WHEN ADRIAN MOODY walked in the front door of the Nashville YMCA on his first day as general executive, he was confronted by the association's accumulation of $395,174 in debt, and a number of ailing family centers, some critically so. One of the first things he did every workday morning was to devote a few minutes to a quiet, private time of prayer, something he had learned from the readings of John Mott, the great YMCA leader of the first half of the twentieth century.[1085]

As so often happens during a time of transition, changes came quickly. In his two years as program director at Northwest, Edward Hargrave had proved his worth. Adrian was happy for Edward when he learned that the Northeast executive had accepted an opportunity to become executive director of the West Broad Street YMCA in Savannah, GA. Still, it hurt to lose him at Northwest at such a crucial time. A compensation that proved huge was the arrival of twenty-nine-year-old Steve Tarver in January to become physical director of the Downtown Fitness Center.

Steve grew up in Jacksonville, Florida, where his mother gave him a YMCA membership for Christmas when he was six years old. When Steve was thirteen, he joined the Y's Junior Leader's Club for teenagers, run by Kent Rea. At fourteen, Steve became a Jacksonville YMCA lifeguard. Years later, when Steve was associate general director and physical director of the Owensboro, KY, YMCA, he named his son, Kenton, for his mentor in Jacksonville, Kent Rea. In 2005, when Steve was CEO of the YMCA of Greater Louisville, he wrote Kent: "You remain a wonderful example and inspiration to me and my work."[1086]

A bank draft program, announced in January 1981 and patterned after one in Houston that Adrian had administered, was a needed step: one that would prove its worth many times over. And even though the women's facilities at the Downtown Center were not yet complete, 130 women were using the facility and there was a waiting list.

In his first month on the job, Adrian was busy meeting business and civic leaders; dealing with problems at the Lebanon YMCA; working with the Association's financial strains; and reorganizing his staff. One change Adrian made was to build a 3 percent contingency figure in each center budget to alleviate possible deficits. Yet, the dynamics of the Nashville YMCA were encouraging to Adrian and he was ready for whatever challenges lay ahead.[1087] In his first year at the helm, the Nashville YMCA had a budget of $2,255,258. Another change made in January was to transfer any center deficits from the previous year to an association account enabling each center to begin the New Year at zero.

President J. P. Foster was pleased with the transition from the Brunson to the Moody regime. In early March, Foster said that the changes were being implemented very smoothly. He also reported at a YMCA Foundation meeting on the 3rd that the ladies' fitness center was complete.

Adrian's very first Metropolitan board meeting was on March 25. Although the contingency fund and the new bank draft plan would have negative impacts on the Association's cash flow for 1981, Adrian was pleased when treasurer Ted Adams said that the association deficit for the first two months of the year was $34,127, significantly less than the $55,000 expected.

The kickoff for the 1981 sustaining membership drive, headed by Bill Wilson, was held the day of the March board meeting. Its goal was $212.000, a 10 percent increase over Walter Knestrick's successful campaign a year earlier. Dr. Jim Hudgins, president of the YMCA Foundation, said that the foundation had set a goal of increasing its assets from $675,000 to $10 million by 1990. That would turn out to be a pipe dream but no one knew it then.

A legal threat arose in the spring that would periodically arise for the next two decades. The State tax-equalization board was studying the exempt tax status of YMCA fitness centers. On the recommendation of the legal committee, the executive committee approved a motion to employ Paul Troutman, Vanderbilt Law School professor, to represent the Nashville and possibly other YMCAs before the board that was expected to make its decision by August. Troutman accepted the offer and began preparing a brief to support the YMCA's exempt status. The result was a reaffirmation that the YMCA was exempt from Federal and State taxes.[1088]

The Harpeth YMCA had raised only $250,000 in pledges on its $2,100,000 capital drive. The April YMCA executive committee meeting was Hugh Hurst Jr.'s last. Described by J. P. Foster as "a total YMCA professional," Hugh would be missed. After serving in Nashville, he became the CEO of the Memphis YMCA from 1983 until 1989. Hugh's father had once been executive director of the Memphis YMCA's Leslie Stratton Branch.[1089]

The 106th annual meeting of the Metropolitan Nashville YMCA was held again at Hillwood Country Club on April 28. Ron Kinnamon, Southeast Region executive of the YMCAs, was the guest speaker. President Foster introduced the officers for the 1981–82 year. They were Robert L. Bibb Jr., president; Walter G. Knestrick, president-elect; Robert Crumby, Ridley Wills II, and William M. Wilson, vice-presidents; Wentworth Caldwell Jr., secretary; and Jack Elisar, treasurer. In May, Ridley, chairman of the long-range planning committee, presided over the corporate planning process at a planning retreat at the DuBose Conference Center in Monteagle. Bo Hardy, a friend of Adrian's, and one of the nation's most outstanding planning consultants, led the process.

Jim Barr succeeded Bill Scott as chairman of the Harpeth Board on July 1. At Downtown, Fitness Center members were anxiously awaiting the arrival of Nautilus equipment. They would have to wait until September.[1090]

Ray Parks resigned as center executive for the Northwest YMCA in June. He left with many friends in the Association. By then, the staff reorganization that Mr. Moody had in mind was complete. Bill Portman, the Southwest Center executive director, was also named associate general director for operations. Jim Rayhab became associate general executive for business and finance and executive director of the Downtown and Urban Services. He also would oversee budget and finances for all the branches. Kent Rea would be associate general executive for human resources and program development.[1091]

The five-year goals developed by the long-range planning committee for the years 1982–1986 were approved at the July 29 board of directors meeting. Goals were set in the areas of programs, family, senior adults, teenagers, outreach, health enhancements, international, and resources.

Adrian Moody's first year as general executive was challenging. With Ray Park's departure, Northwest was without a director until September when John Wright, of Birmingham, Alabama, accepted the position. He would prove to be a strong and entrepreneurial leader. The Lebanon center had a director, Benny Nolan, but the town had not rallied to support the financial needs of the center. If things didn't change quickly, it would have to be closed. The very capable Chuck Harris resigned in September to accept a YMCA position in Memphis. He would later become an outstanding general executive at the South Hampton Roads YMCA in Tidewater, Virginia.

Across the association, membership was down, and, through August, the Metropolitan YMCA had a negative variance of $53,163. Much of the deficit was attributed to the 20 percent membership decline and the fact that membership dues paid by bank draft were deferred. A positive note was that the financial condition was expected to improve in 1982. Another bounce came when Vanderbilt's respected basketball coach, C. M. Newton, became a board member.[1092]

At year-end, the balance sheet for the Metropolitan Nashville YMCA showed assets of $3,819,414.89, down from 1980. The year-end deficit was $89,950 and the sustaining membership enrollment stood at $188,307, 89 percent of its goal. The campaigns fell woefully short in Lebanon and at Northwest where the percentages raised were 32.6 and 36, respectively, Southwest, Metropolitan, and Harpeth were all over 100 percent. As a result, the Association scaled back its 1982 sustaining membership goal to $188,000. The Harpeth capital campaign had picked up, raising $1,015,000 by March 1982.[1093]

A Nashville-Venezuelan Connection

Walter Knestrick, chairman of the financial development steering committee, reported in February that his committee of key community leaders had endorsed a capital campaign of $4 million. The date for the campaign would have to be cleared with the United Way.

In February 1982, general executive Adrian Moody, president Robert Bibb Jr., and chairman of the YMCA's International Committee, Ridley Wills II, wrote Gustavo Espin, National YMCA Federation of Venezuela, suggesting that the Nashville YMCA develop a partnership with one or more YMCAs in Venezuela, and asking that a meeting be held either in Caracas or Nashville to explore the possibilities. Ridley and Bob had no idea where this idea might lead. Adrian, who had first gone to Venezuela in 1966 with a group of South Georgia college students, had an infinitely better idea. The impact of the letter turned out to be enormous as a Nashville-Venezuela partnership not only started but also propelled Nashville into the limelight as a national model for international relationships. Adrian would, over time, become a hero to Venezuelan YMCAs and have a building named for him in Caracas. As of January 2011, he had been to Venezuela forty-five times. William Luers, the attractive ambassador to Venezuela from the United States, visited the Downtown Center on June 11, 1982, and spoke to the Metropolitan board members and others. He encouraged the idea of establishing the Nashville-Venezuelan relationship.

From left to right: Robert L. Bibb Jr., Ridley Wills II, and Adrian M. Moody, ca. 1981

Mr. Moody first met Bob McGaughey, when, as director of the Moultrie, GA, YMCA, he had recruited Bob, then a Bible college student, to work part-time. Bob, who later worked for Adrian in Bristol, arrived in Nashville on May 1 from a Y job in South Dakota to assume the directorship of the Harpeth Center. He would also become an associate general executive. Bob would quickly prove that his reputation for working effectively with young people was no smoke screen.[1094]

The Metropolitan Nashville YMCA paid off in March a $50,000 loan made in 1981 to address the association's cash flow problem. Even better, the budget at the end of February showed a $14,834 surplus and everyone was breathing a sigh of relief that the association had turned the corner financially.

At the March 24 directors meeting, Mr. Moody reviewed some material received from Solon B. Cousins, executive director of the YMCA of the U.S. One of Cousins' recommendations was for the "clustering" of associations. It was decided that Kent Rea would provide leadership for the Tennessee Cluster.[1095]

John Wright, executive director at Northwest, gave an inspirational devotional at the April board of directors' meeting. He spoke of how childhood values carry over into adulthood and closed by reciting the words his mother had taught him in his childhood about Christian values. Chairman Wentworth Caldwell Jr. reported that the sustaining membership campaign was well ahead of its position a year earlier.

In April, the financial development steering committee reported that the association's needs over the next few years were estimated to be $7 million. The committee urged the appointment of a general chairman for the Metropolitan Capital campaign.[1096]

Another name change took place in May when the Southwest board of managers recommended to the Metropolitan Nashville YMCA that the name of the Southwest YMCA be changed to the Green Hills Family

Center. The executive committee approved the change at its May 26 meeting. At the same meeting, a decision was made to expand the Youth in Government program to include a model U.N. Assembly. Bob McGaughey would give outstanding leadership to both programs. The same week a group of Cambodian refugees were meeting at the Downtown YMCA to learn English. Many more foreign visitors would come in the ensuing years.[1097]

The Venezuelan YMCA responded positively to the idea of establishing a Nashville-Venezuelan partnership and invited the Nashvillians to come in August. Consequently, Adrian Moody, Suzanne Briggs, Cecilia Meng, Ted Adams, Ridley and Irene Wills and their son, Morgan, visited Caracas, Valencia, and Maracaibo to establish the relationship.

As many suspected would happen, the Lebanon-Wilson County YMCA closed in the summer as there was not enough local financial support to keep it open. Conversely, John Wright and Bob McGaughey were making their presence felt at Northwest and Harpeth, respectively. John's summer sports program at Northwest was boosted by the involvement of eleven Tennessee State athletes. A generous gift from Metropolitan board member Dr. Bill Wadlington, whose medical practice was in Donelson, encouraged Frank Bellar, chairman of the Donelson board, to think that the center could raise the money to build the long-desired pool at their center.[1098]

Bernard Werthan Jr., joined the Metropolitan YMCA board in August. A worthy representative of one of the city's finest and most philanthropic families, he would serve the Association with distinction during three decades and continue the tradition of other Jewish leaders such as Lee Loventhal and Gerald Averbush who had also appreciated and supported the work of this Christian organization.

Future board chairman William E. Turner Jr. was elected to the Metropolitan Nashville YMCA board in September.[1099] The next month, Bob Bibb announced that Walter Knestrick had accepted the general chairman position for the capital campaign. Walter, a wonderful choice, immediately challenged the board to make a personal commitment to the campaign. Ridley Wills II moved that the YMCA employ Panas and Partners for a six-to-eight-week cultivation program. On an earlier visit, Adrian had introduced Ridley to Panas and suggested that they go to breakfast together. They did so at Swett's Restaurant in North Nashville. Upon their return and after Panas left, Adrian said, "What did you think?" Ridley, who had noticed Jerry's sophisticated ways and monogrammed shirt, said, "He ain't from Owensboro [Adrian's hometown]." After the study, it was anticipated that the board would approve a capital campaign. At this point, Jerold Panas was introduced to the directors.

Mitchell Parks, chairman of the Northwest Center, reported that the branch was in the best financial condition in a long time. Frank Bella, Mitch's counterpart at Donelson, reported that a committee was studying their financial problem, aggravated by a lack of teenagers in that aging community.

• • • • •

That Harpeth was performing well was attested to in 1982, when there were 526 children enrolled in the Harpeth soccer program.[1100]

• • • • •

Jim Love, an educator from Scotland and the president of the World Alliance of YMCAs, visited the Metropolitan Nashville YMCA in mid-October as one of five stops on a tour to promote awareness of the alliance's outreach by urging local YMCA's to form partnerships with other Y's worldwide. Love knew he was preaching to the choir in Nashville as center executive Adrian Moody had long been committed to such relationships. "We can't ignore that we're a very small world," Adrian said, in discussing with Mr. Love the Nashville Y's exchange plans with the Venezuelan YMCA.[1101]

"Changing Lives"

Walter Knestrick reported at the November 24 executive committee that "Changing Lives" would be the theme of the next campaign. He said that John Jingo would be the in-town representative for the Panas Company and asked that he be allowed to step down from the position of president-elect to devote his attention to the campaign. Walter's request was granted and Dortch Oldham replaced him as president-elect. Finally, Walter moved that the Metropolitan Nashville executive committee change the name of the Harpeth Family YMCA Center to the H. G. Hill Jr., Family YMCA Center. This was unanimously approved.[1102] When informed of this honor, Mr. Hill declined to accept it, feeling that the YMCA would be better served by having a name denoting the area to be served. So, the change was rescinded.

At the December board meeting, J. P. Foster presented a proposed slate of officers for 1983. They were Dortch Oldham, president; Walter Knestrick, vice-president; Richard Penuel, secretary; and Jack Elisar, treasurer. The slate was approved.[1103] The new officers assumed office on February 15 at the annual meeting when Bart Starr, Green Bay Packers quarterback, spoke.

An important decision was made in January relative to the site of the Harpeth YMCA Family Center. Because of the limited amount of land for programming at the Franklin Road site earlier given by the H. G. Hill Company and because that land was so valuable, being in the center of the Brentwood business district, Mr. Moody spoke to Mr. Hill to see if he was receptive to the YMCA considering other sites with more acreage and less traffic. Mr. Hill graciously said that the H. G. Hill Co. would be willing to consider making a cash contribution and keeping the Franklin Road property if the YMCA chose another site. The Y had three options: 1) sell the Hill property or return it to the H. G. Hill Co. and buy a new, larger site; 2) build on the Hill site and continue to use the Concord Road site for athletic fields; and 3) build on the Concord Road site even though this was on the fringe of our market area and was partially in the flood plain of the Little Harpeth River.[1104]

Meanwhile, Walter Knestrick had lined up 25 men to make calls on 125 key prospects, and reported that he expected those major calls to be made by February 15. It was imperative, he said, for the entire board to be actively involved in the drive. From the first 15 calls, $1,485,000 was raised—great news.[1105] One thing that wasn't working was the relationship between John Jingo and the campaign staff. After about two weeks on the job, Jingo left and was replaced by Gerry Panas, an exceptional fundraiser. From then on, the campaign was "smooth sailing."

In January, Adrian Moody flew to Houston to take part in the dedication of their greatly expanded Downtown YMCA. Until coming to Nashville in 1981, Adrian had been executive director of that center for four years. During that time, the Houston Downtown branch had gained national recognition as an example of how such a facility should operate. The day before Adrian left for Houston, the *Nashville Banner* published an editorial saluting him for the well-earned honor he would be given in Houston and expressing the thought that Nashville was indeed fortunate to have Adrian in his important position in the community.[1106]

Dortch Oldham, Metropolitan YMCA President 1983

There was good news from the Donelson Family Center. They finally had a contract to sell the pool on Stewart Ferry Pike. The sale would bring $65,000 and culminate a sales effort that lasted more than three years. Approval for architectural drawings for the new inside pool at Donelson was gained in February.

Carey F. Massey Jr. came to East as its new executive director in March when he was a month shy of his thirty-sixth birthday. He had been district executive director of the YMCA of Greater Miami, where he was heavily involved in running possibly the most successful after-school program in the country, being in 42 out of 67 public schools in Dade County. When he left for Nashville, Miami had 2,000 children in the program. Massey had a master's degree from George Williams University in 1974, where he was an honors graduate.

Green Hills was ready to take bids for a new Nautilus and exercise center, and Urban Services, which became a separate center in December, was dedicated to provide outreach services to inner-city Nashville. In 1983, a twenty-nine-member board of managers, two professional staff members, and over two hundred volunteers administrated the Urban Services Center.[1107]

The YMCA lost a potential human resource opportunity when C. M. Newton resigned as a director because his basketball commitment at Vanderbilt and his appointment as coach of the 1984 Olympics basketball team convinced him that he did not have the time to be an active board member.[1108]

The "Changing Lives" Campaign engendered great enthusiasm, something that did not happen in the 1969 and 1976 capital campaigns. On April 13, Walter Knestrick announced to his workers, "You are now over half way toward meeting the objective" of raising $5 million. That night, Walter said, "I'm so proud to be a part of this effort and to be working with you. I know we are going to be successful. It means so much to me to know that the work that you and I are doing now will benefit a generation yet unborn." By then, the drive had six-figure pledges from seven corporations and families. The second largest pledge for $250,000 came from American General Insurance Company, whose chief executive Harold Hook was anxious to make a good impression in Nashville after his company acquired NLT Corporation in a hostile takeover.

YMCA president Dortch Oldham's saying, "The YMCA is the best kept secret in town," encouraged the entire YMCA family to make known its great contributions to the community. More and more prospective donors were learning that the YMCA had inadequate resources to meet the program and financial needs of the inner city, had inadequate or incomplete facilities in the branches serving the suburban areas, and needed an entire facility for the Harpeth YMCA.[1109] Nelson Andrews played a key role as chairman of a communications committee that focused on one-on-one contacts with both newspapers, and radio and TV stations. Mr. Andrews stressed the importance of expressing appreciation to the media for the coverage provided. "Make it easy for the media to tell the story," Nelson would say. He would later tell Bill Wilson to "thank people seven different ways."

In the summer, the death of Dave Rivers at the Birmingham 4th Street YMCA created a vacancy that led the Birmingham YMCA to invite John Wright, a native of that city, to return home to accept the executive directors' position at that branch. John, who was excited about the potential for school-age childcare for African-American youth in Nashville, declined the opportunity, even though he received a letter from the Governor of Alabama encouraging him to accept.[1110]

By August, 110 children had pre-registered for after school child-care in ten schools. Cary Massey anticipated that number to double. It did quickly. By September, the number had nearly tripled to almost 300. This was despite the fact that the sites and staff had to be licensed by the Tennessee Department of Human Services and that there had to be one staff person for every ten children.[1111]

The "Changing Lives" campaign still had plenty of momentum. At the September executive committee meeting, Knestrick reported that the campaign had raised $3,722,000 in gifts and pledges, by far the most ever raised by a YMCA campaign in Nashville. Over at Green Hills, the YMCA Show Chorus, underwritten by flamboyant restaurateur and board member Wayne Oldham and directed by Jay Dawson, was off to a marvelous start with their first performance at the Italian Street Fair.

Dortch Oldham made the point at the October board meeting that the people in the Brentwood area needed "to see something tangible happening" with regard to a building and said, "time is becoming of the essence." There were two choices. One was to build on the Concord Road site that the YMCA already owned. This would work if engineers and architects could satisfy themselves that a building could be constructed there outside the one-hundred-year flood plain. A plus was that an I-65 exchange was projected to be built at Concord Road in 1986. The other possibility was to lease property from the State of Tennessee on Granny White Pike at Murray Lane next to Northside School. This could be a tedious process as the State Attorney General's office would have to prepare an opinion for the State Comptroller on what type of agreement the State could make with the YMCA should it choose the Murray Lane site. As the Tennessee Building Commission still had not heard from the Attorney General's office in November, the YMCA building committee and the Harpeth board of directors opted for the Concord Road site.[1112]

The financial situation in November was that a year-end deficit of between $30,000 and $35,000 was expected. This was covered, however, by an association-wide emergency fund of $70,000, something Ralph Brunson did not have when he was general secretary. At the December board meeting, a proposed 1984 budget of $2,820,326 was discussed, proposed, and unanimously adopted.

The "Changing Lives" campaign continued to go "great guns." Both in the amount of money raised and in the awareness the drive was bringing to the community of the great work done by the YMCA. On December 22,

Walter Knestrick reported to the board that $4,520,000 had been committed. At the same meeting, President Dortch Oldham presented the report of the nominating committee for 1984. The following officers were then nominated and elected. They were president Ridley Wills II, president-elect Walter Knestrick, vice-presidents Wentworth Caldwell and William M. Wilson, and treasurer Jack Elisar. Before adjourning the meeting, Mr. Oldham expressed his opinion that the Nashville YMCA "has the best staff of any in the country."

• • • • •

ADRIAN B. MOODY
General Executive YMCA of Nashville and Middle Tennessee (1981–1987)

Adrian B. Moody grew up in Owensboro, Kentucky, a son of Mr. and Mrs. Allen Moody. While in grammar school, he spent countless hours at the Owensboro YMCA where he had no idea there was a membership fee.

Adrian went on to Owensboro High School, where he excelled in academics and as a varsity basketball player. In 1953, his senior season, he made the All District and All Regional basketball teams. His basketball skills won him an athletic scholarship at Kentucky Wesleyan where the Owensboro YMCA Men's Club paid for this books.

During his senior year at Kentucky Wesleyan in 1955–56, Adrian was physical director at the Owensboro YMCA. That same year, he married Fran Dillehay, who had dropped out of Kentucky Wesleyan and was teaching school.

Following his graduation in 1957, Adrian and Fran moved to Danville, Kentucky, where he became district director of the State YMCA of Kentucky. Fran and Adrian also started a family with the birth of Debbie in 1958.

After three years in Danville with the State YMCA, Adrian accepted, in 1960, a position as associate general secretary of the Augusta, GA, YMCA. There, he made a name for himself by enlisting 350 mothers to give physical fitness tests to 4,000 boys, many of whom later joined the Y. The Moody family also grew with the birth of their son, David, in 1962.

After four wonderful years in Augusta, Adrian was invited by the chairman of the board of the Moultrie, Georgia, YMCA to become their general director. Adrian accepted the challenge. While at Moultrie, he built the largest Hi-Y program in the state, coached a women's volleyball team, got to know all the African-American and white leaders in town, and ran the local United Way campaign. Because of his success working with young people in Augusta and Moultrie, Adrian was asked by the YMCA U.S.A. to help get young adults more interested and active in the Y. Moody ended up taking scores of youth trips to Venezuela, partnering with the Peace Corps and building a strong alliance. Later, he would become Tennessee president of Partners of the Americas and, even later, served on the national YMCA board.

Fran's role as mother expanded a final time, in 1968, when she gave birth to another little girl named Stephanie.

In 1969, Adrian succeeded Frank Marney as general executive at the Bristol, Tennessee/Virginia, YMCA. Two successes there Adrian is proud of were having first woman to serve on the Bristol YMCA board, and having the first woman serve as board chairman. While at Bristol, Adrian prayed for direction, and ended up feeling a clear calling to do international work. During his nearly eight years as general director, the Bristol YMCA hosted 1,200 international guests, and international work became a major program, with 300 host families.

In 1976, Adrian accepted a call to become vice-president of the Houston, Texas YMCA. While in Houston, he was instrumental in establishing the country's largest YMCA refugee center. The Houston YMCA also had the largest Physical Fitness Center in the world. Adrian had responsibility for it, supervised several branch YMCAs, as well as the YMCA camp. After a successful stint of four years in Houston, Adrian accepted the challenge of running the YMCA of Nashville and Middle Tennessee.

• • • • •

Planning for a YMCA trip to Venezuela in November 1984. From left to right: Thomas F. Frist Jr. with back to camera, Dortch Oldham, Ed Temple, unidentified, Walter Knestrick, Bart Bartleson, Adrian Moody, Sandra Fulton, Bob McGaughey, Irene Wills, Ridley Wills II, Jim Barr, and unidentified.

CHAPTER TWENTY-NINE

Moving On!

1984–1985

THE METROPOLITAN NASHVILLE YMCA started 1984 with 20 professional staff members, 54 Metropolitan board members, two honorary board members—Clarence Berson and A. Battle Rodes—and a new president, Ridley Wills II, who was elected at the annual meeting in January. At the first board meeting at which Wills presided, on February 23, his opening remarks were to strongly support a statement made during the "Changing Lives" campaign by Dortch Oldham when Dortch said, "If we are successful, the YMCA could become the greatest force for good in the community." Mr. Wills also said that the Nashville YMCA was recognized as one of the premier YMCAs in the country, and that our goal "should be to have the Nashville YMCA recognized as the very finest in the South."

Walter Knestrick, with his normal exuberance, announced that the "Changing Lives" campaign has raised $5,172,408. Of the total, approximately $480,000 represented deferred giving pledges. Walter's announcement was the highlight of the annual meeting. Under his leadership, the "Changing Lives" campaign completely changed a pattern of unsuccessful capital campaigns extending back to the 1955 drive to build the East YMCA. Senator Howard Baker, who spoke that evening, said, "I have seen a great city on display tonight."

Adrian Moody, now comfortable with his staff and their strengths, realigned a number of staff functions. Jim Rayhab would be in charge of the business, construction, and United Way relations. He would also assist with the administration of the YMCA Foundation, whose chair was Sydney Keeble Jr. Max Cook, former executive director at Donelson, joined the Metropolitan staff and assumed responsibility for citywide maintenance, information management, insurance, and central purchasing. Bill Portman would have line accountability for branch operations with the exception of Downtown, and help with site development. Kent Rea, who already was spending half his time with the YMCA of the USA South, would spend the balance of his time strengthening the Association's wellness and corporate fitness programs. Bob McGaughey would continue with teenage, international, and Christian emphasis programs while devoting most of his time to giving professional leadership to the building of the Harpeth YMCA. Angela Williams assisted him there, focusing on the Youth and Government program.[1113]

Cary Massey would continue to provide staff leadership for program expansion for older adults and also coordinate citywide programs for school-age childcare. John Wright would focus on staff training, government relations, and grants. J. Lawrence would serve as outreach coordinator and work on refugee programs and with college students. Steve Tarver, former assistant Downtown executive, would succeed Max Cook at Donelson. He would work closely with Hart, Freeland and Roberts, the firm selected to design the Donelson natatorium that would hopefully be completed by October at a cost of $400,000.

Jim Barr, the new chairman of the International Committee, reported that the Nashville YMCA had established linkages with YMCAs in Venezuela, West Germany, and Taiwan.[1114] Earlier in the month, Adrian Moody returned from Venezuela, where he enjoyed the pomp and ceremony associated with the inauguration of a new president and saw the wealth created for the upper classes by the oil boom of the mid-1970s. He worked out all sorts of exchange programs, including sending the YMCA Show Choir there, teenage exchanges, a Simon

Bolivar bi-centennial celebration in Bolivar, TN, and clinics led by Tennessee coaches, such as Ed Temple, in Venezuela.[1115] The involvement of Cecilia Meng, a native of China, on the International committee made certain a YMCA trip to Taiwan and China would materialize.

At the March 22 meeting, Jim Rayhab reported that the Brentwood Planning Commission had given the Y clearance to build on the Concord Road site. A survey of Brentwood residents indicated that 61 percent of respondees would be very likely to join the new Harpeth YMCA. Finally, a board retreat was being planned by Nelson Andrews, whose involvement insured that the retreat would be successful.[1116]

John S. Bransford's death was a blow to the YMCA. George Cate Jr. presented a memorial statement regarding Mr. Bransford at the April 22 board meeting. Bransford had been a long-time YMCA friend and an inspirational leader. At the time of his death, he was serving on the Foundation board and the "Changing Lives" steering committee. By June, 100 gifts totaling $4,400 had been donated in his memory, the largest number of memorial contributions made to the YMCA in anyone's memory.[1117]

In 1984, the Urban Services branch was in need of permanent offices. After several meetings, it was decided that the Tolman Roberts property, located at 1913 21st Avenue South, was the best bet. A motion authorizing the Urban Services department to move there was passed. Included in the motion was a decision to review the situation in two years.

• • • • •

A new assignment in 1984 was to provide wellness programs for employees in various enterprises. Kent Rea assumed the leadership in this new program. He started with the Metropolitan Police Department.[1118]

• • • • •

Ann Hogan moved from the Green Hills staff to the Metropolitan office on April 23 to become the Association's communications and public relations chair. She intended to market the Y's core programs, such as childcare, physical fitness, aquatics, various sports, and day camps. She also was responsible for YMCA newsletters in 1984.[1119]

The international partnership was in full flower the summer of 1984. Seventeen members of the Nashville YMCA Show Choir, beautifully directed by Jay Dawson, and fourteen other teenagers went to Venezuela to stay with families in that country. The Show Choir was a smashing success, performing on national TV and at the residence of the governor in Maracaibo. This was particularly meaningful to Nashville businessman Wayne Oldham, whose Southern Hospitality Corporation, Inc., made the Show Choir possible.

Four counselors from Venezuela and two from Germany came to Nashville the same summer to serve on YMCA daycare staffs. Hernan Romero, Maracaibo YMCA executive, made the first of many trips to Nashville. Twenty-one members of the Kaohsiung, Taiwan, YMCA were here for two weeks of intensive English study and home stay experiences. Cecilia Meng, chairman of the Nashville-Taiwan Partnership, would prove to be a dynamo. Earlier in the summer, Barry Watkins, of the Green Hills staff, went to Germany to design a youth exchange program.[1120]

In 1984, the United Way gave the YMCA $169,000, or 6.9 percent of the Association's budget. The Y requested a 19.15 percent increase for 1985 to finance three new childcare programs. The UW came through with an additional $21,000, an 11 percent increase, provided their campaign succeeded.

At mid-year, membership income had increased by an impressive 37 percent over the same period in 1983. The Association's balance sheet for July showed total assets at $7,296,527, up from $4,378,683 a year earlier, thanks largely to the addition of $2,186,371 in pledges receivable from the "Changing Lives" campaign.[1121]

Late in June, seventy-five children from the Nashville YMCA were at the Chattanooga YMCA's resident camp on the Ocoee River. The last time this had happened was in 1972, one year after the last Camp Widjiwagan was held at Standing Stone State Park. Adrian Moody was interested in revising a residence camp program for the Nashville YMCA and asked that a study be made to determine its feasibility.[1122]

Groundbreaking for the Harpeth YMCA was held Saturday, September 8. Nashville's mayor, Dick Fulton, was there to break ground with Adrian Moody, Ridley Wills II, Jim Robinson, and Bob McGaughey. Ridley also attended a meeting of the presidents of the YMCAs in Tennessee in Chattanooga. There he met Clark Baker, the young and dynamic CEO of the Chattanooga YMCA.

When the Tennessee Cluster met in Chattanooga in October, nine other Nashville YMCA board and staff members met the personable Mr. Baker. The Nashville YMCA had just been designated as coordinator for the Tennessee Cluster, and Dr. Jack Tarleton, of Northwest, was elected president and Adrian Moody secretary-treasurer.[1123]

The executive committee approved, at its September meeting, the purchase of Nautilus equipment at the East Branch. The equipment would be paid for by joining fees in 1984 and 1985. The East board was hopeful that a better-equipped and maintained fitness center would slow down or stop the decline in its membership. Of course, the primary reason for the decline was the slow deterioration economically of the East Nashville neighborhoods surrounding the East Family YMCA.[1124]

Setting Goals

Bo Hardy led a Metropolitan Nashville YMCA board retreat at Natchez Trace State Park in October. There, the board reviewed the Association's long-range goals and designed objectives for 1985–86. By the time the retreat met, it was known that the Y Fun Company, the name of the after-school program, was in 21 schools as opposed to 14 in 1983, and that the Nashville YMCA's annual report had been selected as one of 30 winners from over 800 entrants in the Meade Paper Company Annual Contest. There was much to celebrate but much more to do and planning was a key.[1125]

Clifford Love Jr., president of the Nashville YMCA in 1962–63, moved with his wife to Virginia Beach in November. At his last board meeting on October 25, Clifford was recognized with a resolution lauding his efforts on behalf of the local association for more than thirty years.

In November, Nashville Mayor Richard Fulton led a group of Nashville business, civic, and educational leaders on a YMCA-sponsored trip to Venezuela to exchange ideas and strengthen the "partners" program established by the Nashville Y and the YMCAs of Venezuela. The group visited Caracas, Valencia, Maracaibo, and Angel Falls. In Caracas, Dr. Roger Boulton, a member of the World Alliance Board, and a Venezuelan national leader, hosted an elaborate dinner party for the visitors under a beautifully appointed party tent. Making the trip with the Mayor and his wife, Sandra, a YMCA board member, were Dr. Thomas F. Frist Jr. and Dortch Oldham, representing business; Walter Knestrick, representing the arts; Ridley Wills II representing the civic community, his wife, Irene; Tom Ervin, representing the media; Ed Temple, representing sports; and Dr. Roscoe Robinson, representing medicine. Ed Temple, the track coach at Tennessee State University, was well known to Venezuelans because of the unparalleled success the Tigerbelles had in the 1960 summer Olympics. Temple even recruited a high school track star for TSU while in Venezuela.[1126]

Not long before the group made their trip, a bust of Simon Bolivar reached Nashville as a gift from the government of Venezuela to the town of Bolivar, Tennessee. It would be unveiled the next spring.

Russ Young and Bill Portman presented a building proposal from the Green Hills board asking to move the construction schedule for locker rooms and an all purpose room from 1986 to 1985 and also add the construction of three racquetball courts and a fitness-testing lab. The entire cost was projected to be $550,000, of which $300,000 had been approved as part of the "Changing Lives" campaign. The plan was for the Metropolitan YMCA to secure a $250,000 loan to be repaid by increasing joining fees at Green Hills from $50 to $100 and an assessment of a $20 capital improvement fee there. The motion to do this for the fast-growing family center was approved.[1127]

Officers nominated and elected for the new year were Walter Knestrick, president; Dr. Bill Wadlington, president elect; Bill Wilson and Ralph Mosley, vice-presidents; Bill Turner, secretary; and Jack Elisar, treasurer. Committee reports included announcements that the Donelson swimming pool was dedicated December 20, that Buchanan Construction Company had been awarded the contract to build the Harpeth YMCA, and that James Stevens had been chosen as designer/engineer for the Green Hills expansion project. In his executive director's report, Mr. Moody praised Wentworth Caldwell Jr. for his six years of service on the Metropolitan YMCA board, and announced that Kent Rea had accepted a full-time position with the YMCA of the USA. Kent would continue to have his office at the Metropolitan YMCA for his consulting work in four Southern states. Adrian also thanked Ridley Wills II for his leadership and praised the Metropolitan Nashville YMCA as the finest organization he had observed in the YMCA.[1128]

During 1984, the Nashville Association had income of $3,023,970 and a surplus of $35,965. Even the Donelson and Northwest centers operated within their budgets. This was a tribute to Steve Tarver and John Wright. It had taken the Metropolitan Association only three years to move from $2 million to $3 million in income.[1129]

In January, Metropolitan board member Bill Wadlington, M.D. whose medical practice had long been in Donelson, offered to give his indoor tennis center in Donelson to the YMCA. The building's assessed value was $600,000 and the land worth $65,000. The YMCA would assume a note of $92,000 and be responsible for paying $32,000 for the land.

Several committees, having reviewed Dr. Wadlington's offer of his indoor tennis center, enthusiastically approved accepting the gift. The Y would lease the facility until the time was right for Dr. Wadlington to make the gift. On the construction side of things, the Donelson pool was reported as complete and footings had been poured for the Harpeth Center. In response to a request from the YMCA of the USA that the Nashville YMCA identify its service area, a motion was passed to include in the Y's service area the nine counties of Cheatham, Davidson, Dickson, Maury, Robertson, Rutherford, Sumner, Williamson, and Wilson.

International Partnerships

By early 1985, the Y was also preparing for the visit in February of YMCA leaders from Maracaibo.[1130] Walter Knestrick, president, presided at the February 21 board meeting. He and Adrian Moody welcomed Marcel Sambo, president of the Maracaibo YMCA; Eddie Guerra, board member from Maracaibo; Dr. Jose Leon Garcia Diaz, board member and past governor of Maracaibo; and Jorge Garcia Rincon. Sambo, who had worked for the Y in Maracaibo for 31 years, thanked the Nashville YMCA for its assistance to his YMCA.

In February, planning was well underway for a YMCA trip to Taiwan and China. Highlights of the trip would be a formalization of a partnership between the Nashville YMCA and the Kaohsiung, Taiwan, YMCA. Before the meeting adjourned, Adrian described YMCA resident camping as the YMCA's greatest tool. Clearly, he wanted one for Nashville.[1131]

The 1985 sustaining membership goal was $179,500. At the March executive committee meeting, Bill Portman reported that 90 percent of the goal had been achieved. This was well ahead of the pace a few years earlier. Next, Walter Knestrick spoke of the leadership that Joe M. Rodgers had given the YMCA's Youth-in-Government program, and, on Bob McGaughey's suggestion, made a motion that the two Outstanding Statesmen Awards given annually at the Tennessee Youth Legislature be named the "Joe M. Rodgers Awards." Joe had attended the Alabama Youth Legislature in 1951 as a high school student in Montgomery. The motion carried. The annual YMCA Youth Legislature in April was the largest in the program's thirty-two-year history with 528 young people attending.[1132]

Back in August 1984, the Government of Taiwan had extended an invitation to the Nashville YMCA to have representatives visit Taipei the week of October 6 to observe the 75th anniversary of Chinese independence from dynasty rule. Already, the Y had planned a trip to the "Two Chinas" in October that had been orchestrated by Cecilia Meng, whose family was one of the last to flee the mainland after the Communists expelled the Nationalists under Chiang Kai-Shek. Cecilia's grandfather was famous in China for having introduced Sun Yat-sen to Chiang Kai-Shek. Naturally, the invitation from the Government of Taiwan was accepted and 20 YMCA members and friends made the trip, which took place in April 1985. In Taipei, the YMCA group stayed as guests of the government in the Grand Hotel, one of the most magnificent in the Orient.

When the group returned, Jim Barr reported on the fascinating trip. Highlights were a visit in Taipei with vice-president Lee Teng-hui, a friend of Cecilia's. Teng-hui would, in 1988, become the first authentically Taiwanese president of the Republic of China. Because Ann Robinson, wife of board member Dr. Roscoe "Ike" Robinson, Vice-Chancellor for Health Affairs at Vanderbilt, was on the trip, she and a number of the group, including Vanderbilt graduates Ridley Wills II, Walter Knestrick, and Dr. Bill Wadlington, attended a meeting of the Taipei Vanderbilt Club. It turned out that all the club members were graduates of Peabody before it merged with Vanderbilt. The hosts made an endless number of toasts liberally supplied with a strong drink that may have been rice wine. Whatever it was, it almost "put the YMCA group under the table." In responding to one toast, Walter Knestrick intended making a toast to Chiang Kai-shek but couldn't remember his name. Impulsively, he proposed to toast to "Cheky." Dr. Wadlington, president-elect of the Nashville YMCA, could hardly contain his laughter. The Taiwanee hosts also laughed heartily, although the Nashville group was uncertain if they understood Walter.

After arriving in Shanghai, Adrian and Cecilia drove down to her hometown where they visited her first cousin and his family. Despite having an aristocratic heritage, the family was so poor that he was only able to offer tea to his guests. Before leaving Shanghai that morning, Adrian told Ridley to call the local YMCA if he and Cecilia didn't get back by 6 p.m. Because their cab driver had run a police blockade on the way out of town, the police were waiting for them when they returned, delaying their arrival at the hotel until about 8 p.m. Ridley called the Shanghai YMCA at 6 p.m. but that didn't help much because no one there spoke English. Another day, the YMCA group met the head of the YMCA of China, then recently reopened. He suggested that the group walk outside to talk. When the YMCA delegation did so, he explained that his office was bugged. The CEO had one request. He asked the Nashvillians to send him Bibles after they got home. Through the help of the Southern Baptist Sunday School Board, this was done. Chinese food was an interesting experience. At a dinner, hosted by the president of the China Medical Society, fish-eye soup was served. Sandra Fulton and a few others became adept at using chopsticks.[1133]

There were also trips back and forth to Venezuela in 1985. Jack Farrar and Jim Rayhab both visited there. Upon his return, Farrar reported that Elias Polo, a director of the Valencia YMCA was in need of special medical attention unavailable in Venezuela as the result of being shot and paralyzed by a burglar. The man, whom Adrian had known for fifteen years, would be flown to Nashville and diagnosed and operated on at Vanderbilt pro bono, thanks to Dr. Ike Robinson. The operation relieved Polo of much pain and, after recuperating in Nashville for five weeks, he was able to return in a wheel chair to his life's work in Valencia.[1134] When Elias Polo died in August 2010, his son, Elias Jr. succeeded him as executive director of the Valencia YMCA, possibly the finest in Venezuela.[1135]

At the June board meeting, Adrian Moody announced that Barry Watkins had accepted the position of executive director of the Florence, SC, YMCA. Barry had effectively worked with youth in Nashville since 1978 and was presented a plaque for his outstanding achievements.[1136]

City-Wide Membership

The Metropolitan Nashville YMCA implemented a city-wide membership policy that became effective August 1, 1985. Under it,

- Each center determines its own rates;
- A member of one center may use other centers for $3 a visit;
- Any member of one center may join a second center at a 30 percent discount;
- A guest of a member may participate with a member for $4;
- Out-of-town YMCA members are welcomed and accepted without charge.

During the "Changing Lives" campaign, Matt B. Pilcher III expressed an interest in giving the YMCA a portrait of his grandfather, Capt. Matt B. Pilcher, who was president of the Nashville YMCA from 1875 to 1877 and from 1886 to 1895. The unveiling of the portrait in the summer helped to commemorate the 110th anniversary of the Nashville Y. Matt, his wife, and children were present along with members of the executive committee, and several past presidents.[1137]

The Tennessee Cluster of YMCAs met in Nashville on September 25 to share ideas. The cluster consisted of 13 YMCAs in Tennessee at Athens, Bristol, Chattanooga, Clarksville Armed Service YMCA, Cookeville, Greene County (Greeneville), Jackson, Greater Kingsport Family, Knoxville, Memphis, Nashville, Rhea County (Dayton), and the Unicoi County Family (Erwin); one YMCA in Southwest Virginia-Buchanan County, VA, YMCA; one YMCA in North Georgia—the North Georgia YMCA (Rossville); and one in North Mississippi—the Corinth YMCA.

In February, after stepping down as president, Ridley Wills II became the editor of the *VOLUNTEER STATE OF THE Y*, the bi-monthly publication of the Tennessee Cluster of YMCAs. In his first issue, the four-page newsletter included articles from the Athens, Bristol, Chattanooga, Knoxville, Memphis, and Nashville YMCAs, and the South Field Office. In March, J. Ben Casey Jr., National Field Executive, and Bob Ridgeway, chairman of the YMCA's South Field Committee, wrote Ridley Wills II the following note:

> Dear Ridley:
>
> You have done it! Tennessee has garnered the honor of having the finest Cluster Newsletter in the nation. You cannot imagine how proud we are to display this high quality journalistic achievement to other clusters and to other Field areas. You have set the high standards. We are proud of you. Keep it up.

During Ridley's two years as editor, THE VOLUNTEER *STATE OF THE Y* came out ten times thanks to the Third National Corporation underwriting the cost. Ridley learned quickly that he could always count on Clark Baker, the general executive of the Chattanooga YMCA, to provide interesting articles in a timely manner.

The Fun Company in 1985 was in three counties and 37 schools, nine more than in 1984, and had a projected enrollment during the year of between 1,100 and 1,300. Cary Massey was doing exactly what was hoped for when the Nashville YMCA recruited him from the Miami YMCA in 1981.

The next step in the leadership dialogue between the Nashville YMCA and the YMCAs in Venezuela took place in October when Dr. Romulo Quintero, president of the YMCAs in Venezuela, and his wife; Elias Polo, executive director of the Valencia YMCA; Martin Garcia, executive director of the Caracas YMCA; and Hernan Romero, a member of the national staff visited Nashville. They were introduced at the October board meeting. Polo was in a wheelchair, still recovering from his operation at Vanderbilt. He would remain in a wheelchair the rest of his life.

The Venezuelans learned that even in affluent America, YMCAs had to sometimes borrow money. Jack Elizar, the treasurer, stated that it might be necessary to borrow as much as $1 million to cover construction costs while awaiting pledges from Walter Knestrick's "Changing Lives" campaign. A month later, Jack said that the YMCA would use First American National Bank for construction financing. This seemed appropriate since, on January 1, 1986, the YMCA would rotate its account to First American.[1138]

Bill Turner, reporting for the Christian emphasis committee, said that a September prayer breakfast was well attended and that there would be a Christmas breakfast on December 20. John Wright, a member of the data processing committee, reported that, as of October 1, computers had been installed in six family centers. Mr. Knestrick thanked John for his exceptional leadership in this endeavor.

J. Lawrence informed the board that Urban Services had gotten involved with student YMCA programs. He estimated that 150 college students were helping with Urban Services programs.

The Metropolitan Nashville YMCA ended 1985 with a $1,932 surplus, less than the $33,865 surplus in 1984, but still on the right side of the ledger. The 1986 budget, arrived at after two days of discussions, would be a whopping $4,759,639—a 33 percent increase. The addition of expensive facilities and the growth in membership and youth programs accounted for most of the increase. In two years, the budget had grown an astonishing $1,736,000, greater than the entire budget in 1982.

At the December board meeting, Dortch Oldham, reporting for the nominating committee, proposed the following officers for 1986: Dr. Bill Wadlington, president; Bill Wilson, president elect; Sandra Fulton and Ralph Mosley, vice-presidents; Bill Turner, secretary; and Chris Stone, treasurer. These leaders were elected by acclimation. Bill Cochran introduced Gail Wilson, the new Metropolitan communications director, and a motion was passed creating the position of director of financial development to primarily work developing the YMCA Foundation's new philanthropic fund. The YMCA was growing fast and a staff to support that growth was felt essential. For example, a market study showed a strong interest in the fast-growing Hendersonville area for YMCA family fitness and swimming activities.[1139]

One other event in 1985 is worth mentioning. That year, Dr. Arshi Nassef, a refugee from Iran in the 1970s, founded the first YMCA International House. She was also an effective and compassionate counselor for international students at Hillsboro High School. Before the building was sold in 1989 and the program ceased, thousands of international students and refugees in Nashville found friends there. The International House programs included a clothing and furniture bank, emergency shelter, English classes, and youth development activities.

• • • • •

The Fastest Growing YMCA in the Southeast
1986–1987

EIGHT NEW DIRECTORS were nominated at the January 23, 1986, executive committee meeting. They included two future YMCA presidents—Margaret Maddox and James A. Webb III.

In the general executive's report, Adrian Moody reported that Gary Schlansker, general executive of the Evansville, Indiana YMCA, would, on February 17, become the executive director of the Downtown Center and associate general executive. He also stated that Michael Haynes, executive director of the Kentucky State YMCA had accepted the new position of financial development director and associate executive director effective April 1.[1140]

February 21 was a red-letter day for the Harpeth Family YMCA, as that was when the sparkling new center opened. In 1985, center executive Bob McGaughey had projected that Harpeth would have 600 unit memberships when it opened. The number turned out to be 900 and another 300 joined between opening day and March 27. This projected to about 4,000 members. When the groundbreaking had been held for the Harpeth Center, someone asked Mr. Moody and Mr. Wills, then president, why the Metropolitan YMCA was willing to spend so much money building the Harpeth Y. They said the reason was simple. "Someday, the Harpeth YMCA will be our flagship family center and will be able to spin off money to help subsidize our inner city work."[1141]

At Dr. Bill Wadlington's first board meeting as chairman, he heard Adrian report that the YMCA would operate fourteen-day camps that summer with the number of campers expected to exceed 12,000.[1142]

In March, Dean Lackey of the YMCA Law School called Mr. Moody to say that the law school was contemplating moving in the fall and wanted to know if the YMCA would release the school from their lease. The executive committee voted to accede to Dean Lackey's request. One obvious indication of the lack of involvement in the night law school by the YMCA was the fact that, on November 19, 1986, the law school faculty voted to change the name of the school to the "Nashville School of Law."[1143]

Margaret and Dan Maddox at the East Branch YMCA

Sandra Fulton; Adrian Moody; Dr. David Satcher, president of Meharry Medical College; businessman Inman Otey; Dr. Russell Monfort, pastor of West End United Methodist Church; and Dr. E. Aban Oddoye, also of Meharry, visited Zambia and Kenya in April. This resulted

William B. "Bill" Waddlington M.D., Metropolitan Board President, 1986

Dr. Jack Tarleton M.D. of the Northwest YMCA and Bill Wilson, Metropolitan YMCA President, 1987

in student exchanges between the Zambia and Nashville YMCAs.[1144]

The announcement of the completion of the construction projects at the Green Hills Y was made at the May board meeting. At the same meeting, Bill Wilson reported that J. Lawrence had established a Vanderbilt student YMCA with the university furnishing office space, conference rooms, and secretarial help. The agreement was for one year, and would begin in the fall. J. would involve the students in all sorts of work in the inner city. J. also arranged for nine Tennessee State university students to contribute their time in reading power classes. Two months later, Lawrence announced that a dream of his was coming true. The State of Tennessee, he said, had agreed to fund a new Y-CAP program that would link first offenders with Urban Services. The initial grant was for $20,000.

J. was particularly proud that spring of Sok Heng Tok, a seven-year-old Cambodian refugee whom he met in 1983 when she was four. That year, she would tag along with her older brother who was involved in the Y's Junior Striders Track program. Sok displayed an amazing aptitude for running and, in the spring of 1986, finished second in her first grade age group in the Music City 1.6 mile run. Through the Y, the little girl had lost her shyness. J. said, "She feels comfortable now. I guess she has become Americanized."[1145]

The international program was expanding, too. So far in 1986, the Nashville YMCA had hosted 57 young people from several countries and 54 young people from our YMCA had traveled abroad. Some of those young people participated in the Statue of Liberty Celebration in New York before going on to France where U.S. Ambassador to France, Joe M. Rodgers, of Nashville, was their host.[1146]

In the spring, the Metropolitan Nashville YMCA employed Daniel K. Shaddock Jr. as associate general executive and director of financial development. A native Texan, Dr. Shaddock came to Nashville from Dunedin, FL, where he had been pastor of the north Dunedin Baptist Church for nine years. During an earlier pastorate in Moultrie, GA, Dr. Shaddock received the YMCA Service to Youth Award. The YMCA general director in Moultrie at the time was Adrian Moody. Now, they were reunited.[1147]

At the September board meeting, Adrian Moody spoke of the accelerating growth in every major YMCA department, with programs growing 32 percent over the previous year. Day camp enrollment in 26 camps reached almost 12,000 during the summer, doubling the size of the program in two years. Over 1,600 children attended these camps on scholarship. Meanwhile, the Downtown board had finished a strategic planning study that reviewed the center's strengths and weakness, pointed out the proliferation of private fitness centers, and made recommendations for the future. Gary

Schlansker presented a facility planning status report to the executive committee in August. One pressing need, he said, was more permanent parking. In his report, Gary recommended the hiring of an architect to develop cost figures and a draft set of drawings for a pool, a women's center, an aerobic center, a main floor renovation, an elevator, and larger space for Metro offices. Lip Davis' motion to do this passed.[1148]

The record growth was putting a great deal of financial pressure on the association and a year-end deficit seemed inevitable. In September, Chris Stone passed out a statistical report comparing the 22 largest YMCAs in the South. It showed that the Nashville YMCA was the sixth largest with total income of $3,795,275, lagging Charlotte, New Orleans, Metro Atlanta, Louisville, and Birmingham. Of the 22 cities, Nashville received the second smallest percent of income from the United Way (5.8 percent) with only New Orleans having received less. In income growth, between 1984 and 1985, the Nashville YMCA was the fastest growing with an income growth of 25.2 percent.

Children's Programs

Adrian Moody announced in November that Cary Massey, executive director of the East YMCA, would become Metropolitan childcare director, effective January 1. Cary had done such a splendid job with childcare that it simply demanded his entire time. Nashville was, largely because of Cary's leadership, a national role model for childcare and before and after school programs. The childcare program had, in November, 1,600 children under its care at 46 sites in four counties. Bill Portman would succeed Cary at East in addition to continuing as executive director of Southwest. Lip Davis, chairman of the Downtown board of managers, reported, also in November, that membership at Downtown had declined from over 2,100 in 1984 to 1,800 in 1986. His board felt there were three primary reasons: lack of adequate parking, no indoor pool, and increased competition from private fitness centers.

Phil Armor, chairman of Urban Services, introduced Carl Carlson as the new director of the rapidly growing Y-CAP program. Carlson explained that Y-CAP stood for Community Action Project and that it provided first-time juvenile offenders with individual counseling, tutoring, group sessions, and prevocational guidance, using the facilities primarily of East and Northwest. Armor also reported that J. Lawrence was in the process of initiating a program at Vanderbilt known as Alternative Spring Break. Instead of going on vacation during spring break, students would go to some economically distressed area and do volunteer work. This program, suggested by Vanderbilt students, would become so popular that the university would ultimately take it over. In 2011, very few people at Vanderbilt or in the city would know that J. Lawrence was one of the fathers of Vanderbilt's Alternative Spring Break.[1149]

Forty miles south of Nashville, a group of citizens in Columbia founded, on October 7, 1986, a Maury County YMCA. Progress would be slow, as their board did not hold its first meeting until November 1987. The Maury County YMCA was initially independent of the Metropolitan Nashville YMCA.[1150]

• • • • •

In 1986, the Metropolitan Nashville YMCA refined its mission statement to read as follows: "The Young Men's Christian Association of Nashville and Middle Tennessee is a part of a worldwide fellowship united by a common loyalty to Jesus Christ for the purpose of helping persons grow in spirit, mind, and body." This simple statement would be lasting.

• • • • •

In the absence of chairman Nelson Andrews, Ridley Wills II gave the nominating report for 1987 in December. The officers nominated were Bill Wilson, president; Lee Barfield II and Bill Turner, vice president; Olin West III, treasurer; and Jack Elisar, secretary. They were accepted by acclamation. Olin was a second-generation board member. His father, Olin West Jr. had served on the board in the 1960s. The day after the December board meeting, there was a prayer breakfast in the Law School Auditorium, a fitting end to the year.[1151]

As predicted, the year-end financial statement, presented by Olin West III, in January, was not pretty. Total income for 1986 was $4,066,074 while expenses were $4,317,606, a deficit of $231,222.

Expansion for the Y

At the 1987 annual meeting held February 12 at the Opryland Hotel, the new officers were installed at the meeting, and former president Bob Bibb received the Order of the Red Triangle award.

In 1987, the biggest need at the Northwest Family YMCA that winter was for a daycare facility, estimated to cost approximately $440,000. Of this amount, $225,000 was available from the "Changing Lives" campaign. After discussion, the executive committee authorized the building committee to select a contractor on a cost plus plan but not to start construction until the balance of the money had been raised. Quickly, the building committee chose the Walter Knestrick Construction Company, and the center began its effort to raise $50,000.[1152]

By February, Vanderbilt students were involved in tutoring, and volunteering at Y-CAP, Reading Power, Spencer Youth Center, and in various roles at Martha O'Bryan and Bethlehem Center. TSU students were providing leadership for Reading Power and a health awareness program at East Junior High. The Alternative Spring Break program in March included home building in Juarez, Mexico, and youth healthcare and home repair work at the Sioux Indian YMCA in South Dakota. In April, Time magazine published an article on the Alternative spring break program at Vanderbilt. J.'s hard work was paying dividends.[1153]

March saw a feasibility study for a YMCA in Dickson, Tennessee, underway and a growing interest in a relationship with the one in Maury County. Gary Schlansker reviewed the goal of the Downtown board to launch a $1.8 million expansion program to include an indoor pool, locker room, office expansion, and a weight training and exercise component. Bill Wilson stated that, unless the Law School vacated its space on the lower level, the Metropolitan offices would need to be relocated to another building.[1154]

The board of directors of the Metropolitan Nashville YMCA and the board of managers of the Donelson-Hermitage YMCA passed a resolution in April honoring Dr. and Mrs. William B. Wadlington for their steadfastness of character, generosity of spirit, and faithfulness of service, The resolution pointed out Dr. Wadlington's positive influence on the Donelson-Hermitage YMCA and resolved that their Tennis Center be henceforth known as the Wadlington YMCA Tennis Center.[1155]

Bill Wadlington loved the Donelson-Hermitage Center and visited when he could. One summer, when he was there, he noticed children sliding down a temporary water slide on the hillside behind the Y. The slide was simply a long sheet of plastic made slick by water being sprayed on it with a garden hose. Seeing how much fun the children were having, Dr. Wadlington, who was wearing a white suit, decided to join the fun. His momentum propelled him into the grass below the slide. When he stood up, he realized that grass stains had ruined his suit. The beleaguered East YMCA, after flourishing in the sixties and seventies, was on hard times. An East Study Commission was appointed to help chart the declining center's future.

A 1987 market study by Shockley Research at the Harpeth Family YMCA identified tennis courts as the number one activity desired by adult members with an indoor pool their second priority.

Adrian Moody Resigns

Nashvillians read on June 5, 1987 that Adrian Moody, general executive director of the Metropolitan Nashville YMCA since January 1, 1981, had resigned the day before to become a national field executive with the YMCA of the USA. Moody said, "The decision to leave has been very painful. Nashville has become home but I'm excited about the job and particularly about being able to share the things we are doing in Nashville." Under his six years of leadership in Nashville, the Y developed a leading international YMCA program that included partnerships with France, Germany, Taiwan, Venezuela, and Zambia. Also, during Adrian's term of office, the Nashville Association expanded its services to more than 60,000 participants and was operating more than 130 program sites in the area. Moody was one of the most prominent YMCA executives in the country, serving on various regional and national YMCA committees and boards as well as on the National Partners of the Americas Board, Leadership Nashville, and the Governor's Task Force on Daycare.[1156]

Two weeks after Adrian's announcement, president Bill Wilson named former president Ridley Wills II as the chairman of a search committee to recommend a new general executive. The other search committee members were Nelson Andrews, Sandra Fulton, Dortch Oldham, Dr. Ike Robinson, Bill Turner, and president Bill Wilson. One of the first steps the committee took was to meet with Solon Cousins, the respected president of the YMCA of the USA and his deputy director, John Danielson. Ridley didn't know [but should have] that a few weeks earlier, Cousins and Danielson had met with Adrian at his home in Nashville and encouraged him to head the South Field Office. Adrian was ready for a new challenge, feeling that he had accomplished about as much as he could in Nashville and hoping that he could positively impact many YMCAs, just as he had the Nashville Y. He must have been flattered too when Cousins told him that he had talked to YMCA general executives across the South and the prevailing recommendation he received was that Adrian was the right man to head the South Field Office.

John Wright, director of the Northwest YMCA, announced in June that the YMCA would expand its services to families in August when the city's first YMCA-operated daycare center would open at the Northwest YMCA. The $600,000 project included construction of an 8,500 square-foot daycare center connected by a hallway to the community center. The new building included two infant rooms, five classrooms, a kitchen, a special programs room and several offices. All classrooms would feature large windows overlooking the Y's 10 acres of open land. The center was designed to serve 130 children ages 6 weeks to 5 years. Wright said, "Now children can come to us as infants and stay with us through adulthood." Wright also said the program at Northwest was expected to become a prototype for similar centers at Green Hills and Donelson.[1157]

Adrian Moody was not the only senior management member to leave. Bill Hearn had reached retirement age after a long career of faithful service as membership and public relations secretary. Senator Douglas Henry read a resolution of appreciation for what Bill had meant to the Nashville Y.[1158]

One of the many satisfactions that Adrian Moody felt on leaving Nashville was that the YMCA was not only on a firm foundation, but was recognized nationally as a one of the best YMCAs in the country, with possibly the strongest International partnership in the country. Adrian also knew he was leaving a strong staff and a board that he considered as good as anybody's. He predicted that bright days were ahead for the Nashville YMCA. Before heading for Atlanta and his new job, Adrian and Fran decided that they would not sell their Nashville home as they intended to retire in the city they had come to love.

A considerable amount of time was spent in the summer of 1987 compiling a profile of the Nashville and the Metropolitan Nashville YMCA. As part of this process, the selection committee identified 14 former employees of the Nashville YMCA who had gone on to assume positions of YMCA leadership across the country. They were: Tom Blackman, general executive, Ft. Myers, FL, YMCA; Charles Cleveland, general director, Naples, FL, YMCA; Larry Duncan, downtown executive, Jacksonville, FL, YMCA; Claude Frith, executive, Cincinnati Campbell County YMCA; Chuck Harris, operations director, Richmond, VA, YMCA; Craig Heindrichs, executive director, Memphis East Branch YMCA; Hugh Hurst Jr., general executive, Memphis Metropolitan YMCA; Julius Jones, general executive, Pittsburgh YMCA; Bobby Martin, executive director, Jacksonville, FL, Arlington YMCA; Adrian Moody, national field executive, South Field; Kent Rea, national field consultant, South Field; Ralph Reynolds, director of marketing/development, Knoxville, TN, YMCA; Barry Watkins, general executive, Florence, SC, YMCA; and Rusty Yeomans, executive director, Chattanooga Downtown YMCA.

Truly, Nashville's reputation was also that of an incubator for YMCA professional leadership, being one of the first Metropolitan YMCAs that selection committees and the national office looked to when seeking well-qualified candidates for YMCA positions across the country.

More than 40 of Adrian Moody's friends and coworkers gathered at a luncheon on December 1 at the First American Center on Monday to honor this dedicated and beloved leader. Adrian and his wife Fran were presented with an engraved silver service from the YMCA board of directors. Under Moody's six years of leadership, the YMCA had expanded its services to more than 60,000 participants and in December operated at more than 130 program sites in the area. "The Nashville YMCA has experienced more growth than any other YMCA in the South," Moody said. George Cate Jr. credited the success of the wide range of YMCA programs to Moody's foresight and planning. In his new position, Moody would direct the work of YMCA consultants who provide management and program assistance to more than 200 YMCA associations in eleven Southern states.[1159]

• • • • •

TOP: Allen County YMCA BOTTOM: Bellevue YMCA

CHAPTER THIRTY-ONE

A Wise Choice

1987–1989

EARLY IN JULY, general manager selection committee chairman Ridley Wills II met with the Nashville YMCA's senior management staff to answer any questions they might have regarding the selection process. John Wright, Bill Portman, Jim Rayhab, Gary Schlansker, Dan Shaddock, Bob McGaughey, and Jan Scanlan attended the meeting at the Downtown YMCA. Mr. Wills first handed out copies of the recently filed report of vacancy and invited input on the type person they would like to see succeed Adrian Moody. Dan Shaddock said he preferred a general executive with a participatory management style. John Wright agreed with Dan, saying, "I feel that much of what I have been able to accomplish at Northwest has been because Adrian Moody has both supported and encouraged me." Wright asked Wills what he thought the chances of a minority candidate being selected were. Mr. Wills said he thought the odds were slim. John responded by saying he did not think Nashville was ready for an African-American general executive. When asked by Bill Portman if he thought in-house candidates were viable ones this time, Wills said he felt there were in-house candidates qualified to run the Nashville association. Before adjourning, Mr. Wills solicited applications from any staff member who felt qualified to apply for the CEO position. Although he was not at the meeting, Kent Rea submitted two names—Clark Baker, CEO of the Chattanooga YMCA and Bob Gilbertson, CEO of the Tampa YMCA.

At a selection committee meeting on August 7, having already received input from Solon Cousins; John Danielson; Adrian Moody; Ben Casey, Dallas YMCA president; Gene Shaffer, East Field Executive; and Dewitt Smith, Mid-West Field Executive; and having reviewed the resumes of 39 potential candidates, including four from the Nashville YMCA, the committee chose to interview ten candidates, including six from out-of-town. Bob McGaughey, Bill Portman, Kent Rea, and Gary Schlansker, the internal candidates, were also interviewed. By mid-September, the selection committee had narrowed the field to three finalists; Clark Baker, Chattanooga general executive; Norris Lineweaver, Hollywood general executive; and John T. "Jack" Scarborough, executive director and vice-president of the YMCA of Metropolitan Dallas, each of whom was interviewed again.

Following the three interviews on September 21, the selection committee met and voted unanimously to offer the position to Clark Baker. There was also a consensus that each of the three finalists was beautifully prepared to successfully run a metropolitan YMCA and that we were fortunate to be in the enviable position of choosing between three well-qualified men. Ridley was asked to contact Clark and Bill Wilson agreed to formulate the appropriate financial package to offer Clark and to bring the committee's recommendation to the executive committee on September 24.[1160]

At the executive committee meeting, Bill Turner, a selection committee member, moved the adoption of the recommendation to employ Clark Baker. Dr. Ike Robinson seconded the motion. After the motion carried unanimously, several search committee members spoke of the strength of the applicant pool, both those from the Metropolitan Nashville YMCA and those from out-of-town, and of the fact that all the outside candidates seemed to be impressed with the YMCA and Nashville.

The *Chattanooga News-Free Press* broke the news that Clark D. Baker, general director of the Chattanooga Metropolitan YMCA, had resigned to become general director of the Metropolitan Nashville YMCA and that he would assume his new duties on November 30, 1987.

Mr. Clark's YMCA career began in 1969 in Washington, Indiana. Six years later, he became senior associate director of the Orlando YMCA. The *News–Free Press* said, "Not only has he been successful in greatly enlarging the YMCA services, programs and facilities during his years here, but he is a very fine gentleman, who has made many friends. The 'C' in YMCA stands for 'Christian' and Mr. Baker has provided sound leadership in restoring that meaning to Y programs. He is an enthusiastic, personable man who has involved himself constructively in many kinds of community activities, as has his wife, Carolyn, a teacher at Signal Mountain Junior High. The Bakers have served Chattanooga well and will be greatly missed."[1161]

In the announcement in the *Tennessean*, Clark said, "I look forward to the challenge of working with one of the country's truly premier YMCAs. I am excited to be a part of such a dynamic YMCA."[1162]

Meanwhile, Jim Harper, chairman of the Downtown board's property committee, informed the executive committee in September that four contractors had made formal presentations for the planned expansion of the Downtown Y. He said that Walter Knestrick Contractors emerged as the preferred choice and was chosen unanimously. Harper also reported further that architectural drawings were nearing completion.[1163]

Clark Baker was introduced to the Metropolitan Nashville YMCA board on October 22. He, Carolyn, and their two daughters, Caroline and Christen, returned in November to attend the YMCA board reception held for the Baker family at the University Club on the 12th.[1164]

Influenced by the Nashville YMCA's reputation of being, along with the Charlotte YMCA, the strongest YMCA in the South, Clark accepted the call primarily because of the large unmet potential in Nashville. He knew the professional staff of Jim Rayhab, Bill Portman, Gary Schlansker, and Jan Scanlan was top notch. Dortch Oldham and others told him that the board of directors was recognized as being one of the best, if not the best, nonprofit board in town. Dortch also gave Clark some advice: "You will have many opportunities presented to the YMCA while you are here. The genius will be in picking the good ones and leaving the bad ones alone."

Realizing there was a significant amount of time and energy being placed on programs, Clark saw a big potential in membership development. The Y had a Gold Card membership plan designed to allow members access to all the other centers in town. Because all of the branches were not full-service branches, members paid an additional fee to have access to other branches. Clark felt there was a lack of cohesiveness in the branches in that each branch director seemed to run his own show. Clark also saw the need for expanded facilities and sensed that, with six of its centers in Davidson County, there was opportunity for expansion into contiguous counties, if funds could be found.[1165]

Two major decisions were made 10 days after Clark became the CEO. One was one to move the Metropolitan offices to Suite 100 on the first floor of the Doctors' Building on Church Street, one and one-half blocks from the Downtown YMCA—a move precipitated by overcrowding at the Downtown Center. The property, managed by the Charles Hawkins Realty Co., totaled 2,347 square feet. The executive committee, at its December meeting, approved the lease in the Doctors' Building for five years with an average payment of $12.50 per square foot. The other decision was the executive committee's approval to borrow $1.5 million to begin construction of the first phase of the Downtown expansion project, and to raise an additional $168,000 by March 31 so that phase 2 could begin. Phase 1 would include the enlarged women's fitness center and an aerobic and fitness center. Phase 2 would include the eight-lane indoor pool. Clark was authorized to assume Adrian Moody's position as coordinator of the Tennessee Cluster of YMCAs for 1988.

The following financial highlights for 1987 were distributed at the December executive committee meeting:

- Projected revenues were $5,804,087, a 17.9 percent increase over 1986;
- The YMCA funded a maintenance reserve of $45,256 and absorbed $54,500 in operational start-up costs for pre-school childcare centers at Northwest and East;
- The YMCA generated $186,846 in joining fees designated for capital expenditures;
- The sustaining campaign raised $231,309, an 18.65 percent increase over 1986; and
- The Association received $239,000 in government grants, primarily for youth exchange programs and summer youth employment.

Actually, revenues turned out to be $5,891,695, a surplus of $34,979.

At the January board meeting, the finance committee moved the adoption of a $6,815,707 budget for 1988, a 17.4 percent increase over 1987. The rapid growth continued. Before the January meeting concluded, Mr. Baker said the YMCA had 16,259 members as of January 1 and that his first fifty days on the job had been great.[1166]

After 60 days on the job, Clark Baker shared some of his observations. First, he felt that the Metro board was one of the best and most involved he had ever seen. He complimented the five-year plan already in place. The major area of concern, he said, had to do with finances. The incredible growth from $2,033,000 in 1980 to $6,815,7070 for 1988 came with its problems. Clark realized how tight the budgets were. "Either we just balance," he wrote, "or we miss it. Much growth, little net, and few reserves." Clark's intuition was that "without childcare, we would have been flat." He felt childcare rate adjustments needed to be made immediately and that there was great opportunity for building membership. He also wondered if "we are doing too much" in international work. As an example, he said, "We were the second largest contributor to the National YMCA's African Crisis Fund, and have five large exchanges that consume much staff energy." Clark also felt that the Nashville YMCA had the leanest business office staff in the country with a director [Jim Rayhab], an accountant and a clerk, and that we needed to look at the organizational structure. There were eleven people reporting directly to him.[1167]

Clark was still relatively young when he became the Metropolitan Nashville CEO. He dressed as if he were even younger, usually wearing a blue blazer and khaki pants. It did not take the board long, however, to realize that Clark was old enough to get the job done.

The 113th annual meeting of the Metropolitan Nashville YMCA was held, once again, at the Opryland Hotel. The featured speaker was Miss Kellye Cash, Miss America, 1987. Wayne Oldham, wearing his trademark top hat, served as emcee. Sandra Fulton was elected president for two years rather than one, an innovation suggested by Clark. Bill Turner and Lee Barfield were elected vice-presidents; Olin West III, was elected treasurer, and Jack Elisar secretary. Sandra became Clark's best friend.[1168] She would also be only the second female president of the Nashville YMCA in history. Her husband, Richard Fulton, Nashville's mayor, had played a significant role in the establishment of the East Nashville YMCA branch on Gallatin Road in the mid-to-late 1950s when he was in the State Senate.

Sandra Fulton became the Metropolitan YMCA's first Board Chair in 1988.

Clark Baker knew his biggest challenge in Nashville was to strengthen the association's financial strength. This didn't look so good in early April, when a headline in the *Tennessean* read, "East Nashville YMCA's Future Clouded." Financial problems at East, compounded by needed repairs to the Gallatin Road facility, were threatening the future of Nashville's oldest family center. Members of the East Y had been told that the outdoor pool would be closed the following summer because it needed $150,000 in improvements, and the funds to make the repairs were unavailable. Membership at the East Y, at 2624 Gallatin Road, had dropped from around 2,000 households in the mid-1960s by 80 percent to only 400 in March 1988. Jan Scanlan told the reporter that the East operating revenue came from membership and program fees, adding that the budget for the East Nashville facility was only $400,000 in 1987. In contrast, Ms. Scanlan said, the Green Hills YMCA with 2,100 households had an operating budget in 1987 of more than $1 million. Major repairs needed by East's outdoor swimming pool included replacement of the filter and drainage systems and the deck. "The health Department won't let us open it unless we make those repairs," Scanlan said.[1169] Not reported was the telling fact that the East YMCA board had not met in a year.

Because of day camp losses of $70,000 in 1987, daycare fees were restructured and a standardized sliding scale was implemented association-wide. In April, the pool at Northwest was nearly finished, but the women's lockers at Downtown had not arrived. However, pool construction at Downtown had started. At the April executive committee meeting, Clark Baker stated that his intention was to reestablish the Nashville YMCA as a leader in the fitness and aerobic area. He felt we were behind in this area, except, perhaps, at Green Hills.[1170]

• • • • •

Steve Tarver was not only a capable branch executive, but also had a flair for the dramatic. During his years in Nashville, on special occasions and undoubtedly others, he wore a batman outfit, complete with a cape modified to be a Y-man cape, and a mask.

• • • • •

Steve "Y-Man" Tarver, East Center Executive, leading the Fifth Annual Senior Walk Run

Clark addressed the financial problems in tangible way. He hired Bart Bartleson, who became the first professionally trained vice-president of finance at the Nashville Association.

May brought completion of the women's locker room Downtown and the report that the sustaining campaign had raised $218,000 of an Association goal of $228,000, despite East not having kicked off their campaign. Steve Tarver, East center executive, was working hard to repackage the center with emphases on cleanliness, bright lights, and more quality programs.

Bob McGaughey, youth and government director, reported in May that the 1988 Youth Legislature had its highest number of participants ever with over 600 in attendance.[1171]

The full board met on July 6 to receive the results of the recently completed Association evaluation. The overall findings were that the Metropolitan board was held in high esteem, the Y was capable of solving almost any problem and serving any need, and the community was receptive to a major capital campaign. Other observations were that, (1) because of the great growth, there should be an increased emphasis on organizational control and stability, (2) there should be more programming for adults, especially in the fitness area, (3) there was an opportunity for more subsidies from the United Way and sustaining memberships, and (4) with $2 million in debt, a capital campaign was a necessity.

Two more Baker innovations came in the summer. Each center was directed to implement the new corporate color scheme of teal, burgundy, and gray. Clark said, tongue in cheek, "Each center may use these colors in any order they want." The idea was to have a more unified look and a strong visual identity. The other innovation was a change in titles. Effective September, the "general director" title was changed to "president," while the "board chairman" title replaced the "president" title. The "vice-president" title became "vice-chair" while, on the staff side, the "associate general executive" became "senior vice-president" and the "associate general director" became "vice-president." The "finance director" became "vice-president finance." The executive directors" of the branches became "vice-presidents."

Clark Baker announced in July that Dan Shaddock would leave his position in August to join the South Field office in Atlanta. Dan's duties would be assumed by Jim Rayhab and Mr. Baker. He also announced that board member Margaret Maddox and her husband, Dan, who was known to be both wealthy and tight-fisted, generously contributed matching funds to enable Y-CAP to obtain a family therapist. This would be a harbinger of much larger gifts from this couple.[1172]

The Downtown renovation program had more phases than a cat had lives. In August, Gary Schlansker reported that women's membership had almost doubled since the opening of the women's center (phase 1), that phase 2 was complete, that phase 3, including the men's new locker room, and renovated lobby, would be complete shortly and that phase 4, the co-ed weight center would begin once the lower level was vacated by the Nashville School of Law. The Y physical fitness center was praised by Dick Husband, downtown board chairman, as the finest in the city.[1173]

Despite fully realizing that finances could be the Association's Achilles heel, the operating results through August were unsettling. The Association had a $44,893 deficit with only the Green Hills branch above water.[1174]

Work on the YMCA's identity package continued into the fall. At the September executive committee meeting, held for the first time in the sixth floor conference room in the Doctors' Building, Tom Ryan presented the package that included letterhead, envelopes, business cards, etc., supposedly with all using the same format that was used nationally.

With the closing of a health club in Gallatin, a group of citizens there were pressing for the Nashville YMCA to lease the vacated building and open a center in Gallatin. Jack Shockley and Associates was hired to conduct a feasibility study to determine how many people would be willing to pay a $100 fee and $30 a month to be members. Ann Hogan, of the Green Hills staff, was standing by, ready to become vice-president of the Sumner County center should it materialize.[1175]

With the Gallatin community having raised over $50,000 for start-up funds and the building committee vouching for the soundness of the vacated health club building and approving its location, the Metropolitan board approved opening the Gallatin branch. It was also reported in October that the Donelson Center had secured funding for its new fitness center and that the Downtown Y pool should be open by Thanksgiving and the men's locker room and lobby there finished within the week.

Gov. Ned McWherter wrote Cary Massey Jr. on November 18, thanking the Metropolitan Nashville YMCA for pioneering before-and-after school care for children in Tennessee. He said, "Had it not been for the Nashville YMCA, we would not have nearly as many programs in the public schools." He told Carey that his office had asked the Tennessee General Assembly to enact legislation that would allow the public schools to operate before-and-after school care programs directly. He said, "No one entity can solve the problem alone," and he hoped that the YMCA's before-and-after school care programs "would continue and expand."[1176] Collaboration would become much more important in the first decade of the twenty-first century.

In December, Steve Tarver resigned to accept the CEO position at the Clearwater, FL, YMCA. He was ready for the challenge and the board was happy for him. In 2011, Steve would be the CEO of the Louisville, Kentucky YMCA, and still wearing his Y-Man cape. At the December board meeting, it was announced that the Metropolitan Nashville YMCA had been recognized as a premier YMCA, an honor bestowed on 5 of the 195 YMCAs in the South Field.

The year ended with $6,641,495 in income and

$6,640,163 in expenses, another tiny surplus. But with an excellent board and an energetic and able CEO, all was in place for a terrific 1989. Adrian Moody, National Field Executive, was on hand for the February board meeting to present president Sandra Fulton with the YMCA Award of Excellence. He praised the Nashville Y for its amazing growth, its model childcare program, incredible sports programs, teenage programs at the Harpeth Center, and the importance of its International work. He said the Nashville YMCA was setting an example for other South Field YMCAs.[1177]

The leadership development committee reported in February that the following officers had agreed to serve for the current year:

Sandra Fulton, chair
Bill Turner, vice-chair
Lee Barfield, vice-chair
Olin West III, treasurer
Jack Elisar, secretary

These officers would be elected at the 114th annual meeting at the Opryland Hotel on April 4.

Two YMCA stalwarts passed from the scene in 1989. Long-time board member Battle Rodes died while Dr. Jim Hudgins moved to North Carolina. Dr. Hudgins gave the devotional at the February board meeting, making the point that "the strength of all comes only from Christ." He also reminisced about the early days of the East branch. Later in the meeting, George Cate Jr. read tributes to Rodes and Hudgins. In his president's report, Clark announced the employment of Tom Looby from Atlanta's Gwinnett Center, to replace Steve Tarver at the Donelson and East Centers. Tom would prove to be an excellent executive.[1178]

Growing "Like Topsy"

Green Hills was continuing to grow. Their long-range plan and demographic study identified their greatest needs as more parking and 2,000 square feet of additional space for the Nautilus and aerobics workouts. The estimated cost was $175,000. The executive committee authorized an expenditure of $10,000 for design work. The board also approved spending $209,000 to build an all-weather outdoor pool at Harpeth that would include a bubble cover, a heater, and space for bleachers. The hope was to complete the project by June 1. A three-year loan from Sovran Bank, contributions, and a possible allocation from the City of Brentwood if the pool could be used for high school swim meets, would pay for the project.

The two and one-half-year-old Maury County YMCA had made progress, having office space donated, and having received a $15,000 gift from the United Givers Fund of Maury County. In the summer of 1988, the Maury County Y had their first day camp. To take the next few steps in a sure-footed manner, their directors asked for the guidance of the Metropolitan Nashville YMCA. In March, the Metropolitan Nashville executive committee approved a motion to admit the Maury County YMCA as a branch of the Metropolitan Nashville YMCA.[1179]

When you have a YMCA as highly visible and successful as the Metropolitan Nashville YMCA was in the 1980s, other YMCAs naturally looked to it for leadership. That happened twice in June 1989 when Gary Schlansker and Cary Massey were successfully recruited to become the CEOs of the Norfolk, Virginia, and Kansas City, Kansas YMCAs respectively. Both had contributed much to the Nashville YMCA. Within two months, Gary Schlansker decided to return to Nashville and assumed the CEO position at Harpeth. Concurrently, Bob McGaughey was named to fill Carey Massey's vacant position as the Association's new vice president for program and planning.[1180]

At the June meeting, it was reported that the Harpeth pool opened on June 11, and that work would start in the fall to double the size of the Green Hills parking lot and increase the size of their fitness center. As the last order of business, Sandra Fulton appointed a capital campaign steering committee consisting of Nelson Andrews, Walter Knestrick, Dortch Oldham, Ridley Wills II, and Bill Wilson.[1181]

Jim Barr, international committee chairman, reported that a group of board members were planning a trip to Toulouse, France, in October to finalize our partnership with that city's Y and to attend a world Y meeting there. Another group was planning a trip to Zambia in September. Day camp was reported to be going well with over 1,200 day campers at twelve sites.[1182]

A senior adult program kicked off at the Downtown YMCA after Labor Day aimed at adults 55 and older. Dr. Phil Harris' aim was to enlist 200 members at a reduced annual rate of $250. They would be members of the new "200 Club."

Bids were let in September by the City of Nashville to rebuild the Church Street Viaduct. When the construction would begin in the spring off 1990, the YMCA would lose 10' from the south side of its property, not enough to cause any structural changes. The Y benefited in that, by relinquishing its air rights for the bridge, it would receive 20 parking spaces under the viaduct. The H. G. Hill Company also gave the YMCA another 13 spaces across the street from the Downtown Center.[1183]

The low bid for the Green Hills building project, submitted by Knestrick Construction Company, was accepted. The cost would be at a little under $50 per square foot. The contract called for the project to be completed in 80 days.[1184]

A citywide membership plan, designed as one of several steps to improve the YMCA's bottom line, was scheduled for implementation in November. It would feature three kinds of memberships: facility, program, and sustaining. Facility memberships were to be available for adults, individuals, families, youth/teens, senior citizens, and corporations. Membership fees would increase by an average of 15 percent on implementation and up to 40 percent over three years.[1185]

After getting Gary Schlansker back in August, the YMCA lost the services of Jan Scanlan, director of communications, in September to the Nashville YWCA, where she would be their executive. Lori Swann, formerly membership director at Green Hills, replaced Jan.[1186]

Finances were hard to deal with in a YMCA growing as fast as the Metropolitan Nashville YMCA was. Through September, the Association had a $312,000 loss compared to a loss of $146,000 through the comparable period in 1988. The Downtown and Harpeth centers accounted for much of this deficit. The Downtown Center's fall membership drive would be critical in controlling the deficit. With membership renewals in the 4th quarter, a tightening of expenses and a contingency fund of $206,000, the Association hoped to be in a balanced position by year-end. To further shore up the Y's financial staff, Clark employed Bob Ecklund, with the Ashford-Dunwoody YMCA in Atlanta, as the new Metro vice-president for operations. He would start January 2.[1187]

Y-CAP *a Success*

Energetic Y-CAP director Carl Carlson showed the board in October a video from *American Magazine*, a TV show that produced a feature story on Y-CAP. Carl reported that Y-CAP worked with 75 kids in the past three years and, of these, only 8 had come back through the juvenile justice system. He added that YCAP also worked with the families of juvenile offenders through counseling and parenting groups and, in total, was assisting over 200 people.[1188]

To better fund inner city work in Nashville, the Y set up an Inner City Youth Futures Fund to support and enhance inner city programs. Each full-service facility (Donelson, Green Hills, and Harpeth) would set aside 7 percent of their respective membership fees for this purpose.[1189] This had been done in the past but not officially.

Sandra Fulton reported at the November executive committee meeting that the officers for 1990 had been nominated. They were Bill Turner, chairman; Lee Barfield, first vice chair; John Ed Miller, second vice chair; Jack Elisar, secretary; and Doyle Rippee, treasurer. They would be elected at the December board meeting. At the same meeting, Lori Swann reported that the citywide membership program would start on January 1.[1190]

Other news was that fundraiser extraordinaire Jerry Panas would be in town early in December interviewing prominent Nashvillians to assess the perception of the YMCA and test the city's receptiveness to a capital campaign. The Gallatin Y was celebrating its 1st birthday and proud that it had 800 members. Over in Green Hills, the walls were up and the roof almost finished on the new wellness center. November also turned out to provide the greatest amount of revenue in the Association's history—$130,052. Most of this came from membership dues.[1191]

In her last meeting as chair on December 21, Sandra Fulton thanked the board and staff for their support. She said, "The board is the heart of the Y and is the heart of Nashville—its backbone." Clark Baker predictably said, "I lost my best friend."

J. Lawrence, Urban Services Director, introduced Shozo Kawaguchi, who reported that 17 Vanderbilt students would accompany him to Charleston, SC, on Christmas break to work on problems caused by Hurricane Hugo. There were many other 1989 highlights, including 20 young people traveling to Venezuela, Germany, and France, two YMCAs chartered in Columbia and Gallatin, and 2,000 children enrolled in school-age child care at 55 sites. The latter was under Suzanne Spore's direction.[1192]

The introduction of the citywide membership program excited existing members and many new members to join the Y. Membership revenue in the last three months of 1989 totaled $1,061,000 or 32 percent of the Y's total membership revenue for the year. Because of this and by using all of the Association's contingency reserve ($227,000), the budget balanced for the year. All operating units except Downtown, Gallatin, Northwest, and Urban Services recorded surpluses. For East, this was the first surplus in many years.[1193]

TOP: Brentwood YMCA BOTTOM: Turner Dining Lodge

CHAPTER THIRTY-TWO

Upward and Onward

1990–1993

BILL TURNER PRESIDED over his first board of directors meeting on January 25. One of the first decisions made at that meeting was the approval of a very ambitious budget of $9,607,469. Treasurer Doyle Rippee said that revenues had risen 25 percent in 1989 with membership up 40 percent. He projected revenues to grow another 20 percent in 1990, thanks in part to the citywide membership program. He added, "These are aggressive expectations, but achievable."

Clark Baker thanked the Y staff for making 1989 such a successful year and verbalized his hopes for 1990—"a balanced budget, working even harder on program quality and evaluations, raising more sustaining funds, making sure that all we are doing relates to the Y's mission, raising membership retention to 60 percent, a 10 percent growth in new memberships, and development of a comprehensive marketing plan." Clark also reported that Trigg Wilks was named, on January 15, the executive director of the Downtown Center.[1194]

By February, a youth fitness program at Green Hills had been in place for several months. It came about because of the horrifying realization of how unfit American youth were. Scott Reall was running the program at Green Hills as well as at Fun Company sites. Meanwhile, in Columbia, the Maury County YMCA was deep into negotiations to take over an existing childcare center in Columbia, whose respected director was about to retire. This would materialize in August. In his president's report, Clark said that citizens in Bellevue, Lebanon, and Smyrna were anxious to establish YMCAs in their respective areas. Soon Bellevue and Murfreesboro would be added to that list.[1195]

The story at Downtown was reassuring. In April, its board chairman John White reported that the membership had grown to 3,048 with the number of women members having grown to 1,125. Trigg Wilkes was concerned that the center was at near capacity with much resting on whether or not the Nashville School of Law moved to its own facility. It was rumored that this would happen by year-end. Clark Baker reported on March 22 that revenues were up 20 percent over 1989—the exact percentage projected in the budget.[1196]

William E. "Bill" Turner Jr., Metropolitan Board Chair 1990–1991

In April, Clark Baker announced that Becky Weikert had been hired as the new director of development. He said she would be working closely with fundraising guru Jerry Panas to lay the groundwork for the Association's next capital campaign. Clark also reported that the miserable parking problem Downtown would be eased with the news that the Baptist Sunday School Board had made available 210 parking places after 4 p.m. Conversations were also underway, Clark said, with John B. Hardcastle and Wentworth Caldwell Jr. about the Y using H. G. Hill Realty Company space at 900 Church Street for administration offices. The H. G. Hill Realty Co. generously agreed to lease the space for $1 a year; the YMCA moved in during August.[1197] The board also learned in April that senior vice-president Bill Portman would retire later in the year at age 60. Bill had done an outstanding job in many assignments over 37 years.[1198] He was honored with a retirement celebration on July 29.

The spring 1991 issue of *Discovery* YMCA, the official magazine of the YMCA of the USA, had on its cover a picture of inner-city Nashville children, who were members of the Nashville Youth Hockey League thanks to 12 scholarships provided by a YMCA board member. The magazine article said that the children, all African-American and Cambodian, had never had never heard of ice-skating, and, according to J. Lawrence, the Nashville YMCA's Urban Services director, were "basically raising themselves. They aren't doing well in school; their families aren't healthy," J. said. On the Y van taking the kids to Nashville's multi-million-dollar Sportsplex to try on their first skates, J. said they didn't even speak to each other. By the end of the season, the players were pals. One of them, Lemon Jolly, who lived in the Edgehill housing project, said he would like to be a hockey star. The Discovery YMCA article praised J. and the Nashville Y's innovative Urban Services program for giving kids, who face enormous obstacles in their impoverished neighborhoods, opportunities to test their wings in a variety of ways, including a reading power program; compute and shoot, where kids learned basketball and computer skills; and "Ernie, Bert and Me," a preschool for Cambodian children that taught English. One of the Urban Services' most effective volunteers was Arshi Nasseh, a high school guidance counselor and a native of Iran, who led the Y's high school international club that helped assimilate 200 young people from other nations.[1199]

Clark Baker reported that the Maury County YMCA had moved into the donated office on the public square in Columbia and had been given an outdoor pool. Clark stated that some party had an interest in buying the East YMCA building but it had been decided not to give up on the center and to monitor it for two years before even considering such a drastic move. In order to forestall a year-end deficit, cost savings were enacted by the Metropolitan board, the budget revised, and an aggressive marketing plan developed to be implemented as soon as the Law School moved.[1200] Should the deficit continue to grow, the Y was poised to implement another level of cuts in August.

The news finally came from Dean Joe Loser that the Nashville School of Law would be vacating their space on the lower floor of the Downtown YMCA on October 15. As soon as that happened, the Y would start an extensive renovation of the area that would be transformed into a cardiovascular center.[1201]

The Nashville School of Law temporarily leased space in Watkins Institute downtown and at Tennessee State University before settling in a new home at 2934 Sidco Drive in 1991. Thirteen years later, in 2004, the law school would move again, this time to a state-of-the-art campus at 4013 Armory Oaks Drive.[1202]

The legal committee recommended to the board of directors in July that the organization's name be changed to the "YMCA of Nashville and Middle Tennessee" to reflect the fact that the Metropolitan Nashville YMCA was rapidly becoming a regional YMCA. The committee also felt that the chief volunteer officer have the title "chairman," and the chief executive officer would have the title "president." Interestingly, the last named change had already been put in place.[1203] These changes were all approved.

Under Margaret Maddox's enthusiastic leadership, board awareness tours were being made, usually to the East and Northwest centers, Y-CAP, and the Cleveland Park Community Center where a YMCA summer sports camp had 180 youngsters every day. Two of the first to take the awareness tours were Bill Turner and Jimmy Webb III, both of whom spoke of how much the tours meant to them. The tours went so well that Margaret expanded them to include key business leaders who were not affiliated with the YMCA.[1204]

By September, it was perfectly clear that the bank draft plan Adrian Moody brought to Nashville from Houston was a tremendous success. Membership was up 17 percent through August. It was also clear that the attention of YMCAs across the country was on Nashville. That alone made everyone work a little harder.

On November 29, Clark Baker presented an opportunity the YMCA had to acquire the Maryland Farms Downtown Athletic Club located on the top floor of the Third National Financial Center across from the Downtown Presbyterian Church on Church Street. The acquisition was approved by the executive committee in October. It was pointed out that many people in Nashville's financial district could more easily work out in the Third Financial Center than to walk the longer distance to 1000 Church Street. After discussion, a motion was made and seconded to acquire the lease and equipment and operate the facility as a department of the Downtown Center. The motion carried.[1205] Earlier, at the October 25 executive committee meeting, Trigg Wilks said that the Downtown Center would likely get 625 new members with the acquisition of the Maryland Farms Downtown Athletic Club and that the new center should produce a $40,000 to $45,000 surplus. The executive committee voted in October to approve the lease and equipment purchase that cost $60,000. The center would reopen as a YMCA in January.[1206]

Bart Bartleson reported at the December 20 board meeting that the YMCA was almost exactly on budget with revenues up 16 percent for the year. Gallatin was the only center expecting a greater deficit than budgeted. Bob Ecklund, who monitored the budget carefully, reported that the Y had moved from a $300,000 deficit in May to an expected year-end surplus of between $50,000 to $100,000. Bob said the elimination of sixteen full-time positions, greater expense controls, and some price increases had caused the turnaround.

Growth and a New Membership Drive

The leadership development committee recommended that the present slate of officers be re-elected. These were Bill Turner, chairman; Lee Barfield and John Ed Miller, vice chairs; Jack Elisar, secretary; and Doyle Rippee, treasurer. The officers and board members would be elected at the annual meeting on April 16. Before the meeting concluded, president Turner expressed his thanks to the staff and observed that this was the 1,035th meeting of the YMCA board since it was founded in 1875. One wag in the back of the room thought to himself, "only someone claiming to be from Spot, Tennessee, would know that."

On January 15, Doyle Rippee, chair of the finance committee, recommended the approval of a balanced 1991 budget of $10,856,400, a 14 percent increase over 1990. Bart Bartleson made the announcement that the financial results showed a surplus of $11,042 for 1990 with the month of December having a gain of $209,378. For the year, the Y was up 12 percent in contributions and 23 percent in membership.

The "We Build People" sustaining membership campaign kicked off in February under the leadership of Sandra Fulton. Its goal was $395,000.[1207] The drive was greatly aided by the addition of George Goyer, a YMCA veteran from California, to the staff as vice-president for development. George sized up the situation quickly. He concluded that too many metropolitan board members were giving less than $1,000 annually. He encouraged them to elevate their giving by "giving until it hurts," and was instrumental in establishing the Chairman's Roundtable, a donor society that recognized people who gave $1,000 or more annually.[1208]

In February, the Green Hills selection committee named George's son, Scott Goyer, as that center's new executive director, replacing Bill Portman. Scott began work in March. Downtown, the new wellness center helped that branch achieve a growth of 200 percent in three years. The Nashville Y also continued to give leadership to the Tennessee Cluster that was chaired in 1991 by Sandra Fulton.[1209]

At the April 25 board meeting, Sandra reported on the success of the three-week-long "We Build People" campaign. The gifts and pledges totaled $398,000 with 81 donors contributing $1,000 or more. Vice-chair Lee Barfield presented a resolution to approve the issuance of not more than $5 million in industrial revenue bonds. This was something the Nashville Y had never done. Of the amount, 60 percent would be used to refinance existing debt reducing the interest from 11 percent to 8 percent. The remaining 40 percent would be used on new facilities enhancement projects at several branches whose membership revenues were adequate to service the debt. J. C. Bradford & Co. would market the bonds. By April, a New Century Task Fore, chaired by insurance executive Ted Lazenby and co-chaired by Judge Frank Drowota, was planning the Y's upcoming capital campaign.[1210]

The projects at Green Hills consisted of a renovation of the indoor pool, the construction of a second floor over the wellness center, airconditioning of the gym, the construction of an outdoor pool, and work on a youth pavilion. To bring Donelson up to the City-Y standard, their board would enlarge their wellness center, build a new aerobics room, a nursery, and office space, and air-condition the gym. Changes at Harpeth and Downtown would be less extensive. All these projects were approved. The very reliable Knestrick Construction would do the work at Green Hills and Harpeth.

Y-CAP director Carl Carlson reported that the First Church of the Nazarene had offered the Y use of a house on Woodland Street directly across from the church. Since a home situation was the one thing that Y-CAP had been unable to provide, the gift was gratefully accepted and plans were made for minor renovations before 6 to 8 boys moved in early in 1992. With the boys, who would attend public schools, would be house parents and a social worker. Y-CAP would raise the money to make this dream a reality. Fortunately the Department of Human Services would give $64,000 of the $162,000 needed annually to operate the home. By the end of July $120,000 had been raised.[1211]

Clark Baker reported that the Y was in discussion with the City about using the Bellevue Community Center as the temporary home for a Y in that area. He had trouble containing his excitement about better serving that community, the passing of the Industrial Revenue Bonds proposal, and the group home for boys.[1212]

The industrial revenue bond purchase closed on June 28. Of the $5 million, $2.6 would be used to pay off prior debts and the balance would go toward the suburban center projects. J. Lawrence reported at the June 27 board meeting that the YMCA would operate Urban Academy during the day at the home on Woodland Street, serving boys suspended from school. The hope was to change their attitudes so they could go back to a conventional education.

Yet another opportunity to serve a large segment of Davidson County surfaced when the American Fitness Center off Harding Place in Antioch suddenly closed. Fortunately, George Volkert, a former chair of the Downtown Board, owned the building. The executive committee asked that a marketing study be made to see if putting a YMCA in the building would be feasible.

Clark Baker announced at the July executive committee meeting that 1991 was the 100th anniversary of the founding of basketball by Dr. James Naismith at the Springfield, Massachusetts, YMCA.

A special called meeting of the YMCA executive committee was held in August to discuss the Harding Place YMCA. Jimmy Webb III reported that, after much discussion, the negotiated purchase price of $750,000 had been approved. Bart Bartleson reported that, financially, 1992 would be tough but that the opportunity made sense. It would serve an area of 136,000 people living within a 5-mile radius of the center. The committee authorized the board chairman and CEO to purchase the property for $750,000. Bond proceeds would be used to make the needed improvements. Clark Baker would announce at the October board of directors committee meeting that the Y had closed on the Harding Place building. Tom Looby would give half his time to Donelson and the other half to managing the new center.[1213] The Harding Place goal was to have 750 members when the center opened on January 1. To help the new center get through a difficult first year, Green Hills, Brentwood, and possibly one other large center would up part of their surpluses to help make the transition.

J. Lawrence reported to the board in December that Urban Services had launched a new program called Y-Wolf (Youth Working on Leadership and Fitness). This was made possible by an $80,000 grant from the City's Department of Housing and Urban Development. The program would initially involve 12 youngsters with leadership ability who lived in the tough Settle Court area. J. introduced Artrell Harris, a National Y Volunteer of the Year, who would be working with Y-Wolf.

The "We Build People" campaign for 1992, with a goal of $415,000 was well organized and ready under the steady hand of Sandra Fulton. It would be beautifully oversubscribed with a final result of $467,700 being raised.[1214]

Meanwhile, Lee Barfield presided as president of the YMCA of Nashville and Middle Tennessee for the first time at the January 23 executive committee meeting. He thanked his predecessor, Bill Turner, for his steady guidance of the Association for the previous two years. Later in the meeting, treasurer Jack Elisar announced that revenues for 1991 totaled $11,138,200, 24 percent higher than in 1990, and the Association had a surplus of $15,900 by using $92,000 in contingency reserve. Clark Baker reported that the 1992 budget was set at $11,790,200 including $240,000 and $165,000 in contingency and maintenance reserves, respectively.

At the February board meeting, Jimmy Webb III presented a charter to the Harding Place YMCA, represented at the meeting by center executive Tom Looby. Tom announced that Harding Place had close to 500 units or 1,200 members. Clark Baker announced a dollar for dollar matching grant that Margaret Maddox had given the East Y for renovation work there. Lee Barfield reported that the new Y-CAP group home on Woodland Street would open March 22.

Clark reported in March that Gary Schlansker was joining the corporate staff to assist in development and personnel, and would assume Jim Rayhab's duties when Jim retired on January 1, 1993. The New Century planning committee continued to work toward formulating the Association's goal of raising $25 million by 1999. Clark called it "the boldest approach to planning" ever undertaken by the local Y." More than 500 YMCA members, staff and community volunteers were involved in the planning process.[1215]

In April, planning committee co-chairs Fred W. "Ted" Lazenby and Judge Frank Drowota reported that their committee would make a final report in June. Two major needs that had been identified were (1) to be the premier membership organization in Nashville, and (2) to be the #1 agency in teen work in the city.

Much of the May 28 executive committee meeting was devoted to the New Century Plan. Bob Ecklund thoroughly reviewed the 3rd draft of the plan. Two major areas addressed, he said, were (1) work with teens, including those at-risk, and (2) membership and wellness programs in all areas with the same basic quality in all centers. A major maintenance goal was to fully fund the $250,000 reserve by 1994. The top priorities for East and Northwest were for a gym and wellness center at each branch. East also needed an outdoor pool.

Jim Rayhab reported that construction was winding down at Green Hills and Donelson. The new Green Hills pool would open the following weekend. At Donelson, new locker rooms would open soon and new office space was already being used. Work on the Donelson outdoor pool had just started, Rayhab said. Clark Baker passed out a bank draft report that showed a great increase in membership utilizing the plan. For the year, the Y stood 29 percent ahead of 1991 at the same time.[1216]

The 4th draft of the New Century Plan was unveiled at the June board meeting. Final approval was scheduled to take place at the executive committee meeting in July. One aspect of the plan identified the need to develop a regional day camp. This caught the attention of Tom Looby, executive director of the Donelson-Hermitage YMCA. His board wanted to move their day camp from the Donelson center, which the children were [almost] wrecking, to an off-site location, hopefully, with approximately 50 acres and a pond or lake. Having heard that the Nashville Donelson YMCA had leased 55 acres of land on Spencer Creek from the U.S. Army Corps of Engineers for Camp Thunderbird, a day camp, in the 1960s, Tom visited the Corps of Engineers' regional office at Percy Priest Lake to find out why the lease had lapsed. Bill Colvin, the Corps of Engineers' associate resource manager, could not answer that question but told Tom that the Corps was not signing any more leases on Old Hickory Lake. He added, however, that the Corps had several large tracts of land along Percy Priest Lake set aside for recreational purposes. Tom and Colvin looked at a map and immediately targeted a Smith Springs site as most promising. Colvin thought a YMCA youth camp would be an appropriate fit there. Tom told Clark Baker about his promising visit with Colvin and, in February 1993, the two of them, Bob Ecklund, and Ranger Rick of the Corps, visited the site in a pontoon boat. But this is getting ahead of the story.

The July 1992 executive committee meeting opened with a devotional by Margaret Maddox, who told the story of the East Y and its rebirth. Carl Carlson told the story of Y-CAP from its start in 1986 when it had a staff of 2 and served 10 children to July 1992 when it had a staff of twelve who served 1,000 children. Success stories like this are remarkable and inspiring.

The New Century Plan with its $25 million in total requests was approved in July. The plan was broken down into manageable segments to be raised from annual gifts and other sources. The plan's first segment called for $7 million from fundraising and $3 million from borrowing.

Two staff stalwarts from the past were guests at the meeting. They were Chuck Harris, who thanked Jim Rayhab for his help when Chuck started in Nashville 23 years earlier, and Steve Tarver. He stated that his goal, since he first joined the Nashville YMCA, was to be a CEO, a goal he and Chuck both achieved. Steve marveled at how many YMCA volunteers were the same men he worked with earlier in his career.[1217] In anticipation of Jim Rayhab's retirement, the YMCA of Nashville and Middle Tennessee hosted a party for him at the Hillwood Country Club in July. Jim was praised for his 36 years of loyal and dedicated service. During the Brunson years, he had been Ralph's dependable right-hand man.[1218]

In an effort to get young men in inner city Nashville off

the streets on Saturday nights, the Police Athletic League and the Y began holding basketball games at the Downtown YMCA on Saturday evenings for young men between 18 and 25. After each game, there was a 15-minute invitational session on some timely subject, such as AIDS education. The initial crowd of 500 quickly jumped to 700 and police calls went down 15–20 percent near the community centers were the boys were recruited.

Ron Knox reported at the September board meeting that the Vandy Rebounders and Vanderbilt basketball coach Eddie Fogler were working to become involved with Urban Services' "Compute and Shoot" program.[1219] Earlier, former president Bill Wadlington had arranged for J. Lawrence to meet with Fogler. After J. explained the concept of "Compute and Shoot," Coach Fogler said, "That's a great concept," and gave J. his personal check for $500. Then, the enthusiastic Fogler held at luncheon at the University Club to promote the Y program. The luncheon raised $4,000 of the $30,000 needed to fund a staff person. Vanderbilt furnished the gym and other resources. The "Compute and Shoot" staff person turned out to be Eric Reed, a former Vanderbilt basketball player.[1220]

In the fall of 1992, Bill Wilson, chairman of the New Century Vision committee, proposed that the first phase of the capital campaign start in 1993 with the goal of raising $10.3 million by December 1995. He said, "We are going into the inner city when others are leaving it, so our case is strong." Bill also said, "We are going to say 'thanks' more than we say 'please.'" The board approved the campaign at the October board meeting. Someone present commented "There is not a Y in the country doing more for the inner city than we are." The excitement of a new capital campaign extended to euphoria over the fact that, if trends held during the fourth quarter, the Y would have a minimum surplus of $107,000, making 1992 equal to the best year ever in Nashville. Clark Baker then presented J. Lawrence with Fisk University's Humanitarian Award, a richly deserved honor. Lee Barfield said that, before the meeting, he and several others visited Mayor Phil Bredesen to bring him up-to-date on the Y's inner-city work.

Lee Barfield announced in November that Gary Schlansker, director of Metropolitan Services, would be leaving in January to become the CEO of the Greenville, South Carolina YMCA. This would be a great opportunity for Gary, who was ready for the challenge, having performed so well in Nashville.[1221]

The 1993 "We Build People" Campaign had an ambitious goal of $620,000, 53 percent over the Association's 1992 goal. Jimmy Webb III was general chairman.

The 1992 surplus turned out to be $10,017 but, additionally, the Association had been able to set aside $100,000 of reserves. Revenues grew by 24 percent and membership dues were up an astounding 30 percent. A majority of the centers had surpluses with Green Hills recording the largest. By mid-December, the New Century Vision committee had evaluated their top 25 prospects and started making cultivation calls for this enormous fund-raising effort that Bill Wilson had agreed to chair. Jerry Panas had conducted a feasibility study in the city and found that "everyone likes the YMCA but don't really know why."[1222]

"We Build People"

At the December board meeting, Clark Baker said that the Y's newest center, Y-CAP, which was debt-free and had raised more than $250,000, would be its own center in 1993. He also welcomed Julie Sistrunk, the Y's new Communications/PR director and thanked John Wright and Aldorothy Wright for their hard work in launching a Black Achievers program and for a wonderful year at Northwest. Vice-chairman Margaret Maddox concluded the meeting with a prayer that the Lord would be pleased with the Y's accomplishments in 1992 and "give us grace for another year in 1993 that would be pleasing in His sight."[1223]

In January, The YMCA of Nashville and Middle Tennessee learned that it was the 25th largest YMCA in North America. Having grown 100 percent in three years, the board felt that 1993 should be a year in which to stabilize operations. Consequently, the new budget called for a relatively conservative 9 percent increase in revenues to $14,966,700. Treasurer Jack Elisar and the rest of the management team realized that the New Century Vision fund-raising efforts would require a lot of energy but that none of the fund-raising dollars would likely effect operations until 1994 or 1995.[1224]

There was a $25,000 budget deficit at the Columbia YMCA but enthusiasm there was great and their staff would overcome their financial trials. Gallatin was facing a declining membership. To help them, Green Hills donated $15,000 from their surplus for a "facelift" there.

Officers nominated for 1993 were Lee Barfield, chair; Margaret Maddox, chair-elect; John Ed Miller, vice-chair; Jimmy Webb III, secretary; Jack Elisar, treasurer; and Olin West III, assistant treasurer. This was the year that future board chair Cal Turner Jr. joined the board. There was nothing dumb about that move. Clark Baker suggested that board meetings be rotated among the centers so that the members might become better acquainted with them.[1225]

Tom Looby, vice-president, welcomed the board to the Harding Place Center in February and told them that the branch had 1,300 members. Senior vice-president Bob Ecklund reported at the meeting that a feasibility study in Maury County showed the possibility of raising $500,000 and that a market study was underway in Robertson County.

Most of the family centers kicked off their "We Build People" campaigns the latter half of February. The Association goal was $620,000, up 30 percent from 1992.

In March 1993, the YMCA of Nashville and Middle Tennessee submitted a proposal to the Corps of U.S. Army Engineers to lease the undeveloped portion of the Smith Springs Recreational Area for a summer day camp and outdoor center.

The 1993 annual meeting, the 118th since the YMCA was founded, was held at the Opryland Hotel on April 20 in the Chattanooga Ballroom. The meeting began with an unexpected flourish when the Tennessee State Marching Band paraded to the stage. All of a sudden, the drum major took off his high hat to reveal that he was an imposter, none other than YMCA president Lee Barfield. The big crowd howled!

Despite his deceptive trick, Lee was re-elected as chairman, along with the other officers nominated in January. During dinner, the "Vision For A New Century" video was shown. East YMCA daycare children presented a "dessert parade" and Ronald Brown, a Y-CAP participant, gave a moving testimonial on how Y-CAP changed his life. Clark Baker thanked all those who contributed to making the evening a success and praised 1992 as the best year in the history of the YMCA of Nashville and Middle Tennessee.

New Century Vision steering committee chairman Bill Wilson made the dramatic announcement that, although the Y's capital campaign had only recently begun, $2.8 million had already been raised, including a pledge of $1 million from the Potter Foundation to fully equip the Northwest YMCA as a family center. Bill said, "The time to give is now." During the record-setting campaign, Bill and Clark Baker would make at least 100 bus and van trips to show prospective givers and board members various inner-city ministries, including Y-CAP and the Northwest YMCA. Clark started off driving but ended up getting lost in East Nashville. When it was suggested that Julie Sistrunk, not Clark, drive the van, he quipped, "I think I just got fired."[1226]

The YMCA went in a new direction as far as summer camps were concerned in 1993. Thanks to market research, the Y provided a broader range of camping experiences, ranging from more affordable summer camps to more active camps by entering the new arena of specialty camps, specifically horseback riding, backpacking trips, and sports camps.

At the May 27 executive committee meeting, George Goyer reported that the "We Build People" campaign had raised $711,919, or 114 percent of its goal. Over a three-year period, the amount raised had grown, George said, by an astounding 114 percent. Fundraising at the Y was becoming more sophisticated with computers playing a major role in tracking campaign progress.[1227] Clark Baker knew how hard his staff was working in 1993. It was, he thought, "the most exhilarating time but also the scariest time in our history."[1228]

Through May, Jack Elisar reported a surplus of $227,000 in 1993. As family centers were then being allowed to keep 50 percent of their surpluses, their staffs and board members were feeling more empowered. This may well have contributed to the strong bottom line.

Scott Goyer reported in June that Green Hills' challenge was to address the problem of so many teenagers going home, after school, to empty houses. He thought that this was true for more than 50 percent of the teenagers in his service area. The solution, Scott thought, was to establish a separate teen center at Green Hills, with its own lobby, gymnasium, and computer lab. There, teenagers could hang out and relax without adult YMCA members to interact with.

Percy Priest Lake Eyed as Camp Site

June 1993 was the first time most board members ever heard of the possibility of leasing land along Percy Priest Lake from the Corps of Engineers for a summer camp. Tom Looby said that phase 1 of such a project would likely cost $750,000. He and George Goyer were putting together a funding proposal to pay for the exciting project. The board would hear more about this.[1229]

In the 1990s, Williamson and Rutherford counties were

the two fastest growing counties in the state. The Brentwood YMCA was nearing capacity and a market study showed that a full service facility in Franklin would be a blockbuster. One of the two favored sites was on Mack Hatcher Parkway. Time was important as, unless the Y moved quickly, other non-profits might get there first. In Murfreesboro, the market study was equally positive. A YMCA near the intersection of I-24 and State Highway 96 would be a homerun, according to Buck Winfield, of the Winfield Group, who did the study. Such a location would be easily accessible from LaVergne and Smyrna, areas expected to provide 40 percent of the membership. A visit to the Christy-Houston Foundation in Murfreesboro was the next step. There, Clark Baker met Jim Arnhart, the foundation's president. Arnhart told Baker that he was a "scholarship boy," who spent countless hours at the Knoxville YMCA when he was a child during the depression. Arnhart also said, "Murfreesboro needs a "place to belong." Clark and board chair Lee Barfield were elated.[1230] Arnhart told the YMCA delegation that they needed to talk with Murfreesboro mayor Joe Jackson. They did and found him to be equally supportive of having a YMCA in town. Joe grew up at the Chattanooga YMCA on a scholarship.[1231]

To the north, the steering committee in Springfield was fired up about a Y there. Excitement over these expansions was matched by enthusiasm over an overnight summer camp on Percy Priest Lake. A week before the July executive committee meeting, the New Century Vision committee investigated the prospective Corps of Engineers site from a houseboat.[1232]

Laura Jackson Wills sitting in the lap of Rosalyn Simmons at the Downtown YMCA nursery, October 2011. Jackson is the six-month-old daughter of Jessica and Tom Wills and the granddaughter of Irene and Ridley Wills.

A steering committee was formed in Franklin, chaired by George Miller, future Franklin YMCA board chairman. In August, The Metro board approved spending $3 million to build the Franklin Family YMCA subject to approval by the finance, property and executive committees. Moving fast was important as the Franklin area had been identified as the area with the highest potential for development. In anticipation of having a full-service facility in Springfield, in the not distant future, the Y began a before and after school care program there. The Robertson County steering committee's market study projected a growth to 1,700 units in the first year. Because of the groundswell of interest, the YMCA of Nashville and Middle Tennessee board voted to authorize the steering committee to become the Robertson County Family YMCA board and to continue their efforts to raise $1 million to make the Robertson County YMCA in Springfield a reality.

Columbia gained momentum when Dr. Eslick Daniel and his wife, Annie, gave 20 acres on which to build a YMCA. Dr. Daniel, a member of the Maury County YMCA board, also agreed to chair the $750,000 capital campaign.

To fund the Franklin YMCA, including the acquisition of land at 507 South Royal Oaks Boulevard and the building and equipping of the center there, the finance committee recommended using $3 million from the tax-exempt bond issue. The same source would provide $1,375,000 for the Northwest gymnasium, $800,000 for the indoor pool and gymnasium at East, and $500,000 for additional land, an outdoor pool and locker rooms at Harding Place. By handling the financing this way, the Y could accelerate completion of these projects. The intent was to pay this money back later from New Century pledges and membership revenues.

The Rutherford County YMCA was in great shape as the Christy-Houston Foundation awarded the YMCA a $2.5 million grant for the new family YMCA in Murfreesboro. This was the largest gift the YMCA of Nashville and Middle Tennessee had ever received. Among those who were involved in negotiating with Christy-Houston over this magnificent pledge were Lee Barfield, Walter Knestrick, Dortch Oldham, Joe Rodgers, Pat and Bill Wilson. The Murfreesboro facility would be built at 205 North Thompson Lane very close to I-24 and State Highway 96.

The issue of the tax-exempt status for YMCAs was by not by any means a Nashville affair. CEOs and chairs of the other Tennessee YMCAs were concerned. In 1993, John

Ed Miller chaired a statewide committee to preserve the YMCA exemption for property, sales, and income taxes. To fund this statewide effort, the YMCA of Nashville and Middle Tennessee agreed to pay $8,448 of the anticipated cost of $20,000.

There was also inner-city growth in 1993. Clark Baker pointed out the need for addition office space for the corporate staff, Urban Services, the maintenance department, and, perhaps, Y-CAP. Fortunately, a building at 213 McLemore Street, next to the Downtown Center, was available at a reduced price of $200,000. Subject to review by the finance and property committees, a motion was passed to acquire the building. This was a wise move, as a decade later the aging building would be torn down and the space built on for the new and greatly expanded Downtown Center.

Clark's next announcement was a blockbuster. He said the Joe C. Davis Foundation pledged $750,000 to develop a regional outdoor center on the Corps of Army Engineers property on Percy Priest Lake. Clark and Bill Wilson had gone to see Davis Foundation trustees, Bond Davis DeLoache and her husband, Dr. William R. DeLoache, and convinced them of the worthiness of the project. Bond remembered that, when she was a girl, her family did not have enough money to send her to camp. A generation later, when Bond's daughter, Frances, was of camping age, she was able to go only because Bond went too as a counselor.[1233]

George Goyer reported in October that the New Vision Capital Development campaign stood at $7 million. He expressed confidence that the first phase goal of $10.3 million would be raised by December 1994 if not sooner. Separate capital efforts were underway in both Robertson and Maury counties. They were each boosted by Dollar General's pledged $125,000 challenge gift to both efforts.

The Black Achievers program, the idea of John Wright, center executive at Northwest, was off to a great start. This program paired adult African-American men with African-American boys who needed adult guidance and direction.

Another creative program was the colorful new Y-BUS (YMCA Better Urban Street ministry). This was an actual bus, painted by Nashville artist Miles Maille, that would travel to housing projects and other inner-city sites to present puppet shows and information on the evils of drugs and alcohol.[1234]

In October, the "We Build People" campaign established a 1994 goal of $852,000, a 37 percent increase over the 1993 goal. The Metro portion of the goal was $140,000, the largest of any center. The smallest was Uptown with a goal of $20,000. The startling increase in membership numbers propelled the YMCA of Nashville and Middle Tennessee all the way to the 7th position in the country in terms of revenue. Simply amazing!

The December board meeting was held in the newly acquired building on McLemore Street. There, the board approved a record-setting budget of $18,567,000. Bob Ecklund reported that the Y was nearly ready to seek three or four bids for the architectural work on the Franklin and Murfreesboro Family YMCA centers. Before the board meeting, the nominating committee met and proposed at the meeting the following slate of officers for 1994:

Margaret Maddox, board chair
John Ed Miller, chair-elect
Jimmy Webb III, vice chair
Bill Bailey, secretary
Jack Elisar, treasurer
Olin West III, assistant treasurer
Lee Barfield, immediate past chair

The new officers were approved. Clark Baker announced that Cathy Clark had been elected program director of the year by the YMCA of the USA. Finally, president Lee Barfield thanked the board and Clark for their support during two great years for him. He might have added "Two great years for the YMCA," as they were among the best ever.[1235] Lee had performed beautifully.

YMCA president Lee Barfield dressed as the Tennessee State Marching Band drum major

TOP: Cool Springs YMCA BOTTOM: Cookville YMCA

Gone Beyond the Limits
1994–1995

AT THE JANUARY executive committee meeting, Clark Baker reviewed the highlights of 1993, one of the finest years in the history of the local Association. He also announced that Kent Rea would be retiring from his position with the South Field that week. In reflecting on Kent's long service, some of the runners in the room may have remembered times, when running on the 5.8 mile run in Warner Park, Kent would run backwards as he accompanied his less accomplished runners up the long and steep hill beyond Deep Wells. More importantly, Kent had been a great mentor and teacher to younger YMCA executives across the South.

Margaret Maddox, the incoming president, reminded her fellow directors that 1993 didn't happen by accident but was due to the leadership of Lee Barfield, the assistance of a great board, and the work of the indefatigable Clark Baker and his talented staff.

Senator William H. "Bill" Frist with YMCA kids.

In March, vice president Tom Looby reported that a public notice had recently been distributed to people in the Smith Springs recreational area announcing the YMCA's plans for a camp in that area and that there had been a public meeting in February concerning the matter. Although the Y had compromised on virtually all areas of concern to neighbors, a few still opposed the project. One of the most vocal opponents was George Liddle, who lived with his wife on adjourning property. Mr. Liddle had, in the early 1960s, sold land to the Corps of U.S. Army Engineers when the J. Percy Priest Lake was being developed. He felt that, if the Corps of U. S. Army Engineers was going relinquish property, some of which he formerly owned, he should have the right of first refusal.[1236] Mr. Liddle, however, did not voice that argument, as he realized the Corps had no intention of selling the property. Complaints included fears of excessive traffic and the use of the property by poor, inner-city children, who might not respect neighbors' property. A forty-five-day waiting period, during which Liddle and others could express their feelings, was set aside. The Y naturally spent some energy generating calls and letters supportive of the plan that the Corps of U.S. Army Engineers and the MDHA continued to support. Hundreds of supportive letters came in along with seventeen in opposition.[1237] In resolving the issue in favor of the outdoor center, Tennessee's 5th District congressman, Robert N. Clement, was most helpful.[1238]

When the Corps of U.S. Army Engineers signed the lease with the YMCA of Middle Tennessee to develop a day camp and outdoor center on 304 acres at the Smith Springs Recreational area, Clark Baker was both relieved and exhilarated.

The Franklin YMCA had its first board meeting in March. One of the points of discussion was on acquiring a temporary location until a permanent site could be secured. Over in Murfreesboro, a closing on a site south of I-24 near State Highway 96 was expected any time. Thomas Miller was employed to design both buildings that would be similar. There was also construction activity at Northwest (gym and wellness center), East (a pool and gym) and Donelson (weight room and restrooms) all supervised by Tom Looby, the director of both the Downtown and Uptown YMCAs. All in all, there were eight building projects underway or poised to start, including a pool at Harding Place.[1239]

When the 1994 officers were introduced at the annual meeting at the Opryland Hotel, they were recognized with enthusiastic applause. Margaret Maddox was elected chair. Bill Wilson, surrounded by his campaign committee, announced that, since last year's kickoff, the New Century Vision campaign had raised $8,871,396. Bill mentioned specific projects across the association, including a $1.2 million capital campaign in Maury County to build a full-service facility there, and the $2.5 million gift from the Christy-Houston Foundation that would enable the Murfreesboro YMCA to open in March 1995. President Clark highlighted the many accomplishments of 1993 that included a 50 percent growth in the teen leadership program, the YMCA of Nashville and Middle Tennessee becoming the South's first Management Resource Center (MRC), and becoming the third YMCA in the South to join the Urban group that consisted of the 30 largest YMCAs in the country. In terms of revenue, the Nashville Association was, in 1993, the third largest in the Southeast, trailing Charlotte and Atlanta.[1240]

Another sign of the vitality of the Nashville Association came in April when the astonishing results of the 1994 "We Build People" campaign were published. Ron Knox's team raised $1,039,478—22 percent more than the $854,000 goal.[1241]

Because of the unprecedented amount of construction going on across the Association, Margaret Maddox, who was big on tours, took the YMCA executive committee to visit three or four YMCA family centers on June 1. Although a new teen center was on hold at Brentwood, their new wellness center was highly visible from Concord Road. Green Hills' expansion was on schedule, while Northwest's was not. Although rain had delayed the pool construction at East, their members were excited that it was actually happening. Construction was set to begin in August on the Franklin and Murfreesboro YMCAs, the same month the free weight area was expected to be completed at Donelson.

There were a few bumps in the road in July as far as capital projects were concerned. There was now a slight delay on the wellness center expansion at Green Hills due to weather. Health department requirements regarding outdoor toilets at Harding Place slowed down progress on the outdoor pool there. East's pool was behind because of delays in receiving steel shipments. Better news came from Donelson where the wellness center was completed a month ahead of schedule. Costs were a concern at Franklin and Murfreesboro. At the August executive committee meeting, three new center heads were introduced—Mike Heilbronn at Donelson, Baron Doherty at Rutherford County, and Dan Ryan at Robertson County. Board chair Margaret

Maddox continued to push for more awareness tours for directors and business leaders. Included in her sights were members of the Memorial Foundation.[1242]

There were two crucial meetings that would go a long way in determining the fate of the regional outdoor center, one on August 29 at the mayor's office and the other on September 13 when the Metropolitan Development and Housing Agency (MDHA) board met in public session. Both went well. At the MDHA meeting, the vote was unanimous to approve the lease of the land from the Corps of Engineers to the MDHA. By the September board meeting, the lease had been forwarded to Washington, DC, for signatures by the Corps and the MDHA. Upon its return the MDHA would sublease it to the Y. During these negotiations, Congressman Bob Clements continued his supportive. Still, there was uncertainty as the opposition group' attorney said he intended to file a lawsuit. Nevertheless, the property committee voted to move ahead with a site engineering master plan.

Gary Hunt, chairman of the property committee, had a full plate. A property update in October showed wellness centers completed at Brentwood and Green Hills and a weight room and day camp addition complete at Donelson. Five projects were under construction, the largest being the Franklin and Rutherford County Ys. A Harding Place water park was expected to be complete by May 1995 while the East project was well underway with completion expected by November 27. Because of a delay in steel delivery, the Northwest gym project opening was pushed back to mid-January.

In collaboration with the City of Springfield, the Robertson County YMCA was planning an outdoor pool and water park on 15 acres of land, half of which would be dedicated wetlands and was a gift from the city. The other half would cost $100,000. The land was at 3332 Tom Austin Highway. Y-CAP, that had been in the old Juvenile Justice building on Second Avenue for eight years, was hoping to build a new facility on Rosebank Avenue in East Nashville. Finally, design was underway for a Brentwood teen center.

Bill Wilson reported in October that the New Century Vision committee had raised $10.3 million, while John Wright reported that the first annual Black Achievers banquet was held October 8 at the Opryland Hotel with 500 people attending. Seventeen corporations sent black achievers to the affair. Clark Baker announced that the Heritage Club dinner at the Belle Meade Country Club, hosted by Dortch and Sis Oldham, had eighty attendees, each of whom had included the YMCA in their estate planning.[1243]

Great Year-End Achievements

The Rutherford County YMCA executive director Baron Dougherty reported at the November executive committee meeting that his Y currently had 500 children in before and after-school care at 15 sites. Their center was still under construction with an expected opening date of May 15.[1244]

When the Corps of U.S. Army Engineers signed the lease with the YMCA of Middle Tennessee to develop a day camp and outdoor center on 304 acres at the Smith Springs Recreational area, Clark Baker was both relieved and exhilarated.

At the December executive committee, Jack Elisar announced that Tim Weill had been employed as the new comptroller. Gary Hunt reported that the Maury County YMCA had raised $1.4 million and that their new center on the Hampshire Pike three miles west of Columbia should be open by June 15. He said the projected cost of the 33,000 square foot Robertson County Y was $3 million, and that the outdoor center on Percy Priest Lake could be open for partial use by the following summer. The Murfreesboro and Franklin centers, Hunt said, should be open by April and May, respectively with both within budget.

Chair Doyle Rippee reported that the 1995 "We Build People" campaign would kick off in January with an overall goal of $1.3 million. George Goyer reported that the New Century Vision campaign had raised $10,909,087 and was ahead of schedule toward its $16,885,000 goal slated to be achieved in 1995.

Bob Ecklund projected a strong year-end financially. He was correct. For the year, income totaled $19,346,819, exceeding expenses by $83,705, and $164,000 was added to the contingency fund. Twelve centers had surpluses. Bob also announced that the December meeting would be the last official board meeting for executive vice president George Goyer, who was retiring after 38 years with the YMCA. The Y held a reception in February at the Springhouse Golf Club to honor George for his wonderful service to the YMCA of Nashville and Middle Tennessee. George's legacy would include his saying, "donors should give until it hurts."[1245]

Jack Elisar proposed at the January executive committee meeting a 1995 budget of $23,324,000. After discussion, it was approved. The three largest centers were Green Hills, with a 1995 budget of $1,141,536, followed by Donelson with a $870,625 budget, and Brentwood, whose 1995 budget was $815,479. As a boost to the new Franklin YMCA, John Ed Miller arranged for the Franklin phone book cover to have a color photograph of the new center. Over 250 membership units had been sold in January.[1246]

The Northwest YMCA held a grand opening on February 21.[1247] Their campaign leaders were grateful for all the support that made this possible, including a leadership gift made by Jane and Richard Eskind.

The Search for More Land

At the March executive committee meeting, Lori Swann gave a final report on the annual membership campaign. The total memberships sold during the drive were 3,024, a 16 percent increase over 1994. An operations update included the news that, with Peter Oldham's help, an additional 3.09 acres had been donated to the Rutherford YMCA scheduled to open in mid-May. Fundraising was continuing at the Maury and Robertson County YMCAs with the former having passed the $1 million mark. Franklin was also scheduled to open in mid-May, according to Bob Ecklund.[1248]

The YMCA/Percy Priest Day Camp Task Force learned in the spring that George Liddle and the Cheatham Pointe Homeowners Association had sued the Corps of Engineers for signing a lease with MDHA. The plaintiffs claimed the Corps had violated both the National Environmental Policy Act and the First Amendment, had exceed their authority, and would create a nuisance because of camp traffic flow, noise and pollution. The YMCA had to decide whether to proceed with construction while the lawsuit was pending, and whether to intervene as a party in the lawsuit. On the recommendation of legal counsel, the YMCA did not intervene but did go ahead with phase 1 construction, including pavilion, restrooms, dock, barn, and airasium (if that is a real word).[1249]

Peter Oldham and Alex Fardon reviewed the details of the lawsuit filed by the homeowners against the Corps of Engineers at the May executive committee meeting. [1250]

The annual meeting at the Opryland Hotel took place in April with Margaret Maddox presiding. After the election of new members, Nelson Andrews introduced the new officers. The program ended with the appearance of a spectacular flying space ship (the starship Y0) which had come to seek out Bill Wilson to tell him what an important part he would play in the future of the YMCA and to wish him well on his mission. Earlier, Wilson, chair of the New Century Capital Development drive, had announced that the drive had raised over $11 million.

In mid-1995, the YMCA of Nashville and Middle Tennessee was a dynamic and changing organization with unprecedented growth through the year-to-date of 24 percent with the strong likelihood that the growth rate would accelerate to 30 percent in 1996. Program revenue was growing by 28 percent and annual giving by 12 percent. Operations were solid with a six-figure surplus predicted for year-end. Franklin opened with a flourish and Murfreesboro was right behind, opening in May. Over the past five years, the YMCA budget had grown by 300 percent and the number of centers jumped from seven to fifteen. The Maury County YMCA was under construction and the Robertson County YMCA would break ground that month.

A market study for a YMCA in Hendersonville showed a very high demand. The next steps were to create a board and commission a capital feasibility study. The new mayor of Shelbyville had contacted the Nashville Association about it operating a $4.2 million city recreation center then under construction. After much study, it was determined that this would not be feasible. A center in Bellevue was on hold. The consensus was "In the long term, we need to be there. In the short term, it would be a "high risk." Mt. Juliet had been courting the Y for several years. A market study would be launched there imminently.

The YMCA in Clarksville had been providing programs as an Armed Services YMCA since the 1970s. In 1995, their board wanted to either become an independent YMCA or affiliate with the YMCA of Nashville and Middle Tennessee. A Panas study revealed that they could raise $2 million and a market study showed a maximum demand for 3,900 units. Clarksville was a promising market but, with its plate full, the YMCA of Nashville and Middle Tennessee did not pursue the matter. The result was that the Clarksville YMCA was chartered as an independent YMCA.[1251]

Personnel changes were being made in response to the tremendous growth. The Y would create a position of vice president of membership and marketing for Lori Swann in hopes that she could duplicate the tremendous success of the Franklin Family Center. Tom Looby would redirect East and make needed changes there, while, in the near future, the Y needed to hire a new MRC director, a full-time director of human resources, and develop a capital development resource office. The YMCA of Nashville and Middle Tennessee was the only YMCA in the country of its size that did not have a full-time director of human resources.

Peter Oldham and Alex Fardon said that the chance of the plaintiff prevailing against the Corps of Engineers was very small, and that it would still be premature to intervene.[1252]

The April 15–June 30 membership campaign had as its goal to sell 2,300 total membership units. The campaign ended with 3,897 units sold, 167 percent of the goal. Other good news was that the Y's retention rate of 70 percent was one of the highest in the country.[1253]

In August, Bob Ecklund reported that, effective January 1, 1996, Urban Services and the Downtown YMCA would merge with Michael Brown being an associate executive downtown. Simultaneously, a community development office was being created as a department of the Metro Y for citywide, statewide, and international work. J. Lawrence would head it. The Y had a very successful summer with regard to summer day camps—45 sites with 90 schools being served in six counties and 2,200 in daily attendance.

At the same meeting, Clark Baker gave the board an update on the physical condition of George Goyer, who was seriously ill. He called George "a hero" and asked everyone to pray for him. Clark also said that he had asked Ridley Wills II, soon to be officially named the YMCA historian, to write a brief history of the YMCA of Nashville and Middle Tennessee. Senator Henry had agreed to write the preface. Ridley would accomplish this in 1996. The paperback book's title was *A Brief History of the YMCA of Nashville and Middle Tennessee*.[1254]

Clark Baker announced the reorganization of his senior management team in September. Bob Ecklund would be executive vice-president, Tom Looby and Lori Swann senior vice-presidents, and Tim Weill director of finance. Tom and Lori would be moving to the corporate office on January 1, the date the promotions would be effective. Clark also reported that Y-CAP celebrated its 10th anniversary earlier in the month and raised over $26,000.[1255]

• • • • •

At the Heritage Club dinner on October 17, Dortch and Sis Oldham were presented with the first H. G. Hill Jr. Philanthropy Award given by H .G. Hill Company. Clark reported at the October board meeting that the Gallatin Y board and the Sumner County steering committee had merged to create the Sumner County YMCA boards. At the same meeting, Aldorothy Wright spoke enthusiastically about the Black Achievers banquet on October 18 at the Opryland Hotel. There were over 700 people there, excited about the growth of this important program.

• • • • •

In November, the executive committee approved the purchase from the State of Tennessee of the unsightly and deteriorating building at 211 McLemore Street for $75,000. It would be torn down and the space converted into badly needed parking spaces. The executive committee also approved a new pricing schedule for 1996. Rates, effective January 1, would increase to:

Family, $30.00/mo.
Individual, $20.00/mo.
Teen/college, $20.00/mo.
Youth, $10.00/mo.
Sr. Family, $22.50/mo.
Sr. Individual, $15.00/mo.[1256]

In his report, Clark stressed the importance of staff training. He reported that in October 125 staff members attended a staff training session at Lake Barkley, and that, in November, 140 people were trained for the 1996 "We Build People" campaign. Because of the Y's enormous growth, it had been difficult to maintain the needed staff support.[1257]

Jack Elisar reported at the December board meeting that the finance committee had approved a budget of $28,055,155 for 1996. Jack also said that the finance committee was continuing to work on a loan in the $2 million to $2.5 million range to complete all capital projects, including finishing the Green Hills renovation, and replacing the building on McLemore Street with parking spots.

Bob Ecklund gave an operations report for 1995. Here are the highlights:

- Balanced budget;
- 25 percent growth;
- East and Northwest became full-service facilities;
- Franklin and Murfreesboro opened in May;
- Brentwood, Donelson, Franklin, Green Hills, and Murfreesboro all did well financially;
- Increased debt payments by $476,100; and
- Greater emphasis on teen work.

Senior vice-president Tom Looby reported that four new

Clarksville YMCA

executives had been hired to fill the vacancies at Brentwood, Downtown, East, and Harding Place. The new center executives were Kim Looby at Brentwood, Mike Brennan at Downtown, Charlie Willingham at East, and David Reeves at Harding Place.

Nelson Andrews, chair of the leadership development committee, recommended to the board that the following officers be elected for 1996: John Ed Miller, board chair; Jimmy Webb III, chair-elect; Jack Elisar, treasurer; Olin West III, assistant treasurer; and Ron Knox, secretary. The board quickly approved Nelson's motion. Clark Baker then reported that the New Century Vision campaign total was close to $13 Million with $3.5 million out "in asks." Next, Clark asked Lori Swann to read a poem she wrote in tribute to Margaret Maddox for her two incredible years as board chair. After Lori finished, Margaret was given a standing ovation. This petite lady thanked Dortch Oldham for encouraging and convincing her years earlier to become involved in the YMCA. She then thanked everyone in the room for their hard work and support.[1258]

The Frist Teen Center at Green Hills opened the end of February. Funded by Dr. and Mrs. Thomas F. Frist Jr., and the Frist Foundation. It was a model for YMCAs nationally.[1259] Already, it was having a touching impact on teenagers.

Ridley Wills II finished his book on the YMCA in 1995 and it was in the hands of interested members the next year.

Early in 1995, the Metropolitan office extended its lease with the H. G. Hill Company at 900 Church Street for five years.[1260]

• • • • •

Clark Completes a Decade as CEO
1996–1997

IN NASHVILLE, you could almost hear the jubilation coming from Hampshire Pike in Maury County when that YMCA opened on January 22. The beautiful building was surrounded by a serene countryside dotted with cattle and deer. There were over 1,500 people enrolled. Campaign leaders Eslick Daniel, Waymon Hickman, Tiny Jones, Joe Lancaster, Sydney McClain, Dan Batey, Dr. Jim Richardson, and others were ecstatic. The campaign would raise $3.3 million, with leadership gifts of $500,000 from Mr. and Mrs. Keith Baker and a $1 million from Maury Regional Medical Center, thanks to their CEO Bill Walter. The latter gift, made in October 1996, was for an indoor aquatic complex at the Y that the hospital could use for its rehabilitation services. The new building was dedicated to the Baker family. Until the Maury County YMCA campaign, which was the largest in Maury County history, benevolence dollars in Columbia had primarily benefited the James K. Polk home, the APTA, and other local historical sites. The situation got even better when the membership quickly jumped to 3,000 in March 1996.[1261] Columbia's first executive director was Angela Williams, who would later leave the YMCA of Middle Tennessee to become interim director of the Cheyenne River Reservation Sioux YMCA in Dupree, South Dakota.

In 2011, Angela Williams was chair of the Sioux YMCA board, on the board of Blue Ridge Assembly and, in her spare time, assisting Bob McGaughey at the Montgomery, Alabama, YMCA.[1262]

John Ed Miller
Board chair
1996–1997

The new YMCA board chair, John Ed Miller, Clark Baker and his senior staff reorganized the Association's committee structure early in January, eliminating or combing five committees. In his report, Clark Baker thanked Margaret and Dan Maddox for their lead gift to furnish the Frist Teen Center at Green Hills. It would open in February. Clark also thanked everyone for making 1995 such a grand year. Thinking about the future, he told the executive committee, "Let's do it again."[1263]

Alex Fardon gave a brief report of the outdoor center situation, saying that the Corps filed for a summary judgment in September, asking the judge to rule in the Corps' favor without going to trial. The judge referred the motion to a Magistrate Court judge who had not yet ruled. The trial date was postponed indefinitely. Alex felt confident that the Corps would win the lawsuit. After discussion, the executive committee voted to proceed with infrastructure improvements.

Tom Looby reported that Northwest center executive John Wright had resigned. The March executive committee minutes described his decision as "difficult and emotional." Wright had done an outstanding job at the child-care driven Y that, because of its difficult environment, would test any executive. Extremely entrepreneurial, he would go on to serve for seven years as a very effective vice-president for campus management at American Baptist College before prematurely dying of cancer in 2009.[1264]

Bob Ecklund reported in March that the Y experienced a 24.5 percent growth in revenue, a 27.8 percent growth in membership revenue, and a 28.9 percent increase in program revenue in 1995.

Melanie Easterly, new YMCA MIS director, gave an overview of the computer environment. She said that e-mail had been installed citywide, software standardized, access established via ISDN lines to all centers, hardware and software upgraded in 7 centers with 74 Pentium 120s installed.

The assets of the YMCA Foundation stood at $1,954,712.51 as of March 31, 1996. Nearly 75 percent of this, $1,462,124, was invested in securities (both stocks and bonds) managed by Lee, Danner & Bass. The next largest holding, totaling $306,817, was in a money market fund at J. C. Bradford & Company.

The 1996 annual meeting was held at, of all places, the Ryman Auditorium. Appropriately, a local gospel group led everyone in the song "Will the Circle Be Unbroken." Ron Knox introduced the officers for 1996 elected earlier, as well as new board members. The highlight of the meeting was the presentation of "The 13 Million Dollar Man Award" to Bill Wilson, chair of the New Century Vision Capital Development program that raised $13 million in phase 1. The three-year goal for phase was $10.3 million. In his state of the "Reunion" address, Clark Baker reported a balanced budget, 25 percent growth, the creation of two full facility inter-city YMCAs, the opening of two new YMCAs, the beginning of construction on two more YMCAs, a successful $1.3 million "We Build People" campaign, and the $13 million raised in capital development—enough said.

Singer Ricky Skaggs' performance ended with a final song in tribute to Margaret Maddox and the volunteers who served under her in 1995.[1265]

Effective June 1, vice president Beth Boord headed the financial development office while vice-president Julie Sistrunk, became vice-president for capital development. The communications and marketing departments merged at the same time to be supervised by Lori Swann.

May was Sumner County's opportunity to make the case for a new YMCA there affiliated with the YMCA of Nashville and Middle Tennessee. An independent Gallatin

Clark Baker, Sandra Fulton, J. P. Foster, Russell W. Brothers Sr., Ridley Wills II, and Bill Turner. Brothers was president in 1957 when that title went with the chief volunteer officer. Foster was president in 1980–81 while Fulton, Wills and Turner were board chairs.

YMCA had failed in 1995 after only five years of operation. This time, a Hendersonville group financed a market study that had been positive. A subsequent feasibility study indicated that $1 million could be raised in Sumner County for a Y at Hendersonville. The next steps would be to launch a capital campaign and seek 1-to-1 debt financing for a partial facility. Although a site had not been obtained, the executive committee approved taking these steps.

In May, Clark Baker reported that the Memorial Foundation had made a $1.7 million gift to Y-CAP and that the Frist Teen Center at Green Hills was dedicated a week earlier.[1266]

June brought summer camp with kids by the busloads. The Y served 550 kids per day in six sites in four counties. Summer daycare was much bigger—1,800 kids per day at 43 sites.

The Robertson County YMCA opened July 3, praised by the Chamber of Commerce as having played an important part in raising the quality of life for local citizens. Their capital campaign garnered $3.3 million.[1267]

At the June board meeting, Clark Baker reported that W. C. "Bill" Weaver III had started a program at Montgomery Bell Academy called "Time to Rise." It would bring inner-city boys to the school for athletics and academics. Charlie Willingham, the East Y director, was helping, Clark said.[1268]

An effort to duplicate the Green Hills Teen Center at the Brentwood Y was well underway with $600,000 of the needed $1 million secured. Members of the executive committee met with Northwest board members to improve that relationship, that had probably been impaired by the resignation of John Wright, who was very popular in the Bordeaux area. The executive committee was also receptive to seriously considering expanding to Clarksville, whose director was interested in an affiliation with the Nashville Y.[1269]

During the Clark Baker years, International partnerships continued to be important. In 1996, the YMCA of Nashville had six partnerships: Toulouse, France; Detmold, Germany; Bryansk, Russia which Sandra Fulton, Scott Goyer, Jimmy Webb III, and Clark Baker visited in May; Kaohsiung, Taiwan; the Zambia YMCA; and the YMCA of Venezuela where a Nashville Y delegation participated in the 50th anniversary celebration of the Venezuelan YMCA. Tim Stewart was the Nashville YMCA's international director.[1270]

Doyle Rippee, YMCA of Middle Teneessee board chairman 2000-2001 with Clark D. Baker, president

Work with teenagers continued to be a priority in 1996 when the YMCA of Nashville and Middle Tennessee had teen centers at Green Hills and Maury County and were close to opening one at Brentwood. J. Lawrence reported at the August executive committee meeting that the National YMCA planned to establish six regional resource centers across the nation, including one in Nashville. This materialized and lasted for a number of years.[1271]

The development work in Sumner County was stalled with hopes for a gift of land in the Hendersonville area. Exploratory steps were still being taken in Clarksville, Dickson, and Wilson County. In Franklin, a $2.1 million grant from the Kellog Foundation, of Battle Creek, Michigan, was the largest program grant anyone could remember.[1272]

The ground breaking for the Brentwood Teen Center was set for Thanksgiving with Knestrick Construction Company having received the bid, which was the lowest by $50,000. Clark Baker predicted in September that the association would end the year with a balanced budget. He did have some disquieting news. He expected to lose $250,000 in funding from the United Way.[1273]

One of the challenges in 1996 was competition from privates companies anxious to carve out a significant part of the YMCA's school age childcare program. Managing the budget continued to be a challenge as the YMCA of Nashville and Middle Tennessee had, for five years, maintained a growth rate higher than 21 percent.

Tom Looby reported in October that the road to the outdoor camp on Percy Priest Lake should be completed in two weeks and that W. R. Newman had been named general contractor. There was also movement in Clarksville where the board of the Clarksville YMCA agreed, in November, to merge with the YMCA of Nashville and Middle Tennessee. The new affiliation might also include the Armed Forces Y as a third party. The Clarksville community had already raised $884,000 and BellSouth had greed to a $20,000 gift contingent on the merger. A motion to approve the merger was approved at the October 24 board meeting.

After serving as interim director of the Northwest YMCA since John Wright left, Tom Looby relinquished those duties when Lyndon Murray, of Washington, DC, became executive director effective January 6, 1997. Another person, who helped hold Northwest together during the difficult interim period was Dr. Aldorothy Wright, who served six years as Northwest chair before moving to the Metropolitan board in 1997.[1274]

Bob Ecklund announced that Scott Goyer had accepted the position of senior vice-president of the St. Paul, Minnesota, YMCA. Bob said he would fill Scott's shoes after he left on December 20 until a replacement could be found.

A possible stumbling block to the Outdoor Center arose in December when the Metro Codes Department decided that before a building permit could be issued for the Outdoor Center, a conditional use permit must be granted by the Board of Zoning Appeals and this would involve a public hearing. The Corps of Engineers said this was absolutely wrong in that Federal property was exempt from all local zoning and regulations. The YMCA property committee decided not to proceed with the project until the issue was decided.[1275]

At the December board meeting, treasurer Jack Elias asked for, and received, approval of the 1997 budget of $32.9 million. He had earlier assured the members that the 1996 budget would be balanced. Bob Ecklund reported that he had met with Steve Turner about the possibility of establishing a YMCA in Scottsville, Kentucky. He also said that the State had provided a ten-acre site on Ben Allen Road for a new Y-CAP Center, and that 2/3 of the $3 million needed to build the center had been raised.

The articles of merger of the Clarksville Area YMCA with and into the YMCA of Nashville and Middle Tennessee was executed December 11, 1996, bringing the YMCA of Nashville and Middle Tennessee into the state's fifth largest city.[1276]

Vice-president Julie Sistrunk reported to the board in December that capital dollars raised since 1992 totaled $18,887,877 and that annual fund dollars raised over the same period of time totaled $5,255,097, for an impressive total of $24,142,974. December was also a good time for Bill Wilson, who had chaired the New Century Vision committee for four years to step down. He agreed to remain active as vice-chair under Margaret Maddox. Bill told the board that he would never forget the words of wisdom given him by Nelson Andrews when he accepted the development assignment. Nelson said, "You need to say thank you more than please." Bill then thanked all those who helped him in the magnificently successful development effort, and was, in turn, thanked by Mrs. Maddox.

Clark Baker next introduced Jay Mullins, the new center director of the Robertson County YMCA. At the same meeting, John Ed Miller reported that he felt that the YMCA of Nashville and Middle Tennessee should shorten its name to "The YMCA of Middle Tennessee." Although some were reluctant to drop "Nashville" from the Association's name, his recommendation was approved by the board. Before adjourning, Mr. Miller presented departing Scott Goyer with a plaque in recognition to his hard work and success at the YMCA of Middle Tennessee. The year ended with a slight surplus of $19,499 on the 1996 budget. Revenues for 1996 hit $28,750,469.[1277]

A New Identity for the YMCA

At the January 23 executive committee meeting, Clark Baker asked all the current board officers and all executive committee members to serve another term. Beth Boord gave the financial report. She said the kickoff for the 1997 "We Build People" campaign would be that evening at Planet Hollywood, that the goal was $1,865,000 and that Jim D'Agostino would serve as chair.

There were also reports on Sumner County, Clarksville, and Dickson. Julie Sistrunk said that the Y was working on possible land gifts in Sumner County and Dickson, and that we had asked the Memorial Foundation for a $1.5 million grant for Sumner County. Buck Winfield reported that a marketing study in Dickson showed 7,000 potential members. The capital campaign in Clarksville had raised almost $1 million.

There was also progress at the Outdoor Center. Tom

Looby said that the Y had received a conditional use permit and that the road from the street to the camp would be laid out, graded and smoothed. The first employee of the Outdoor Center was Bob Copeland, who would be in charge of maintenance. Looby reported at the meeting that the camp would be fully operational by the summer of 1998.

Lori Swann was next on the program. She reported that the local Association experienced a 28 percent membership revenue growth in 1996 and that our retention rate was 71 percent. Clark Baker said that we were in the 90th percentile in the country in this respect.

Clark Baker reminded the executive committee members that H. Hill Jr. had made a pledge of $500,000 before his death and that the H.G. Hill Company intended to honor the outstanding balance of $285,000. The H. G. Hill Company, Clark said, had agreed to lease the 900 Church Street building to the YMCA Foundation for five years at $1 per year. The foundation would then sublease the building to the YMCA. In turn, the YMCA would pay $58,000 per year in rent to the foundation with the money designated for inner-city work through Urban Services. This proposal would, Clark said, be presented, in the form of a resolution, at the February board meeting. Clark also announced that the Y's new identity package would be released on February 14 and thanked the Bill Hudson Agency for their help on this. Elizabeth Talsky reported that community leaders in Scottsville were raising money for a market study there. Before adjourning, chair John Ed Miller thanked everyone and said his motto for 1997 was Clark's "Let's do it again."[1278]

Walter Knestrick held a dinner at his home on January 28 to honor Bill Wilson for his outstanding work as chair of the New Century Vision capital campaign and to welcome Margaret Maddox as the new campaign chair.

As for operations, it was reported that the Brentwood Teen Center construction was underway and on time, and that Green Hills was still looking for a center executive. It was also reported that the New Century Vision plan had to be updated. The original plan called for reaching $25 million by 1999. Because of the great progress that number was revised upward to $42 million and 18 centers by 1999. Jessica Willingham unveiled the new identity package to a round of applause. Lori Swann then took center stage to introduce a new Genesis program that would be tested under the auspices of the Franklin YMCA at a separate location. The program was designed to help individuals begin on a variety of goals, ranging from losing weight, learning a foreign language, or studying the Bible. Clark Baker then reported that he would meet that afternoon with eight people from Scottsville, KY, about building a Y in that small town. President John Ed Miller announced that Bob Ecklund had accepted the position of executive vice president of the Detroit YMCA. Bob, whose strength was his ability to analyze and work with numbers, would leave on April 4. He had been, in Clark's words, "a tremendous asset."[1279] Clark told the executive committee in March that he would divide Bob Ecklund's responsibilities between senior vice-presidents Tom Looby and Lori Swann at least through the end of the year.

Tom then gave a report on the outdoor center. He said there was a road to the waterfront and that steel had been ordered for the Airnasium (an open-sided gymnasium) and that he was setting up times for individuals to visit. The cost for phase one was, he said, $1.6 million. He also reported that YMCA officials were talking to the Davis Foundation trustees regarding funding. The New Century Vision campaign was going strong, with the total amount raised over $20 million, $1.2 million of which had been raised since January.

Clark's daughter, Caroline, was invited to the March 1997 meeting to talk about her YMCA experiences. The 1997 St. Cecilia senior spoke enthusiastically of her experiences with YMCA youth sports, Youth-in-Government, and a trip to Germany where she worked as a counselor at a YMCA camp. Do you suppose her dad was proud?[1280]

With Bob Ecklund gone, Clark's senior management team consisted of senior vice-presidents Lori Swann and Tom Looby, who shared responsibility for the branches; vice-president MRC Liz Talsky; vice-president finance Tim Weill; vice-president financial development Beth Boord; and vice-president capitol development Julie Sistrunk.[1281] The Management Resource Center (MRC) was providing consultative services to 31 YMCAs in Tennessee, Western Kentucky, Southern Indians, Virginia, and Illinois.

One of the new board members elected at the annual meeting on April 24 was future board chair Rich Ford. Another was future U.S. Senator Bob Corker. Clark Baker gave the State of the Y address. He reported the YMCA of Middle Tennessee was the 10th largest Y in the United States, having grown in membership and budget more than 20 percent in 1996. The YMCA of

Middle Tennessee had also opened new family centers in Springfield and Columbia, and the Frist Teen Center in Green Hills. Clark also reported that the New Century Vision campaign had passed the $19 million mark in capital contributions. Of course, awards were presented. On April 24, the Order of the Red Triangle went to Margaret Maddox.[1282]

The ever-alert Clark Baker became aware that the old Russell Street Baptist Church building at 1020 Russell Street came on the market. Partially renovated with 12,754 square feet, the building was listed for $875,000 and an adjoining parking lot for another $110,000. The executive committee in May authorized Jimmy Webb and Tom Looby, who had been supervising Y-CAP since Carl Carlson resigned in April, to work with the Y-CAP facility committee toward purchasing the property that seemed to be superior to property on Ben Allen Road that Y-CAP had been negotiating with the State of Tennessee to acquire.

Tom Looby, who wore many hats, gave a report on the Outdoor Center. He said the boat dock was built, the main road in, construction on the Airnasium underway, and electricity in the process of being installed. The Y had two new center executives—Lyndon Murray, who came to Northwest in January, and Mark Bachman, who came to Green Hills in April. Both had encouraging starts. Clark also had a national search underway for an associate senior wellness director for the Downtown Y.[1283]

Great news came in June when it was reported that the Davis Foundation would give the YMCA $1 million to complete the first two phases of work at the Outdoor Center. It was also reported that Carrie Phelps, from the Denver YMCA, would be the new associate senior wellness director. Y-CAP was reported to be close to purchasing the Russell Street building, and the Margaret Burnett Turner Teen Center at Brentwood to open on July 24 would honor Mrs. Cal Turner and the success of Brentwood's $1 million campaign. Sumner County had not, Looby reported, acquired a site.

In Murfreesboro, Bob Miflin and Baron Hardelin-Doherty, chair and president, respectively, of the Rutherford County YMCA obtained a $1 million grant from the Christy-Houston Foundation to add a teen and program center to the Y and expand the nursery. Three one million dollar gifts in a short span of time wasn't bad!

Meanwhile, summer programs were going well. Lisa Beck, Fun Company director, said the Y had 2,216 children enrolled in daycare programs at 47 sites, and that of these children, 1,036 were on some type of financial assistance. The program had grown 30 percent over 1996, she added. We additionally had, Lisa continued, 570 enrolled in the Y's day camp program of whom 157 were on financial assistance. This program had grown 5 percent over the past year.[1284]

The executive committee approved the purchase by Y-CAP of the church and house on Russell Street for $930,000, and the 4,900 square foot expansion at the Donelson-Hermitage to increase the wellness and mutlipurpose areas, as well as build an outdoor play pool there. Also approved was the purchase of a house on the Percy Priest Outdoor Center property that would be used as a caretaker's home.

After several visits to the Outdoor Center by Joe C. Davis Foundation board members, that foundation gave the YMCA of Middle Tennessee an additional million dollars.[1285] The center needed an executive direction and that search was on. The boat dock was complete and the roof was on the Airnasium, which was a reality, if not a legitimate word.

Susan Moriarty, program director, introduced a new program at the August board meeting. Called Nashville Youth Leadership, it was a program sponsored by the Frist Foundation and administered by the YMCA. Its charge was to provide leadership training for a select group of Nashville high school sophomores. The program's kickoff event was held at BellSouth in November.

Good News for Several Programs

Board awareness tours, initiated by Margaret Maddox, continued during John Ed Miller's tenure. After several visits to the Outdoor Center by Joe C. Davis Foundation board members, that foundation gave the YMCA of Middle Tennessee an additional million dollars.[1286]

The executive committee learned in September that the YMCA of Middle Tennessee was the fasting growing YMCA in the country, the sixth largest in the country in campaign funds raised, and 10th largest in budget. Over five years, the annual "We Build People" campaign contributions grew from $400,000 to $1,911,000, a 377 percent growth. Clark recommended at the September executive committee meeting that Jeff Jowdy be employed to fill the new position of senor development director. This was approved.[1287]

Y-CAP got an executive director in October to go with its new center—Jim Palmer. The Y-CAP annual dinner was a huge success, raising $37,000, an amount graciously matched by Anne and Dick Ragsdale.

Another success, the October 7 Black Achievers event at Northwest on the 7th raised $76,000.

The Genesis program was going well and was scheduled to be implemented in every center by January 1, 1998. Ralph Mosley, who had chaired the Brentwood capital campaign, was a guest at the October board meeting. He shared the Brentwood story and showed his pride having been involved with the Brentwood Y since its beginning. The center had 12,000 members in a community whose population was 22,000. That, friends, is an outstanding marketshare.[1288]

The best news in October was that Judge Thomas A. Higgins, of Nashville, had issued a summary judgment dismissing the Chatham Pointe Homeowners Association lawsuit. The YMCA had a green light to proceed with construction.[1289]

In the fourth quarter of 1997, the Green Hills YMCA was the largest in the Association and growing at 12 percent. With strong growth expected to continue, a new site master plan had been developed to better manage growth.

Clark reported that a center in Madison would open in mid-December and the exciting news was that the Turner family had offered $5 million to build a facility in their hometown if the Scottsville community could raise $650,000.[1290]

Clark Baker, who had pushed himself relentlessly ever since coming to the YMCA of Middle Tennessee eleven years earlier, took a well-deserved thirty-day leave "retreat" to "reflect, refuel, and renew." He returned on December 27 after spending more time with Caroline and their two daughters and enjoying a Christmas in Arizona.

At the December board meeting, treasurer Jack Elisar reported that the Association had a favorable operating record through November and proposed, for the finance committee, that the Y adopt a $37,585,415 budget for 1998.

Marshall "Shag" Polk reported that the 1998 "We Build People" campaign goal was $2 million. Margaret Maddox reported that the New Century Vision committee raised $3.7 million in 1997 and that the campaign total was close to $24 million. Madison Interim director Laurie Goode said that center would open on the 22nd. And finally, officers were elected for 1998.

Jimmy Webb III, chair
Doyle Rippee, chair-elect
Jack Elisar, treasurer
Olin West III, assistant treasurer
Ron Knox, secretary
Lucille Nabors, assistant secretary[1291]

The YMCA of Middle Tennessean ended 1997 with a modest surplus of $56,827 and revenues of $33,916,123. Total membership revenue was $15,498,128, a 15.3 percent growth.

Columbia YMCA

TOP: Franklin YMCA BOTTOM: Green Hills YMCA

CHAPTER THIRTY-FIVE

The Fastest Growing YMCA in North America

1998–1999

THE NEW YEAR was barely two weeks old when the devastating news reached Nashville that Dan and Margaret Maddox had been killed on the 14th in a Louisiana boating accident. They were on the back deck of a 28-foot fishing boat with friends when, all of a sudden, in a dense, early morning fog, their craft was hit by a 110-foot supply vessel on Freshwater Bayou, causing it to overturn and sink. Dan, who was 87 when he died, was an ardent outdoorsman, and was one of the world's biggest game hunters. He was also a conservationist, a retired financier, and a philanthropist. Margaret, Dan's second wife, was one of the YMCA of Middle Tennessee's brightest stars. She was chair of the local Association in 1994 and 1995 and had a special love for the East Nashville Family Center as she grew up in East Nashville and attended Bailey Junior High School and East High, the latter with another YMCA president, George H. Cate Jr. Margaret and Dan gave substantial amounts of money to the YMCA and fully funded the new gym and wellness center at the East Nashville YMCA. Dan taught Margaret to hunt and fish, while Margaret taught him the joy of philanthropy. They were also long-time supporters of Belmont University and took great pleasure in getting to know Belmont students on Presidential Scholarships made possible by the Maddoxes and their foundation. At the time of her death, Margaret was leading the YMCA's New Vision Capital Campaign.[1292]

Jack Elisar's financial report in January was highlighted by his announcement that the Association ended the year with a surplus of $56,800. The operational highlights for 1997 included a new nursery at Franklin, a wellness center expansion completed at Donelson, and 3,700 membership units at Downtown. There were very positive reports from Y-CAP, Green Hills and other centers. Northwest had a challenging year in 1977 and 65 percent of the memberships at the Madison Center were senior citizens. Lori Swann reported that 1977 membership revenue was $15,498,128, a 15.3 percent growth. Jessica Willingham, communications director, reported that the Association had been successful in increasing its media coverage. In 1977, there were 315 newspaper clips about the Y and 159 photographs, publicity worth $388,226. Tom Looby radiated excitement when he announced the employment in December of Mark Weller as executive director of the Joe C. Davis Outdoor Camp. Mark had been recruited by Clark Baker, Looby and Dan Ryan, vice president of human resources. Weller had been associate executive director of the YMCA of the Ozarks in Potasi, MO, where he ran an overnight camp and a lodge.

Mark arrived in January and, using a double-wide trailer as his office, began working out plans for the lodge that would be named the Joe C. Davis Outdoor Center, an equestrian center, the Bank of America Alpine Tower, a team tree house, a central pavilion, and a bath house. He would include camp features that he had at the YMCA of the Ozarks overnight camp, such as the equestrian center, horse trails, and various waterfront activities. Mark's first job as executive director was to name the camp. After learning from Jim Rayhab that previous summer camps had been named "Camp Widjiwagan." It was an easy decision. The new summer camp at the outdoor center would be "Camp Widjiwagan."[1293]

J. Lawrence, director of community development, reported that the Y was looking at the possibility of making Y-CAP a statewide program. Y-CAP was, J. said, "nationally recognized as one of the best early intervention programs of the past decade." In his report, Clark introduced

Liz Dubuque, who reported the results of a recent staff satisfaction survey. The results were that 90 percent of the Y employees were satisfied with their employment. Clark described 1997 as a challenging year and predicted the same for 1998. He expressed his conviction that the Y's staff was the strongest since he arrived.[1294]

Tom Looby reported to the board in February that Y-CAP would move to its new facility on Fatherland Street the end of the month and would be open for business March 1. Lori Swann reported that Laurel Wilson had been named the new executive director of the East Family YMCA, that Madison was up to 720 units, and that the Genesis program was doing particularly well at Brentwood, Franklin, and Maury County. Tom also reported that the Y was starting a new planning process that would carry the Association through 2001. With both the Brentwood and Franklin YMCAs at capacity and growing rapidly, Lori Swann was working on a proposal for a Cool Springs YMCA. Clark also said that he was talking to Dr. and Mrs. William DeLoache about the possibility of the Davis Foundation building a lodge at the Joe C. Davis Camp.[1295]

"If you are good enough, people will knock on your door." That maxim was true in the first quarter of 1998 when the Putnam County YMCA in Cookeville voted to enter a management agreement with the YMCA of Middle Tennessee. Founded in 1978, the Putnam County Y had opened a 23,450 sq. ft. facility in 1993 on ten acres. This involved a lot of debt ($1.2 million) that caused their board to devote time and energy to debt service that might otherwise gone to program and membership growth. A "troubled YMCA" almost from day one, the Association had been without an executive director since December. With the assistance of the Management Resource Center at the YMCA of Middle Tennessee, the Putnam County directors dropped the idea of selling their building to the city, and, instead, became determined to "save the YMCA" by affiliating with the YMCA of Middle Tennessee. At the March 26 executive committee meeting, Clark Baker explained the situation and recommended that a management agreement be approved. Mike Heilbronn, Donelson executive director, would head the effort and the Putnam County YMCA would compensate the YMCA of Middle Tennessee with payments of $1,000 each month.

Thanks to a gift from Dan and Margaret Maddox, given before their deaths, the East center was being renovated. Lori Swann recommended that the name of the East Y be changed to the Margaret Maddox Family YMCA East Center. This was unanimously approved.

President Clark Baker reported that Mike Heilbronn and Baron Herdelin-Doherty had been promoted to vice-presidents. Everyone left the meeting in a good mood as the statement of operating income and expenses through February showed an operating gain of $605,000 compared to a budgeted gain of $35,000.[1296]

A tornado struck parts of Nashville on Thursday afternoon, April 16, with startling intensity. The most severe storm moved through the city in about thirty minutes, starting at 3:14 p.m. The storm was reminiscent of the 1933 tornado in that both storms followed a nearly identical path, sweeping down Charlotte Avenue, slamming downtown before crossing the river and continuing out Main and Woodland streets across Porter Road and Rosebank to Cornelia Fort Airport. Although no YMCAs were damaged, the Y-CAP group home in East Nashville was, forcing it to temporarily move. Minutes before it was hit, the Y's community development building at 213 McLemore, next door to the Downtown Center, was struck. The damage disrupted the renovation going on there, slowing the project by an estimated two months.[1297]

John Ed Miller was the master of ceremonies at the 123rd annual meeting of the Association held at the Renaissance Hotel. Nelson Andrews introduced the officers for 1998: James A. Webb III, chairman; Doyle R. Rippee, vice chairman; Jack A. Elisar, treasurer; Olin West III, assistant treasurer; Ronald F. Knox Jr., secretary; and Lucille Neighbors, assistant secretary. Also nominated for reelection for a second three-year term were past and future stars: Chuck Elkin, Bill Hudson, Peter Oldham, Marshall "Shag" Polk, and Bernard Werthan. They were promptly elected.

John Ed presented the 1998 chairman's Leadership Award to Jack Elisar, the treasurer and chair of the finance committee. He had been treasurer since 1981 with the exception of six years. There was a round of applause for Jack's longstanding leadership and financial acumen. There were many highlights from 1997. One of those was that the Association served more than 100,000 people, including 88,000 members, of whom 40,100 were children. Another was that the YMCA of Middle Tennessee continued as the fastest growing YMCA in North America, operating 18 centers and 209 program locations in 7 counties. The Y employed more than 1,800 people, raised over $2 million in the "We Build People" campaign, and raised $4 million in new capital dollars, bringing the New Century Vision total to over $24 million.

Clark Baker welcomed the Clarksville Area YMCA as the newest branch in the YMCA of Middle Tennessee, and announced plans to build a new Sumner County Family YMCA on eight acres of land in Hendersonville, thanks to the generosity of the Memorial Foundation. That was a lot to take in. The last order of business of the year came when Sandra Fulton presented the 1998 Order of the Red Triangle Award to Lee Barfield.[1298]

Personnel Changes

There were a number of key personnel changes in the spring of 1998. Jessica Willingham left to accept a position with the St. Louis YMCA and Laurie Goode left the Y while Carrie Phelps took over responsibility for corporate wellness. Mary Mossing was hired from the St. Louis Y as a group vice president to supervise Scottsville and Robertson County, while Baron Herdelin-Dohery added to his duties at Rutherford County by additionally supervising the East and Madison YMCAs. Mossing was introduced at the June board meeting.

Tom Looby reported at the May executive committee meeting that the Joe C. Davis Outdoor Center would have an open house on May 30 and open on June 8. Tom also expressed his excitement over the additional $1.2 million gift and matching challenge from the Davis Foundation that would enable the Y to build the lodge.[1299]

At the June board meeting, Lori Swann announced that the Memorial Foundation had donated 8 acres of land on Gallatin Road for a new Sumner Country YMCA. She also said that the Y was still researching the prospect of a YMCA in Cool Springs. Tom Looby reported that the Y had 46 Fun Company summer care sites and a daily enrollment of 3,000.

Chuck Elcan, a member of the New Century Vision committee, who would play an important volunteer role at the

Sandra Fulton wins the Red Triangle Award. From left to right: Alan Brunson, Clark D. Baker, Tom Looby, Sandra Fulton, Ralph Brunson, and Ralph's wife, Willie Belle

Joe C. Davis Center, reported that the capital campaign had raised nearly $35 million, having recently received the $1.2 million challenge grant from the Davis Foundation. Ridley Wills II, chair of the Foundation board, said that its board was working to revitalize the foundation and had just revised the bylaws to increase the number of board members. He also announced that J. Lawrence had been with the YMCA of Middle Tennessee for twenty years, and thanked him for his effectiveness in making a difference in so many inner-city lives.[1300]

With the YMCA still growing at a fast rate, the question of having adequate reserves warranted attention. Accordingly, a new reserve policy was endorsed by the finance committee and presented to the executive committee in July. Under the new policy, 100 percent of center surpluses were retained by the Association and invested. Operating deficits would be forgiven each year-end but responded to with aggressive management improvement plans. A goal was to fund $5 million in reserves over a four-year period. The new policy was approved.

• • • • •

The Joe C. Davis Outdoor Center experienced a very successful first summer with 802 campers, of whom 195 received financial assistance. The high Alpine Tower was a great hit with 1,059 climbers. This was possible because over 4,000 kids were at the outdoor camp from June through August 31.

• • • • •

Clark Baker commented on a wonderful "thank you" event, the Y held to thank David K. "Pat" Wilson for his strong support of the Y. Nelson Andrews, one of Pat's closest friends, was the host. Clark also shared the news that honorary board member Clarence Berson had died. Like Battle Rodes, who died a little earlier, Clarence faithfully attended meetings in his declining years.[1301] Years earlier, he had convinced Ridley Wills II to join the Downtown YMCA on Union Street.

With overcrowding already a problem at Green Hills and Brentwood, it was natural that the Y began exploring the possibility of converting the Maryland Farms Athletic Club facility into a YMCA. As a first step, Jimmy Webb met Brad Reed, who represented the Massey Foundation, and learned that the property was available for purchase. Quickly, the Y did its due diligence. An environmental impact study came back positive, and an engineering study found the building to be in decent condition. The estimate was that it would cost between $700,000 and $1 million to bring the building up to Y standards. After a demand study showed a first year loss of $188,000 and a positive cash flow in four years, Clark and Jimmy were ready to bring the matter to a board task force appointed to consider the matter. That happened in September. Chairman Webb brought the group up to date and said that the offer would be between $5.3 and $5.5 million with an additional $1 million for renovation, Following a full discussion, during which John Ed Miller expressed confidence that the Y could exceed the pro forma, and Ron Knox pointed out that Maryland Farms only served 1,600 members, the executive committee authorized Chairman Webb to make the offer contingent on executive committee approval. That came at an executive committee meeting three days later.[1302] At that meeting, treasurer Jack Elisar gave a report from the finance committee. He said that the committee had recommended that the previous loans be refinanced and packaged with the next bond issue that would be an estimated $52 million of which an estimated $14 million was expected to be paid from pledges. After discussion, the executive committee approved the bond issue.

Lori Swann reported that the Y was operating out of an interim location in Cool Springs, sharing space with "Let It Shine" gymnastics. Lori went on to explain that plans for a capital campaign were underway in Sumner County, and that the renovation of the Margaret Maddox Center would begin soon. Lori also spoke about a partnership with St. Thomas Hospital under which the hospital would commit $6 million to work with the YMCA on various community projects, including corporate wellness programs. These funds would also help the new Cool Springs and Sumner County YMCAs.

Vice president Liz Dubuque reported that the Fun Company was fifteen years old, and had grown to 6,395 children enrolled daily at 119 sites, serving 142 schools in seven counties. She also announced that J. Lawrence had accepted the position of statewide Y-CAP director. Jeff Jowdy announced that, with the help of Judge Frank Drowota, the Frist Foundation had agreed to fund the $350,000 water park at the Joe C. Davis Outdoor Center.

Clark reported that John Ed Miller had been elected the state public policy chairman for the South Field, and that construction of the waterpark and lodge at the Joe C. Davis Center would begin immediately, thanks to the generosity of the Frist and Joe C. Davis foundations.[1303]

Jimmy Webb convened a special board meeting on October 8 to advise the members that the Y had submitted a successful bid of $5.6 million to the Massey Foundation earlier in the week. Jimmy said that he felt that the Maryland Farms land alone was worth the price of the facility that included 136,000 square feet on 17 acres. Lori Swann reviewed the pro forma and disclosed that a number of former Maryland Farms Health Club members were skeptical about swapping their membership to a more egalitarian YMCA. Lori shared a press release to be released that afternoon and said the close date would be December 1. The board was enthusiastic.

Phase 1 of the Joe C. Davis Outdoor Center cost approximately $2 million. Remarkably, it had been completely funded by the Davis Foundation.

A New Millennium Plan

At the October 27 board meeting, Tom Looby announced that the first draft of the New Millennium Plan would be unveiled on November 2. There were three meetings at the YMCA Corporate office to review the first draft of the New Millennium strategic plan. The YMCA's mission and purpose was at the front of the plan. It read, we are "a worldwide charitable fellowship united by a common loyalty to Jesus Christ for the purpose of helping persons grow in spirit, mind, and body." The plan had four major sections: Our mission and purpose, our values, our vision, and our strategic priorities.

The nominating committee, chaired by Nelson Andrews, met on November 18 to discuss the 1999 slate of officers. Their recommendations were to reelect Jimmy Webb III, as chair, Jack Elisar as treasurer, and Olin West III, as assistant treasurer. Doyle Rippee would move from vice chair to chair-elect with Ron Knox Jr., taking his place as vice chair. Elaine McReynolds would succeed Knox as secretary, and the assistant secretary slot would be left unfilled.

The Cool Springs YMCA opened in October and the parking expansion project at Green Hills started the next month. At the November executive committee meeting, plans for the water park and lodge at the Joe C. Davis Outdoor Center were approved. That month, the high ropes course there was completed. Jeff Jowdy reported that the Farmers National Bank had given $75,000 for the Scottsville Y and Rich Ford was named as chairman of the 1999 "We Build People" campaign that would seek to raise $2 million.

In the fall, Northwest YMCA members enjoyed listening to NBA star Isiah Thomas speak. There were 400 people there to hear him.[1304]

Jack Elisar presented the 1999 budget at the December board meeting. It totaled approximately $45 million and was approved. Similarly, the nominees for 1999 officer positions were approved and the meeting moved on to the Operations reports traditionally given by senior vice presidents Tom Looby and Lori Swann. Tom began by saying that, earlier in December, 900 high school students attended the Model U.N. Conference in Nashville. This was, he said, the second largest Model U.N. conference in the country. Tom also reported that the Anne Ragsdale Recreation Center was under construction and due for a spring completion. Lori reported that construction was underway on the renovation at East, hopefully to be supported by a Maddox Foundation gift. J. Lawrence reported that the statewide Y-CAP program was operational in Knoxville, Memphis, Chattanooga, and Springfield. Naturally, the New Millennium Plan was discussed, after which it was approved. Lori Swann then introduced the Y staff at Maryland Farms that had a membership of 1,200, virtually all of whom were Maryland Farm Athletic Club members. Lori said that John Ed Miller would head the interim board.

Clark Baker closed the meeting by thanking Tim Weill for his outstanding work on securing the bond issue, and reporting that Frank Drowota had agreed to chair the Joe C. Davis board. The Association had yet another outstanding year, having a surplus of $64,518 on revenues of $38,300,922, and fully funding all reserves. The Association grew by 12.6 percent. The most spectacular contributions were a $4.9 million pledge from the Turner family for the Scottsville YMCA, a $3.3 million program grant from the State of Tennessee to expand the Y-CAP program, and the gift of land in Hendersonville worth $1.2 million from the Memorial Foundation. Three new centers opened during the year—Cool Springs, Madison and Maryland Farms.

Skate Park at Murfreesboro

Murfreesboro was the first family center in the YMCA of Middle Tennessee to have a skate park. By January, Maryland Farms membership was up to 1,500 and members were beginning to feel excited about YMCA ownership. The "We Build People" campaign reached its goal of $2 million and $13.5 million was raised in the New Century Vision capital campaign. Newspaper coverage of the YMCA increased an amazing 350 percent since 1997.

Clark Baker announced at the January executive

committee that Melanie Easterly, Lisa Beck and Carrie Phelps had all been named assistant vice presidents. Michael Brown had been so named a little earlier. The best news was the last. Thanks to an additional gift of $530,000 from the Maddox Foundation, the renovation at East was completely paid for.[1305]

By February, all kinds of fundraising was going on. Having just raised over $3 million, Clarksville would have a groundbreaking on March 1. Scottsville had raised $380,000 of the $650,000 needed to match the Turner family gift, Green Hills was in the preliminary stages of a fund-raising campaign, Sumner County board members had given over $550,000 on a campaign that totaled $2 million, and the Joe C. Davis Center was close to matching the gift from the Davis Foundation. Also, Camp Widjiwagan already had 472 campers enrolled and the goal for the summer was 1,400. By then, the Bell South bell tower and water park should be completed.

Board members were elected and officers introduced at the annual meeting at the Renaissance Hotel in April. Chair Jimmy Webb presented the 1999 Community Leadership Award to Judge Frank Drowota III, who was serving as first chairman of the new Joe C. Davis Outdoor Center board, and on the YMCA board where he was on the executive committee. Jude Drowota's insight, strong value system and wisdom were enormously beneficial. Later, Lee Barfield, recipient of the 1998 Order of the Red Triangle, presented the 1999 award to John Ed Miller, who had started his YMCA career at the Brentwood Y, where he was on the building committee. He went on to chair the YMCA of Middle Tennessee Board in 1996 and 1997, where he played a key role in adding new YMCA branches and completing the merger with the Clarksville YMCA. In 1998, John Ed became interim chair of the new Maryland Farms Family YMCA Conference & Tennis Center.

During 1998, the YMCA of Middle Tennessee served nearly 120,000 people, of whom 107,351 were members. The Y provided childcare for 6,461 children through the Fun Company, 25 percent of whom received financial assistance. In total, the Y provided $7 million in charitable subsidies during the year. The Joe C. Davis YMCA Outdoor Center was named the #1 day camp in Nashville, and the Y operated 21 centers and 250 program locations in seven counties. The "We Build People" campaign surpassed its $2 million goal and the capital campaign raised $13.9 million, bringing the New Century Vision total to $37.5 million.

In May, in preparation for the opening of Camp Widjiwagan, the Joe C. Davis Outdoor Center Board met with the 54 counselors in training. Board chair Judge Frank Drowota announced that the bell tower was almost complete and that footings had been poured for the lodge.

At the May executive committee meeting, Tom Looby had lots to report. The Y-CAP Ragsdale Recreational Center would be dedicated June 8; consideration was being given to building a second YMCA in Rutherford County since the Y there was growing so fast (25 percent in 1998); and the Bellevue YMCA had received an anonymous gift of $1 million and was actively looking for a site; Green Hills was expected to break ground in September on their 23,000 sq. ft addition. Lori Swann reported that Maryland Farms now had 2,050 membership units, more than the private Maryland Farm Athletic Center ever had before the sale.

In his report, Clark Baker said that Lyndon Murray had done a wonderful job at Northwest and would be missed. He had accepted a position with the Baltimore YMCA. Clark spoke about the critical point the YMCA was rapidly reaching in Sumner County. The Memorial Foundation's gift of land worth $1.2 million was contingent on construction beginning by the end of 1999. The Sumner County Y had raised $1 million and hoped to double that.

There was more good news across the Association in June. Scottsville had raised over $500,000 toward meeting the Turner match, and Sumner County was working hard to meet the December 31 deadline for construction to begin there. Clarksville had some big gifts pending, and a market study was underway in north Rutherford County. Tom Looby's report on Camp Widjiwagan included the news that the water park was open and would be dedicated July 7.[1306] This year, Camp Widjiwagan would have 1,586 campers, 15 percent over the goal.

At mid-year, the budget looked good with an operating gain of $802,500.

In 1997, the tax complaint was against the Downtown YMCA. By 1999, it had been expanded to all YMCAs in Middle Tennessee except Y-CAP. The Y's attorney, Jim Bass, of Bass, Berry and Sims, expressed confidence that the YMCA of Middle Tennessee would win. A national search for a new executive at Northwest bore fruit when it was announced in July that Cedric Thomas, executive of the Downriver Branch of the Detroit, Michigan, YMCA, would become the executive director of Northwest, effective August 9.

Good news kept coming. The Bellevue YMCA had made an offer to buy a site for its new Y, and the Christy-Houston Foundation was so pleased with the success of the fast-growing Rutherford County YMCA that they would be receptive to making a major gift for a second YMCA in the county. Jeff Jowdy reported that Anne and Dick Ragsdale had made a $104,000 gift to the YMCA Foundation, designated for Y-CAP. He also said the Clarksville YMCA had received a $450,000 gift from Montgomery County Commission to fund a gymnasium.

Clark Baker reported that the dedication of the newly-renovated Margaret Maddox Family YMCA East Center was well-attended. Those on hand saw how effectively the center had Margaret's YMCA T-shirt collection displayed on the walls.

In addition to having 1,600 children at the Joe C. Davis Outdoor Center during the summer, there were 3,000 guests. In August, Vanderbilt held freshman orientation there and Columbia/HCA held their company picnic on the grounds.

At the August executive committee meeting, the Bridge Program director Jerry Brest reported that there were 139 rising 7th and 8th graders involved in the program. Sandra Fulton gave the capital update, passing on the wonderful news that Scottsville, KY, had raised nearly $800,000 well over its $650,000 goal. That translated into over $180 in gifts per person from the 4,327 people in the small but fired-up Allen County town.

Susan Moriarty, executive director of the YMCA's Youth Leadership program, explained to the board that the program was a nine-month affair under which 40 high school students from 22 schools were exposed to business leaders and community leaders. The Frist Foundation funded the program. Then Joyce Royce reported on the steady success of the Youth-in-Government program, which had grown to become the fourth largest in the country. In 1999, components included YMCA Model United Nations, YMCA Youth Legislature, YMCA Middle School Youth-in-Government, and the YMCA Model Metropolitan Government Conference.

Clark Baker welcomed Adrian Moody back to Nashville and announced that he would serve as staff chaplain. Adrian had retired for the second time, having spent the five previous years as CEO of the Greater Miami YMCA that had been in an almost moribund condition when Adrian moved there. With the help of wise old retired YMCA executive from across the country, who Adrian lovingly called "viejos sabios," Adrian brought the Y back to a stable position, when he decided, in 1999, that he had done all he could. It may have been his greatest accomplishment.

At the September 23 executive committee meeting, Tom Looby reported that Camp Widjiwagan at the Joe C. Davis Outdoor Center would be at its capacity of 400 the following summer. Phase 1 was fully complete and phase 2, also fully funded, continued under construction. Mark Weller emphasized the importance of moving ahead with phase 3, a $3.5 million project that would include sports and athletic fields, an amphitheater, an arts and outdoor education center, as well as an infirmary, an office, and maintenance area. September also saw the Joe C. Davis Foundation offer a third challenge gift of $1.5 million to the Joe C. Davis Center.[1307] The completion date for the lodge at the Joe C. Davis Outdoor Center was set for May 31.

Three Groundbreakings

The last four months of 1999 was a time for groundbreaking. The first was on September 22 at the Green Hills YMCA for their expansion. The next happened the following week when the skate park groundbreaking was held in Murfreesboro. Groundbreaking for the Scottsville YMCA was held on October 21, while the Sumner County YMCA groundbreaking would be held at year-end. The search for a suitable site in Bellevue appeared nearly over as negotiations were underway to buy a prime site near the intersection of Highway 100 and Old Hillsboro Road.

Space constraints at the Cool Springs center caused it to become an adult/teen center with childcare. Programming focused on adults. The leased facility had a half-court gym, community meeting rooms, a café run by a Christian non-profit organization, and a rocks and ropes course for corporate team building.[1308]

Something exciting was happening at Green Hills where, in 1997, senior wellness director Scott Reall founded Restore ministries, a Christian wellness ministry designed to bring healing and wholeness to people struggling with life's problems. Scott's pilot program at Green Hills was very promising.

The Black Achievers dinner would be held in November with Martin Luther King III as speaker. It would draw 430 in attendance.

In November, Sandra Fulton reported that Scottsville had raised $7,087,240, including the Turner family gift.

Ridley Wills, II, reported that the foundation's assets had increased to $2.7 million. Marshall Polk reported that the 2000 "We Build People" goal would be $2.3 million. He would chair that campaign, after leading the 1999 campaign that raised $2,142,000.

Clark Baker said that the Y would end 1999 with a balanced budget.[1309] At the December board meeting, Jack Elisar reviewed and asked approval of the 2000 budget of $51,511,000. His motion was seconded and passed.

Tom Looby's report included the news that a site in Smyrna seemed likely for the second Rutherford County YMCA, and that the Fun Company was operating at 131 sites, sixteen more than in 1998. He also said that Time To Rise would become a YMCA program beginning in January.

Nelson Andrews presented his committee's slate of officers for 2000. The slate was a follows:

Doyle Rippee, chair
Ron Knox, chair-elect
Elaine McReynolds, secretary
Jack Elisar, treasurer
Olin West III, assistant treasurer

The executive committee voted to elect these officers, who would begin serving on January 1.

Bill Wilson, once again capital committee chair, reported that, in 1999, the Y raised $10.8 million and the total raised to date in the New Century Vision campaign had reached $49.2 million, almost doubling the original goal of $25 million. Bill then said that the 2,400-member Clarksville Family YMCA Center would open in a week. It would be named the Kimbrough Family YMCA in honor of Mr. and Mrs. Ben Kimbrough, who had been the major benefactors in the drive. Another $5.5 million had been raised to date for the Joe C. Davis Center, Bill reported. He then revealed that volunteers in Sumner County had raised $3.5 million of the $5 million they sought.

Clark Baker called 1999 an incredible year and covered many of the highlights. The very first was that the YMCA had balanced a $45 million budget and fully funded all reserves. The Association grew by 17.3 percent with a revenue growth of 19.8 percent. The Y signed a $5 million contract with St. Thomas Hospital to provide health and disease management programs for Association members. Yes, the Sumner County Y did meet its goal of breaking ground for their new $50,000 sq. ft. facility in Hendersonville. The Bellevue Y got big boost with an anonymous gift of $1 million for the purchase of the land on Highway 100 as the site of their new Y.[1310]

Clark ended the last year of the 20th century by making a presentation to board chair Jimmy Webb in appreciation of his two years of outstanding leadership. How envious other YMCAs were of Nashville's enormous success. Often Clark Baker's name was mentioned as a possibility for some of the very largest YMCA positions in the country including the national YMCA's CEO position. Jimmy Webb must have been thankful that "We kept Clark on my watch."

Other highlights of 1999 were raising $10,8549,000 in capital dollars, having completed phase 1 at Camp Widjiwagan, and welcoming the Clarksville Area YMCA Kimbrough Family Center and the YMCA of Scottsville and Allen County to the YMCA of Middle Tennessee, and celebrating the 30th anniversary of the Urban Services program that reached out to over 5,000 youth and served seven inner-city housing developments. In 1999, the YMCA of Middle Tennessee operated 21 centers and 311 program locations in eight area counties.[1311]

Donelson Hermitage YMCA

On the Radar Screen
2000–2001

IN THE FIRST EXECUTIVE committee meeting of the year, Clark Baker highlighted the achievements of 1999 and reviewed the operating objectives of 2000. He said he fully expected 2000 to be as outstanding as had been 1999. The Clarksville YMCA had 1,234 units and 3,168 members. Scottsville had 488 memberships sold toward a goal of 1,000 when the facility would open the following September. And the Nashville Chamber of Commerce had awarded the Joe C. Davis Outdoor Center the "Excellence in Development" award. This was an appropriate time for Frank Drowota, the center's first board chair, to turn over those responsibilities to Chuck Elcan. When the Green Hills expansion was complete, that branch would have 80,000 sq. feet of space.[1312]

The announcement of the signing of a contract to purchase 20 acres of land on Highway 100 just east of the Pasquo community for a YMCA was made at the February 24 board meeting. Robin Costa and Tommye Maddox of the Maddox Foundation made this possible. Tom Looby reported that the ribbon cutting for the 5,100-member Kimbrough Family YMCA in Clarksville was held a week earlier.

A focus in 2000 would be personal physical fitness. The YMCA had designed programs in all areas of wellness. Goodness knows it was needed. In a study of 13 cities comparable to Nashville, Nashvillians ranked 13th in high blood pressure and cholesterol and 9th in the percentage of citizens who smoked.

The results of the 2000 membership satisfaction survey showed ratings of 8.42, 8.45, and 8.59 in 1997, 1998, and 1999 on a ten-point scale where "10" is extremely satisfied. The survey also showed that 77 percent of those who responded in 1999 visited the YMCA at least twice a week, that 56 percent were female and 44% male, and that 41 percent of the 1,541 telephone responders had been members for 1–3 years.[1313]

At the April executive committee meeting, Clark Baker reported that Julie Sistrunk would be leaving after eight years with the Nashville YMCA to accept a position with the Seattle YMCA. Julie, who would leave the end of April, had made a great contribution, Clark said. Chair Doyle Rippee congratulated Clark on being the recipient of two prestigious awards.[1314]

At the 2000 annual meeting in April, John Ed Miller presented the Order of the Red Triangle Award to Miss Rebecca Thomas, a member of the first YMCA Foundation board in 1969. One of Nashville's first female attorneys, she never missed a foundation meeting.

Site grading was underway in May for the new 45,000 square foot facility to be built in Bellevue in connection with a 15,000 square foot Senior Citizens Center in the same building. A shallow rock ledge that lay under most of the YMCA building site and under the entire Senior Citizens' site would cause problems. The main floor of the YMCA and the Senior Citizens' Center would be elevated approximately 5 feet due to the possibility of flooding. Preliminary cost estimates were that the entire project would cost $1,370,400.

Tom Looby's report to the executive committee on May 25 included the announcement that Steve Tammaro, of the Rochester, NY, YMCA, had been named executive director of the Rutherford County YMCA and that the Brentwood Y was still in a CEO search mode. Tom also announced a ribbon-cutting ceremony at the Cool Springs YMCA and the opening in August of a Hermitage extension of the Donelson/Hermitage Y. At the same meeting, Peter Oldham, legal committee chair, reviewed the terms of the ten-year management agreement with the YMCA of Scottsville and Allen County. The agreement was unanimously approved.[1315]

In June, the senior YMCA staff members moved from 900 Church Street to the fourth floor of the old Doctors' Building [FirstStar Bank Bldg.] at 814 Church Street. As a significant number of departments stayed at 900 Church, it was decided not to change the mailing address.

The June board meeting was held at the Joe C. Davis Outdoor Center. All reports were mailed in advance so that the meeting could quickly adjourned in order that the board could walk over to the dedication of the Clark D. Baker Lodge. Clark and Caroline were present for the wonderful occasion that allowed the staff and board to publicly thank Clark for his amazing leadership over nearly thirteen years. Clark's first budget in Nashville in 1988 was $6,815,707. The YMCA of Middle Tennessee's 2000 budget was $51,548,388, more than 8 times greater. Unprecedented growth like that does not occur by chance!

July saw the completion of the Bridgestone/Firestone Waterfront Park and expanded ski dock at the Joe C. Davis Center.

John Ed Miller, having served as chairman of the public policy committee of the National Board of the YMCA of the USA, was elected to serve a three-year term on the National Board. He may well have been the first member of the Nashville Association ever elected to that board.[1316]

Tom Looby announced at the July executive committee meeting that Mark Bachman, executive director of the Green Hills YMCA, had accepted a district vice president position with the Charlotte YMCA. Lori Swann reported that the campaign at the Joe C. Davis Center to match the $1.5 million challenge gift from the Joe C. Davis Foundation was still $200,000 short despite a generous $250,000 gift from the Maddox Foundation. A month later, Lori would report that the challenge gift had been met, thanks to Chuck and Trisha Elcan and many others.[1317] July also saw the completion of the Bridgestone/Firestone Waterfront Park and expanded ski dock at the Joe C. Davis Center.

Jim Palmer, executive director of Y-CAP, gave the devotional at the board meeting on August 24. He also announced that he would be leaving the YMCA soon to join an international ministry. Tom Looby reported that the Y closed on the Bellevue YMCA property earlier that day, thanks in large part to a Maddox Foundation gift.

President-elect Ron Knox welcomed the board to the Maryland Farms YMCA and gave a brief history of the property. He said that James Truman Ward began buying land where the YMCA was newly located in 1937 and built the horse barn there in 1939, followed by his home in 1941. In 1946, Ward stopped showing horses but continued to train horses for other people. In 1970, his son, Jim Ward, along with partners Jack Massey and John Neff, started developing the property. In December 1978, the fitness facility was built. Originally named Maryland Farms Racquet and Country Club, the name was changed to the Athletic Club of Maryland Farms. At that time, the property was connected only with Granny White Pike.[1318] The branch staff reported that the final phase of the renovation would be completed by Labor Day and that currently there were 3,900 members in the Association's most affluent community where the median household income was $87,594. The center was a great success and would be serving nearly 11,000 people by the fall.

• • • • •

Rich Ford reported that the 2000 "We Build People" campaign had been a great success and it would surpass its $2,365,000 goal. By October, it was reported that the campaign raised over $2.4 million with 700 Roundtable members.

• • • • •

Camp board chair Chuck Elcan shared the good news that the 2000 camp had 2,229 campers, a 40 percent increase over 1999. Scholarships also increased by 40 percent to 484.

That Nashville continued to be on the radar screen of YMCAs all across the country, if not the world, was pointed out by the presence of Mark Dini, development director of the Houston YMCA, at the August executive committee meeting and that visitors from YMCAs in Tampa and Japan were expected soon. Additionally, the local Association would host a public policy conference on August 29–30.[1319]

Clark announced that the dedication of the Scottsville and Allen County YMCA would be held October 19. The new building would be named for Laura and Cal Turner Sr. The Scottsville Association, Clark said, had 2,632 members in a county of only 12,000. Clark also reported that the *Nashville Parent Magazine* named Camp Widjiwagan the best day camp in Nashville for the third straight year. Some of the neighbors, who had originally objected to the camp's presence in their neighborhood, including George Liddle, softened their feelings. He graciously agreed to allow, at no charge, the YMCA to quarter horses on twelve acres of his property if the Y would enclose the acreage with a fence. Because Liddle's mother, who lived in a house beside the fenced-in lot, enjoyed watching the horses so much, Mr. Liddle also suggested that the YMCA move the fence closer to her house so she could have a closer better view. The YMCA obliged and later, in October 2002, would purchase the fifteen acres from Liddle, bringing the entire camp property to 318 acres.[1320]

John Ed Miller, back from the YMCA of the USA board meeting in Chicago, said that the YMCA of Middle Tennessee was mentioned several times, and not by him. He also spoke about a new YMCA of the USA structure that would close all MRCs,[1321] including the one in Nashville, but would bring the organizational structure into the 21st century. The first week in November saw two big events. The first was the Association's 18th annual Model UN conference with over 1,000 students from 34 high schools and 340 middle school students from across the state in attendance. On the 3rd, the Y hosted the 7th annual Black Achievers dinner at the Renaissance Hotel with over 400 expected.

The October 31 board meeting was hosted by the Green Hills Family Center and its board chair and center executive, Gracie Allen and Gene deManincor. He reported that the center had 12,000 members, a $6 million budget, 600 volunteers, and 22 program locations. That budget was considerably larger than the entire Chattanooga YMCA budget was in 1988 and only $800,000 less than the Metropolitan Nashville YMCA was in 1988, Clark's first year in Nashville.

Another indication of the sterling reputation of the YMCA of Middle Tennessee came in the form of 12 YMCA visitors from Taiwan who where in the United States for a model UN Conference. Clark reported at the October meeting that the Association was working to increase its cash reserve to $5 million, that growth in 2000 would be around 13 percent, and that the 2001 budget would be $51 million. He also said that a YMCA/St. Thomas partnership would be announced by year-end. This would be possible because of a $5 million gift from St. Thomas. Earlier in the month, Jeff Jowdy had reported that, thanks to a $1 million gift from Orin Ingram and an NDHA grant, the Y would collaborate with the Boys and Girls Club on a project in the Preston Taylor Homes that would include a program center.[1322]

An intriguing announcement made at the October 31 board meeting was that the Y was exploring the possibility of a partnership with Senior Citizens, Inc. at the Bellevue Y. There was, Tom Looby said, "great compatibility between the missions of our two organizations."

Vice President Lisa Beck reported in November that the Fun Company program was in its 17th year and was operating in 134 sites in six counties. She said that 6,300 children attended daily. Their 2000 theme was "Learning through Discovery."

Progress of the Joe C. Davis Center

There was much discussion about the Putnam County YMCA and its two-year management agreement with the YMCA of Middle Tennessee that would expire December 31, 2000. Because certain conditions had not been met by the Putnam County YMCA, the board voted to not extend the agreement beyond 2000.

Because Clark Baker decided to combine the December board meeting with the 2001 "We Build People" kickoff meeting, the business portion of the meeting was abbreviated. Tom Looby gave the Operations report. He said the Sumner County YMCA had 940 charter members enrolled, having almost made their goal of 1,000 members prior to opening. He then reported that the satellite Y in Hermitage, an extension of the Donelson YMCA, opened December 1. By year-end Tom's goal was to enroll 500 members there. Tom moved on to discuss the good problem that Franklin had. With 3,500 members, there was a need there for additional space. The Franklin Y board and their executive director, Dan Dummermuth, were, Tom said, working on an expansion plan. The Joe C. Davis Center had projects under design or under construction that totaled $1.5 million. They included athletic fields and an arts & outdoor education center. Both were expected to be completed for the following summer.

Active capital campaigns continued at the Joe C. Davis Outdoor Center and at Sumner County. At the Davis Center, there was a July 31, 2001 deadline for the second $750,000 match while Sumner County had raised $4.8 million on a goal of $5.5 million.[1323]

In Clark Baker's December 8 memo to the board announcing the combined meeting, he wrote, "Pray for a strong December and, indeed, that will make me have a very happy New Year!"

The YMCA had a strong December with an operating surplus of $81,000, allowing the Association to end the year in the black with a modest surplus of $21,000. The Franklin Family YMCA had trouble ending the year in the black. Their 37,000 square foot family YMCA facility was full to bursting. That was not the problem. The problem was the separate 15,000-square-foot Genesis Center that primarily served adults. It was a financial disaster, having been a serious financial drain from the beginning, averaging between $180,000 and $220,000 in deficits for the past three years. The Franklin board recommended that it be closed prior to the end of the five-year lease that would expire March 31, 2002. The board further recommended that the Family YMCA facility be expanded at an estimated cost of $450,000. The recommendation was approved both by the finance and executive committees.

Tom Looby reported on a number of new staff assignments. Gene deManincor would give up supervision of the Sumner County Y to have time to pursue the possibility of opening a YMCA in Dickson and to supervise the Bellevue Y. Mike Heilbron would give up Donelson to assume responsibility for Sumner County, Clarksville, Robertson County, Madison, and the Margaret Maddox East Family Center. David Reeves would become executive director at Donelson and give up his Harding Place duties. Bob Holland, operations director at Uptown, would become the new Harding Place executive.

The 2000 "We Build People" campaign finished with a 15 percent increase over the previous year. The YMCA Foundation received nearly $500,000 in cash gifts in 2000 and had 21 new Heritage club members.

A YMCA-St. Thomas Hospital Collaboration

Clark Baker reviewed the 2000 highlights and announced that Dan Ryan, vice president of Human Resources, had left the Y to accept a position in the business world and that Liz Dubuque, senior vice president and MRC director, had accepted a position with the Suncoast Family YMCA in Clearwater, Florida.

Lori Swann then gave a report on the YMCA–St. Thomas partnership under which the hospital would give the Y $1 million a year for five years. Under the collaboration, St. Thomas and the YMCA of Middle Tennessee would provide joint programming, marketing and wellness services governed by a board consisting of four representatives from the YMCA and four from St. Thomas. The executive committee approved the concept.[1324]

Construction on the athletic complex at the Joe C. Davis Outdoor Center was well underway in February. By March, the roof over the hockey pavilion was being installed, and infield clay was being spread on the baseball diamonds. Most of the work would be completed by summer with the Arts and Outdoor Education Village expected to come online in June. Registration for the 2001 camp was available online.

It was announced in March that a new outreach would come in July when Josias Arteaga would join the YMCA of Middle Tennessee as program director for special populations. Mr. Arteaga would be a hands-on program director working directly with children and families, mostly Hispanic, along the Murfreesboro Road/Nolensville Road corridor in Southeast Nashville.

As inevitably happens, the Downtown Y, twenty-eight years old, was beginning to look frayed, particularly when compared to the new facilities and improvements at Green Hills and Maryland Farms. Plans were underway for an upgrade, using an architect who was a member of the Downtown Center.

In May, an amended charter of the YMCA of Middle Tennessee was filed with the State of Tennessee. The new charter changed the name of the Association from the "YMCA of Middle Tennessee" to the "Young Men's Christian Association of Middle Tennessee." Due to the on-going tax challenge, it was important that the charter reflect the Association's full name that emphasizes that the YMCA is a Christian organization. At the May meeting, Jack Elisar, reporting for the financial committee recommended that the YMCA purchase for $267,500 a house at 1706 Eastland Avenue to replace the Y-CAP group home in Madison that was then being rented by Y-CAP. Most of the cost would be financed over three years. The balance would be paid from current Y-CAP funds. The recommendation was approved.

Senior vice president Tom Looby told the board that Hastings Architectural Associates had been selected to design the North Rutherford YMCA and Everton Askew had been hired to design the Bellevue YMCA. Camp Widjiwagan would open, Tom said, on May 29 with 1,882 campers enrolled.

Following the completion of the Scottsville and Allen County YMCA, the mayor of Franklin, Kentucky, approached the YMCA of Middle Tennessee about the possibility of building a YMCA there. A few miles to the north, the struggling Bowling Green, Kentucky, YMCA also asked to be absorbed by the YMCA of Middle Tennessee. The Nashville Association was cautious, agreeing only to consult with the Bowling Green YMCA. Tom also said that a new membership satisfaction survey found an overall increase in satisfaction to 8.7 on a scale in which 10 was perfect.

At the 126th annual meeting, held at the Renaissance Hotel, Nelson Andrews introduced the officers for 2001: Doyle R. Rippy, chairman; Ron Knox, chair-elect; Rich Ford, vice chair; Jack A. Elisar, treasurer; Olin West III, assistant treasurer; and Peter Oldham, secretary. Board members were also elected for three-year terms. Chair Doyle Rippee introduced the guest speaker of the evening, Ken Gladish, Ph.D., national executive director of the YMCA of the USA. Bill Hudson, 2001 "We Build People" chair reported that the 2000 campaign, led by Rich Ford, had been extremely successful, raising a total of $2,507,979, well over its $2,365,000 goal.

Dan Harbison, CEO of Farmers National Bank of Scottsville, paid tribute to the late Cal Turner Sr., the 2001 recipient of the Order of the Red Triangle. Harbison shared the fact that Mr. Turner, who died November 14, 2000, had been the pioneer of the dollar-store industry and the founder of Dollar General Corporation. In 1977, Mr. Harbison said that Mr. Turner helped convince Scottsville community leaders to seek a YMCA for their county. To ensure the project's success, he pledged to match community dollars through the Laura G. Turner Foundation, named after his wife of 52 years and operated by his four children. Cal Turner Jr. accepted the YMCA's highest honor for his father. Several months later, the YMCA learned that, prior to Mr. Turner's death, he had made a $2.5 million gift to the YMCA of Middle Tennessee and St. Thomas Hospital in honor of Dr. and Mrs. Roy Elam. At that time, the Turner family had given over $10 million to the YMCA of Middle Tennessee. The board, obviously grateful for the gift, hoped to honor Mr. Turner's wishes by naming a center for the Elams. They empowered Clark and Doyle to make that decision.[1325]

Clark Baker spoke of the many accomplishments of 2000, including the opening of the beautiful YMCA of Scottsville and Allen County and the Sumner County Family. He also mentioned the opening of the Y-CAP Academy and his appreciation for the Clark Baker Lodge at the Joe C. Davis Outdoor Center being named for him.

During the summer, all centers held two-hour planning sessions with their boards and key staff members as one step in the process of implementing a strategic plan for 2002–2004. At the end of August, a half-day planning retreat was held to assimilate all the information gathered. This would be followed by a final review and recommendations to the board in December. A guiding light in this process was Tom Massey, a former national consultant for the YMCA of the USA, who worked with the Y on the development and implementation of the plan.[1326]

Mark Weller reported at the June board meeting that the Camp Widjiwagan was at 87 percent of capacity and that construction was also going well with the arts and education center and the athletic fields almost complete. Two innovations would be a senior camp, to open in the fall, and a horseback riding program for children with disabilities.

Tom Looby passed on the good news that the Joe C. Davis Outdoor Center had been accredited by the American Camping Association. Congratulations were extended to

Mark Weller and his staff. "Only 1 in 4 camps across the country receive this recognition," Looby said.

Peter Oldham reported that St. Thomas Health Services and the YMCA of Middle Tennessee had formed a separate entity to cooperatively develop programs and services to heal the whole person. The executive committee authorized Doyle Rippee and Clark Baker to execute the operating agreement.

The Robertson County YMCA received good news in 2001 when the Draughon Foundation made a grant that allowed the Y to creatively use a wetlands area on the back of their property to build an outdoor walking/running trail and an observation deck. This would become part of the City of Springfield's Greenway.[1327]

By August 30, 2001, the "We Build People" campaign had passed its goal with $2.78 million raised. Bill Hudson had given the drive great leadership. Jeff Jowdy also announced that the Great Hall in the Clark D. Baker Lodge had been named in memory of Ralph Brunson, who had passed away. Brunson had been general secretary of the Metropolitan Nashville YMCA for sixteen years before his retirement in 1980. He served longer than any other general secretary except for Ernest Spain, who served 28 years, from 1921 to 1948. The best news was that the $750,000 challenge grant from the Davis Foundation had been met.

The End of an Era

The inevitable news that, sooner or later, Clark Baker would decide the time was right for him to consider another YMCA opportunity, came in early September when Clark wrote chairman Doyle Rippee saying that he had accepted the position of President/CEO of the YMCA of Greater Houston, the sixth largest YMCA in the country. In his letter, Clark wrote Doyle that he would be replacing "my friend, mentor, and coach Bill Phillips, who will retire March 1, 2002." His resignation would be effective January 31, 2002.[1328]

At the September board meeting, Doyle made the official announcement. After complimenting Clark on the terrific job he had done in Nashville and wishing him well in his new assignment, Doyle said, "We are prepared to go forward and know that this will be a 'very sought after' position because of the high profile of this Y and the strength of our board and staff." He then appointed a search committee chaired by Ron Knox, to recommend a successor. Other members who agreed to serve were Nelson Andrews, Kenny Blackburn, Florence Davis, Bill DeLoache, Sandra Fulton, Peter Oldham, Jimmy Webb III, Ridley Wills II, and Bill Wilson.

Jimmy Webb III
Board Chair
1998–1999

Jack Elisar reported in September that the financial situation had worsened over the summer with a deficit of $337,000 through August. Tom Looby announced the development of a new young adult membership category to go in effect January 1, 2002. For this age group, that represented only 7 percent of total membership, membership fees would drop from $53 to $39 per year. Tom also reported that Dan Dummermuth, executive director of the Franklin YMCA, had resigned to accept a position with the Phoenix YMCA. Moving on to the North Rutherford YMCA, Looby reported that the City of Smyrna had given the Y seven acres of land but that the Y was requesting at least three additional acres. Tom's last report was on the rave reviews schools in East Nashville were giving Y-CAP Academy that was in its second year with 24 at risk students in grades 5 and 6.

Clark Baker shared with the executive committee how fulfilling and wonderful the past 14 years as CEO had been, and what a difficult decision he had made. Clark said he felt the decision was the right thing for him personally and for the Y. He then thanked everyone for their continuous support, loyalty and dedication.[1329]

At the October board meeting, Tom Looby announced two staff changes: Gail Sonia had been named district director of the Franklin and Cool Springs YMCAs, and Bill Powell had been named executive director at Harding Place. He said the expansion projects at Franklin and Clarksville were a little behind original schedules but should be completed by January. Rich Ford reported that the 2001 "We Build People" campaign had gone even higher, cresting at $2.95 million with 8,200 donors, 854 of whom gave at the Chairman's Roundtable level. Other good news was that Robin Costa of the Maddox Foundation had announced a $1 million gift to the YMCA Foundation in honor of Florence Davis.[1330]

The results of the YMCA staff satisfaction survey reported the satisfaction ratio to be 89 percent, five percent above the national average and better than the YMCA's rating two years earlier.

Clark spoke to the board about his decision to go to Houston, and expressed confidence that the YMCA of Middle Tennessee would attract an outstanding CEO. He was given a standing ovation.[1331]

The Strategic Planning team, chaired by Ron Knox Jr. unveiled the Y's priorities for 2002 through 2004. Core areas addressed in the plan were member involvement, aging boomers, teens, mission awareness, wellness, endowment, and capital projects. The plan was approved at the November board meeting.[1332] Also approved at that meeting was the construction of an outdoor pool at the Sumner County YMCA. Tim Weill reported on this and on the news that the H. G. Hill Company had offered to sell their property at 900 Church Street to the YMCA for approximately $190,000, less than the market value. The executive committee also approved this.

Tom Lobby's operations report included the news that the Y and the Jackson Foundation had mutually agreed to drop the idea of collaborating on a YMCA in Dickson and that the possibility of taking on the struggling Bowling Green YMCA was nearly dead.

Jeff Jowdy reported that Bill Turner would chair the 2002 "We Build People" campaign. Its goal was set at $3 million.

Clark Baker reported that the Madison YMCA was having severe financial problems and there were serious discussions about closing it. He also reported that Lori Swann had stepped down as marketing director but would continue working on the YMCA/St. Thomas Alliance project. Lori would remain a senior vice president.[1333]

David Roddy reported for the finance committee in December that the 2002 budget would total $61,031,000, an 8 percent increase over the projected 2001 expenses. His recommendation to approve the budget was approved.

Tom Looby made his customary operating report at the December meeting. He reviewed the Bellevue project and asked approval for a YMCA negotiations committee, chaired by John Ed Miller, to negotiate with Senior Citizens, Inc. to develop a plan to share the facility, programs and personnel, as appropriate, at the center to be built in Bellevue. This was approved.

Doyle Rippee reported for the nominating committee that their officer choices for 2002 were Ron Knox Jr., board chair; Rich Ford, chair-elect, Jack Elisar, treasurer; Olin West III, assistant treasurer; and Peter Oldham, secretary. It was moved that the slate of officers, to be elected at the Association's annual meeting in April, be approved. This motion passed.

Clark Baker recognized Jim Rayhab for having completed 54 years of service to the YMCA and presented him with a fifty-year service pin. He also announced that Adrian Moody had agreed to become the new YMCA International Director on a volunteer basis and thanked him for his long years of service. Clark also thanked the selection committee that brought him to Nashville fifteen years earlier, and recognized center executives and senior staff members for their outstanding work and dedication. He also thanked all the volunteers for helping make the YMCA of Middle Tennessee one of the finest in the country. He spoke of his love for this Y and Nashville and said that he and Carolyn planned to retire in Nashville after an anticipated six years in Houston.[1334]

Harding Place YMCA

TOP: Maryland Farms YMCA BOTTOM: Mount Juliet YMCA

CHAPTER THIRTY-SEVEN

A Fast Start
2001–2003

IN LATE FALL, the CEO search committee, led by Ron Knox Jr., and aided by Charles Cleveland of the national office, narrowed its focus on the YMCA CEOs of two major cities, Cincinnati and Richmond. The committee visited both YMCAs and hosted both candidates, Jerry Haralson of Cincinnati, and John Mark "Journey" Johnson of the YMCA of Greater Richmond, and their wives in Nashville. On December 20, Ron Knox Jr., on behalf of his committee, offered Journey Johnson the presidency of the YMCA of Middle Tennessee subject to approval of the board.[1335] On January 2, 2002, after the YMCA of Middle Tennessee board ratified the committee's recommendation, Journey officially accepted the opportunity to continue his YMCA ministry in Middle Tennessee. To help with the transition, he and his wife, Sharon, came to Nashville in January for four days so Journey could meet with Clark Baker and the executive committee, and so they could look at houses and schools for their children. Journey pledged to Ron that he would do his absolute best to build on the rich tradition of such dedicated YMCA leaders as Ralph Brunson, Adrian Moody, and Clark Baker.[1336] The search committee was confident that he would do exactly that, as it was clear to them that the people in Richmond, inside and outside the YMCA, admired Journey's "energy, commitment and ability to inspire others to do their best."[1337]

Ron Knox
Board Chair
2002-2003

One of the things Journey learned from his trips to Nashville was that three important senior staff members leaders—Lori Swann, Mary Mossing, and Tom Looby—had either left or would leave soon. Senior vice-president Lori Swann was leaving to work for the Triangle YMCA in North Carolina; Mary Mossing would soon be named CEO of the YMCA of Collier County in Naples, Florida, and senior vice president Tom Looby was hoping for a call from the Triangle/Central North Carolina Region YMCA to become its CEO. Realizing what an operational void their absences would cause, Journey quickly called his friend, David Byrd, the exceptionally capable president and CEO of the YMCA of Greater Durham, North Carolina, and arranged to meet him halfway between Richmond and Durham. Journey knew that David had been instrumental in merging the YMCA of Greater Durham with the Raleigh Capital Area YMCA to form a $50 million regional YMCA serving six counties and with 13 operating centers. David and Tom Looby, the COO of the YMCA of Middle Tennessee, were the two finalists for the CEO position in Raleigh. Realizing he was not going to be chosen for the Raleigh position, David was receptive to the opportunity Journey offered him to come to Nashville with him as COO of the YMCA of Middle Tennessee, a $56.5 million operation and the 8th largest YMCA in the Country. David accepted the challenge and assumed his COO responsibilities in Nashville on April 15.[1338]

Journey Johnson, 46, started his YMCA career in 1978 as a program director with the Altavista, Virginia, Area YMCA. He next was named executive director of the new Bedford, Virginia Area YMCA. At one of his very first board meetings there, Journey was attired in a pair of running shorts and a T-shirt, having just run eight miles. After the meeting, Eliza Mount Thomas, a board member and one of the Grande Dames of Bedford, wrote a letter to the chairman of the board, expressing her displeasure at Journey's inappropriate dress. Her point was that, in a business setting with ladies and gentlemen present, "you don't show up wearing running shorts and a T-shirt." She then asked that the twenty-four-year-old Journey order a new suit. Journey and Mrs. Thomas soon became friends. Shortly thereafter she gave him her deceased husband's office furniture. When it was installed in his modest office, Journey had hardly enough room to get around the table. He was not about to complain, however, as he had learned a valuable lesson in appropriate business attire.[1339]

Successful in Bedford, Journey attracted the attention of the YMCA director in Richmond, who, in 1983, invited him to join the YMCA of Greater Richmond as executive director of the Tuckahoe Family Branch. Journey's mission there was to grow the membership and reduce the center debt. His success led to him being named president and CEO of the YMCA of Greater Richmond in September 1991. Once, at a board meeting in Richmond, Journey slipped back a bit. He forgot to wear socks. Nevertheless, he proved himself to be a charismatic leader, skillful fundraiser, and a strong supporter of the YMCA's beliefs and programs.[1340]

With an operating budget of over $27 million, the YMCA of Greater Richmond would, in 2002, be one of the thirty largest YMCAs in the United States, with 10 branches and an outdoor center, 200 full-time and 1,400 part-time staff members.[1341]

Journey received both his undergraduate degree and an M.Ed (master's in education) from Lynchburg College. He later earned an M.B.A. from the E. Claiborne Robins School of Business at the University of Richmond. In the spring of 2000, Journey was honored as the Distinguished Alumni of the Year from Lynchburg College.

Journey and Sharon have four children: Jeni, Bobby, Katie, and Jack. Before accepting the CEO position in Nashville, he had just been elected as chair of the board at the fast-growing Gayton Road Christian Church.

Journey Johnson was introduced to the executive committee of the YMCA of Middle Tennessee at its meeting on January 23. In his introduction, Ron Knox said that Journey would begin on a part-time basis effective February 1 and would be full-time on March 18. Journey expressed how excited and honored he was "to have been selected to carry on the leadership of this great organization."

Tom Looby then gave the operations report. He congratulated Walter Knestrick Contractors for the good jobs that company did in building the Clarksville and Franklin YMCA expansions, and reported that, in its 5th season, Camp Widjiwagan would be full with 550 children per week. Clark also announced that Maria Wolfe would replace Lori Swann as vice-president of membership/marketing. Clark reported that the Madison Y had been struggling financially and that the finance committee had recommended that it be closed. Clark said that Senior Citizens, Inc. was willing to work with the Y to provide a program for seniors at their location. The executive committee approved the recommendation. Clark then reviewed the highlights of 2001 and discussed some of the current issues that the Y and the new CEO would face in 2002. As this was his last executive committee meeting, Clark thanked everyone for their loyalty, dedication, and support.[1342]

At the February board meeting, Peter Oldham explained some proposed amendments to the YMCA charter and bylaws that had not been amended since the mid-90s. The first change was to add as one of the YMCA's purposes "to build strong kids, strong families and strong communities." Another was to increase the number of voting members at the annual meeting from 275 to "up to 1,000 voting members." A third change was to delete the references to "vice chairman" as an elected office. The Association had not used this title since 1998. The final change was to change the number of voting members each center could have from "up to 27" to "up to 50." At the time, the largest center had 30 board members, simply ignoring the bylaws restriction. The changes to the charter and bylaws were approved and ratified at the annual meeting in April.

Ron Knox gave an international update, saying that the YMCA of Middle Tennessee ran one of the largest international programs in the country, having partnerships with YMCAs in six countries. The following month, the local Association would host a YMCA delegation from China, Ron said.

To help Journey Johnson make the transition from the 28th largest YMCA in the country to the 8th largest, he was assisted by Tom Massey, of Triangle2, a consulting firm. Tom's three objectives were 1) to help Journey learn as much as possible about the YMCA and the Nashville area; 2) assist the staff, board and community leaders to learn more about Journey; and 3) to gather preliminary information to better address immediate issues, and develop a plan for the balance of 2002.[1343]

At the March board meeting, group vice president Gene deManincor announced that Tom Looby had been named CEO of the Triangle/Central North Carolina YMCA and would start on April 1 and that Mary Mossing had already begun her new assignment as CEO of the Collier County, Florida YMCA. Fortunately, David Byrd would be on board in less than three weeks. Gene also announced that the Madison YMCA would close on May 31 and that 69 members had transferred to other centers. Tom Looby was ready for his new assignment, having performed well in Nashville. His leadership in the establishment of the Joe C. Davis Outdoor Center was particularly impressive.

Rich Ford, development committee chairman, reported that the "We Build People" annual campaign had raised $1.96 million or 63.47 percent of its $3,099,000 goal and that the YMCA Foundation had assets of $3.5 million plus a commitment of $1 million from the Maddox Foundation, putting it on target to achieve its goal of $5 million by 2004. Rich also reviewed the status of eight current or impending capital campaigns then underway in various centers.

Jeff Jowdy reported that the YMCA was partnering with the Boys & Girls Club to operate a joint facility next door to McKissack School to serve the Preston Taylor Homes area of Nashville. The program would use a new building on the school campus. The Metro School System would pay for utilities, and the projected annual budget of $180,000 would be a joint responsibility of the YMCA and the Boys and Girls Club. The YMCA would serve as a lead partner for two years, responsible for operations. Once an anonymous donor made the project feasible, the executive committee approved the partnership.

During the winter, Journey spent much of his time meeting board and foundation members in small groups and visiting all the centers meeting with staff, key volunteers, and potential donors. He spoke of how impressed he had been with the high caliber of the YMCA staff and volunteers.

The 127th annual meeting of the YMCA of Middle Tennessee was held April 25, 2002 at the Renaissance Hotel in Nashville. Nelson Andrews initiated the program by introducing the new officers and nominating new board members Leilani Boulward and Bill Hudson. He also nominated for re-election, for a second three-year term, seven board members. After the election, the new slate of officers and the newly elected board members received a round of applause. Awards were then presented to the "Volunteers of the Year" for their outstanding service. Ridley Wills II presented the Order of the Red Triangle Award to Senator Douglas Henry, who had been recruited by Horace Hill Jr. to serve on the YMCA board. Bill Hudson reported on the successful "We Build People" campaign and said that, of the 8,413 gifts made the previous year, 889 were Chairman's Roundtable gifts of $1,000 or more. Doyle Rippee, after serving as board chairman for 2000 and 2001, handed the gavel over to new chair Ron Knox Jr. Doyle received a standing ovation for a job well done.

Clark Baker came from Houston for the meeting. He expressed pleasure at being in Nashville and reflected on how much he enjoyed his 15 years as CEO of the YMCA of Middle Tennessee. Clark presented a "master key" to Journey Johnson that he hoped would continue to unlock the joy of the YMCA and signify the opening of doors and hearts of the Nashville community to the Y. Journey graciously accepted the key and the meeting was adjourned at the early hour of 8:35 p.m.[1344]

The grand opening of The Institute for Healing Arts (IHA), the joint venture between St. Thomas Health Services and the YMCA of Middle Tennessee, was held in May at the institute's 10,000 square foot facility inside the Maryland Farms YMCA Carol and Roy Elam Family Center. After a VIP dedication and ribbon cutting, there was an open house for YMCA members followed by a grand opening for the general public. The center introduced a new concept of health and wellness by providing integrative medicine services with a holistic approach. The cost to build and furnish the center was $930,000.[1345]

The Genesco Footpath at the Joe C. Davis Center was dedicated in June. It would immediately become the main artery for campers walking from the central lawn to the equestrian center and athletic complex.[1346]

• • • • •

A YMCA of Middle Tennessee Employee Handbook was published in July. The handbook provided employees with a single source of information about "your Association, how it operates, what you can expect from us and what we expect from you." It including employment and separation information, a section on compensation section, a description of employee benefits, safety issues, a code of conduct, and a section on staff development and recognition. Nancy Reese and Suzanne Dooley spearheaded this effort.

• • • • •

In his first ninety days, Journey had individual or small group meetings with 70 community leaders, met with YMCA board members in small groups, visited every center, and had numerous staff meetings. In June, he gave an update on the "Vision for the Future" strategic plan. For each of the six priority areas, there were, he said, an overall goal, three-year objectives and specific actions to be completed by the end of 2002.[1347]

In July, Journey, David Byrd, Jeff Jowdy, Steve Tammaro, and Jan Berry met to discuss strategy for the proposed North Rutherford Center. The goal was to raise $3 million in pledges from the LaVergne and Smyrna communities by year-end and then begin submitting proposals to the Christy-Houston Foundation and others asking for matching gifts.

On Sunday afternoon, July 21, the YMCA hosted its second annual staff appreciation day at the Joe C. Davis Outdoor Center, More than 1,000 employees and their families attended. Over the Fourth of July holiday, the staff had moved into the new camp office. The double-wide trailer was gone.[1348]

Rich Ford reported at the July executive committee meeting that the "We Build People" campaign stood at 99.23 percent of the $3,099,000 goal. Journey Johnson reported on having attended, with David Byrd, Rich Ford and Ron Knox, a YMCA Leadership Summit in Colorado and that the Association had received a letter from the IRS validating the YMCA of Middle Tennessee as a not-for-profit charitable organization.

A program quality survey, a year in the making, was announced in August. Based on a 100 percent scale, it showed satisfaction percentages for swim lessons at 88.5 percent, group fitness at 93.8 percent, membership at 90.18 percent, and nursery at 93.15 percent.

Mike Heilbronn headed the program in the Association office.[1349]

Now with 30,000 members walking through the doors of the YMCA's 20 centers every day, it became clear, after a eight month study, that automated external defibrillators (AEDs) were not a luxury but a necessity. On July 17, the YMCA and the American Heart Association held a press conference at the Green Hills YMCA to announce that every center would have an AED.

Rich Ford brought good news in August that the Y had exceeded its 2002 "We Build People" goal of $3,099,000. At the Chairman's Roundtable dinner in September, the theme was "Fantasy Island: Where philanthropists make dreams come true." Some 350 people were in attendance. By then, there were 841 Chairman's Roundtable donors and total pledges and gifts of $3,147,211. Marty Dickens, the campaign chairman had done a fine job. Thanks also went to Sam Bartholomew, who had agreed to chair the 2003 campaign.[1350]

In the first three months of its operation, the Institute for the Healing Arts had generated total revenue of $61,815 with average daily sales of approximately $700. Due to low activity on Friday evenings and Saturdays, the hours of operation were shortened. This caused the Y to reevaluate its overall delivery system.[1351]

If the IHA had a shaky start, the Bellevue Family YMCA Center was "raring to go." Here was its situation in mid-September. The Y owned 20 acres of land off Highway 100 that had been purchased with a $1 million gift from the Maddox Foundation. Senior Citizens, Inc., the Y's projected partner, had committed $2 million to the project. Two market studies were extremely positive and a funding plan was in place. It worked this way. The total cost would be $9 million. In addition to the two lead gifts, the Y needed to raise $1.5 million, which would cover half the expected cost. Internal funding of $1.5 million and debt financing of $3 million would get the Y to the $9 million needed. The timeline was to break ground in October 2003 and open in October 2004. The center was projected to break even by year two with a target of 2,730 household memberships by the end of the year.

2010 Vision Plan Introduced

During the fall, there were a series of focus group meetings to introduce a 2010 Vision of what the YMCA would be in 2020. This was a process to bring all planning and activities of the YMCA into a coordinated effort. The board members were exposed to a three-fold challenge to determine:

- What the YMCA of Middle Tennessee can be best at?
- What our leaders are passionate about accomplishing?
- What is the best economic engine for this vision?

The 2020 vision would encompass all aspects of the YMCA of Middle Tennessee and would drive all other planning processes. An important by-product was the adoption of an open-door rate scale by the Association. One of the most interesting efforts initiated early in Journey Johnson's tenure was one to conduct a marketing and communications audit to identify "gaps" between the community's perceptions of the YMCA and how the Y wanted to be perceived. With the results of this audit, the Y intended to develop an awareness campaign to help position the YMCA of Middle Tennessee as a "caring, competent, mission-driven force worthy of charitable support." Journey reported on this in a six-month report he sent to the executive committee. He also spoke of the 2020 Vision plan, the Institute for the Healing Arts and the transition in his senior staff with David Byrd as the new chief operating officer

and Peter Oldham as senior vice president and general counsel. Peter would also serve as planned giving officer. Just as David brought financial and operating acumen to the YMCA of Middle Tennessee, Peter brought stability and a thorough understanding of the Nashville community and local relationships.[1352]

After a thorough discussion of the Bellevue Family YMCA, a motion was passed at the September executive committee meeting to proceed with the $1.5 million fundraising effort in Bellevue, and, once those funds were raised, to approve the $9 million project there.[1353]

Buzz and Florence Davis hosted the Foundation Board at their home on September 25. Through October 24, the foundation had raised $398,874 in current year gifts and pledges toward a $500,000 goal. The goal was to reach $5 million in assets by year-end 2003 with a long-term goal of having assets equal to the YMCA's operating budget, then $61 million. At the Heritage Club dinner in November, a record 117 Heritage Club members were present.[1354]

In October, the YMCA redesigned the services offered by the Institute of the Healing Arts. Beginning in January, a "Stay Well" slogan would begin to appear in the family centers. The new offerings at the various YMCA branches would center around weight management, nutrition, stress management, and Restore Ministries. The current Institute for the Healing Arts would serve as an incubator for new program development. Four of the most popular programs at the center would be continued—cardiac rehab, movement education, stress, and weight reduction. Journey stressed the fact that the partnership with St. Thomas was continuing to evolve. A little later, it was decided that "Stay Well" resident nurses would be available at five family centers.[1355]

Roy Elam, director of the Institute for Healing Arts, spoke at the October board meeting. He said that the IHA was the only place in Nashville where people could find help in making a lifestyle change. Scott Reall, director of Restore Ministries, also spoke. He said that someone finds hope every day at Restore. These talks fired up Lee Barfield so much that he announced that he intended to lose 20 pounds by year-end.[1356]

By November, VISION 2020 had solidified the following goals:

- Increasing availability to all;
- Developing youth and teens;
- Inspiring healthier lifestyles;
- Deepening member and community involvement; and
- Ensuring our legacy.

Bob Napier reported at the November 22 executive committee meeting that the Joe C. Davis Outdoor Center Long-Range Planning Task Force, headed by Frank Drowota, was developing a vision and business plan for camping and outdoor programs at the center. One of the objectives was to determine the need for a resident and year-round camp at this location. Bob said the timeline for this project was from January 2002 through November 2003. Journey announced that Dewey Branstetter and his sister, Jane Branstetter Stranch, would co-chair the Bellevue Capital campaign. Their involvement and support and that of their father, Cecil, would be keys to the Bellevue Family Center becoming a success.

The operations report of December 19 reported that, following a national trend, the YMCA of Middle Tennessee had significantly reduced its joining fees to $100, $75, and $50 depending on the center. Although only operational since the last week of November, the YMCA was proud to be able to say that it had reversed a two-year trend of declining membership growth when compared to the previous year.

A winter marketing campaign kicked off in December. For 2003, 35 percent of marketing dollars of $190,000 would go to TV, 26 percent to radio, 16 percent to direct mail, 12 percent to billboards, and 11 percent to newspaper print.[1357]

The 2003 "We Build People" campaign kicked off officially at the December 2002 board meeting. The goal was established at $3,343,000 and every effort was promised to accomplish that goal by the April annual meeting. At the same meeting, Ron Knox presented the final version of Vision 2020. Before adjourning, Journey Johnson and Ron Knox reflected on the fact that it was exactly one year earlier that Journey first talked with the YMCA of Middle Tennessee search committee about the CEO vacancy. Both men agreed that it had been "a fast, unforgettable and exciting first year on the job!"

Good News for a New Year

Good news came in January. One was that the Tennessee State Board of Equalization voted to uphold the YMCA of Middle Tennessee's property-tax exemption on the Y's wellness centers. Thanks to December's operating surplus of $235,000 and an association contingency of $2 million ($525,000 great than in 2001), the YMCA had an operating surplus of $17,000 for the calendar year 2002.[1358]

At the January board meeting, it was announced that senior vice president for development Jeff Jowdy would be leaving at the end of April. Journey Johnson reported that the Capital Development Task Force, chaired by Bill DeLoache, would focus on prioritizing the YMCA's projects when the committee met in February.[1359]

In February, the YMCA of Middle Tennessee brought in Bruce Roberts, a seventeen-year YMCA veteran, to become Stay Well executive director. His responsibilities would include supervision of HIS and providing leadership to the Stay Well program partnership with St. Thomas Hospital and the YMCA of the USA Total Health initiative. Phase I of the Stay Well program was launched a week earlier with the introduction of St. Thomas nurses at Green Hills, Brentwood, Donelson-Hermitage, Downtown, and Maryland Farms.

The school-age childcare program, Fun Company, continued to be strong during the 2002–2003 school year when it was serving almost 7,000 children in 137 sites.

In February, the Y began to gear up for the summer season when it would open 28 outdoor pools. Of course, the association's 19 indoor pools were open year-round. Always aware of the importance of safety, the Y would have approximately 500 lifeguards in 2003 and 125 swim instructors.[1360]

Jeff Parsley, most recently CEO of the Shreveport YMCA and earlier CEO of the Maury County YMCA, rejoined the staff as director of the annual fund and regional development director. In the latter role, he would provide consulting support to the Robertson County, Sumner County, Scottsville and Clarksville YMCAs. George Crook Jr., and Jan Berry would do the same as regional development directors for Williamson County (George), and Rutherford County, Donelson-Hermitage, and Maury County (Jan). In March, Jeff would be promoted to vice president of financial development and Peter Oldham would serve as planned giving officer and work with the YMCA Foundation. Michael Brown would become vice president for community resources.[1361]

Out at the Joe C. Davis Center, March saw construction underway with the rope swing dock going in at the beach and two 150-foot slides into the lake under construction. It was obvious that 2003 would be a blockbuster year as over 1,000 campers had enrolled for summer day camp, up from over 460 in 2002. Group sales were also going well with Enterprise Rent-a-Car, Vanderbilt's freshman orientation camp, and Cracker Barrell having signed up. At the March executive committee meeting, an invited guest was John Stanley with Triangle2. He was in Nashville to conduct interviews to determine the interest for a resident camp. Plans were also shaping up for visits in the summer to resident camps in Michigan, North Carolina, and Virginia. Y-CAP also had a new executive director, Jim Finchum. Naturally, one of his first tasks was to meet with County Juvenile Justice system officials. In his president's report, Ron Knox moved that the executive committee approve a lease with the City of Smyrna for land on which to locate the North Rutherford YMCA. It passed.[1362]

At the annual meeting in April, Nelson Andrews introduced the 2003 officers—Ronald F. Knox Jr., chairman; Rich Ford, chair-elect; Jack Elisar, treasurer; Olin West, assistant treasurer; and Sam Batholomew, secretary. Nelson also nominated Billy Frist and Bob Knestrick as new board members each to serve a three-year term. Because of Nelson's visionary leadership, the YMCA of Middle Tennessee continued to have an extraordinarily strong board. Senator Douglas Henry Jr., the last year's winner, and Bill Wilson, the 1989 winner, presented the Order of the Red Triangle to Jimmy Webb III. During Jimmy's seventeen years of providing leadership on the board, he had served as secretary, vice-chair, chair-elect and chair as well as chairing the "We Build People" drives in 1992 and 1993.

On May 21, the Bowling Green, KY. YMCA board of directors voted to dissolve their YMCA and return the charter to the YMCA of the USA. This ended the idea, proposed in 2000, that the YMCA of Middle Tennessee take over the Kentucky organization that had constantly struggled for financial support.[1363]

By the latter part of May, Mark Weller and his team at Camp Widjiwagan had completed hiring the summer staff of 44 counselors, 12 lifeguards, 9 ropes instructors, 5 wranglers, and 5 support staff. Group sales were far ahead of 2002 and the two waterslides were ready. The U-dock with its lake swing and slide were on target for completion by the summer. In the fall, construction would begin on the amphitheater.

Membership was also healthy. The YMCA of Middle Tennessee had, at the end of April, 48,689 total units with new unity sales at 8,535, 15 percent over the 2003 goal.[1364]

In June, David Byrd introduced Don Jones, the Y's new senior vice president of property management. Don came from the YMCA of Greater Richmond, where he had responsibility for both operations and facilities. His addition would complete Journey's senior management team, the other members being David Byrd and Peter Oldham.

The North Rutherford YMCA moved a step closer to reality when the executive committee voted to commit $1.5 million of reserve funds to the North Rutherford project. It was hoped that the Smyrna and LaVergne communities would contribute $3 million. At the time, they had given $860,000. The City of Smyrna had leased 10.86 acres of land at $1 a year for 50 years, contingent on the Y breaking ground by December 4, 2003. So, the pressure was on.

Peter Oldham reported that the plaintiffs in the tax-exemption case before the State Board of Equalization had filed an appeal on the last possible day to do so. Peter said that the Y would file its answer immediately but that the trial would likely be from 8 to 12 months away in the court of Chancellor Irvin Kilcrease, a 1966 YMCA Night Law School graduate. Ron Knox reported that the 2006 national meeting of the YMCA of the USA would be held at the Opryland Hotel with more than 5,000 expected.[1365]

Frank Drowota, resident camp task force chair, announced the results of the market study for the resident camp in June. It showed there was a high demand for an overnight component at Camp Widjiwagan. The survey found that 84 percent of the 500 general public respondents would be very interested in sending their children to a one-week camp. Over half of the general population respondents would be more likely to be interested in the new camp if they knew it was developed and managed by the YMCA. The next step, Frank Drowota said at the June board meeting, was for his committee to present a business plan and vision for the camp by November 20.[1366]

Focusing on the Future

Jim Finchum, on board since February as executive director of Y-CAP, reported on the program's focuses. They were 1) to strengthen the juvenile justice program, that already included programs six days a week; 2) to strengthen the board; 3) to offer, in addition to those at the juvenile justice center, preventative programs for youth through the summer and on weekends; and 4) to seek more grant funding.

The Y-CAP Academy, which had been in operation for two years, was returned to the Metro School System as the school system decided not to contract out those services for the 2003–2004 school year. The Group Home was still functional with Anne Ragsdale leading a committee dealing with issues related to its operation.[1367]

The "We Build People" campaign ended up being successful. Campaign chair Sam Bartholomew announced on June 26, that it had exceeded its $3,343,000 goal by $39,053.

Progress on the Bellevue project was particularly encouraging. Secured funding of $7,525,000 had materialized even though a capital steering committee was just then being formed. The Springfield Family Center got a boost when the HCA Foundation announced it would give $100,000 toward the wetland project that would include trails and an observation landing.[1368]

The YMCA received another boost in June when two $100,000 gifts came in for the North Rutherford YMCA. Journey Johnson announced this at the June board meeting. He also said that Boot Camp would have 150 kids in its summer sessions, and that, if funding could be secured, he hoped to expand that to a year-round program. Journey also said that, since grant funding for a statewide Y-CAP program had ended, J. Lawrence would return to lead the Association's Urban Services efforts.[1369]

Because of the rapidly growing number of Spanish-speaking people moving to Nashville, the YMCA responded by starting a Hispanic Achievers program in partnership with Habitat for Humanity and with many other local organizations assisting in providing housing, English classes, mental health services, and other programs to the economically-challenged Hispanic community clustered largely in the Nolensville and Murfreesboro Road areas. The Hispanic Achievers committee had eleven members in July 2003.

Turn No Camper Away

Enrollment at Camp Widjiwagan stood at 2,532 on July 22, compared with 1,934 in 2002 and 2,161 in 2001. Over $126,000 had been given away for financial assistance, insuring that no camper was turned away because of financial need. The children enjoyed for the first time an expanded dock, a giant lake swing, and two 150' "Wet

Willie" waterslides. While the kids were having fun, the camp's long-range planning committee visited nine camps in five states earlier in the summer. In total there would be four trips to camps in thirteen states. Dr. Thomas Frist Jr. and his son, Billy, were pilots for two of those trips.[1370]

Youth development programs active in 2003 were the Time to Rise program; the bridge program, that saw college students teaching more than 120 middle school children; and the eleventh annual Urban Services School of Academics and Athletics (USSAA) boot camp, where 150 young people maximized their leadership and athletic skills at the Army National Guard Base in Smyrna. This was a YMCA program that board member Shag Polk took enormous interest in.[1371]

At a YMCA board meeting at Camp Widjiwagan, Journey Johnson, David Byrd and board member Marty Dickens, all active Christians, brainstormed about the idea of starting a new committee to promote Christian values in all the YMCA centers. The Richmond YMCA had such a committee and Journey wanted to bring the idea to Nashville. The session led directly to the establishment in 2003 of the Christian emphasis committee that Dickens, then President and CEO of Bell South Tennessee, would chair until 2009. Dickens hosted the committee regularly for breakfast at the Bell South Tower. David Byrd, Sam Bartholomew, Bill Lee, and Jimmy Pickel were among the committee members who came from all the centers. The Christian emphasis committee worked hard to insure that all YMCA of Middle Tennessee members knew that the YMCA was a Christian organization that welcomed everyone. Because the "C" in the letters "YMCA" was taken so seriously by the YMCA of Middle Tennessee, it was well-known as one the country's leading YMCAs with a Christian emphasis.[1372] Later, Journey would invite Larry Yarbrough to become chaplain of the YMCA of Middle Tennessee. Having a chaplain was another idea Journey brought from Richmond.[1373]

The 2003 staff satisfaction survey had a response rate of 29 percent, consistent with the national average. Overall, 93 percent of 747 responders were either satisfied or very satisfied with their jobs. This compared extremely well with the national average of 85 percent.

The Green Hills Family YMCA, producing surpluses between $750,000 and $800,000 annually, had been the "cash cow" of the Association for a long time, by funneling money to the inner city mission work. Because of a serious parking problem and overcrowding, the Green Hills board proposed spending $750,000 to add 90 additional parking spaces, "building out two floors of the facility where the tennis courts were" and adding 7,000 square feet to the wellness center ($1.25 million). Funding for the wellness area would come from surpluses over the next seven years, and the parking lot expense would come from major maintenance. With the blessing of the finance committee, the executive committee approved the expenditure of the $2 million.

David Byrd reported on the IHA agreement with St. Thomas Hospital. He said the program, started in 2001 through the vision of Dr. Roy Elam and others, was having financial difficulty. Only one institute had been built (at Maryland Farms) while three others had been on hold because of financial instability. While the vision was "right on," the Y could not get the business plan to work. There were, David continued, discussions taking place with St. Thomas to end the LLC. If this happened, the YMCA would lose about $900,000. David said the hope was to continue the IHA in some fashion.[1374]

In August, Neysa Taylor was named the new director of the Association's Black Achievers Program (BA). A graduate of one of the country's premier Black Achievers programs in Louisville, Neysa had been a longtime BA volunteer in Nashville.

The Sumner County Family YMCA hosted the August 28 board meeting of the YMCA of Middle Tennessee. Executive director Carole Carter spoke of a time in 1994 when a group in Gallatin and another group in Hendersonville had dreams for a YMCA in the area. That dream materialized and, in 2003, there were 175 staff members, of whom 65 worked in childcare, the YMCA's largest program. The center had 9,200 members with 1,000 visiting the facility every day. Fun Company served 950 children daily, Carole said. Lisa Beck pointed out that the Fun Company was twenty years old and had 139 sites in six counties, serving 7,000 children daily.

On September 1, 2003, the YMCA of Middle Tennessee and Saint Thomas signed a contract ending the LLC partnership but providing for Saint Thomas to operate cardio/rehab units within certain YMCAs and coordinating certain of their marketing efforts with those of the YMCA. Under the new agreement, the YMCA would continue to operate a reorganized Institute for the Healing Arts (IHA) under the banner of Total Health. The YMCA would lease the services of five Stay well nurses and half of Dr. Elam's time from St. Thomas. St. Thomas would continue paying off its $5 million pledge annually over seven years and the Y paid St. Thomas $109,000 for its 50 percent share of the LLC operating loss.[1375]

• • • • •

In September, the executive committee adopted a Diversity Commitment Statement that stated, "In member service, we need the ability to work with different cultures, age groups, all people. We must model the behavior of Jesus, treating all with respect and dignity, living out our core values of respect, responsibility, honesty and caring."

• • • • •

Journey reported at the same meeting that he, and key players, Bill DeLoache, Leilani Boulware, Chuck Elcan and Mark Weller, had met with officials from MDHA and the Corps of Engineers at which time the Corps of Engineers agreed to extend the YMCA's lease to 50 years. A Corps official said, "This project is a great example of a good collaboration." Don Jones announced that Green Hills had accepted a low bid from R. C. Matthews to begin its wellness center/parking lot expansion. It was expected to be complete by mid-February.[1376]

At the October board meeting, held at the ten-year-old Harding Place YMCA, the branch executive director Bill Powell welcomed the Metropolitan board members and spoke of his YMCA's diversified membership and unique community. Journey Johnson spoke of how much the YMCA had to be thankful for: (1) securing funding for a year-round USSAA boot camp, (2) the $1 million grant to the North Rutherford YMCA by the Christy-Houston Foundation, (3) and the $600,000 the Y would receive over three years from Cal Turner to fund the Y's Positive Beginnings program.[1377]

In November, construction began on the 750-seat amphitheater at the Joe C. Davis Outdoor Center. The doubling of the beachfront and a maintenance building would all completed by May. This work completed Phase I of the overall camp vision.[1378]

Susan Moriarty, Youth-in-Government director, spoke at the November executive committee. She reported that more than 1,500 students from across the state attended the two sessions of the Y's Model United Nations program in Nashville the previous weekend. The big news, however, was the report given by Frank Drowota, chair of the camp task force. He, Mark Weller, John Stanley of Triangle2, and Joe Hodgson, of Hogdson and Douglas, all spoke about various aspects of their recommendations. Mark said that the final plan called for a camp for boys and girls, with two-week sessions planned over an eight-week camping season. Day camp, Mark continued, would be scaled back to about 365 campers, with resident camp capacity at 286 by the end of 2011. A total of 22 cabins were envisioned and the total cost was estimated at $12,665,000. Joe Hodgson reported that the entrance to the resident camp would be past the equestrian center and that the plan would open up views of the lake. Journey Johnson said that the next steps would include sharing the business plans with key stakeholders, finalizing the site plan, getting approval of the board of Zoning Appeals, a feasibility study and campaign planning. The business plan was then unanimously approved and everyone left the meeting with a feeling of excitement.[1379]

Late in the year, detailed planning had been initiated with architects and engineers to design the new facilities in North Rutherford and at Bellevue. The schedule called for construction documents to be completed in May, groundbreaking in June, if fundraising was completed, and opening of both centers by Memorial Day 2005.

The last formal event of the year was the board meeting in December that was also the kickoff of the 2004 "We Build People" campaign. The campaign chair-elect Bob Knestrick announced that the 2003 campaign raised a record breaking $3,455,042 with 9,506 donors and 1,195 campaign volunteers. Everyone, particularly Sam Bartholomew and Jeff Parsley, were thanked and awards were given, including one for highest membership participation, won by the Maury County Family YMCA. Joyce Cook was introduced as chair of the 2004 campaign that would seek to raise $3,836,000. Treasurer Jack Elisar assured the members that the YMCA would finish the year with a surplus and asked approval of a $62.7 million budget for 2004. This would be a 3.6 percent increase in revenues. The budget was approved. Journey Johnson then gave his president's report. On behalf of everyone, Journey thanked Ron Knox for his two years of wonderful leadership and welcomed Rich Ford as chair for 2004–2005.[1380]

• • • • •

CHAPTER THIRTY-EIGHT

Vision 2020 Quiet Phase
2004–2005

NEW YEAR'S DAY 2004 was a splash as over 125 Middle Tennesseans joined in the annual New Year's Day Polar Bear jump into Percy Priest Lake at Camp Widjiwagan. The temperature was 45 degrees.

Tennessee Titans fans, even in January, were aware that Bridgestone/Firestone contributed $500 to send deserving kids to summer camp for every touchdown the Titans scored in the 2003 season. The number was 62.

The financial picture for 2003 closely resembled that for 2002. In both years, the YMCA ended the year with a surplus between $17,000 and $18,000.[1381]

There was a 12 percent increase in new membership sales in 2003. The new and extremely successful open doors income-based rate scale contributed to the increase to 18,768 in new sales. Because of dropouts, the membership gain was 582, an improvement over 2002, Financial assistance memberships comprised 25 percent of the total.[1382]

Bill DeLoache announced at the January executive committee meeting that the Y was beginning planning for a comprehensive development campaign. A task force he headed was evaluating potential major projects, the scope of the campaign, and the community interest in supporting it.

The parking deck at Green Hills was completed on February 20, on schedule and within budget. The 7,000 square foot wellness center would open by April 5. By the spring, a maintenance center, enlargement of the beachfront and a state of the art 750 seat amphitheater, all at the Joe Davis Center, would be complete. A marketing update reminded members that billboards advertising the YMCA were posted from Scottsville to Columbia. It was also announced that the YMCA Country Music Marathon and a kid's marathon would happen on April 24. Twelve thousand runners were expected for the marathon and 800 for the kid's marathon.[1383]

At the February board meeting, David Byrd introduced board member and architect David Allard who presented a master plan for a major expansion of the Downtown Center. The existing building would remain, with a parking deck built in and below the current parking area and where the McLemore Building stood. A new four-story addition with mostly glass walls would be built to the above the parking levels. The new building would include terraced lounges, racquetball courts and the gym on the street level, and a huge wellness area on the second floor. A new indoor track would encircle the wellness area on the third level while Metropolitan offices would occupy the entire fourth floor. Journey Johnson spoke of the incredibly warm welcome he received two years earlier, and commented on some of the highlights of his first two years. Ranking high on that list would be working with Frank Drowota, Leilani Boulware, and the camp task force in developing a vision for an exciting Joe C. Davis YMCA Resident Camp.[1384]

The annual Heritage Club dinner was held at the Belle Meade Country Club in November. Highlights of the evening were the presentation of the H.G. Hill Jr. Philanthropic Award to Frank Burkholder and his sister, Linda. The Burkholders generously contributed the lead gift for the expansion and renovation of the Downtown YMCA, where, for three decades or longer, Frank played handball. It was appropriate that Bill Turner, chair of the foundation, recognized George Cate Jr., Homer B. Gibbs, Roupen Gulbenk, and Sydney Keeble Jr. as the four "cornerstone" members of the YMCA Foundation of Middle Tennessee.[1385]

At the annual meeting held in April, Sandra Fulton, past recipient of the Order of the Red Triangle, presented the 2004 award to Anne Ragsdale for her many years of leadership and dedication to Y-CAP. Anne, a former president of Y-CAP, had literally kept the program alive through the creation of the Dick and Anne Ragsdale Recreation Center at Y-CAP, and their Anne and Dick Ragsdale Fund in the YMCA Foundation, the income from which was designated for Y-CAP.

On the eve of Camp Widjiwagan opening, Mark Weller felt he had the best camp waterfront anywhere. Don Jones, who had come from the Richmond YMCA in 2002, was senior vice president of property. As such, he was heavily involved in all the YMCA's expansion projects, including those at Camp Widjiwagan. Under a staff realignment, Don also assumed responsibility for risk management, which meant the YMCA was serious about taking a proactive position with regard to child molestation, drowning, and transportation accidents.

• • • • •

In 2004, the YMCA of Middle Tennessee maintained relationships with the Guangzhou, Hangzhou and Shanghai YMCAs in China; Toulouse, France; Detmold-Lippe, Germany; Bryansk, Russia; Lasaka, Zambia; and Valencia and Caracas, Venezuela YMCAs.[1386] While not as engaged with International work as during the 1980s when this was at or near the top of the association's priority list, the YMCA's International work would continue through the first decade of the 21st century as one of the top ten such programs in the country.

• • • • •

During the spring of 2004, the YMCA of Middle Tennessee and the YMCA of Putnam County reviewed the possibility of expanding the service area of the Nashville-based YMCA to include Putnam County. The conclusion was that the Putnam County YMCA needed to hire the right executive director who could implement high quality member services and programs. The Y also needed to reduce its debt, and build the addition needed for a health and wellness space. Were these criteria met, the YMCA of Middle Tennessee would be agreeable to expand its services to include the Putnam County YMCA. This had been a stressful exercise for both the Putnam County YMCA and for those from the YMCA of Middle Tennessee who had been providing management services to the Putnam County Y for two years.

The North Rutherford YMCA had raised $5.3 million by June with only $680,000 remaining. This gap disappeared when an anonymous donor agreed in June to donate $2 million to the North Rutherford YMCA if the YMCA of Middle Tennessee would agree to name it in honor of Ronald Reagan. At the June executive committee meeting, the YMCA was officially renamed North Rutherford YMCA–Ronald Reagan Family Center.

There was at the same meeting more discussion about the Putnam County YMCA. Their board chair said that it would help them in their $750,000 fundraising effort, if the YMCA of Middle Tennessee would pre-approve the merger, pending their success in their campaign. The YMCA of Middle Tennessee executive committee agreed to this under certain guidelines, including one that all pledges must be secured by September 1, 2004. At a board meeting the same morning, Leillani Boulware reported that Camp Widjiwagan had the largest enrollment ever with 2,700 campers, and that it had been rated the #1 day camp in Nashville for the sixth year in a row. Mike Blevins, program director, reported that the U.S.S.A.A. had 150 kids in its 12th year of operation. State YMCA Youth in Government director Susan Moriarty reported that Tennessee had the second largest YIG program in the country.

On July 15, Richard H. Dinkins, Chancellor of the Twentieth Judicial District, Davidson County, ruled that "the final decision and order of the Board of Equalization is affirmed in all respects and this matter is dismissed." Costs were assessed to the plaintiffs. The YMCA of Middle Tennessee would continue to be a non-profit organization in all its operations.[1387] This was a tremendous victory!

Joyce Cook, chair of the 2004 "We Build People" campaign announced in July that the drive had recorded pledges of $3,836,000 exceeding the goal of $3,380,524, and an increase of $455,523 over 2003. There were 8,982 donors, including 957 who gave $1,000 or more to qualify for the Chairman's Roundtable.[1388] By year-end, the total amount raised had topped out at $3,925,646.[1389]

On August 24, construction documents were distributed to six general contractors to provide bids on the North

Rutherford YMCA–Ronald Reagan Family Center. Groundbreaking was set for October with completion a year later. The project was designed at 35,500 square feet with a total budget of $6,400,000 excluding land cost. At Bellevue, Everton Architects was working with Turner Construction to finalize cost estimates. The project's budget was anticipated to be $9 million to construct a 50,000-square-foot facility in collaboration with Senior Citizens. When an anonymous donor bumped the amount pledged for the Bellevue Center to $7,668,050 with a $100,000 pledge, the campaign leaders realized, "This is going to happen." Over at Franklin, Paul Bianchi came on board as the new center executive, while Carole Carter was the new group vice president for Green Hills.

Camp Widjiwagan was reaccredited by the American Camping Association, missing on only one standard out of hundreds required to be an accredited camp.[1390]

Laurel Wilson was promoted to become the district executive of the Sumner County YMCA in September. This left her former position as executive director of the Maddox YMCA open. It was also announced that month that the YMCA of Middle Tennessee had won the YMCA's Beginning Diversity initiatives award from the YMCA of the USA. The YMCA of Middle Tennessee began the initiative in 2002. A diversity implementation task force had been continuously working on this important undertaking.[1391]

Journey Johnson had fabulous news at the September board meeting. He announced that the Davis Foundation had given the Y a $4.5 million challenge grant toward the resident camp, and that Frank Burkholder and his sister, Linda, had made a $5 million gift to the planned Downtown YMCA expansion. Frank's forty-year love affair with the YMCA led to this magnificent gift. Undergirded by the Burkholder pledge and the 1 for 1 match offered by the Davis Foundation, the comprehensive development task force adopted the following resolution at their September 21 meeting: "Resolved that the YMCA of Middle Tennessee pursue plans for a comprehensive development program with an initial goal in the range of $51 million to $58 million. This will include the YMCA's 'We Build People,' and endowment programs over a five-year period. The YMCA should commit the resources and energy needed to successfully complete the campaign to serve community needs as outlined in the Vision 2020 goals." The resolution was adopted unanimously. With its mission complete, the comprehensive development task force disbanded. Its members, Bill DeLoache, Billy

Frist, Lee Barfield, Florence Davis, Rich Ford, Jimmy Granbery, Ron Knox, Bill Turner, Cal Turner, Jimmy Webb III, and Bill Wilson had provided great vision and leadership.[1392]

More Staff Changes

More operational progress was made in October when the Tri-Star Construction began work on the North Rutherford YMCA-Ronald Reagan Family Center located on Sam Ridley Parkway in Smyrna.[1393]

With twenty-three operating units, management succession was always a challenge. In October, the YMCA of Middle Tennessee welcomed four new senior staff members—Donnie Cohen, executive director of the Maddox YMCA; Rob Gray, group vice president of the Donelson-Hermitage YMCA; Eric Nelson, group vice president of the Rutherford, North Rutherford and Harding Place YMCAs; and Suzanne Iler, planned giving officer. Donnie had been CEO of the Unicoi County YMCA. Rob was district vice president of the Louisville YMCA while Eric was district vice president of the Greenville, SC, YMCA. Suzanne was a veteran development officer, most recently with Centerstone in Nashville. All would start that fall.

Rich Ford
Board Chair
2004–2005

After thirteen fruitful years with the Clarksville YMCA, Betsy Shelton left in November. David Shipman took her place as interim director. Freda Herndon was named district executive responsible for the Robertson County and Scottsville centers. Laurel Wilson, who had been with the Maddox Y for eight years, would oversee Sumner County and Maddox as district executive. Mike Brennan was named group vice president responsible for the Downtown District and Maury County YMCAs, while Dawana Wade was selected vice president of community development.[1394]

Programming was in full swing at the Youth Development Center with a dazzling array of programs, many of which were new. They included Black Achievers, the Bridge, Boys and Club YMCA at McKissack School, Buffalo Soldiers, the Seal team, and Youth in Government.[1395]

At the October board meeting, Journey Johnson announced that Jeff Parsley had been promoted to senior vice president for financial development and that he would serve as Vision 2020 campaign director. Lee Barfield reported that the YMCA endowment had reached $4 million. He, Peter Oldham, and Suzanne Iler were working hard, as a team, to get all the board member to include the YMCA in their estate plans.[1396]

In November, construction was underway at the Robertson County YMCA where an outdoor pool bathhouse was being converted into a youth and teen space and the interior was being adapted to expand the wellness space and add a cycling room. The Donelson-Hermitage and Brentwood Ys were also renovating space for indoor cycling and wellness activities. International partnerships were active with visitors from the Jerusalem International YMCA and the Detmold-Lippe, Germany, YMCA coming in July.[1397]

Scott Reall, director of Restore ministries, spoke to the YMCA executive committee members in November. His said his program, that started in the basement of the Green Hills YMCA in 1999, had grown to 400 participants in the past year. This life-changing program was supported by the "We Build People" campaign, the support of fifteen churches, and small participant fees. Scott also mentioned that other YMCAs across the country were asking for the Christ-centered program.

At the December meeting, Jeff Parsley introduced 2005 "We Build People" vice-chair Wood Caldwell, and announced a preliminary goal of $4,090,000. Bob Knestrick was the campaign chair.[1398] The "We Build People" campaign kickoff was held at the Union Station Hotel, a new venue. The hotel's Christmas decorations provided a festive feeling among those in attendance. The first order of business was for chair Rich Ford to congratulate Joyce Cook and her team on the splendid 2004 "We Build People" campaign. In response, Joyce was proud to mention that Northwest had the highest membership participation as well as the greatest increase in the number of donors. Journey Johnson announced that the Vision 2020 Campaign co-chairs would be Lee Barfield and Bill Turner, two tried and true YMCA volunteer leaders. The Vision 2020 organizational chart included Florence Davis and Jimmy Granbery, vice chairs for the Joe C. Davis Outdoor Center; Marshall Polk and Hunter Adkins, vice chairs for Downtown; Sandra and Dick Fulton, vice chairs for Maddox Family Center; Billy Frist, vice chair for youth and development; and Ron Knox and Ridley Wills II, vice chairs for planned giving. In all, 2004 had been a great year.

YMCA *of Putnam County Achieves Its Goal*

January saw the 2005 "We Build People" campaign goal of $4,145,000 officially announced, and the arrival of B. J. Davis as associate executive director of Camp Widjiwagan. At the executive committee meeting, Olin West reported that the Y ended the year with revenues of $63,206,490, a modest surplus of $4,521, thanks to contingency funding. The Chairman's Round Table goal was also met with 1,011 members.[1399]

Anxious to help the Putnam County YMCA raise the remaining $176,000 to reach its $600,000 fundraising goal, the YMCA of Middle Tennessee sent Rob Gray and George Crook Jr., to Cookeville in January to work with that Y's campaign team. By late February, the checklist of tasks needing to be accomplished was looking better. The total documented pledges had reached $642,000, an outstanding bill was settled for a discounted amount, and the YMCA of the USA agreed to forgive a debt of $42,000 when the merger was completed. There was a growing optimism that the merger would work.[1400]

On March 17, the executive committee of the YMCA of Middle Tennessee adopted a resolution approving the plan of merger by and between the YMCA of Putnam County and the YMCA of Middle Tennessee. Under the terms of the resolution, the YMCA of Putnam County would cease to exist and the YMCA of Middle Tennessee would continue as the surviving corporation. The only remaining tasks were for the members of the two associations to vote on the merger. This was scheduled to be completed by mid-June.

The Vision 2020 campaign received its third multi-million dollar pledge in four months in February 2005 when Cal Turner made a $5 million challenge gift to the drive. A group of children from the Y preschool entered the meeting, held at Northwest, to personally thank Mr. Turner for his gift. In addition to thanking Cal, Journey Johnson called the board's attention to an article in The Tennessean on February 22 about a remarkable young man named Robert Hudson, who had lived in the YMCA group home for more than five years, and was a graduate of boot camp. A B student at Hillsboro, where he was starting point guard, Robert had just learned that he had earned an academic scholarship to attend Emory & Henry College in Virginia where he would play Division III basketball. Before the YMCA changed his life, Robert had been in considerable trouble because of poor decisions.[1401] This was one of many examples over the years of how much impact the organization had on the lives of its members.

The Vision 2002 Campaign completed its campaign cabinet with the addition of Bernard Werthan Jr. and Brenda Gilmore as vice-chairs for Northwest. Already Sam Bartholomew, Jimmy Pickel, Jimmy Webb, and Bill Wilson had been named cabinet advisory members. Rich Ford, Leilani Boulware, Bill DeLoache, and Cal Turner were also members, along with the campaign co-chairs and vice-chairs. By June, the Vision 2020 campaign, although in the silent phase, passed the $20 million mark.[1402]

In March, David Byrd shared with the executive committee the story of his visit to Jerusalem with six YMCA volunteers and five staff members. He spoke of the incredible beauty of the Jerusalem YMCA and the fact that it was the one place in the world where Jewish, Christian, and Muslim people could come together in peace. A discussion was held regarding the Bellevue YMCA. Following that, Jimmy Webb made a motion that the Y proceed. Later in the meeting, Jimmy Webb moved that the Y proceed with the Bellevue project on June 1 contingent on receiving a $750,000 challenge grant. The motion passed. Journey Johnson announced that Gary Cobbs had been selected as executive director of the North Rutherford YMCA, and that Florence and Buzz Davis had pledged a lead gift to the Vision 2020 campaign.[1403]

Rich Ford announced each center's volunteer of the year award at the annual celebration meeting on April 14 at the Gaylord Entertainment Center. Nelson Andrews presented the officers for 2004–2005. Returning to the board after an absence were Frank Drowota, Joe Kelley, Marshall "Shag" Polk, and Bernard Werthan Jr. Anne Ragsdale, immediate past recipient of the highest YMCA award, presented the Order of the Red Triangle to Florence Davis, who had played so many leadership roles over five decades.

The YMCA passed a bond resolution on May 19 authorizing the issuance of bonds, notes or other indebtedness to finance six projects in an amount not to exceed $28,200,000. The four largest of these projects were $12,500,000 for the Downtown expansion, $7,500,000 for the Bellevue YMCA facility, $3,500,000 for the north

Rutherford County facility, and $2,500,000 for the Northwest Aquatics center.

The Association welcomed Mark Dengler as vice president. He started in May and would assume responsibilities for membership, Bellevue, and North Rutherford. Mark had formerly been with the YMCA of Los Angeles. The Sumner County YMCA's 3,600 square foot youth pavilion was completed by June 1. Construction on Cookeville's new 5,000 square foot wellness center began June 15.

The May executive committee meeting brought the good news that the $750,000 challenge grant that Cal Turner had been working on for Bellevue had materialized. A more global announcement, made by John Ed Miller, was that the YMCA's General Assembly would be held at the Opryland Hotel on July 26–29, 2006.

At a special meeting of the voting members of the YMCA of Middle Tennessee on May 23, Peter Oldham announced that 215 members had voted by proxy for the merger of the YMCA of Middle Tennessee and the Putnam County YMCA. One person voted no and one other abstained. The merger had been approved, but not without a lot of hard work by the Cookeville leadership.

Soon after, the groundbreaking for the Bellevue YMCA was celebrated on June 16, 2005. Mayor Bill Purcell joined officials of the YMCA of Middle Tennessee and Senior Citizens at the site a week earlier to rejoice with co-campaign chairmen Dewey Branstetter and Jane Stranch that a center dreamed of since the mid-1980s would be a reality in July 2006.[1404]

A record number of 2,881 campers were enrolled for Camp Widjiwagan in 2005. Through proceeds from the "We Build People" campaign, 20 percent of those attending would receive financial assistance. With an overnight residence camp on the horizon, it was important to visit some of the best such camps in the country to see their facilities, their dining halls in particular. Dr. Thomas F. Frist Jr. flew Leilani Boulware, Bill DeLoache, Jimmy Granbery, Lawson Allen, Frank Drowota, Journey Johnson, Don Jones, and Mark Weller to visit such facilities in late June. On the trip to Seagull, the Triangle YMCA camp on the North Carolina coast twenty-five miles east of New Bern, the Nashville visitors were invited to join testimonial by a camp counselor, who spoke to the young campers about scars, both physical and emotional. At the end, everyone, including the visitors had a chance to speak. Dr. Frist spoke of having met Judge Drowota when they were campers at Camp Highlake. Putting his arm around Frank, Dr. Frist said that they had, ever since, been best friends. That friendship led Dr. Frist to take a great interest in Camp Widjiwagan. He flew out to the camp so regularly that Mark Weller had a sign saying "Hi Tommy" painted on the roof of a camp building. One Sunday morning, Dr. Frist flew out to the camp and landed his seaplane in the cove. As he sat in the cockpit reading the newspaper, he could hear the sounds of a Sunday morning worship service drifting across the water from the camp. He thought to himself, "This camp is doing things right," and he made sure that the HCA Foundation made a generous grant.[1405]

Dawana Wade was named executive director of the Northwest YMCA in July 2005. And Downtown, Peter Oldham and Suzanne Iler had made an astounding 320 planned giving visits during the year. Their hard work showed as that summer, the YMCA Foundation had in excess of $7 million in planned gifts.

The groundbreaking for the new wellness center at Cookeville, held July 16, was a great event with everyone there thrilled to be officially a part of the YMCA of Middle Tennessee.[1406]

Other programs were also hitting the mark. Urban Services' Y Build Program was a year old in July. This unique program, based at the old Tennessee Preparatory School, was a 12-month program to provide training in construction skills to young men between 18 and 24. J. Lawrence and Eddie Phillips, former president of Beazer Homes, dreamed up the idea. Eric Evans, campus life director, said that in twelve months, 12 young men had been placed in full-time jobs with various companies in Nashville.[1407]

The Bridgestone Firestone Trust Fund was now donating $750 to Camp Widjiwagan every time a Tennessee Titan scored a touchdown. Since 1999, the trust fund had donated $108,500 to Camp Widjiwagan and a total of $279,500 to the YMCA of Middle Tennessee.

In August, the resident camp building committee selected Hastings Architecture Associates as the lead architect to design the new facilities. Other partners would include Hodgson & Douglas, Littlejohn Engineering, and Schmidt-Copeland. Other good camp news was that Phil and Pam Pfeffer made the lead gift for the future sailing marina.[1408]

In October, the YMCA of Middle Tennessee welcomed

two new center executives—Todd Ramsey at Putnam County and Rick Canada at Rutherford County. The Y also welcomed Mark Dengler, the new vice president for special initiatives.[1409]

Board chair Betsy Waldron welcomed everyone who attended the opening of the North Rutherford–Ronald Reagan Family Center on November 3. The ribbon cutting ceremony for the North Rutherford–Ronald Reagan Family Center took place on the 14th. This was a dream come true for many, including center executive Gary Cobbs and development director, Jan Berry.[1410]

There was also excitement at Cookeville. The Putnam County YMCA's new wellness center was completed six weeks ahead of schedule, opening on November 12. Nailing down the complicated details of the financial arrangement between the YMCA of Middle Tennessee and Senior Citizens (SCI) was taking a lot of time, particularly for David Byrd and Peter Oldham. They had no model to follow. The concept was for SCI to pay the YMCA $2 million up front and, in turn, receive the right to use the facility for 12.5 years. During the 12.5-year period, the YMCA would receive all revenues and, with certain exceptions, would incur all expenses.[1411]

The "We Build People" campaign surpassed its goal in mid-November. As of December 15, there were commitments of $4,164,410. The total 2006 budget was set at $71,168,902, with a $1 million contingency, an 8.2 percent increase over the projected 2005 annual budget. The three new facilities—North Rutherford, Putnam, and Bellevue accounted for $2,934,000 of the anticipated increase in revenue.[1412]

In his last executive committee meeting as board chair, Rich Ford introduced 2006 "We Build People" chair Wood Caldwell and vice-chair Jim Shaub. Wood announced that the goal would be $4,488,500. Rich also thanks everyone who reached out to him during his two years as chair, and especially thanked Ron Knox. Journey, in turn, thanked Rich for his leadership and for having given so much of himself to the Y.[1413]

Ron and Journey had much to celebrate, including the fact that the YMCA of Middle Tennessee reached out to 200,873 lives in 2005, 1 in 8 people in its 12-county service area through 25 centers and 343 program locations.[1414]

Maddox YMCA

TOP: Northwest YMCA MIDDLE: Oakwood Commons YMCA BOTTOM: Y-Cap YMCA

CHAPTER THIRTY-NINE

The General Assembly Comes to Town

2006–2007

LEE BARFIELD AND BILL TURNER reported in January that, although the 2020 Vision campaign would still be in its quiet phase for another year or two, firm commitments were in hand, as of December 31, 2005, of $35,548,256. What a start![1415] Bill and Lee would always keep in mind, throughout the campaign, that the YMCA's mission continued to be "a worldwide charitable fellowship united by a common loyalty to Jesus for the purpose of helping people grow in spirit, mind and body."[1416] A membership update written in January showed that the YMCA of Middle Tennessee exceeded its membership sales goal for 2005 by a whopping 29 percent. New sales for the year were 29,319 with a net of 7,187. The year-old corporate membership program also worked, bringing in 2,009 units with revenues of $694,000. The theme of the 2006 marketing program was "Begin, Become, Belong." Radio, billboards, ads, and direct mail flooded the market with this message.[1417]

• • • • •

For thirteen years, the Urban Services School of Academics and Athletics (USSAA) had targeted young men and women between 8 and 18 with athletic skills through a program that instilled in them discipline, hard work and a sense of purpose. In the spring of 2005, 100 percent of the USSAA seniors graduated from high school and were, in the 2005–2006 school year, enrolled in college.[1418]

• • • • •

In February, three hot spots for future YMCA development were at Cool Springs, Spring Hill, and Mt. Juliet. The second issue of the YMCA's new newsletter, *Y-Life*, was mailed to 30,000 subscribers.[1419]

The highlight of the February board meeting came when Vision 2020 campaign co-chair Lee Barfield invited Bernard Werthan Jr., Kevin Jones, Dawana Wade, Yolanda Darville, and Journey Johnson to the podium to congratulate them on the recent $1.5 million challenge grant from the Ingram Foundation for the Northwest YMCA. Journey then shared the news that the gift was the eleventh gift of one million or more in the Vision 2020 Campaign.[1420]

After many joint meetings, the YMCA and Senior Citizens, Inc., staffs reached an informal agreement on how to jointly operate what would be known as the Bellevue Family YMCA and J. L. Turner Center for Lifelong Learning. Under the agreement, CSI had the right to occupy their space for an initial term of 20 years, plus four options of five years each. There would be one membership with seniors taking part in SCI programs at the Bellevue facility becoming members of the YMCA at regular rates. The Bellevue Center board would be comprised of both YMCA and SCI representatives. Both parties would work on the annual "We Build People" campaign with the YMCA receiving 80 percent of the

funds and SCI keeping 20 percent. These terms and others would, it was thought, provide wins for the YMCA, SCI, and the Bellevue community.[1421]

Hastings Architecture had architectural and engineering plans for the resident camp and year-round outdoor center by March 10. The timeline called for the grand opening to be held in April 2008. All this news was challenging and exciting. Lawson Allen, Joe C. Davis board chair, made the point in March that, over the past half century, only three YMCA resident camps had been built, giving the YMCA of Middle Tennessee an opportunity to "set the bar" for the next 50 years.[1422]

With Tennessee continuing to rank near the bottom in obesity among children, the YMCA announced in March that "YMCA Healthy Kids Day" would run throughout April with activities at all centers.[1423]

At the annual meeting, which was held at the Nashville Convention Center on April 27 with Rich Ford presiding, the 2006 officers were presented, new board members elected, and those rotating off the board thanked. Volunteer of the Year awards were presented for each center and Ron Knox received the Order of the Red Triangle for 2005. After Bill Turner led the audience of more than 1,150 in a spirited rendition of "Take Me Out to the Ballgame," Journey Johnson spoke of the importance of helping kids to succeed. The meeting concluded with four-time Grammy nominee, Restless Heart, presenting two songs. Everyone was asked to join in on the second one, "Lean on Me," as it exemplified what the YMCA does for so many.

A May 2006 property update showed expansion projects underway at North Rutherford, Brentwood, and Maddox in addition to the continuing construction at the Bellevue Center. Plans were progressing on expansion projects at Downtown, Maddox, Northwest, and the Joe C. Davis Center. A record 2,925 campers had enrolled for Camp Widjiwagan, including campers from Salvation Army homeless shelter, Youth Encouragement Services, Y-CAP, Boys & Girls Club, Martha O'Bryan Center, Rape and Sexual Abuse Center, Preston Ministries, Corner Stone, Habitat for Humanity, and Renewal House. Campers from these agencies attended without charge. The YMCA had a vigorous aquatics program in 2006, operating out of 36 swimming pools spread across Middle Tennessee. Zack Tolbert, who had 18 years of aquatic experience with YMCAs in Raleigh and Atlanta, came on board in May to assume responsibility for the program.[1424]

Frank Drowota
Board Chair
2008–2009

The goal for the Bellevue capital campaign was successful reached and the grand opening was planned for August 26, and the ribbon cutting set for September 15.[1425] Although opening of the resident camp was somewhere down the road, plans were materializing. Mark Weller reported in June that each of the 14 cabins would have 1,600 square feet with back porches and 7 bunks to house 14 campers as well as an elevated counselor area to accommodate 2 counselors. Each cabin would have a restroom as well as heat and air conditioning. Frank Drowota mentioned the appropriateness of the name "Widjiwagan," an Indian word for "close lifelong friends." He also recalled that the camp visioning committee was nearly four-years old, and that its members had conducted 13 benchmarking trips to the best camps in the country. Mark Weller praised the leadership of the committee, particularly that of Judge Drowota and Florence Davis. Florence's battle cry was, "make visiting the camp a priority and bring as many friends as possible."[1426]

The long-awaited YMCA General Assembly meeting opened on July 28 at Opryland Hotel. John Ed Miller, chair of the event, was as busy as a switch engine with 5,000 delegates and myriad meetings. The theme of the meeting was "In tune together." The highlight for the YMCA of Middle Tennessee delegates and many others was the induction of Adrian Moody into the YMCA Hall of Fame. In his honor, the YMCA of the U.S.A. renamed its international endowment fund the "Adrian Moody International Endowment Fund." At a reception for Adrian Sunday evening, friends and admirers from across the county were there to honor the man who had done more for "Worldwide charitable fellowship" than anyone else.[1427]

Peter Oldham and Suzanne Iler reported in August on the progress made by the Vision 2020 planned giving campaign, co-chaired by Ron Knox and Ridley Wills II. Their report said that, since January 1, 2005, 1,232 planned giving visits had been made, that total expectancies exceeded $10 million and that audited assets and expectancies exceed $15 million. Pretty good!

On July 31, the 2006 "We Build People" campaign crossed the threshold of its goal of $4,488,500. By year-end, the total pledged hit $4,621,984, which was 103 percent of the goal. By then, the 2007 goal had been established at $4,801,000.[1428]

A New Center in Bellevue

With 4,200 full and part-time staff members, there were always changes. On August 14, Mark Dengler became the new senior vice president of people and operations, Mike Heilbronn was named vice president of operations, and Rob Gray assumed responsibility for supervising the Harding Place, Robertson County, and Scottsville YMCAs. Berry Brooks, formerly executive director of the Bridge Program, became the new executive director of the Margaret Maddox YMCA. Effective the end of September, Mark Dengler resigned to accept a position with SEER Analytical. Coming on board, on October 9, would be Rebecca Walker. Her new role would be Regional Human Resource director.[1429]

The YMCA board held its August board meeting at the beautiful, soon-to-be-opened Bellevue Center. Laurel Wilson, executive director, and Jane Stranch, Bellevue board chair, welcomed everyone. There were so many people to thank, including Jane, her brother, Dewey Branstetter, their father, Cecil Branstetter, and the Bellevue board. Jane and Dewey grew up in Bellevue watching their parents campaign for a YMCA in their community so they made sure the Y became a reality there. Lee Barfield thanked them and others, including the Joe C. Davis Foundation trustees for their $4.5 million challenge grant for the camp, and the Steve Turner Family Foundation for a wonderful lead gift of $1 million for a teen center at the Margaret Maddox Family YMCA.[1430]

At the Bellevue Family YMCA opening on September 15, chair Cal Turner and president Journey Johnson were right there, lending their support. Before arriving in Bellevue, Cal told Journey he was going down the indoor pool water slide and challenged Journey to do the same. Boxed in a corner, Journey agreed. At the appropriate time, Cal took off his shoes and went down the slide in his business suit. Journey did the same. When they were showering afterward, Cal admitted that he had worn his "expendable" suit. Journey claimed he did not have a throw away suit. The 300 people at the ceremony probably thought Mr. Turner was wearing a Brooks Brothers suit. That was not true.

Realizing that construction costs at the Joe C. Davis Outdoor center were escalating, the trustees of the Joe C. Davis Foundation increased their $4.5 million challenge grant to $5 million. The challenge deadline was just around the corner—December 31, 2006, and it was heavy on the minds of Journey Johnson and Cal Turner. Journey said, "We have 67 days to raise $4 million. On January 1, 2007 we will celebrate or cry." He wanted to build a sense of urgency and focus. Journey also announced the appointment of Remizer Seals as the YMCA's senior regional development director. Not long after, Amy Kerr was promoted to executive director for the Harding place YMCA.[1431]

At the September executive committee meeting, David Byrd itemized the expected costs associated with the new Downtown building. The total cost of the project was estimated at $18.4 million. He hoped to break ground on May 15, 2007 and estimated the project would take 16 months.

The Fun Company celebrated its 24th birthday, proud that they were at 152 locations in eight counties serving 7,500 students per day. Anyone driving to the Green Hills YMCA in October immediately realized that its entrance had been realigned to meet the new street light on Hillsboro Circle and the new street of retail shops built by the Hill Company.

Journey Johnson, president, 2002–present

As you might imagine, James W. "Jimmy" Granbery, the CEO of the Hill Company, helped get this done.

Black Achievers and Hispanic Achievers were both active in 2006. Their goals were similar—to help children in the African-American and Hispanic communities to achieve their educational goals. During Black History month in February, there would be an essay-writing contest help in connection with Vanderbilt University. With fall in the air, it was also time for the annual Model UN session for the Tennessee Youth in Government program. November would be the silver anniversary of this program.[1432]

The Vision 2020 campaign closed 2006 having crossed the $50 million milestone. The total raised as of December 14 was $51.5 million. The December board meeting was also the kickoff for the 2007 "We Build People" campaign, headed by Stewart Bronaugh.[1433] Its goal was $4,801,000. For the 12-month period ending December 30, 2006, the Y had an operating surplus of $526,100 compared to a $4,300 surplus for the previous 12 months. Jack Elisar said 2006 was definitely the best financial year the YMCA had ever had. The YMCA Foundation of Middle Tennessee gained 20 new members during 2006 and added nearly $5 million in documented planned gifts, bringing total assets plus expectances to $16.5 million.

The Association's total number of members grew from 119,651 in 2004 to 135,904 in 2005 and 150,821 in 2006. In the last named year, 20,171 members received some form of financial assistance.[1434] The best news was, thanks to the leadership of Florence Davis and James W. Granbery, the Joe C. Davis Challenge grant of $5 million was exceeded. Three major gifts were instrumental in this happening—$250,000 from the Hendrix Foundation, $250,000 from Bailey and Sue Robinson, and a $1 million grant from Dollar General. The resident camp was now certain to become a reality.[1435]

A Splendid Choice

The New Year brought Keith Coss on board as senior vice president of people and strategy. Keith had been a consultant with the Y-USA. Larry Yarbrough, D.D., also joined the staff as chaplin. Journey Johnson had approached Larry two years earlier about this possibility. Larry made the move after a long career with Lifeway. What a splendid move that turned out to be, both for the YMCA and for Larry. Michael Check was named executive director of Y-CAP YMCA, while David Stryjewski was promoted to executive director of Sumner County YMCA. Check had worked with Y-CAP ten years earlier. Meanwhile, farewells were said to David Snow, executive director of the Brentwood Family YMCA and Todd Ramsey executive director of the Putnam County YMCA. David left to accept a senior vice president position with the YMCA of Greater Houston, while Todd accepted the position of executive director of the Clinton County YMCA in Albany, KY.[1436] A month later, Journey Johnson announced that Maury County executive Chad Randall was leaving the Y as was Linda Forceno, recording secretary, who had nearly twenty years of service.[1437]

The February board meeting was held at Y-CAP YMCA. Members present were reminded that Urban Services Youth Development Center had six core programs: Seal Team, Lil' Sisters/Buffalo Soldiers, Youth-in-Government, Y-Build, Time to Rise, and The Bridge.

By March, 100 new parking spaces had been completed at the Margaret Maddox Center, and site work had begun for the new resident camp at the Joe C. Davis Outdoor Center.[1438] One of the most generous corporate sponsors of the camp was the Bridgestone Firestone Trust Fund that had worked for the six years ensuring that dozens of Middle Tennessee children were able to attend camp on financial assistance. In 2007, the trust fund donated $32,250 to allow 73 campers to experience Camp Widjiwagan at no cost.[1439] Since 1999, Bridgestone Firestone had donated $177,500 to Camp Widjiwagan and $277,500 to the YMCA of Middle Tennessee.[1440]

The 2007 annual celebration was held at the Schermerhorn Symphony Center on April 23 where Ron Knox, a past recipient of the Order of the Red Triangle presented the 2006 award to Jackie Guthrie, who first became involved with the YMCA when she was a member of Y-Teens. Over her years on the Robertson County and the YMCA of Middle Tennessee boards, Jackie was a perfect example of the "joyful giver." With the current Vision 2020 campaign total at $60,041,266, Lee Barfield and Bill Turner announced that the "quiet phase" of the campaign had ended, and that the YMCA's campaign goal was $75 million. The campaign theme would be "Every Kid Deserves a Y." Vince Gill entertained the crowd with two songs, one of which was "What You Give Away."[1441]

The May 23 update on the Downtown YMCA capital project indicated that cost estimates from Mathews Construction were $3 million over budget. This was an incentive for the staff to work even harder with David Allard, the architect, to bring the project within the $18.9 million revised budget that was approved by the executive committee. To accomplish this, the square feet in the new addition was reduced from 68,759 square feet to 66,578, and other changes made.

In February and again in April, the YMCA Foundation held luncheons for professional legal advisors in town so that they would be more attuned to YMCA programs, and more aware of its mission. All were invited to become members of the Association's professional advisory committee. Sixteen financial advisors did so.[1442]

The late Charlie Rhea was memorialized April 20 at the dedication of "Mr. Charlie's Playplace," a new $100,000 indoor playground at the Putnam County Family YMCA. Mr. Rhea had been a beloved twenty-seven-year volunteer at the Y before his death in 2006. He loved the YMCA, Putnam County, and children.[1443]

Then on May 26, the Joe C. Davis YMCA Outdoor Center celebrated its 10th anniversary and the groundbreaking for the overnight resident camp. The NewsChannel 5 helicopter landed at the camp, bringing a birthday card for Florence Davis. The event was an opportunity for Florence and Jimmy Granbery to thank all those who made this special day possible. First on the list were members of the DeLoache family and the Joe C. Davis Foundation. Charles Elliott, former president of Harvard, spoke. He said, "A few weeks spent in a well organized summer camp may be of more value educationally than a whole year of formal school work." Tom Edwards, project manager for American Constructors, said that his company was on schedule to complete the camp by May 1, 2008. Not everyone there saw Frank Drowota show off his colorful argyle socks. He did so in an effort to compete with Cal Turner, who customarily wore colorful striped socks.[1444]

The capital campaign for Downtown hit a milestone by reaching the $8 million mark in late June. This qualified the Y for a $1 million matching gift and provided momentum for reaching the $10 million goal. Frank and Linda Burkholder were recognized on the 27th by co-chairs Shag Polk and Hunter Adkins as were others who helped pave the way for what Don Jones called "a world-class project."[1445] It was announced that the new center would be named the Downtown YMCA Burkholder Center. Journey Johnson expressed his pleasure and satisfaction that the YMCA of Middle Tennessee had celebrated two major events in a span of 48 hours, and that the Downtown Center had been able to remain open during construction.

Aquatics classes were offered over the summer at 18 centers that taught 15,422 children to swim.

Out at the Joe C. Davis Center, Camp Widjiwagan classes were filled to capacity. Summer enrollment climbed to a new high of 2,941 campers.[1446]

The August meeting of the board of the YMCA of Middle Tennessee met at Northwest, where the directors were welcomed by Rita McDonald, board chair, and Dawana Wade, center executive. Brenda Gilmore and Don Jones were also on hand to talk about the Vision 2020 pool project at Northwest. Brenda said that pool construction costs had increased. She then said that the Northwest campaign goal was $3.7, with $500,000 for endowment, $500,000 for the learn-to-swim program, and $2.7 million for construction costs. Wood Caldwell reported that the roof was on one cabin at Camp Widjiwagan and work was on schedule for a May opening. Wood also said that the Downtown project was the largest one ever undertaken by the YMCA of Middle Tennessee.[1447]

And for the fourth consecutive summer, Jimmy Granbery took Campers of the Year on seaplane flights over J. Percy Priest Lake and Camp Widjiwagan. This fourth generation board member of the YMCA of Middle Tennessee and CEO of H. G. Hill Realty, loved Camp Widjiwagan, describing it as "the greatest treasure in the entire Middle Tennessee Y portfolio."[1448]

The 2007 "We Build People" campaign reached the promised land in September when it was announced that the campaign total had climbed above $5 million, easily surpassing the goal of $4,801,000. The success story was celebrated and as part of the entertainment, Cal Turner rode a tricycle accompanied by three unicyclists.[1449]

In less than a year, the artEMBRACE program grew enormously and was incorporated in programs at 57 Fun Company sites. In the fall, artEMBRACE was recognized by the YMCA of the USA and the Gibson Foundation as one of the leading arts-friendly Y programs in the country. Some of the workshops offered by artEMBRACE were Origami, introductory guitar, ballroom dance, capoeira (a type of African dance), wall mural painting, and hip-hop dance.[1450]

Feeling that it was becoming more difficult to secure land for future YMCA centers, Journey Johnson had earlier appointed a task force to (1) identify capital projects for the next ten years, (2) to secure future sites quietly and quickly, (3) to determine which projects to fast track, (4) to establish criteria for capital projects, and (5) to create a comprehensive funding model. In September, Bill DeLoache reported for the task force that contracts were being written to acquire 10 acres at $130,000 per acre in Sumner County, 10 to 12 acres in Mt. Juliet, and a lease of land in Spring Hill.

In the fall, the YMCA of Middle Tennessee opened a fitness center in a Mt. Juliet shopping center. By the following February, it had 400 members. This was the YMCA of Middle Tennessee's first presence in Wilson County since the Wilson County YMCA closed in 1982.[1451]

The October board meeting was held at the Y-CAP building at 1021 Russell Street. Y-CAP board chair, Rob Blagojevich, welcome the group and thanked Lisa Beck for bringing new life into Y-CAP with all the building improvements she had made. Lisa, vice president of school age services, reported the Y had been in the school age services business for 25 years and had grown, during that period, to 150 sites in eight counties, serving 8,000 children. Marsha Warden, Metro Nashville Public Schools board chair, and Dr. Pedro Garcia, Metro Nashville Public Schools Director, were both present and thanked the YMCA for how effectively it had partnered with the Metro Nashville Public Schools for a quarter of a century.

At the Heritage Club dinner held in November at Hillwood Country Club, the big news was that Foundation assets exceeded $6 million. Bond DeLoache received the H. G. Hill Jr. Award. The younger sister of Joe C. Davis had been instrumental in the Davis Foundation gifts that made the Joe C. Davis Regional Center one of the finest such centers in the country. That night, on the recommendation of Suzanne Iler, the Foundation board engaged the services of Thompson & Associates to assist high net worth YMCA members ascertain the most appropriate way to transfer wealth to heirs, make a difference in the community, and by-pass taxes.[1452]

By November, the site work for the new resident camp was nearly complete, and all 15 cabins were under roof. Construction of the dining lodge was underway. In addition to the major construction there and at Downtown, there were expansion projects at Bellevue, Margaret Maddox, Rutherford County, and Northwest.[1453]

And by year-end, the "We Build People" campaign had commitments totaling $5,061,691, and the Vision 2020 campaign had raised $66,939,243 of its $75 million goal.[1454]

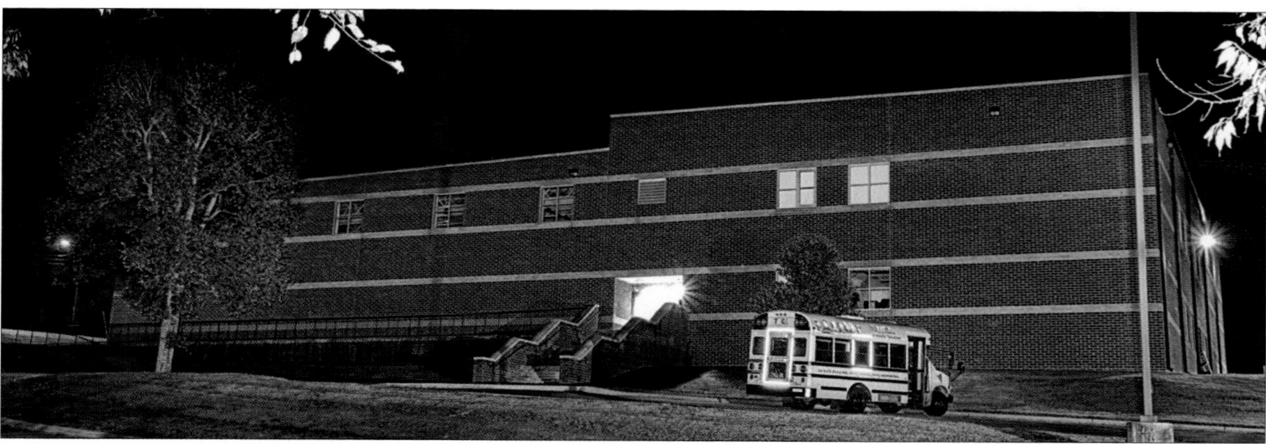

YMCA Preston Taylor Boys and Girls' Club

CHAPTER FORTY

Overnight Camp a Reality

2008–2009

IN JANUARY, there was a great deal of property activity. Bellevue opened their expanded wellness center in December and expected to open a new gym by month's end. Demolition was complete on a major renovation of the outdoor pool at Maryland Farms that would include a family play pool and water park. The YMCA, having long realized Nelson Andrews' leadership contributions, had, in 2006, established the Nelson Andrews Leadership Center. In January, design documents were being developed for the 15,000 square foot facility to be built at the Joe C. Davis YMCA Outdoor Center.[1455]

New staff members included Rebecca Walker, director of staffing and recruitment; Ken Strawbridge, new executive at Rutherford County; and John Schlansker, new executive at Clarksville. John was the son of former Nashville YMCA executive, Gary Schlansker.[1456]

After a great "We Build People" campaign in 2007, Stewart Bronaugh and George Yowell were working hard to meet the 2008 goal of $5,602,000. Meanwhile, Bill Turner and Lee Barfield announced that they intended to meet the $75 million Vision 2020 goal by year-end. Already, their campaign was at $68,675,208.[1457]

At the January executive committee meeting, Cal Turner reflected on his two years as board chair. He said that he loved the YMCA when he accepted the assignment and that, as he turned the chair's gavel over to incoming chair, Frank Drowota, he loved the Y and its mission even more. His two years had been incredible ones, a point that Judge Drowota stressed. Frank's leadership team consisted of Leilani Boulware, chair-elect; Joyce Cook, secretary; Randy Laszewski, treasurer; DeCosta Jenkins, assistant treasurer; and Cal Turner, past chair.[1458] It was an ending of an era with Jack Elisar stepping down as treasurer. Jack had first served as treasurer in 1981 and, except for six years when he was secretary, between 1986 and 1991, had efficiently performed the treasurer's duties that entire time.

One of the brightest stars in the YMCA galaxy in the winter of 2008 was Leilani Boulware, secretary of the YMCA board and past chair of the Joe C. Davis Outdoor YMCA Center. Asked why she was so involved, Leilani said, "When I think about when Christ was here on this earth, his teachings that he left us were to love each other and to help where you can. That's what the Y does in so many different ways. Being able to be a volunteer, as well as to contribute my talents in any way I can, is really quite a privilege for me."[1459]

With the assistance of the Professional Advisory Committee, the YMCA Foundation offered a wealth Management Seminar Series beginning in March 2008. Two of the seminars were "How to Make Charitable Gifts and Maintain Control," presented by James Gooch and "Financial Fitness for Women," presented by Stephanie Edwards, Carl Lovell, Gail Bradford, and Christy Cole.

Total documented planned gifts benefiting the Association plus cash contributions rose to $2,875,315 at year-end 2007. Peter Oldham and Suzanne Iler were the muscle behind this project. Helping them by making calls for deferred gifts were co-chairs Ron Knox and Ridley Wills II. During the winter and spring, Jeremy Pharr, of Thompson and Associates, spent one day a month meeting with YMCA members assisting them in estate planning. In June, he would report that, based on conversations with 7 couples, the YMCA Foundation would receive in excess of $5 million in bequests or trust over the next decade or so.[1460]

To further consolidate the YMCA's youth offerings and make them more consistent and cohesive, the Y consolidated supervision of all flagship youth programs in 2008 under Dawane Wade, senior vice president of community outreach. She began overseeing Y-CAP YMCA, the Urban Services/Youth Development center, U.S.S.A.A., the new Center for Civic Engagement (formerly the Youth in Government program), and the Center for Asset Development. The idea was to standardize, reorganize, and brand all youth development work for years to come.

"12 Days of Opportunity"

With much cold weather still ahead, all 19 buildings at the resident camp were under roof and work was underway on the camp director's home. Lawson Allen, in his third year as camp board chair, was determined to see the resident camp come to fruition. The expectation was for the camp to have a ribbon cutting on May 17. The new gym and group exercise studio at Bellevue opened on January 25 as hoped for. A child watch area was completed at the Rutherford County Y.[1461]

In 2008, the Harding Place Family YMCA was a far different place than it was when it opened 16 years earlier. Then, it served a largely middle-class white clientele. By 2008, Mexicans, Kurds, Vietnamese, Laotians, Arabs, Sudanese, and Somalis all frequented the Y. The center's 2008 membership numbered 5,500 with 51.5 percent receiving financial help. Among the members were people from 28 foreign countries. Speaking of international relationships, the YMCA of Middle Tennessee visited Caracas in February in hopes of rekindling the program that reached a zenith when Adrian Moody and a group of YMCA and Nashville leaders visited there twenty-five years earlier.[1462]

The executive committee approved in April a $2.5 million expansion at Green Hills that would add 100 more parking spaces and add 6,000 square feet of program space. The construction would be financed through debt but would be very manageable to pay, said Don Jones.[1463] The Green Hills YMCA was sort of like the old Harvey's Department Store downtown. In the 1940s and 1950s, Harvey's owner, Fred Harvey, would brag about his, saying, "Harvey's—The store that never knows completion."

The Downtown YMCA Center closed for 12 days in early April. YMCA leaders referred to this down period as "12 Days of Opportunity," because of the amazing amount of work done then with crews on the expansion working 24 hours a day. At noon on Monday April 14, YMCA officials unveiled a new sign and LED reader board that said, "We Love You Frank and Linda," and a frame depicting the new name "Burkholder Center."

Linda and Frank were grateful for the recognition but declined to have the center named for them.[1464]

Scott Reall, executive director of Restore ministries, gave an update on the ministry at the April executive committee meeting. He said that Restore had expanded to 5,000 participants and 300 sessions per month. A few weeks early, a national summit for Restore Ministries was held in Brentwood with representatives from 18 cities and 2 foreign countries. The Lord was clearly working through Scott and Restore Ministries. Larry Yarborough, YMCA chaplain, spoke next. He made the interesting observation that Nashville was hosting more National Day of Prayer events in 2008 than any city in the country. The YMCA of Middle Tennessee was clearly doing one of the best jobs in the country in uplifting the "C" in YMCA.

Finally, after years of dreaming and planning, the Camp Widjiwagan Overnight Camp became a reality on June 8 when over 100 campers signed in and made their way to their respective cabins to meet their counselors. The first camper registered was Samantha Kearns of Forrest City, Arkansas. The first meal was held in the beautiful Turner Dining Lodge named for immediate past president Cal Turner. Following dinner, the children enjoyed a theater production and an opening campfire. It had been six years of insightful planning and hard work by the task force of volunteers under Frank Drowota that made the dream a reality. The project was completed on time and within the budget, thanks to a great architect, Hastings, and builder, American Constructors. Even better, the Joe C. Davis YMCA Outdoor Center became the first camp in the South to implement, with the Tennessee Resources Agency, the Spirit of America Foundation's award-winning boating safety educational program.[1465]

Also complete were the HCA Sayahh Center, Florence Field, named for Florence Davis, the Pheffer Marinas, and an addition to the Jimmy Webb III guesthouse. Elsewhere in town, the family play pool and water park at Maryland Farms were completed in May, and construction projects were being considered at a handful of other centers.[1466]

The accidental drowning of a seven-year-old boy on June 8 in the pool at the Donelson-Hermitage family YMCA was the worst experience that David Byrd had ever experienced as a YMCA senior executive. A third party investigation determined that the child went down the water slide and was under water for no more than 62 seconds when lifeguards rescued him. Finding a pulse, a nurse performed CPR before emergency personal arrived in 5 to 7 minutes. The little boy died that afternoon in a local hospital. Journey Johnson, David Byrd, Gary Cobbs, and Chaplain Larry Yarborough attended his funeral. The YMCA paid the funeral costs and his father's travel expenses. The Y also offered counseling to the lifeguards and all others involved, including several of the deceased child's friends and his family. The situation, while tragic, was handled compassionately and skillfully by the Y,[1467] particularly by Larry Yarbrough and David Byrd, who were most involved. As a result of the loss of the child, the YMCA staff rose to the challenge of creating a safer environment for all in hopes that the Y would not experience another such loss in the future.[1468]

Kevin Watkins felt he had come full circle when he was named executive director of the Margaret Maddox YMCA in June. He had been a teenage volunteer there in 1995. By 2005, he had become senior program director. He next worked as associate director at the Green Hills YMCA before moving to Los Angeles. Three years later, he was back in Nashville where he started. Kevin shared his goal for the Maddox Y. "I'd love for us to have a significant increase in the number of members served. I'd love for this to be known as the place to go in East Nashville."[1469] Kevin sounded very much like Comer Teal did when Comer, who was executive director of the East Nashville YMCA in the 1960s, expressed similar dreams.

Residential camperships were inaugurated in 2008. The first was funded in honor of Lee Barfield. Others were established to honor Bond DeLoache and Jim Rayhab. Patrick Hale, Tommy Maddox, Bill Wilson, and Lawson Allen funded scholarships.

Some of the YMCA programs active in 2008 were YMCA MedCorps; the Bridge program; the Millennium Leadership Academy; Positive Beginnings, a three week life skills cap for boys; Smart Kids Update; Y-Build, a 12-month career development program; and Warren House where, in 2008, there were four young men in residence.[1470]

In September, it was announced that Carole Carter, Laurel Wilson, Bob Knestrick, and Gary Cobbs had all been promoted to group vice presidents, each responsible for multiple family centers. Jodi Schroer would become the new executive director of the Franklin YMCA, and Mike Heilbronn, senior vice president of operations, would have all membership centers reporting to him.[1471]

By the end of the year, the two-year-old, 8,500-square-foot storefront YMCA in Mt. Juliet, had nearly 700 households represented in its membership. The nineteen-member Mt. Juliet YMCA board was looking ahead toward having a full facility in this fast-growing city. In November, the executive committee approved a lease agreement with the City of Mt. Juliet for a full-service family center although there were still some problems that Wilson County and Mt. Juliet officials would have to work out before the dream of a facility could come true.[1472]

In December, the Association submitted a balanced budget for 2009 totaling $91,749,415—a 3.9 percent increase over the projected revenues for 2008. The budget included thirty centers. In 2008, the YMCA of Middle Tennessee ranked 7th largest in the United States in terms of revenue. Here are the top ten YMCAs in the country in that ranking. Keep in mind that the Nashville MSA population was smaller than that of any city in the top ten.

1. YMCA of Greater New York
2. YMCA of San Diego County
3. YMCA of the Greater Houston Area
4. YMCA of Metropolitan Atlanta, Inc.
5. YMCA of Metropolitan Los Angeles
6. YMCA of Metropolitan Chicago
7. YMCA of Middle Tennessee
8. YMCA of Greater Charlotte
9. YMCA of Silicon Valley
10. YMCA of San Francisco

Just as promised, the 2008 "We Build People" campaign exceeded its goal of $5,602,000. Stewart Bronaugh and George Yowell, chair and vice chair, pushed hard to make this possible. Both deserved and received a special thanks! The grand total was $5,943,000. Following the December board meeting, there was a tour of the renovated and expanded Downtown YMCA.[1473] Board members were stunned at how functional and beautiful it was. The Vision 2020 campaign also met its goal of raising $75 million by December 31, 2008. Co-chairs Lee Barfield and Bill Turner were naturally thrilled. On December 18, the figures looked like this:

Capital/current giving endowment: $40,415,212
Planned giving expectancies: $15,349,885
We Build People: $20,508,534
Total: $76,273,632[1474]

Downtown YMCA Dedicated

Frank Drowota recognized Nelson Andrews at the February executive committee meeting for having been named Nashvillian of the Year for 2008. At that meeting, he also asked everyone to keep Peter Oldham and his family in their prayers as Peter's father, Dortch Oldham, died in January. After a successful business career as president of the Southwestern Company, Dortch devoted the balance of his life giving back to his community and state in many ways. One of his major interests was the YMCA of Middle Tennessee, which he guided as president in 1983, when the Changing Lives campaign successfully concluded. A memorial resolution commemorating the life of Dortch would be passed at the August board meeting.[1475] Bill Wilson, chairman of the YMCA Foundation board also announced that the YMCA surpassed its planned giving goal of $15 million. He thanked Ron Knox and

Ridley Wills II, who co-chaired the planned giving component, for their tireless efforts to make this possible. In the successful effort they worked closely with Suzanne Iler, who also deserved much credit.[1476]

Over the winter, a task force consisting of Jack Elisar, chair; Wood Caldwell; John Eakin; Randy Laszewski; and Jim Shaub stayed busy was studying possible expansion and other Phase II Vision 2020 projects. They had eight potential new YMCAs to evaluate, including ones in Crossville and Sparta, both on the eastern fringe of the YMCA of Middle Tennessee's service area.[1477]

The 2009 annual meeting of the YMCA of Middle Tennessee on April 30 was also the celebration of the Downtown YMCA dedication. Former general executive Adrian Moody and Alan Brunson, son of former General Executive Ralph Brunson, helped place the cornerstone that was the same one that was outside the former home of the YMCA at 7th and Union. On it were the words of Ephesians 2:20, reminding us that the legacy of our YMCA was that we always considered "Jesus Christ Himself as the chief corner stone."[1478] Earlier, Rich Ford introduced the Association officers for 2009: Frank Drowota III, chair; Leilani Boulware, chair-elect; Joyce Cook, Secretary; Randy Laszewski, treasurer; DeCosta Jenkins, assistant secretary; and Cal Turner, past chair. Volunteers of the Year were recognized for their contributions and board members elected and Cal Turner received the Order of the Red Triangle Award from 1991 recipient Nelson Andrews. Bill Turner, co-chairman of the Vision 2020 Campaign, and Ron Knox then updated the crowd on the success of the success of the Vision 2020 campaign that had raised in excess of $78 million.

Staff officers of the YMCA of Middle Tennessee were elected in May. They were: Mark "Journey" Johnson, president and CEO; David Byrd, chief operating officer; Tim Weill, chief financial officer; Jeff Parsley, senior vice president development; Michael Heilbronn, senior vice president operations; Keith Cross, senior vice president strategy and people; and Don Jones, senior vice president property management. In May 2009, the YMCA also officially relocated its address from 900 Church Street to the Downtown YMCA Association office at 1000 Church Street, Nashville, TN 37203.[1479]

Nelson Andrews Dies

Only six weeks after presenting the Order of the Red Triangle to Cal Turner, Nelson Andrews died at age 82. One of Nashville's greatest civic leaders of the 20th century, he had a remarkable capacity to build consensus among people of different interests and persuasions. A renaissance man, Nelson founded Leadership Nashville, the Davidson Group, and, although he shunned alcohol, led the effort to obtain liquor by the drink in Nashville. He served for nine years as chairman of the Tennessee State Board of Education and was a mentor to many, including civic leader David K. Wilson, with whom he served on the boards of Vanderbilt University and Montgomery Bell Academy. Always willing to serve, Nelson focused on what would be best for the city and state he loved. Through many years of service as chairman of the YMCA's leadership development committee, Nelson made certain that the board of the YMCA of Middle Tennessee was always as strong as any in the city.[1480] The YMCA of Middle Tennessee wasted little time in honoring Nelson. In the summer, the Y announced that it would establish a Nelson Andrews Leadership and Interpretative Center at the Joe C. Davis YMCA Outdoor Center. There, youths and adults could grow and learn through a cadre of leadership development programs facilitated by experienced trainers.[1481] Groundbreaking for the center took place in a beautiful grove of trees on August 31, 2011, with Nelson's widow, Sue Adams Andrews, and other family members present.

Another YMCA stalwart, James M. Ward, died in 2009. After resigning as general manager of WLAC in 1978, Jim and his father, Truman Ward, developed the greater Nashville area's first successful suburban office park, Maryland Farms. Eight years earlier, in 1970, Jim became president of the Metropolitan Nashville YMCA. During his term of office, the YMCA sold its old building at 7th and Union and broke ground on a new Downtown YMCA at 1000 Church Street. Jim received the Order of the Red Triangle in 1977 and continued to serve responsibly and caringly on the YMCA board until his death at age eighty.[1482]

Journey Johnson told the board in June about two recent gifts, one of which was approximately $1.8 million worth of programs and services from Microsoft. He then updated the board on the current Vision planning process. He said that he had visited with 750–800 volunteers and staff, received 500, responses and held 26 forums. The feedback he received was that leaders were passionate about making a difference in the lives of children, making a bigger impact on health, and being a hub for the community. Mark Weller reported that overnight camp was running 5 percent ahead of 2008 and 11 percent better than the national average.[1483] By July 27, overnight camp enrollment skyrocketed to a 27 percent increase over the previous summer.

July saw the Harding Place Family YMCA help to reopen the aquatics center at Glencliff High School, which had closed earlier in the year when the school couldn't afford to continue operating it. Under the supervision of the Harding Place YMCA, the pool was again open to the public on a fee per-use basis and swim lessons and other aquatics programs were once again made available to the public. A YMCA fall soccer league was also being organized at Glencliff.[1484] At the July executive committee meeting, Journey Johnson shared the news that he had the privilege of serving on the board of the Blue Ridge Assembly, representing Tennessee.

At the August board meeting, Larry Yarborough, YMCA chaplain, explained the stained glass window above the door of the Downtown YMCA Chapel. The window was a gift of Sydney McClain, longtime YMCA volunteer and benefactor. At the center of the window is the YMCA emblem. The inner circle symbolizes completeness and unity of the total life and God. The outer circle symbolizes love without end. Both circles together represent the eternal union of all YMCA members brought together in Christian fellowship. Within the circles are the letters "Chi" and "Rho" representing Christ. The red triangle represents the trinity of God, Son and Holy Spirit combined with the reminder to grow in spirit, mind and body. The Bible opened to John 17:21 expresses the YMCA's ideal "that they may all be one." The colors are also symbolic. Purple stands for our heritage of faith. Red expresses caring, yellow stands for respect. Green represents responsibility and blue stands for honesty. The two globes stand for our worldwide fellowship in Jesus Christ.[1485]

Cal Turner Jr.
Board Chair
2006–2007

"Hope for Life"

In 2009, a YMCA Vision Council was formed to determine how the Association could best address the most critical issues facing it over the next decade. The ten-year Hope For Life plan called for the YMCA to expand partnerships and collaborations with other organizations to achieve significant, measurable results in the following areas: inspiring youth, improving health, experiencing community, and serving others.[1486]

The Dollar General Boathouse Lounge and the Turner Dining Lodge at Camp Widjiwagan were dedicated in October to the Dollar General Corporation and Cal Turner Jr., respectively, for their generous lead gifts. The lodge was both big and beautiful.[1487]

The *Tennessean* informed its readers in November of the depth of the recession the country was in. In Davidson County, the article said, "poverty rates rose from 15.2 percent of residents in 2007 to 16.9 percent last year. The same rate for children grew from 24.2 to 25.7 percent. Nationwide, poverty rose from 12.5 percent in 2007 to 13.2 percent in 2008, its highest level in more than a decade,"[1488] The YMCA, acutely aware of the steep economic downturn, announced two programs to alleviate the problems. One was the Y's Open Doors Program that helped members facing catastrophic personal crises, such as job loss, divorce, or death, keep their YMCA memberships. The YMCA saw an alarming increase in financial assistance requests with about one-third of members seeking aid. In Green Hills, Associate Executive Director Lisa Ellis said about 33 percent of her YMCA's 19,000 members had income-based memberships.[1489]

A key area of growth in this tough period was Restore Ministries, a service for members to receive individual and group counseling for issues such as depression, grief, anxiety, and self-esteem. "So many people out there are hurting right now," Ellis Fain said, "We had to open two new rooms just to handle the counseling here." Fain added that the YMCA of Middle Tennessee had 57 YMCA Restore Ministries groups operating area-wide in 2008. "So far, in 2009, there were 103 groups meeting throughout Middle Tennessee," he said.

• • • • •

Scott Reall, the founder of Restore Ministries, wrote a popular book, *Journey to Living with Courage: Freedom From Fear*, in 2008.[1490]

• • • • •

J. Lawrence retired from the YMCA of Middle Tennessee on October 30 after more than thirty years of dedicated service. J.'s ministry focused almost entirely on the helping the youth of inner city Nashville break through the cords of poverty that enveloped them. Soon after arriving in Nashville, he was walking down a street in the Preston Taylor Homes, one of the city's tough inner-city housing projects late in the day, dressed informally and wearing a beard. A young African-American girl, sitting on the stoop in front of her apartment, saw J. and thought to herself: "This is either Jesus Christ or a crazy white man." J. was neither but people began to view him as the YMCA's Jesus in tennis shoes. Not long thereafter, J., who long headed the YMCA's Urban Service YMCA, helped establish the first spring break of community service in deprived areas of the country for Vanderbilt University undergraduates. The Y held a retirement party for J. on November 30. Attended by people from all walks of life, there was, nevertheless, a common thread. J. had positively impacted the lives of every person there, young or old, black or white, rich or poor.

On that same day, Cal Turner announced at the October board meeting that the Vision Council job was complete and it was time for the board to approve the Hope For Vision plan and authorize the YMCA management team to proceed with planning and implementation of the plan. The motion was seconded and unanimously passed. Journey responded by saying that Cal had been the best possible teacher to guide the Hope for Life Vision planning process and identified the staff members responsible for implementation.[1491]

There was nothing passive about the November executive committee meeting. The board approved the expansion of the Margaret Maddox YMCA branch by utilizing capital reinvestment funds over a five-year period so that construction could begin promptly. The project would add 9,000 square feet to the existing 44,000 square foot facility. Projections were that, when the addition was complete, an additional 900 member units could be expected, and that, by 2013, the branch should stop running a deficit. Journey Johnson announced that the Y had received a $100,000 pledge from the Dan and Margaret Maddox Charitable Trust exclusively for the proposed teen center there. Hardaway Construction Co. was the contractor. Their bid for the total project was $2.5 million. In addition to the teen center, the center would have a full facelift, a fitness center, a new outdoor pool, and additional parking.[1492] The executive committee also approved the estimated $5 million expansion of the Northwest Family YMCA branch by agreeing to build the long-awaited indoor pool and an expansion of the indoor fitness center. The renovation would include staining the brick on the front and one side of the building. At the time, $2.6 million had been raised. Another $2.6 million would be funded through the capital reinvestment fund. The Northwest YMCA had an operating deficit of approximately $400,000. When the renovation and expansion was completed, the deficit was expected to grow to $760,000 but should decrease back to $350,000 by 2013.[1493]

On November 30, the Uptown YMCA closed. Its proximity to the Downtown Center, only five blocks away, was a drawback in that it attracted members who would otherwise be likely to join the greatly expanded Downtown Center that was dedicated on April 30, and that had the capacity to handle the members of both centers.[1494]

At the December 17 board meeting and 2010 "We Build People" kickoff, new board members were elected and those rotating off the board were thanked. Chair Frank Drowota then presented the slate of officers for 2010 as proposed by the leadership development committee. The new officers were Leilani Boulware, chair; Marty Dickens, chair-elect; Joyce Cook, secretary; Randy Laszewski, treasurer; and DeCosta Jenkins, assistant treasurer. George Yowell, 2009 "We Build People" chair, reported that the Y had raised $5,476,927 with the help of 9,680 contributors and 857 volunteer solicitors. Jeff Parsley announced that the "We Build People" goal for 2010 would be $5,608,000. After thanking Frank Drowota for two years of incredible volunteer leadership as chair, and thanking George Yowell, Journey Johnson called on chaplain Larry Yarborough to give a closing prayer.[1495]

The year 2009 was the 135th year of service for the YMCA of Middle Tennessee. And though it was a tough year financially for many in the community, many milestones were achieved. One of the highlights was that the Y reached 284,162 lives during the year, or 1 in every 6 people in the YMCA's twelve-county service area. This happened at 30 centers and 297 program locations. Serving people in all walks of life, the Y provided financial assistance to 28 percent of its members. The lives of 111,370 youth and teens were enriched by providing them with safe, caring places, where they could grow spiritually, mentally, and physically.

The "We Build People" annual giving campaign raised $5,462,011 thanks to the leadership of Sydney McClain and George Yowell. The greatly expanded, renovated Downtown YMCA continued the Association's storied legacy of service in the heart of Nashville. Those and so many other success stories speak to the outstanding volunteer leadership provided by Association board chair Frank Drowota III and Foundation board chair Bill Wilson. Finally, the YMCA of Middle Tennessee ended the year with a balanced budget of $88,108,339.[1496]

• • • • •

TOP: Robertson YMCA MIDDLE: Sumner YMCA BOTTOM: Rutherford YMCA

The Sky Is the Limit!
2010–2011

GOOD NEWS is always welcomed in a cold month. At the January executive committee meeting, Jeff Parsley explained that five YMCA regions had joined hands to apply for a student mentoring grant and were approved. The YMCAs were San Francisco, Oakland, Baltimore, Cincinnati, and the YMCA of Middle Tennessee. Of the total money awarded, the YMCA of Middle Tennessee would receive approximately $1 million over three years. Stephenie Smith would oversee the local mentoring program. She said that we would begin by working with current programs to identify students who most needed mentors in their lives, and that the YMCA would partner with other organizations to identify program volunteers.

The Association ended the year with an operating surplus of $19,400 compared to a $474,000 surplus for 2008. Farsheed Ferdowski was introduced at the meeting as the new chair of the people services committee and a member of the executive committee. Before adjourning, Frank Drowota passed the gavel to oncoming chair Leilani Boulware, who thanked Judge Drowota for mentoring her and for his wonderful contributions to the YMCA. Leilani, who became the fourth woman and the first person of African-American descent to serve as president, would do so with grace and intelligence.[1497] The officers who were elected to serve with Leilani during 2010 were Marty Dickens, chair-elect; Joyce Cook, secretary; Randy Laszewski, treasurer; and DeCosta Jenkins, assistant treasurer.

Mike Heilbronn introduced David Shipman, vice president of membership and program development at the February board meeting. David, who was leading the learn-to-swim efforts, reported that a pilot program for learn-to-swim began at Glencliff High School on February 8. He anticipated that the YMCA would be working with 300–400 youth in 2010–2011 and that, by the 2011–2012 school year, the Y's learn-to-swim program should be available to all first graders in the Metropolitan Nashville School System.[1498]

During the winter, the Margaret Maddox Family YMCA-East Center was extremely busy with nearly 1,800 members under 18. Unfortunately, space at the center dedicated to teen programming was limited to just one small hallway, but that was about to change. Construction on a 6,000-square-foot Teen Center began in late December, and youth could anticipate utilizing the space as early as June 2010. Maddox campaign chair Sandra Fulton said the new space designed specifically for teens would enable the Y to make a significant positive impact

in the lives of East Nashville youth. "A Teen Center will be a special place for young people to enjoy programs and facilities developed just for them in a wholesome environment." The Teen Center would be named for Sandra and Dick Fulton, long-time patrons of the East Family YMCA. As a sixteen-year-old student at East High School in the summer of 1944, Dick was employed by the YMCA to direct playground activity at East Park on Woodland Street between 6th and 7th streets. In 2011, Dick remembered nailing a cordless rim on a tree in the park to serve as a basketball goal. Sandra was chair of the Nashville YMCA in 1988–89.[1499] The new Richard and Sandra Fulton Teen and Senior Center at the Margaret Maddox Family YMCA would be dedicated on September 9, 2010, with a large crowd. How appropriate that the center was named for the Fultons, who had been so closely identified with and supportive of the Maddox YMCA for decades.[1500]

Features at the new Teen Center would include a learning lab, lounge and game room, separate rooms for studying, tutoring and classes, community space for meetings, etc., a catering kitchen and additional space for job-skills training, music and art programs, concerts, and more.[1501]

On February 26, the Bridgestone Americas Trust Fund presented the YMCA of Middle Tennessee with a check for $36,000. This was the ninth year that Bridgestone Americas and the Tennessee Titans had given generously to enable deserving children to enjoy summer camping experiences at Camp Widjiwagan.[1502]

The groundbreaking for the indoor pool and wellness expansion at Northwest was held March 23. Many people in attendance had tears in their eyes as they thought about how long they had hoped and dreamed of having such a facility.[1503]

The 2010 annual celebration meeting was held at Glencliff High School, the first time the event was ever held at a public school, where the Order of the Red Triangle was presented to the 2009 winner, Wood Caldwell for his many years of service and leadership to the YMCA of Middle Tennessee.[1504]

The record flood of May 2010 changed the Cumberland River basin landscape dramatically, damaging homes and businesses across Middle Tennessee, including the homes of many YMCA members. Nine YMCA facilities sustained damage. At the Joe C. Davis Outdoor Center, floodwaters reached 15 feet above the lake's summer pool level, washing away trails, damaging sailboats and leaving piles of driftwood along the shoreline. Hardest hit was the Green Hills Family YMCA where 18 inches of floodwater covered much of the first floor resulting in $800,000 having to be spent on flood repairs, and causing the center to be closed for three weeks. The Bellevue community was particularly hard hit and the Bellevue Family YMCA and Fifty Forward J. L. Turner closed for two days because of a flooded parking lot and power outage. Senior vice president of property Don Jones was amazed with the response of the YMCA's staff and volunteers, who worked tirelessly to keep most YMCAs open. There were many unsung heroes.[1505]

There were also a number of staff changes in May. Brian Hunter was appointed as executive director of the Cool Springs YMCA. Robin Graham, after many years of service at Cool Springs, assumed responsibility as executive director of the Maury County YMCA. Mark Thomas, formerly of the Y-CAP staff, was named executive director of a branch of the Tulsa, Oklahoma, YMCA.[1506]

The biggest loss was that of David Byrd. The YMCA of Middle Tennessee hosted a reception at the Clark Baker Lodge at Camp Widjiwagan on May 27 in honor of David who left the following week for Kansas City, MO, where he became CEO of the YMCA of Kansas City. David was in Nashville eight years as COO having been persuaded by Journey Johnson to come there from the Durham, NC, YMCA where he had been CEO. During his years in Nashville, David did a splendid job as he and Journey complemented each other's skills beautifully. While realizing the great loss David would be for the YMCA of Middle Tennessee, his Nashville friends were confident that he would also excel in Kansas City. In his remarks, David said that the Nashville YMCA was the best one he had ever seen and that its success was due to the fact that the YMCA of Middle Tennessee had traditionally been Christ-centered.

The YMCA of the USA proposed eight amendments to its constitution in March. Each YMCA in the country was asked to vote for or against the constitutional amendments proposed. The proposal that drew the most controversy was one that gave the Y-USA the right to revoke a local Y's charter in the event the local Y did not comply with the new Y branding standards. The staff of the YMCA of Middle Tennessee felt comfortable that the brand revitalization efforts, that would include calling the YMCA the "Y," would be very positive for membership growth and financial development and that the YMCA of Middle Tennessee would not lose its identity, its mission focus, or its focus on the C in YMCA. Accordingly, the YMCA of Middle Tennessee cast all its 54 votes for each of the eight matters presented on March 27.[1507]

In May 2010, the Urban Land Institute's Nashville District Council announced its architectural awards of excellence and named five winning buildings, one of which was the beautiful Downtown YMCA. Here is what the judges said about the building: "A winning display of reinvestment by a non-profit; the original and new buildings blend seamlessly; a valuable resource for the community; and the redesign is sensitive to its context/neighbors."[1508]

In June, the Y-Build program honored its fourteenth class of graduates at a ceremony. The 19 class members had just completed a nine-month career development program that the Y first launched in 2004. The program works in partnership with local contractors to provide education, support, and job skill training for young men in the inner city ages 18–24. Over the past six years, 160 men had completed the course.[1509]

June also saw the dedication of the marina at the Joe C. Davis Outdoor Center to Pam and Phil Pfeffer who had given a handsome gift to enhance water sports and promote safety at the camp. Phil had also introduced Mark Weller to Spirit of America, a fifteen-year-old organization that promoted water safety, working with organizations such as the YMCA.[1510]

With the departure of David Byrd, Journey Johnson needed to realign his leadership team. He did so in June. The new senior team consisted of Mike Heibronn, executive vice president and COO; Peter Oldham, executive vice president and CAO; Tim Weill, CFO; Suzanne Iler, senior vice president for philanthropy; Gary Cobbs, senior vice president of organizational advancement; Maria Wolfe, senior vice president for brand strategy; Rob Gray, senior vice president of facilities and new communities; Lisa Beck, senior vice president for youth development; and Keith Cross, senior vice president for leadership development.[1511]

Positive Beginnings is a camp for youth whose offenses range from theft and assault to truancy and drug possession. In June, 21 boys and 17 girls, most of whom had some gang affiliation, elected to attend the YMCA camp in lieu of spending three to six months in a juvenile detention center. Held at the Tennessee National Guard Armory in Smyrna, this camp must be the best prevention program in Nashville where gangs had, in 2010, an estimated 5,000 members.[1512]

More Changes in Store

There was an update on the Mt. Juliet YMCA at the July executive committee meeting. Staffer Rob Gray spoke of the hard work that had been expended to find a suitable site in Mt. Juliet for a full service YMCA. Wood Caldwell, a YMCA of Middle Tennessee board member followed up by saying that the search was, hopefully, nearing its conclusion as the finance committee had approved spending up to $2 million to acquire the Chandler property of 14.5 acres with the understanding that an additional fifty acres would be donated. Later in the year, an acquisition agreement for the entire 64.5 acres was

Leilani Boulware, Board Chair, 2010–11

executed. Chair Leilani Boulware reported in July on the 2010 General Assembly meeting in Salt Lake City. She said that, at the meeting, the YMCA of Middle Tennessee was mentioned several times as an example of a "cause" driven YMCA, meaning that the this YMCA takes very seriously its mission of being part of a worldwide charitable fellowship united by a common loyalty to Jesus Christ. Christian mission has long been a central focus at the YMCA of Middle Tennessee.[1513]

Don Jones planned to retire from the YMCA of Middle Tennessee in July 2011. When the president of the South Hampton Roads YMCA in Norfolk heard of his plans, he contacted Don and asked if he would delay his retirement for two years and help that YMCA with three major building projects. Don agreed to do this and would report to the South Hampton Roads YMCA on April 1, 2011. This would be the eighth anniversary of Don coming to the YMCA of Middle Tennessee from the Greater Richmond YMCA. While in Nashville, Don presided over $79 million of new construction in the form of new YMCAs or additions to existing facilities.[1514]

Fighting obesity was still a priority in the summer of 2010. In July, the YMCA of Middle Tennessee launched pilot programs for obese mothers in the East Nashville, Northwest/Bordeaux, Maury County, and Robertson County communities. The program, Journey reported, would target entire families, not just mothers.[1515]

• • • • •

The YMCA of Middle Tennessee's SMARTKids program is an after school endeavor with an emphasis on academics. The program provides tutoring, individual, and group counseling as well as a structured recreation component. The youth in this Y-CAP program excel in school. In 2010, eighty percent of the children involved maintained a 2.8 GPA or higher.[1516]

• • • • •

Suzanne Iler reported in August on the three primary philanthropic goals of the Association. They were to increase philanthropic support from 7 percent to 20 percent by 2020, to increase member donors from 7 percent to 50 percent by 2020, and to strengthen the endowment so that the foundation's assets plus documented expectancies would equal the annual operating budget by 2020. Part of the strategy, Suzanne said, would be to seek more funding from foundations and corporate sponsors.[1517]

Leigh Ann Landreth, the executive director at the Putnam County YMCA was promoted to district executive in August. Her new responsibility would be to lead the capital campaign in Mt. Juliet and build a full service YMCA there. Obee O'Bryant was moving from the Harding Place YMCA to Clarksville, where, on September 1, she would become executive director.[1518]

Americans who have traveled to the Orient usually remember encountering people of all ages performing Tai Chi exercises in public parks and elsewhere. The usual response was how strange this seemed. It was less strange in 2010 at the Bellevue YMCA where aquatic exercises moved way beyond water aerobics to include everything from Ai Chi (similar to Tai Chi in water) to hydro riding, a Latin-inspired dance routine performed in the pool. Dawn Fears, an aqua Zumba instructor with the YMCA of Middle Tennessee, spoke of the stigma with which aqua class instructors have to deal. "People think they're all for seniors or people with injuries." These people learn better if they have attended one of Dawn's aqua Zumba classes in the Bellevue YMCA pool, where students burn from 500 to 800 calories in one workout. "Because water is twelve times more resistant to motion than air, people have to work harder to move in the water and, consequently, burn more calories than when they do similar exercises on land. In addition, the cooling effects of water and the reduced impact on joints usually allow people to work out harder and longer," said Dave Horn, a personal trainer.

Vicki Carter struggled to walk when she started taking Ai Chi classes at Bellevue in 2009 as a result of the deterioration of bones in her ankle. Carter, who did Ai Chi twice a week throughout 2010, said it helped her ankle heal more quickly because the workouts allowed her to exercise her ankle without putting a lot of weight on it. Working out in water is especially beneficial to those who are obese and those with arthritis or other forms of muscle or joint pain. For those in good physical condition, "aquatic exercise is a great way to cross train," said Leah Murtagh, associate group fitness director for the YMCA of Middle Tennessee.[1519]

The search for a successor to Tim Weill, who would retire as CFO in January 2011, bore fruit in October. Journey Johnson introduced Rob Ivy at that month's board meeting. Rob's start date was November 29. He was one of ten finalists and one of 167 applicants for the position.[1520]

The highlight of the November executive committee was Bob Knestrick's announcement of the new Christ Church YMCA that opened November 1 at 15354 Old Hickory Boulevard in the Nolensville Road area. Bob introduced Dan Scott, pastor of Christ Church that served so many refugees. The Y was partnering with his church, Scott said, in managing the church's gymnasium. Knestrick, Maryland Farms YMCA Group vice president, said that the Christ Church YMCA center had sold 150 memberships in their first three weeks.

Journey Johnson spoke of the Hope for Life Vision Plan and the five-year strategic plan. His senior strategy team met at Evins Mill Retreat at month-end to fine-tune the plans. Hope For Life's vision is to inspire youth, improve health, serve others, and create a community.

Chair Leilani Boulware then surprised some by reporting that, earlier in the year, McLemore Street's name had been changed to YMCA Way, and that there would be a formal celebration of the change in February.[1521] The name change came about through the persistence of Nashville City Council member Erica Gilmore, who grew up at the Northwest Family Center when John Wright was executive director. Peter Oldham was also helpful in making the name change possible.[1522]

Just two weeks earlier, the YMCA of Middle Tennessee hosted the first Philanthropy University with 190 staff members and 50 volunteers in attendance. Jerry Panas, one of the nation's foremost fundraisers, facilitated two sessions, one of which was an interview with Cal Turner, held in the Cal Turner Lodge at the Joe C. Davis Center.[1523]

The Preston Taylor Boys & Girls Club/YMCA, started in 2002, continued to provide positive influences in 2010 to about 85 boys and girls from ages 6 to 18 primarily from lower income and single parent homes. The program, based at Pearl/Cohn School, operated from 2 to 7 p.m. weekdays with an eight-week summer program at the Preston-Taylor center. Programs offered were character & leadership development, education and career development, health and life skills, the arts and sports, and fitness and recreation. Students from Tennessee State University and Montgomery Bell Academy provided volunteers during the 2010–2011 school year.[1524]

The December board meeting on the 16th was special. For one thing, most attendees had never been to the Hilton Garden Inn Hotel, where the meeting was held. Second, chair Leilani Boulware gave a beautiful prayer to begin the meeting. Although there was business to be discussed, most of the meeting was devoted to the kickoff of the 2011 "Annual Giving Campaign." Leilani announced that this would be the new campaign name after, for so many years, calling the annual drive the "We Build People" campaign.

There were Christmas boxes with red bows on each table, which, when opened, contained streamers, hats and horns. Earlier chair George Yowell and Suzanne Iler announced that the 2010 "We Build People" campaign had surpassed its $5,608,500 goal by $3,000. That wonderful news set the stage for the next act. Shag Polk and Sydney McClain came on stage to be introduced as co-chairs of the 2011 campaign. That's when the fireworks started with a cannon inside the biggest Christmas box, that was on the stage, was tilted and began firing streamers, a number of which seemed to be aimed at Cal Turner. The noise was near deafening.

Earlier in the meeting, Cal announced that board chair Leilani Boulware, chair-elect Marty Dickens, treasurer Randy Laszewski, secetary Farsheed Ferdowski, and assistant treasurer DeCosta Jenkins would be the officers for 2011. He also thanked retiring board members, including Bernard Werthan Jr., who first came on the board in 1982, and announced the names of new board members. Journey announced that the Y had received an early Christmas present—a $1.1 million pledge from an anonymous "joyful giver" for the next expansion at Bellevue.[1525] The amazing success story of the YMCA of Middle Tennessee continues.

The New Year 2011 opened with fanfare, particularly in Bordeaux where the Northwest Family YMCA unveiled its long-awaited—and spectacular—indoor aquatics center. Kenny Alonzo, Dwana Wade, Cavondus Cross, and Henry Smith spent New Year's Day welcoming the northwest community back to their YMCA home. Project manager Don "Papa" Jones was equally happy to have completed the last project in the YMCA's Vision 2020 campaign.[1526]

Looking back, certainly Captain Matt Pilcher, a charter member and director of the YMCA of Nashville and Edgefield when it organized on May 15, 1875, would be dumfounded by the size, scope, and energy of the YMCA of Middle Tennessee if he could see it 136 years later. He would, hopefully, recognize the new logo, and would certainly appreciate the fact that YMCA he helped found was still attributing much of its strength and vitality to its mission of being a worldwide charitable fellowship united by a common loyalty to Jesus Christ for the purpose of helping persons grow in spirit, mind, and body.

The Amazing Journey Johnson

It is never easy to follow a superstar, and that is exactly what Journey Johnson did when he left his beloved Virginia to succeeded Clark D. Baker as president of the YMCA of Middle Tennessee on January 1, 2002. In his board reports for the next eight years, Journey often shared the joy he felt as the organization he is so capably leading continues to do the Lord's work.

There were many accomplishments the YMCA of Middle Tennessee had achieved since Journey arrived. Life-changing programs were implemented; record-shattering amounts of funding were raised, donated, and pledged; new Ys were opened and others renovated; and both financial and literal storms were weathered as a community. Still, the YMCA of Middle Tennessee remained, at year-end 2010, the seventh largest YMCA in the country.

When knowledgeable YMCA people across the country speak of the YMCA of Middle Tennessee, they use such phrases as "remarkable," "amazing," or "off the charts." The board and staff of this wonderful, Christ-centered YMCA look forward to upholding and even enhancing its reputation of being one of the country's finest YMCAs in the decades to come.

The amazing success story of the YMCA of Middle Tennessee continues.

James A. Rayhab of the Nashville YMCA with a group of campers

TOP and BOTTOM: Smyrna YMCA

APPENDIX I: **YMCA Presidents/Board Chairs**

1875–1877	Matt B. Pilcher
1877–1880	Mitchell L. Blanton
1880–1881	Joseph B. O'Bryan
1881–1882	John Thomas Jr.
1882	Mitchell L. Blanton
1882–1883	A. D. Wharton
1883–1886	James Bowron
1886–1896	Matt B. Pilcher
1896–1901	Henry Sperry
1901–1904	Edgar M. Foster
1904–1914	Dr. Matt G. Buckner
1915–1918	Willard O. Tirrill
1919–1921	J. P. W. Brown
1921–1933	Horace G. Hill
1934–1938	William C. "Will" Weaver
1939–1941	W. J. O'Callaghan
1942–1944	Dudley Gale
1945–1947	Edmund W. Turnley Sr.
1948–1950	Ferriss C. Bailey
1951–1953	Horace G. Hill Jr.
1954	Ennis E. Murrey
1955–1956	Stirton Oman
1957	Russell W. Brothers Sr.
1958–1959	George M. Green Jr.
1960–1961	Mark Bradford
1962	Harold U. Buchi
1963–1964	Clifford Love Jr.
1969–1970	George H. Cate Jr.
1965–1967	Horace G. Hill Jr.
1967–1969	Roupen M. Gulbenk
1969–1970	George H. Cate Jr.
1970–1971	James M. Ward
1971–1972	Robert L. Freeman
1972–1973	Thomas E. Baldridge
1973–1974	Sydney F. Keeble Jr.
1974–1975	Homer B. Gibbs Jr.
1975–1976	Charles L. Cornelius Jr.
1976–1977	Rev. Robert H. Spain
1977–1978	William I. Henderson
1978–1979	Dr. Elbert Brooks
1979–1980	Florence Davis
1980–1981	J. P. Foster
1981–1982	Robert L. Bibb Jr.
1983	Dortch Oldham
1984	Ridley Wills II
1985	Walter Knestrick
1986	William B. Wadlington, M.D.
1987	William M. Wilson

Effective September 1988, the title of "president" was changed to "board chair."

1988–1989	Sandra Fulton
1990–1991	Bill Turner
1992–1993	H. Lee Barfield II
1994–1995	Margaret Maddox
1996–1997	John Ed Miller
1998–1999	James A. Webb III
2000–2001	Doyle Rippee
2002–2003	Ron Knox
2004–2005	Rich Ford
2006–2007	Cal Turner
2008–2009	Frank Drowota
2010–2011	Leilani Boulware

APPENDIX II: **Recipients of The Order of the Red Triangle**

1964	H. G. Hill Jr.
1965	Clifford Love Jr.
1966	Edmund W. Turnley Sr.
1967	Mark Bradford Jr.
1968	Roupen M. Gulbenk
1969	Harold U. Buchi
1970	George H. Cate Jr.
1971	Russell W. Brothers Sr.
1972	James M. Hudgins, M.D.
1973	Robert L. Freeman
1974	D. H. Vardell
1975	Thomas E. Baldridge
1976	Homer B. Gibbs Jr.
1977	James M. Ward
1978	Charles L. Cornelius
1979	A. Battle Rodes, William C. "Bill" Weaver Jr.
1980	William Henderson
1981	Sydney F. Keeble Jr.
1982	J. P. Foster
1983	Ridley Wills II
1984	Walter Knestrick
1985	Dortch Oldham
1986	Jack Elisar
1987	Robert L. Bibb Jr.
1988	William B. Wadlington, M.D.
1989	William M. Wilson
1990	E. M. "Bert" Haywood
1991	Nelson Andrews
1992	Sandra Ford Fulton
1993	William E. Turner Jr.
1996	Margaret H. Maddox
1997	H. Lee Barfield

1998	John Ed Miller
1999	Rebecca Thomas
2000	Cal Turner Sr.
2001	Senator Douglas Henry Jr.
2002	James A. "Jimmy" Webb III
2003	Anne E. Ragsdale
2004	Florence Davis
2005	Ron F. Knox Jr.
2006	Jacquelyn Draughon Guthrie
2007	William R. DeLoache Jr.
2008	Cal Turner Jr.
2009	Wood S. Caldwell
2010	Brenda Gilmore

APPENDIX III: **H. G. Hill Philanthropic Award Winners**

1995	Sis and Dortch Oldham
1996	Margaret and Dan Maddox
1997	Ann and Walter Knestrick
1998	Cathy and William E. "Bill" Turner Jr.
1999	Anna and Bill Wadlington
2000	Anne and Dick Ragsdale
2001	Florence and H. Lipscomb "Buzz" Davis Jr.
2002	Honey and Joe Rogers
2003	Irene and Ridley Wills II
2004	Marshall Polk
2005	Frank and Linda Burkholder
2006	Lolly and Senator Douglas Henry Jr.
2007	Bond DeLoache
2008	Kaye and Ron Knox
2009	Mary and H. Lee Barfield II
2010	Barry and Homer Gibbs Jr.
2011	Frances Caldwell Jackson, Anne Caldwell Parsons, and Wentworth Caldwell Jr.

APPENDIX IV: **YMCA General Secretaries**

1875–1879	Frank P. Hume (recording secretary)
1879–1881	John H. Elliott
1881	Frank P. Hume
1881–1882	Raymond Rolph
1882	Frank P. Hume, C. C. Emery, and J. O. Friend Jr.
1883–1884	Wesley T. Dunley
1884–1889	Frank P. Hume
1889–1891	Charles E. Thomas
1891–1900	Edgar S. McFadden
1900	B. G. Alexander
1900–1903	Walter B. Abbott
1903–1906	Burtt S. Fenn
1906–1909	William S. Frost
1910–1919	Samuel W. McGill
1919–1921	Charles W. Bush
1921–1949	Ernest L. Spain
1949–1964	Charles M. Gray
1964–1980	Ralph Brunson
1981–1987	Adrian M. Moody
1987–2002	Clark D. Baker
2002–present	Journey Johnson

*In 1966, the title of general secretary was changed to executive director. In February 1968, the title was changed again, this time to general executive. In September 1988, the title was changed for the third time to president.

APPENDIX V: **Nashville-Grown YMCA Leaders and Their Subsequent Positions**

Baker, Clark, CEO Houston
Barcado, Jan, CEO Lexington, KY, YMCA USA Mid-size Group (Donelson)
Blackman, Tom, OD Director Lexington (East)
Byrd, David, CEO Kansas City, MO
Cleveland, Charles, CEO Naples
Criswell, George, CEO Charlotte
Daugher, Byron, CEO San Diego
Goyer, Scott, CEO Cleveland, YMCA USA National Field Consultant
Harris, Chuck, CEO South Hampton Roads
Heindrichs, Craig, OD Director Indianapolis (Donelson)
Hume, Frank P., General Secretary Montgomery, AL, YMCA
Hurst, Hugh Jr., CEO Memphis Metropolitan
Jones, Julius, CEO Pittsburg
Looby, Kim, YMCA USA Field Consultant
Looby, Tom, CEO Tampa
McGaughey, Bob, CEO Montgomery, AL
Massey, Cary, YMCA USA National Field Consultant Montgomery, AL, CEO Norfolk
Moody, Adrian, CEO South Field, CEO Miami
Morris, Jack, Wilmington, Delaware
Mossing, Mary CEO Naples, FL
Rayhab, Jim, YMCA USA Risk Consultant
Rea, Kent, YMCA USA National Field Consultant
Tarver, Steve, CEO Clearwater, FL, CEO Louisville
Schlansker, Gary, CEO Greenville, SC, CEO St. Louis
Shaddock, Dan, YMCA USA National Field Consultant
Watkins, Barry, YMCA USA National Field Consultant, CEO Florence
Wilks, Trigg, CEO Jacksonville, FL
Woods, Lloyd, CEO Chevy Chase, MD, OD Director
Yeomans, Rusty, CEO Mobile

NOTES

Chapter 1

1. Andrea Hinding, *Proud Heritage: A History in Pictures of the YMCA in the United States* (Norfolk and Virginia Beach: The Donning Company, 1988), 15.

2. *The Daily Journal 1851–1899*, YMCA of Middle Tennessee archives.

3. *Nashville Men*, Vol. 4, No. 2, October 23, 1903.

4. Ibid., "Sir George Williams," Vol. 3, No. 11, April 24, 1903.

5. *Better Nashville*, June 4, 1920.

6. "History of the YMCA," Wikipedia.

7. Hinding, *Proud Heritage*, 15–16.

8. W.W. Clayton, *History of Davidson County, Tennessee* (Philadelphia, Pa.: W. Lewis and Co., 1880), 343; "The Quarterly Report," (Cincinnati, Ohio: The Confederation of the North American YMCAs, 1856); "Sixty Years of Service," YMCA archives, Nashville; "100th Anniversary of the YMCA Founding to Be Observed Here, " *The Nashville Tennessean*, June 2, 1944.

9. *Better Nashville*, January 10, 1913.

10. Ibid., "Creed of the YMCA. Adopted 1855," June 4, 1920.

11. Bess White Cochran, *All Together: A History of the Nashville YMCA 1875–1975* (Nashville: Metropolitan Board of the YMCA), 1.

12. Frank Burns, *Phoenix Rising: The Sesquicentennial History of Cumberland University 1842–1992* (Lebanon, Tn., Cumberland University, 1992), 42.

13. "The Quarterly Reporter," National YMCA office.

14. "Anniversary Addresses," *Nashville Daily Gazette*, December 11, 1856; "The Quarterly Reporter, National YMCA office.

15. Cochran, *All Together*, 3.

16. Clayton, *History of Davidson County*, 343.

17. *Better Nashville*, January 10, 1913; typed recollections of Frank P. Hume, undated, YMCA of Middle Tennessee archives.

18. Clayton, *History of Davidson County*, 343.

19. Edward R. Crews, *The Richmond YMCA 1854–2004* (YMCA of Greater Richmond, 2004), 47.

20. "MAGGIE" *Maggie Lindsley's Journal* (privately published in Southbury, CT, 1977), 30.

21. *Better Nashville*, January 10, 1913; "Nashville YMCA Celebrates Sixtieth Anniversary," *The Nashville Tennessean and The Nashville American*, January 2, 1916. A china plate in the archives of the First Lutheran Church in Nashville is decorated with an etching of the First Lutheran Church Building on the east side of Summer Street near Union. The plate also has an inscription on the back that reads, "The local YMCA was reorganized after the war in this building in 1867."

22. Clayton, *History of Davidson County*, 343.

23. Robert Weidensall (1836–1922) was a graduate of Gettysburg College. In 1867, he established a YMCA there. He served the YMCA as national field secretary from 1868 until his retirement in 1918. Robert Weidensall Collection, Gettysburg College, 300 North Washington Street, Gettysburg, PA 17325.

24. Robert Weidensall's annual report for 1872, Kautz Family Archives, University of Minnesota Libraries.

25. Typed reminiscences of Frank P. Hume, undated, YMCA of middle Tennessee archives.

26. "F. P. Hume," *Better Nashville*, Vol. XI, No. 8, October 22, 1920.

27. Typed reminiscences of Frank P. Hume, undated, YMCA of Middle Tennessee archives.

28. Clayton, *History of Davidson County*, 343.

29. *Better Nashville*, January 10, 1913; Kautz Family YMCA Archives, University of Minnesota Libraries.

30. "Nashville YMCA Celebrates Sixtieth Anniversary," *The Nashville Tennessean* and *The Nashville American*, January 2, 1916.

31. Ibid; typed reminiscences of Frank P. Hume, YMCA of Middle Tennessee archives.

Chapter 2

32. A copy of the act of the General Assembly of the State of Tennessee passed on 3/19/1875 to provide for the organization of a YMCA and YWCA, YMCA of Middle Tennessee Archives.

33. "The Religious Awakening," *Republican Banner*, May 15, 1875.

34. Ibid., "YMCA," May 18, 1875.

35. "Ibid., "YMCA—The Meeting at the Cumberland Presbyterian Church Last Night," May 16, 1875.

36. Clayton, *History of Davidson County*, 343.

37. "YMCA—A Board of Ten Directors Elected Last Night," *Republican-Banner*, May 23, 1975.

38. *Better Nashville*, January 10, 1913; "Nashville YMCA Celebrates Sixtieth Anniversary," *The Nashville Tennessean* and *The Nashville American*, January 2, 1916.

39. Littell J. Rust, *Eighty-One Years of Service: A History of the Nashville YMCA* (Nashville: 1935), n.p.

40. "YMCA, Reports of Delegates from the International Convention Submitted,'" *Republican Banner*, June 6, 1875.

41. *Association Bulletin*, December 15, 1879, p. 3.

42. Typed reminiscences of Frank P. Hume, YMCA of Middle Tennessee archives.

43. Ibid.

44. Clayton, *History of Davidson County*, 344.

45. "The Young Men's Christian Association," *Association Bulletin*, Vol. 1, No. 6, March 1, 1880.

46. "Nashville YMCA Celebrates Sixtieth Anniversary," *The Nashville Tennessean and The Nashville American*, January 2, 1916.

47. Cochran, *All Together*, 11.

48. "Our Annual Meeting," *Association Bulletin*, Vol. 1, No. 10, May 1, 1880.

49. Ibid., "Officers of the Association," Vol. 1, No. 1, December 15, 1979; "Nashville YMCA Celebrates Sixtieth Anniversary," *The Nashville Tennessean and The Nashville American*, January 2, 1916; "F. P. Hume," *Better Nashville*, Vol. XI, No. 8, October 22, 1920.

50. "The 'Association Bulletin,'" *Association Bulletin*, Vol. 1, No. 1, December 1, 1879; Ibid., "The Association Bulletin," Vol. III, No. 1, January 1882.

51. H. W. Crew, *History of Nashville, Tenn.* (Nashville: Publishing House of the Methodist Episcopal Church, South, 1890), 161.

52. Hinding, PROUD HERITAGE, "A Period of Beginnings," 34–35.

53. "Members Parlor," *Association Bulletin*, Vol. 1, No. 4, January 15, 1880.

54. Ibid., "A Glance at the Association Work Throughout the World," Vol. 1, No. 8, April 1, 1880.

55. Ibid., "House Cleaning," Vol. 1, No. 15, July 15, 1880.

56. Ibid., "How Shall The Association Be Sustained?," Vol. 1, No. 17, August 15, and "Privileges the YMCA of Nashville Offers to Its Members This Season 1880–81," Vol. 1, No. 21, October 15, 1880.

57. Ibid., "Young Men's Meeting," Vol. II, No. 4, February 1, 1881.

58. Ibid., "Noonday Meetings," Vol. II, No. 4, February 1, 1881.

59. Ibid., Vol. II, No. 7, March 15, 1881.

60. "Officers and Committees," *The Lyceum*, Vol. 1., No.1, February 1881.

61. "Our General Secretary," *Association Bulletin*, Vol. II, No. 9, April 15, 1881.

62. Ibid., "Personal," Vol. II, No. 10, May 1, 1881.

63. Ibid., "The Annual Meeting," Vol. II, No. 10, May 1, 1881; "Officers of the Association," Vol. II, No. 15, July 15, 1881.

64. Ibid., "Our General Secretary," Vol. II, No. 21, October 15, 1881.

65. "Nashville YMCA Celebrates Sixtieth Anniversary," *The Nashville Tennessean and The Nashville American*, January 2, 1916.

66. Ibid.

67. "Chattanooga YMCA," *Association Bulletin*, Vol. III, No. 3, March 1882.

68. "The New Assistant Secretary," *Association Bulletin*, Vol. III, No. 5, May 1882.

69. Ibid., "Annual Meeting," Vol. III, No. 6,

NOTES

June 1882.

70. Ibid., "Items," Vol. III, No. 11, November 1882.

71. Ibid., "The 'Watchman,'" Vol. III, No. 7, July 1882.

72. Typed reminiscences of Frank P. Hume, YMCA of Middle Tennessee archives.

73. Rust, *History of the Nashville YMCA*.

74. "Nashville YMCA Celebrates Sixtieth Anniversary," *The Nashville Tennessean and The Nashville American*, January 2, 1916.

75. Ibid.

76. Resolution signed February 10, 1885 by James Bowran, John F. Wheless Jr., and J. B. O'Bryan, YMCA of Middle Tennessee archives; typed reminiscences of Frank P. Hume, undated, YMCA of Middle Tennessee archives.

77. "Resigned, E. S. McFadden, General Secretary YMCA," *Nashville Banner*, June 7, 1900.

78. "Nashville YMCA Celebrates Sixtieth Birthday," *The Nashville Tennessean*, January 2, 1916; program of the 1st anniversary of the opening of the new YMCA in 1912, YMCA of Middle Tennessee archives.

Chapter 3

79. Typed reminiscences of Frank P. Hume, YMCA of Middle Tennessee archives.

80. "Nashville YMCA Celebrated Sixtieth Anniversary, " *The Nashville Tennessean and The Nashville American*, January 2, 1916.

81. Ryman and others interested in building Union Gospel Tabernacle did not raise money immediately for the project as they knew the YMCA was in the midst of a campaign to raise money for their new building. Charmaine B. Gossett, ed. And comp., *Captain Tom Ryman His Life and Legacy* (Franklin, TN: Hillsboro Press, 2001), 61, 67.

82. Ibid., 76–77.

83. Typed reminiscences of Frank B. Hume, YMCA of Middle Tennessee archives.

84. *Better Nashville*, January 10, 1913; "YMCA Celebrates Sixtieth Anniversary," *The Nashville Tennessean and The Nashville American*, January 2, 1916.

85. "Eleventh Annual Meeting of the Nashville Branch," *Nashville Banner*, May 31, 1886.

86. *All Together*, 15; certified copy of Davidson County Deed, Book No. 96, page 584; "YMCA Celebrates Sixtieth Anniversary," *The Nashville Tennessean and The Nashville American*, January 2, 1916.

87. Typed reminiscences of Frank P. Hume, undated, YMCA of Middle Tennessee archives; Davidson County Deed Registered Oct. 18, 1886, book No. 96, page 584, copy in YMCA of Middle Tennessee archives.

88. Cochran, *All Together*, 16.

89. Crew, *History of Nashville, Tennessee*, 568.

90. Program, Twelfth Anniversary Meeting of the YMCA of Nashville, Tenn., Sunday, May 1, 1887, YMCA of Middle Tennessee archives.

91. "News Summary," *The Daily American*, June 24, 1887; Invitation to "Laying the Corner Stone," June 23, 1887, YMCA of Middle Tennessee archives.

92. Typed reminiscences of Frank P. Hume, undated, YMCA of Middle Tennessee archives.

93. *Better Nashville*, January 2, 1916; "YMCA Celebrates Sixtieth Anniversary," *The Nashville Tennessean and The Nashville American*, January 2, 1916.

94. "Resigned, E. S. McFadden, General Secretary YMCA," *Nashville Banner*, June 7, 1900.

95. Solon Cousins, *The Incredible YMCABIRD and Other Stories* (Old Dominion Books, 1992), 30.

96. Ridley Wills II, *The YMCA: A Brief History* (Nashville: YMCA of Nashville and Middle Tennessee, 1996), 6.

97. "YMCA Celebrates Sixtieth Anniversary," *The Nashville Tennessean and The Nashville American*, January 2, 1916.

98. Cochran, *All Together*, 17.

99. Hinding, *Proud Heritage*, 57; Cochran, *All Together*, 17–18.

100. Hinding, *Proud Heritage*, 35.

101. Crews, *The Richmond YMCA 1854–2004*, 60–61.

102. "Our Third Quarter in the New Building, YMCA, Nashville, Tenn., 1889, YMCA of Middle Tennessee archives.

103. Typed reminiscences of Frank P. Hume, undated, YMCA of Middle Tennessee archives.

104. Ibid.

105. Cochran, *All Together*, 18; *Nashville Banner*, June 7, 1900.

106. Cochran, *All Together*, 18.

107. Ibid., 19; *The Comet* [Vanderbilt], 1898.

108. W. J. Keller came to the Nashville Association from the School for Christian Workers in Springfield, MA. In October 1891. He stayed until September 1892, when he resigned to study medicine. Typed reminiscences of Frank P. Hume, undated, YMCA of Middle Tennessee archives.

109. Cochran, *All Together*, 20.

110. Ibid.

111. "What Advantage Does the Association Offer?" membership brochure undated [1893–94], YMCA of Middle Tennessee archives.

112. Cochran, *All Together*, 19.

113. Ibid.; Littell R. Rust, *Eighty-One Years of Service: A History of the Nashville YMCA*, 1935.

114. "In Ruins," *Nashville American*, October 5, 1894; Ibid., "Temple of Ruins," October 6, 1894.

115. Ibid.

116. "In Ruins," *Nashville American*, October 5, 1894.

117. Ibid.

118. "The YMCA, Meetings at the Temporary Headquarters Were Well Attended," *Nashville Banner*, October 8, 1894.

119. "The Door of Opportunity, YMCA, Don't Knock," 1909, YMCA archives.

120. "YMCA Celebrates Sixtieth Anniversary," *The Nashville Tennessean and The Nashville American*, January 2, 1916.

121. "Boys Are You In for a Good Time?" Here You Have It at the YMCA," undated [1896] Brochure, YMCA of Middle Tennessee archives.

122. Printed list of Nashville YMCA officers for 1896, YMCA of Middle Tennessee archives.

123. "Director's Meeting," *Nashville Banner*, January 8, 1898.

124. "The YMCA's Century with Youth, 1844–1944, "YMCA of Middle Tennessee Archives; Rust, *Eighty-One Years of Service: A History of the Nashville YMCA*, 1935.

125. "YMCA Notes," *Nashville Banner*, January 13, 1899; Ibid., "At the YMCA," January 25, 1899.

126. Ibid., "Resigned," June 7, 1900.

Chapter 4

127. Printed names of Directors of the Nashville YMCA, 1900, YMCA of Middle Tennessee archives.

128. "Fourth of a Series," *Nashville Banner*, March 12, 1900.

129. Ibid. "YMCA Notes," March 10, 1900.

130. Ibid. "Pleasant Evening," January 24, 1900.

131. Rau-wood Retreat Center, 8687 Old Harding Pike, Nashville, TN.

132. "YMCA Boys' Camp," *Nashville Banner*, June 19, 1900.

133. Ibid. "Resigned, E. S. McFadden, General Secretary, YMCA," June 7, 1900.

134. "Gone to Richmond," *Nashville Men*, October 17, 1901, and "Gone to Knoxville," April 10, 1902.

135. "General Secretary," *Nashville Banner*, November 17, 1900.

136. Cochran, *All Together*, 22.

137. "Eighty One Years of Service," YMCA of Middle Tennessee archives.

138. Roy M. Neel, *Dynamite! 75 Years of Vanderbilt Basketball* (Nashville: Burr-Oak Publishers), 25.

139. Cochran, *All Together*, 22.

140. "Membership Items," *Nashville Men*, May 2, 1901.

141. Ibid., "Our Mortgage," November 21, 1901; "Dormitories," January 2, 1902.

142. Ibid., "Gymnasium," July 25, 1901.

143. Ibid., "Boys' Department," February 27, 1902.

144. Ibid., "Gymnasium," October 10, and "Nashville Boys," October 24, 1901.

145. Cochran, *All Together*, 24.

146. "Physical Department Notes," *Nashville Men*, November 21, 1901.

147. 1901–1902 Physical Department Brochure, YMCA of Middle Tennessee archives.

148. "What Is It," *Nashville Men*, January 16, 1902.

149. Ibid.

150. Ibid.

151. Ibid.

152. "Sam Jones," *Nashville Men*, April 3, 1902.

153. Cochran, *All Together*, 26.

154. "A. Allen Jamison," *Nashville Men*, April 3, 1902.

155. Cliff Downey, *Tennessee Central Railway* (Lynchburg, VA: TLC Publishing, Inc., 2005), 13, 16.

156. "Boys' Camp," *Nashville Men*, Vol. 2, No. 18, May 15, 1902; Ibid., "Camp Thomas J. Felder," Vol. 2. No. 19, May 22, 1902.

157. "Home Again," *Nashville Banner*, July 11, 1902.

158. "Membership Report Nashville YMCA," *Nashville Men*, February 6, 1902.

159. Cochran, *All Together*, 24.

160. Ibid., "New Addition," October 9, and "Our New Addition," December 25, 1902.

161. Ibid.

162. "YMCA Basketball League," *Nashville Banner*, January 10, 1903.

163. "Men's Calendar," NASHVILLE MEN, February 5, 1903.

164. Ibid., "Notes," March 19, 1903.

165. "Secretary Abbott Accepts Call," *Nashville Banner*, June 26, 1903.

166. "Notes," March 19, 1903.

167. "New Secretary Of YMCA," *Nashville Banner*, September 17, 1903.

168. Ibid., "Secretaryship of Local YMCA," July 30, 1903.

169. "Walter Brooks Abbott," *Nashville Men*, Vol. 3, No. 22, August 14, 1903.

170. Ibid.

Chapter 5

171. "Walter Brooks Abbott," *Nashville Men*, August 14, 1903.

172. Ibid., "Interested Visitors," January 22, 1904.

173. Isidore Newman School history, www.newmanschool.org.

174. "YMCA Officers," *Nashville Banner*, January 27, 1904.

175. "Contest for YMCA Cup," and "Basketball at YMCA," *Nashville Banner*, January 14 and 22, 1904.

176. Ibid., "City Basketball League," Vol. 4, No. 14, January 22, 1904, and "Basketball," Vol. 4, No. 19, February 26, 1904.

177. Ibid., "Preparatory School Baseball League," Vol. 4, No. 22, March 18, 1904. The athletic carnival may have happened but it did not on April 15, 1904.

178. Ibid., "Masquerade Exhibition," Vol. 4, No. 32, May 27, 1904.

179. Ibid., "Preparatory School Basketball" Vol. 4, No. 20, March 4, 1904.

180. Ibid., "City Basketball League," Vol. 4, No. 12, January 1, 1904.

181. "At YMCA," *Nashville Banner*, February 20, 1904.

182. Ibid., "Resignation of President Foster," Vol. 4, No. 35, June 24, 1904.

183. "Tenders His Resignation," *Nashville Banner*, June 21, 1904.

184. Ridley Wills II, *Elizabeth and Matt: A Love Story* (privately published, 2007), 4–6.

185. "Physical Examinations," *Nashville Men*, Vol. 5, No. 12, December 2, 1904.

186. Ibid., "Camp Felder 1904," Vol. 4, No. 33, June 3, 1904; "YMCA Work in Tennessee," *Nashville Banner*, July 19, 1904.

187. "Vallie C. Hart, Jr.," *Nashville Men*, Vol. 5, No. 4, September 30, 1904; "YMCA Work in Tennessee," *Nashville Banner*, July 14, 1904.

188. "J. G. Hamaker," *Nashville Men*, Vol. 5, No. 1, September 9, 1904.

189. "Ibid., "The Newman Baths," Vol. 5, No. 1, September 9, 1904.

190. "Convention Hears Reports," *Nashville Banner*, October 15, 1904.

191. "Mr. James H. Anderson," *Nashville Men*, Vol. 5, No. 7, October 21, 1904.

192. Ibid.

193. Ibid., "Handball," Vol. 5, No. 17, January 13, 1905.

194. Ibid., Vol. 5, No. 8, October 28, 1904.

195. Ibid., "Night School," Vol. 5, No. 10, November 11, 1904

196. Ibid., "Basketball," Vol. 5, No. 16, December 30, 1904.

197. Ibid., "Annual Meeting."

198. Ibid. "YMCA Orchestra."

199. Ibid., "Board Meeting," Vol. 5, No. 29, April 7, 1905.

200. Ibid., "The Women Auxiliary Officers for 1906," Vol. VII, No. 5, January 19, 1906.

201. Ibid., "Physical Department Work," Vol. 5, No. 23, February 24, 1905.

202. Ibid., "Outdoor Sports," Vol. 5, No. 32, April 28, 1905.

203. Ibid., "1905 Boys' Camp June 21–30," Vol. 5, No. 38, June 9, 1905.

204. Vernon was the first county seat of Hickman County. In 1823, the courthouse moved to Centerville. Tennessee Historical Commission Historic Marker, State Highway 230, Vernon, TN.

205. "450 Railroad Men—3,000," *Nashville Men*, Vol. 5., No. 31, April 21, 1905.

206. Ibid., "The Membership Club," Vol. VII, No. 7, February 16, 1906.

207. Ibid.," Our New Constitution," Vol. 7, No. 12, March 23, 1906.

208. Ibid., "New Directors," Vol. VII, No. 12, March 23 and "New Directors," Vol. VII, No. 15, April 13, 1906.

209. Ibid., "Physical Department," Vol. VII, No. 2, January 12, 1906.

210. Ibid., "The Purpose Club," Vol. VII, No. 2, January 12, 1906.

211. Ibid., Vol. VII, No. 25, June 22, 1906; there was no notice in the *Nashville Banner* of the boys actually going to camp on July 9, 10, or 11.

212. Ibid., "Danger! Warning!" Vol. VIII., No. 2, March 2, 1907.

213. Ibid., "Vol. VIII, No. 1, February 23, 1907.

214. Ibid.

215. "State Committee of the Y.M.C.A.," *Nashville Banner*, October 12, 1906.

216. Ibid., "New General Secretary Y.M.C.A.," October 17, 1906.

217. Ibid.

Chapter 6

218. "The Door of Opportunity, YMCA, Don't Enter," 1909, YMCA of Middle Tennessee archives.

219. Cochran, *All Together*, 27; Rust, *History of the Nashville YMCA*, 1935, YMCA of Middle Tennessee archives; *Better Nashville*, January 10, 1913, and September 18, 1914.

220. "Occupying New Quarters," *Nashville Banner*, January 2, 1907.

221. The lot purchased was part of lot 124 in the original plan of Nashville.

222. Cochran, *All Together*, 29; "Last Work in the Old YMCA," *Nashville Banner*, January 1, 1907.

223. "Chattanooga Wins," *Nashville Men*, Vol. VIII, No. 13, May 18, 1907.

224. "Handsome New Home for the YWCA," *Nashville Banner*, April 5, 1907.

225. Cochran, *All Together*, 27.

NOTES

226. "The YMCA Subscription," *Nashville Banner*, April 22, 1907.

227. Ibid.

228. Report of the general secretary at the annual meeting of the Nashville YMCA, May 9, 1908. YMCA of Middle Tennessee archives.

229. "For the Boys," *Nashville Men*, Vol. VIII, No. 15, June 1, 1907; Vol. VIII, No. 16, June 8; and "Assistant Secretary Thomas Promoted," Vol. VIII, No. 17, June 15, 1907.

230. Report of the general secretary, annual meeting of the Nashville YMCA, May 9, 1908, YMCA of Middle Tennessee archives.

231. "Farewell to Mr. Hamaker," *Nashville Men*, Vol. VIII, No. 14, May 25, 1907; "Assistant Secretary Thomas Promoted," Vol. VIII, No. 17, June 15, 1907.

232. "Campaign for YMCA Funds," *Nashville Banner*, December 12, 1907.

233. Ibid., "Handsome New Home of YMHA," December 17, 1907.

234. *Nashville Men*, "Railroad Meeting, Vol. 2, No. 19, May 22, 1902; Report of the general manager at the annual meeting of the Nashville YMCA, May 9, 1909, YMCA of Middle Tennessee archives; 1909–1910 Year Book of the YMCA of North America, pp. 11, 67, YMCA of Middle Tennessee archives.

235. Report of the general secretary, annual meeting of the Nashville YMCA, May 9, 1908, YMCA of Middle Tennessee archives.

236. Mr. Frost later became the general secretary of the Huntsville, Alabama YMCA. "YMCA Celebrates Sixtieth Anniversary," *The Nashville Tennessean and The Nashville American*, January 2, 1916.

237. "YMCA Celebrates Sixtieth Anniversary," *The Nashville Tennessean and The Nashville American*, January 2, 1916.

238. Cochran, *All Together*, 32.

239. "Interesting History," *Better Nashville*, Vol. 1, No. 2, February 17, 1911.

240. Ibid.

241. Cochran, *All Together*, 29.

242. "Brownies Win From the YMHA," *Nashville Banner*, January 3, 1909; Ibid., "YMCA Wins 13–12," February 19, 1909.

243. Ibid., "City League Reorganized," February 15, 1909; Ibid., "YMCA to Play Knights of Columbus," February 23, 1909.

244. "Interesting History," *Better Nashville*, Vol. 1, No. 2, February 17, 1911.

245. Ibid., "$25,000 for New Building," March 13, 1909.

246. Cochran, *All Together*, 32.

247. "YMCA Subscription Tide at a Booming Stage," *Nashville Banner*, March 26, 1909.

248. Ibid., "Magnificent Success of YMCA Campaign," April 1, 1909.

249. Ibid.

250. "Interesting History," *Better Nashville*, Vol. 1, No. 2, February 17, 1911.

251. When Gould left the firm in 1912, the company took back its old name, Foster & Creighton Company.

252. "Many Bidders After YMCA," *Nashville Banner*, August 14, 1909.

253. Ibid., "No Contracts Were Awarded," August 17, 1909.

254. Cochran, *All Together*, 34.

255. "Interesting History," *Better Nashville*, Vol. 1, No. 2, February 17, 1911.

256. "YMCA Plans Found to Fill Requirements," *Nashville Banner*. February 19, 1910.

257. Cochran, *All Together*, 34.

258. "New YMCA Gym Almost Complete," *Nashville Banner*, January 6, 1910.

259. In 1910, as in much of the 19th century, the term "evangelical churches" still applied broadly to Protestant churches in general, as opposed to Roman Catholic. It was not until after WWII that the more modern sense of a separate "evangelical" identity began to emerge within the Protestant community, characterized by an emphasis on personal conversion and theological conservatism.

260. "Second Game in Prep Basketball League," *Nashville Banner*, February 7, 1910.

261. Ibid., "New YMCA Gym Almost Complete," January 6, 1910.

262. "Interesting History," *Better Nashville*, February 17, 1911.

263. "YMCA's Make Good Getaway," *Nashville Banner*, February 11, 1910, and "Nashville Easily Defeats YMCA," March 9, 1910.

264. Ibid., "Cornerstone," September 9, 1910.

265. The by-laws of Cumberland Lodge No. 8 F. and A.M., YMCA of Middle Tennessee archives.

266. Ibid, "Most Important Meeting Held," November 16, 1910; "Making History in Brick and Stone," December 1, 1910. The stonework was by Foster-Herbert Cut Stone Company while Fulcher Brick Company supplied the brick.

267. "William Jennings Bryan," *Better Nashville*, Vol. 1, No. 2. February 17, 1911.

268. "Original Ramblers Present an Interesting Study to Cage Fans," *Nashville Banner*, December 12, 1920.

269. Ibid.

270. Ibid., "Commodores Swamp YMCA," February 4, 1911

271. Ibid., "Tennis and Baseball," Vol. 1, No. 7, March 31, 1911.

272. "Going," *Better Nashville*, Vol. 1, No. 6, March 17, 1911.

273. Ibid. "A Boys' Camp," Vol. 1, No. 11, May 5, 1911.

274. Ibid., "A Proposed Program," Vol. 1, No. 16, June 9, 1911; "Report of Year's Work at YMCA By Secretary McGill," *Nashville Banner*, March 16, 1912.

275. "Board Meeting," *Better Nashville*, Vol. 1, No. 18, June 23, 1911.

276. E. Thomas Wood, *Profiles in Tenacity: A Century of Stories from Nashville School of Law* (Beckon Books, 2011), 11.

277. "Meeting of Directors," *Better Nashville*, Vol. 1, No. 23, September 22, 1911.

278. Ibid., "Meeting of Directors," Vol. 1, No. 26, October 13, 1911.

279. Ibid., "Meeting of Directors," Vol. 1, No. 23, September 22, 1911.

280. Ibid., "The Association Emblem," Vol. 1, No. 29, November 3, 1911.

281. Ibid., "Educational Classes," *Better Nashville*, Vol. 1, No. 33, December 1, 1911.

282. Ibid.

283. Ibid., "Association Apartment Applications," Vol. 1, No. 37, December 29, 1911.

Chapter 7

284. Waller Raymond Cooper, *Southwestern at Memphis, 1848–1948* (Richmond, VA: John Knox Press, 1949), 74; "Ten Day Opening," *Better Nashville*, Vol. 1, No. 41, January 26, 1912; "Wilson's Visits to Nashville," *Nashville Banner*, February 5, 1924.

285. "We Are In," *Better Nashville*, Vol. 1, No. 38, January 5, 1912.

286. Ibid., Vol. 1, No. 39, January 12, 1912.

287. Ibid., "January Board Meeting," Vol. 1, No. 41, January 26, 1912,

288. "New Secretary for Boys' Work," *Nashville Banner*, January 2, 1912.

289. "Campaign Started for 2,000 Members," *Nashville Men*, Vol. 1, No. 39, January 12, 1912; Ibid., "The Membership Campaign," Vol. 1, No. 41, January 26, 1912.

290. Ibid., "Membership Thermometer," Vol. 1, No. 42, February 2, 1912.

291. "Responsible Men Direct the Work," undated [1912] Nashville YMCA brochure, YMCA of Middle Tennessee archives.

292. "Basketball League Will Begin To-night," *Nashville Banner*, February 10, 1912.

293. Ibid., January 12, 1912; "Ladies' Day At YMCA," February 19, 1912.

294. Ibid., "Woodrow Wilson Guest of YMCA Today," February 24, 1912.

295. "A Statement by the Board of Directors of the Nashville Young Men's Christian Association," *Nashville Banner*, February 26, 1912.

296. Ibid., "Campaign for the Y.M.C.A.," February 26, 1912.

297. Ibid., "Banquet Was A Great Success," March 4, 1912.

298. *Better Nashville*, Vol. II, No. 40, January 10, 1913; "To Continue the Campaign," *Nashville Banner*, March 13, 1912.

299. Cochran, *All Together*, 39.

300. "Plan of Organization," *Better Nashville*, Vol. II, No. 18, June 7, 1912.

301. Ibid., "The Turkish Baths," Vol. II, No. 7, March 22, 1912.

302. Ibid., "Work for Colored Men," Vol. II, No. 12, April 26, 1912.

303. Ibid., "Join Now," Vol. II, No. 14, May 10, 1912.

304. Lois Barnes Binkley, *The Deserted Sycamore Village of Cheatham County* (privately published, 1980), 72, 188.

305. "Camp at Sycamore, June 12 to 26, on Mr. A. P. Jackson's Estate," *Better Nashville*, Vol. II, No. 17, May 31; Ibid., "Summer Camp," Vol. II, No. 18., June 7, 1912.

306. Ibid, "The Club," Vol. II, No. 11, April 19, 1912.

307. Wood, *Profiles in Tenacity: A Century of Stories from Nashville School of Law*, 5,6.

308. *Better Nashville*, October 18, 1912; "Dedication," *Nashville Banner*, October 18, 1912.

309. "Addresses Local Manufacturers," *Better Nashville*, Vol. II, No. 28, October 18, 1912; "Ladies Auxiliary of the YMCA, Vol. II, No. 32, November 15, 1912.

310. Ibid., "Notes," Vol. II, No. 35, December 6, 1912; "Commodores Leave for Kentucky Trip," *Nashville Banner*, February 17, 1913.

311. "The YMCA and the Boulevard," *Better Nashville*, Vol. II, No. 34, November 29, 1912.

312. "Opening of the Library," *Better Nashville*, Vol. II, No. 41, January 17, 1913.

313. Ibid., "Association Abandons Pool Room," Vol. II, No. 48, March 7, 1913.

314. Ibid., "Board Meeting."

315. Ibid., "The Building Fund," Vol. III, No. 37, May 16, 1913.

316. Postcard of baseball diamond in the collection of the author; "The Second Annual Boys' Summer Camp Will be held at Sycamore June 12 to 26," *Better Nashville*, June 6, 1913.

317. Ibid., "Our Creed," Vol. IV., No. 1, September 5, 1913.

318. Ibid, "The Outdoor Gymnasium," Vol. IV, No. 2, September 12, 1913.

319. Ibid., "Business Law," Vol. IV, No. 5. October 3, 1913.

320. Ibid., "Shall They Be Sued?" Vol. IV, No. 8, October 24, 1913.

321. Ibid., "Generous Directors," Vol. IV, No. 11, November 14, 1913. A. M. Shook was a bank president and coal and iron magnate. Warner was president of the Nashville Railway and Light Company, while Thompson was president of the Nashville Trust Company.

322. Ibid., "The Campaign," Vol. IV, No. 16, December 19, 1913. Sometime during the campaign, the original goal of $80,000 had been increased to $85,000.

323. Nashville YMCA Anniversary Statement, January 4, 1914, YMCA of Middle Tennessee Archives.

324. April 1914 Session minutes, Davidson County Quarterly Court.

325. *Better Nashville*, Vol. IV, No. 19, "Election of Officers," January 9, and Vol. IV, No. 22, January 30, 1914.

326. Ibid., "A Personal Letter to Every Member Important!" November 13, 1914.

327. Ibid., Vol. IV, No. 27, March 6, 1914.

328. Ibid., "Colored Men's YMCA Building," April 3, 1914.

329. Ibid., Vol. IV, No. 36, May 8, and Vol. IV, No. 42, June 19, 1914.

330. YMCA Southern Student Conference brochure, June 12–21, 1914, YMCA of Middle Tennessee archives.

331. *Better Nashville*, Vol. V, No. 5, October 2 and Vol. V, No. 9. October 30, 1914.

332. Ibid., November 13, 1914.

333. Ibid., "Mr. W. O. Tirrill," Vol. V, No. 20, January 15, 1915; "W. O. Tirrill Heads Y.M.C.A.," *Nashville Banner*, January 13, 1915.

334. "W-alkingall O-vertown Tirrill," Vol. VI, No. 18, *Better Nashville*, December 31, 1915.

335. Ibid., "What the Emblem Said to Him," Vol. V, No. 19, January 8, 1915.

336. Ibid., "Secretarial Leadership," Vol. V, No. 21, January 22, 1915.

337. Ibid., "Colored Men's Branch," Vol. V, No. 22, January 29, 1915.

Chapter 8

338. "W. O. Tirrill Heads YMCA," *Nashville Banner*, January 13, 1915.

339. Ibid.

340. Ibid., "YMCA," December 26, 1914.

341. Ibid., "The Home Games of the Ramblers," January 20, 1915; Ibid., "Commodores Are City Champions," March 4, 1915.

342. "Welcome Rotary," *Better Nashville*, Vol. V, No. 25, February 19, 1915.

343. Ibid., "The Central Committee," Vol. V, No. 23, February 5, 1915.

344. Ibid., "Major C. T. Cheek," Vol. V, No. 28, March 12, 1915.

345. Ibid., "Forty Years in the YMCA," Vol. V, No. 31, April 2, 1915.

346. Ibid., "Making History," Vol. V, No. 28, March 12, 1915.

347. Ibid., "Boys' Summer Camp—June 11–24," Vol. V, No. 39, May 28 1915.

348. Ibid., "Camp Peyton," Vol. V, No. 42, June 18, 1915.

349. Ibid., "Nashville's Hart to Work Among Boys in India," Vol. VI, No. 4, September 24, 1915.

350. Ibid, "Central 'Y' Changes," Vol. VI, No. 1, September 3, 1915.

351. Ibid., "Gymnasium Attendance," Vol. VI, No. 12, November 19, 1915.

352. Ibid., "Boys' Baseball League," Vol. VI, No. 14, December 3, 1915.

353. Ibid., "Debating Club," Vol. VI, No. 16, December 10, 1915.

354. "Nashville YMCA Celebrates Sixtieth Anniversary," *The Nashville Tennessean and The Nashville American*, January 2, 1916.

355. "Ramblers," Vol. VI, No. 19, January 7, 1916, and "Outweighed but not Outplayed," *Better Nashville*, Vol. VI, No. 27, March 3, 1916.

356. Ibid., "President Tirrill Offers $1,000 to Finish the New Hand Ball 'Gym,'" Vol. VI, No. 42, June 16, 1916.

357. Ibid., "New Men," Vol. VI, No., 22, January 28, 1916.

358. Ibid., "Nashville Junior Baseball League," Vol. VI, No. 32, April 7 and "Indoor Baseball League," Vol. VI, No. 33, April 14, "Telegraph Swimming Meet—Nashville vs. Memphis, Vol. VI, No. 36, May 5, 1916.

359. Ibid., "Report from Henry Hart," Vol. VI, No. 29, March 17, and "Nashville YMCA's Lucknow Branch," Vol. VI, No. 43, June 23, 1916.

360. Ibid., "Do Cigarettes Help?" Vol. VI, No. 37, May 12, 1916.

361. Ibid., "Boys' Summer Camp June 15–29," May 19, "Boys' Camp," Vol. VI, No. 41, June 9, and "Dance Goes to Norfolk," Vol. VII, No. 15, December 8, 1916. There is the possibility that the summer camp was not held as it was not mentioned in *Better Nashville* issues for June 16, and 23, 1916, or in the *Nashville Banner* from July 1 until July 15.

362. Ibid., "Dixie-Jackson Highway," Vol. VII, No. 5, September 29, "An Open Letter to YMCA Members," Vol. VII, No. 7, October 13, 1916.

363. Ibid., "The Negro YMCA," Vol. VII, No. 18, December 29, 1916, and "Colored YMCA Building," Vol. VII, No. 36, May 4, 1917.

364. Ibid., "YMCA Budget," Vol. VII, No. 20, January 12, 1917.

365. Ibid., "President Tirrill," Vol. VII, No. 21, January 19, 1917; Conversation, John B. Tirrill with the author, February 22, 2010.

366. "Ministerial Cooperative Board," *Better Nashville*, Vol. VII, No. 20, January 12, 1917.

367. Ibid., "A Question of Community Pride," Vol. VII, No. 26, February 23, 1917.

368. Ibid., "Ramblers Vs. Georgia," Vol. VII, No. 25, February 16, and "Rambler Basketball Team of the Nashville YMCA," Vol. VII, No.

30, March 23, 1917.

369. Ibid., "The Campaign."

370. Ibid., "The Negro YMCA," Vol. VII, No 18, December 29, 1916; "Will You Work?" Vol. VII, No. 29, March 17, 1917.

371. Ibid., "The YMCA Mobilizing," Vol. VII, No. 34, April 20, 1917; "The Secretarial Staff Responds to the Call," Vol. VII, No. 38, May 18; "$100,000,000 Nation Wide War Fund Campaign," Vol. VII, No. 42, June 15, "Our Handicap But Your Opportunity," Vol. VII, No. 43, June 22, and "Nashville YMCA Doing Its Bit," Vol. VIII, No. 1, September 7, 1917.

372. Ibid, "Big Summer Camp," Vol. VII, No. 39, May 25 and "Our Handicap But Your Opportunity," Vol. VII, No. 42, June 22, 1917. Beasley later served in France.

373. George W. Perkins, "To the Contributors of the War Work Funds of the YMCA," *Association Men*, June 1919, Vol. XLIV, No. 10.

374. "Nashville YMCA Doing Its Bit," *Better Nashville*, Vol. VIII, No. 1, September 7, 1917.

375. Ibid., "Robert S. Henry Writes About Army YMCA," Vol. VIII, No. 12, November 23, 1917.

376. Ibid., "In Nashville," Vol. VIII, No. 13, November 30 and "Tippens New Boys' Secretary," Vol. VIII, No. 15, December 14, 1917."

377. Ibid., "Nashville—A Reserve City and the Opportunity City of the South," Vol. VIII, No. 16, December 21, 1917.

378. "New Year Program By Local YMCA," *Nashville Banner*, January 2, 1918.

379. Typed list of officers, directors, advisory directors, and executive officers of the Nashville YMCA, October 15, 1918, YMCA of middle Tennessee archives.

380. "Ramblers Down Memphis Five," *Nashville Banner*, January 19, 1918.

381. "Sunday Musicale In YMCA Lobby," *Better Nashville*, Vol. VIII, No. 25, February 22, 1918.

382. Ibid., "Social Committee of YMCA Meets," Vol. VIII, No. 24, February 15, 1918.

383. Ibid., "Big Gym Show at YMCA To-night," Vol. VIII, No. 29, March 22, 1918.

384. "YMCA to Settle Debt By Bond Issue," *Nashville Banner*, February 23, 1918.

385. *Nashville Banner*, June 28, 1918.

386. "Murray E. Hill Gets New Post," *The Nashville Tennessean*, April 25, 1944.

387. Ibid., "Fair Shatters Record of 1917," September 22, 1918.

388. Ibid., "Want Funds for Colored YMCA," August 22, 1918.

389. "Light in Darkness," *Nashville Globe*, August 30, 1918.

390. "YMCA Man There with His Huge Pack," *Nashville Banner*, September 18, 1918.

391. *Better Nashville*, Vol. IX, No. 7, October 25, 1918.

392. Ibid., Vol. IX, No. 15, December 20, 1918.

393. Ibid., June 21, 1918; printed list of Nashville YMCA officers, directors, and executive officers, October 15, 1918, YMCA of Middle Tennessee archives.

Chapter 9

394. "Local Board No. 3 Thanks 'Y,'" *Better Nashville*, Vol. IX, No. 17, January 3, 1919.

395. Resolution on John P. W. Brown adopted by the Electric Power Board of the City of Nashville, January 10, 1940, copy in the collection of the author.

396. Ibid.

397. "Free Membership to Soldiers," *Better Nashville*, Vol. IX, No. 20, January 24, and "A Trip Through Nashville's Character Factory," Vol. IX, No. 41, June 20, 1919.

398. Ibid., "Baths Open Last Sunday," Vol. IX, No. 31, April 11, 1919.

399. Ibid., "Nashville Boys' Camp June 23rd to July 19th," Vol. IX, No. 33, April 25, "Latest Camp News," Vol. IX, No. 37, May 23, and "Beautiful Lake Calls Nashville Boys to 'Y' Camp," Vol. IX, No. 40, June 13, 1919.

400. Ibid., "McGill Back in America," June 27, 1919; Ridley Wills II, *Elizabeth and Matt—A Love Story* (Nashville: Ridley Wills II, 2007), 60.

401. "YMCA Vacation School," *Better Nashville*, Vol. IX, No. 18, May 30, 1919.

402. Letter, John Randle, assistant librarian, National Council of the YMCA of the United States, to Mrs. Bess White Cochran, March 28, 1972, YMCA of middle Tennessee archives.

403. "YMCA Makes Great Progress," *Nashville Banner*, January 1, 1920.

404. Cochran, *All Together*, 40, 42, 44.

405. "Meet Mr. Baggett," *Better Nashville*, Vol. X, No. 7, October 17, 1919.

406. Ibid., "Open House at Y On New Year's Eve."

407. "High Caliber Officiating Assured For T.I.A.A. Meet," *Nashville Banner*, February 20, 1927.

408. Ibid., "Ramblers Victorious in First of Series," January 28, 1920.

409. "Y Board Takes Up 1920 Budget," *Nashville Banner*, December 29, 1919.

410. "Great Forward Movement of the Federated YMCAs of Nashville," BETTER NASHVILLE, Vol. X, No. 24, February 13, 1920; Ibid., "Results of the Campaign," Vol. X, No. 29, March 19, 1920.

411. Ibid.

412. Ibid., "YMCA Is 76 Years Old Sunday," Vol. X, No. 40, June 4, 1920.

413. Cochran, *All Together*, 43, 58.

414. "How About This for a Regular Camp?" *Better Nashville*, Vol. X, No. 42, June 18, 1920; Ibid., "About the 'Y' Boys' Camp," Vol. X, No. 43, June 25, 1920.

415. Ibid., "1920 YMCA Vacation School," Vol. X, No. 38, May 21, 1920; "Over 200 in 'Vacation School,'' Vol. X, No. 42, June 18, 1920.

416. Wood, *Profiles in Tenacity*, 13.

417. Ibid., "F. P. Hume," Vol. XI, No. 8, October 22, 1920.

418. "Six New Directors of YMCA Chosen," *The Nashville Tennessean*, December 8, 1920.

419. "Men from Many States at YMCA," *The Nashville Tennessean*, January 7, 1920.

420. Ibid.

421. "Inter-Racial Work of State YMCA," *Nashville Banner*, January 22, 1921.

422. Roy Neel, *DYNAMITE, Seventy-five Years of Vanderbilt Basketball* (Nashville: Burr- Oak Publishers, 1975), 40.

423. Conversation, Lallie Richter Jr. with the author, September 13, 2010. Lallie's father, Lallie Richter Sr., was one of the Hume-Fogg players and later a Rambler player and coach.

424. "The Radio Club," *Better Nashville*, Vol. XI, No. 29, March 18, 1921.

425. Ibid., "Nashville Radio Club," Vol. XI, No. 31, April 1, and "The Radio Club," Vol. XI, No. 32, April 8, 1921.

426. "1921 Season State YMCA Boys' Camp on the Collins River, Rock Island, Tenn," *Better Nashville*, Vol. XI, N. 30, March 25, and "Vacation Camp for Boys," Vol. XI, No. 39, May 27, 1921.

427. "New Committee Controls YMCA," *The Nashville Tennessean*, June 8, 1921.

428. Ibid.

429. Cochran, *All Together*, 43.

430. Bobby L. Lovett, *The African-American History of Nashville, Tennessee 1780–1930* (Fayetteville: The Univ. of Arkansas Press, 1999), 122.

431. Rust, *Eighty-One Years of Service: History of the Nashville YMCA*.

Chapter 10

432. Ibid., "Ramblers Come from Behind and Defeat Vandy," February 1, 1922; "Single Goal Margin of Win Over Vandy's Quint," February 15, 1922; and "Ramblers in Easy Win Over 'Peps,'" February 28, 1922.

433. Ibid., 'Hi-Y Clubs to Enjoy Banquet," April 26, 1922.

434. Ibid., "Select Site For 'Y' Boys' Camp," May 24, 1922.

435. Ibid., "Southern Men at 'Y' Meeting," July 19, 1922.

436. Ibid., "YMCA Issues Report for July," August 7, 1922.

437. Reminiscences of R. Sydney Smith, "New

Light in the Old Y," *The Nashville Tennessean*, June 6, 1970.

438. "YMCA to Elect New Board," November 22, 1922; "Hill Again Heads YMCA," January 12, 1923, *Nashville Banner*.

439. Ibid.

440. "Prep Partisans Seek Pugilistic Honors After Cage Battle," *The Nashville Tennessean*, March 23, 1923.

441. Tennessee Historical Commission historic marker, State Highway 49 at Sycamore Creek.

442. "YMCA Camp at Sycamore," *Nashville Banner*, June 17, 1923; "Forty Boys at Camp Sycamore," *Nashville Banner*, June 23, 1923; Cheatham County deed, book 97, pp. 183–84.

443. "Forty Boys at Camp Sycamore," *Nashville Banner*, June 23, 1923; "South's Finest Insurance Building," *Nashville Banner*, February 22, 1924; "Kids all Happy at YMCA Camp," *Nashville Banner*, June 19, 1924.

444. Cheatham County, Tennessee Deed, book 29, p. 629.

445. "Ramblers Have Attractive Schedule Arranged for Present Cage Season," *Nashville Banner*, December 9, 1923; Neal, *Dynamite*, 41, 223.

446. "Mexico's Splendid Team Is Defeated By Rambler Five," *Nashville Banner*, January 8, 1924.

447. *Nashville Banner*, "Notes on Basketball," January 13, and "Notes on Basketball," January 17, 1924.

448. Ramblers 1923–24 team picture, collection of Lallie Richter Jr.

449. "350 Youngsters Dine As Debutants Serve," *The Nashville Tennessean*, February 9, 1924.

450. "YMCA Officers Hold Election," *Nashville Banner*, February 9, 1924.

451. Ibid. "YMCA Makes Monthly Report," March 14, 1924.

452. Ibid., "YMCA to Have Open House Tuesday," May 26, 1924.

453. Ibid., 'Improvements Made at YMCA Camp," June 5, 1924.

454. Ibid., "New Launch at YMCA Camp," June 6, 1924.

455. Ibid.

456. Ibid., "Boyd Lesvr For YMCA Summer Camp," June 18, and "Kids All Happy at YMCA Camp," June 19, 1924.

457. Ibid., "Kids All Happy at YMCA Camp," June 19, 1924.

458. Ibid., "Swim Trials at YMCA Friday Night," June 11, 1924.

459. YMYWHA News, Dedication number, October 1924, copy in collection of the author.

460. Ibid, "Turkey Loop at YMCA Looking Good," November 16, 1924.

461. Ibid. "YMCA Basketball Team Is Impressive in Debut Game," December 21, 1924; "Vanderbilt Quintet Wins City Title," February 27, 1925.

462. Coverdale went on to teach and coach at Castle Heights Military Academy and to become the president of BGA in 1950. For many years, he ran Camp Hi Lake near McMinnville, where he later retired. Conversation, author with John Bragg, March 15, 2010; Neel, *Dynamite 75 Years of Vanderbilt Basketball*, 44–45; *Nashville Banner*, January 13, 1925.

463. "Ramblers Easy Winners," *Nashville Banner*, January 13, 1925.

464. Ibid., "Hill Heads Y for Fourth Term," January 15, 1925.

465. Ibid., "YMCA Reports Successful Year," January 18, 1925.

466. Ibid., "Women's Auxiliary."

467. Ibid., "Boys' Division of 'Y' Is Busy," November 23, 1924.

468. "Monthly Report on YMCA Activities Made," *The Nashville Tennessean*, March 20, 1925.

469. Ibid., "Dr. Mott Cites World's Needs," March 24, 1925.

470. "Local Water Teams Meet at YMCA," May 13, 1925, and "YM-YWHA Play Wednesday," May 26, 1925, *Nashville Banner*.

471. Ibid., "All in Readiness at Y.M.C.A. Camp," June 14, 1925.

472. Ibid.

473. Ibid., "Sycamore Camp Gets Going Monday," June 21, 1925.

474. Ibid; "Camp Sycamore Invaded by 95 Y Boys," June 23, 1925, "YMHA Boys Will Go to Camp," July 9, 1925.

475. Ibid., "Y Camp Plans Patriotic Program," July 2, 1925.

476. Ibid., "Plan for State YMCA Convention September 18–20," August 5, 1925.

477. Ibid., "Ramblers Win 34–12 over Union," December 12, 1925.

478. Ibid., "Boys' Leagues Are Formed at YMCA," January 6, 1926.

479. Ibid., "YMCA Will Launch Drive," February 21, 1926.

480. Ibid., "YMCA Boys' Work Impressive," February 22, and "Goal Is 1,000 New Members, February 23, 1926.

481. Ibid., "Y Campaign Nets 429 New Members," February 24, 1926.

Chapter 11

482. "State Cage Champs Defeated," *Nashville Banner*, January 20, 1926; "Ramblers in Title Race," February 24, 1926.

483. Ibid., "Celtics' Wonderful Passing Features Appearance Here," February 13, 1926.

484. Ibid., "City Basketball Race Ends," March 2, 1926.

485. Ibid., "Camp Sycamore to Be Opened Monday by YMCA. Many Reservations Made," June 20, 1926.

486. Ibid., "Businessmen to Visit Camp," July 15, 1926.

487. Ibid., "Winners at YMCA Camp Announced," June 29, 1926; "Camp Sycamore Enjoys Stunts," July 8, 1926.

488. Ibid., "Ramblers Ready," November 30, 1926; "High Caliber Officiating Assured for T.I.A.A. Meet," February 20, 1927.

489. Ibid., "YMCA to War on the Flapper," December 13, 1926.

490. Ibid., "Roberts Leads Ramblers to Win Over Chattanoogans," January 12, 1927; "Ramblers Continue Winning Streak in Game at Memphis," January 16; "Ramblers Rally to Capture Series from Atlanta," January 23; "Ramblers Beat Memphis Five," January 30; and "Cody Quintet Beats Y Five," February 2, 1927.

491. Ibid., "H. G. Hill Reelected Head of YMCA, January 12, 1927.

492. Ibid.

493. Ibid., "YMCA Reports an Active Year," January 16, 1927.

494. Ibid., "George C. Appleby Dies Suddenly," January 27, 2917; "YMCA Honors George Appleby," January 30, 1927.

495. Ibid., "High Caliber Officiating Assured for T.I.A.A. Meet," February 20, 1927; "Castle Heights Wins State TIAA Basketball Title, March 13, 1927.

496. Ibid., "Terrors Beat Keim Quintet," March 16, 1927.

497. Ibid., "Noon Volley Ball Class at YMCA," April 3, 1927.

498. Ibid., "Camp Bon Air Soon to Open," January 30, 1927; "Rifle Championship Matches to Be Held in YMCA Gym in May," April 3, 1927; "Camp Bon Air to Open June 6," May 22, 1927.

499. Cochran, *All Together*, 47–48.

500. "Boys Leave for Y Camp at Sycamore," *Nashville Banner*, June 22, 1927; Ibid., "Camp Sycamore Closes," July 20, 1927.

501. Ibid., "George R. Gillespie Dies," July 25, 1927.

502. Ibid., "The Ramblers Impatient," December 12, 1927.

503. Ibid., "Ramblers Win Championship," March 1, 1928.

504. Ibid., "Ramblers Win 25–14," January 26, 1928.

505. Ibid., "Winners of 'Y' Basketball League Championship," March 18, 1928.

506. Ibid., "MBA Wins State Championship in Banner's TIAA Meet," March 4, 1928; "Purdy Wins Cage Tournament," March 11, 1928.

507. Ibid., "Eighty Boys at Camp Sycamore,"

June 19, 1928.

508. Ibid., "Youngsters Enjoy Camp Activities," June 24, 1928.

509. Ibid., "YMCA School to Award Diplomas," June 20, 1928.

510. Ibid., "Ramblers Win Over Sewanee in First Game," December 9; "Ramblers Beat Louisville By Large Score, December 16; "Mississippi Aggies Lose to Ramblers," December 21, 1928.

Chapter 12

511. Ibid., "Hill Reelected YMCA Head," January 10, 1929.

512. Ibid.

513. Ibid.

514. Ibid., "Ramblers Win 25–14," January 26; "Ramblers in Title Chase," February 3, 1329.

515. Ibid., "Chattanoogans Are Victorious 55–27," March 7, 1929.

516. Ibid., "Dr. A. S. Keim Will Open New Health Club on Fifth Avenue," February 24, 1929.

517. Ibid., "Entrance Period to State Event Closes at Midnight," March 3, 1929; March 6, 1929.

518. Ibid., "CMI Victor in Boys' Meet at YMCA," March 27, 1929; "Ralph McGill Joins Staff of Atlanta Constitution," March 31, 1929.

519. Ibid., "YMCA Night Law School Will Close," June 12, 1929.

520. Ibid., "Y Activities at Camp Sycamore," June 30, 1929.

521. Ibid., "Boys' Club Members Will Have Outing," July 7, 1929.

522. Ibid., "Hill Again Heads Nashville YMCA," January 15, 1930.

523. *Nashville Banner*, "Full Program in Y Urged," February 8, 1930; "Swimmers Meet at Y Wednesday," February 24, 1930.

524. Ibid., "Ideal Aces Beat Rambler Quintet," March 6, 1930; "TIAA State Tournament Open," March 6,1030; "Two Cage Games Carded at YMCA," March 31, 1930.

525. Ibid., "Exchangites Honor Spain," June 4, 1930; "YMCA Secretary School Is Opened," June 24, 1930.

526. Ibid., "Tribes Compete at Camp Sycamore," June 26, 1930.

527. Ibid., "Camp Sycamore Program Active," July 2, 1930.

528. Ibid., "YMCA Secretary School Is Opened," June 24, 1930.

529. Ibid., "Four Teams Ready for Annual City Cage Struggle," November 30, 1930; photograph f Ideal Aces, December 14, 1930.

530. Ibid., "Hill Is Again YMCA Head," December 18, 1930.

531. Ibid., "State YMCA Delegates Meet," January 18, 1931.

532. Ibid., "Father Ryan Quintet Wins TIAA Cage Crown," March 8, 1931.

533. Ibid., "Cloverdale Goes to Castle Heights," June 25, 1931; "2 Castle Heights Men to Head BGA Management," January 5, 1950.

534. Ibid., "Camp Sycamore Schedule Full," July 1, 1931.

535. Ibid., "Lions to Send Boys to YMCA Camp," June 26, 1931.

536. *Nashville Banner*, "YMCA Gym May Be Closed to Major Quints," January 9, 1932.

537. *The Nashville Tennessean*, December 13, 1931.

538. Ibid., "Death Comes to Rosenwald," January 7, 1932.

539. Ibid., "Community Chest Initial Gifts Leaders," October 16, 1932; Ibid., "Lambeth Will Direct City's Chest Efforts," October 9, 1932.

540. Ibid., "Aquatic Tryouts Held in YMCA," October 9, 1932.

541. Ibid., "YMCA Officials Reelected," January 17, 1933.

542. *Nashville Banner*, "YMCA Officials Reelected," January 17, 1933.

Chapter 13

543. "Weaver Heads Nashville YMCA," *Nashville Banner*. January 25, 1934.

544. Ibid., "Hermitage Defeats Ramblers 36–26 to Tie for Lead," January 17, 1934; "Ramblers Clout Kay See Outfit in League Tilt," January 26, 1934.

545. Ibid., "DuPont Retains Court Supremacy," March 8, 1934.

546. Ibid., "TSSAA Cage Tournament to be Four-Day Affair," February 2, 1934.

547. Ibid., "YMCA Boxers Not Trained for Tournament," March 8, 1934; "Finals Tonight in Basketball," March 17, 1934.

548. "Sixteen Admitted to Hardwood Net Instead of Eight," *Nashville Banner*, April 1934.

549. Ibid., "Judge Aust to Address 'Y' Law School Seniors," June 10, 1934.

550. "Eighty-one Years of Service: History of the Nashville YMCA," 1935, YMCA Archives.

551. Ibid.

552. "Capacity Crowd Sees 'Mitt' Show," *Nashville Banner*, January 15, 1935.

553. Ibid., "Nashville Wins Water Carnival," February 10, 1935; "Pingpong Meet Begins Tonight," March 25, 1935; "Peterson, Folk Meet for Title," March 30, 1935.

554. "Camp Overton Plans for Several Groups," *Nashville Banner*, June 16, 1935.

555. Ibid.

556. Ibid., "Crown Champs in 'Y' Tournament," March 1, 1936.

557. Ibid., "Property of YMCA School Is Taken Over by Vanderbilt," July 2, 1936.

558. Wills, *All Together*, 48.

559. Interview, George Cate Jr. with the author, August 21, 2009.

560. Only when the Federal Fair Labor Standards Act of 1938 was passed, did the practice of young boys working long hours as street newspaper vendors cease.

561. "Youths Return Home after Week at Camp," *Nashville Banner*. June 16, 1937; "YMCA Opens Camp Sycamore," June 24, 1937; "Nashville Newsboys Frolic at Camp Sycamore," August 15, 1937.

562. "City Cage Circuit Not to Function," *Nashville Banner*, December 7, 1937; Ibid., "City Cage Loop Drafts Schedule," January 3, 1938.

563. Ibid., "YMCA Wrestlers Beat Wesley House," March 1, 1938.

564. Ibid., "East Wins," March 19, 1938.

565. Ibid., "Three Linden Players Named on All-Star Quint For Meet," March 21, 1938.

566. Ibid., "Table Tennis Title," April 8, 1938.

567. Ibid., "Gym Exhibition Slated For 'Y,'" April 7, 1938.

568. Ibid., "YMCA Fellowship Group Hears Dr. Dobbs," April 20, 1938.

569. "Night Law School Begins 29th Year," *The Nashville Tennessean*, August 6, 1939

Chapter 14

570. "Ramblers Upset DuPont With Rally," *Nashville Banner*, January 6, 1939.

571. Ibid., "Dr. J. W. O'Callaghan Hailed as Scholar," January 5, 1927.

572. Three four-wall handball courts and one squash court were added. Ibid., October 20, 1941.

573. Ibid., "YMCA Board Elects Officers," January 27, 1939.

574. Ibid., "YMCA To Present Annual Carnival," May 15, 1939.

575. Wood, *Profiles in Tenacity*, 13.

576. "Community Chest Aids Work at 'Y,'" *Nashville Banner*, August 11, 1939.

577. Ibid., "Local 'Y' to Join in U.S. Observance," October 10, 1939.

578. Ibid., "Riflery Club Will Organize at YMCA," January 9, 1940.

579. "Hi-Y Council," *The Nashville Tennessean*, December 17, 1939.

580. "A Resolution, The Electric Power Board of the City of Nashville, Wednesday, January 10, 1940," copy in the collection of the author; "J. P. W. Brown's Rites Today at Westwood," *The Nashville Tennessean*, December 29, 1939.

581. "Nashville YMCA Elects Officers," *Nashville Banner*, January 22, 1940.

582. Ibid., "Boys Offered Free Swimming Instruction," June 8, 1940.

583. "Dr. O'Callaghan Is Reelected YMCA Head," *The Nashville Tennessean*, January 15, 1941.

584. "Bombs, Fire Ruin Spot Where YMCA Was Established," *Nashville Banner*, January 22, 1941.

585. "Boys and Girls to Talk About Boys and Girls," *The Nashville Tennessean*, March 2, 1941.

586. Ibid., "'Y' Will Permit First Dances In History for Visiting Soldiers," April 25, 1941.

587. Ibid., "YMCA Plans For Summer Work," June 4, 1941.

588. "Prof. J. A. Tate, Veteran Educator, to Teach at YMCA," *Nashville Banner*, June 19, 1941.

589. Ibid., "Camp Sycamore," June 25, 1941.

590. Ibid., "YMCA Personnel, Program for Year Are Announced," October 21, 1941.

591. Ibid. "Local YMCA Plans Tribute to Founder," October 15, 1941.

592. Ibid., "YMCA council Plans Soldiers' Yule Programs," December 18, 1941.

593. "W.D. Gale Named YMCA President," *The Nashville Tennessean*, December 17, 1941.

594. Ibid.

595. "City's Universal Prayer Week Begins at Noon on Monday," *Nashville Banner*, January 3, 1942.

596. Ibid., "YMCA Housing 75 Air Base Engineers," February 2, 1942.

597. Ibid., "YMCA First Floor to Be Service Club," May 9, 1942.

598. Ibid., "YMCA Learn-to-Swim Campaign Set Monday," June 12, 1942.

599. Ibid., "Y Law School in 32nd Year," July 26, 1942.

600. "Horace G. Hill Funeral Held This Afternoon," *Nashville Banner*, October 18, 1942.

601. Ibid., "Gale Again Heads YMCA," January 4, 1943.

602. Ibid., "YMCA Lounge Hostesses Solve Service Men's Varied Problems," March 18, 1943.

603. Ibid., "Funeral Set Tomorrow for W. C. Weaver," June 15, 1943.

604. Ibid., "Boys' Day Camp Opens Monday at Central School," June 18, 1943.

605. Ibid., "YMCA Night School Graduates Three," June 16, 1943.

606. Ibid., "H. G. Hill Jr. to YMCA Board," July 19, 1943.

607. Ibid., "YMCA Lounge Program For Week Announced," July 21, 1943.

608. Ibid. "Personal Counsel Seminar Opens Here Tomorrow," September 27, 1943.

609. Ibid., "YMCA Housing Service Gives Timely Aid," October 1, 1943.

610. Ibid., "Club Planned as Curb on Delinquency," November 15, 1943.

611. Ibid., "Mrs. Thompson New YMCA-USO Lounge Hostess," November 6, 1943.

612. Ibid., "YMCA Open House Set Thursday for World War Vets, November 9, 1943.

613. Wills, *All Together*, 51.

614. "YMCA Sends Gifts to Americans in German Prisons," *Nashville Banner*, November 23, 1943.

Chapter 15

615. "Dudley Gale YMCA president," *The Nashville Tennessean*, January 26, 1944.

616. Ibid., "East Nashville YMCA Formed," March 28, 1944.

617. Ibid., "Schools Adopt Own Pay Plan," April 25, 1944.

618. "YMCA Observing 100th Birthday with Open House," *Nashville Banner*, May 6, 1944.

619. "100th Anniversary of YMCA Founding to Be Observed Here," *The Nashville Tennessean*, June 2, 1944; "YMCA Observing 100th Birthday with Open House," *Nashville Banner*.

620. Ibid., "YMCA Sets Up Centralized Branch in East Nashville," June 30, 1944.

621. Ibid., "Campers Leave For Mountains," August 24, 1944

622. Ibid., "YMCA-USO Fetes 2,000,000th Guest, Overseas Veteran, With Seven-Hour Party," October 5, 1944.

623. Ibid., "East YMCA Opens Monday; Program Set," November 19, 1944.

624. "New East Nashville YMCA Off to Good Start," *The Nashville Tennessean*, February 8, 1945.

625. "Dr. Buckner, Prominent Physician Dies," *Nashville Banner*, April 10, 1945.

626. Ibid., "YMCA-USO Club to Honor Two Service Branches," July 29, 1945.

627. Wills, *A Brief History*, 16.

628. "YMCA-USO Plans Programs," November 5, 1945, *Nashville Banner*; November 19, 1944.

629. Ibid., "New Year's Eve Dance Slated at YMCA-USO Club," December 29, 1945.

630. Ibid., "YMCA Used By 2,291,201 Service Men," January 22, 1946.

631. Reminiscences of Stanley E. Hime, copy in collection of the author.

632. Ibid., "Peabody Dean Addresses Hi-Y Parley," February 2, 1946.

633. Ibid., "YMCA Secretary Retires After 30 Years of Service," October 31, 1949.

634. Interview, Ralph Brunson with the author, 1969.

635. Wood, *Profiles in Tenacity*, 29.

636. "Service Men's Activities Listed," *Nashville Banner*, September 23, 1946.

637. *By the Grace of God*, Vol. 1, Issue 5, October 20, 2003, YMCA archives.

638. Ibid., "Phalanx Fraternity Elects First Officers," January 25, 1947.

639. Cochran, *All Together*, 52–53.

Chapter 16

640. "Five to Be Installed Tonight on 'Y' Board of Directors," *Nashville Banner*, December 12, 1961.

641. Ibid., "25,000 Troop Joint Army Air Force Maneuvers Set at Campbell in May," March 13, 1948.

642. Ibid., "Community Y Organized in East Nashville," July 28, 1948.

643. "11 Y Law Students Presented with Degrees," *The Nashville Tennessean*, June 15, 1948.

644. Ibid., "333 Boys End Swim Course at YMCA Pool," June 20, 1948.

645. Ibid.

646. Ibid.

647. Ibid.

648. "YMCA Health Club Director," *Nashville Banner*, May 13, 1949.

649. Ibid., "East YMCA Seeks Local Financing," May 17, 1949.

650. Ibid., "Conduct Tests in National Swim Program," June 26, 1949.

651. "YMCA Secretary Retires After 40 Years of Service," *Nashville Banner*, October 31, 1949.

652. Ibid.

653. Ibid.

654. Ibid.

655. Conversation, Forrest Cooper [grandson of E. L. Spain] with the author, August 28, 2010.

656. Letter, E. L. Spain to Ferriss C. Bailey, November 18, 1949, copy in the collection of Forrest Cooper.

657. "YMCA Secretary Retires After 40 Years of Service," *Nashville Banner*, October 31, 1949.

658. 1950 YMCA Yearbook.

659. Ibid., "YMCA Swim Classes Will Start Tomorrow," May 28, 1950.

660. "East YMCA to Launch First Summer Day Camp for Boys," *Nashville Banner*, June 12, 1950.

661. "New YMCA Directors Will Be Installed," *Nashville Banner*, January 24, 1951.

662. Ibid. "YMCA Board Names Officers," January 30, 1951.

663. "YMCA Opens Annual Drive for New Members Tuesday," *The Nashville Tennessean*,

NOTES

April 22, 1951.

664. "Gray Named Official At YMCA Meet," *Nashville Banner*, August 25, 1951.

665. "'Y' Observing 100th Birthday; Churches Join in Program," *Nashville Banner*, November 13, 1951.

666. Ibid.

667. "E. L. Spain, Former YMCA Official Dies," *The Nashville Tennessean*, February 3, 1951.

668. Ibid.

669. Solon Cousins, *The Incredible YMCABIRD and Other Stories* (Old Dominion Books, 1992), 29.

670. "YMCA Planning Broader Program, *Nashville Banner*, January 27, 1952.

671. Ibid.

672. "Nashville 'Y' Officers Chosen," *Nashville Banner*, January 29, 1953.

673. E-mail, Edgar Evins Jr., to Lawrence "Larry" Stumb, February 8, 2011.

674. "Indian 'War' Slated at Camp Widjiwagan," *The Nashville Tennessean*, June 7, 1953.

675. Ibid., "'Y' Readies Drive For Capital Fund," May 10, 1953.

676. "Drive Launched For 'Y' Improvements," *Nashville Banner*, May 12, 1953.

677. Ibid., "Building for the Future," May 14, 1953.

678. Ibid., "YMCA Drive Nets $17,213 In New Funds," May 29, 1953.

679. *Nashville Banner*, May 2, 1953.

680. Ibid., "Browning Visited by Four Boy Governors," June 30, 1949.

681. Ibid., "You Wouldn't Believe It, Mother: Your Boy Likes Camp Discipline," July 29, 1953.

682. *The Nashville Tennessean*, "'Y' Swimming Teams Hold First Practice," September 25 and October 3, 1953.

Chapter 17

683. "Officers Named to YMCA Board," *The Nashville Tennessean*, January 29, 1954.

684. "Water Safety Classes Slated at YMCA Pool," *Nashville Banner*, February 13, 1954.

685. Ibid., "Ban on Unused Ice Boxes Passed by Youth Legislature," April 3, 1954.

686. Ibid., "Alabama 'Y' Leader Joins Staff Here," April 19, 1954; *The Nashville Tennessean*, June 13, 1954.

687. Ibid., "YMCA Launches Swim Campaign," May 24, 1954.

688. Ibid., "Youth Center Near Completion," June 10, 1954.

689. Written reminiscences of L. D. Hobbs, who lived in the YMCA in the late 1940s and early 1950s.

690. "Stirton Oman New YMCA Head," *The Nashville Tennessean*, January 27, 1955.

691. "UGF Agencies Find I Drive Best," *The Nashville Tennessean*, February 4, 1955; "3 Nashvillians to Attend YMCA Paris Conference," *Nashville Banner*, August 8, 1955.

692. Ibid., "750 Midstate Scouts Attend Summer Camp," August 10, 1955; "YMCA Enrolls 500 Beginners in Swim Class," *The Nashville Tennessean*, June 6, 1955.

693. Ibid., "City Teen-agers Gather for New 'Y' Party Series," August 5, 1955.

694. "YMCA Director to Be Hospitalized," *Nashville Banner*, June 24, 1955.

695. Ibid., "Handball Fast Becoming Popular Sport at YMCA," February 2, 1959.

696. Ibid., "Vital Role Expected for New Teen Town," November 17, 1955.

697. Ibid., "Billy Cooper Scholarship Fund Set Up at YMCA Night Law School," November 26, 1955.

698. Ibid.

699. Ibid., "YMCA Night Law School Alumni to Meet Saturday," June 15, 1956.

700. Ibid., "'Y' News Notes," June 23, 1956.

701. Ibid., "'Y' News Notes," June 2 and June 23, 1956.

702. Ibid., "'Y' News Notes," November 10, 1956.

703. Ibid.. "'Y' News Notes," November 10 and November 24, 1956.

704. Ibid., "New Officers Elected by WMCA Board," January 26, 1957.

705. Ibid., "New Official Hopes to Form 'Y' Indian Guides Group Here," February 8, 1957.

706. Ibid., "'Y' Father-Son Indian Guides Meet Thursday," November 5, 1958.

707. Ibid., "Camps Provide Fresh Summer Fun For Thousands of Area Youngsters," June 15, 1957.

708. "Sylvan Park Meets Gra-Y All-Stars at MBA Tonight," *Nashville Banner*, November 16, 1957; "YMCA News Notes," November 30 and December 7, 1957.

709. Ibid., "YMCA Directors Elect Officers," January 21, 1958.

710. Ibid., "YMCA Board Names 7 Members, Reelects 4," January 20, 1958.

711. Ibid., "Plans for Expanded YMCA in East Nashville Outlined," February 11, 1958.

712. Ibid., "YMCA Ready for Boys' Visit Registration," September 1, 1958.

713. Ibid.

714. Ibid., "'Y' Gets OK on Expansion Site Purchase," October 6, 1958.

715. Ibid., "Comer M. Teal Named Exchange Man of the Year," October 10, 1958

716. Ibid.

717. "Handball Fast Becoming Popular Sport at YMCA," *Nashville Banner*, February 2, 1959.

718. Ibid.

719. "'Y' Day Camp Opens June 15," *Nashville Banner*, May 21, 1959.

720. "1st Camp Trip Tougher on Parents, Ball," *Nashville Banner*, June 22, 1959.

721. Ibid., "Boys' Division of Y Slates Fall Program," September 9, 1959.

722. "Hill Interests to Help YMCA," *The Nashville Tennessean*, September 19, 1959.

723. "Man on a Tightrope," *The Nashville Tennessean*, November 15, 1959.

724. "First 'Family-Type' YMCA Plans Announced by Group," *Nashville Banner*, November 17, 1959.

725. "First 'Family-Type' YMCA Plans Announced by Group," *Nashville Banner*, November 17, 1959.

726. Ibid., "East Nashville's $675,000 YMCA Gets Step Closer," December 15, 1959.

Chapter 18

727. Ibid., "YMCA Sets Drive in E. Nashville," January 15, 1960; "Sunday YMCA Day: Time to Pause, Reflect on Work," January 8, 1960; "TV Stations Tell Story of City's 'Y,'" January 13, 1960.

728. Ibid.

729. Ibid., "Fulton Lauds Family Plan of YMCA," January 26, 1960.

730. "East Nashville Y Fund Over One Half Way," *The Nashville Tennessean*, January 29, 1960.

731. Ibid., "$396,813 Pledged for East Nashville Y," February 3, 1960.

732. "Community Y Drive Extended," *Nashville Banner*, February 8, 1960.

733. Ibid., "YMCA Board OK's Plans For Expanded Program," March 26, 1960.

734. Don H. Doyle, *Nashville Since the 1920s* (Knoxville: University of Tennessee Press, 1985), 249.

735. "YMCA Law School Rejects Negro," *The Nashville Tennessean*, October 5, 1960.

736. Wood, *Profiles in Tanacity*, 50.

737. "YMCA to Set up Legislature Here Today," *The Nashville Tennessean*, April 8, 1961.

738. Ibid., "YMCA to Run Camp Widjiwagan," April 9, 1960.

739. Ibid., "Unique Camp Sessions Set at Widjiwagan," June 9, 1960.

740. Ibid., "German to Join Staff of Widjiwagan," June 1, 1960.

741. Ibid., "YMCA Camp Opens July 11 for First Session," July 7, 1960.

742. Ibid., "YMCA Official Slated for 40-Year Certificate," August 11, 1960.

743. White, *All Together*, 59.

744. "Nashville YMCA Elects 5 New Board Members," *Nashville Tennessean*, November 28, 1960.

745. "YMCA Rated in Top 50," *The Nashville Tennessean*, December 10, 1960.

746. "To Remodel for YMCA Athletic Club," *Nashville Banner*, December 12, 1960.

747. "YMCA Has Openings in Gym Classes," *Nashville Banner*, November 29, 1960.

748. "East Nashville YMCA Work Starts March 1," *Nashville Banner*, February 15, 1961.

749. Ibid., "Groundbreaking Held Foe East Y," March 20, 1961.

750. Ibid., "Trimble Joins YMCA Law School Faculty," February 17, 1961.

751. "West Nashville YMCA Slates Summer Events," *Nashville Banner*, June 17, 1961.

752. "YMCA Camp Counselors Are Named," *The Nashville Tennessean*, May 6, 1961.

753. Nelson Andrews, Autobiography, pp. 137–38, copy in collection of the author.

754. Conversation, Frank Burkholder with the author, June 19, 2009.

755. Conversation, Walter Knestrick with the author, May 9, 2009.

756. "Handball Called Best Conditioner for All Athletes," *Nashville Banner*, February 2, 1962.

757. "New YMCA Club Opens," *Nashville Banner*, September 21, 1961.

758. "YMCA Adds 2 New Staff Members in New Program," *Nashville Banner*, October 2, 1961.

759. "YMCA Officers Elected," *The Nashville Tennessean*, December 13, 1961.

760. White, *All Together*, 56–57.

761. *Suburban News*, February 24, 1972, YMCA archives.

762. "10-Day Canoe Trip Offered in North Woods," *Nashville Banner*, February 10, 1962.

763. Ibid., "YMCA Secretary Takes New Post," August 20, 1962.

764. Ibid., "Ready for Camp Thunderbird," May 12, 1962.

765. "YMCA Swimming Lessons To Start," *The Nashville Tennessean*, July 4, 1962.

766. "Grady Looney Assumes YMCA Position Here," *Nashville Banner*, November 20, 1962.

767. Ibid.

768. Ibid.

769. "Negroes Plan Church Move," *The Nashville Tennessean*, October 23, 1962.

770. "Trial Of Four In 'Y' Sit-In Attempt Set," *Nashville Banner*, February 12, 1963.

771. "60 Marchers Urge YMCA to Integrate," February 25, 1963.

772. In 1963, the year John Lewis was arrested at the Nashville YMCA, he was elected president of the Southern Christian Leadership Council. A soft-spoken young man, Lewis was beaten badly several times, including at Montgomery and Selma. In 2010, John Lewis was a United States Congressman from Atlanta. He remained optimistic about America and our form of government.

773. "'Y' Café integration Termed 'Mistake,'" *The Nashville Tennessean*, March 2, 1963.

774. "Course on Guns Offered at YMCA," *The Nashville Tennessean*, March 6, 1963.

775. "Many Firms Desegregate Facilities," *Nashville Banner*, June 11, 1963.

776. Conversation, James Rayhab, September 8, 2009.

777. Nashville YMCA Board of Directors with the author, Nashville YMCA board meeting minutes, February 26, 1964, YMCA Archives.

Chapter 19

778. "Teal's Dream Reaches Half Way Mark," *Nashville Banner*, January 24, 1964.

779. Nashville YMCA board of directors meeting minutes, January 15, 1964, Nashville YMCA archives.

780. "YMCA Buys State Acreage," *The Nashville Tennessean*, February 24, 1964; Nashville YMCA Board of directors meeting minutes, March 18, 1864, Nashville YMCA archives.

781. Ibid., June 17, 1964.

782. Ibid., May 20, 1964.

783. *The Tennessean*, April 21, 2010.

784. Nashville YMCA board of directors meeting minutes, March 18, 1964, Nashville YMCA Archives.

785. Ibid., April 15, 1964.

786. "Kentucky Man Takes Nashville YMCA Post," *Nashville Banner*, May 11, 1964.

787. Nashville YMCA board of directors meeting minutes, May 20, 1964, YMCA archives.

788. Ibid.

789. "Retiring Nashville YMCA General Secretary," *Nashville Banner*, July 28, 1964.

790. Nashville YMCA board of directors meeting minutes, April 15, 1964.

791. Ibid., July 25, 1964.

792. Conversation, George Cate Jr. with the author, August 22, 2009.

793. Nashville YMCA board of directors meeting minutes, August 19, 1964.

794. White, *All Together*, 61.

795. Nashville YMCA board of directors meeting minutes, August 19, 1964.

796. *All Together*, 61; Conversation, George Cate Jr. with the author, August 21, 2009.

797. Wills, *A Brief History*, 17.

798. "YMCA Plans Large Center," *Nashville Banner*, September 2, 1964.

799. Donelson-Hermitage YMCA History, published July 2000, Nashville YMCA Archives.

800. Ibid.

801. Ibid.

802. Nashville YMCA membership committee minutes, November 5, 1964, Nashville YMCA Archives.

803. "News About Your YMCA," 1964, YMCA Archives.

804. Ibid.

805. Ibid.

806. Ibid., "YMCA Plans Two Suburban Branches," May 20, 1965.

807. Ibid.

808. Ibid., "Hill Takes Office as 'Y' President, July 1, 1965.

809. "New Southwest 'Y' Board Organized," *The Nashville Tennessean*, September 23, 1965.

810. "$5 Million Y Plan Urged," *Nashville Banner*, October 2, 1965

811. "Kiwanis Gives Payment on Southwest 'Y,'" *Nashville Banner*, October 2, 1965.

812. NEWS ABOUT YOUR YMCA, September 1965, Metropolitan Nashville YMCA Board Reports, September 1965.

813. Metropolitan Nashville YMCA board of directors meeting minutes, November 24, 1965.

Chapter 20

814. Nashville YMCA Downtown Branch board of managers meeting minutes, February 15, 1966.

815. "NEWS ABOUT YOUR YMCA," Nashville YMCA Board Reports, 1966.

816. "NEWS ABOUT YOUR YMCA," Nashville YMCA Board Reports, 1966.

817. Nashville YMCA business-finance committee minutes, April 7, 1966.

818. Nashville YMCA long-range development committee minutes, April 20, 1966,

819. Special committee minutes, April 22, 1966.

820. "NEWS ABOUT YOUR YMCA," Nashville YMCA Board Reports, 1966.

821. Nashville YMCA property committee minutes, April 26, 1966.

822. Ibid.

823. Ibid.

824. Nashville YMCA property committee minutes, June 20, 1966.

825. Ibid.

826. Letter, T. D. Boyd Jr., President of the board of directors of the Colored YMCA, to Ralph L. Brunson, executive secretary, Metro-

politan Nashville YMCA, July [1966]; "YMCA Plans New Branch," *Nashville Banner*, September 14, 1966.

827. "Now Recorded on Film, Memories of 'the Black Y' Provokes Smiles and Tears," *New York Times*, July 8, 2010.

828. Ibid.

829. Ibid.

830. Donelson Branch YMCA board of managers meeting minutes, October 17, 1966,

831. Nashville YMCA Statement to United Givers' Fund Relative to the 1967 Budget. YMCA Board Reports, 1967.

832. Nashville YMCA board of directors meeting minutes, November 30, 1966, Nashville YMCA Board Reports, 1966.

833. "Metropolitan Nashville YMCA Voting Members to Meet December 5," in "News About Your YMCA," Nashville YMCA Board Reports, 1966.

834. "NEWS ABOUT YOUR YMCA," Board Reports, 1967.

835. Metropolitan Nashville YMCA board of directors meeting minutes February 22, 1967.

836. Cochran, *All Together*, 59.

837. Ibid.

838. "New East 'Y' Pool Dedicated Sunday," *Nashville Banner*, May 20, 1967.

839. 92nd Annual Report of the Metropolitan Nashville YMCA, Nashville YMCA Board Reports, 1966.

840. Ibid.

841. Nashville YMCA board of directors meeting minutes, May 23, 1967, Board Reports, 1967.

842. "Ennis Murrey Dies; Banking, Civic Leader," *Nashville Banner*, May 18, 1967.

Chapter 21

843. No one was more thrilled with Roupen's election than his father, Reuben Gulbenk, who had left Turkey for America in 1912 as a penniless fourteen-year-old Armenian a day before his father was killed by the Turks for being a Christian.

844. Nashville YMCA board of directors meeting minutes, June 28, 1967.

845. NEWS ABOUT YOUR YMCA, Nashville YMCA Board Reports, 1967.

846. Nashville YMCA branch relations committee minutes, October 17, 1967, Nashville YMCA Board Reports, 1967.

847. Nashville YMCA executive committee minutes, August 16, 1967.

848. Nashville YMCA board of directors meeting minutes, September 27, 1967.

849. Ibid., October 25, 1967, Nashville YMCA Board Reports, 1967.

850. NEWS ABOUT YOUR YMCA, page 5, Nashville YMCA Board Reports, 1967; Ibid., 1968.

851. Ibid., 5A, 5B, and 5C.

852. "YMCA Gets Land Gift For New Branch," *Nashville Banner*, December 22, 1967.

853. Ibid., "For YMCA A Notable Gift," December 23, 1967.

854. "NEWS ABOUT YOUR YMCA," Nashville YMCA Board Reports, 1967.

855. Nashville YMCA property committee minutes February 1, 1968, Nashville YMCA Board Reports, 1968.

856. Ibid., March 27, 1968.

857. "Who's Who on the Staff," Nashville YMCA Board Reports, 1968.

858. Letter, Ralph L. Brunson to Judge Richard Jenkins, April 11, 1968, Nashville YMCA Board Reports, 1968.

859. "$175,000 Pledged by Hookers," *The Nashville Tennessean*, May 22, 1968.

860. Ibid.

861. Ibid.

862. "Special committee meeting minutes, September 20, 1968.

863. Ibid.

864. Conversation, Jim Rayhab with the author, September 8, 2009.

865. Ibid.

866. "NEWS ABOUT YOUR YMCA," reprinted from the *Nashville Banner*, December 13, 1968.

867. Nashville YMCA board of directors meeting minutes, January 22, 1969.

868. Ibid.

869. Ibid.

870. Donelson Branch YMCA board of managers meeting minutes, April 28, 1969.

871. "NEWS ABOUT YOUR YMCA," Board Reports 1969.

872. Ibid.

873. Ibid.

874. Ibid.

875. Ibid.

Chapter 22

876. Conversation, Roupen Gulbenk with the author, July 10, 2010.

877. Ibid.

878. "NEWS ABOUT YOUR YMCA," Nashville YMCA Board Reports, 1969.

879. Ibid.

880. "NEWS ABOUT YOUR YMCA," Nashville YMCA Board Reports, 1969.

881. Ibid.

882. Ibid.

883. Ibid.

884. Nashville YMCA board of directors meeting minutes, October 22, 1969.

885. Ibid., November 13, 1969.

886. Ibid., December 30, 1969.

887. "NEWS ABOUT YOUR YMCA," Nashville YMCA Board Reports, 1970.

888. Ibid., March 25, 1970; Nashville YMCA property meeting committee, March 27, 1970.

889. Ibid., April 22, July 23, and August 19, 1970.

890. "NEWS ABOUT YOUR YMCA," Board Reports, November, 1971.

891. Metropolitan Nashville YMCA board of directors meeting minutes, June 24, 1970; YMCA of Middle Tennessee Philanthropic Update, September 30, 2010.

892. "NEWS ABOUT YOUR YMCA," Board Reports, 1970.

893. "Why a Full Facility YMCA in Sumner County," May 13, 1996, YMCA of Nashville and Middle Tennessee Board Reports, 1996.

894. Metropolitan Nashville YMCA Board Reports, June 1971.

895. Ibid.

896. Metropolitan Nashville YMCA new building committee minutes, September 23, 1970.

897. Metropolitan Nashville YMCA board of directors meeting minutes, October 29, 1970.

898. Metropolitan Nashville YMCA long-range development minutes, October 27, 1970.

899. "NEWS ABOUT YOUR YMCA," Nashville YMCA Board Reports, 1970.

900. Attachment to Nashville YMCA board of directors meeting minutes, February 24, 1971.

901. "NEWS ABOUT YOUR YMCA," Nashville YMCA Board Reports, 1971.

902. Nashville YMCA board of directors meting minutes, February 24, 1971.

903. "NEWS ABOUT YOUR YMCA," Nashville YMCA Reports, February 1971.

904. "NEWS ABOUT YOUR YMCA," Nashville YMCA Reports, June 1971.

905. Ibid.

906. Ibid., June 1971.

Chapter 23

907. Metropolitan Nashville YMCA board of directors meeting minutes, July 7, 1971.

908. "NEWS ABOUT YOUR YMCA," YMCA Board Reports, June 1971.

909. Metropolitan Nashville YMCA joint meeting executive-finance committees minutes, August 5, 1971.

910. Metropolitan Nashville YMCA board of

directors meeting minutes August 25, 1971.

911. "NEWS ABOUT YOUR YMCA," YMCA Board Reports, October 1971.

912. Conversation, Kent Rea with the author, November 3, 2010.

913. The following July, Blackwelder was named executive director of the Southwest Family YMCA.

914. Metropolitan Nashville YMCA Christian emphasis committee minutes, September 30, 1971.

915. Metropolitan Nashville YMCA board of directors meeting minutes, September 22, 1971.

916. Metropolitan Nashville YMCA board of directors meeting minutes, October 27 1971.

917. Ibid.

918. YMCA Foundation board of directors meeting minutes, November 9, 1971.

919. Metropolitan Nashville YMCA executive committee minutes, January 19, 1972.

920. "NEWS ABOUT YOUR YMCA," YMCA Board Reports, December 1971.

921. "Downtown 'Y' Successful Bid $1,074 Million," *The Nashville Tennessean*, February 16, 1972.

922. Metropolitan Nashville YMCA executive committee minutes, February 22, 1972.

923. "NEWS ABOUT YOUR YMCA," Nashville YMCA Board Reports, March 1972.

924. Ibid.

925. Conversation, Kent Rea with the author, November 3, 2010.

926. Nashville YMCA Board Reports, May 1972.

927. Ibid.

928. Metropolitan Nashville YMCA board of directors meeting minutes, June 28, 1972.

929. Contract Tennessee Division of Vocational Rehabilitation and Nashville YMCA Urban Village, Nashville YMCA Board Reports, July 1974.

930. Ibid.

931. Nashville YMCA Executive Committee meeting minutes, July 20, 1972, Nashville YMCA Board Reports, July 1972.

932. Metropolitan Nashville YMCA board of directors meeting minutes, July 27, 1972.

933. Ibid.

934. "NEWS ABOUT YOUR YMCA," Nashville YMCA Executive committee minutes, September 14, 1972, and Metropolitan Nashville YMCA board of directors minutes, September 28, 1972.

935. Letter, Sydney Keeble Jr. to Andrew Benedict, September 28, 1972, Nashville YMCA Board Reports, September 1972.

936. "NEWS ABOUT YOUR YMCA," Nashville YMCA Board Reports, November 1972.

937. Metropolitan Nashville YMCA board of directors meeting minutes, November 18, 1972.

938. "Cornerstone Opening Brings Back Year 1910," *The Tennessean*, November 4, 1972.

939. Approved 1973 budget, Nashville YMCA Records, January 1973.

940. Ibid.

941. "NEWS ABOUT YOUR YMCA," Nashville YMCA Board Reports, January 1973.

942. Ibid.

943. Ibid.

944. NEWS ABOUT YOUR YMCA," Nashville YMCA Board Reports, February 1973.

945. "Past 'Key' To Future," *The Tennessean*, November 17, 1974.

946. Cochran, *All Together*, 75–76.

947. Conversation, Wentworth Caldwell Jr. with the author, October 5, 2010.

948. Ibid.

949. Metropolitan Nashville YMCA nominating committee minutes, April 18, 1973.

950. Ibid.

951. Ibid.

952. "NEWS ABOUT YOUR YMCA," Nashville YMCA Board Reports, September 1973.

953. Ibid.

954. Conversation, Kent Rea with the author, November 3, 2010.

955. "NEWS ABOUT YOUR YMCA," Nashville YMCA Board Reports, August 1973.

956. "NEWS ABOUT YOUR YMCA," Nashville YMCA Board Reports, September 1973.

957. Metropolitan Nashville YMCA board of directors meeting minutes, October 24, 1973.

958. Ibid.

959. Ibid.

960. Report of Hal Gibbs to the YMCA executive committee, Nashville YMCA Board Reports, February 1974.

961. "NEWS ABOUT YOUR YMCA," Nashville YMCA Board Reports, May 1974.

962. Ibid.

963. Metropolitan Nashville YMCA financial development council minutes, July 18, 1974.

964. Ibid.

965. Ibid., September 11, 1974.

966. Metropolitan Nashville YMCA executive committee minutes, September 19, 1974.

967. Metropolitan Nashville YMCA executive committee minutes, September 19, 1974.

968. Recommendations to the Downtown board of manager from the Urban Services committee, Nashville YMCA Board Reports, September 1975.

969. Program services council Report to the executive committee, October 17, 1974.

970. Southwest Family YMCA board of managers minutes, October 10, 1974.

971. Ibid.

972. "Past 'Key' to Future," *The Tennessean*, November 17, 1974.

973. 1974 End of the Year membership and program statistical report, Nashville YMCA Board Reports, January 1975.

Chapter 24

974. Nashville YMCA executive committee minutes, January 16, 1975.

975. Nashville YMCA executive committee minutes, March 20, 1975, Nashville YMCA Board Records, March 1975; "NEWS ABOUT YOUR YMCA."

976. Conversation, Kent Rea with the author, November 3, 2010.

977. Nashville YMCA executive committee minutes, March 21, 1975.

978. Memorandum, Ralph L. Brunson to professional staff, March 17, 1975, Nashville YMCA Board Reports, March 1975.

979. 100th Anniversary Citywide Membership Enrollment Report, March 31, 1975.

980. "NEWS ABOUT YOUR YMCA," Nashville YMCA Board Reports, May 1975.

981. Letter, Sam J. Friedman to Charles L. Cornelius Jr., July 29, 1975, Nashville YMCA Board Reports, July 1975.

982. Ibid.

983. Ibid.

984. Metropolitan Nashville YMCA executive committee minutes, October 16, 1975.

985. NEWS ABOUT YOUR YMCA, Nashville YMCA Board Reports, November 1975.

986. Ibid.

987. Nashville YMCA Board of Directors meeting, December 31, 1975, Nashville YMCA Board Reports, December 1975.

988. Tri-Gra-Y programs were ones for girls.

989. "NEWS ABOUT YOUR YMCA," Board Reports, January 1976.

Chapter 25

990. Nashville YMCA executive committee minutes, January 15, 1976, Board Reports, January 1976.

991. "NEWS ABOUT YOUR YMCA," Board Reports, March 1976.

992. Nashville YMCA Foundation meeting minutes, April 7, 1976.

NOTES

993. "NEWS ABOUT YOUR YMCA," April 1976.

994. Centennial Capital Campaign Final Report, May 20, 1976.

995. "NEWS ABOUT YOUR YMCA," Board Reports, May 1976.

996. "NEWS ABOUT YOUR YMCA," Board Reports, August 1976.

997. Metropolitan Nashville YMCA Its Purpose and Operating Goals 1977–1981, Board Reports, July 1976.

998. Nashville YMCA executive committee minutes, August 16, 1976.

999. "Bar Test Upsets 'Y' Students," *Nashville Banner*, September 15, 1976.

1000. "NEWS ABOUT YOUR YMCA," Board Reports, October 1976.

1001. Program Activity Report to the Metropolitan YMCA Board, October 20, 1976.

1002. Nashville YMCA executive committee minutes, October 27, 1976.

1003. Nashville YMCA financial development committee minutes, October 27, 1976.

1004. Nashville YMCA long range planning committee minutes, October 28, 1976.

1005. "NEWS ABOUT YOUR YMCA," Board Reports, November 1976.

1006. YMCA Foundation of Metropolitan Nashville meeting minutes, December 1, 1976; YMCA board of directors meeting minutes, December 29, 1976.

1007. "NEWS ABOUT YOUR YMCA," Board Reports, December 1976.

1008. YMCA Statement of operating income and expenses, December 31, 1976; Analysis of 3-year study of membership, programs and activities by Kent Rea, attached to Nashville YMCA board of directors meeting minutes, March 23, 1977.

1009. Ibid.

1010. Conversation, Kent Rea with the author, August 9, 2010.

1011. "NEWS ABOUT YOUR YMCA," March 1977.

1012. Ibid., April 1977.

1013. Ibid.

1014. Nashville YMCA resolution attached to Nashville YMCA executive committee minutes, April 20, 1977.

1015. Conversation, Krent Rea with the author, November 3, 2010.

1016. "NEWS ABOUT YOUR YMCA," YMCA Board Reports, April 1977.

1017. Ibid.

1018. "NEWS ABOUT YOUR YMCA," Board Reports, June 1977.

1019. Nashville YMCA executive committee minutes, June 15, 19776.

1020 Ibid.

1021. Nashville YMCA executive committee minutes, August 17, 1977.

1022. Report of ad hoc committee to consider expanding programs and services of the Metro Physical Fitness Center, July 21, 1977.

1023. Ibid.

1024. Ibid.

1025. Ibid.

1026. "NEWS ABOUT YOUR YMCA," Board Reports, October 1977.

1027. "Growth and Progress," year-end report from William I. Henderson, President, Metropolitan Nashville YMCA, Board Reports, December 1977.

Chapter 26

1028. Nashville YMCA executive committee minutes, January 1, 1978.

1029. Ibid.

1030. Program activity council report, Board Reports, April 26, 1978.

1031. Letter, board managers of the Bordeaux-North YMCA Family Center to Mr. William I. Henderson, chairman, Metropolitan Nashville YMCA board of directors, March 13, 1978.

1032. United Way Allocation an Request, Board Reports, March 1978.

1033. Metropolitan Nashville board of directors meeting minutes, March 22, 1978; Metropolitan Nashville YMCA 103rd annual meeting, April 20, 1978.

1034. Ibid.

1035. Program Activity Council Report to the executive committee, April 26, 1978.

1036. Ibid.

1037. Ibid.

1038. Ibid.

1039. Conversation, J. Lawrence with the author, August 24, 2010.

1040. Metropolitan Nashville YMCA 104th annual meeting committee minutes, July 12, 1978.

1041. "NEWS ABOUT YOUR YMCA," June 1978.

1042. Metropolitan Nashville YMCA board of directors meeting minutes, October 25, 1978.

1043. Metropolitan Nashville YMCA executive committee minutes, September 20, 1978.

1044. Ibid.

1045. Metropolitan Nashville YMCA executive committee minutes, October 18, 1978.

1046. "NEWS ABOUT YOUR YMCA," November 1978.

1047. Ibid., December 1978.

1048. Metropolitan Nashville YMCA executive committee minutes, November 15, 1978; Metropolitan Nashville YMCA voting members meeting minutes, December 13, 1978.

1049. Letter, Ralph L. Brunson to Mrs. W. Lipscomb Davis, November 3, 1978.

1050. Metropolitan Nashville YMCA long-range planning committee minutes, November 28, 1978.

1051. "Some YMCA Highlights of 1978," YMCA Reports, 1978.

1052. 1979 "Communications Emphases," Board Reports, January 1979.

1053. "NEWS ABOUT YOUR YMCA," March 1979.

1054. Ibid., May 1979.

1055. Ibid., June 1979.

1056. Ibid.

1057. Metropolitan Nashville YMCA board of directors meeting minutes, July 25, 1979.

1058. Metropolitan Nashville YMCA executive committee minutes, August 15 and September 19, 1979;

1059. "NEWS ABOUT YOUR YMCA," September 1979.

1060. Ibid., October 1979.

1061. Metropolitan Nashville YMCA executive committee minutes, October 17, 1979.

1062. "NEWS ABOUT YOUR YMCA," October 1979.

1063. YMCA Foundation of Greater Nashville minutes, December 12, 1979. The fist time this title was officially used was at the September 26, 1979 board meeting.

1064. Ibid.

1065. Metropolitan Nashville YMCA executive committee minutes, November 21, 1979.

1066. Metropolitan Nashville YMCA voting members' meeting, December 5, 1979.

1067. Ibid.

Chapter 27

1068. Metropolitan Nashville YMCA board of directors meeting minutes, August 20, 1980.

1069. "NEWS ABOUT YOUR YMCA," YMCA Board Reports, January 1980.

1070. Ibid., February 20, 1980.

1071 Ibid.

1072. Metropolitan Nashville YMCA board of directors meeting minutes, March 26, 1980.

1073. "NEWS ABOUT YOUR YMCA," YMCA Board Reports, March 1980.

1074. Ibid., YMCA Board Reports, April 1980.

1075. Ibid., YMCA Board Reports, May 1980.

1076. "NEWS ABOUT YOUR YMCA," YMCA Board Reports, July 1980.

1077. Ibid.

1078. Metropolitan Nashville YMCA board of directors meeting minutes, July 3, 1980.

1079. Ibid., August 20, 1980.

1080. Ibid.

1081. "NEWS ABOUT YOUR YMCA," YMCA Board Reports, September 1980.

1082. "NEWS ABOUT YOUR YMCA," YMCA Board Reports, October 1980.

1083. Metropolitan Nashville YMCA executive committee minutes, October 15, 1980.

1084. "NEWS ABOUT YOUR YMCA," YMCA Board Reports, December 1980.

Chapter 28

1085. "NEWS ABOUT YOUR YMCA," January 1981.

1086. Bob Hill, *150 Years: The YMCA of Greater Louisville* (The YMCA of Greater Louisville, 2005), flyleaf and page 11; conversation, Kenton "Kent" Rea with the author, December 29, 2010.

1087. Metropolitan Nashville YMCA executive committee minutes, January 21, 1981.

1088. Ibid.

1089. Ibid.

1090. Ibid.

1091. Ibid.

1092. Metropolitan Nashville board of directors meeting minutes, September 23, 1981; executive committee minutes, October 28, 1981.

1093. Metropolitan Nashville YMCA Board Reports, December 1981.

1094. Conversation, Adrian Moody with the author, September 16, 2010.

1095. Ibid.

1096 Ibid.

1097. Metropolitan Nashville executive committee minutes, May 26, 1982.

1098. Ibid., July 28, 1982.

1099. Ibid.

1100. Metropolitan Nashville board of directors meeting minutes, October 27, 1982.

1101. "YMCA Leader Here To Share Global Efforts," *The Nashville Tennessean*, October 14, 1982.

1102. Metropolitan Nashville YMCA executive committee minutes, November 24, 1982.

1103. Ibid.

1104. Metropolitan Nashville YMCA executive committee minutes, January 18, 1983.

1105. Ibid., Metropolitan Nashville YMCA board of directors meeting minutes, February 15, 1983.

1106. "YMCAs Thrive under Mr. Moody," *Nashville Banner*, January 20, 1983.

1107. "Urban Services YMCA Making a Difference in Nashville" newsletter, collection of J. Lawrence.

1108. Metropolitan Nashville YMCA executive committee minutes, March 15, 1983.

1109. "Changing Lives—A Compelling Case," Metropolitan Nashville YMCA Board Reports, April 1983.

1110. Metropolitan Nashville YMCA board of directors meeting minutes, August 18, 1983.

1111. Metropolitan Nashville executive committee minutes, September 21, 1983.

1112. Ibid., November 23, 1983.

Chapter 29

1113. E-mail, Angela Williams to the author, February 15, 2011.

1114. Metropolitan Nashville board of directors meeting minutes, February 23, 1984.

1115. Partners of the Americas Trip Report by Adrian Moody and Fay Kilgore, YMCA Board Reports, February 1984.

1116. Metropolitan Nashville YMCA executive committee minutes, March 22, 1984.

1117. Metropolitan Nashville YMCA board of directors meeting minutes, June 28, 1984.

1118 Metropolitan Nashville YMCA board of directors meeting minutes, April 26, 1984.

1119. Ibid., March 22, 1984.

1120. Ibid., June 28, 1984.

1121. Nashville YMCA Balance Sheet, July 1984, YMCA Board Reports, 1984.

1122. Metropolitan Nashville YMCA board of directors meeting minutes, June 28, 1984.

1123 Ibid.

1124. Metropolitan Nashville YMCA executive committee minutes, September 27, 1984.

1125. Ibid.

1126. Metropolitan Nashville YMCA board of directors meeting minutes, October 25, 1984.

1127. Metropolitan Nashville YMCA executive committee minutes, November 29, 1984.

1128. Ibid.

1129. Metropolitan Nashville YMCA Proposed Budget for 1985, Nashville YMCA Board Reports, 1985.

1130. Metropolitan Nashville YMCA executive committee minutes, January 24, 1985.

1131. Metropolitan Nashville board of directors meeting, February 21, 1985.

1132. Ibid.

1133. Metropolitan Nashville executive committee minutes, August 28, 1986; "YMCA tour group finds trip to China fun, educational," *Nashville Bannner*, April 13, 1985.

1134. Metropolitan Nashville YMCA executive committee minutes, May 21, 1985.

1135. Conversation, Adrian Moody with the author, August 31, 2010.

1136. Metropolitan Nashville YMCA board of directors meeting minutes, June 27, 1985.

1137. Ibid., August 12. 1985.

1138. Metropolitan Nashville YMCA executive committee minutes, November 20, 1985.

1139. Ibid.

Chapter 30

1140. Metropolitan Nashville YMCA executive committee minutes, January 23, 1986.

1141. Ibid., March 27, 1986.

1142. Metropolitan Nashville YMCA board of directors meeting minutes, February 27, 1986.

1143. Metropolitan Nashville YMCA executive committee minutes March 27, 1986; YMCA of Nashville and Middle Tennessee board of directors meeting minutes, September 27, 1990; Wood, *Profiles in Tenacity*, 65.

1144. Metropolitan Nashville YMCA executive committee minutes, March 27, 1986.

1145. Joe Biddle, "Running Freer," *Nashville Banner*, April 24, 1986.

1146. Ibid., July 24, 1986.

1147. VOLUNTEER STATE OF THE Y, May 1986.

1148. Ibid., September 25, 1986.

1149. Ibid., November 20, 1986.

1150. Metropolitan Nashville YMCA executive committee minutes, March 30, 1989.

1151. Ibid.

1152. Metropolitan Nashville YMCA executive committee minutes, January 22, 1987; Metropolitan Nashville YMCA board of directors meeting minutes, February 26, 1987.

1153. Metropolitan Nashville YMCA board of directors, meeting minutes, April 23, 1987.

1154. Metropolitan Nashville YMCA executive committee minutes March 26, 1987.

1155. Resolution adopted at the Metropolitan Nashville YMCA board of directors meeting April 23, 1987.

1156. "YMCA's Moody Leaves For National Job," *Nashville Banner*, June 5, 1987.

1157. "YMCA to Open Daycare Center," *The Tennessean*, June 10, 1987.

1158. Metropolitan Nashville YMCA board of directors meeting minutes, June 18, 1987.

1159. "Ex-Nashville YMCA Leader Adrian Moody Is Honored," *Nashville Banner*, December 1, 1987.

Chapter 31

1160. Metropolitan Nashville YMCA selection committee minutes, September 22, 1987.

NOTES

1161. *Chattanooga News-Free Press*, September 27, 1987.

1162. Ibid.

1163. Metropolitan Nashville YMCA executive committee minutes, September 24, 1987.

1164. Metropolitan Nashville YMCA board of directors meeting, October 22, 1987.

1165. Laura H. Newsom, "Yeah, yeah, yeah…So What's the Big Deal?" pp. 4–5.

1166. Ibid.

1167. "Observations/Concerns, Nashville YMCA, February 1, 1988, Metropolitan Nashville YMCA Board Report, 1988.

1168. Ibid.

1169. "East Nashville YMCA's Future Clouded," *The Tennessean*, April 8, 1988.

1170. Metropolitan Nashville YMCA executive committee minutes, April 21, 1988.

1171. Metropolitan Nashville YMCA board of directors meeting minutes, May 26, 1988.

1172. Metropolitan Nashville YMCA executive committee minutes, July 28, 1988.

1173. Metropolitan Nashville YMCA board of directors meeting minutes, August 18, 1988.

1174. Metropolitan Nashville YMCA balance sheet, August 31, 1988.

1175. Metropolitan Nashville YMCA executive committee minutes, September 29, 1988.

1176. Letter, Gov. Ned McWherter to Carey F. Massey Jr., November 18, 1988, Metropolitan Nashville YMCA Board Report, 1988.

1177. Metropolitan Nashville YMCA board of directors meeting minutes, February 15, 1989.

1178. Ibid.

1179. Metropolitan Nashville YMCA executive committee minutes, March 30, 1989.

1180. Ibid.

1181. Ibid. June 15, 1989.

1182. Ibid.

1183. Ibid.

1184. Ibid.

1185. Metropolitan Nashville YMCA executive committee minutes, September 28, 1989.

1186. Ibid.

1187. Metropolitan Nashville YMCA board of directors meeting minutes, October 17, 1989.

1188. Ibid.

1189. Inner City Youth Futures Fund, attachment to Metropolitan Nashville YMCA board of directors meeting minutes, October 17, 1989.

1190. Ibid.

1191. Metropolitan Nashville YMCA executive committee minutes November 30, 1989.

1192. Metropolitan Nashville board of directors meeting minutes, December 21, 1989.

1193. Metropolitan Nashville YMCA Statement of Operating Income and Expense, 1989.

Chapter 32

1194. Ibid.

1195. Metropolitan Nashville YMCA executive committee minutes, February 21, 1990.

1196. Ibid.

1197. Laura H. Newsom, "Yeah, Yeah, Yeah… So What's the Big Deal?" 10.

1198. Metropolitan Nashville executive committee minutes, April 26, 1990.

1199. Christine Scheele, "In Flight with Urban Pilots," *Discovery YMCA*, Spring 1991, Number 39.

1200. Metropolitan Nashville board of directors meeting minutes, May 31, 1990.

1201. Metropolitan Nashville executive committee minutes, June 28, 1990.

1202. Wood, *Profiles in Tenacity*, 67–69.

1203. Ibid.

1204. Ibid.

1205. The YMCA of Nashville and Middle Tennessee voting members meeting, November 29, 1990.

1206. Newsom, "Yeah, Yeah, Yeah…So What's the Big Deal?" 8.

1207. YMCA of Nashville and Middle Tennessee executive committee minutes, January 24, 1991.

1208. Newsom, "Yeah, Yeah, Yeah…So What's the Big Deal?" 11.

1209. YMCA of Nashville and Middle Tennessee board of directors meeting minutes, February 27, 1991.

1210. Ibid., April 25, 1991.

1211. YMCA of Nashville and Middle Tennessee executive committee minutes, July 25, 1991.

1212. Ibid., May 23, 1991.

1213. YMCA of Nashville and Middle Tennessee board of directors meeting minutes, October 24, 1991; "'We Build People' Campaign, 1993," YMCA of Nashville and Middle Tennessee Board Report, 1992.

1214. Ibid., December 19, 1991.

1215. YMCA of Nashville and Middle Tennessee executive committee minutes, March 26, 1992.

1216 Ibid.

1217. YMCA of Nashville and Middle Tennessee executive committee minutes, July 23, 1992.

1218. Conversation, James Rayhab with the author, November 19, 2010.

1219. YMCA of Nashville and Middle Tennessee board of directors meeting minutes August 27, 1992.

1220. YMCA of Nashville and middle Tennessee executive committee minutes, September 24, 1992; conversation, J. Lawrence with the author, March 4, 2011.

1221. Ibid.

1222. Conversation, "William M. "Bill" Wilson with the author, February 16, 2011.

1223. Ibid.

1224. 1993 Operational Goals, Draft #1 January 26, 1993, YMCA of Nashville and Middle Tennessee Board Report 1992.

1225. Ibid.

1226. YMCA of Nashville and Middle Tennessee annual meeting, April 20, 1993; conversation, William R. "Bill" Wilson with the author, February 16, 2011.

1227. YMCA of Nashville and Middle Tennessee executive committee minutes, May 27, 1993.

1228. Newsom, "Yeah, Yeah, Yeah…So What's the Big Deal?" 16.

1229. Ibid.

1230. Ibid., 17.

1231. Ibid.

1232. YMCA of Nashville and Middle Tennessee executive committee minutes, July 22, 1993.

1233. YMCA of Nashville and Middle Tennessee executive committee minutes, September 23, 1993; conversation, William R. DeLoache Jr. with the author, January 8, 2011.

1234. YMCA of Nashville and Middle Tennessee board of directors meeting minutes, October 21, 1993.

1235 YMCA of Nashville and Middle Tennessee board of directors meeting minutes, December 23, 1993.

Chapter 33

1236. Conversation, Mark Weller with the author, January 6, 2011.

1237. YMCA of Nashville and Middle Tennessee executive committee minutes, March 10, 1994; board of directors meeting minutes, August 25, 1994.

1238. Conversation, Robert N. Clement with the author, January 11, 2011.

1239. YMCA of Nashville and Middle Tennessee executive committee minutes, March 10, 1994.

1240. YMCA of Nashville and Middle Tennessee annual meeting minutes, April 25, 1994.

1241. Ibid.

1242. Ibid.

1243. YMCA of Nashville and Middle Tennessee board of directors meeting minutes, October 27, 1994.

1244. Ibid.

1245. YMCA of Nashville and Middle Tennessee board of directors meeting minutes, December 22, 1994.

1246. YMCA of Nashville and Middle Tennessee executive committee minutes, January 19, 1995.

1247. YMCA of Nashville and Middle Tennessee board of directors meeting minutes, February 21, 1995.

1248. Ibid.

1249. Confidential memo, Harwell Howard Hyne & Manner, P. C. to YMCA/Percy Priest Day Camp Task Force, May 16, 1995, YMCA of Nashville and Middle Tennessee, 1995 Board Reports.

1250. YMCA of Nashville and Middle Tennessee executive committee minutes, May 25, 1995.

1251. History of the Clarksville YMCA, March 28, 2000, copy in collection of the author.

1252. Ibid.

1253. Summer campaign summery, April 15–June 30, 1995, YMCA of Nashville and Middle Tennessee Board Reports, 1995.

1254. YMCA of Nashville and Middle Tennessee board of directors meeting minutes, August 24, 1995.

1255. YMCA of Nashville and Middle Tennessee executive committee minutes, September 28, 1995.

1256. YMCA of Nashville and Middle Tennessee executive committee minutes, November 16, 1995, 1995.

1257. Ibid.

1258. YMCA of Nashville and Middle Tennessee board of directors meeting minutes, December 21, 1995.

1259. Green Hills Family YMCA History, July 2000, copy in the collection of the author.

1260. YMCA of Nashville and Middle Tennessee board of directors meeting minutes, February 22, 1996.

Chapter 34

1261. Conversation, Eslick Daniel, M.D. with the author, October 2, 2010; YMCA of Nashville and Middle Tennessee board of directors meeting minutes, December 19, 1996.

1262. Conversation, Angela Williams with the author, December 12, 2010.

1263. Ibid.

1264. Ibid.

1265. YMCA of Nashville and Middle Tennessee annual meeting minutes, April 9, 1996.

1266. YMCA of Nashville and Middle Tennessee, executive committee minutes, May 16, 1996.

1267. "Robertson County Family YMCA History," July 2000, copy in collection of the author.

1268. Ibid.

1269. YMCA of Nashville and Middle Tennessee executive committee minutes, July 23, 1996.

1270. International Update, August 1996, YMCA of Nashville and Middle Tennessee Board Reports, 1996.

1271. Conversation, J. Lawrence with the author, March 3, 2011.

1272. YMCA of Nashville and Middle Tennessee board of directors meeting, August 19, 1996.

1273. YMCA of Nashville and Middle Tennessee, executive committee minutes, September 24, 1996.

1274. YMCA of Nashville and Middle Tennessee board of directors meeting minutes, October 24, 1996.

1275. Ibid.

1276. Articles of Merger of the Clarksville Area YMCA with and into the YMCA of Nashville and Middle Tennessee, executed December 17, 1996, YMCA of Nashville and Middle Tennessee Board Reports 1996.

1277. YMCA of Nashville and Middle Tennessee board of directors meeting minutes, December 19, 1996.

1278. Ibid.

1279. YMCA of Middle Tennessee board of directors meeting minutes, February 27, 1997.

1280. YMCA of Middle Tennessee executive committee minutes, March 27, 1997.

1281. Ibid.

1282. Annual meeting of the YMCA of Middle Tennessee minutes, April 24, 1997.

1283. YMCA of Middle Tennessee executive committee minutes, May 22, 1997.

1284. Ibid.

1285. Typed recap of significant events in the history of the Joe C. Davis Center (1991–-2008), Joe C. Davis Center archives.

1286. Ibid.

1287. YMCA of Middle Tennessee executive committee minutes, September 27, 1997.

1288. YMCA of Middle Tennessee, board of director meeting minutes, October 23, 1997.

1289. Typed recap of significant events in the history of the Joe C. Davis Center (1991–2008), Joe C. Davis Center archives.

1290. Ibid.

1291. Ibid.

Chapter 35

1292. "Generous and Genuine, Mrs. Maddox Was Leader," *Nashville Banner*, January 15, 1998.

1293. Conversation, Mark Weller with the author, January 6, 2011; typed recap of significant events n the history of the Joe C. Davis Center, Joe C. Davis Center archives.

1294. YMCA of Middle Tennessee executive committee minutes, January 22, 1998.

1295. Ibid., March 26, 1998.

1296 Ibid.

1297. "Tornadoes," special report, *The Tennessean*, April 19, 1998; YMCA of Middle Tennessee executive committee minutes, May 28, 1998; YMCA of Middle Tennessee board of directors meeting minutes, June 25, 1998.

1298. YMCA of Middle Tennessee annual meeting minutes, May 4, 1998.

1299. YMCA of Middle Tennessee executive committee minutes, May 28, 1998.

1300. Ibid.

1301. Ibid.

1302. Ibid.

1303. Ibid.

1304. YMCA of Middle Tennessee executive committee minutes, November 19, 1998.

1305. YMCA of Middle Tennessee executive committee minutes, January 26, 1999.

1306. YMCA of Middle Tennessee board of directors meeting minutes, June 24, 1999.

1307. Typed summary of significant events in the history of the Joe C. Davis Center, Joe C. Davis Center archives.

1308. YMCA of Middle Tennessee executive committee minutes, September 23, 1999.

1309. Ibid., November 18, 1999.

1310. YMCA of Middle Tennessee 1999 Highlights, Board Reports, 1999.

1311. 1999 Highlights, YMCA of Middle Tennessee Board Reports, 2000.

Chapter 36

1312. YMCA of Middle Tennessee executive committee minutes, January 27, 2000; typed summery of significant events in the history of the Joe C. Davis Center, Joe C. Davis Center archives.

1313. YMCA of Middle Tennessee Member Satisfaction Survey, February 2000, YMCA of Middle Tennessee Board Reports 2000.

1314. Ibid.

1315. Ibid.

ccclviii316 Elizabeth Dubuque's report to the board of the YMCA of Middle Tennessee, June 2000, Board Reports 2000.

1317. Ibid.

1318. Maryland Farms history given at the August 24, 2000 meeting of the YMCA of Middle Tennessee.

1319. YMCA of Middle Tennessee board of directors meeting minutes, August 24, 2000.

1320. Conversation, Mark Weller and Bob Copeland with the author, January 6, 2011.

1321. Ibid.

1322. Ibid.

1323. Ibid.

1324. Ibid.

1325. YMCA of Middle Tennessee board of directors meeting minutes, August 30, 2001.

1326. YMCA of Middle Tennessee 2002–2004 Strategic Plan, Board Reports 2001.

1327. Robertson County History, copy in the collection of the author.

1328. Letter, Clark D. Baker to Doyle Rippee, September 4, 2001.

1329. Ibid.

1330. Development Report, Rich Ford, chairman, December 18, 2001, YMCA of Middle Tennessee Board Reports 2001.

1331. Ibid.

1332. YMCA of Middle Tennessee executive committee minutes, November 15, 2001.

1333. YMCA of Middle Tennessee executive committee minutes, November 15, 2001.

1334. YMCA of Middle Tennessee board of directors meeting, December 18, 2001.

Chapter 37

1335. Letter, Ronald F. Knox Jr. to Ridley Wills II, December 26, 2001.

1336. Letter, John Mark "Journey" Johnson to Ronald F. Knox Jr., January 2, 2002.

1337. Edward R. Crews, *The Richmond YMCA 1854–2004* (YMCA of Greater Richmond, 2004), 165.

1338. Curricular vita, David E. Byrd, 2010; conversation, David Byrd with the author, May 18, 2010.

1339. Conversation, Douglas Cruickshank with the author, October 27, 2010. Doug heard this story from Mrs. Thomas when they served together on the board of Popular Forest, Thomas Jefferson's home; conversation, Journey Johnson with the author, January 13, 2011.

1340. Crews, *The Richmond YMCA 1854–2004*, 165.

1341. Curriculum Vita for John Marks "Journey" Johnson, 2002.

1342. YMCA of Middle Tennessee executive committee minutes, January 23, 2002.

1343. YMCA of Middle Tennessee board of directors meeting, February 28, 2002; Transition report, May 20, 2002, YMCA of Middle Tennessee Board Reports, 2002.

1344. YMCA of Middle Tennessee annual meeting minutes, April 25, 2002.

1345. Institute for the Healing Arts press release, YMCA of Middle Tennessee Board Reports, 2002.

1346. Typed summary of significant events in the history of the Joe C. Davis Center, Joe C. Davis Center archives.

1347. YMCA of Middle Tennessee board of directors meeting minutes, June 27, 2002.

1348. YMCA of Middle Tennessee operations report, July 26, 2002.

1349. YMCA of Middle Tennessee Operations Report, August 22, 2002.

1350. Development Update, September 27, 2002, YMCA of Middle Tennessee Board Reports 2002.

1351. YMCA of Middle Tennessee Operations Report, September 27, 2002, 2002 Board Reports.

1352. Memorandum from Journey Johnson to executive committee, September 12, 2002, YMCA of Middle Tennessee Board Reports, 2002.

1353. YMCA of Middle Tennessee executive committee minutes, September 27, 2002.

1354. Ibid.

1355. YMCA of Middle Tennessee Operations Report, October 24, 2002.

1356. YMCA of Middle Tennessee board meeting, October 24, 2002.

1357. 2003 Winter Marketing Campaign Goals, YMCA of Middle Tennessee Board Reports, 2002.

1358. Memorandum from Journey Johnson to the Board of Directors and others, January 17, 2003; YMCA of Middle Tennessee Statement of Operating Income and Expense for the twelve months ended December 31, 2002, YMCA of Middle Tennessee Board Reports 2002.

1359. YMCA of Middle Tennessee executive committee minutes, January 24, 2002.

1360. YMCA of Middle Tennessee Operations Report, February 27, 2003.

1361. Ibid.

1362. YMCA of Middle Tennessee Operations Report, March 25, 2003; YMCA of Middle Tennessee executive committee minutes, March 25, 2002.

1363. YMCA of Middle Tennessee 2003 Priorities, Reports and Updates, May 21, 2003.

1364. Ibid.

1365. Ibid.

1366. Joe C. Davis YMCA Outdoor Center, June 2003, YMCA of Middle Tennessee Board Reports, 2003; YMCA of Middle Tennessee board meeting minutes, June 26, 2003.

1367. YMCA of Middle Tennessee Operations Report, June 20, 2003.

1368. Development Update, June 26, 2003, Board Reports 2003.

1369. YMCA of Middle Tennessee board meeting minutes, June 26, 2003.

1370. Typed summary of significant events in the history of the Joe C. Davis Center, Joe C. Davis Center archives.

1371. YMCA of Middle Tennessee Operations Report, July 22, 2003.

1372. Conversation, Marty Dickens with the author, January 29, 2011.

1373. Conversation, Journey Johnson with the author, February 2, 2011.

1374. YMCA of Middle Tennessee executive committee minutes, July 24, 2003.

1375. YMCA of Middle Tennessee-St. Thomas Contract Agreement, September 1, 2003, Board Reports 2003; Executive resolutions, May 27, 2004, YMCA of Middle Tennessee Board Report; Operations report, May 27, 2004.

1376. Ibid.

1377. Ibid.

1378. Development Update, November 20, 2003, Board Reports 2003.

1379. YMCA of Middle Tennessee executive committee minutes, November 20, 2003.

1380. YMCA of Middle Tennessee board meeting minutes, December 18, 2003.

Chapter 38

1381. YMCA of Middle Tennessee Statement of Operating Income and Expense for the twelve months ended December 31, 2003.

1382. Ibid.

1383. YMCA of Middle Tennessee Operations Report, February 26, 2004.

1384. YMCA of Middle Tennessee board meeting minutes, February 26, 2004.

1385. "Heritage," Winter 2006.

1386. YMCA of Middle Tennessee Operations Report, My 27, 2004, Board Report 2004.

1387. Ibid.

1388. Development Update, December 16, 2004; YMCA of Middle Tennessee executive committee minutes, July 22, 2004.

1389. Development Update, October 28, 2004, YMCA of Middle Tennessee Board Report, 2004.

1390. YMCA of Middle Tennessee Operations Report, August 26, 2004.

1391. Ibid.

1392. YMCA of Middle Tennessee executive committee minutes, September 23, 2004; Development Update, October 28, 2004.

1393. Ibid.

1394. Ibid.

1395. Ibid.

1396. YMCA of Middle Tennessee board meeting minutes, October 28, 2004.

1397. YMCA of Middle Tennessee Operations Report, November 18, 2004.

1398. YMCA of Middle Tennessee executive committee minutes, November 18, 2004.

1399. YMCA of Middle Tennessee and Putnam County YMCA Merger Checklist, January 27, 2005; YMCA of Middle Tennessee executive committee minutes, January 27, 2005.

1400. YMCA of Middle Tennessee and Putnam County YMCA Merger Checklist, February 23, 2005.

1401. The YMCA of Middle Tennessee board meeting minutes, February 24, 2005.

1402. Ibid.

1403. YMCA of Middle Tennessee executive committee minutes, March 17, 2005.

1404. "Bellevue YMCA Starts to Rise Just North of County Line," *The Tennessean*, June 21, 2005.

1405. Conversation, Mark Weller with the author, January 6, 2011.

1406. Development Update, July 21, 2005, YMCA of Middle Tennessee Board Report 2005.

1407. "Y Build Program Helps Young Men Build a Future," *The Tennessean*, Board Report 2005.

1408. Ibid.

1409 Ibid.

1410. YMCA of Middle Tennessee executive committee meeting, November 17, 2005.

1411. Executive summary, YMCA/Senior Citizens, Inc., Bellevue Center, November 17, 2005.

1412. YMCA of Middle Tennessee 2006 Budget, Association Summary, Board Report 2005.

1413. YMCA of Middle Tennessee executive committee minutes, December 15, 2005.

1414. "2005 Milestones, Our 130th Year of Service," 2006 Board Report.

Chapter 39

1415. Development Update, January 26, 2006, YMCA of Middle Tennessee Board Report, 2006.

1416. Development Update, January 26, 2006, YMCA of Middle Tennessee Board Report, 2006.

1417. Ibid., January 26, 2006.

1418. USSAA Urban Services School of Academics and Athletics, Board Report, 2006.

1419. YMCA of Middle Tennessee Operations Report, February 23, 2006.

1420. YMCA of Middle Tennessee board meeting, February 23, 2006.

1421. Executive summary, Bellevue YMCA/Senior Citizens Agreement, March 13, 2006.

1422. Resident Camp & Year-Round Outdoor Center Executive Summary, March 18, 2008.

1423. YMCA of Middle Tennessee Operations Report, March 16, 2006.

1424. Ibid., May 25, 2006.

1425. Development Update, June 22, 2006.

1426. YMCA of Middle Tennessee board meeting minutes, June 22, 2006; Operations Report, July 27, 2006.

1427. YMCA of Middle Tennessee executive committee minutes, July 27, 2006.

1428. Development Update, December 14, 2006.

1429. YMCA of Middle Tennessee Operations Report, August 24 and September 28, 2006.

1430. YMCA of Middle Tennessee board meeting minutes, August 24, 2006.

1431. YMCA of Middle Tennessee board meeting minutes, October 26, 2006.

1432. YMCA of Middle Tennessee Operations Report, November 16, 2006.

1433. YMCA of Middle Tennessee board meeting minutes, December 14, 2006.

1434. YMCA of Middle Tennessee Statement of Operating Income and Expense for the Twelve Months Ended December 31, 2006; YMCA of Middle Tennessee Foundation Update, year-end 2006; Membership comparison year-end 2004-2006, Board Reports 2007.

1435. Development Update, January 24, 2007; YMCA of Middle Tennessee executive committee meeting minutes, January 24, 2007.

1436. YMCA of Middle Tennessee Operations Report, January 24, 2007.

1437. YMCA of Middle Tennessee board meeting minutes, February 22, 2007.

1438. YMCA of Middle Tennessee Operations Report, March 29, 2007.

1439. Ibid.

1440. YMCA of Middle Tennessee Operations Report, June 28, 2007.

1441. YMCA of Middle Tennessee 2007 Annual Celebration Meeting, April 23, 2007.

1442. Foundation Update, May 23, 2007.

1443. "The Way Mr. Charlie Would Have Wanted It," *Cookeville Herald-Citizen*, April 15. 2007.

1444. YMCA of Middle Tennessee Operations Report, June 28, 2007, YMCA of Middle Tennessee board meeting minutes, June 28, 2007.

1445. Development Report, June 27, 2007.

1446. YMCA of Middle Tennessee Operations Report, August 23, 2007.

1447. Ibid.

1448. "Widjiwagan Campers of the Year May Go Along for the Ride," *The Tennessean*, August 8, 2007.

1449. Development Report, September 20, 2007.

1450. YMCA of Middle Tennessee Operations Report, September 20, 2007.

1451. "Old Mt. Juliet School Site May Become YMCA Facility," *The Tennessean*, February 27, 2008.

1452. Ibid.

1453. YMCA of Middle Tennessee Operations Report, November 14, 2007.

1454. Development Report, December 13, 2007.

Chapter 40

cdlxxvi455 YMCA of Middle Tennessee Operations Report, January 17, 2008.

1456. Ibid.

1457. Ibid.

1458. Ibid.

1459. Ibid.

1460. Ibid.

1461. Ibid.

1462. YMCA of Middle Tennessee executive council minutes March 27, 2008.

1463. Ibid.

1464. YMCA of Middle Tennessee Operations Report, April 24, 2008.

1465. YMCA of middle Tennessee Operations Report, July 24, 2008.

1466. YMCA of Middle Tennessee Operations Report, June 19, 2008.

1467. Ibid.

1468. Ibid.

1469. "New Director Returns to His YMCA Roots," *The Tennessean*, June 11, 2008.

1470. YMCA of Middle Tennessee Operations Report, August 21, 2008.

1471. Ibid.

1472. YMCA of Middle Tennessee board minutes, October 30, 2008; executive committee minutes, November 20, 2008.

1473. YMCA of Middle Tennessee board meeting minutes, December 18, 2008.

1474. YMCA of Middle Tennessee Development Update, January 29, 2009.

1475. YMCA of Middle Tennessee Association Board Resolution, August 20, 2009.

1476. Ibid.

1477. YMCA of Middle Tennessee executive committee minutes, March 11, 2009.

1478. Journey's Journal, May 12, 2009.

1479. YMCA of Middle Tennessee executive committee resolutions, May 19, 2009.

1480. "Nashville Visionary United People, Spurred Progress," *The Tennessean*, June 14, 2009.

1481. "Trails & Tales," Camp Widjiwagan Newsletter, Fall, 2009.

1482. A Resolution commemorating the late James M. Ward's legacy of service to the YMCA of Middle Tennessee, adopted October 29, 2009.

1483. YMCA of Middle Tennessee board meeting minutes, June 25, 2009.

1484. *YMCA TIMES*, Fall 2009.

1485. YMCA of Middle Tennessee board of directors meeting minutes, August 20, 2009.

1486. Ibid.

1487. Ibid.

1488. "Reduced Fees Help YMCA Members," *The Tennessean*, November 27, 2009.

1489. Ibid.

1490. Ibid.

1491. Ibid.

1492. Ibid.

1493. Ibid.

1494. E-mail, Journey Johnson to the author, March 3, 2011.

1495. Ibid.

1496. Ibid.

Chapter 41

1497. YMCA of Middle Tennessee executive committee minutes, January 21, 2010.

1498. YMCA of Middle Tennessee board meeting minutes, February 25, 2010.

1499. Conversation, Sandra and Richard "Dick" Fulton with the author, January 22, 2011.

1500. YMCA of Middle Tennessee Philanthropy Update, September 30, 2010.

1501. "Teen Center Construction Underway at Margaret Maddox YMCA," *YMCA TIMES*, Winter 2010.

1502. "Trails & Tales," a newsletter for Friends of the Joe C. Davis Outdoor Camp, Spring 2010.

1503. YMCA of Middle Tennessee executive committee minutes, March 25, 2010.

1504. YMCA of Middle Tennessee executive committee minutes, March 25, 2010.

1505. "YMCA Pool Reopens," *The Tennessean*, July 21, 21010; *YMCA TIMES*, Fall 2010.

1506. YMCA of Middle Tennessee executive committee minutes, May 27, 2010.

1507. Ibid.

1508. "Nashville's Best New Buildings Honored," *The Tennessean*, May 28, 2010.

1509. Ibid.

1510. YMCA of Middle Tennessee executive committee minutes, June 24, 2010.

1511. Ibid.

1512. Ibid., "Camp for Young Offenders Offers Clean Slate," June 21, 2010.

1513. Ibid.

1514. E-mail from Journey Johnson to YMCA Board members, November 25, 2010.

1515. YMCA of Middle Tennessee executive committee minutes, July 29, 2010.

1516. Letter, Michael Check, executive director Y-CAP YMCA to the author, August 17, 2010.

1517. Ibid.

1518. Ibid.

1519. Ibid.

1520. YMCA of Middle Tennessee board meeting minutes, October 28, 2010.

1521. YMCA of Middle Tennessee executive committee minutes, November 23, 2010.

1522. Conversation, Journey Johnson with the author, January 21, 2011.

1523. YMCA of Middle Tennessee executive committee minutes, November 23, 2010.

1524. Preston Taylor outreach changes lives of youth, *The Tennessean*, December 7, 2010.

1525. Ibid.

1526. E-mail, Journey Johnson to YMCA of Middle Tennessee leaders, January 1, 2011.

INDEX

INDEX

I WANT TO THANK my editor, Alice Sullivan, for her hard work, accomplished under pressure. The book is much better because of her good help.

One of the last tasks in the publication of any book is the design of the cover. I am grateful to Mary Sue Englund for her choice of an etching of the four-story Nashville YMCA building of Kentucky sandstone, the cornerstone of which was laid June 25, 1887. With the title in red, the cover is both simple and effective.

Throughout the many months I worked on *The YMCA of Middle Tennessee: Three Centuries of Service*, a constant was my close communications with Suzanne Iller, Senior Vice President of Philanthropy at the YMCA of Middle Tennessee. Invariably, Suzanne was upbeat about the book, helpful with her suggestions, and encouraging to me. Thanks, Suzanne, for your friendship and assistance in all sorts of meaningful ways. —RIDLEY WILLS II